everything's an argument

Fifth Edition

EVERYTHING'S AN argument

Andrea A. Lunsford
STANFORD UNIVERSITY

John J. Ruszkiewicz
UNIVERSITY OF TEXAS AT AUSTIN

BEDFORD / ST. MARTIN'S
BOSTON ◆ NEW YORK

For Bedford/St. Martin's

Senior Developmental Editor: John Elliott
Production Editor: Jessica Skrocki Gould
Senior Production Supervisor: Nancy Myers
Marketing Manager: Molly Parke
Art Director: Lucy Krikorian
Text Design: Anna Palchik
Copy Editor: Rosemary Winfield
Photo Research: Sue McDermott Barlow
Cover Design: Donna Dennison
Cover Photos: (clockwise from top) Veer, Collection: Photodisc Photography; Veer, Collection: Digital Vision Photography; Everett Kennedy Brown/epa/ Corbis; Veer, Collection: Brand X Photography; Original image by Matt Krueger at DVICE; Courtesy of Lexus; Getty Images, Inc., Photographer/ Artist: Tom Schierlitz
Composition: Six Red Marbles
Printing and Binding: R.R. Donnelley & Sons Company

President: Joan E. Feinberg
Editorial Director: Denise B. Wydra
Editor in Chief: Karen S. Henry
Director of Development: Erica T. Appel
Director of Marketing: Karen R. Soeltz
Director of Editing, Design, and Production: Marcia Cohen
Assistant Director of Editing, Design, and Production: Elise S. Kaiser
Managing Editor: Shuli Traub

Library of Congress Control Number: 2009939557

For information, write: Bedford/St. Martin's, 75 Arlington Street, Boston, MA 02116   (617-399-4000)

ISBN 10: 0–312–53862–6
ISBN 13: 978–0–312–53862–0

Acknowledgments

PREFACE

In each previous edition, we have described *Everything's an Argument* as a labor of love for us, and it remains so. Our affection for the book derives in part from knowing that it helps students to make persuasive and ethical arguments in a world where that ability grows ever more essential. *Everything's an Argument* first appeared just as new media and technologies were beginning to reshape the ways persuasive writing could be framed and shared, and we have enjoyed tracking those developments— offering fresh arguments and provocative visual images in each new edition to illuminate the ways we all use language to assert our presence in the world. A best-seller in its field since its debut, *Everything's an Argument* apparently strikes a chord with students and instructors who expect a book on persuasion to be candid, balanced, and attuned to everyday events. We now offer a fifth edition, carefully revised to meet those standards and to offer writers and instructors important new tools for reading and making arguments.

The purposefully controversial title of this text sums up three key assumptions we share. First, language provides the most powerful means of understanding the world and of using that understanding to help shape lives. Second, arguments seldom if ever have only two sides: rather, they present a dizzying array of perspectives, often with as many "takes" on a subject as there are arguers. Understanding arguments, then, calls for carefully considering a full range of perspectives before coming to judgment. Finally, and most important, all language—including that of sounds and images or of symbol systems other than writing—is in some way persuasive, pointing in a direction and asking for a response. Texts of every kind beckon for reactions, from the dyed finger of a voter in Zimbabwe to the latest Twitter feed, from the American flag to Sarah Palin's shoes, from the latest reggaeton hit to the brand identity of the new Tata Nano. People walk, talk, and breathe persuasion very much as they breathe the air: everything is a potential argument.

So our purpose in *Everything's an Argument* is to present argument as something that's as everyday as an old sweater, as something we do almost from the moment we are born (in fact, an infant's first cry is as poignant a claim as we can imagine), and as something worthy of careful attention and practice. In pursuing this goal, we try to use ordinary language whenever possible and keep specialized terminology to a minimum. But we also see argument, and want students to see it, as a craft both delicate and powerful. So we have designed *Everything's an Argument* to be itself an argument for civil persuasion, with a voice that aims to appeal to readers cordially but that doesn't hesitate to make demands on them when appropriate.

To that end (and in response to numerous requests), we have written a new chapter, "Academic Arguments," to explain precisely how the arguments students encounter and write in school might differ from those they meet in other arenas of life. The chapter examines the special demands and conventions of scholarly writing and provides two extended examples, one by a student and one by a faculty member. In addition, because academic writing crosses all genres, we highlight its variety with a box in each chapter of Part II that illustrates how it's used in the chapter's genre, such as a definition or proposal.

The new essays in the "Academic Arguments" chapter are among six new full-length arguments—on topics ranging from Chris Rock to what to do with the International Space Station to the role music has played in U.S.-China diplomacy—that provide engaging, topical new readings for students. All of the essays in the book that use MLA documentation style have been updated to conform to the newest (2009) edition of the *MLA Handbook for Writers of Research Papers*, and Chapter 20, "Using Documentation," has been thoroughly revised to offer guidelines and examples reflecting those in both the new *MLA Handbook* and (for APA style) the new 2009 edition of the *Publication Manual of the American Psychological Association*.

In another major improvement, and again in response to users' requests, we have expanded our chapter on "Structuring Arguments" to show better how assumptions embedded within the structures of arguments shape what makers of arguments are likely to say. We use the classical oration to represent traditional thesis-driven patterns of organization and introduce Rogerian argument as a less-oppositional alternative. The chapter concludes with our thorough presentation of Toulmin argument, but now that familiar strategy is set into a fuller context. We are confident that the revised chapter offers writers better-considered choices for organizing a piece of writing.

As always, in the new edition we aim to balance attention to the critical reading of arguments (analysis) with attention to the writing of arguments (production). Once again, we have tried to demonstrate both activities with lively—and realistic—examples, on the principle that the best way to appreciate an argument may be to see it in action. We have kept the best materials from previous editions, but we have also found many new examples and arguments—including visual ones—that we believe capture the spirit of the times, a period of rapid, sometimes frightening, and yet exciting change. As always, we want students to page through the book to find the next intriguing argument or to discover one of their own.

Here is a summary of the key features that continue to characterize *Everything's an Argument* and of the major new features in this edition:

Key Features

- A fresh and winning approach, going beyond traditional pro/con assumptions to show that argument is everywhere—in essays, rap lyrics, news articles, scholarly writing, poems, advertisements, cartoons, posters, bumper stickers, billboards, Web sites, blogs, text messages, and other electronic environments.

- Student-friendly explanations in simple, everyday language, with many brief examples and a minimum of technical terminology.

- Fifteen full-length essays, including seven by student writers, that provide engaging models of extended verbal arguments in academic contexts and over questions of fact, definition, evaluation, cause and effect, and proposals, as well as an extended model of rhetorical analysis.

- A handsome full-color design that brings the images in the text to life.

- Boxed discussions of "Cultural Contexts for Argument" that alert students to the fact that ways of arguing differ from culture to culture and make this book more useful to both native and non-native speakers of English.

New to This Edition

- A new chapter on "Academic Arguments" that defines the genre, explains its conventions, and provides full-sized examples.

- A box in each chapter of Part II highlighting the use of academic argument in that chapter's genre.

- Six new full-length arguments in Part II—on topics ranging from Chris Rock to what to do with the International Space Station to the role music has played in U.S.–China diplomacy—that provide engaging, topical new readings for students.

- New material on the classical oration and Rogerian argument in Chapter 7, "Structuring Arguments."

- Guidelines and examples for the latest (2009) versions of MLA and APA styles in Chapter 20, "Documenting Sources."

You Get More Digital Choices for
Everything's an Argument

Everything's an Argument doesn't stop with a book. Online, you'll find both free and affordable premium resources to help students get even more out of the book and your course. You'll also find convenient instructor resources, such as downloadable sample syllabi, classroom activities, and a nationwide community of teachers. To learn more about or order any of the products below, contact your Bedford/St. Martin's sales representative, email sales support (sales_support@bfwpub.com), or visit the Web site at bedfordstmartins.com/everythingsargument/catalog.

Everything's an Argument Student Center at bedfordstmartins .com/everythingsargument

Send students to free and open resources, provide them with an online chapter of readings that include multimedia, or upgrade to an expanding collection of innovative digital content—all in one place.

Free and open resources provide students with easy-to-access reference materials, exercises, and downloadable content.

- *TopLinks* gives links to reliable online sources that students can use to further explore topics introduced in the book.

- *Bedford Bibliographer* helps students with the process of collecting source information and making a bibliography in MLA, APA, and *Chicago* styles.

- *Exercise Central* offers over eight thousand grammar and writitng exercises with immediate scoring, linked to a gradebook that you can access from the Instructor Resources tab in *Re:Writing*.

An e-chapter of readings, updated each fall, provides students with an opportunity to analyze arguments in dynamic electronic formats, including audio, video, and hypertext. The initial e-chapter includes such multimedia selections as well as traditional verbal and visual arguments on the topic of foreign attitudes toward the United States and Americans. The e-chapter is available for free only when packaged with the book. An activation code is required. To order the e-chapter packaged with the book, use ISBN-10: 0-312-64256-3 or ISBN-13: 978-0-312-64256-3.

Re:Writing Plus, **now with** *VideoCentral,* gathers all of Bedford/ St. Martin's premium digital content for composition into one online collection. It includes hundreds of model documents, the first ever peer-review game, and *VideoCentral*, with more than fifty brief videos for the writing classroom. *Re:Writing Plus* can be purchased separately at the *Student Center* or packaged with the book at a significant discount. An activation code is required. To order *Re:Writing Plus* packaged with the book, use ISBN-10: 0-312-62436-0 or ISBN-13: 978-0-312-62436-1.

Instructor Resources at bedfordstmartins.com/ everythingsanargument/catalog

You have a lot to do in your course. Bedford/St. Martin's wants to make it easy for you to find the support you need—and to get it quickly.

Instructor's Notes for Everything's an Argument is available in PDF format that can be downloaded from the Bedford/St. Martin's online catalog or the *Student Center*. For each chapter in the text, the *Instructor's Notes* outlines some of the challenges you might face while teaching the chapter, suggests solutions, and provides answers and teaching suggestions for the chapter exercises, ending with ideas for extending those exercises beyond the text.

TeachingCentral offers the entire list of Bedford/St. Martin's print and online professional resources in one place. You'll find landmark reference works, sourcebooks on pedagogical issues, award-winning collections, and practical advice for the classroom—all free for instructors.

Bits collects creative ideas for teaching a range of composition topics in an easily searchable blog. A community of teachers—leading scholars, authors, and editors—discuss revision, research, grammar and style, technology, peer review, and much more. Take, use, adapt, and pass the ideas around. Then, come back to the site to comment or share your own suggestion.

Content cartridges for the most common course management systems—Blackboard, WebCT, Angel, and Desire2Learn—allow you to easily download Bedford/St. Martin's digital materials for your course.

Even More Options for Students

Add more value and flexibility to your textbook with one of the following resources, free when packaged with *Everything's an Argument*. To learn more about package options or any of the products below, contact your Bedford/St. Martin's sales representative or visit the Web site at bedfordstmartins.com/everythingsanargument/catalog.

i•series on CD-ROM includes multimedia tutorials in a flexible CD-ROM format—because there are things you can't do in a book.

- *ix visual exercises* helps students visualize and put into practice key rhetorical and visual concepts.

- *i•claim visualizing argument* offers a new way to see argument—with six tutorials, an illustrated glossary, and over seventy multimedia arguments.

- *i•cite visualizing sources* brings research to life through an animated introduction, four tutorials, and hands-on source practice.

Acknowledgments

We owe a debt of gratitude to many people for making *Everything's an Argument* possible. Our first thanks must go to the students we have taught in our writing courses for nearly four decades, particularly first-year students at the Ohio State University, Stanford University, and the

University of Texas at Austin. Almost every chapter in this book has been informed by a classroom encounter with a student whose shrewd observation or perceptive question sent an ambitious lesson plan spiraling to the ground. (Anyone who has tried to teach claims and warrants on the fly to skeptical first-year students will surely appreciate why we have qualified our claims in the Toulmin chapter so carefully.) But students have also provided the motive for writing this book. More than ever, they need to know how to read and write arguments effectively if they are to secure a place in a world growing ever smaller and more rhetorically challenging.

We are grateful to our editors at Bedford/St. Martin's who contributed their talents to our book, beginning with Joan Feinberg, who has enthusiastically supported the project and provided us with the resources and feedback needed to keep us on track. Most of the day-to-day work on the project has been handled by the ever patient, perceptive, and good-humored John Elliott. We said this in the last edition, but the claim remains as true as ever: he prevented more than a few lapses of judgment yet understands the spirit of this book—which involves, occasionally, taking risks to make a memorable point. We have appreciated, too, his meticulous line editing as well as his ability to find just the right example when we were struggling to do so.

We are similarly grateful to others at Bedford/St. Martin's who contributed their talents to our book: Kristin Bowen, senior development editor; Jessica Skrocki Gould, project editor; Nancy Myers, senior production supervisor; Lucy Krikorian, art director; Molly Parke, marketing manager; Sue McDermott Barlow, art researcher; Rosemary Winfield, copyeditor; and Cecilia Seiter, editorial assistant.

We'd also like to thank the astute instructors and students who reviewed the fourth edition: Kristin Arola, Washington State University; Diann L. Baecker, Virginia State University; Amy Becker-Chambless, University of Texas Pan-American; Julia Bleakney, Saddleback College; Lois Lake Church, Southern Connecticut State University; Chris Diller, Berry College; Karen R. Dwyer, Arizona State University; Katherine Gossett, Old Dominion University; April Green, University of Tennessee, Chattanooga; Judith Griffith, Wartburg College; Kim Gunter, University of North Carolina, Pembroke; Heather Hoyt, Arizona State University; Gregory Johnson, Kennesaw State University; Dana Kinnison, University of Missouri; Joy Langford, Blinn College; Sonja Lynch, Wartburg College; Linda Macri, University of Maryland; Eric Mason, Nova Southeastern

University; Mary Ellen Muesing, University of North Carolina, Charlotte; Kathryn Pitrone, Lakeland Community College; Jeff Rice, University of Missouri; and Jacqueline Wheeler, Arizona State University.

Thanks, too, to Keith Walters, our coauthor for *Everything's an Argument with Readings*, who contributed many useful suggestions in the drafting of the new "Academic Arguments" chapter, and to John Kinkade, who once again has prepared the instructor's notes for this fifth edition. Finally, we are grateful to the students whose fine argumentative essays appear in our chapters: Milena Ateya, Claire Liu, Michael Osofsky, Sayoh Mansaray, Jack Chung, Lia Hardin, and Manasi Deshpande.

We hope that *Everything's an Argument* responds to what students and instructors have said they want and need. And we hope readers of this text will let us know how we've done: please share your opinions and suggestions with us at bedfordstmartins.com/everythingsanargument.

Andrea A. Lunsford

John J. Ruszkiewicz

CONTENTS

Preface   *v*

Part 1:
Reading Arguments   1

1.   Everything Is an Argument   3

Purposes of Argument   *5*

NOT JUST WORDS   *6*

Arguments to Inform   *8*
Arguments to Convince   *9*
Arguments to Persuade   *10*
Arguments to Explore   *11*
Arguments to Make Decisions   *12*
Arguments to Meditate or Pray   *14*
Academic Arguments   *15*

Occasions for Argument   *15*

Arguments about the Past   *16*
Arguments about the Future   *17*
Arguments about the Present   *18*

Kinds of Argument   *21*

Did Something Happen? Arguments of Fact   *21*
What Is the Nature of the Thing? Arguments of Definition   *22*
What Is the Quality or Cause of the Thing? Arguments of Evaluation
and Causality   *23*
What Actions Should Be Taken? Proposal Arguments   *25*

STASIS QUESTIONS AT WORK *26*

Audiences for Arguments *27*
Considering Contexts *30*

CULTURAL CONTEXTS FOR ARGUMENT *32*

Appealing to Audiences *33*
Emotional Appeals: Pathos *33*
Ethical Appeals: Ethos *34*
Logical Appeals: Logos *34*
Arguments and Their Rhetorical Situations *35*

Respond *36*

2. **Arguments Based on Emotion: Pathos** 38
Understanding How Emotional Arguments Work *40*

NOT JUST WORDS *43*

Using Emotions to Build Bridges *44*
Using Emotions to Sustain an Argument *46*
Using Humor *48*
Using Arguments Based on Emotion *50*
Respond *51*

3. **Arguments Based on Character: Ethos** 52

NOT JUST WORDS *54*

Understanding How Arguments Based on Character Work *57*
Claiming Authority *57*
Establishing Credibility *59*

CULTURAL CONTEXTS FOR ARGUMENT *64*

Coming Clean about Motives *65*
Respond *67*

4. Arguments Based on Facts and Reason: Logos 69

NOT JUST WORDS 71

Providing Hard Evidence 73
  Facts 76
  Statistics 78
  Surveys and Polls 79
  Testimonies and Narratives 82

Using Reason and Common Sense 84
  Cultural Assumptions and Values 87

Providing Logical Structures for Argument 88
  Degree 88
  Analogies 90
  Precedent 91
Respond 93

5. Rhetorical Analysis 95

Composing a Rhetorical Analysis 97
Understanding the Purpose of Arguments You Are Analyzing 99
Understanding Who Makes an Argument 99
Identifying and Appealing to Audiences 101
Examining Arguments Based on Emotion: Pathos 103
Examining Arguments Based on Character: Ethos 105
Examining Arguments Based on Facts and Reason: Logos 107
Examining the Arrangement and Media of Arguments 109
Looking at Style 111

NOT JUST WORDS 112

Examining a Rhetorical Analysis 117
  Derek Bok, *Protecting Freedom of Expression at Harvard* 118
  Milena Ateya, *A Curse and a Blessing* (student essay) 121

GUIDE TO WRITING A RHETORICAL ANALYSIS 124

Respond 130

Part 2:
Writing Arguments 131

6. Academic Arguments 133

Understanding What Academic Argument Is *133*

NOT JUST WORDS *140*

Developing an Academic Argument *141*
Respond *147*

Two Sample Academic Arguments *150*
Claire Liu, *Music in U.S.-China Diplomacy* (student essay) *150*
Lan Xue, *China: The Prizes and Pitfalls of Progress* *164*

7. Structuring Arguments 170

The Classical Oration *172*

Rogerian Argument *176*

NOT JUST WORDS *181*

Toulmin Argument *182*
Making Claims *182*
Offering Evidence and Good Reasons *184*
Determining Warrants *186*
Offering Evidence: Backing *192*
Using Qualifiers *194*
Understanding Conditions of Rebuttal *196*
Outline of a Toulmin Argument *199*
A Toulmin Analysis *200*
Alan M. Dershowitz, *Testing Speech Codes* *201*
What Toulmin Teaches *204*

CULTURAL CONTEXTS FOR ARGUMENT *205*

Respond *206*

8. Arguments of Fact 208

Understanding Arguments of Fact *209*

NOT JUST WORDS *214*

Characterizing Factual Arguments *215*
Developing a Factual Argument *217*
Identifying an Issue *218*

FACTS AND ACADEMIC ARGUMENTS *220*

Researching Your Hypothesis *220*
Refining Your Claim *221*
Deciding Which Evidence to Use *223*
Presenting Your Evidence *225*

Considering Design and Visuals *226*

Key Features of Factual Arguments *227*

GUIDE TO WRITING AN ARGUMENT OF FACT *229*

Respond *234*

Two Sample Factual Arguments *236*
Michael Osofsky, *The Psychological Experience of Security Officers Who Work with Executions* (student essay) *236*
Jess Henig and Lori Robertson, *What Is a Civil Union?* *243*

9. Arguments of Definition 249

Understanding Arguments of Definition *250*

NOT JUST WORDS *254*

Kinds of Definition *256*
Formal Definitions *256*
Operational Definitions *257*
Definitions by Example *258*
Other Issues of Definition *259*

Developing a Definitional Argument *260*
Formulating Claims *260*

DEFINITIONS AND ACADEMIC ARGUMENTS *261*

Crafting Definitions *263*
Matching Claims to Definitions *264*
Considering Design and Visuals *265*

Key Features of Definitional Arguments *265*

GUIDE TO WRITING AN ARGUMENT OF DEFINITION *268*

Respond *274*

Two Sample Definitional Arguments *276*
Sayoh Mansaray, *The Offbeat Allure of Cult Films*
(student essay) *276*
Lynn Peril, *Pink Think* *280*

10. Evaluations *284*

Understanding Evaluations *285*

EVALUATIONS AND ACADEMIC ARGUMENTS *288*

Criteria of Evaluation *289*
Characterizing Evaluation *292*
Quantitative Evaluations *293*
Qualitative Evaluations *293*

NOT JUST WORDS *294*

Developing an Evaluative Argument *297*
Formulating Criteria *297*
Making Claims *300*
Presenting Evidence *301*
Considering Design and Visuals *302*

Key Features of Evaluations *304*

GUIDE TO WRITING AN EVALUATION *305*

Respond *311*

Two Sample Evaluations *313*
Jack Chung, *The Burden of Laughter: Chris Rock Fights Ignorance
His Way* (student essay) *313*
Tom Hodgkinson, *With Friends Like These . . .* *326*

11. Causal Arguments 335

Understanding Causal Arguments *336*
Characterizing Causal Arguments *342*

CAUSAL CLAIMS AND ACADEMIC ARGUMENTS *343*

NOT JUST WORDS *346*

Developing Causal Arguments *348*
Formulating a Claim *348*
Developing the Argument *350*
Considering Design and Visuals *354*

Key Features of Causal Arguments *356*

GUIDE TO WRITING A CAUSAL ARGUMENT *357*

Respond *363*

Two Sample Causal Arguments *365*
Lia Hardin, *Cultural Stress Linked to Suicide* (student essay) *365*
Elisabeth Rosenthal, *Stinging Tentacles Offer Hint of Oceans' Decline* *369*

12. Proposals 373

Understanding and Categorizing Proposals *374*
Characterizing Proposals *378*
Developing Proposals *380*
Defining a Need or Problem *381*
Making a Strong and Clear Claim *383*
Showing That the Proposal Addresses the Need or Problem *384*

PROPOSALS AND ACADEMIC ARGUMENT *386*

Showing That the Proposal Is Feasible *387*
Using Personal Experience *387*
Considering Design and Visuals *388*

Key Features of Proposals *389*

NOT JUST WORDS *390*

GUIDE TO WRITING A PROPOSAL *392*

Respond *398*

Two Sample Proposals *399*
Manasi Deshpande, *A Call to Improve Campus Accessibility for the Mobility Impaired* (student essay) *399*
Michael Benson, *Send It Somewhere Special* *411*

Part 3: Style and Presentation in Arguments 415

13. **Style in Arguments** 417

Style and Word Choice *418*

NOT JUST WORDS *420*

Sentence Structure and Argument *421*
Punctuation and Argument *423*
Special Effects: Figurative Language and Argument *426*
Tropes *428*

CULTURAL CONTEXTS FOR ARGUMENT *432*

Schemes *437*
Respond *439*

14. **Visual Arguments** 441

The Power of Visual Arguments *442*

NOT JUST WORDS *445*

Shaping the Message *446*
Analyzing Visual Elements of Arguments *446*

Using Visuals in Your Own Arguments *451*
  Visual Arguments That Appeal to Emotion *452*
  Visual Arguments Based on Character *455*
  Visual Arguments Based on Facts and Reason *459*
Respond *463*

15. Presenting Arguments 466

Print Presentations *467*
Oral and Multimedia Presentations *468*
  Oral Arguments in Discussions *468*

  NOT JUST WORDS *469*

  CULTURAL CONTEXTS FOR ARGUMENT *470*

  Formal Oral and Multimedia Presentations *470*
  Arguments to Be Heard *471*
  Arguments to Be Remembered *475*
  The Role of Visuals in Oral and Multimedia Arguments *476*
  Some Oral and Multimedia Presentation Strategies *484*
  A Note about Webcasts: Live Presentations
  over the Web *485*
Web-Based Presentations *486*
  Web Sites *486*
  Blogs *488*
Respond *489*

Part 4:
Conventions of Argument 491

16. What Counts as Evidence 493

Evidence and the Rhetorical Situation *494*
Firsthand Evidence and Research *496*

Observations   *496*
Interviews   *498*
Surveys and Questionnaires   *500*
Experiments   *502*
Personal Experience   *503*

CULTURAL CONTEXTS FOR ARGUMENT   *504*

Secondhand Evidence and Research   *505*
Library Sources   *505*

NOT JUST WORDS   *506*

Online Sources   *509*

Using Evidence Effectively   *510*

CULTURAL CONTEXTS FOR ARGUMENT   *510*

Considering Audiences   *511*
Building a Critical Mass   *512*
Arranging Evidence   *513*

Respond   *513*

17.   **Fallacies of Argument**   515

Fallacies of Emotional Argument   *516*
Scare Tactics   *517*
Either-Or Choices   *517*

NOT JUST WORDS   *519*

Slippery Slope   *520*
Sentimental Appeals   *521*
Bandwagon Appeals   *522*

Fallacies of Ethical Argument   *523*
Appeals to False Authority   *523*
Dogmatism   *524*
Ad Hominem Arguments   *525*

Fallacies of Logical Argument   *526*
Hasty Generalization   *526*
Faulty Causality   *527*

Begging the Question   *529*
Equivocation   *530*
Non Sequitur   *531*
The Straw Man   *532*
Faulty Analogy   *533*
Respond   *534*

18. Intellectual Property, Academic Integrity, and Avoiding Plagiarism   536

Crediting Sources in Arguments   *537*
Citing Sources and Recognizing Plagiarism   *538*
Inaccurate or Incomplete Citation of Sources   *539*

NOT JUST WORDS   *540*

Acknowledging Your Use of Sources   *544*
Using Copyrighted Internet Sources   *545*

CULTURAL CONTEXTS FOR ARGUMENT   *547*

Acknowledging Collaboration   *547*
Respond   *548*

19. Evaluating and Using Sources   549

Evaluating Sources   *551*
Print Sources   *551*
Electronic Sources   *553*
Field Research   *555*

Using Sources   *555*
Signal Words and Introductions   *556*
Quotations   *557*

NOT JUST WORDS   *558*

Paraphrases   *561*

Summaries   *562*

CULTURAL CONTEXTS FOR ARGUMENT   *563*

Visuals   *563*

Respond   *565*

20. Documenting Sources   566

MLA Style   *567*

In-Text Citations   *567*

Explanatory and Bibliographic Notes   *571*

List of Works Cited   *572*

Sample First Page for an Essay in MLA Style   *584*

Sample List of Works Cited for an Essay in MLA Style   *585*

NOT JUST WORDS   *586*

APA Style   *587*

In-Text Citations   *587*

Content Notes   *590*

List of References   *590*

Respond   *598*

Glossary   *599*

Acknowledgments   *609*

Index   *615*

everything's an argument

PART 1

READING arguments

1
Everything Is
an Argument

On January 30, 2005, when Iraqis voted for the first time following the fall of Saddam Hussein, photographs of proud citizens brandishing fingers dyed purple to prevent double-balloting flashed around the world. The raised purple digits were variously interpreted as gestures of support for democracy, defiance to terrorist threats, or even resistance to U.S. occupation.

On June 27, 2008, voters in Zimbabwe went to the polls to vote for a single candidate on a run-off ballot for president—the incumbent Robert Mugabe, who was widely regarded as the loser of the initial balloting. Now Mugabe was forcing his way into yet another term by a corrupt and violent election. If Zimbabweans voted, their fingers were dyed red. If they dared to resist, they faced consequences at the hands of government agents. So when photographs of fingers were again sent around the world, this time they made different and more somber arguments from those of the Iraqis in 2005. But they did make arguments, some of which could be spoken only outside the African dictatorship.

The caption to this image from the *New York Times* made a clear claim about the Zimbabwean election: "Some people said they feared punishment or even death unless they could produce a finger colored by red ink as evidence they had cast their ballot."

You already know that raised fingers can make statements. But so can many other images, gestures, and activities that you take for granted. There may be an argument on the T-shirt you don in the morning, in the sports column you read on the bus, in the prayers you utter before a quiz, in the off-the-cuff political remarks of a teacher lecturing, even in the assurances of a health center nurse that "this won't hurt one bit."

The clothes you wear, the foods you eat, and the groups you join are everyday things that make nuanced, sometimes unspoken arguments about who you are and what you value. So an argument can be any text—written, spoken, or visual—that expresses a point of view. Sometimes arguments can be blunt and aggressive and are composed deliberately to change what people believe, think, or do. At other times, your goals may be subtler, and your writing is designed to convince yourself or others that specific facts are reliable or that certain views should be considered—or at least tolerated.

In fact, some theorists claim that language is itself inherently persuasive and hence that every text is also an argument that is designed to influence readers. (When you say "Hi, how's it going?," for instance, in one sense you're arguing that your hello deserves a response.) Even humor makes an argument when it causes readers to recognize—through bursts of laughter or just a faint smile—how things are and how they might be different.

More obvious as arguments are those that make a direct claim based on or drawn from evidence. Such writing often moves readers to recognize problems and to consider solutions. Persuasion of this kind is usually easy to recognize:

> A country that displays an almost ruthless commitment to efficiency and performance in every aspect of its economy—a country that switched to Japanese cars the moment they were more reliable, and to Chinese T-shirts the moment they were five cents cheaper—has loyally stuck with a health-care system that leaves its citizenry pulling out their teeth with pliers.
> —Malcolm Gladwell, "The Moral Hazard Myth"

> [W]omen unhappy in their marriages often enter full-time employment as an escape. But although a woman's entrance into the workplace does tend to increase the stability of her marriage, it does not increase her happiness.
> —The Popular Research Institute, Penn State University

> We will become a society of a million pictures without much memory, a society that looks forward every second to an immediate replication of what it has just done, but one that does not sustain the difficult labor of transmitting culture from one generation to the next.
> —Christine Rosen, "The Image Culture"

Purposes of Argument

Although in some ways all language has an argumentative edge that aims to make a point, not all language use aims to win out over others. In contrast to the traditional Western concept of argument as being about disputation or combat, communication theorists such as Sonja Foss, Cindy Griffin, and Josina Makau describe an invitational argument, the kind that aims not to defeat another person or group but to invite others to enter a space of mutual regard and exploration. In fact, as you'll see, writers and speakers have as many purposes for arguing as for using language, including—in addition to winning—to inform, to convince, to explore, to make decisions, and even to meditate or pray.

Not Just Words

Can something as innocuous as a hoodie branded with your school's logo be an argument? And would it make a difference if that apparel were being sold by Victoria's Secret—as is the Arizona State item shown here? Spend some time working with one other student in your class to analyze the argument that a branded piece of clothing like this might make. Then write a paragraph that elaborates on that claim.

Of course, many arguments *are* aimed at winning. Such is the purpose of much writing and speaking in the political arena, business world, and law courts. Two candidates for office, for example, vie for a majority of votes; the makers of one soft drink try to outsell their competitors by appealing to public tastes; and two lawyers try to outwit each other in pleading to a judge and jury. In your college writing, you may also be called on to make an argument that appeals to a "judge" and "jury" (your instructor and classmates). You might, for instance, argue that peer-to-peer music file sharing is legal because of the established legal precedent of fair use. In doing so, you may need to defeat your unseen opponents—those who regard such file sharing as theft.

At this point, it may help to acknowledge a common academic distinction between argument and persuasion. In this view, the point of *argument* is to use evidence and reason to discover some version of the truth. Argument of this sort leads audiences toward conviction—an agreement that a claim is true or reasonable or that a course of action is desirable. The aim of *persuasion* is to change a point of view or to move others from conviction to action. In other words, writers or speakers argue to discover some truth; they persuade when they think they already know it.

In practice, this distinction between argument and persuasion can be hard to maintain. It's unnatural for writers or readers to imagine their minds divided between a part that pursues truth and a part that seeks to persuade. And yet you may want to reserve the term *persuasion* for writing that's aggressively designed to change opinions through the use of reason and other appropriate techniques. For writing that sets out to persuade at all costs—abandoning reason, fairness, and truth altogether—the term *propaganda* (with all its negative connotations) is often used. Some suggest that the term *advertising* often works just as well.

As we've already suggested, arguing isn't always about winning or even about changing others' views. In addition to invitational argument, another school of argument—called *Rogerian argument* (after the psychotherapist Carl Rogers)—is based on approaching audiences in nonthreatening ways and on finding common ground and establishing trust among those who disagree about issues. Writers who follow Rogerian approaches seek to understand the perspectives of those with whom they disagree, looking for "both/and" or "win/win" solutions (rather than "either/or" or "win/lose" ones) whenever possible. Many writers of successful arguments today follow such principles, whether consciously or not (for more on Rogerian strategies, see Chapter 7).

The risks of Rogerian argument.

"You say it's a win–win, but what if you're wrong–wrong and it all goes bad–bad?"

Some other purposes or goals of argument are worth considering in more detail.

Arguments to Inform

Many arguments—including street signs, notices of meetings, and newspaper headlines—may not seem especially "argumentative" because their main purpose is to tell members of an audience something they didn't know. Other informative arguments are more obviously designed to persuade. For example, an essential step in selling anything, especially something new, is to advise customers that it exists. The classic poster announcing the first *Batman* film in 1989 carried only two words: *June 23.* Political campaigns can be comparably blunt. Think of all the bumper stickers you've seen that merely identify a candidate, an office, and maybe a year: "Obama '08," "Jindal 2012." Such simple arguments

give a candidate "name recognition" by telling voters
who is available for an
office.

Arguments to Convince

As a form of argument,
many reports, white papers,
and academic articles typically aim to convince readers rather than win out over
opponents. For instance, if
you are writing a report on
the safety record of nuclear
plants for a college course,
you would likely present
evidence to demonstrate to
general readers (including
an instructor and fellow
students) that the issue
merited their attention. You
would not likely expect to
win over activist partisans

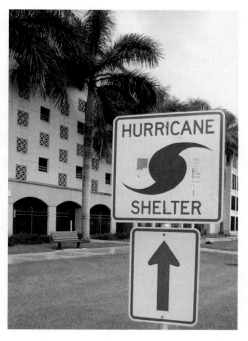

A visual argument to inform in Key West, Florida

who already reject atomic power as an energy alternative. Yet the presence of those who might disagree is always implied in an argument, and
it inevitably shapes a writer's strategies. In the following passage, for
example, controversial political scientist Charles Murray uses intelligence quotient (IQ) correlations to raise questions about higher education that many readers of the *Wall Street Journal*, where his article
appeared, may find troubling:

> There is no magic point at which a genuine college-level education
> becomes an option, but anything below an IQ of 110 is problematic. If
> you want to do well, you should have an IQ of 115 or higher. Put
> another way, it makes sense for only about 15% of the population, 25%
> if one stretches it, to get a college education.
>
> —Charles Murray, "What's Wrong with Vocational School?"

Murray uses numbers to draw a seemingly objective conclusion about
who should attend college, hoping to convince some readers to consider

In an argument to convince, opponents' viewpoints aren't addressed directly, but they are always implied ("Hold the electricity." "No toaster.").

RUDY PARK   **BY DARRIN BELL & THERON HEIR**

RUDY PARK: © Darrin Bell and Theron Heir/Dist. by United Feature Syndicate, Inc.

his point. But he's also arguing against those—perhaps a majority of his audience—who prefer to believe that higher education should be encouraged for all.

Arguments to Persuade

In many situations, writers unabashedly want to move audiences enough to provoke action, whether that involves buying a product, voting for a candidate, or supporting a policy. Advertisements, political blogs, and newspaper editorials use all the devices of rhetoric to motivate action, produce change, or win a point. Here Daniel Ben-Ami drives home his argument at the conclusion of a long essay on the London-based Web site Spike examining "Why people hate fat Americans":

> By focusing on fat Americans the critics of consumption are saying, implicitly at least, that people should consume less. They are arguing for a world in which Americans become more like those who live in the poorer countries of the world. From such a perspective equality means levelling everyone down rather than raising the living standards of the poor. It means giving up on the battle to resist hurricanes or to reclaim land from the sea.
>
> Yet implementing such a viewpoint is a super-size mistake. Our aspiration for the world should be to give the poor the advantages of

affluence enjoyed by those in the West. Living standards in countries such as Ethiopia and Niger should be, at the very least, as high as those in America today. In that sense we should all aim to be fat Americans.

In these two paragraphs, Ben-Ami dramatizes his point by balance and repetition in the structure of his sentences, by reminders in the final paragraph of poverty in Ethiopia and Niger, and by a final ironic call for others to grow as fat as Americans. With these rhetorical moves, he pushes the lengthy article from analysis toward action, which is typical of most persuasive writing.

Arguments to Explore

Many important subjects call for arguments that take the form of exploration. If there's an "opponent" in such a situation at all (often there is not), it's likely the status quo or a current trend that—for one reason or another—is puzzling. Exploratory arguments may be deeply personal, such as E. B. White's often reprinted essay "Once More to the Lake," in which the author's return with his young son to a vacation spot from his own childhood leads him to reflect on time, memory, and mortality. Or the exploration may be aimed at addressing serious problems in society. Writing in 2005, James Fallows presciently explored what he saw as "America's coming economic crisis" by projecting himself forward to the election of 2016—and then looking back to speculate on what might happen between 2005 and 2016. Along the way, he considered changes that might occur in education:

> . . . we could have shored up our universities. True, the big change came as early as 2002, in the wake of 9/11, when tighter visa rules . . . cut off the flow of foreign talent that American universities had channeled to American ends. In the summer of 2007 China applied the name "twenty Harvards" to its ambition, announced in the early 2000s, to build major research institutions that would attract international talent. It seemed preposterous (too much political control, too great a language barrier), but no one is laughing now. . . . The Historic Campus of our best-known university, Harvard, is still prestigious worldwide. But its role is increasingly that of the theme park, like Oxford or Heidelberg, while the most ambitious students compete for fellowships at the Har-Bai and Har-Bei campuses in Mumbai and Beijing.
>
> —James Fallows, "Countdown to a Meltdown"

A student from India chats with one from Romania at the University of Nottingham, England. Since 9/11, the United States has been issuing fewer visas to international students; as a result, these students are increasingly enrolling in non-American universities.

Perhaps the essential argument in any such piece is the writer's assertion that a problem exists (in this case, the damage that tighter visa rules do to American economic competitiveness) and that the writer or reader needs to solve it.

Arguments to Make Decisions

Closely allied to argument that explores is argument that aims at making good, sound decisions. In fact, the result of many exploratory arguments may be to argue for a particular decision, whether that decision relates to the best career path to follow in a tight economy or the "right" person to choose as your life partner. For college students, choosing a major is a momentous decision, and one way to go about making that decision is to argue your way through several alternatives in your own mind as well as with friends, colleagues, and even your parents. By the time you've examined the pros and cons of each alternative, you should be a little closer to a good decision.

Arguments to make decisions occur all the time in the public arena, as well. In a college essay, Elizabeth Wong explored the pros and cons of extending copyright protection to designers of apparel who wanted protection from fashion pirates and knock-off artists. But Wong came down on the opposing side, deciding that the 2007 legislation would do more harm than good. Here's a passage from her paper that makes that point:

> If this act is passed, it opens the floor for legal battles of designer against designer. The larger names, like Chanel or Louis Vuitton, will be able to hire endless lawyers and consultants to take care of these cases for them. But what is the young and struggling designer to do? If someone were to sue him, he would not likely have the resources to hire a legal team and fight the suit. Money aside, young designers simply do not have the time for lawsuits. While more established designers often have teams of design assistants doing the work, a new designer has to keep up with the grueling fashion cycle almost completely alone. With younger designers put in jeopardy by the threat of lawsuits, the field of design would narrow, and fashion itself would suffer. In this situation, the industry doesn't profit; the lawyers do.
>
> —Elizabeth Wong, "Unnecessary Precaution: Extending Copyright to Fashion Design"

You probably know that people make and sell cheap knock-offs of Louis Vuitton's high-fashion handbags, shoes, and accesssories. But a designer pretending to be a knock-off artist? Model Eva Herzigova and designer Marc Jacobs examine real Vuitton bags at a party space made up to look like a stall selling counterfeit luxury goods. What argument might this peculiar shopping space make?

Arguments to Meditate or Pray

Sometimes arguments can take the form of prayer or intense meditations on a theme. In such cases, the writer or speaker is most often hoping to transform something in him- or herself or to reach a state of
equilibrium or peace of mind. If you know a familiar prayer or mantra,
think for a moment of what it "argues" for and how it uses quiet medita-
tion to accomplish that goal. Such meditations don't have to be formal
prayers, however. Look, for example, at an excerpt from Michael Lassell's
poem "How to Watch Your Brother Die." This poem, which evokes the
confusing emotions of a man during the death of his gay brother, uses a
kind of meditative language that allows the reader to reach an understanding of the speaker and to evoke meditative thought in others:

> Feel how it feels to hold a man in your arms
> whose arms are used to holding men.
> Offer God anything to bring your brother back.
> Know you have nothing God could possibly want.
> Curse God, but do not
> abandon Him.
>
> —Michael Lassell, "How to Watch Your Brother Die"

The Tree of Jesse window in France's Chartres Cathedral

Another sort of meditative argument can be found in the stained-glass windows of churches and other public buildings. Dazzled by a spectacle of light, people pause to consider a window's message longer than they might if the same idea were conveyed on paper. The window engages viewers with a power not unlike that of poetry.

Academic Arguments

To the public, describing an argument as "academic" usually means it's pointless, endless, arcane, or silly. If you've written one too many research papers, you may feel the same. But an academic argument is simply one that is held to the standards of a professional field or discipline, such as psychology, engineering, political science, or English. It is an argument presented to knowledgeable people by writers who are striving to make an honest case that is based on the best information and research available, with all of its sources carefully documented. Though we'll examine all types of arguments in this book, we'll focus on the kinds that you'll make in professional and academic situations. Such arguments typically follow patterns that are defined by their disciplines (consider the research paper again or journal articles you have read) and adhere to precise standards for handling evidence. As you'll see, the style of academic writing also tends to be more formal and impersonal than arguments in the public arena, but there are exceptions. For more about academic writing, see Chapter 6.

Occasions for Argument

Another way of thinking about arguments is to identify the public occasions that call for them. In an ancient textbook of *rhetoric* (the art of persuasion), the philosopher Aristotle provides an elegant scheme for classifying the purposes of arguments. His formula is based on issues of time—past, future, and present. It is easy to remember and helpful in its strategies for making convincing cases. But because all classifications overlap with others to a certain extent, don't be surprised to encounter many arguments that span more than one category—arguments about the past with implications for the future, arguments about the future with bearings on the present, and so on.

Arguments about the Past

Debates about what has happened in the past are called *forensic arguments*; such controversies are common in business, government, and academia. For example, in many criminal and civil cases, lawyers interrogate witnesses to establish exactly what happened at an earlier time: *Did the defendant sexually harass her employee? Did the company deliberately ignore evidence that its product was deficient? Was the contract properly enforced?* The contentious nature of some forensic arguments is evident in this excerpt from a letter to the editor of the *Atlantic Monthly*:

> Robert Bryce's article on the U.S. military's gas consumption in Iraq ("Gas Pains," May *Atlantic*) is factually inaccurate, tactically misguided, and a classic case of a red herring.
> —Captain David J. Morris

In replying to this letter, the author of the article, Robert Bryce, disputes Morris's statements, introducing more evidence in support of his original claim. Forensic arguments rely on evidence and testimony to recreate what can be known about events that have already occurred.

Forensic arguments also rely heavily on precedents—actions or decisions in the past that influence policies or decisions in the present—and on analyses of cause and effect. Consider the ongoing controversy over Christopher Columbus: are his expeditions to the Americas events worth celebrating, or are they unhappy chapters in human history—or a mixture of both? No simple exchange of evidence will suffice to still this debate; the effects of Columbus's actions beginning in 1492 may be studied and debated for the next five hundred years. As you might suspect from this example, arguments about history are typically forensic.

Forensic cases may also be arguments about character, such as when someone's reputation is studied in a historical context to enrich current perspectives on the person. Allusions to the past can make present arguments more vivid, as in the following selection from an essay about the reputation of Ernesto ("Che") Guevara, an Argentinian Marxist who aided several Latin American revolutions in the 1960s and whose image still appears across the globe:

> Rebels and activists the world over still take inspiration from Guevara. But the image has lost something; Che's face on a poster in 1968 isn't quite the same thing as it is on a mousepad 40 years later. Perhaps it is precisely that loss—the shedding of Che's radicalism and ideological rigor—that renders him so supremely marketable today. Things

Theodor de Bry's 1594 engraving tells one version of the Christopher Columbus story.

are not going well these days. Kids don't want revolution so much as, um, something different.
　　　　　　　—Ben Ehrenreich, "Capitalizing on Che Guevara's Image"

Such writing can be exploratory and open-ended, the point of argument being to enhance and sharpen knowledge, not just to generate heat or score points.

Arguments about the Future

Debates about what will or should happen in the future are called *delib-erative arguments*. Legislatures, congresses, and parliaments are called *deliberative bodies* because they establish policies for the future: *Should two people of the same sex be allowed to marry? Should the U.S. Treasury Department bail out failing banks and businesses in times of economic chaos?* Because what has happened in the past influences the future, delibera-tive judgments often rely on prior forensic arguments. Thus, deliberative arguments routinely draw on data and testimony, as in this passage from a college essay using precedents from the United Kingdom to argue for a system of national health care in the United States:

> Studies have long proven preventive health care to be more cost-effective than simply treating illnesses as they appear. According to Andrew Light, "starting in 1990, the [British] government added a new element to the [general practitioner] contract—lump sums or bonuses for carrying out preventive measures on a high percentage of the patient panel" (26). This policy has resulted in a high number of preventive measures being taken in the UK and a reduction in overall illness. So in addition to the cost benefits, more UK citizens do not have to be treated for cancer, heart-conditions, and any number of illnesses that can be prevented with vaccines.
>
> —Ryan Thomas, "The Critical Condition of Health Care"

But since no one has a blueprint for what's to come, deliberative arguments also advance by means of projections, extrapolations, and reasoned guesses (If X is true, then Y may be true; if X happens, then so may Y; if X continues, then Y may occur):

> In 2000, according to a World Health Organization assessment, 1.1 billion people worldwide had no regular access to safe drinking water, and 2.4 billion had no regular access to sanitation systems. Lack of access to clean water leads to four billion cases of diarrhea each year. Peter Gleick, an expert on global freshwater resources, reveals that even if we reach the United Nations' stated goal of halving the number of people without access to safe drinking water by 2015, as many as 76 million people will die from water-borne diseases before 2020.
>
> —Pacific Institute for Studies in Development, Environment, and Security

Arguments about the Present

Arguments about the present are often arguments about contemporary values—that is, the beliefs and assumptions that are widely held (or debated) within a society. Sometimes called *epideictic arguments* or *ceremonial arguments* because they tend to be heard at public occasions, they include inaugural addresses, sermons, eulogies, graduation speeches, and civic remarks of all kinds. Ceremonial arguments can be passionate and eloquent, rich in anecdotes and metaphor. President Ronald Reagan was a master of ceremonial discourse, and he was particularly adept at defining the core values of the American way of life:

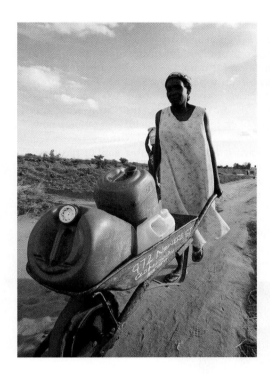

A woman carries drums of water from a well that has been a major source of cholera in Harare, Zimbabwe. Proposals to protect and clean up the world's water supply are a common form of deliberative argument by international organizations like the United Nations.

Ours was the first revolution in the history of mankind that truly reversed the course of government, and with three little words: "We the people." "We the people" tell the government what to do, it doesn't tell us. "We the people" are the driver, the government is the car. And we decide where it should go, and by what route, and how fast. Almost all the world's constitutions are documents in which governments tell the people what their privileges are. Our Constitution is a document in which "We the people" tell the government what it is allowed to do.
—Ronald Reagan, "Farewell Address"

Reagan directs the American people to the founding documents of the nation to find their values. But not all ceremonial arguments reach quite this far. More typical are values arguments that explore contemporary culture, praising what's admirable and blaming what's not. In the following argument, student Latisha Chisholm looks at rap after Tupac Shakur—and doesn't like what she sees:

When I think about how rap music has changed, I generally associate the demise of my appreciation for the industry with the death of Tupac. With his death, not only did one of the most intriguing rap rivalries of all time die, but the motivation for rapping seems to have changed. Where money had always been a plus, now it is obviously more important than wanting to express the hardships of Black communities. With current rappers, the positive power that came from the desire to represent Black people is lost. One of the biggest rappers now got his big break while talking about sneakers. Others announce retirement without really having done much for the soul or for Black people's morale. I equate new rappers to NFL players that don't love the game anymore. They're only in it for the money. . . . It looks like the voice of a people has lost its heart.

—Latisha Chisholm, "Has Rap Lost Its Soul?"

As in many ceremonial arguments, Chisholm here reinforces common values such as representing one's community honorably and fairly.

Are rappers since Tupac Shakur only in it for the money? Many epideictic arguments find fault with contemporary culture.

Kinds of Argument

Yet another way of categorizing arguments is to consider their status or stasis—that is, the kinds of issues they address. This categorization system is called *stasis theory*. In ancient Greek and Roman civilizations, rhetoricians defined a series of questions by which to examine legal cases. The questions would be posed in sequence because each depended on the question(s) preceding it. Together, the questions helped determine the point of contention in an argument, the place where disputants could focus their energy, and hence the kind of argument they should make. A modern version of those questions might look like the following:

- Did something happen?
- What is its nature?
- What is its quality or cause?
- What actions should be taken?

As you can see, each stasis question explores a different aspect of a problem and uses different evidence or techniques to reach conclusions. You can use stasis theory to explore the aspects of any topic you're considering. We use the stasis issues to define key types of argument in Part 2.

Did Something Happen? Arguments of Fact

An argument of fact usually involves a statement that can be proved or disproved with specific evidence or testimony. Although relatively simple to define, such arguments are often quite subtle, involving layers of complexity that are not apparent when the question is initially posed.

For example, the question of pollution of the oceans—is it really occurring?—might seem relatively easy to settle. Either scientific data prove that the oceans are being polluted as a result of human activity, or they don't. But to settle the matter, writers and readers first have to agree on a number of points, each of which has to be studied and debated: How will pollution be defined and measured? Over what period of time? Are current deviations in water quality unprecedented? Can any deviations be attributable to human action? Nevertheless, questions of this sort can be argued primarily on the facts, complicated and contentious as they may be. (For more on arguments based on facts, see Chapter 4.)

Mark Cadena and Stuart Hata in San Francisco's City Hall after their wedding on November 3, 2008, the day before a California ballot referendum ended several months of legalized marriage ceremonies between same-sex couples in the state. The debate over this issue involves arguments of fact (does a "civil union" or "domestic partnership" provide the same benefits as a "marriage"?) as well as more basic arguments of definition (are these forms of legal recognition the same thing? must "marriage" involve two people of the opposite sex?).

What Is the Nature of the Thing? Arguments of Definition

Just as contentious as arguments based on facts are questions of definition. An argument of definition often involves determining whether one known object or action belongs in a second—and more highly contested—category. One of the most hotly debated issues in American life today involves a question of definition: is a human fetus a human being? If one argues that it is, then a second issue of definition arises: is abortion murder? As you can see, issues of definition can have mighty consequences—and decades of debate may leave the matter unresolved.

Bob Costas used an important definitional distinction to eulogize Mickey Mantle, a great New York Yankee baseball player who had many human faults:

> In the last year, Mickey Mantle, always so hard upon himself, finally came to accept and appreciate the distinction between a role model and a hero. The first he often was not, the second he always will be.
>
> —Bob Costas, "Eulogy for Mickey Mantle"

But arguments of definition can be less weighty than these, though still hotly contested: Is playing video games a sport? Is Batman a tragic figure? Is President Obama a liberal or a moderate? (For more about arguments of definition, see Chapter 9.)

What Is the Quality or Cause of the Thing? Arguments of Evaluation and Causality

Arguments of definition lead naturally into arguments of quality—that is, to questions *about* quality. Most auto enthusiasts, for example, wouldn't be content merely to inquire whether the Corvette is a sports car. They'd prefer to argue whether it's a *good* sports car or a better sports car than, say, the Nissan GT-R. Or they might want to assert that it's the best sports car in the world, perhaps qualifying their claim with the caveat *for the price.*

Arguments of evaluation move forward typically by presenting criteria and then measuring individual people, ideas, or things against those standards. Both the standards and the measurement can be explored argumentatively, or they can be implied by the sheer weight of evidence. For instance, writer Molly Ivins praises Barbara Jordan by making explicit the qualities and achievements that make the woman a "great spirit":

> Barbara Jordan, whose name was so often preceded by the words "the first black woman to . . ." that they seemed like a permanent title, died Wednesday in Austin. A great spirit is gone. The first black woman to serve in the Texas Senate, the first black woman in Congress (she and Yvonne Brathwaite Burke of California were both elected in 1972, but Jordan had no Republican opposition), the first black elected to Congress from the South since Reconstruction, the first black woman to sit on major corporate boards, and so on. Were it not for the disease

that slowly crippled her, she probably would have been the first black woman on the Supreme Court—it is known that Jimmy Carter had her on his short list.

And long before she became "the first and only black woman to . . ." there was that astounding string of achievements going back to high school valedictorian, honors at Texas Southern University, law degree from Boston University. Both her famous diction and her enormous dignity were present from the beginning, her high school teachers recalled. Her precise enunciation was a legacy from her father, a Baptist minister, and characteristic of educated blacks of his day. Her great baritone voice was so impressive that her colleagues in the Legislature used to joke that if Hollywood ever needed someone to be the voice of the Lord Almighty, only Jordan would do.

—Molly Ivins, "Barbara Jordan: A Great Spirit"

In examining a circumstance or situation, we are often led to wonder what accounts for it: *how did Barbara Jordan achieve what she did, or what happened as a result of her work?* Though not strictly one of the classical stases, the question of *causality* certainly plays a role in many political, social, and scientific controversies. We want to know why something has happened, what factors have shaped the situation we are in, or what

Barbara Jordan addressing fellow members of Congress in 1978

might happen in the future as the result of actions we take now. For instance, nailing down the causes of global warming would certainly make a difference in how we define, evaluate, or act on the problem. Consider the reactions of bloggers at *Popular Science* reading yet another causal examination of the phenomenon:

> Wait, now pollution is preventing global warming? That's the conclusion of a recent study in the journal *Geophysical Research Letters*, which says rising temperatures seen in Europe over the last few years result as much from the reduction of air pollution as from the creation of it. The research, which looked at the effects of aerosols on climate, confirms an older concept known as global dimming, and complicates our understanding of how mankind affects the climate.
>
> According to the study, temperatures in Europe have risen over the past 28 years far faster than could be explained by the greenhouse effect alone. After looking at the aerosol concentrations in the atmosphere in six spots, the authors of the paper realized the temperature rise was assisted by more sunlight penetrating the newly pollution free skies. It seems that the stricter pollution standards, adopted in part to slow global warming, may have sped it up.
>
> —Stuart Fox, "Is Pollution Slowing Global Warming?"

Consider, too, how many different implications this study of causality raises and how many ways its findings can be interpreted. (For more about arguments of evaluation, see Chapter 10; for causal arguments, see Chapter 11.)

What Actions Should Be Taken? Proposal Arguments

In arguments that propose action, writers first have to describe a problem so well that readers ask: *What can we do?* So a proposal argument typically begins by proving that there is a problem. For example, in developing an argument about rising tuition at your college, you might use all the prior stasis questions to study the issue and establish how much and for what reasons tuition is rising. But the final question—*What actions should be taken?*—will be the most important, since it will lead you to develop proposals for action. In examining a nationwide move to eliminate remedial education in four-year colleges, John Cloud offers a moderate proposal:

> Students age 22 and over account for 43% of those in remedial classrooms, according to the National Center for Developmental Education.

[. . . But] 55% of those needing remediation must take just one course. Is it too much to ask them to pay extra for that class or take it at a community college?

—John Cloud, "Who's Ready for College?"

Americans tend to see the world in terms of problems and solutions. Indeed, many expect that almost any difficulty can be overcome by the proper infusion of technology and money. So proposal arguments seem especially appealing to Americans, even though quick-fix attitudes may themselves constitute a problem. (For more about proposal arguments, see Chapter 12.)

STASIS QUESTIONS AT WORK

Suppose that you have an opportunity to speak at a student conference on the issue of global warming. The Campus Young Republicans are sponsoring the conference, but they've made a point of inviting speakers with varying perspectives. You are tentatively in favor of strengthening industrial pollution standards aimed at reducing global warming trends. But you decide that you'd like to learn more about the issue. So you use the stasis questions to get started.

- **Did something happen?** Does global warming exist? Many in the oil and gas industry and some reputable scientists insist that global warming isn't a worldwide phenomenon or that evidence for its existence remains inconclusive. But most scientists who've studied the issue and most governments argue that the phenomenon is real and that it has reached serious proportions. In coming to your own conclusion about global warming, you'll weigh the factual evidence carefully. When you reach your conclusion, whatever it is, you should be able to identify problems with opposing arguments.

- **What is the nature of the thing?** Looking for definitions of global warming also reveals great disagreement. Global warming skeptics tend to define it in terms of naturally occurring events (such as periodic long-term fluctuations in climate), while most scientists and governments base their definition on human causes (emissions of carbon dioxide and methane). Thus, you begin to consider competing definitions very carefully: *How do the definitions these groups use foster the goals of each group? What's at stake for skeptics in the oil industry in promoting their definition of global warming? What's at stake*

(continued)

for the scientists and governments who put forth the opposing definition? Exploring this stasis question should help you understand how the contexts of an argument shape the claims people and groups make.

- **What is the quality of the thing?** This question will lead you to examine claims that global warming is—or is not—causing harm to the environment. Again, you quickly find that these charges are hotly contested. Exploring these differing assessments of damage done by climate change should lead you to ask who stands to gain in these analyses. *Do oil executives want to protect their investments? Do scientists want government money for grants? Where does evidence for the dangers of global warming come from? Who benefits if the dangers are accepted as real and present, and who loses?*

- **What actions should be taken?** Once again, you find wide disagreement. If global warming is occurring naturally or causing little harm, then arguably nothing needs or can be done. Or perhaps those who have made such arguments ought to sponsor a new study of global warming to prove once and for all that their assessment is correct. If, on the other hand, global warming is caused mainly by human activity and poses a clear threat to the environment, then the government and industry are bound to respond to such danger (although not everyone may agree on what such responses should be). As you investigate the proposals being made and the reasons behind them, you come closer to developing your own argument.

Audiences for Arguments

No argument, even one that engages stasis questions thoroughly, can be effective unless it speaks well to others—to what we describe as the *audiences* for arguments. Audiences cross a full range of possibilities—including the flesh-and-blood person sitting across a desk when you negotiate a student loan, the "friends" who join you in a social network, and the ideal readers that you imagine for a paper or editorial you write.

The figure on the following page may help you appreciate how many dimensions an audience can have as writers and readers negotiate their relationship to a verbal or visual text.

Readers and writers in context

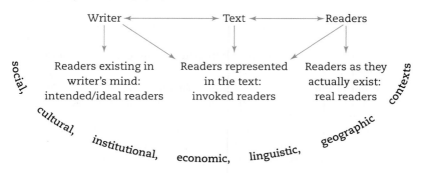

As a writer, you'll almost always be addressing an *intended* reader who exists in your own mind. As we write this textbook, we're certainly thinking of those who will read it: you are our intended reader, and ideally you know something and might even care about the subject of this book. Though we don't know you personally, we see you in our minds, for we *intend* to write for you. In the same way, the editors of *Rego: The Latino College Magazine* have a clear sense of whom they want to reach with their publication, even providing a graphic to define that audience:

Mission and Vision

- The leading lifestyle publication for the Latino collegiate, postcollegiate, and college-bound demographic
- Expand the minds of the college-age demographic

Rego, a campus magazine

- Cover the best and most pertinent issues affecting our culturally diverse target audience
- Exposure to positive role models; American, world, and popular culture; self-improvement tools; and poignant political issues

So texts have intended readers whom the writer consciously wants to address. But texts, whether visual or verbal, also have *invoked* readers—those who are represented in the text. Later in this chapter, for example, "you" (our audience) are invoked as people who recognize the importance of respecting readers. For another example, look at the second and third paragraphs of this chapter; they call on readers who should be interested in the goals of argument, whether overt or subtle. Even the cover of *Rego* invokes an audience—hip Latinos and Latinas who are intrigued by music, travel, and romance.

Writers often establish their relationships to intended and evoked audiences through their choice of pronouns, sometimes addressing favored readers as *you*, *we*, or *us*. Although such personal pronouns can help readers connect with a writer, using them can be dicey: if readers don't fit into the *us*, they may feel excluded from a text and thus less receptive to its argument. Such is the risk that writer bell hooks takes in the passage below:

> **The most powerful resource any of us can have as we study and teach in university settings is full understanding and appreciation of the richness, beauty, and primacy of our familial and community backgrounds.**
> **—bell hooks, "Keeping Close to Home: Class and Education"**

This sentence reflects hooks's intention of talking to a certain *us*—"we [who] study and teach in university settings." Readers who don't fit into such an *us* may feel excluded from this group and thus from hooks's essay. Such readers have suddenly become *they* or *them*.

In addition to intended and invoked readers, an argument will also have "real" readers—who may not be among those a writer originally imagined or called forth. You might pick up a letter written to a sibling, for instance, and read it even though it's not intended for you. Even more likely, you may read email not sent to you but rather forwarded (sometimes unwittingly) from someone else. Or you may read a legal brief prepared for a lawyer and struggle to understand it, since you're neither the intended reader nor the knowledgeable legal expert invoked in the text. As these examples suggest, writers can't always (or even usually) control who the real readers of any argument will be. As a writer, you want to think carefully about these real readers and to summon up what you do know about them, even if that knowledge is limited.

Considering Contexts

No consideration of audiences can be complete without understanding how *context* shapes and colors the perspectives readers bring to an argument. Reading always takes place in a series of contexts that move outward like concentric circles from the most immediate situation (the specific circumstance in which the reading occurs) to broader environments (including local and community contexts; institutional contexts such as school, church, or profession; and economic, cultural, and linguistic contexts).

When reporter Louise Story of the *New York Times* wrote a front-page story in 2006 saying that many women attending prestigious colleges planned to abandon their professional careers when they had children, she set off a firestorm of controversy that provoked different responses from various audiences. Some journalists challenged the integrity of Story's article and the prominence the paper gave it. Jack Schafer of Slate.com, for example, found it full of slippery and evasive qualifying terms, such as *many* and *seems*, that made its claims meaningless:

> While bogus, "Many Women at Elite Colleges Set Career Path to Motherhood" isn't false: It can't be false because it never says anything sturdy enough to be tested. So, how did it get to Page One? Is there a *New York Times* conspiracy afoot to drive feminists crazy and persuade young women that their place is in the home?
>
> —Jack Schafer, "Weasel-Words Rip My Flesh!"

Faculty members at the schools Story examined brought a different perspective to the piece. Some, like Deborah Belle, a professor of psychology at Boston University, depicted it to an interviewer for the campus newspaper, *BU Today*, as sadly emblematic of the dilemma professional women still face:

> I think the thing that resonates so badly with me about the *New York Times* article is that the onus is always on the woman, and that's not where it should be. . . . Of course there are superheroes who can do it all, but that's not the point. The point is that none of us should be forced to be in these positions.
>
> —Deborah Belle, qtd. in "The Do-It-All Dilemma"

And female students themselves—from a different generation than their professors—placed the story in their own contexts, thinking about the careers they faced. Here's Alana Steinhardt from that same *BU Today* article, bringing personal values to bear on the controversy:

> Why have kids if you can't see them grow up, and be there for the experience? . . . At BU, I'm preparing myself to be a more well-rounded person. That doesn't necessarily mean I have to work.

As you can see, arguments are created and read in complicated environments. As you compose arguments of your own, you need to think carefully about the contexts that surround your readers—and to place your topic in its context as well.

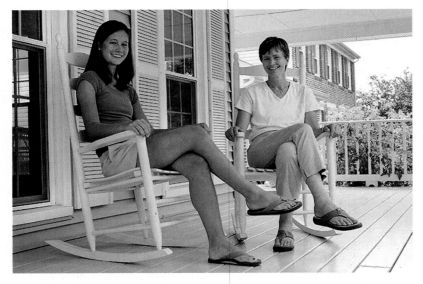

Yale student Emily Lechner, left, is one of the subjects of a controversial *New York Times* article on young women attending prestigious colleges who say their career plans will take a backseat to raising children. A variety of readers— journalists, older professional women, and other female college students— found fault with the article when viewing it in the context of their own experiences.

CULTURAL CONTEXTS FOR ARGUMENT

Considering What's "Normal"

If you want to communicate effectively with people across cultures, then learn something about the traditions in those cultures—and examine the norms guiding your own behavior:

- Explore the assumptions that guide your ways of making a point. Most of us regard our ways of thinking as "normal" or "right." Such assumptions also guide our judgments about what works in persuasive situations. But just because it may seem natural to take aggressive stands or speak bluntly in arguments, consider that others may find such aggression startling or even alarming.

(continued)

- Remember that ways of arguing are influenced by contexts that differ widely across cultures. Pay attention to how people from groups or cultures other than your own argue, and be open to the different paths of thinking you'll no doubt encounter. And be sensitive to differences in language.

- Don't assume that all people share your cultural values, ethical principles, or political assumptions. People across the world have different ways of defining *family, work*, or *happiness*. And as you present arguments to them, consider that they may be content with their different ways of organizing their lives and societies.

- Respect the differences among individuals *within* a given culture or group. Don't expect that every member of a community behaves— or argues—in the same way or shares the same beliefs. Avoid thinking, for instance, that there is a single Asian, African, or Hispanic culture or that Europeans are any less diverse or more predictable than Americans or Canadians in their thinking. In other words, be skeptical of stereotypes.

Appealing to Audiences

Twenty-five hundred years ago, Aristotle identified three key ways that writers can appeal to their audiences in arguments; he labeled these appeals *pathos, ethos*, and *logos*. These general appeals are as effective today as they were in Aristotle's time, though we usually think of them in slightly different terms.

Emotional Appeals: Pathos

Human beings often respond strongly to emotional appeals, or *pathos*. Such arguments generate emotions (such as anger, fear, jealousy, empathy, pity, and love) in readers to shape their responses and dispose them to accept a claim. For instance, while facts and figures (or logical appeals) may convince us that the AIDS epidemic in Africa is real and serious, what elicits an outpouring of support is the emotional power of televised images and newspaper accounts of suffering people. Concrete and descriptive language can similarly paint pictures in readers' minds, thus building an emotional appeal and perhaps a bond between writer and readers. For more about emotional appeals, see Chapter 2.

A starkly visual emotional appeal: a mother holds her ill daughter at a Doctors Without Borders clinic in Sudan, where violence and disease are killing tens of thousands.

Ethical Appeals: Ethos

Equally important to an argument's success is the writer's *ethos*, or presentation of self. When writers or speakers seem trustworthy, audiences are likely to listen to their arguments and accept them. You can make an ethical appeal to an audience simply by proving that you know what you're talking about. Or you can build credibility by emphasizing that you share values with your audience, by demonstrating that you're even-handed, and by showing that you respect both your audience and your opponents. Even visual items can make ethical appeals: consider how flags, logos, or badges convey respectability and authority. For more about ethical appeals, see Chapter 3.

Logical Appeals: Logos

Appeals to logic, or *logos*, are often given prominence and authority in U.S. culture: "Just the facts, ma'am," a famous early television detective used to say. Indeed, audiences respond well to the use of reasons and evidence—to the presentation of facts, statistics, credible testimony, cogent examples, or even a narrative or story that embodies a sound reason in support of an argument. For more about logical appeals, see Chapters 4 and 7.

Arguments and Their Rhetorical Situations

In this chapter, we've been examining elements of argument one at a time, identifying the purposes and kinds of arguments, the crux of any argument (its stasis), and ways to formulate arguments that appeal to audiences. This discussion has emphasized the social nature of argument: even if we're arguing with ourselves, there's some give-and-take involved, and the argument exists in a particular context that influences how it can be shaped and how others will receive it. The *rhetorical situation* is a shorthand phrase for this entire set of concerns, and it can be depicted as a simple triangle. (See the figure below.)

It's important to regard any rhetorical situation as dynamic, since each element of it has the potential to affect all the other elements. A change of audience in a project, for example, can lead you to reconsider all of your appeals; a change in topic may require rethinking your audience. If you begin to think in this critical way, you'll be developing a rhetorical turn of mind. You'll find yourself habitually viewing any topic from a number of perspectives and hence develop greater critical engagement with the issues and ideas important to you. Such a rhetorical frame of mind might even lead you to challenge the title of this textbook: is everything *really* an argument?

The rhetorical triangle

Topic/Message
(Logical Appeals)

CONTEXT

Audience/Readers
(Emotional Appeals)

Speaker/Writer
(Ethical Appeals)

RESPOND●

1. Can an argument really be any text that expresses a point of view? What kinds of arguments—if any—might be made by the following items?

    the embossed leather cover of a prayer book

    a Boston Red Sox cap

    a Livestrong bracelet

    the "explicit lyrics" label on a best-selling rock CD

    the health warning on a package of cigarettes

    a belated birthday card

    the nutrition label on a can of soup

    the cover of a science fiction novel

    a colored ribbon pinned to a shirt lapel

    a Rolex watch

2. Write six short paragraphs describing times in the recent past when you've used language to inform, to convince, to persuade, to explore, to make decisions, and to meditate or pray. Be sure to write at least one paragraph for each of these six purposes. In class, trade paragraphs with a partner, and decide whether his or her descriptions accurately fit the categories to which they've been assigned. If they don't, work with your partner to figure out why. Is the problem with the descriptions? The categories? Both? Neither?

3. In a recent newspaper or periodical, find three editorials—one that makes a forensic argument, one a deliberative argument, and one a ceremonial argument. Analyze the arguments by asking these questions: *Who is arguing? What purposes are the writers trying to achieve? To whom are they directing their arguments?* Then consider whether the arguments' purposes have been achieved in each case. If they have, offer some reasons for the arguments' success.

4. What common experiences—if any—do the following objects, brand names, and symbols evoke and for what audiences in particular?

    a USDA organic label

    the Nike swoosh

    the golden arches

    the Sean John label as seen on its Web site

    a can of Coca-Cola

    Sleeping Beauty's castle on the Disney logo

Oprah Winfrey

the Vietnam Veterans Memorial

Ground Zero at the World Trade Center site

a dollar bill

5. Read the main editorial in three or four issues of your campus newspaper. Then choose the most interesting one, and consider how the editor creates credibility, or ethos, in the editorial.

6. Take a look at the bumper sticker below, and then analyze it. What is its purpose? What kind of argument is it? Which of the stasis questions does it most appropriately respond to? What appeals does it make to its readers, and how?

2
Arguments Based on Emotion: Pathos

What makes you glance at a magazine ad long enough to notice a product? These days, it's probably an image or boldfaced words promising pleasure (a Caribbean beach), excitement (extreme diving on Maui), beauty (a model in low-rise jeans), technology (a glossy high-tech phone), or good health (more models). In the blink of an eye, ads can appeal to your emotions, intrigue you, and perhaps even seduce you. Look closer, and you might find logical reasons given for buying a product or service. But would you have even gotten there without an emotional tug to pull you into the page?

Emotional appeals (sometimes called *appeals to pathos*) are powerful tools for influencing what people think and believe. We all make decisions—even important ones—based on our feelings. We rent funky apartments or buy worn-out cars because we fall in love with some

This image parodies ads that exploit one of the most powerful of emotional appeals.

small detail. On impulse, we collect whole racks of shirts or shoes that we're later too embarrassed to wear. We date and maybe even marry people that everyone else seemed to know are wrong for us—and sometimes it works out just fine.

That may be because we're not computers that use cost-and-benefit analyses to choose our friends or make our political decisions. Feelings belong in our lives. There's a powerful moment in Shakespeare's *Macbeth* when the soldier Macduff learns that his wife and children have been executed by the power-mad king. A well-meaning friend urges Macduff to "dispute it like a man." Macduff responds gruffly, "But I must also feel it as a man" (*Mac.* 4.3.219–21). As a writer, you must learn like Macduff to appreciate legitimate emotions, particularly when you want to influence the public. When you hear that formal or academic arguments should rely solely on facts, remember that facts alone often won't carry the day, even for a worthy cause. The civil rights struggle of the 1960s is a particularly good example of a movement that persuaded people equally by means of the reasonableness and the passion of its claims.

You don't have to look hard for less noble campaigns that are fueled with emotions such as hatred, envy, and greed. Democracies suffer when people use emotional arguments (and related fallacies such as personal attacks and name-calling) to drive wedges between groups, making them fearful or hateful. For that reason alone, writers should not use emotional appeals casually. (For more about emotional fallacies, see Chapter 17.)

Understanding How Emotional Arguments Work

You already know that words, images, and sounds can arouse emotions. In fact, the stirrings they generate are often physical. You've likely had the clichéd "chill down the spine" or felt something in the "pit of the stomach" when a speaker (or photograph or event) hits precisely the right note. On such occasions, it's likely that the speaker has you and people like you in mind and is seeking to rouse an emotion that will make you well disposed toward a particular message.

But sometimes speakers are called on to address not a particular group (such as a gathering of political supporters) but an entire nation or even the entire world. Such was the case during World War II when Prime Minister Winston Churchill spoke to the British House of Commons on June 4, 1940, seeking to raise British spirits and strengthen the country's resolve in resisting the German attacks:

> **We shall not flag or fail. We shall go on to the end. We shall fight in France, we shall fight on the seas and oceans, we shall fight with**

Hearing Barack Obama speak following a primary victory in Wisconsin, journalist Chris Matthews declared, "My, I felt this thrill going up my leg. I mean, I don't have that too often." Even some professionals can't resist a good emotional appeal.

> growing confidence and growing strength in the air, we shall defend our island, whatever the cost may be, we shall fight on the beaches, we shall fight on the landing grounds, we shall fight in the fields and in the streets, we shall fight in the hills. We shall never surrender.
> —Winston Churchill, "We Shall Fight on the Beaches"

When writers and speakers find the words and images that evoke certain emotions in people, they might also move their audiences to sympathize with ideas that they connect to those feelings and even to act on them. Make people be aware of how much they owe to others, and they'll acknowledge that debt; persuade people to hate an enemy, and they'll rally against it; help people to imagine suffering, and they'll strive to relieve it; make people feel secure or happy (or insecure or unhappy), and they'll buy products that promise such good feelings. In 2008, Barack Obama jump-started an entire presidential campaign by appealing to a single emotion—hope.

Arguments based on emotion probably count more when you're persuading than when you're arguing. When arguing, you might use reasons and evidence to convince readers something is true—for instance, that preserving wetlands is a worthy environmental goal. When persuading, however, you want people to take action—to join an environmental boycott, contribute money to an organization dedicated to wetlands protection, or write a well-researched op-ed piece for the local paper about a local marsh that is threatened by development.

The practical differences between being convinced and acting on a conviction can be enormous. Your readers may agree that contributing to charity is a noble act, but this conviction may not be enough to persuade them to part with their spare change. You need a spur that is sharper than logic, and that's when emotion might kick in. You can embarrass readers into contributing to a good cause (*Change a child's life for the price of a pizza*), make them feel the impact of their gift (*Imagine the smile on that little child's face*), or tell them a moving story (*In a tiny village in Central America . . .*). We've all seen such techniques work.

A March 20, 2008, cover of *Rolling Stone* presented Barack Obama as an emblem of hope, even giving him an aura. Later that election year (July 21, 2008), a *New Yorker* cover presented him and his wife, Michelle, in a different light, suggesting how his opponents would depict the Obamas to evoke the politics of another emotion—fear.

Not Just Words

Take a look at this image, which at first glance depicts the familiar stars and stripes of the American flag. But a second glance reveals corporate logos rather than stars. Study the picture carefully and write for two or three minutes about the emotions that the image arouses in you. Do you respond first to the flag and then to the logos? What clash of emotional appeals do you see here, and how do you feel about that conflict? Try your hand at creating one or two possible titles or captions for this image.

Using Emotions to Build Bridges

You may sometimes want to use emotions to connect with readers to assure them that you understand their experiences or, to use President Bill Clinton's famous line, "feel their pain." Such a bridge is especially important when you're writing about matters that readers regard as sensitive. Before they'll trust you, they'll want assurances that you understand the issues in depth. If you strike the right emotional note, you'll establish an important connection. That's what Apple founder Steve Jobs does in a 2005 commencement address in which he tells the audience that he doesn't have a fancy speech, just three stories from his life:

> My second story is about love and loss. I was lucky. I found what I loved to do early in life. Woz [Steve Wozniak] and I started Apple in my parents' garage when I was twenty. We worked hard and in ten years, Apple had grown from just the two of us in a garage into a $2 billion company with over 4,000 employees. We'd just released our finest creation, the Macintosh, a year earlier, and I'd just turned thirty, and then I got fired. How can you get fired from a company you started? Well, as Apple grew, we hired someone who I thought was very talented to run the company with me, and for the first year or so, things went well. But then our visions of the future began to diverge, and eventually we had a falling out. When we did, our board of directors sided with him, and so at thirty, I was out, and very publicly out. . . .
>
> I didn't see it then, but it turned out that getting fired from Apple was the best thing that could have ever happened to me. The heaviness of being successful was replaced by the lightness of being a beginner again, less sure about everything. It freed me to enter one of the most creative periods in my life. During the next five years I started a company named NeXT, another company named Pixar and fell in love with an amazing woman who would become my wife. Pixar went on to create the world's first computer-animated feature film, *Toy Story*, and is now the most successful animation studio in the world.
>
> —Steve Jobs, "You've Got to Find What You Love, Jobs Says"

In no obvious way is Jobs's recollection a formal argument. But it prepares his audience to accept the advice he'll give later in his speech, at least partly because he's speaking from meaningful personal experiences.

A more obvious way to build an emotional tie is simply to help readers identify with your experiences. If, like Georgina Kleege, you were blind and wanted to argue for more sensible attitudes toward blind people, you might ask readers in the first paragraph of your argument to confront their prejudices. Here Kleege, a writer and college instructor, makes an emotional point by telling a story:

> I tell the class, "I am legally blind." There is a pause, a collective intake of breath. I feel them look away uncertainly and then look back. After all, I just said I couldn't see. Or did I? I had managed to get there on my own—no cane, no dog, none of the usual trappings of blindness. Eyeing me askance now, they might detect that my gaze is not quite focused. . . . They watch me glance down, or towards the door where someone's coming in late. I'm just like anyone else.
>
> —Georgina Kleege, "Call It Blindness"

Given that the way she narrates the first day of class, readers are as likely to identify with the students as with Kleege, imagining themselves sitting in a classroom, facing a sightless instructor, confronting their own prejudices about the blind. Kleege wants to put them on edge emotionally.

Let's consider another rhetorical situation: how do you win over an audience when the logical claims that you're making are likely to go against what many in the audience believe? Once again, a slightly risky appeal to emotions on a personal level may work. That's the tack that Michael Pollan takes in bringing readers to consider that "the great moral struggle of our time will be for the rights of animals." In introducing his lengthy exploratory argument, Pollan uses personal experience to appeal to his audience:

> The first time I opened Peter Singer's *Animal Liberation*, I was dining alone at the Palm, trying to enjoy a rib-eye steak cooked medium-rare. If this sounds like a good recipe for cognitive dissonance (if not indigestion), that was sort of the idea. Preposterous as it might seem to supporters of animal rights, what I was doing was tantamount to reading *Uncle Tom's Cabin* on a plantation in the Deep South in 1852.
>
> —Michael Pollan, "An Animal's Place"

In creating a vivid image of his first encounter with Singer's book, Pollan's opening builds a bridge between himself as a person trying to enter into the animal rights debate in a fair and open-minded, if still skeptical, way and readers who might be passionate about either side of this argument.

A visual version of Michael Pollan's rhetorical situation

THE BIRTH OF A VEGETARIAN

Using Emotions to Sustain an Argument

You can also use emotional appeals to make logical claims stronger or more memorable. That is the way that photographs and other images add power to arguments. In a TV attack ad, the scowling black-and-white photograph of a political opponent may do as much damage as the claim that he bought his home on the cheap from a financier convicted of fraud. Or the attractive skier in a spot for lip balm may make us yearn for brisk, snowy winter days. The technique is tricky, however. Lay on too much emotion—especially those like outrage, pity, or shame, which make people uncomfortable—and you may offend the very audiences you hoped to convince.

But sometimes a strong emotion such as anger adds energy to a passage, as it does when writer Stuart Taylor and history professor K. C. Johnson react in outrage when Mike Nifong, a prosecutor charged with deliberately lying about evidence in an emotionally charged rape case at Duke University, received only a twenty-four-hour sentence for his misconduct. In an op-ed in the *Washington Post*, the authors review the wider dimensions of the biased prosecution and turn their ire especially on faculty who were too eager to pillory three white student athletes at Duke for an alleged crime against a minority woman that subsequent investigations proved never occurred. As you read the following excerpt, notice how the authors' use of emotional language might lead some readers to share their anger and others to resent it.

> To be sure, it was natural to assume at first that Nifong had a case. Why else would he confidently declare the players guilty? But many academics and journalists continued to presume guilt months after

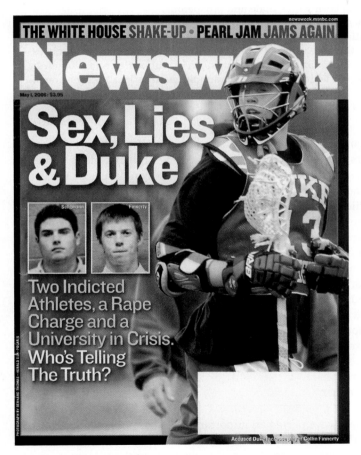

What is the emotional impact of a *Newsweek* cover like this one, which appeared on May 1, 2006, following initial indictments in what became known as the Duke University rape case? Does the magazine seem to be taking sides?

massive evidence of innocence poured into the public record. Indeed, some professors persisted in attacks even after the three defendants were declared innocent in April by North Carolina Attorney General Roy Cooper—an almost unheard-of event.

Brushing aside concern with "the 'truth' . . . about the incident," as one put it, these faculty ideologues just changed their indictments from rape to drunkenness (hardly a rarity in college); exploiting poor black women (the players had expected white and Hispanic strippers); and being born white, male and prosperous.

This shameful conduct was rooted in a broader trend toward subordinating facts and evidence to faith-based ideological posturing. Worse, the ascendant ideology, especially in academia, is an obsession with the fantasy that oppression of minorities and women by "privileged" white men remains rampant in America. Its crude stereotyping of white men, especially athletes, resembles old-fashioned racism and sexism.

—Stuart Taylor and K. C. Johnson, "Guilty in the Duke Case"

In using language this way, writers can generate emotions by presenting arguments in their starkest terms, stripped of qualifications or subtleties. Readers or listeners are confronted with core issues or important choices and asked to consider the consequences.

It's difficult to gauge how much emotion will work in a given argument. Some issues—such as racism, rape, abortion, and gun control—provoke strong feelings and, as a result, are often argued on emotional terms. But even issues that seem deadly dull—such as funding for Medicare and Social Security—can be argued passionately when proposed changes in these programs are set in human terms: cut benefits and Grandma will have to eat cat food; don't cut benefits and Social Security will surely go broke, leaving nothing for later generations of seniors. Both alternatives might scare people into paying enough attention to take political action.

Using Humor

Humor has always played an important role in argument, sometimes as the sugar that makes the medicine go down. You can slip humor into an argument to put readers at ease, thereby making them more open to a proposal you have to offer. It's hard to say no when you're laughing. Humor also makes otherwise sober people suspend their judgment and even their prejudices, perhaps because the surprise and naughtiness of wit are combustive: they provoke laughter or smiles, not reflection. That may be why TV sitcoms like *Sex and the City* and *Will & Grace* became popular with mainstream audiences, despite their sometimes controversial subjects. Similarly, it's possible to make a point through humor that might not work in more sober writing. Consider the gross stereotypes about men that humorist Dave Barry presents here, tongue in cheek, as he explains why people don't read the instructions that come with the products they buy:

> The third reason why consumers don't read manuals is that many consumers are men, and we men would no more read a manual than we would ask directions, because this would be an admission that the person who wrote the manual has a bigger . . . OK, a bigger grasp of technology than we do. We men would rather hook up our new DVD player in such a way that it ignites the DVDs and shoots them across the room—like small flaming UFOs—than admit that the manual-writer possesses a more manly technological manhood than we do.
>
> —Dave Barry, "Owners' Manual Step No. 1: Bang Head against the Wall"

Our laughter testifies to a kernel of truth in Barry's observations and makes us more likely to agree with his conclusions.

A writer or speaker can use humor to deal with especially sensitive issues. For example, sports commentator Bob Costas, given the honor of eulogizing the great baseball player Mickey Mantle, couldn't ignore problems in Mantle's life. So he argues for Mantle's greatness by admitting the man's weaknesses indirectly through humor:

> It brings to mind a story Mickey liked to tell on himself and maybe some of you have heard it. He pictured himself at the pearly gates, met by St. Peter who shook his head and said, "Mick, we checked the record. We know some of what went on. Sorry, we can't let you in. But before you go, God wants to know if you'd sign these six dozen baseballs."
>
> —Bob Costas, "Eulogy for Mickey Mantle"

Similarly, politicians use humor to admit problems or mistakes they couldn't acknowledge in any other way. Here, for example, is President George W. Bush at the 2004 Radio and TV Correspondents Dinner discussing his much-mocked intellect:

> Those stories about my intellectual capacity do get under my skin. You know, for a while I even thought my staff believed it. There on my schedule first thing every morning it said, "Intelligence briefing."
>
> —George W. Bush

Not all humor is well intentioned. In fact, among the most powerful forms of emotional argument is ridicule—humor aimed at a particular target. Eighteenth-century poet and critic Samuel Johnson was known for his stinging and humorous put-downs, such as this comment to an aspiring writer: "Your manuscript is both good and original, but the part that is good is not original and the part that is original is not good." Today, even bumper stickers can be vehicles for succinct arguments:

But ridicule is a two-edged sword that requires a deft hand to wield it. Humor that reflects bad taste discredits a writer completely, as does ridicule that misses its mark. Unless your target deserves assault and you can be very funny, it's usually better to steer clear of humor.

Using Arguments Based on Emotion

You don't want to play puppetmaster with people's emotions when you write arguments, but it's a good idea to spend some time early in your writing or designing process thinking about how you want readers to feel as they consider your persuasive claims. For example, would readers of your editorial about campus traffic policies be more inclined to agree with you if you made them envy faculty privileges, or would arousing their sense of fairness work better? What emotional appeals might persuade meat eaters to consider a vegan diet—or vice versa? Would sketches of stage props on a Web site persuade people to buy a season ticket to the theater, or would you spark more interest by featuring pictures of costumed performers?

Consider, too, the effect that a story can have on readers. Writers and journalists routinely use what are called *human-interest stories* to give presence to issues or arguments. You can do the same, using a particular incident to evoke sympathy, understanding, outrage, or amusement. Take care, though, to tell an honest story.

RESPOND•

1. To what specific emotions do the following slogans, sales pitches, and maxims appeal?

   "Just do it." (ad for Nike)

   "Think different." (ad for Apple Computers)

   "Reach out and touch someone." (ad for AT&T)

   "Yes we can!" (2008 presidential campaign slogan for Barack Obama)

   "Country first." (2008 presidential campaign slogan for John McCain)

   "By any means necessary." (rallying cry from Malcolm X)

   "Have it your way." (slogan for Burger King)

   "You can trust your car to the man who wears the star." (slogan for Texaco)

   "It's everywhere you want to be." (slogan for Visa)

   "Know what comes between me and my Calvins? Nothing!" (tag line for Calvin Klein jeans)

   "Don't mess with Texas!" (antilitter campaign slogan)

2. Bring a magazine to class, and analyze the emotional appeals in as many full-page ads as you can. Then classify those ads by types of emotional appeal, and see whether you can connect the appeals to the subject or target audience of the magazine. Compare your results with those of your classmates, and discuss your findings. For instance, do the ads in newsmagazines like *Time* and *Newsweek* appeal to different emotions and desires from the ads in publications such as *Cosmopolitan*, *Spin*, *Sports Illustrated*, *Automobile*, and *National Geographic*?

3. How do arguments based on emotion work in different media? Are such arguments more or less effective in books, articles, television (both news and entertainment shows), films, brochures, magazines, email, Web sites, the theater, street protests, and so on? You might explore how a single medium handles emotional appeals or compare different media. For example, why do Internet newsgroups seem to encourage angry outbursts? Are newspapers an emotionally colder source of information than television news programs? If so, why?

4. Spend some time looking for arguments that use ridicule or humor to make their point: check out your favorite Web sites; watch for bumper stickers, posters, or advertisements; and listen to popular song lyrics. Bring one or two examples to class, and be ready to explain how the humor makes an emotional appeal and whether it's effective.

3
Arguments Based on Character: Ethos

It was a moment many had been waiting for: on January 10, 2008, Ratan N. Tata, head of India's Tata Motors, unveiled Nano, "the people's car" designed to be affordable for those who had never dreamed of owning an automobile. Saying he hoped the Nano will bring "pride and joy" to millions of new owners, Tata stood aside to showcase the tiny car, reputed to sell for $2,500.

In describing the Nano, Tata Motors focuses not simply on its low cost but on what you might think of as its character: this people's car will be dependable, safe, fuel efficient, and low on emissions. In short, it is a car for everyone and can be counted on to serve its owners as well as its country's environment.

To be successful in selling the Nano, Tata Motors depends to a large extent on the character or ethos of the company itself. Writers and speakers (and companies) create ethos in at least two ways—through the reputation they bring to the table and through the language, evidence, and images they use. Tata Motors's homepage, for example, focuses on

The Tata Nano, said to be the world's cheapest car

its ethos, beginning with its carefully worded motto "Green matters" and then drawing on its reputation in its opening statement:

> True to the tradition of the Tata Group, Tata Motors is committed in letter and spirit to Corporate Social Responsibility. It is a signatory to the United Nations Global Compact, and is engaged in community and social initiatives on labour and environment standards in compliance with the principles of the Global Compact. In accordance with this, it plays an active role in community development, serving rural communities around its manufacturing locations.

In making an argument based on the character of the company, Tata Motors is also creating an ethos that it promises the Nano will live up to, perhaps even exceed, as the company works to improve the car's performance, durability, and green qualities. In doing so, Tata is appealing to the values of many today who believe that humans must reduce our carbon footprints and save energy if we are to avoid irrevocable damage to our shared planet.

Audiences pay attention to ethos and to the values that it represents. Before we accept the words (or image) of others, we must usually respect

WHAT MAKES THE TATA NANO SO CHEAP?

Windows wind down by hand

No air conditioning on standard model

Height 1.6m (5ft)

624cc two-cylinder engine in boot giving max speed of 70km/h (43mph)

Manual steering, no air bag

Plastic and adhesive replaces welding

TATA nano

Bodywork made of sheet metal and plastic

Width 1.5m (5ft)   Length 3.11m (10ft)

Not Just Words

Someone browsing the Web for information about the Tata Nano will quickly come across images like the one on page 53—and also like the one above. This second, annotated image points out that the company can build and sell the Nano cheaply for good reasons. Some reasons, like the use of plastic, might worry those who have concerns about safety. Others may be disappointed at the lack of air conditioning or the hand-crank windows. This annotated image therefore can raise questions about some of the claims made for the Nano.

Others investigating the car and the company that produces it might note the home page claim that Tata is a "signatory to the United Nations Global Compact" and decide to find out what that means. They would soon find the logo of this UN group, which has strong suggestions of global harmony and peace:

The logo image is reinforced on the homepage of the United Nations Global Compact, which focuses on the organization's "ten principles in the areas of human rights, labour, the environment and anti-corruption [that] enjoy universal consensus." Together, the logo and images of the natural world featured on the Web site create an ethos of responsibility, openness, and trust. But readers and writers must examine issues of ethos carefully. If you looked further, for example, you would likely identify some critics of the ethos of the Global Compact. In fact, a group called Global Compact Critics uses another powerful symbol to do just that—by superimposing a big question mark on the Global Compact logo:

Look at the Web site for Tata Motors (http://www.tatamotors .com) or the Web site for the United Nations Global Compact (http://www.unglobalcompact.org):

- What specific issues of ethos can you find addressed on the homepage for either group? How is ethos created through the use of images as well as words?

- Now look at the Web site for Global Compact Critics (http:// globalcompactcritics.blogspot.com), noting the way that this group uses images to question the ethos of the UN Global Compact.

- Working with a group, create some images that could help build a positive ethos for either the Tata Nano, the UN Global Compact, or Global Compact Critics.

their authority, admire their integrity and motives, or at least acknowledge what they stand for. Potential buyers of the Nano will know something of the ethos of Tata Motors since it is the largest manufacturer of automobiles in India and one of the country's ten top corporations. But Tata's advertising campaign will also make sure that buyers know a great deal about the way that the new Nano reflects the ethos of Tata's "Green matters": its very low cost, very high mileage ratio (fifty-four miles to the U.S. gallon), and high safety standards all help to build trust and a strong consumer base.

Character alone may not carry an argument, however, and the character of Tata Motors and its Nano probably won't speak to everyone. In fact, soon after its launch, several prospective customers interviewed by the news media said the Nano's low price could backfire on the company, driving away customers who look for status rather than fuel efficiency in an automobile. As one person said, "I still like big cars." In creating arguments based on character or ethos, writers must remember that a particular character will not appeal to every kind of audience.

Nevertheless, establishing ethos is important in arguments, whether the argument is made by a company (like Tata Motors), a person (such as a presidential candidate), a group (like the American Civil Liberties Union or Students for Academic Freedom), or an institution (such as a corporation, newspaper, or college). We observe people, groups, or institutions making and defending claims all the time and ask ourselves: *Should we pay attention to them? Can we trust them?* But establishing a persuasive ethos requires not simply seeming honest or likable but also affirming an identity and sharing parts or all of it with an intended audience. For example, while Tata, Porsche, and Tesla all hope to sell lots of automobiles, they are attempting to reach different audiences. Tata, as we've seen, is targeting the millions of everyday Indians who today are riding bicycles or motorscooters; Porsche aims for drivers who want the status of a beautifully designed, powerful, and expensive car; while Tesla wants to sell to those willing to pay big bucks for a zero-emissions electric car.

If a company (or anyone building an argument from character) is well known, liked, and respected, that reputation will contribute to its persuasive power. If its character is problematic in any respect, it may have to use argument to reshape an audience's perception. The fact that Tata Motors also produces heavy trucks, for example, could call into question some of its "Green matters" claim, leading consumers to question its ethos.

Understanding How Arguments Based on Character Work

Because life is complicated, we often need shortcuts to help us make choices. We can't weigh every claim to its last milligram or trace every fragment of evidence to its original source. And we have to make such decisions daily: *Which brand of clothing should I buy? Whom should I vote for in the next election? Which reviews of an Academy Award nominee for best film should I believe? What are the real risks in taking prescription painkillers?* To answer serious questions, people typically turn to professionals—doctors, lawyers, teachers, pastors—for wise, well-informed, and frank advice. But people look to equally knowledgeable individuals to guide them in less momentous matters as well. An expert can be anyone with knowledge and experience, from a professor of nuclear physics at an Ivy League college to a short-order cook at the local diner.

Readers give the people (or institutions) they know a hearing they might not automatically grant to a stranger or someone who hasn't earned their respect or affection. That trust indicates the power of arguments based on ethos or character and accounts for why people will often take the word of the "car guy" in their neighborhood more seriously than the reviews in *Consumer Reports*. And they'll believe *Consumer Reports* more readily than the SUV ads in *People*. Appeals or arguments about character often turn on claims such as the following:

- A person (or group) does or does not have the authority to speak to this issue.
- A person (or group) is or is not trustworthy or credible on this issue.
- A person (or group) does or does not have good motives for addressing this subject.

Claiming Authority

When you read an argument, especially one that makes an aggressive claim, you have every right to wonder about the writer's authority: *What does he know about the subject? What experiences does she have that make her especially knowledgeable? Why should I pay attention to this writer?*

When you offer an argument, you have to anticipate pointed questions like these and be able to answer them, directly or indirectly. Sometimes the claim of authority will be bold and personal, as it is when writer and activist Terry Tempest Williams attacks those who poisoned the Utah deserts with nuclear radiation. What gives her the right to speak on this subject? Not scientific expertise, but gut-wrenching personal experience:

> I belong to the Clan of One-Breasted Women. My mother, my grandmothers, and six aunts have all had mastectomies. Seven are dead. The two who survive have just completed rounds of chemotherapy and radiation.
>
> I've had my own problems: two biopsies for breast cancer and a small tumor between my ribs diagnosed as a "borderline malignancy."
> —Terry Tempest Williams, "The Clan of One-Breasted Women"

We are willing to listen to Williams's claims because she has lived with the nuclear peril she will deal with in the remainder of her essay.

Writers usually establish their authority in other and less striking ways. When they attach academic and professional titles to their names, for example, they're subtly building their authority by saying "this is how I've earned the right to be heard"—they are medical doctors, have law degrees, or have been state certified to work as psychotherapists. Similarly, writers can assert authority by mentioning their employers (their institutional affiliations) and the number of years that they've worked in a given field. Bureaucrats often identify themselves with their agencies, and professors with their schools. As a reader, you'll likely pay more attention to an argument about global warming if it's offered by someone who identifies herself as a professor of atmospheric and oceanic science at the University of Wisconsin–Madison, than by your Uncle Sid, who sells tools at Sears. But you'll prefer your uncle to the professor when you need advice about a reliable rotary saw.

When your readers are apt to be skeptical of both you and your claim, you may have to be even more specific about your credentials. That's exactly the strategy Richard Bernstein uses to establish his right to speak on the subject of teaching multiculturalism in American colleges and universities. At one point in a lengthy argument, he challenges those who make simplistic pronouncements about non-Western cultures, specifically "Asian culture." But what gives a New York writer named Bernstein the authority to write about Asian peoples? Bernstein tells us in a sparkling example of an argument based on character:

> The Asian culture, as it happens, is something I know a bit about, having spent five years at Harvard striving for a Ph.D. in a joint program called History and East Asian Languages and, after that, living either

as a student (for one year) or a journalist (six years) in China and Southeast Asia. At least I know enough to know there is no such thing as the "Asian culture."

—Richard Bernstein, *Dictatorship of Virtue*

Bernstein understates the case when he says he knows "a bit" about Asian culture and then mentions a Ph.D. program at Harvard and years of living in Asia. But the false modesty may be part of his argumentative strategy, too.

When you write for readers who trust you and your work, you may not have to make an open claim to authority. But you should know that making this type of appeal is always an option. A second lesson is that it certainly helps to know your subject when you're making a claim.

Even if an author doesn't make an explicit effort to assert it, authority can be conveyed through fairly small signals that readers may pick up almost subconsciously. On his blog, educator and writer Mike Rose responds to "In the Basement of the Ivory Tower," an *Atlantic Monthly* article that he says "offers a disheartening portrait of the 'non-traditional' (or 'remedial' or just run-of-the-mill) college student, a portrait common in mass media, and in high-brow media particularly." In the passage below, we've italicized self-assured prose that Rose uses in criticizing this essay:

> *It is certainly accurate* that a number of people do enter higher education poorly prepared. And *we do need to think hard* about what the current push for "college for all" truly means, how it can be enacted in an effective way, and whether or not it offers the best remedy for past educational inequality. These are *important questions*. Articles like "In the Basement of the Ivory Tower" *don't help us answer them.*
>
> —Mike Rose, Mike Rose's Blog

Establishing Credibility

Whereas authority is a measure of how much command a writer has over a subject, credibility speaks to a writer's honesty, respect for an audience and its values, and plain old likeability. Sometimes a sense of humor can play an important role in getting an audience to listen to you: it's no accident that all but the most serious speeches begin with a few jokes or stories. The humor puts listeners at ease and helps them identify with the speaker. In fact, a little self-deprecation can endear writers or speakers to the toughest audiences. We'll often listen to people confident enough to make fun of themselves, because they seem clever and yet aware of their own limitations.

Take, for example, the opening scene of *An Inconvenient Truth*, the documentary on the dangers of global warming. Al Gore, who later won an Academy Award for this film, takes the stage dressed in a dark suit, holding a PowerPoint clicker, and looking urgent. The Global Warming Slideshow for which he has become so well known occupies the huge screen behind him as he prepares to address a large group of students. There's a pause, and then Gore says, "Hello, my name is Al Gore, and I used to be the next president of the United States." The students erupt with roars of laughter, cheers, and whistles at this very effective piece of self-deprecating humor.

But humor alone can't establish credibility. Although a funny anecdote may help dispose an audience to listen to you, you will need to move quickly to make reasonable claims and then back them up with evidence and documentation—or, in electronic environments, to link your claims to sites with reliable information. That is, showing your authority on a topic is itself a good way to build credibility.

But there's even more to it than that. Consider that a number of studies over the years have shown that tall, slender, good-looking people have an advantage in getting a job or getting a raise. Apparently, employers make assumptions about such people's competence based on nothing more than good looks. You probably act the same way in some circumstances, even if you resent the practice.

You might recall these studies when you make an argument, knowing that like it or not, readers and audiences are going to respond to how you present yourself as a person. In other words, be sure that your writing visually conveys your message as effectively as possible. Choose a medium that shows you at your best. Some writers love a written text garnished with quotations, footnotes, charts, graphs, and a bibliography. Others can make a better case online or in some purely visual form. Choosing a medium carefully will help you design arguments that assure readers they can trust you.

You can also establish credibility by connecting your own beliefs to core principles that are well established and widely respected. This strategy is particularly effective when your position seems to be—at first glance, at least—a threat to traditional values. For example, when author Andrew Sullivan (who is himself a conservative) argues in favor of

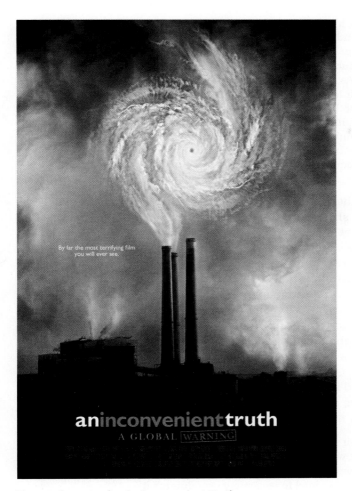

The movie poster for *An Inconvenient Truth*

legalizing same-sex marriages, he does so in language that echoes the themes of family-values conservatives:

Legalizing gay marriage would offer homosexuals the same deal society now offers heterosexuals: general social approval and specific legal advantages in exchange for a deeper and harder-to-extract-youself-from commitment to another human being. Like straight marriage, it would foster social cohesion, emotional security, and economic prudence. Since there's no reason gays should not be allowed to adopt or be foster parents, it could also help nurture children. And its introduction would not be some sort of radical break with social custom. As it has become more acceptable for gay people to acknowledge their loves publicly, more and more have committed themselves to one another for life in full view of their families and their friends. A law institutionalizing gay marriage would merely reinforce a healthy social trend. It would also, in the wake of AIDS, qualify as a genuine public health measure. Those conservatives who deplore promiscuity among some homosexuals should be among the first to support it.

—Andrew Sullivan, "Here Comes the Groom"

Yet another way to affirm your credibility as a writer is to use language that shows your respect for readers, addressing them neither above nor below their capabilities. Citing trustworthy sources and acknowledging them properly prove, too, that you've done your homework (another sign of respect) and suggest that you know your subject. So does presenting ideas clearly and fairly. Details matter: helpful graphs, tables, charts, or illustrations may carry weight with readers, as will the visual attractiveness of your work (or your Web site, for that matter). Again, even correct spelling counts.

Writers who establish their credibility in this way seem trustworthy. But sometimes, to be credible, you have to admit limitations, too: *This is what I know; I won't pretend to understand more.* It's a tactic used by people as respected in their fields as the late biologist Lewis Thomas, who in this example ponders whether scientists have overstepped their bounds in exploring the limits of DNA research:

Should we stop short of learning some things, for fear of what we, or someone, will do with the knowledge? My own answer is a flat no, but I must confess that this is an intuitive response and I am neither inclined nor trained to reason my way through it.

—Lewis Thomas, "The Hazards of Science"

When making an argument, many people would be reluctant to write "I suppose" or "I must confess," but those are the very concessions that might increase a reader's confidence in a scientist and writer like Lewis Thomas.

In fact, a powerful technique for building credibility is to acknowledge outright any exceptions, qualifications, or even weaknesses in your argument. For example, a Volkswagen ad with the headline "They said it couldn't be done. It couldn't," shows pro basketball star Wilt Chamberlain, who at seven feet, one inch, tall just can't fit inside the bug. This ad is one of a classic series in which Volkswagen pokes fun at itself and admits to limitations while also promoting the good points about the car, gaining credibility in the bargain.

Making such concessions to objections that readers might raise, called *conditions of rebuttal*, sends a strong signal to the audience that you've scrutinized your own position and can therefore be trusted when you turn to arguing its merits. Speaking to readers directly, using *I* or *you*, for instance, also enables you to come closer to them when that strategy is appropriate. Using contractions and everyday or colloquial language can have the same effect. In a 2008 commencement address, Oprah Winfrey argues that the graduates need to consider how they can serve others. To build her case, she draws on her own experience—forthrightly noting some mistakes and problems that she has faced in trying to live a life of service:

> I started this school in Africa . . . where I'm trying to give South African girls a shot at a future like yours. And I spent five years making sure

Oprah Winfrey in South Africa

that school would be as beautiful as the students. . . . And yet, last fall, I was faced with a crisis I had never anticipated. I was told that one of the dorm matrons was suspected of sexual abuse.

That was, as you can imagine, devastating news. First, I cried—actually, I sobbed. . . . And the whole time I kept asking that question: What is this here to teach me? And, as difficult as that experience has been, I got a lot of lessons. I understand now the mistakes I made, because I had been paying attention to all of the wrong things. I'd built that school from the outside in, when what really mattered was the inside out.

—Oprah Winfrey, Stanford University Commencement Address

In some situations, however, you may find that a more formal tone gives your claims greater authority. Choices like these are yours to make as you search for the ethos that best represents you in a given argument.

CULTURAL CONTEXTS FOR ARGUMENT

Ethos

In the United States, students writing arguments are often asked to establish authority by drawing on personal experiences, by reporting on research that they or others have conducted, and by taking a position for which they can offer strong evidence and support. But this expectation about student authority is by no means universal.

Some cultures regard student writers as novices who can most effectively make arguments by reflecting on what they've learned from their teachers and elders—those who are believed to hold the most important knowledge, wisdom, and, hence, authority. Whenever you're arguing a point with people from cultures other than your own, therefore, you need to think about what kind of authority you're expected to have:

- Whom are you addressing, and what is your relationship with that person?

- What knowledge are you expected to have? Is it appropriate or expected for you to demonstrate that knowledge—and if so, how?

- What tone is appropriate? If in doubt, always show respect: politeness is rarely if ever inappropriate.

Coming Clean about Motives

When people are trying to sell you something, it's important (and natural) to ask: *Whose interests are they serving? How will they profit from their proposal?* Such suspicions go to the heart of ethical arguments. It's no accident that Jonathan Swift ends his satirical *A Modest Proposal* with his narrator claiming he will benefit in no way from what he suggests—that the people of eighteenth-century Ireland end their poverty by selling their infant children to be used for food:

> I profess, in the sincerity of my heart, that I have not the least personal interest in endeavoring to promote this necessary work, having no other motive than the public good of my country, by advancing our trade, providing for infants, relieving the poor, and giving some pleasure to the rich. I have no children by which I can propose to get a single penny; the youngest being nine years old, and my wife past child-bearing.
>
> —Jonathan Swift, *A Modest Proposal*

Even this monster of a narrator appreciates that his idea will gain no traction if his motives are suspect in the least. He's also smart enough to discuss his potential conflicts of interest (his own children and his wife). This is always a sensible strategy whenever your motives for offering an idea might seem driven by its potential advantage to yourself or by your attachment to a particular class, gender, faction, or other group.

Here, for example, someone posting on the Web site Serious Eats, which is "focused on celebrating and sharing food enthusiasm" online, acknowledges—in a footnote—that his attention to Martha Stewart, her Web site, and a *Martha Stewart Living* cookbook may be influenced by his employment history:

> Martha Stewart* has been blipping up on the Serious Eats radar lately.
>
> First it was this astronaut meal she chose for her longtime Microsoft billionaire friend Charles Simonyi, "a gourmet space meal of duck breast confit and semolina cake with dried apricots." Talk about going above and beyond.
>
> Then official word comes that marthastewart.com has relaunched with a fresh new look and new features. The site, which went live in its new form a few weeks before this announcement, is quite an improvement. It seems to load faster, information is easier to find, and the recipes are easier to read—although there are so many brands,

magazines, and "omnimedia" on offer that the homepage is a little dizzying at first.

Third, while reading Apartment Therapy's Kitchen blog, I ran across a review of the *Everyday Food* cookbook, which was released recently by Martha Stewart Living Omnimedia: "Guests said that the dinner cooked from this book tasted like 'restaurant food' and we'll take the compliment. There is a fullness of flavor in these recipes that is not found in other quick fix recipes. . . ."

* *Full disclosure: I used to work at* Martha Stewart Living *magazine.*

—Adam Kuban, "Martha, Martha, Martha"

Especially in online venues like the one Kuban uses here, writers have to expect that readers will hold diverse views and will be quick to point out unmentioned affiliations as serious drawbacks to credibility. In fact, attacks on such loyalties are common in political circles, where it's almost a sport to assume the worst about an opponent's motives and associations. But we all have connections and interests that represent the ties that bind us to other human beings. It makes sense that a woman might be concerned with women's issues or that investors might look out for their investments. So it can be good strategy to let your audiences know where your loyalties lie when such information does, in fact, shape your work.

There are other ways, too, to invite readers to regard you as trustworthy. Nancy Mairs, in an essay entitled "On Being a Cripple," wins the attention and respect of her readers by facing her situation with a riveting directness:

First, the matter of semantics. I am a cripple. I choose this word to name me. I choose from among several possibilities, the most common of which are "handicapped" and "disabled." I made the choice a number of years ago, without thinking, unaware of my motives for doing so. Even now, I am not sure what those motives are, but I recognize that they are complex and not entirely flattering. People—crippled or not—wince at the word "cripple," as they do not at "handicapped" or "disabled." Perhaps I want them to wince. I want them to see me as a tough customer, one to whom the fates/gods/viruses have not been kind, but who can face the brutal truth of her existence squarely. As a cripple, I swagger.

—Nancy Mairs, "On Being a Cripple"

The paragraph takes some risks because the writer is expressing feelings that may make readers unsure how to react. Indeed, Mairs herself admits that she doesn't completely understand her own feelings and motives. Yet the very admission of uncertainty helps her to build a bridge to readers.

RESPOND•

1. Consider the ethos of each of the following public figures. Then describe one or two public arguments, campaigns, or products that might benefit from their endorsements as well as several that would not.

   Oprah Winfrey—TV celebrity

   Margaret Cho—comedian

   Kate Winslet—actress

   Colin Powell—former chair of the Joint Chiefs of Staff and Secretary of State in the George W. Bush administration

   Sarah Palin—former governor of Alaska and Republican vice-presidential candidate

   Dave Chappelle—humorist and columnist

   Jeff Gordon—NASCAR champion

   Nancy Pelosi—speaker of the U.S. House of Representatives

   Bill O'Reilly—TV news commentator

   Marge Simpson—sensible wife and mother on *The Simpsons*

   Jon Stewart—host of *The Daily Show* on Comedy Central

2. Voice is a choice. That is, writers modify the tone and style of their language depending on whom they want to seem to be. In the excerpts from this chapter, Mike Rose wants to appear fair yet confident; his language aims to convince us of his expertise. Andrew Sullivan wants to seem mature, objective, and unthreatening to traditional family values. Nancy Mairs wants to come across as frank and brutally honest about herself and her situation. In different situations, even when writing about the same topics, Rose, Sullivan, and Mairs would likely adopt different voices. Rethink and then rewrite the Sullivan passage on pp. 61–62 from a more personal, subjective viewpoint, taking on the voice (the character) of someone who is gay or has gay friends or family members and using the pronoun *I* if appropriate. Or rethink and rewrite the Mairs passage on p. 66, taking on the voice of someone, either "crippled" or not, who uses *I* much less frequently than Mairs does—perhaps not at all. You may also need to change the way that

Public figures try to control their images for obvious reasons. Would you buy a used car from any of these distinguished men and women?

you claim authority, establish credibility, and demonstrate competence as you try to present a different and a more personal or a less personal ethos.

3. Opponents of Richard Nixon, the thirty-seventh president of the United States, once raised doubts about his integrity by asking a single ruinous question: *Would you buy a used car from this man?* Create your own version of the argument of character. Begin by choosing an intriguing or controversial person or group and finding an image online. Then download the image into a word-processing file. Create a caption for the photo that is modeled after the question asked about Nixon: *Would you give this woman your email password? Would you share a campsite with this couple? Would you eat lasagna that this guy fixed?* Finally, write a serious 300-word argument that explores the character flaws or strengths of your subject(s).

4. A well-known television advertisement from the 1980s featured a soap-opera actor promoting a pain-relief medication. "I'm not a doctor," he said, "but I play one on TV." Today, many celebrities—from athletes like Venus Williams to actors like Leonardo DiCaprio—use their fame in promoting products or causes. One way or another, each case of celebrity endorsement relies on arguments based on character. Develop a one-page print advertisement for a product or service you use often—anything from soap to auto repair to cell-phone service— or a political position. There's one catch: your advertisement should rely on arguments based on character, and you should choose a spokesperson who seems the *least* likely to use or endorse your product or service. The challenge is to turn an apparent disadvantage into an advantage by exploiting character.

4
Arguments Based on Facts and Reason: Logos

SPOCK: Logic and practical information do not seem to apply here.

McCOY: You admit that?

SPOCK: To deny the facts would be illogical, Doctor.
—from *Star Trek* episode "A Piece of the Action"

When writers need to persuade, they usually try their best to provide readers with good reasons to believe them. When the choice is between logic and emotion, many of us will side with *Star Trek*'s Dr. McCoy rather than the stern Mr. Spock. Most of us respect *appeals to logos*—arguments based on facts, evidence, and reason—but like the good doctor, we're inclined to test the facts against our feelings and against the ethos of those making the appeal. Aristotle, among the first philosophers to write about persuasion, gives us a place to begin. He divided proofs based on facts and reason into two kinds—those derived from what we call *hard evidence* (Aristotle described these as *inartistic appeals*—facts, clues, statistics, testimonies, witnesses) and those based on *reason and common sense* (what Aristotle termed *artistic appeals*). These categories overlap and leak (what, after all, is *common sense?*), but they remain useful even today.

The differences can be observed in two arguments presented forty years apart at the United Nations when American representatives charged other nations with harboring weapons of mass destruction. On October 25, 1962, Adlai Stevenson, U.S. ambassador to the UN, asked, "Do you, Ambassador Zorin, deny that the U.S.S.R. has placed and is placing medium and intermediate range missiles and sites in Cuba?"—knowing that he had the hard evidence of spy photographs to prove his claim. The images showed the alleged construction beyond a reasonable doubt in an era when doctoring photographs was not an easy process.

Forty years later, on February 5, 2003, U.S. Secretary of State Colin Powell did not have the same kind of open-and-shut case when he argued to the UN Security Council that Iraq was harboring weapons of mass destruction in contravention to UN resolutions. Instead, he had to assure his worldwide audience that "what you will see is an accumulation of facts and disturbing patterns of behavior." None of his materials—including some photographs—had the immediacy or transparency

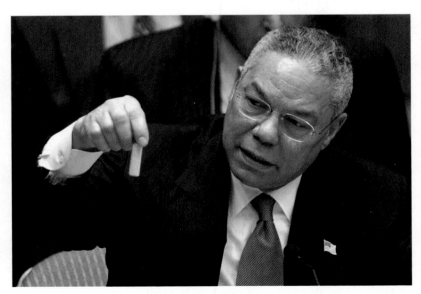

Colin Powell lost some credibility after his claim that Iraq had weapons of mass destruction proved untrue.

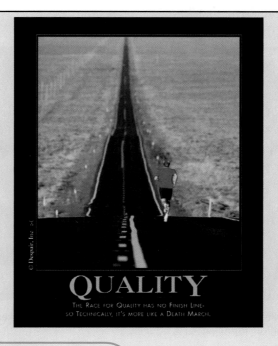

QUALITY

THE RACE FOR QUALITY HAS NO FINISH LINE-
SO TECHNICALLY, IT'S MORE LIKE A DEATH MARCH.

Not Just Words

Sometimes the difference between appeals isn't immediately self-evident. What one person considers an appeal to reason may look like an emotional or ethical argument to another. Add in the element of irony or parody, and the categories scramble even more. Take a look at the image above. At first glance, this may look like a serious poster, one that uses pathos and ethos (the title "Quality" and the picture, which implies that the poster's creator is committed to the long, lonely journey necessary to achieve this admirable goal) to argue that high standards are worth the effort. But the (logical?) caption cleverly undercuts that message. Dig a little deeper, and you will find that this is part of a series of parodies in poster form found at http://motivationalpostersonline.blogspot.com. What do you think this poster's overall point is? How do words and image work together to make that point? Who is the intended audience? Finally, working within a group, discuss whether the poster represents an appeal to logic and reason, and why.

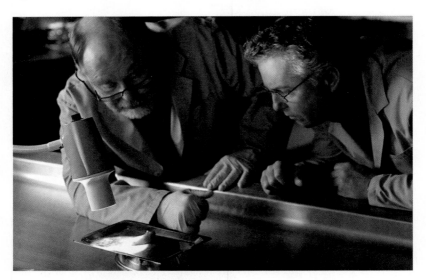

As the storylines on *CSI* suggest, hard evidence almost always makes the strongest logical argument.

of the 1962 Cuban missile crisis images. So Powell had to hope that the pattern and weight of evidence offered in a lengthy presentation would make his claim—"that Saddam Hussein and his regime are concealing their efforts to produce more weapons of mass destruction"—seem compelling. Since no such weapons were found after Western troops invaded Iraq, one might infer (logically) that hard evidence is superior to reasoning aided by less-than-compelling inferences and probabilities. In fact, Powell came to regret his dependence on the assortment of reasons he had been offered by other members of the Bush administration to back up the claims he made. Eighteen months later, he called his presentation a "blot" on his record and said that he felt "truly terrible" about being misinformed by the less-than-hard evidence he had been given.

As this example shows, hard evidence won't always be available, nor will it always be as overwhelming as the photographs that Adlai Stevenson displayed. And even when hard evidence is available, it must be carefully tested. While Stevenson could trust the veracity of the photographs that he displayed nearly fifty years ago, he probably would be more skeptical today. On July 9, 2008, a photo of Iranian missile tests was published in newspapers around the world. The photo showed four missiles being fired, but it was called into question when other photos of the tests showed only three missiles. Where had the fourth missile come from? Even after extensive examination, experts disagreed about whether the three-missile image had simply been digitally changed or whether a fourth missile had actually been fired at a later time and then composited into the original photo. In short, even the hardest of evidence needs to be scrutinized with great care before being accepted as clear and compelling proof.

Providing Hard Evidence

As the Stevenson and Powell examples suggest, even when hard evidence is contested or hard to come by, people usually prefer arguments based on facts and testimony to those grounded in reasoning alone. In a

Iranian missile test: Where did the fourth missile (second from right in the top photo) come from? Does this photo constitute "hard evidence"?

courtroom as well as in the popular media, for example, lawyers or reporters look for the "smoking gun"—the piece of hard evidence that ties a defendant to a crime. It might be an audiotape, a fingerprint, an email, or, increasingly, DNA evidence. Popular crime shows such as *CSI: Crime Scene Investigation* focus intensely on gathering this sort of "scientific" support for a prosecution. Less dramatically, the factual evidence in an argument might be columns of data carefully collected over time to prove a point about racial profiling or the effects of climate change on populations of fish and other wildlife. If you live in a state where you can be ticketed after a camera catches you running a red light, you know what hard evidence means.

Factual evidence, however, takes many forms. The ones that you use will depend on the kind of argument you're making. In fact, providing appropriate evidence ought to become a habit whenever you write an argument. The evidence makes your case plausible; it may also supply the details that make writing interesting. Consider Aristotle's claim that all arguments can be reduced to just two components:

Statement + Proof

Here's another way of naming those parts:

Claim + Supporting Evidence

In a scholarly article, you can see this connection between statements and proof in the text and the notes. As an example, we reprint a single page from a much-cited review of Michael Bellesiles's *Arming America: The Making of America's Gun Culture* by James Lindgren published in the *Yale Law Review* (see facing page). Bellesiles used evidence gathered from eighteenth-century documents to argue that gun ownership in frontier America was much rarer than advocates of the right to bear arms believed. After publication, *Arming America* was hailed by gun critics for weakening the claim of gun advocates today that the ownership of weapons has always been a part of American culture. But Lindgren, as well as many other critics and historians, found so many evidentiary flaws in Bellesiles's arguments that questions were soon raised about his scholastic integrity. Lindgren's review of *Arming America* runs for more than fifty meticulous pages (including an appendix of errors in Bellesiles's work) and contains 212 footnotes. You can see a factual argument in action just by looking at how Lindgren handles evidence on a single page. You may never write an argument as detailed as Lindgren's review, but you should develop the same respect for evidence.

This selection from James Lindgren's review of Michael Bellesiles's *Arming America: The Making of America's Gun Culture* first appeared in the *Yale Law Review*, volume 111 (2002).

LINDGRENFINAL.DOC   APRIL 26, 2002 4/26/02 12:34 PM

2002]   *Arming America*   2203

B. *How Common Was Gun Ownership?*

The most contested portions of *Arming America* involve the book's most surprising claim, that guns were infrequently owned before the mid-1800s. As I show below, the claim that colonial America did not have a gun culture is questionable on the evidence of gun ownership alone. Compared to the seventeenth and eighteenth centuries, it appears that guns are not as commonly owned today. Whereas individual gun ownership in every published (and unpublished) study of early probate records that I have located (except Bellesiles's) ranges from 40% to 79%; only 32.5% of households today own a gun.[44] This appears to be a much smaller percentage than in early America—in part because the mean household size in the late eighteenth century was six people,[45] while today it is just under two people.[46] The prevailing estimate of 40% to 79% ownership differs markedly from Bellesiles's claim that only about 15% owned guns.[47] In the remainder of this Section, I explain why.

1. *The Gun Censuses*

Bellesiles bases his claims of low gun ownership primarily on probate records and counts of guns at militia musters.[48] He also discusses censuses of all guns in private and public hands, but on closer examination, none of these turns out to be a general census of all guns.

The trend is set in Bellesiles's first count of guns in an American community—the 1630 count of all the guns in the Massachusetts Bay Colony of about 1000 people. Bellesiles's account is quite specific: "In 1630 the Massachusetts Bay Company reported in their possession: '80 bastard musketts, . . . [10] Fowlinge peeces, . . . 10 Full musketts . . . .' " There were thus exactly one hundred firearms for use among seven towns

---

44. This results from my analysis of the March 2001 release of the National Opinion Research Center's *General Social Survey, 2000* [hereinafter 2000 NORC GSS]. The data are also available at Nat'l Opinion Research Ctr., General Social Survey, *at* http://www.icpsr.umich.edu/GSS/ (last visited Apr. 8, 2002). According to the survey, 32.5% of households owned any gun, 19.7% owned a rifle, 18.6% owned a shotgun, and 19.7% owned a pistol or revolver. 2000 NORC GSS, *supra*. Only 1.2% of respondents refused to respond to the question. *Id.*

45. Inter-Univ. Consortium for Political & Soc. Research (ICPSR), Census Data for the Year 1790, http://fisher.lib.virginia.edu/cgi-local/censusbin/census/cen.pl?year=790 (last visited Aug. 10, 2001).

46. 2000 NORC GSS, *supra* note 44.

47. BELLESILES, *supra* note 3, at 445 tbl.1.

Facts

"Facts," said John Adams, "are stubborn things," and so they make strong arguments, especially when readers believe they come from honest sources. Gathering such information and transmitting it faithfully practically define what we mean by professional journalism in one realm and scholarship in another. We'll even listen to people that we don't agree with if they can overwhelm us with evidence. Below, for example, a reviewer for the conservative magazine *National Review* praises the work of William Julius Wilson, a well-known liberal sociologist, because of how well he presents his case:

> In his eagerly awaited new book, Wilson argues that ghetto blacks are worse off than ever, victimized by a near-total loss of low-skill jobs in and around inner-city neighborhoods. In support of this thesis, he *musters mountains of data, plus excerpts from some of the thousands of surveys and face-to-face interviews that he and his research team conducted among inner-city Chicagoans.* It is a book that deserves a wide audience among thinking conservatives.
>
> —John J. Dilulio Jr., "When Decency Disappears" (emphasis added)

In this instance, the facts are respected even when the reviewer (Dilulio) has a very different political stance from that of the author of the book (Wilson).

When your facts are compelling, they may stand on their own in a low-stakes argument, supported by little more saying where they come from. Consider the power of phrases such as "reported by the *Wall Street Journal*," "according to MSNBC," or "in a book published by Cambridge University Press." Such sources gain credibility if they have, in readers' experience, reported facts accurately and reliably over time. In fact, one reason that you document the sources you use in an argument is to let the credibility of those sources reflect positively on you.

But arguing with facts also sometimes involves challenging the biases of even the most reputable sources if they lead to unfair or selective reporting. You don't have to search hard to find critics of the *Wall Street Journal* or MSNBC these days. In recent years, bloggers and other online critics have enjoyed pointing out the biases or factual mistakes of what conservatives like to call "mainstream media" (MSM) outlets (some liberals prefer "corporate media" or "traditional media"). These criticisms often deal not just with specific facts and coverage but with the overall way that an issue is presented or "framed."

In the following passage, for example, blogger Andrew Sullivan, who unlike many of his fellow conservatives strongly opposes using waterboarding and other extreme interrogation techniques against suspected terrorists, takes on the *New York Times*. Conservatives often accuse the *Times* of having a liberal bias in its news coverage, but in this case Sullivan attacks the newspaper for framing the issue in what he considers an unjustifiably *neutral* way:

> The front-page piece in the NYT today on Obama's thorny task in staffing the CIA, after seven years of its violation of the Geneva Conventions, is revealing in many ways. Like many in the MSM, the NYT cannot bring itself to describe the techniques that the CIA has used as "torture." And yet we *know* that the CIA has tortured prisoners under the plain legal definition of torture, and we *know* that this was the whole point of giving the CIA explicit legislative permission for this in 2006. [Yet], the only time the word "torture" is used in the NYT piece is to describe techniques practiced by other countries. This is an important point because it shows how the NYT is now actively *deceiving* its readers about this matter. Here is the NYT's locution on waterboarding, a torture technique used for centuries:
>
> > the near-drowning tactic considered by many legal authorities to be torture.
>
> Can the NYT cite *one* legal authority . . . that says waterboarding is *not* torture? Can they cite one instance in American legal history in which is was *not* so defined? If not, why this absurd avoidance of *the truth* in the paper of record? . . .
>
> This is the strategy of the torture defenders: render this debate once again a red-blue, right-left ding-dong, culture war struggle. It isn't. It's a foundational, moral and constitutional issue that transcends all those categories. And the NYT does its readers a disservice in occluding that.
>
> —Andrew Sullivan, "The NYT and the T-Word"

In an ideal world, good information would always drive out bad. But you already know that we don't live in an ideal world, so sometimes bad information gets repeated in an echo chamber that amplifies the errors: if reputable media say that waterboarding or similar techniques may not constitute torture, how long will it take for people to begin to believe this?

And many media have no pretenses at all about being reputable. During the 2008 presidential campaign, the Internet buzzed with statements proclaiming that Barack Obama was Muslim, even after dozens of sources, including many people with whom Obama had worshipped, testified to his Christianity. As a reader and researcher, you should look beyond headlines, bylines, reputations, and especially rumors that fly about the Internet. Scrutinize any facts you collect before passing them on yourself. Test their reliability, and admit any problems at the start.

Statistics

Let's deal with a cliché right up front: figures lie and liars figure. Like most clichés, it contains a grain of truth. It's possible to lie with numbers, even those that are accurate, because numbers rarely speak for themselves. They need to be interpreted by writers—and writers almost always have agendas that shape the interpretations.

For example, suppose the crime rate in the city where you live has fallen from one hundred crimes per thousand residents four years ago to fifty per thousand this year. The mayor and the police chief, who are running for reelection, crow *The crime rate has been cut in half during our time in office!* But their opponents spin the figure another way—*One out of every twenty citizens of Springfield will be a crime victim this year!*—and point out that the crime rate in a nearby city has fallen by two-thirds over the same period. Suddenly that fifty per thousand looks like a sobering number. Sometimes the same statistic can be cited as a cause for celebration or for alarm.

We're not suggesting that numbers are meaningless or that you have license to use them in any way that serves your purposes. Quite the contrary. But you do have to understand the role you play in giving numbers a voice and a presence. Consider the way Armen Keteyian, writing for the *Sporting News*, raises serious questions about the safety of aluminum bats in high school and college sports, despite the insistence by many sports officials that they're safe. Keteyian makes his case by focusing on statistics and numbers—which we've italicized—suggesting otherwise:

> Bat companies point to the NCAA's *annual injury report* ranking baseball as one of the safest collegiate sports. The report also shows "there is *no . . . significant increase in batted ball injuries.*" But last December, after an 18-month study, the U.S. Consumer Product Safety Commission released a report that called the NCAA's *injury statistics* "inconclusive . . . and not complete enough" to determine whether current aluminum bats are more dangerous than wood.

"Let's be honest," says Anderson. "Bat manufacturers have been wonderful for college baseball. So you get caught up in that, the free product, the fact it's saving you money. But all of a sudden I see my young man lying on the ground, and I'm going, 'Is this the right thing?'"

[Many college players have been] struck—and in some cases nearly killed—by balls hit off aluminum bats certified by the NCAA and the national high school federation. To be approved, an aluminum bat must not cause *a batted ball to travel any faster than the best wood bat does*. But there's a catch: Bats are tested in a laboratory on a machine set at a *70 mph pitch speed and a 66 mph swing speed*. Why not test at far more realistic numbers, say, *85 mph pitches and 80 mph swings?*

Simple, says MacKay: "It would scare people to death."

Why? Reaction time. Experts say *the fastest batted ball a pitcher can defend against is about 97 mph.* Translation: *Less than four-tenths of a second.*

Ninety-seven mph also is the fastest a ball can be hit by a certified bat in the lab test. Sounds safe, right? But what about on the field? Well, it turns out nobody officially tests balls hit by aluminum bats under game conditions.

"We've seen some things on our radar gun—*108 miles per hour, 110 at different times,*" says Anderson. "*I've witnessed 114 myself.* Makes you question whether we are doing the right thing."

—Armen Keteyian, "Bats Should Crack, Not Skulls" (emphasis added)

This is hardly the last word on aluminum bats. In fact, since Keteyian's article was published, the Little League has pronounced that aluminum bats are as safe as wooden bats even as high school leagues across the country were banning them. Nor is the controversy likely to end any time soon, unless a persistent spike in injuries brings about consensus.

Surveys and Polls

Some of the most influential forms of statistics are those produced by surveys and polls. These measures play so large a role in people's social and political lives that writers, whether interpreting them or fashioning surveys themselves, need to give them special attention.

When they verify the popularity of an idea or proposal, surveys and polls provide persuasive appeals because, in a democracy, majority opinion offers a compelling warrant: a government should do what most people want. Polls come as close to expressing the will of the people as anything short of an election—the most decisive poll of all. (For more on

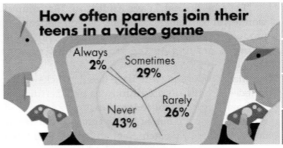

Fathers are more likely than mothers (33% vs. 26%) to say they sometimes play video games with their teens ages 12 to 17.

How often parents join their teens in a video game

Always 2%
Sometimes 29%
Rarely 26%
Never 43%

By Michelle Healy and Sam Ward, USA TODAY
Source: Pew Internet & American Life Project

USA Today is famous for the tables, pie charts, and graphs it creates to present statistics and poll results. What claims might the evidence in this graph support? How does the design of the item influence your reading of it?

warrants, see Chapter 7, pp. 186–92.) However, surveys and polls can do much more than help politicians make decisions. They can also provide persuasive reasons for action or intervention. When surveys show, for example, that most American sixth-graders can't locate France or Wyoming on a map—not to mention Turkey or Afghanistan—that's an appeal for better instruction in geography. When polls suggest that con-sumer confidence is declining, businesses may have reason to worry about their bulging inventories.

It always makes sense, however, to push back against any poll num-bers reported—especially when they support your own point of view. Ask who commissioned the poll, who is publishing its outcome, who was surveyed (and in what proportions), and what stakes these parties might have in its outcome.

Are we being too suspicious? No. In fact, this sort of scrutiny is ex-actly what you should anticipate from your readers whenever you do surveys of your own to explore an issue. You should be confident that you've surveyed enough people to be accurate, that the people you chose for the study were representative of the selected population as a whole, and that you chose them randomly—not selecting those most likely to say what you hoped to hear.

On the other hand, as with other kinds of factual evidence, don't make the opposite mistake by discounting or ignoring polls whose find-ings are *not* what you had hoped for. In the following excerpts from a column in the *Dallas News*, conservative Rod Dreher forthrightly faces up to the results from a poll of registered Texas voters after the 2008 election—results that he finds ominous for his Texas Republican Party:

> The full report, which will be released today, knocks the legs out from under two principles cherished by the party's grassroots: staunch social conservatism and hard-line immigration policies. At the state level, few voters care much about abortion, school prayer and other hot-button issues. Immigration is the only conservative stand-by that rates much mention – and by hitting it too hard, Republicans lose both the Hispanics and independents that make up what the pollster defines as the "Critical Middle." . . .
>
> This is not going to go down well with the activist core of the Texas GOP, especially people like me: a social conservative with firm views on illegal immigration. But reality has a way of focusing the mind, forcing one to realize that political parties are not dogma-driven churches, but coalitions that unavoidably shift over time.
>
> —Rod Dreher, "Poll's Shocking SOS for Texas GOP"

Dreher's frank acknowledgment of findings that were unpleasant to him—which included his pointing out that the poll was conducted by a Republican polling firm—also helps him to create a positive ethos, presenting himself as a trustworthy, credible writer who follows the facts wherever they lead.

The meaning of polls and surveys is also affected by the way that questions are asked. Recent research has shown, for example, that questions about same-sex unions get differing responses according to how they are worded. When people are asked whether gay and lesbian couples should be eligible for the same inheritance and partner health benefits that heterosexual couples receive, a majority of those polled give positive responses—unless the word *marriage* appears in the question; then the responses are primarily negative. As a result, you need to be careful in constructing questions for any poll or survey you want to conduct.

You often also need to read beyond headlines and journalists' (or pollsters') summaries of poll results to be sure that you understand all the details of the findings and the ways that they are being interpreted. In a blog posting in which Dreher discusses the column excerpted above, for example, he notes:

> The news is actually even worse for Republicans than I was able to indicate in the space constrictions of a newspaper column. The

support Democrats have is strong, according to the poll, whereas those who back the GOP are lukewarm.

—Rod Dreher, "Is Texas Going Democratic?"

Finally, always keep in mind that the date of a poll may strongly affect the results—and their usefulness in an argument. On July 31, 2008, for example, the *Orange County* (California) *Registrar* carried an article with the headline "Poll: Californians Now Favor Offshore Drilling." The article reported that 51 percent of those polled favored offshore drilling for oil, which a majority of California residents had previously opposed, and noted that this was an increase of ten percentage points from a survey done a year earlier. But it also noted that the poll was conducted at a time of sharply rising gasoline prices. Within a few months, prices were falling dramatically amid the global economic recession, so an argument in favor of drilling would have to take into account the possibility that public sentiment might have shifted significantly again.

Testimonies and Narratives

Numbers and statistics are not the only good evidence that writers need. You can support arguments with all kinds of human experiences, particularly those that you or others have undergone or reported. In a court,

A drilling platform off the California coast. Polls on allowing offshore drilling tend to track fluctuations in oil prices.

for example, decisions are often based on detailed descriptions of what happened. Following is a reporter's account of a court case in which a panel of judges decided, based on the testimony presented, that a man had been sexually harassed by another man. The narrative, in this case, supplies the evidence:

> The Seventh Circuit, in a 1997 case known as *Doe v. City of Belleville*, drew a sweeping conclusion allowing for same-sex harassment cases of many kinds. Title VII was sex-neutral, the court ruled; it didn't specifically prohibit discrimination against men or women. Moreover, the judges argued, there was such a thing as gender stereotyping, and if someone was harassed on that basis, it was unlawful. This case, for example, centered on teenage twin brothers working a summer job cutting grass in the city cemetery of Belleville, Ill. One boy wore an earring, which caused him no end of grief that particular summer—including a lot of menacing talk among his co-workers about sexually assaulting him in the woods and sending him "back to San Francisco." One of his harassers, identified in court documents as a large former marine, culminated a verbal campaign by backing the earring-wearer against a wall and grabbing him by the testicles to see "if he was a girl or a guy." The teenager had been "singled out for this abuse," the court ruled, "because the way in which he projected the sexual aspect of his personality"—meaning his gender—"did not conform to his co-workers' view of appropriate masculine behavior."
> —Margaret Talbot, "Men Behaving Badly"

Personal experience carefully reported can also support a claim convincingly, especially if a writer has earned the trust of readers. In the following excerpt, Christian Zawodniak describes his experiences as a student in a first-year college writing course. Not impressed by his instructor's performance, Zawodniak provides specific evidence of the instructor's failings:

> My most vivid memory of Jeff's rigidness was the day he responded to our criticisms of the class. Students were given a chance anonymously to write our biggest criticisms one Monday, and the following Wednesday Jeff responded, staunchly answering all criticisms of his teaching: "Some of you complained that I didn't come to class prepared. It took me five years to learn all this." Then he pointed to the blackboard on which he had written all the concepts we had discussed that quarter. His responses didn't seem genuine or aimed at improving

his teaching or helping students to understand him. He thought he was always right. Jeff's position gave him responsibilities that he officially met. But he didn't take responsibility in all the ways he had led us to expect.

—Christian Zawodniak, "Teacher Power, Student Pedagogy"

This portrait of a defensive instructor gives readers details by which to assess the argument. If readers believe Zawodniak, they learn something about teaching. (For more on establishing credibility with readers, see Chapter 3.)

Using Reason and Common Sense

In the absence of hard facts, claims may be supported with other kinds of compelling reasons. The formal study of principles of reasoning is called *logic*, but few people (except perhaps mathematicians and philosophers) use formal logic to present their arguments. Many people might recognize the most famous of all *syllogisms* (a vehicle of deductive reasoning), but that's about the extent of what they know about formal logic:

All human beings are mortal.

~ Socrates is a human being.

Therefore, Socrates is mortal.

In valid syllogisms, the conclusion follows logically—and technically—from the premises that lead up to it. Many have criticized syllogistic reasoning for being limited, and some say that the conclusion of a syllogism is really only a restatement of the premises. Others have poked fun at the syllogism, as in the cartoon on the facing page, which demonstrates an error in reasoning known as the *undistributed middle term* (in this case, the term is "black and white").

Even as gifted a logician as Aristotle recognized that most people argue perfectly well using informal rather than formal logic. Consciously or not, we are constantly stating claims, drawing conclusions, and making and questioning assumptions whenever we read or write. People mostly rely on the habits of mind and cultural assumptions that they share with their readers or listeners.

Logic: another thing that penguins aren't very good at.

In Chapter 7, we describe a system of informal logic that you may find useful in shaping credible arguments—Toulmin argument. Here, we briefly examine some ways that people use informal logic in their daily lives. Once again, we begin with Aristotle, who used the term *enthymeme* to describe an ordinary kind of sentence that includes both a claim and a reason but depends on the audience's agreement with an assumption that is left implicit rather than spelled out. The following sentences are all enthymemes:

We'd better cancel the picnic because it's going to rain.

Flat taxes are fair because they treat everyone the same.

I'll buy a PC laptop instead of a Mac because it's cheaper.

NCAA football needs a real play-off to crown a real national champion.

On their own, enthymemes can be persuasive statements when most readers agree with the assumptions on which they're based. Perhaps that's why enthymemes lie at the heart of many humorous statements, like this one from Will Rogers:

> **I am not a member of any organized political party. I am a Democrat.**

Rogers is counting here on his audience filling in what is implicit: because historically the Democrats have been diverse and given to fighting among themselves, they are a "disorganized" rather than an "organized" party.

Sometimes enthymemes seem so obvious that readers don't realize that they're drawing inferences when they agree with them. Consider the first example on p. 85:

> **We'd better cancel the picnic because it's going to rain.**

Let's expand the enthymeme a bit to say more of what the speaker may mean:

> **We'd better cancel the picnic this afternoon because the weather bureau is predicting a 70 percent chance of rain for the remainder of the day.**

Embedded in this brief argument are all sorts of assumptions and fragments of cultural information that are left implicit but that help to make it persuasive:

> **Picnics are ordinarily held outdoors.**
>
> **When the weather is bad, it's best to cancel picnics.**
>
> **Rain is bad weather for picnics.**
>
> **A 70 percent chance of rain means that rain is more likely to occur than not.**
>
> **When rain is more likely to occur than not, it makes sense to cancel picnics.**
>
> **The weather bureau's predictions are reliable enough to warrant action.**

For most people, the original statement carries all this information on its own; it's a compressed argument, based on what audiences know and will accept.

But sometimes enthymemes aren't self-evident:

> **Be wary of environmentalism because it's religion disguised as science.**

iPods are undermining civil society by making us even more focused on ourselves.

It's time to make all public toilets unisex because to do otherwise is discriminatory.

In those cases, you'll have to work much harder to defend both the claim and the implicit assumptions that it's based on by drawing out the inferences that seem self-evident in other enthymemes. And you'll likely also have to supply credible evidence. A simple declaration of fact won't suffice.

Cultural Assumptions and Values

Some of the assumptions in an argument will be based on shared values derived from culture and history. In the United States, for example, few arguments work better than those based on principles of fairness and equity. Since the Declaration of Independence announces these principles, they are deeply inscribed in U.S. culture and represent a cherished value. As a result, most Americans will say that they believe all people should be treated the same way, no matter who they are or where they come from.

Because fairness is so deeply endorsed in American culture, enthymemes that rely on principles of fairness and equity need less formal support than those that challenge them. That's why, for example, both sides in debates over affirmative-action programs seek the high ground of fairness: proponents claim that affirmative action is needed to correct enduring inequities from the past; opponents suggest that the preferential policies should be overturned because they cause inequity today. Here, Linda Chavez assumes that her audience will value principles of equity:

> Ultimately, entitlements based on their status as "victims" rob Hispanics of real power. The history of American ethnic groups is one of overcoming disadvantage, of competing with those who were already here and proving themselves as competent as any who came before. Their fight was always to be treated the same as other Americans, never to be treated as special, certainly not to turn the temporary disadvantages they suffered into permanent entitlement. Anyone who thinks this fight was easier in the earlier part of this century when it was waged by other ethnic groups does not know history.
> —Linda Chavez, "Towards a New Politics of Hispanic Assimilation"

Chavez expects Hispanics to accept her claims because she believes that they don't wish to be treated differently from other ethnic groups in the society.

Societies in other times and places have held their own cultural values and principles derived from them. Medieval Europe, for example, valued aristocratic birth, and the effectiveness of many arguments in that time and place counted on widespread consensus on that principle. Other cultures, including some in Africa, have valued cooperation and community rather than individualism and based arguments on such a value.

Writers need to understand the values and cultural assumptions held by their audiences, but even an assumption that seems pervasive—like that of equity and fairness—will still be open to interpretation. In the case of Linda Chavez's argument, for instance, many citizens—whether Hispanic or not—disagreed vehemently with her arguments against affirmative action because they held different definitions of what *fair* and *equal* mean.

Providing Logical Structures for Argument

Some arguments are not tied to cultural assumptions but rather depend on particular logical structures to make their points. In the following pages, we identify a few of these logical structures.

Degree

Arguments based on degree are so common that people barely notice them. Nor do people pay much attention to how they work because they seem self-evident. Most audiences will readily accept that *more of a good thing or less of a bad thing is good*. In her novel *The Fountainhead*, Ayn Rand asks: "If physical slavery is repulsive, how much more repulsive is the concept of servility of the spirit?" Most readers immediately comprehend the point Rand intends to make about slavery of the spirit because they already know that physical slavery is cruel and would reject any forms of slavery that were even crueler on the principle that *more of a bad thing is bad*. Rand still needs to offer evidence that "servility of the spirit" is, in fact, worse than bodily servitude, but she has begun with a

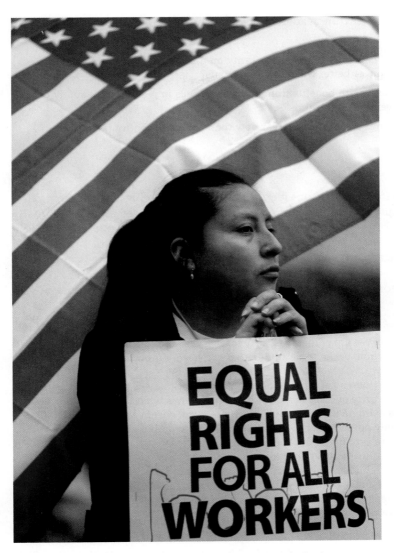

A demonstrator at an immigrant-rights rally in New York City in 2007. Arguments based on values that are widely shared within a society—such as the idea of equal rights in American culture— have an automatic advantage with audiences.

logical structure readers can grasp. Here are other arguments that work similarly:

> If I can get a ten-year warranty on a humble Kia, shouldn't I get the same or better warranty from Lexus?
>
> The health benefits from using stem cells in research will surely outweigh the ethical risks.
>
> Better a conventional war now than a nuclear confrontation later.

Analogies

Analogies explain one idea or concept by comparing it to something else. People understand comparisons intuitively. Indeed, people habitually think in comparative terms, through similes and metaphors: *he is as slow as molasses; love is never having to say you're sorry; war is hell.* An analogy is typically a complex or extended comparison. Following is an excerpt from an extended analogy in a *New York Times* op-ed column by Thomas Friedman, entitled "9/11 and 4/11" (the 4/11 refers to the price of gas, then at $4.11):

> We don't have a "gasoline price problem." We have an addiction problem. We are addicted to dirty fossil fuels, and this addiction is driving a whole set of toxic trends that are harming our nation in different ways. . . .
>
> When a person is addicted to crack cocaine, his problem is not that the price of crack is going up. His problem is what that crack addiction is doing to his whole body. The cure is not cheaper crack, which would only perpetuate the addiction and all the problems it is creating. The cure is to break the addiction.
>
> Ditto for us. Our cure is not cheaper gasoline, but a clean energy system. And the key to building that is to keep the price of gasoline and coal—our crack—higher, not lower, so consumers are moved to break their addiction to these dirty fuels and inventors are moved to create clean alternatives.
>
> —Thomas L. Friedman, "9/11 and 4/11"

Many would resist Friedman's analogy here, perhaps arguing that it oversimplifies a complex issue and challenging his details of the analogy. And analogies of argument are routinely abused, so much so that faulty analogy (see p. 533) is one of the most familiar fallacies of argument.

Precedent

Arguments from precedent are related to arguments of analogy in that they both involve comparisons. Sometimes an argument of precedent focuses on comparable institutions. Consider an assertion like the following:

> If motorists in most other states can pump their own gas safely, surely the state of Oregon can trust its own drivers to be as capable. It's time for Oregon to permit self-service gas stations.

You could pull a lot of inferences out of this claim to explain its reasonableness: people in Oregon are as capable as people in other states, people with equivalent capabilities can do the same thing, pumping gas is not hard, and so forth. But you don't have to because most readers get the argument simply because of the way it is put together.

Here's an excerpt from an extended argument by a columnist for the student newspaper of the University of Massachusetts at Amherst calling for "bathroom reform." Note the ways in which this student calls on a number of precedents in making her case:

> Several semesters ago, transgender students began to protest the bathroom situation at UMass, demanding gender-neutral bathrooms in many dorms. This was so students who do not identify with their assigned gender at birth or with either gender could feel comfortable entering the bathrooms without going into the "wrong" bathroom. This movement filled *The Massachusetts Daily Collegian* with many columns for and against doing so, along with a table that was always manned by someone in the Campus Center. Since then, the movement for a "restroom revolution" to transform the way we think about bathrooms has died down, either due to the UMass administration's unwillingness to bend or lack of energy and time.
>
> Often I find male bathrooms to be empty while a long line stretched out the door from female bathrooms. This is due to the evident fact that males are quicker than females at relieving themselves; yet, whenever bathrooms are built, both the female and male bathrooms are built of an equal size. . . .
>
> Just several decades ago, UMass dorms were either all-female or all-male, and females could attend a male dorm only one Sunday a month, in which case the dormitory room door had to stay open and three feet had to be on the ground at all time. Today's co-ed dorms are an idea that was unheard of at that time, an idea as strange as co-ed bathrooms are today. Today, schools such as Harvard University and

As more and more restrooms go gender-neutral, they provide precedents for future arguments. This one, at Kent State University in Ohio, accommodates transgendered people, designated by the symbol at the bottom right.

the University of New Hampshire, as well as many others, have co-ed bathrooms with no problems.

At UMass, sexual assault does remain a problem and an issue that needs to be dealt with. The fact is that gender-specific bathrooms have not shown in the past to prevent sexual assaults and a perpetrator is not prevented from entering such a bathroom simply by a "no men allowed" sign. Statistically, most assaults on women are not done by complete strangers, but rather by someone that the victim already knew. By creating gender-neutral bathrooms, a greater number of people would be allowed to enter these facilities, making them less empty and isolated. . . .

Fifty years ago, women wearing men's clothing, such as pants, was taboo and unthinkable, and co-ed gym classes was an inconceivable concept. Imagine how ridiculous a notion those ideas must have been then. I don't think society will crumble now if we allow all genders to use the same bathrooms in college. Gender-segregated bathrooms are an example of an attempt to hold onto the past, but we are in a new age of equality. Why not create some equally accessible bathrooms?

—Gilad Skolnick, "A Plea for Bathroom Reform"

Other precedents deal with issues of time. For example, what courts have decided in the past often determines how courts will rule on a similar or related issue. The near avalanche of lawsuits brought by the Recording Industry Association of America (RIAA) in an attempt to stop online file sharing has over the last decade aimed at establishing a set of legal precedents that would make it harder for consumers to share music, films, and so on. In this case, opponents of the RIAA are working to establish their own legal precedents, and experts expect this argument to go on for years.

You'll encounter additional kinds of logical structures as you create your own arguments. You'll find some of them in Chapter 7 on Toulmin argument and still more in Chapter 17, "Fallacies of Argument."

RESPOND ●

1. Discuss whether the following statements are examples of hard evidence or rational appeals. Not all cases are clear-cut.

   The bigger they are, the harder they fall.

   Drunk drivers are involved in more than 50 percent of traffic deaths.

   DNA tests of skin found under the victim's fingernails suggest that the defendant was responsible for the assault.

   Polls suggest that a slim majority of Americans favor a constitutional amendment to ban same-sex marriage.

   A psychologist testified that teenage violence could not be blamed on video games.

   An apple a day keeps the doctor away.

   History proves that cutting tax rates increases government revenues because people work harder when they can keep more of what they earn.

   "The only thing we have to fear is fear itself."

   Air bags ought to be removed from vehicles because they can kill young children and small-frame adults.

2. Take a look at comedian Rita Rudner's fairly complicated enthymematic argument:

   I was going to have cosmetic surgery until I noticed that the doctor's office was full of portraits by Picasso.

Working with two other students, analyze this enthymeme. What information is left implicit? What inference or conclusion does Rudner ask us to draw from this enthymeme? What causes the humor in this statement?

3. We suggest in this chapter that statistical evidence becomes useful only when responsible authors interpret the data fairly and reasonably. As an exercise, go to the *USA Today* Web site or to the newspaper itself and look for the daily graph, chart, or table called the *USA Today* snapshot. (On the Web site, you'll have a series of these items to choose from.) Pick a snapshot, and use the information in it to support at least three different claims. See if you can get at least two of the claims to make opposing or very different points. Share your claims with classmates. (The point is not to learn to use data dishonestly but to see firsthand how the same statistics can serve a variety of arguments.)

4. Testimony can be as suspect as statistics. For example, check out the newspaper ads for some recent movies. How lengthy are the quotes from reviewers? A reviewer's stinging indictment of a violent action film—"this blockbuster may prove to be a great success at the box office, but it stinks as filmmaking"—could be reduced to "A great success." Bring to class a full review of a recent film that you enjoyed. (If you haven't enjoyed any films lately, select a review of one you disliked.) Using testimony from that review, write a brief argument to your classmates explaining why they should see that movie (or why they should avoid it). Be sure to use the evidence from the review fairly and reasonably, as support for a claim that you're making. Then exchange arguments with a classmate, and decide whether the evidence in your peer's argument helps to change your opinion about the movie. What's convincing about the evidence? If it doesn't convince you, why not?

5. Choose an issue of some consequence, locally or nationally, and then create a series of questions designed to poll public opinion on the issue. But design the questions to evoke a range of responses. See if you can design a reasonable question that would make people strongly inclined to favor or approve an issue, a second question that would lead them to oppose the same proposition just as intensely, a third that tries to be more neutral, and additional questions that provoke different degrees of approval or disapproval. If possible, try out your questions on your classmates.

5
Rhetorical Analysis

When the thirty-second spot first aired in late March 2004, many viewers reacted with disbelief: What the . . . ?! The guy with the mustache . . . and a sexy underwear model . . . it couldn't be . . . could it?

But it was—counterculture folk legend pop icon Bob Dylan crooning "Love Sick" in a TV ad for Victoria's Secret, a purveyor of women's underclothes. Dylan, who had never before pitched a product other than his own recordings, now traded glances with an alluring young woman in wings and high heels. The bard who'd penned "The Times They Are A-Changin'" and "Blowin' in the Wind" had sold his birthright, disillusioned critics charged, for—yikes—a bra and blue panties. (Check YouTube for a series of related ads and videos.)

Media critic Seth Stevenson, writing in *Slate*, devoted a full column to analyzing this particular pitch, trying first to figure out why an artist of Dylan's stature would do a commercial: For money? Whimsy? Exposure?

Pitchman Bob Dylan and Victoria's Secret model Adriana Lima

But then he turns to another intriguing question—how ads manage to work their persuasive magic:

> Why would a brand that's about sexiness, youth, and glamour want any connection at all with a decrepit, sixtysomething folksinger? The answer, my friend, is totally unclear. The answer is totally unclear.
>
> Even if Victoria's Secret hopes to bring in more boomer women, do those women want their underwear to exude the spirit and essence of Bob Dylan? Or, conversely, is Bob Dylan the sort of man they're hoping to attract? Even if you're of the belief that men frequently shop at VS for their ladies, I still don't see the appeal of this ad. I, for instance, am a man, and I can assure you that Bob Dylan is not what I'm looking for in a woman's undergarment. (And if I found him there—man, would that be disturbing.)
>
> Victoria's Secret wouldn't return my calls, but media reports say the idea of putting Dylan's face in the ad (they'd been using his song— "Love Sick"—in ads for the past year or so) came straight from corporate chief Les Wexner. To the company's surprise, Dylan accepted their offer. It's at this point that someone at Victoria's Secret should have stopped the madness. Just because you can hire Bob Dylan as the figurehead for your lingerie line, doesn't mean you should. Perhaps

no one was willing to say no to the big boss, or perhaps they fully expected Dylan to say no. Joke's on them.
—Seth Stevenson, "Tangled Up in Boobs"

To pose the sort of questions that Stevenson asks here is to perform a brief rhetorical analysis—a close reading of a text to find how and whether it works to persuade. In these few paragraphs from a longer piece, Stevenson considers some of the basic strategies of argument that are explored in this book's preceding chapters. He first identifies the ethos of the company making the appeal ("sexiness, youth, and glamour") and finds it hard to reconcile it with the ethos of the celebrity that he sees in the ad ("decrepit, sixtysomething"). He considers the emotional pull that the TV commercial might have (maybe enticing older men to buy expensive underwear for women) but then rejects the logic of that approach: even men who shop for underwear at Victoria's Secret certainly don't want to think about Dylan when they do.

Then Stevenson takes a step beyond the ad itself to consider the rhetorical world in which it might have been created—one in which it would seem so cool to have a superstar spokesperson like Bob Dylan that you don't think about the messages you might be sending. Stevenson's conclusion? "Joke's on them."

Whenever you encounter a similarly puzzling, troubling, or even successful appeal, try subjecting it to a rhetorical analysis of your own. Ask yourself what strategies the piece employs to move your heart, win your trust, and change your mind—and why it does or doesn't do so. Here's how.

Composing a Rhetorical Analysis

Exactly how does a Bose ad make you want to buy new speakers, or how does an op-ed piece in the *Washington Post* suddenly change your thinking about school vouchers? A rhetorical analysis might help you understand. You perform a rhetorical analysis by analyzing how well the components of an argument work together to persuade or move an audience. You can study arguments of any kind—advertisements (as we've seen), editorials, political cartoons, and perhaps even movies or photographs. Because arguments have many aspects, you will need to focus your rhetorical analysis on elements that stand out or make the piece intriguing or problematic. You could begin by exploring issues such as the following:

- What is the purpose of this argument? What does it hope to achieve?
- Who is the audience for this argument?
- What appeals or techniques does the argument use—emotional, logical, ethical?
- What type or genre of argument is it, and how does the genre affect the argument? (You'd have every right to challenge an argument in an editorial if it lacked sufficient evidence; you'd look foolish making the same complaint about a bumper sticker.)
- Who is making the argument? What ethos does it create, and exactly how does it do so? What values attach to the ethos? How does it try to make the writer or creator seem trustworthy?
- What authorities does the argument rely on or appeal to?
- What facts are used in the argument? What logic? What evidence? How is the evidence arranged and presented?
- What claims are advanced in the argument? What issues are raised, and which ones are ignored or, perhaps, evaded?
- What are the contexts—social, political, historical, cultural—for this argument? Whose interests does it serve? Who gains or loses by it?
- What shape does the argument take? How is the argument organized or arranged? What media does the argument use?
- How does the language or style of the argument work to persuade an audience?

Questions like these should get you thinking. But don't just describe techniques and strategies in your rhetorical analysis. Instead, show how the key devices in an argument actually make it succeed or fail. Quote language freely from a written piece, or describe the elements in a visual argument. (Annotating a visual text is one option.) Show readers where and why an argument makes sense and where it seems to fall apart (just as Stevenson does in the Victoria's Secret ad). If you believe that an argument startles audiences, challenges them, insults them, or lulls them into complacency, explain precisely why that's so, and provide evidence. Don't be surprised when your rhetorical analysis itself becomes an argument. That's what it should be.

Understanding the Purpose of Arguments You Are Analyzing

To understand how well any argument works, ask what its purpose might be: To sell shoes? To advocate Social Security reform? To push a political agenda? In many cases, that purpose may be obvious. A conservative newspaper will likely advance right-wing causes on its editorial page; ads from a baby food company will show happy infants delighted with stewed prunes and squash.

But some projects may be coy about their persuasive intentions or blur the lines between types of argument. Perhaps you've responded to a mail survey or telephone poll only to discover that the questions are leading you to switch your cell-phone service. Does such a stealthy argument succeed? That may depend on whether you're more intrigued by the promise of cheaper phone rates than offended by the bait-and-switch. The deception could provide material for a thoughtful rhetorical analysis in which you measure the strengths, risks, and ethics of such strategies.

Understanding Who Makes an Argument

Knowing *who* is claiming *what* is key to any rhetorical analysis. That's why you'll usually find the name of a person or an institution attached to an argument or persuasive appeal. Do you remember the statements included in TV ads during the last federal election campaign: "Hello, I'm Candidate X—and I approve this ad"? Federal law requires such statements so that viewers can tell the difference between ads endorsed by candidates and those sponsored by groups that are not affiliated with the campaigns. Their interests and motives might be very different.

Funny, offensive, or both?

Knowing an author's name is just a starting place for a serious analysis. You need to dig deeper whenever you don't recognize the author of an argument or the institution sponsoring it—and sometimes even when you do. You could do worse than to Google the Internet to discover more about such people or groups. What else have they produced? By whom have they been published—the *Wall Street Journal*, the blog Daily Kos, *Spin*, or even 4chan? If a group has a Web site, what can you learn about its goals, policies, contributors, and funding?

The blogger bio: required reading for rhetorical analysis

Contact

Email Address: **Email Me**

One-Line Bio

I am a citizen journalist, public policy consultant and political commentator.

Biography

I am a citizen journalist, public policy consultant, and political commentator. I am particularly interested in the intersection of technology and civic engagement.

I share my insights, as well as news and information that resonate with African American voters, political influentials and thought leaders.

My blog is included in the Harvard University Web Archiving Collection, "Capturing Women's Voices," a project of the Schlesinger Library at the Radcliffe Institute for Advanced Study.

During the 2008 presidential election, posts to Anderson@Large were cross-posted to "The Ruckus," a collaboration between Newsweek.com and the Media Bloggers Association.

Identifying and Appealing to Audiences

Most arguments are composed with specific audiences in mind, and their success depends, in part, on how well their strategies, content, tone, and language meet the expectations of readers or viewers. In analyzing an argument, you must first identify its target audience(s), remembering how complex that notion can be (see Audiences for Arguments on pp. 27–33). But you can usually make an educated judgment because most arguments have contexts that, one way or another, describe whom they intend to reach and in what ways.

Both a photocopied sheet stapled to a bulletin board in a college dorm ("Why You Should Be a Socialist") and a forty-foot billboard for Bud Lite might be aimed at the same general population—college students. But each will adjust its appeals for the different moods of that group in different moments. The political screed will likely be deliberately simple in layout and full of earnest language ("We live in a world of obscene inequality") to appeal to students in a serious vein, while the liquor ad will be visually stunning and virtually text-free to connect with students when they aren't worried about uniting the workers of the world. Your rhetorical analysis might make a case for the success or failure of such audience-based strategies.

You might also examine how a writer or an argument establishes credibility with an audience. One effective means of building credibility, you will discover, comes through a seven-letter word made famous by Aretha Franklin—*respect*. Respect is crucial in arguments that invoke audiences who don't agree on critical issues or who may not have thought carefully about the issues presented. In introducing an article on problems facing African American women in the workplace, editor in chief of *Essence* Diane Weathers considers the problems that she faced with respecting all her potential readers:

> We spent more than a minute agonizing over the provocative cover line for our feature "White Women at Work." The countless stories we had heard from women across the country told us that this was a workplace issue we had to address. From my own experience at several major magazines, it was painfully obvious to me that Black and White women are not on the same track. Sure, we might all start out in the same place. But early in the game, most sisters I know become stuck—and the reasons have little to do with intelligence or drive. At some point we bump our heads against that ceiling. And while White women may complain of a glass ceiling, for us, the ceiling is concrete.

So how do we tell this story without sounding whiny and paranoid, or turning off our White-female readers, staff members, advertisers and girlfriends? Our solution: Bring together real women (several of them highly successful senior corporate executives), put them in a room, promise them anonymity and let them speak their truth.
—Diane Weathers, "Speaking Our Truth"

Both paragraphs affirm Weathers's determination to treat audiences fairly *and* to deal honestly with a difficult subject. The strategy would merit attention in any rhetorical analysis.

Look, too, for signals that writers share values with readers or at least understand an audience. In the following passage, writer Jack Solomon is clear about one value that he hopes readers have in common—a preference for "straight talk":

There are some signs in the advertising world that Americans are getting fed up with fantasy advertisements and want to hear some straight talk. Weary of extravagant product claims and irrelevant associations, consumers trained by years of advertising to distrust what they hear seem to be developing an immunity to commercials.
—Jack Solomon, "Masters of Desire: The Culture of American Advertising"

Retailers like Walmart build their credibility by simple "straight talk" to shoppers: our low prices make your life better.

It's a pretty safe assumption that consumers don't like doubletalk or duplicity, isn't it? But writers or advertisers can manage even more complex appeals to values by targeting specific groups and their experiences, values, and perceptions. Here's media critic Seth Stevenson again, first summarizing ads in a new antismoking campaign directed at teens:

> The spots: *They appear to be episodes of a sitcom called* Fair Enough. *In this series of 30-second segments, a team of tobacco executives brainstorms new ways to market to teens. Among their ideas: fruit-flavored chewing tobacco, tobacco in the form of a gum ball, and an effort to win influence with the "hipster" crowd by giving them free packs of smokes.*
>
> —Seth Stevenson, "How to Get Teens Not to Smoke"

Then he does a rhetorical analysis, explaining why the particular TV spot will resonate with its target audience. The creators of the ad clearly knew what might motivate teens to give up cigarettes—insecurity:

> In fact, the ultimate adolescent nightmare is to appear in any way unsavvy—like an out-of-it rookie who doesn't know the score. These *Fair Enough* ads isolate and prey on that insecurity, and they do a great job. With a dead-on, rerun sitcom parody (jumpy establishing shot; upbeat horn-section theme song ending on a slightly unresolved note; three-wall, two-camera set; canned laugh track), the ads first establish their own savvy, knowing coolness before inviting us to join them in ridiculing big tobacco's schemes. The spots are darkly comic, just the way teens like it. And rather than serving up yet more boring evidence that smoking is deadly (something that all teens, including the ones who smoke, already know) the ads move on to the far more satisfying step: kicking big tobacco in the groin.

Examining Arguments Based on Emotion: Pathos

Some emotional appeals are just ploys to win over readers with a pretty face, figurative or real. You've seen ads promising an exciting life and attractive friends if only you drink the right soda or wear a particular brand of clothes. Are you fooled by such claims? Probably not, if you pause to think about them. But that's the strategy—to distract you from thought just long enough to make a bad choice. It's a move worth commenting on in a rhetorical analysis.

Yet emotions can add real muscle to arguments, too, and that's worth noting. For example, persuading people not to drink and drive by making them fear death, injury, or arrest seems like a fair use of an emotional appeal. That's exactly what the Texas Department of Transportation did when it created a memorable ad campaign (see the figure below) featuring the image of a formerly beautiful young woman who has been horribly scarred in a fiery accident caused by a drunk driver. In a rhetorical analysis, you might note the effect of the headline right above the gut-wrenching image: "Not everyone who gets hit by a drunk driver dies."

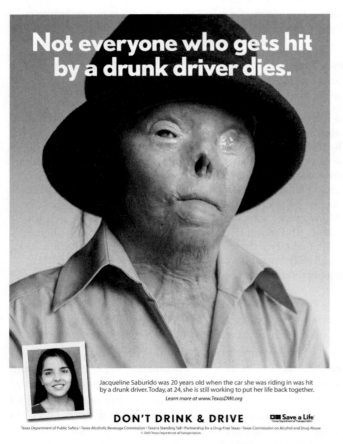

Images and words combine to create an unforgettable emotional appeal.

In analyzing emotional appeals, judge whether the emotions raised—anger, sympathy, fear, envy, joy, or love—advance the claims offered. For example, consider how British newspaper columnist and novelist Lionel Shriver (who changed her first name from Margaret Ann when she decided men had easier lives than women) uses concrete and graphic language to evoke disgust with SUVs—and anyone who owns one—at a time of soaring gas prices:

> Filling the tank of an SUV in the U.S. has now crossed the psychologically traumatizing $100 mark. The resale value of these monsters is plummeting, and many owners are getting stuck with the things, like holding the Old Maid in cards. I greet this news with sadistic glee. People who bought SUVs were fools and I want them to suffer. Not just because I'm a sanctimonious greenie, but because I'm an aesthete. Sure, SUVs are petro-pigs, and they side-swipe cyclists into the curb. Yes, they emblemize everything about Americans the rest of the world detests: greedy, wasteful, and oblivious to the future. But on top of all that, they're ugly.
>
> —Lionel Shriver, "If the U.S. Election Were a Novel"

Does the use of pathos ("monsters," "petro-pigs") convince you, or does it distract from or undermine the claim that SUVs are ugly? Your task in a rhetorical analysis is to study an author's words, the emotions they evoke, and the claims they support and then to make such a judgment.

Examining Arguments Based on Character: Ethos

It should come as no surprise: readers believe writers who seem honest, wise, and trustworthy. So in examining the effectiveness of an argument, look for evidence of these traits. Does the writer have the experience or authority to write on this subject? Are all claims qualified reasonably? Is evidence presented in full, not tailored to the writer's agenda? Are important objections to the author's position acknowledged and addressed? Are sources documented? Above all, does the writer sound trustworthy?

Take a look at the following paragraph from a blog posting by Timothy Burke, a teacher at Swarthmore College and parent of a preschool child who is trying to think through the issue of homework for elementary school kids:

So I've been reading a bit about homework, and comparing notes with parents. There is a lot of variation
across districts, not just in the amount of homework
that kids are being asked to do, but in the kind of
homework. Some districts give kids a lot of time-
consuming busywork, other districts try to concentrate
on having homework assignments be substantive work
that is best accomplished independently. Some give a
lot from a very early point in K–12 education, some
give relatively little. As both a professional educator
and an individual with personal convictions, I'd tend to
argue against excessive amounts of homework and
against assigning busywork. But what has ultimately
interested me more about reading various discussions
of homework is how intense the feelings are swirling
around the topic, and how much that intensity strikes
me as a problem in and of itself. Not just as a symptom
of a kind of civic illness, an inability to collectively and
democratically work through complex issues, but also
in some cases as evidence of an educational failure in
its own right.

Burke establishes his ethos by citing his reading and his talks with other parents.

Burke shows that he is considering alternatives (though he then states his tentative preference).

He criticizes immoderate arguments as "a kind of civic illness" (and suggests that he will demonstrate the opposite of such an approach).

In considering the role that ethos plays in rhetorical analyses, you need to pay attention to the details, right down to the choice of words or, in a visual argument, the shapes and colors. The modest, tentative tone that Burke uses in his blog is an example of the kind of choice that can shape an audience's perception of ethos. But these details need your interpretation. Language that's hot and extreme can mark a writer as either passionate or loony. Work that's sober and carefully organized might suggest that an institution is either competent or excessively cautious. Technical terms and abstract phrases can make a writer seem either knowledgeable or pompous.

Examining Arguments Based on Facts and Reason: Logos

In analyzing most arguments, you'll have to decide whether an argument makes a plausible claim and offers good reasons for you to believe it. Not all arguments will package such claims in a single neat sentence, or *thesis*—nor should they. A writer may tell a story from which you have to infer the claim. Think of the way that many films make a social or political statement by dramatizing an issue like political corruption, government censorship, or economic injustice. Visual arguments may work the same way: viewers have to assemble the parts and draw inferences before they get the point.

In some conventional arguments (like those that you might find on an editorial page), arguments may be perfectly obvious. Writers may first stake out a claim and then present reasons that you should consider, or they may first present reasons and lay out a case that leads you toward a conclusion. Consider the following examples. The first comes from the conclusion of an August 22, 2008, editorial in the *New York Times*; the second is the lead paragraph of a July 1, 2008, editorial in the *St. Petersburg* (Florida) *Times*.

> To win the right to host [the Olympic] Games, China promised to honor the Olympic ideals of nonviolence, openness to the world and individual expression. Those promises were systematically broken, starting with this spring's brutal repression in Tibet and continuing on to the ugly farce of inviting its citizens to apply for legal protest permits and then arresting them if they actually tried to do so. . . .
>
> Surely one of the signature events of these Games was the sentencing of two women in their late 70s to "re-education through labor." Their crime? Applying for permission to protest the inadequate compensation they felt they had received when the government seized their homes years ago for urban redevelopment.
>
> A year ago, the I.O.C. predicted that these Games would be "a force for good" and a spur to human-rights progress. Instead, as Human Rights Watch has reported, they became a catalyst for intensified human-rights abuse.
>
> Mr. Bush has taken some note of China's appalling human-rights record this summer—privately meeting with Chinese dissidents in Washington just before his visit to the Games and gently nudging his hosts on religious freedom while in Beijing. With these repression-

scarred Olympics now drawing to a close, Mr. Bush and other world leaders must tell Beijing that its failure to live up to its Olympic commitments will neither be ignored nor forgotten.

The medal count and DVD sales cannot be the last word on the Beijing Games.

—"Beijing's Bad Faith Olympics," *New York Times*

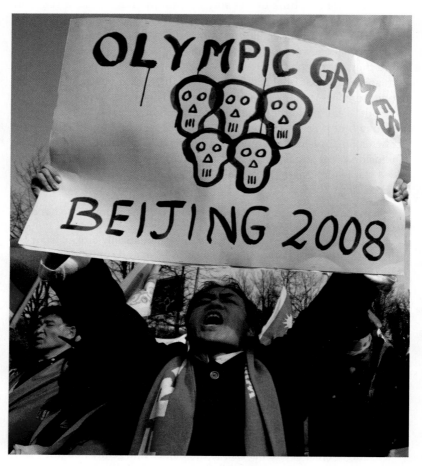

Tibetans opposed to holding the 2008 Summer Olympic Games in Beijing demonstrate in front of the International Olympic Committee headquarters in Lausanne, Switzerland. In contrast to newspaper editorials, protest signs usually concentrate on emotional rather than logical arguments.

Florida's congressional delegation should stand firm against President Bush's increased pressure to allow offshore oil drilling. That would not immediately lower the price of gasoline or produce more oil, as even the president acknowledged Tuesday. It would jeopardize the foundation of Florida's economy, no matter how many assurances the oil companies make about better drilling techniques and safety.
—"Hold the Line on Offshore Drilling," St. *Petersburg Times*

When you encounter explicit claims like these, rhetorical analysis calls for you to look at how they are supported by good reasons and reliable evidence. A lengthy essay may, in fact, contain a series of claims, each developed to support an even larger point. Indeed, every paragraph in an argument may develop a specific and related idea. In a rhetorical analysis, you need to identify all these separate propositions and examine the relationships among them. Are they solidly linked? Are there inconsistencies that the writer should acknowledge? Does the end of the piece support what the writer said (and promised) at the beginning?

Since many logical appeals rely heavily on data and information from sources, you'll also need to examine the quality of the information presented in an argument, assessing how accurately such information is reported, how conveniently it's displayed (in charts or graphs, for example), and how well the sources cited represent a range of *respected* opinion on a topic. (For more information on the use of evidence, see Chapter 16.)

Knowing how to judge the quality of sources is more important now than ever before because the electronic pathways are clogged with junk. In some ways, the computer terminal has become the equivalent of a library reference room, but the sources available online vary widely in quality and have not been evaluated by a library professional. As a consequence, you must know the difference between reliable, firsthand, or fully documented sources and those that don't meet such standards. (For more on using and documenting sources, see Chapters 19 and 20.)

Examining the Arrangement and Media of Arguments

Arguments have a structure. Aristotle carved the structure of logical argument to its bare bones when he observed that it had only two parts:

- statement
- proof

What argument does this editorial cartoon make? What elements come together to constitute the claim? What good reasons would be needed to support it?

© Mike Lester/The Mike Lester Studio

You could do worse, in examining an argument, than to make sure that every claim a writer makes is backed by sufficient evidence. Most arguments that you read and write, however, will be more than mere statements followed by proofs. Some writers will lay their cards on the table immediately; others may lead you carefully through a chain of claims toward a conclusion. Writers may even interrupt their arguments to offer background information or cultural contexts for readers. Sometimes they'll tell stories or provide anecdotes that make an argumentative point. They'll qualify the arguments they make, too, and often pause to admit that other points of view are plausible.

In other words, there are no formulas or acceptable patterns that fit all successful arguments. Many are written on the fly in the heat of the moment. In writing a rhetorical analysis, you'll have to assess the organization of a persuasive text on its own merits.

It's fair, however, to complain about what may be *absent* from an argument. Most arguments of proposal (see Chapter 12), for example, include a section that defends the feasibility of a new idea, explaining how it might be funded or managed. In a rhetorical analysis, you might fault an editorial that supports a new stadium for a city without addressing feasibility issues. Similarly, analyzing a movie review that reads like off-the-top-of-the-head opinion, you might legitimately ask what criteria of evaluation are in play (see Chapter 10).

Rhetorical analysis also calls for you to look carefully at an argument's transitions, headings and subheadings, documentation of sources, and overall tone or voice. Don't take such details for granted, since they all contribute to the strength—or weakness—of an argument.

Nor should you ignore the way a writer or an institution uses media. Would an argument originally made in a print editorial, for instance, work better as a spoken presentation (or vice versa)? Would a lengthy paper have more power if it included more images? Or do you find that images distract from a written argument and diminish its substance? These are important issues that you might comment on or connect to other aspects of an argument, such as its style, as you work toward a rhetorical analysis.

Finally, be open to the possibility of new or nontraditional structures of arguments. The visual arguments that you analyze may defy conventional principles of logic or arrangement—for example, making juxtapositions rather than logical transitions between elements or using quick cuts, fades, or other devices to link ideas. Quite often, these nontraditional structures will also resist the neatness of a thesis, leaving readers to construct at least a part of the argument in their heads. Advertisers are growing fond of these sorts of soft-sell multimedia productions that can seem more like games or entertainments than what they really are—product pitches. We're asked not just to buy a product but also to live its lifestyle. Is that a reasonable or workable strategy for an argument? Your analysis might entertain such possibilities.

Looking at Style

Even a coherent argument flush with evidence may not connect with readers if it's dull, off-key, or offensive. Readers naturally judge the credibility of arguments in part by how stylishly the case is made—even when they don't know exactly what style is. Consider how these simple, blunt sentences from the opening of an argument shape your image of

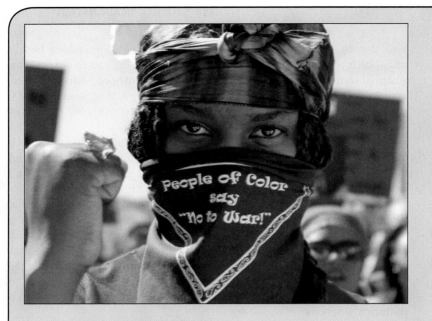

Not Just Words

Web sites and blogs now practically make a sport out of critiquing the stories and other arguments in older media such as newspapers, magazines, and TV news shows. It's no surprise that traditional mainstream media have pushed back, providing readers with lively examples of rhetorical analyses as part of the daily news.

In September 2005, the *San Francisco Chronicle,* regarded by conservatives as a liberal news source, included in its coverage of an anti–Iraq War demonstration the photograph above, with the following caption: "Jasmine Williams, 17, a student with the leadership group Youth Together, joins the Iraq war protest in San Francisco." The image provoked the ire of a presumably more conservative blogger at zombietime.com. Zombie, who had also photographed the event and even the same girl, but at a wider angle, found the *Chronicle's* shot disingenuous because it omitted details such as Palestinian flags in the background. Here are some of Zombie's photographs and commentary:

Now we can see that the girl is just one of several teenagers, all wearing terrorist-style bandannas covering their faces. But, as you'll notice, the bandannas are all printed with the same design. Was this a grassroots protest statement the teenagers had come up with all by themselves? To find out, let's take a look at another photo in the series, taken at the same time:

Oops—it looks like they're actually being stage-managed by an adult, who is giving them directions and guiding them toward the front of the march. But who is she? The last picture in the series reveals all. It turns out that the woman giving directions belongs to one of the Communist groups organizing the rally—if her T-shirt is to be believed, since it depicts the flag of Communist Vietnam, which has been frequently displayed by such groups at protest rallies in the United States for decades. The *San Francisco Chronicle* featured the original photograph on its front Web page in order to convey a positive message about the rally—perhaps that even politically aware teenagers were inspired to show up and rally for peace, sporting the message, "People of Color say 'No to War!'" And that served the *Chronicle*'s agenda. But this simple analysis reveals the very subtle but insidious type of bias that occurs in the media all the time. The *Chronicle* did not print an inaccuracy, nor did it doctor a photograph to misrepresent the facts. Instead, the *Chronicle* committed the sin of omission: it told you the truth, but it didn't tell you the *whole* truth.

Shortly after Zombie's photos and observations made their way around the Web, the *Chronicle* offered a rebuttal. Here's a brief portion of that newspaper's rhetorical analysis of the situation, offered by "readers' representative" Dick Rogers:

> So the *Chronicle* photo didn't exactly shout "Middle America." It was far more dramatic and displayed the protester in far more detail. If the newspaper was setting out to "de-radicalize" the scene, it did a pretty

lame job. If the paper wants to sanitize a protest, it should forget tight shots of radicals in disguise and go for pictures of suburban moms with young children. Now that's centrist.

The accompanying story, by the way, noted the Palestinian angle, the arrests of members of an anarchist group and the presence of counter-demonstrators, one of whom called for "patriotism instead of a socialist revolution."

Readers should ponder what they don't see in pictures, just as they should critically judge what they do see. Photographs are representations of reality, and small slices of it at that.

But a wide-angle view isn't necessarily a bigger slice of reality. It's true that, in some cases, a story is told in more detail by stepping back. In other cases, an image is more powerful and vivid by coming in close.

—Dick Rogers, "Picturing the Debate"

Study the photographs and the contrary rhetorical analyses here. Might one of Zombie's images more accurately represent the protest than the one published in the *Chronicle*? Can you make such a judgment without more information? How could you find out more about this controversy?

Apply what you learn from this exercise to your own analysis of several news photographs selected from current newspapers, newsmagazines, or Web sites. Do the images you've chosen provide the facts you need to make a judgment about a story, or do you suspect something may have been left out of them? Do the images provoke strong emotional responses because of their careful composition, or do they manipulate your feelings? Do you have reason to trust the source offering the images, or might the ethos of that source be suspect? Select one or two of the images, and present your rhetorical analysis of them to your class.

the author and probably determine whether you're willing to continue to read the whole piece:

> We are young, urban and professional. We are literate, respectable, intelligent and charming. But foremost and above all, we know what it's like to be unemployed.
> —Julia Carlisle, "Young, Privileged and Unemployed"

Now consider how you'd approach an argument that begins like the following, responding to a botched primary election in Florida following the electoral disaster of 2000:

> The question you're asking yourself is: Does South Florida contain the highest concentration of morons in the entire world? Or just in the United States? The reason you're asking this, of course, is South Florida's performance in Tuesday's election.
> —Dave Barry, "How to Vote in One Easy Step"

Both styles probably work, but they signal that the writers are about to make very different kinds of cases. In this case, style alone tells readers what to expect.

Manipulating style also enables writers to shape readers' responses to their ideas. Devices as simple as repetition and parallelism can give sentences remarkable power. Consider this passage from liberal blogger Kevin Drum, who argues that both major U.S. political parties share in the blame for the 2008 financial meltdown:

> I haven't been able to work up quite the level of partisan outrage over the fall of Wall Street that some people have. You see, when it comes to environmental regulation, Democrats are mostly on the side of the angels. When it comes to workplace regulation, they're on the side of workers. When it comes to consumer regulation, they're on the side of consumers. But when it comes to financial regulation, they're. . . . um—well, they've been mostly on about the same side as Republicans.
> —Kevin Drum, "Bipartisan"

Or look at this sentence from a profile of Chief Justice John Roberts of the U.S. Supreme Court in the *New Yorker*:

> In every major case since he became the nation's seventeenth Chief Justice, Roberts has sided with the prosecution over the defendant, the state over the condemned, the executive branch over the legislative, and the corporate defendant over the individual plaintiff.
> —Jeffery Toobin, "No More Mr. Nice Guy: The Supreme Court's Stealth Hard-Liner"

In a rhetorical analysis, you can explore many stylistic choices. Why does a formal style work for discussing one type of subject matter but not for another? How does a writer use humor or irony to underscore an important point or to manage a difficult concession? Do stylistic choices, even something as simple as the use of contractions or personal pronouns, bring readers comfortably close to a writer, or do a highly technical vocabulary and an impersonal voice signal that an argument is for experts only?

To describe the stylistic effects of visual arguments, you may use a different vocabulary and talk about colors, camera angles, editing, balance, proportion, fonts, perspective, and so on. But the basic principle is this: the look of an item—whether a poster, an editorial cartoon, or a film documentary—can support the message that it carries, undermine it, or muddle it. In some cases, the look will *be* the message. In a rhetorical analysis, you can't ignore style.

Examining a Rhetorical Analysis

On the following pages is an argument in defense of free speech that was written by Derek Bok, a distinguished scholar and past president of Harvard University—credentials that certainly add to his ethos. Responding to it with a detailed analysis is Milena Ateya, a college student who reveals in her piece that she, too, brings unique credentials to this case.

Protecting Freedom of Expression at Harvard

DEREK BOK

For several years, universities have been struggling with the problem of trying to reconcile the rights of free speech with the desire to avoid racial tension. In recent weeks, such a controversy has sprung up at Harvard. Two students hung Confederate flags in public view, upsetting students who equate the Confederacy with slavery. A third student tried to protest the flags by displaying a swastika.

These incidents have provoked much discussion and disagreement. Some students have urged that Harvard require the removal of symbols that offend many members of the community. Others reply that such symbols are a form of free speech and should be protected.

Different universities have resolved similar conflicts in different ways. Some have enacted codes to protect their communities from forms of speech that are deemed to be insensitive to the feelings of other groups. Some have refused to impose such restrictions.

It is important to distinguish between the appropriateness of such communications and their status under the First Amendment. The fact that speech is protected by the First Amendment does not necessarily mean that it is right, proper, or civil. I am sure that the vast majority of Harvard students believe that hanging a Confederate flag in public view— or displaying a swastika in response—is insensitive and unwise because any satisfaction it gives to the students who display these symbols is far outweighed by the discomfort it causes to many others.

I share this view and regret that the students involved saw fit to behave in this fashion. Whether or not they merely wished to manifest their pride in the South—or to demonstrate the insensitivity of hanging Confederate flags, by mounting another offensive symbol in return—they must have known that they would upset many fellow students and ignore the decent regard for the feelings of others so essential to building and preserving a strong and harmonious community.

To disapprove of a particular form of communication, however, is not enough to justify prohibiting it. We are faced with a clear example of the conflict between our commitment to free speech and our desire to foster a community founded on mutual respect. Our society has wrestled with this problem for many years. Interpreting the First Amendment, the Supreme Court has clearly struck the balance in favor of free speech.

While communities do have the right to regulate speech in order to uphold aesthetic standards (avoiding defacement of buildings) or to protect the public from disturbing noise, rules of this kind must be applied across the board and cannot be enforced selectively to prohibit certain kinds of messages but not others.

Under the Supreme Court's rulings, as I read them, the display of swastikas or Confederate flags clearly falls within the protection of the free speech clause of the First Amendment and cannot be forbidden simply because it offends the feelings of many members of the community. These rulings apply to all agencies of government, including public universities.

Although it is unclear to what extent the First Amendment is enforceable against private institutions, I have difficulty understanding why a university such as Harvard should have less free speech than the surrounding society—or than a public university.

One reason why the power of censorship is so dangerous is that it is extremely difficult to decide when a particular communication is offensive enough to warrant prohibition or to weigh the degree of offensiveness against the potential value of the communication. If we begin to forbid flags, it is only a short step to prohibiting offensive speakers.

I suspect that no community will become humane and caring by restricting what its members can say. The worst offenders will simply find other ways to irritate and insult.

In addition, once we start to declare certain things "offensive," with all the excitement and attention that will follow, I fear that much ingenuity will be exerted trying to test the limits, much time will be expended trying to draw tenuous distinctions, and the resulting publicity will eventually attract more attention to the offensive material than would ever have occurred otherwise.

Rather than prohibit such communications, with all the resulting risks, it would be better to ignore them, since students would then have little reason to create such displays and would soon abandon them. If this response is not possible—and one can understand why—the wisest course is to speak with those who perform insensitive acts and try to help them understand the effects of their actions on others.

Appropriate officials and faculty members should take the lead, as the Harvard House Masters have already done in this case. In talking with students, they should seek to educate and persuade, rather than resort to ridicule or intimidation, recognizing that only persuasion is likely to produce a lasting, beneficial effect. Through such effects, I believe that we act in the manner most consistent with our ideals as an educational institution and most calculated to help us create a truly understanding, supportive community.

A Curse and a Blessing

MILENA ATEYA

In 1991, when Derek Bok's essay "Protecting Freedom of Expression at Harvard" was first published in the *Boston Globe*, I had just come to America to escape the oppressive Communist regime in Bulgaria. Perhaps my background explains why I support Bok's argument that we should not put arbitrary limits on freedom of expression. Bok wrote the essay in response to a public display of Confederate flags and a swastika at Harvard, a situation that created a heated controversy among the students. As Bok notes, universities have struggled to achieve a balance between maintaining students' right of free speech and avoiding racist attacks. When choices must be made, however, Bok argues for preserving freedom of expression.

In order to support his claim and bridge the controversy, Bok uses a variety of rhetorical strategies. The author first immerses the reader in the controversy by vividly describing the incident: two Harvard students had hung Confederate flags in public view, thereby "upsetting students who equate the Confederacy with slavery" (51). Another student, protesting the flags, decided to display an even more offensive symbol—the swastika. These actions provoked heated discussions among students. Some students believed that school officials should remove the offensive symbols, whereas others suggested that the symbols "are a form of free speech and should be protected" (51). Bok establishes common ground between the factions: he regrets the actions of the offenders but does not believe we should prohibit such actions just because we disagree with them.

The author earns the reader's respect because of his knowledge and through his logical presentation of the issue. In partial support of his position, Bok refers to U.S.

Supreme Court rulings, which remind us that "the display of swastikas or Confederate flags clearly falls within the protection of the free speech clause of the First Amendment" (52). The author also emphasizes the danger of the slippery slope of censorship when he warns the reader, "If we begin to forbid flags, it is only a short step to prohibiting offensive speakers" (52). Overall, however, Bok's work lacks the kinds of evidence that statistics, interviews with students, and other representative examples of controversial conduct could provide. Thus, his essay may not be strong enough to persuade all readers to make the leap from this specific situation to his general conclusion.

Reference to First Amendment serves as warrant for Bok's claim.

Comments critically on author's evidence.

Throughout, Bok's personal feelings are implied but not stated directly. As a lawyer who was president of Harvard for twenty years, Bok knows how to present his opinions respectfully without offending the feelings of the students. However, qualifying phrases like "I suspect that," and "Under the Supreme Court's rulings, as I read them" could weaken the effectiveness of his position. Furthermore, Bok's attempt to be fair to all seems to dilute the strength of his proposed solution. He suggests that one should either ignore the insensitive deeds in the hope that students might change their behavior, or talk to the offending students to help them comprehend how their behavior is affecting other students.

Examines how Bok establishes ethical appeal.

Identifies qualifying phrases that may weaken claim.

Analyzes author's solution.

Nevertheless, although Bok's proposed solution to the controversy does not appear at first reading to be very strong, it may ultimately be effective. There is enough flexibility in his approach to withstand various tests, and Bok's solution is general enough that it can change with the times and adapt to community standards.

Raises points that suggest Bok's solution may work.

In writing this essay, Bok faced a challenging task: to write a short response to a specific situation that represents a very broad and controversial issue. Some people may find that freedom of expression is both a curse and a blessing because of the difficulties it creates. As one who has lived under a regime that permitted very limited,

Returns to personal experience in conclusion.

censored expression, I am all too aware that I could not have written this response in 1991 in Bulgaria. As a result, I feel, like Derek Bok, that freedom of expression is a blessing, in spite of any temporary problems associated with it.

WORK CITED

Bok, Derek. "Protecting Freedom of Expression on the Campus." *Current Issues and Enduring Questions.* Ed. Sylvan Barnet and Hugo Bedau. 6th ed. Boston: Bedford, 2002. 51–52. Print. Rpt. of "Protecting Freedom of Expression at Harvard." *Boston Globe* 25 May 1991.

GUIDE to writing a rhetorical analysis

● Finding a Topic

A rhetorical analysis is usually assigned work: you're asked to describe how an argument works and to assess its effectiveness. When you're free to choose your own subject for analysis, look for one or more of the following qualities:

- a verbal or visual argument that challenges you—or disturbs, excites, amazes, or impresses
- a verbal or visual argument with lots to analyze
- a text that raises current or enduring issues of substance
- a text that you believe should be taken more seriously

Obvious places to look for arguments to analyze include the editorial and op-ed pages of any newspaper, political magazines such as *The Nation* or *National Review*, Web sites of organizations and interest groups, political blogs such as DailyKos.com or Powerline.com, corporate Web sites that post their TV ad spots, videos and statements posted to YouTube, and so on.

● Researching Your Topic

Once you've selected a text to analyze, find out all you can about it. Use the library or resources of the Web to explore

- who the author is and what his or her credentials are
- if the author is an institution, what it does, what its sources of funding are, who its members are, and so on
- who is publishing or sponsoring the piece, and what the organization typically publishes
- what the leanings or biases of the author and publisher might be
- what the context of the argument is—what preceded or provoked it and how others have responded to it

● Formulating a Claim

Begin a rhetorical analysis with a hypothesis in mind. A full thesis might not become evident until you're well into your analysis, but your final thesis should reflect the complexity of the piece that you're studying, not just state that "the editorial has good pathos and ethos but lousy logos." In developing a thesis, consider questions such as the following:

- How can I describe what this argument achieves?
- What is the purpose, and is it accomplished?
- What audiences does the argument seem to address?
- For what audiences does it work or not work?
- Which of its rhetorical features will likely influence readers most: Audience connections? Emotional appeals? Style?
- What aspects of the argument work better than others?
- How do the rhetorical elements interact?

Here's the hardest part for most writers of rhetorical analyses: whether you agree or disagree with an argument doesn't matter in a rhetorical analysis. You've got to stay out of the fray and pay attention only to how—and to how well—the argument works. That's tough to do, but keep your distance!

● Examples of Possible Claims for a Rhetorical Analysis

- Many people who admire the inspiring language and elevated style of Barack Obama's speeches might be uneasy with some of the claims that he makes.
- Today's editorial in the *Daily Collegian* about campus crimes may scare first-year students, but its anecdotal reporting doesn't get down to hard numbers—and for a good reason. Those statistics don't back the position taken by the editors.
- The imageboard 4chan has been called an "Internet hate machine," yet others claim it as a great boon to creativity. A close analysis of its home-page can help to settle this debate.
- The original design of New York's Freedom Tower, with its torqued surfaces and evocative spire, made a stronger argument about American values than its replacement, a fortress-like skyscraper stripped of imagination and unable to make any statement except "I'm 1,776 feet tall."

● Preparing a Proposal

If your instructor asks you to prepare a proposal for your rhetorical analysis, here's a format you might use:

- Provide a copy of the work that you intend to analyze, whether it's a printed text or something available in another medium. You might have to furnish a photograph, digital image, or URL, for instance.

- Offer a working hypothesis or tentative thesis.

- Indicate which rhetorical components seem especially compelling and worthy of detailed study. Also note where you see potential connections between elements. For example, does the piece seem to emphasize facts and logic so much that it becomes disconnected from potential audiences? If so, hint at that possibility in your proposal.

- Indicate the background information—about the author, institution, and contexts (political, economic, social, and religious) of the argument—that you intend to research.

- Define the audience that you imagine for the analysis. If you're responding to an assignment, you may be writing primarily for a teacher and classmates. But they make up a complex audience in themselves. If you can do so within the spirit of the assignment, imagine that your analysis will be published in a local newspaper, on a Web site, or in a blog.

- Suggest the media that you might use in your analysis. Will a traditional paper work? Could you use highlighting or other word-processing tools to focus attention on stylistic details? Would it be possible to use balloons or other callouts to annotate a visual argument?

- Conclude by briefly discussing the key challenges you anticipate in preparing your analysis.

● Thinking about Content and Organization

Your rhetorical analysis may take various forms, but it's likely to include the following:

- Facts about the text you're analyzing: Provide the author's name; the title or name of the work; its place of publication or its location; the date it was published or viewed.

- Contexts for the argument: Readers need to know where the text is coming from, to what it may be responding, in what controversies it might be embroiled, and so on. Don't assume that they can infer the important contextual elements.

- A synopsis of the text that you're analyzing: If you can't attach the original argument, you must summarize it in enough detail so that a reader can imagine it. Even if you attach a copy of the piece, the analysis should include a summary.

- Some claim about the rhetorical effectiveness of the work: It might be a straightforward evaluative claim or something more complex. The claim can come early in the paper, or you might work toward it steadily, providing the evidence that leads toward the conclusion you've reached.

- A detailed analysis of how the argument works: Although you'll probably analyze rhetorical components separately, don't let your analysis become a dull roster of emotional, ethical, and logical appeals. Your rhetorical analysis should be an argument itself that supports a claim; a simple list of rhetorical appeals won't make much of a point.

- Evidence for every part of the analysis.

- An assessment of alternative views and counterarguments to your own analysis.

● Getting and Giving Response

If you have access to a writing center, discuss the text that you intend to analyze with a writing consultant before you write the paper. Try to find people who agree with the argument and others who disagree, and take notes on their observations. Your instructor may assign you to a peer group for the purpose of reading and responding to one another's drafts; if not, share your draft with someone on your own. You can use the following questions to evaluate a draft. If you're evaluating someone else's draft, be sure to illustrate your points with examples. Specific comments are always more helpful than general observations.

The Claim

- Does the claim address the rhetorical effectiveness of the argument itself and not the opinion or position that it takes?

- Is the claim significant enough to interest readers?

- Does the claim indicate important relationships between various rhetorical components?

- Would the claim be one that the author or creator of the piece might regard as serious criticism?

Evidence for the Claim

- Is enough evidence furnished to explain or support all claims you make? If not, what kinds of additional evidence are needed?

- Is the evidence in support of the claim simply announced, or are its significance and appropriateness analyzed? Is a more detailed discussion needed?

- Do you use the right kind of evidence, drawn either from the argument itself or from other materials?

- Do you address any objections that readers might have to the claim, criteria, or evidence or to the way the analysis is conducted?

- What kinds of sources might you use to explain the context of the argument? Do you need to use sources to check factual claims made in the argument?

- Are all quotations introduced with appropriate signal phrases (such as "As Peggy Noonan points out"), and do they merge smoothly into your sentences?

Organization and Style

- How are the parts of the argument organized? How effective is this organization? Would some other structure work better?

- Will readers understand the relationships among the original text, your claims, your supporting reasons, and the evidence you've gathered (from the original text and any other sources you've used)? If not, what could be done to make those connections clearer? Are more transitional words and phrases needed? Would headings or graphic devices help?

- Are the transitions or links from point to point, paragraph to paragraph, and sentence to sentence clear and effective? If not, how could they be improved?

- Is the style suited to the subject and appropriate to your audience? Is it too formal? Too casual? Too technical? Too bland?

- Which sentences seem particularly effective? Which ones seem weakest, and how could they be improved? Should some short sentences be combined, or should any long ones be separated into two or more sentences?

- How effective are the paragraphs? Do any seem too skimpy or too long? Do they break the analysis at strategic points?

- Which words or phrases seem particularly effective, accurate, and powerful? Do any seem dull, vague, unclear, or inappropriate for the audience or your purpose? Are definitions provided for technical or other terms that readers might not know?

Spelling, Punctuation, Mechanics, Documentation, and Format

- Check the spelling of the author's name, and make sure that the name of any institution involved with the work is correct. Note that the names of many corporations and institutions use distinctive spelling and punctuation.
- Get the name of the text you're analyzing right.
- Are there any errors in spelling, punctuation, capitalization, and the like?
- Does the assignment require a specific format? Check the original assignment sheet to be sure.

RESPOND •

1. Describe a persuasive moment that you can recall from a speech, an article, an editorial, an advertisement, a video clip, or your personal experiences. Alternatively, research one of the following famous moments of persuasion, and describe the circumstances of the appeal—the historical situation, the issues at stake, the purpose of the argument, and the reasons it is memorable:

    Abraham Lincoln's "Gettysburg Address" (1863)

    Elizabeth Cady Stanton's draft of the "Declaration of Sentiments" for the Seneca Falls Convention (1848)

    Franklin Roosevelt's first inaugural address (1933)

    Winston Churchill's addresses to the British people during the early stages of World War II (1940)

    Martin Luther King Jr.'s "Letter from Birmingham Jail" (1963)

    Ronald Reagan's tribute to the *Challenger* astronauts (1986)

    Toni Morrison's speech accepting the Nobel Prize (1993)

    Barack Obama's "A More Perfect Union" speech on race (2008)

2. Find a written argument on the editorial page or op-ed page in a recent newspaper. Analyze this argument rhetorically, drawing on the principles discussed in this chapter. Analyze the elements of the argument that best explain why it succeeds, fails, or does something else entirely. Perhaps you can show that the author is unusually successful in connecting with readers but then has nothing to say. Or perhaps you discover that the strong logical appeal is undercut by a contradictory emotional argument. Be sure that the analysis includes a summary of the original essay and basic publication information about it (its author, place of publication, and publisher).

3. Browse YouTube or another Web site to find an example of a powerful emotional argument that's made visually, either alone or using words as well. In a paragraph, defend a claim about how the argument works. For example, does an image itself make a claim, or does it draw you in to consider a verbal claim? What emotion does the argument generate? How does that emotion work to persuade you?

4. Find a recent example of a visual argument, either in print or on the Internet. Even though you may have a copy of the image, describe it carefully in your paper on the assumption that your description is all readers may have to go on. Then make a judgment about its effectiveness, supporting your claim with clear evidence from the "text."

PART 2

WRITING arguments

6

Academic Arguments

Much of the writing you will do in college (and some of what you may do later in your professional work) is called *academic discourse* or *academic argument*. Although this kind of writing has many distinctive characteristics that we explore in this chapter, in general terms this writing is addressed to an audience that is well informed about the topic, that attempts to convey a clear and compelling point in a somewhat formal style, and that follows agreed-upon conventions of usage, punctuation, formats, and so on. Milena Ateya's rhetorical analysis in Chapter 5 is an example of a brief academic argument, and you will find many other examples of academic arguments throughout this book.

Understanding What Academic Argument Is

As this definition suggests, *academic argument* covers a wide range of writing. Take a look at the following statements about migraine, the subject of a great deal of academic (especially medical) writing.

An advertisement for a drug, Weleda Migraine Remedy:

An excerpt from an article in the magazine *Body + Soul*: Hillarie Dowdle, "Fighting Migraines"

> For me, it's like this: I catch a whiff of perfume, or the weather shifts, or I get overtired—and boom. My fingers and toes start to burn and my vision blurs, while my hearing and sense of smell become painfully sharp. Dizzy and nauseated, I feel myself telescoping inward as the entirety of my consciousness shrinks to a hot dot of agony that takes up residence behind my right eyeball for 72 hours, never more, never less. Migraine.

A cartoon from the Web site http://www.migraine-aura.org:

© Linda Causey

An excerpt from an article in *Scientific American* (August 2008): David W. Dodick and J. Jay Gargus, "Why Migraines Strike"

At the moment, only a few drugs can prevent migraine. All of them were developed for other diseases, including hypertension, depression and epilepsy. Because they are not specific to migraine, it will come as no surprise that they work in only 50 percent of patients—and, in them, only 50 percent of the time—and induce a range of side effects, some potentially serious.

Recent research on the mechanism of these antihypertensive, antiepileptic and antidepressant drugs has demonstrated that one of their effects is to inhibit cortical spreading depression. The drugs' ability to prevent migraine with and without aura therefore supports the school of thought that cortical spreading depression contributes to both kinds of attacks. Using this observation as a starting point, investigators have come up with novel drugs that specifically inhibit cortical spreading depression. Those drugs are now being tested in migraine sufferers with and without aura. They work by preventing gap junctions, a form of ion channel, from opening, thereby halting the flow of calcium between brain cells.

Infographic: The root of migraine pain

MORE TO EXPLORE

Migraine. Oliver Sacks. Vintage, 1999.

"Migraine—New Molecular Mechanisms." Daniela Pietrobon in *Neuroscientist,* Vol. 11, No. 4, pages 373–386; 2005.

Receptor, Transporter, and Ion Channel Diseases. J. Jay Gargus in *Encyclopedia of Molecular Cell Biology and Molecular Medicine*. Edited by Robert A. Myers. Wiley, 2005.

Chronic Daily Headache. David W. Dodick in *New England Journal of Medicine*, Vol. 354, No. 2, pages 158–165; January 12, 2006.

Recent Advances in Understanding Migraine Mechanisms, Molecules and Therapeutics. Peter J. Goadsby in *Trends in Molecular Medicine*, Vol. 13, No. 1, pages 39–44; January 2007.

ABOUT THE AUTHOR(S)

David W. Dodick and J. Jay Gargus share a deep interest in understanding and ameliorating migraine. Dodick, a professor of neurology at the Mayo Clinic in Arizona, received his medical degree at Dalhousie University in Halifax, Nova Scotia. He studies the central nervous system abnormalities behind migraine and other forms of headache. Gargus, a professor of physiology, biophysics and human genetics at the University of California, Irvine, received his medical degree and doctorate at Yale University. He is studying the genetic underpinnings of migraine and other ion channel disorders.

An excerpt from an article in the journal *Trends in Molecular Medicine*: Peter Goadsby, "Recent Advances in Understanding Migraine Mechanisms, Molecules and Therapeutics."

Peter J. Goadsby, Institute of Neurology, The National Hospital for Neurology and Neurosurgery, Queen Square, London, UK WC1N 3B

Abstract

Migraine is a complex, disabling disorder of the brain that manifests itself as attacks of often severe, throbbing head pain with sensory sensitivity to light, sound and head movement. There is a clear familial tendency to migraine, which has been well defined in a rare autosomal dominant form of familial hemiplegic migraine (FHM). FHM mutations so far identified include those in CACNA1A (P/Q voltage-gated Ca(2+) channel), ATP1A2 (N(+)-K(+)-ATPase) and SCN1A (Na(+) channel) genes. Physiological studies in humans and studies of the experimental correlate—cortical spreading depression (CSD)—provide understanding of aura, and have explored in recent years the effect of migraine preventives in CSD. Therapeutic developments in migraine have come by targeting the trigeminovascular system, with the most-recent being the proof-of-principle study of calcitonin gene-related peptide (CGRP) receptor antagonists in acute migraine. To understand the basic pathophysiology of migraine, brain imaging studies have firmly established reproducible changes in the brainstem in regions that include areas that are involved in sensory modulation. These data lead to the view that migraine is a form of sensory dysmodulation—a system failure of normal sensory processing.

Introduction

Migraine is an episodic brain disorder that affects ~15% of the population [1]; it can be highly disabling, and has been estimated to be the most costly neurological disorder in the European Community at >27 billion per year [2]. Migraine is a familial episodic disorder, the key marker of which is headache with certain associated features (Table 1). By studying its component parts, one can gain insights into potential molecular mechanisms that might direct the development of new therapies. For a more-general clinical account of the disorder and its treatments, texts are available [3, 4 and 5].

Table 1. International Headache Society features of migraine [18]

Repeated episodic headache (4–72 hrs) with the following features:

Any two of:	Any one of:
• Unilateral	• Nausea and/or vomiting
• Throbbing	• Photophobia and phonophobia
• Worsened by movement	
• Moderate or severe	

References

1 R.B. Lipton *et al.*, Prevalence and burden of migraine in the United States: data from the American Migraine Study II, *Headache* **41** (2001), pp. 646–657.

2 P. Andlin-Sobocki *et al.*, Cost of disorders of the brain in Europe, *Eur. J. Neurol.* **12** (2005) (Suppl 1), pp. 1–27.

3 J. Olesen *et al.*, The Headaches, Lippincott, Williams & Wilkins (2005).

4 J.W. Lance and P.J. Goadsby, Mechanism and Management of Headache (7th ed.), Elsevier (2005).

5 P.J. Goadsby *et al.*, Migraine—current understanding and treatment, *N. Engl. J. Med.* **346** (2002), pp. 257–270.

It's pretty easy to tell that the article in *Trends in Molecular Medicine* is the "most academic" of these examples. But the essay from *Scientific American* also qualifies as academic argument, and the other examples (an ad, a cartoon, and an article in a popular magazine) might be used as illustration or evidence in such an argument. Each of these texts presents an argument, but the differences among them are striking.

The two visuals—the cartoon and the advertisement—use few words and rely on the image to carry a large part of the message: they are short and to the point, make implicit claims without offering support for them, and draw on emotional appeals. The article from *Body & Soul* is easy to read and to follow: it uses a narrative structure grounded in personal experience (again, note the use of pathos) that testifies to the claim. Also note its dramatic opening, fairly short sentences with simple structure, and tone of urgency and immediacy. While you might use one or more of these features in some of your college writing, especially on informal assignments, this is not an example of an academic argument.

Now compare this excerpt with the one from the end of the article in *Scientific American*. Here, we find a more nuanced and cautious tone ("At the moment, only a few drugs can prevent migraine"). The article carefully establishes the ethos of the authors to demonstrate that they are responsible and credible ("About the Authors") and provides a brief review of what is known about the topic (an overview of prior research and background information on migraine).

In addition, note that the authors' clear, direct style uses somewhat longer sentences than the popular article, with more complex structure and some technical vocabulary ("induce," "antihypertensive"), and it avoids personal information or use of first person. Finally, the article features careful presentation of evidence (the "infographic") and a focus on logical appeals (because drugs were developed for treating diseases other than migraine, they work in only 50 percent of the cases), along with references for further reading ("More to Explore").

This article, which argues that migraine is "imaginary" no longer, is written in academic style, with one major exception. Because it is intended for the broad audience that reads *Scientific American*, including many people who are not scientists but have a general interest in scientific topics, and because it adheres to the style of that particular magazine, it does not contain traditional academic citations and a list of works cited.

The final example on migraine, from a scientific journal, establishes the credentials of the author (his ethos) at the very beginning of the article by giving his institutional affiliation. It contains many citations and a long list of references, the first five of which we show here along with part of the introduction. This is a full-blown academic argument that is addressed to other physicians and scientists. In addition to the extensive citations and references, all of which contribute to the logical appeals of the article, note the review of earlier research about migraine and the use of a table, clearly labeled.

This article also features precise and sometimes highly technical language ("a rare autosomal dominant form of familial hemiplegic migraine (FHM)") and a clear, direct style that takes an authoritative stance while highlighting the importance of the topic ("Migraine is an episodic brain disorder that affects ~15% of the population [1]"). The author uses *one* rather than the more personal *I* except when he gives an overview of what he does in the article. And the careful, evenhanded tone he establishes ("These data lead to the view that migraine is a form of sensory dysmodulation") makes clear that the author's data (and not his feelings about the topic) are what are intended to convince his audience. These are all key features of academic argument.

One professor we know defines *academic argument* as "carefully structured research," and that seems to us to be a pretty good definition. In addition, we can sum up the characteristics of academic argument in a brief list. Academic argument

- is authoritative (written by experts who are addressing an audience of their peers and therefore need to establish a strong ethos)
- reviews what is known about a topic and creates new knowledge about it
- focuses on issues (facts, definitions, evaluations, or causes and effects) that are important to the writer's academic peers
- includes logical appeals based on careful research (such as field, lab, and library research)
- cites every source carefully and provides full bibliographical references so that others can find the sources
- is written in a clear and formal style
- has an evenhanded tone, deals fairly with any opposing points of view, and avoids appeals to emotion

Not Just Words

You've already seen that academic arguments often include visuals, such as the table on page 137. (The article from *Trends in Molecular Medicine* includes a second important table that we do not show here.) In *Scientific American*, which is printed in color and aims for a highly engaging design, readers see many visuals at work. In addition to the "infographic," the article excerpted on pages 135–36 includes eight other visuals, some of them as large as a full page. Charts, photographs, and drawings are included, such as this page from a twelfth-century illuminated manuscript.

The drawings help readers who have never suffered from migraine experience a few symptoms of this kind of headache. Here, the intense blues and deep reds seem to bore inward, while the aura surrounds the pain and intensifies it.

Take a look at a piece of academic writing that you are working on or have recently done, and find a passage that would be enhanced considerably by the addition of a strong visual image. What do you gain by adding the image?

Developing an Academic Argument

This chapter intends to get you thinking about academic arguments and to describe the features of these arguments in general. Not all academic arguments are similar, however, and not every academic argument includes each of the features we've presented here. Indeed, academic arguments cover a broad range—a brief note in a journal like *Nature* that announces a major breakthrough and promises more to come, short papers on important topics featured in *Physical Review Letters*, a poster presentation given at a conference on linguistics, a full research report in biology, or an undergraduate honors thesis in history. In addition, scholars today are pushing the envelope of traditional academic discourse in a number of fields. The use of narrative in medicine, for example, is on the rise as physicians try to communicate more effectively with other medical personnel.

In your first couple of years of college, the academic arguments you make may take a number of forms, but most will probably include the features we've discussed above. You'll see plenty of examples of academic argument throughout this book (including the two sample academic arguments at the end of this chapter), so keep these in mind when you get assignments in your classes; you may be able to use some of these examples as models. In addition, you can work toward making a good strong academic argument by following some time-tested techniques.

Choose a topic you want to explore in depth. Unless you are assigned a topic (and remember that even assigned topics can be tweaked to match your own interests), look for a subject you have been intrigued by—one you want to know a lot more about. In college writing, one of the hardest parts of producing an academic argument is finding a topic that can sustain your interest over a period of time but that can be narrowed enough to be manageable in the time you have to work on it. Begin by talking with friends about possible topics and explaining to them why you'd like to pursue research on this issue. Browse through books and articles that interest you, make a list of potential topics, and then zero in on one or two top choices.

Get to know the conversation surrounding your topic. Once you've chosen a topic, you need to do a lot more browsing. Start by searching on the Internet using key terms that are associated with your topic, but remember that you have access to a number of databases through your library that are not available to you on Google or other search engines. You're trying to familiarize yourself with what's been said about this topic and especially with what controversies surround it. Where do scholars agree, and where do they disagree? What key issues seem to be at stake?

Assess what you know and what you need to know. As you read and talk with others about your topic, begin to keep notes on what you have learned, including what you already know about the topic. Such notes should soon reveal where the gaps in your knowledge are. You may find that you need to read about relevant legal issues and thus end up in a law school library doing research there. Or you may find that you need to consult some experts about your topic. Instructors on your campus may have such expertise, so do some browsing on your college Web site to find faculty you might want to talk with. You can then make an appointment to visit during office hours, bringing along specific questions with you. You also may find that you need to conduct some field research—a survey, for example, or a set of observations. (See Chapter 19 for information on conducting field research.)

Begin formulating a claim about your topic. Chapter 5 provides a lot of guidance in formulating a claim, which every academic argument must have. Remember that good claims are debatable. After all, you can't argue effectively about something that everyone agrees on or accepts. In addition, your claim needs to be significant and say something meaningful about an important or controversial topic. Good claims can be supported with strong evidence and good reasons (see Chapter 16 for more information on the use of evidence). Here's the claim that the authors of the *Scientific American* article make: "Scientists and physicians are finally coming to see migraine for the complex, biologically fascinating process it is and to recognize its powerfully debilitating effects. The disorder is 'imaginary' no longer." Each piece of evidence that they present works to support that claim.

Consider your rhetorical stance and purpose. Begin by asking yourself where you are coming from in terms of this topic and how you want to represent yourself to those reading your academic argument. You may find that your stance is primarily that of a critic: you want to point out the problems and mistakes associated with some view of your topic. Or you may take the stance of a reporter—reviewing what has been said about your topic, analyzing and evaluating contributions to the conversation surrounding it, coming up with a synthesis of the most important strands of the conversation, and drawing conclusions based on them. On other occasions, your stance might be that of an advocate—one whose research strongly supports a particular view on your topic. Whatever your stance, remember that in academic arguments you want to be especially careful to come across as fair and evenhanded. In each case, your stance will be closely related to your purpose. In most of your college writing of academic arguments, your purpose will be at least two-fold—to do the best job you can in fulfilling an assignment for one of your courses and to introduce, establish, and support the claim you are making to the fullest extent possible. Luckily, these two purposes work well together.

Think about your audience(s). Here again, you will often find that you have at least a dual audience. First, you will be writing to the instructor who gave you this assignment, so make sure to take careful notes in class when the assignment is given and, if possible, set up a conference with your instructor so that you can know as much as possible about his or her expectations: what will it take to convince this audience that you have done a terrific job of writing an academic argument? Beyond your instructor, you should think of your classmates as members of your audience—informed, intelligent peers who will be interested in what you have to say. Again, what do you know about this audience, and what will they expect from your academic argument? Finally, consider yet another audience—people who are already engaged in discussing your topic. These will include the authors whose work you have read and the larger academic community of which they are a part.

Concentrate on the material you are gathering. Any academic argument is only as good as the material it presents in its support, so you need to be careful as you search for evidence. With each major piece of evidence (a lengthy article, say, that addresses your topic directly), take the time to summarize the main points, to analyze how those points are made, to evaluate their effectiveness, to synthesize the results of your analysis and evaluation, and to articulate what you think about this article. In this way, you are testing each piece of evidence and deciding which to keep—and which to throw out. In doing so, remember that you do not want to gather only material that favors your take on the topic. You want to look at all legitimate perspectives on the topic, and in doing so, you may even change your mind. That's what good research for an academic argument can do, so keep yourself open to change.

Remember that you will probably be gathering or creating visual materials as well as text materials. You may find a drawing that perfectly illustrates an aspect of your topic, or you may create a pie chart that shows the results of a questionnaire you distributed. Whether you find or create visuals for your academic argument, you need to give them the same careful scrutiny you give to articles, books, and so on. Remember that the graphic representation of data always involves an interpretation of the data: numbers can lie and pictures distort. (For more information on evaluating visuals, see Chapter 14.)

Take special care with documentation. As you gather material for your academic argument, be scrupulous in recording where you found each source so that you can cite it accurately. Remember that different academic fields use different systems of documentation, so if your instructor has not recommended a style of documentation to you, ask in class about it. Scholars have developed these systems over a long period of time. Using them carefully and accurately shows that you understand the conventions of your field of study and that you have done your homework, and this helps to establish your credibility as a knowledgeable member of the academy. (For more detailed information on documentation, see Chapter 20.)

Think about organization. As you work on design and survey the materials that you have gathered, you are beginning the work of drafting your academic argument. At this point, look at the organization of some of the articles you have gathered. The article in *Trends in Molecular Medicine* begins with an abstract that is followed by a formal introduction. The author then organizes the rest of his article by using a series of ten subheadings (such as "The Genetics of Migraine" and "Familial Hemiplegic Migraine"). The *Scientific American* article does not have an abstract, though a box on the first page announces "Key Concepts":

Key Concepts

- Migraine is more than a headache: it is intensely painful and has distinct phases.
- The disorder used to be considered a vascular one, but recent research reveals it to be neurological, related to a wave of nerve cell activity that sweeps across the brain.
- The root of migraine may reside in brain stem malfunctioning.
- Although debate swirls about the precise cause of migraine, discoveries are already permitting the development of new treatments.

The authors of this article also make effective use of subheadings (such as "Aura's Origin," "From Aura to Ache," and "What the Future May Hold") to guide readers. Sometimes, a field will use an established set of headings for organization—abstract, introduction, materials and methods, results, discussion, conclusion, references. As you organize your academic argument, check with your instructor to see if there is a recommended pattern to follow—or create a scratch outline or storyboard for how your essay will proceed. And remember that your organization needs to take into account the placement of visuals—charts, tables, photographs, and so on.

Consider style and tone. The examples from *Scientific American* and *Trends in Molecular Medicine* demonstrate traditional academic style, which strives for clarity and directness. Such a style leans toward the formal, using the third person and avoiding a focus on *I*; avoiding colloquialisms, slang, or contractions; and using technical vocabulary where necessary. Most academic argument adopts the tone of a reasonable, fair-minded, careful thinker who is interested in coming as close to the truth about a topic as possible.

Consider design and visuals. Most college academic arguments look more like the article in *Trends in Molecular Medicine* than the one in

Scientific American—that is, they are usually black on white, use a traditional font size and type (like 11-point Times New Roman), and lack any conscious design other than inserted tables or figures. But such conventions are changing as more and more students have access to sophisticated software that allows for the kind of design elements on display in the *Scientific American* piece. In addition to columns and boxed sidebars, the authors use a number of powerful visuals, including this one on the left that accompanies the opening of the article.

Indeed, student writers today may now go well beyond print, creating digital documents that include sound and video to go along with visuals such as photographs, charts, and so on. Writers of academic arguments need to consider what kind of design is most appropriate for their topic, their purpose, and their audience and then act accordingly. As you think about the design of your academic argument, you may want to consult your instructor—and to try out your design on friends or classmates.

Reflect on your draft and get responses. As with any important piece of writing you do, an academic argument calls for careful reflection on your draft. Now may be the time to do a formal outline so that you can "see" whether you establish the logical links you intended. In addition, you will want to judge the effectiveness of your argument, assessing what each paragraph adds and what may be missing. Turning a critical eye to your own work now can save a lot of grief in the long run. In addition to your own critique, make sure to get some response from classmates and friends. To make sure that they give you helpful responses, come up with a set of questions you have about the draft, and ask them to refer to the questions as they read. Now's the time to find out what is confusing or unclear to others, what needs further support, and so on.

Edit and proofread your text. If you are writing for publication, you will almost always get responses from a copyeditor and a proofreader, who go through your text and question you about any discrepancies, including missing references, typos, wrong words, and so on. Students don't usually get the benefit of such experts, however, so you need to be prepared to do these jobs for yourself. Proofread the piece at least three times—one time to make sure that all your ideas and main points make sense (that you haven't left out a key word, for instance); another time word for word (some people like to read backwards since that focuses attention at the word level); and a final time to check that every source mentioned in the academic argument appears in the references list and that every citation is correct. This is also the time to make any final touch-ups to your design. Remember that how the document looks is part of what establishes its credibility.

RESPOND ●

1. Working with another student in your class, find examples of academic arguments from two or three different fields that strike you as being well written and effective. Spend some time looking closely at them. Do they exemplify the key features of academic arguments discussed in this chapter? What other features do they use? How are they organized? What kind of tone do the writers use? What use do they make of visuals? Draw up a brief report on your findings (a list will do), and bring it to class for discussion.

2. Look closely at the following five passages, each of which is from an opening of a published work, and decide which ones provide examples of academic argument. How would you describe each one, and what are its key features? Which is the most formal and academic? Which is the least? How might you revise them to make them more— or less—academic?

During the Old Stone Age, between thirty-seven thousand and eleven thousand years ago, some of the most remarkable art ever conceived was etched or painted on the walls of caves in southern France and northern Spain. After a visit to Lascaux, in the Dordogne, which was discovered in 1940, Picasso reportedly said to his guide, "They've invented everything." What those first artists invented was a language of signs for which there will never be a Rosetta stone; perspective, a technique that was not rediscovered until the Athenian Golden Age; and a bestiary of such vitality and finesse that, by the flicker of torchlight, the animals seem to surge from the walls, and move across them like figures in a magic-lantern show (in that sense, the artists invented animation). They also thought up the grease lamp—a lump of fat, with a plant wick, placed in a hollow stone—to light their workplace; scaffolds to reach high places; the principles of stenciling and Pointillism; powdered colors, brushes, and stumping cloths; and, more to the point of Picasso's insight, the very concept of an image. A true artist reimagines that concept with every blank canvas—but not from a void.

—Judith Thurman, "First Impressions," *The New Yorker*

I stepped over the curb and into the street to hitchhike. At the age of ten I'd put some pretty serious mileage on my thumb. And I knew how it was done. Hold your thumb up, not down by your hip as though you didn't much give a damn whether you got a ride or not. Always hitch at a place where a driver could pull out of traffic and give you time to get in without risking somebody tailgating him.

—Harry Crews, "On Hitchhiking," *Harper's*

Coral reef ecosystems are essential marine environments around the world. Host to thousands (and perhaps millions) of diverse organisms, they are also vital to the economic well-being of an estimated 0.5 billion people, or 8% of the world's population who live on tropical coasts (Hoegh-Guldberg 1999). Income from tourism and fishing industries, for instance, is essential to the economic prosperity of many countries, and the various plant and animal species present in reef ecosystems are sources for different natural products and medicines. The degradation of coral reefs can therefore have a devastating impact on coastal populations, and it is estimated that between 50% and 70% of all reefs around the world are currently threatened (Hoegh-Guldberg). Anthropogenic influences are cited as the major cause of this degradation, including sewage, sedimentation, direct trampling of reefs, over-fishing of herbivorous fish, and even global warming (Umezawa et al. 2002; Jones et al. 2001; Smith et al. 2001).

—Elizabeth Derse, "Identifying the Sources of Nitrogen to Hanalei Bay, Kauai, Utilizing the Nitrogen Isotope Signature of Macroalgae," *Stanford Undergraduate Research Journal*

Some of my best friends are women—heck, I am a woman—but I've come to the conclusion that we've seen too much of the fairer sex. For me, the final straw came last month when Britney Spears jauntily revealed her waxed nether regions to waiting photographers as she exited her limo. Britney's stunt made her the Internet smash of the season. But in providing America's workers with this cubicle distraction, Britney was doing a lot more than making her own privates public.

—Kay S. Hymowitz, "Scenes from the Exhibitionists," *Wall Street Journal*

From the richest high school to the poorest high school in America, students are being told that employment in the computer industry is nothing less than salvation from the indignities of the jobs those others have to do to survive. If you don't learn your computer skills well, if by some chance you're bored sitting in front of that screen, day after day under buzzing fluorescents, pecking at a vanilla keyboard, clicking a mouse, it's your problem, and there will be no excuse for your fate in this new economy: you will be doomed to menial, manual labor. That dirty, anybody-can-do-that work. Poor income, low prestige. Pues, así va la vida, compa, that's life if you don't get your stuff right.

—Dagoberto Gilb, "Work Union," *Gritos* [a book]

3. Read the following paragraphs, and then list changes that the writer might make to convert them into an academic argument:

Every well-traveled cosmopolite knows that America is mind-numbingly monotonous—"the most boring country to tour, because everywhere looks like everywhere else," as the columnist Thomas Friedman once told Charlie Rose. Boston has the same stores as Denver, which has the same stores as Charlotte or Seattle or Chicago. We live in a "Stepford world," says Rachel Dresbeck, the author of *Insiders' Guide to Portland, Oregon*. Even Boston's historic Faneuil Hall, she complains, is "dominated by the Gap, Anthropologie, Starbucks, and all the other usual suspects. Why go anywhere? Every place looks the same." This complaint is more than the old worry, dating back to the 1920s, that the big guys are putting Mom and Pop out of business. Today's critics focus less on what isn't there—Mom and Pop—than on what is. Faneuil Hall actually has plenty of locally owned businesses, from the Geoclassics store selling minerals and jewelry, to Pizzeria Regina ("since 1926"). But you do find the same chains everywhere.

The suburbs are the worst. Take Chandler, Arizona, just south of Phoenix. At Chandler Fashion Center, the area's big shopping mall, you'll find P. F. Chang's, California Pizza Kitchen, Chipotle Mexican Grill, and the Cheesecake Factory. Drive along Chandler's straight, flat boulevards, and you'll see Bed Bath & Beyond and Linens-n-Things; Barnes & Noble and Borders; PetSmart and Petco; Circuit City and Best Buy; Lowe's and Home Depot; CVS and Walgreens. Chandler has the Apple Store and Pottery Barn, the Gap and Ann Taylor, Banana Republic and DSW, and, of course, Target and Wal-Mart, Starbucks and McDonald's. For people allergic to brands, Chandler must be hell—even without the 110-degree days.

—Virginia Postrel, "In Praise of Chain Stores"

4. Choose two pieces of your college writing, and examine them closely. Are they examples of strong academic writing? How do they use the key features that this chapter identifies as characteristic of academic arguments? How do they use and document sources? What kind of tone do you establish in each? After studying the examples in this chapter, what might you change about these pieces of writing, and why?

5. Go to a blog that you follow, or check out one like the *Daily Kos*. Spend some time reading the articles or postings on the blog, and look for ones that you think are the best written and the most interesting. What features or characteristics of academic argument do they use, and which ones do they avoid?

Music in U.S.-China Diplomacy

CLAIRE LIU*

The introduction to the general topic stresses the importance of the power of music.

Music is often referred to as a universal language. Humans express their thoughts, emotions, and aspirations through various media of music, which can manifest individual and collective identities and can unite people. But music can also express the differences that separate people. The power of music to unify and divide is nowhere more apparent than between the peoples of two countries that have striven to understand each other for over a century.

The author provides an overview of U.S.-Chinese musical interactions.

China and the United States have a lengthy history of musical interactions accompanying their diplomatic history. One could even argue that for most Chinese, exposure to Western music preceded encounters with Americans themselves. China's introduction to American music stems from a general introduction to Western culture and music by Roman Catholic Jesuit missionaries during the sixteenth and seventeenth centuries, since music was fundamental to missionary education. After foreign powers defeated China in the first of three Opium Wars, the Treaty of Nanjing in 1842 forced China to surrender control of select "treaty ports," one of which was Shanghai.[1] Having a unique geographic status and

___

*Claire Liu wrote this essay for a course at Stanford University on the history of U.S.-China relations. A major in international relations, Liu also is studying at the Shanghai Conservatory of Music. Note that she uses her interest in music to help create a strong academic argument about U.S.-China relations. She introduces the three-part structure of her essay in a thesis paragraph on p. 151 and then uses subheadings to guide readers through the three major episodes she traces in this relationship. This essay is documented using the style recommended in *The Chicago Manual of Style*, which is widely used in the field of history.

Chicago style is followed for footnotes and bibliography.

1. Sheila Nelson and Jindong Cai, *Rhapsody in Red: How Western Classical Music Became Chinese* (New York: Angora, 2004), 26.

exemption from domestic Chinese policies, Shanghai became a hub for foreign economies, cultures, and music. In fact, Shanghai developed a reputation for being the "Paris of the East."

In the early twentieth century, the fall of the Qing dynasty marked the end of the imperial form of government in China and widespread social ferment led to the May Fourth Movement to reform society and build a renewed nation-state.[2] At the same time, another reform effort was started by a new generation of musicians and educators, many of whom were trained in music schools in Europe and Japan or had listened to Western music. They aimed to build a modern infrastructure in China, complete with Western music education. This movement was shaped by influential figures such as Xiao Youmei, Li Delun, and Li Jinhui.

This essay seeks to identify interactions between Americans and Chinese through music during the twentieth century, interactions that carry significance for U.S.-China relations. Three episodes are worth examining to highlight the function that music played in this exchange—the Chinese jazz age of the 1920s and 1930s; Chinese-American diplomacy through Western music during the time of President Richard Nixon and Secretary of State Henry Kissinger; and cultural exchanges after the United States officially recognized Beijing. Although music and politics are very different means of discourse, these episodes reveal that they may be used for similar purposes. Moreover, as China and the United States grow politically and economically more interdependent, music has increasingly been used as an agent for promoting relations between the two nations.

Note the use of an evenhanded, serious tone that characterizes academic argument.

Fairly formal language is used throughout, another characteristic of much academic argument.

A thesis paragraph announces the three-part focus for the essay.

---

2. Andrew F. Jones, *Yellow Music: Media Culture and Colonial Modernity in the Chinese Jazz Age* (Durham: Duke University Press, 2001), 101.

A subheading signals the first part: a major U.S.-Chinese musical encounter through jazz.

THE ROAD TO JAZZ

One of the first direct musical encounters between Americans and Chinese came through the advent of a quintessential American musical form—jazz. The Chinese jazz age resulted from internal and external influences on Shanghai musicians to modernize that coincided with the political, intellectual, and social revolution spawned by the May Fourth Movement. Many elite musicians preferred Western culture to what they viewed as the obsolete traditions of Chinese society. Among this elite was Xiao Youmei. A native of Guangdong province, he was the son of a respected Confucian scholar, grew up in the Portuguese colony of Macao, and was educated in Germany. He was also influenced by friends and neighbors, including a Portuguese minister who introduced him to classical music and Sun Yat-Sen, the revolutionary who introduced him to politics and nationalism.[3] With Sun's help, Xiao received a scholarship to study piano and composition at the Leipzig Music Academy in Germany beginning in 1912. He returned to China in 1921, where he supported the May Fourth Movement.

The author creates an academic ethos with evidence of her careful research on Youmei and the May Fourth Movement and uses logical appeals to argue her points.

Xiao Youmei believed that Chinese music was a stale product of "a thousand years of stagnation," a tradition "at a standstill."[4] He defined Chinese music in terms of what it lacked, which included a tempered scale, functional harmony, counterpoint, orchestration, standardized notation, and engineered instruments such as the piano.[5] These were all qualities of Western music that Xiao found worthy of emulation. Western music, according to Xiao and his supporters, was the result of superior technology, better institutions, and higher standards for practice and performance. A select population in China,

---

3. Nelson and Cai, *Rhapsody in Red*, 93.
4. Jones, *Yellow Music*, 25.
5. Ibid.

he felt certain, was ready to embrace new sounds—especially foreign ones.

At the same time, the musicians and intellectuals of the May Fourth Movement, including Xiao himself, desired to preserve Chinese culture. For example, the musicians modernized traditional Chinese instruments using Western technologies, rather than replacing them with new instruments altogether. Xiao believed that music should help construct a modern, national identity for China. Even Liang Qichao, a cautious intellectual, considered music a means of "aesthetic education, a method by which the intellectual and moral quality of citizenry could be elevated to advance the nationalistic cause."[6]

When Chinese musicians listened to foreign music, they observed and favored polyphonies, functional harmonies, and orchestration of particular genres because these represented what the musicians saw as "forward thinking." This is how American jazz became popular in China in the 1920s and 1930s.

This popularity first developed in Shanghai, the treaty port where Russians, French, Germans, Italians, Japanese, and Americans had carved out colonial territories and established businesses. A Frenchman named Labansat introduced the gramophone to the streets of Shanghai, earning money from passersby who paid to listen to a sampling from this curious machine. In 1908, Labansat set up a recording company called Pathé Orient, which initially manufactured and sold recordings of Peking opera, a traditional Chinese musical genre. The company began recording and selling a new genre of music in the form of popular songs.[7] By turning music into a portable, material object, the success of Pathé Orient created an alternative context for music and musicians that was

Additional evidence from a scholarly book is introduced to support the popularity of jazz in China and help establish the author's credibility or ethos.

---

6. Ibid., 34.
7. Ibid., 53–54.

perfect for the rich sounds of jazz. Soon, major recording companies such as RCA Victor began recording and manufacturing in Shanghai. Mass music culture evolved as department stores and street retailers played a wide range of music, including jazz. The private enterprises and symbols of upward class mobility that were widely despised elsewhere in China were highly popular in Shanghai, and thus they played a crucial role in exposing Chinese people to new ideas embedded in music.

Li Jinhui, an icon of modern Chinese popular music, is widely credited for bringing jazz to China. Born in 1891, Li loved Western music from an early age. In addition to studying and teaching music, he listened to jazz on the gramophone, or "talking box" (hua xiazi). Experimenting with blending sounds from jazz with traditional folk tunes, he recorded hundreds of "modern songs" between 1927 and 1936. He also composed songs for fifteen popular films and led the first all-Chinese jazz band at a posh Shanghai nightclub that had traditionally employed only foreigners. He had great ambitions—to enlighten the masses with this nonelitist music, which he likened to the literature of the common people.[8]

In pursuing these goals, Li was working within a larger setting of early multicultural encounters. The Chinese jazz age in Shanghai resulted from two unconventional populations—jazz musicians and Shanghai residents—that attracted one another. Shanghai was a mosaic of many cultures assembled from the shards of colonialism, and its residents manifested their dynamic, multicultural, capitalist qualities through their affinity for progressive music, literature, and lifestyles.

The author summarizes China's encounter with jazz.

Jazz responded perfectly to these needs. At upscale nightclubs and dance halls, American bands frequently performed live for audiences, who included foreigners, Chinese people involved in the city's modern commercial economy, and traditional Chinese. Created by African

_____

8. Ibid., 73–79.

A Shanghai dance club in 1926. (Photograph courtesy of Bettman/CORBIS.)

Americans, jazz was an active form of music that liberated its performers and listeners both physically and emotionally. Jazz represented creation, improvisation, and the individual voice. And just as jazz fed the desires of newer Shanghai residents, older Chinese audiences also appreciated an inherent cultural diversity in jazz, a quality that Hollywood and conservative Americans often disregarded. It's no surprise that James Stanley, an American musician, lauded Shanghai for being a "Seventh Heaven for the jazz musician."[9]

REAL MUSIC DIPLOMACY

Social unrest caused by World War II changed the Shanghai music scene significantly, making it difficult for conservatories and other music institutions to function. Security deteriorated in Shanghai, and Xiao Youmei moved his school every few months to a new sanctuary. Many students and faculty fled Shanghai for safer areas

A subheading signals a second stage in U.S-Chinese musical encounters and helps to provide clear structure for the essay.

---

9. Ibid., 148.

at the request of worried families. But at a sad and troubling time for the country and for the music institutions, a young man named Li Delun enrolled at the Shanghai Conservatory in 1940. He came from a well-to-do Muslim family plagued by social scandal. Taking solace in Western classical music, Li began taking piano lessons in Beijing when he was a teenager. At the same time, he seized every opportunity to attend concerts, take in Hollywood movies, and listen to music shows on the radio that were intended for foreigners. After entering the Shanghai Conservatory, he attended Shanghai Municipal Orchestra concerts and studied conducting.

Chronological order is used to trace cultural events from the 1940s to the 1960s.

While Li Delun fortified his cultural education, China followed a different path. In 1949, Mao Zedong led his Communist followers to power over the Nationalists. Ensuing policy disasters (like the Great Leap Forward) and hardline leaders (like those later labeled the Gang of Four) resulted in political turmoil and international isolation for China. During the 1960s, Mao claimed it was time to get rid of the "liberal bourgeoisie" who he believed contaminated Communist thought and class struggle. He launched the Cultural Revolution, during which intellectuals, revolutionary elders, and artists—including musicians—were officially denounced and purged from leadership positions.[10]

A strong topic sentence helps guide readers.

The impact of the Cultural Revolution on music institutions in China was certainly negative. However, in an attempt to control the arts without completely destroying them, the Communist Party, largely influenced by Mao's wife Jiang Qing, established the so-called Hundred Flowers movement (based on the notion that the party should "let a hundred flowers bloom"—allow different ideas to exist—so long as each was compatible with Communist thought). Thus, the government created the Central Philharmonic Society in 1965 in response to Jiang

---

10. Warren I. Cohen, *America's Response to China* (New York: Columbia University Press, 2000), 34.

Qing's call for cultural and arts education through the Party. Li Delun was appointed its conductor.[11] Li was, as I have indicated above, strategically poised for music diplomacy, but during China's period of isolation, which lasted for two decades, communication between the People's Republic of China and the United States ceased. Not until the early 1970s did the leaders of both nations envision rebuilding a relationship, one in which music would again play a role.

Henry Kissinger and Richard Nixon began establishing a diplomatic dialogue with Mao Zedong and Chinese premier Zhou Enlai in 1971. In an October 5, 1970, article in *Time*, Nixon said that he wanted to improve relations with Beijing: "Maybe that role won't be possible for five years, maybe not even ten years. But in 20 years it had better be, or the world is in mortal danger. If there is anything I want to do before I die, it is go to China. If I don't, I want my children to."[12] Zhou Enlai's warm reception of the American team at the World Table Tennis championship in Japan marked the beginning of "ping-pong diplomacy." Receiving a surprising invitation from the premier for a paid visit to the People's Republic, the U.S. ping-pong team became the first American group allowed into the country since 1949.

But if sports paved the way for the first visit by an American president to Beijing, music also had a role to play. Zhou Enlai suggested to Li Delun that the Central Philharmonic should perform for Henry Kissinger during an October 1971 visit and even suggested that because "Kissinger's German[, y]ou should play Beethoven."[13] Zhou was eager to appeal to Kissinger's tastes and hoped that playing a German composer's work for the German American Secretary of State would do the trick. He believed that music could help represent the common

Sources are used to stress the role of music in bringing U.S. and Chinese leaders together.

---

11. Nelson and Cai, *Rhapsody in Red*, 215.
12. "I Did Not Want the Hot Words of TV," *Time*, October 5, 1970, 16.
13. Nelson and Cai, *Rhapsody in Red*, 266.

interests and values of American and Chinese leaders. But while the Central Philharmonic excelled at Beethoven's Fifth Symphony, Jiang Qing and her musical adviser were opposed to the idea of its performance. According to the adviser, Yu Huiyong, the doomed fatalist theme of the Fifth seemed inappropriate for Communist China. Eventually, the Central Philharmonic settled on Beethoven's Sixth Symphony, since it was reportedly about land and nature, though Maestro Li understood that it was actually about a landlord's property.

Nixon's visit in 1972 also called for a personalized repertoire, which included a unique version of none other than "Home on the Range." And like Kissinger, who had been treated to a Peking opera performance that he later described as "an art form of truly stupefying boredom,"[14] Nixon was taken by Jiang Qing to an opera, *The Red Detachment of Women*. While Nixon reported being impressed by its "dazzling technical and theatrical virtuosity," he was also well aware of its propagandistic ambitions.[15] Together, these interactions suggest that though diplomatic exchange occurred cordially and with good intentions, Americans and Chinese still had much to learn about each other.

In the long run, however, these visits laid the foundation for furthering what a joint U.S.-Chinese communiqué called "people-to-people contacts and exchanges in such fields as science, technology, culture, sports, and journalism" that were mutually beneficial.[16] And once again, music would be part of this effort of opening up to the West, as Zhou Enlai advocated a series of measures promoting musical discourse.

Quotations provide vivid detail.

The author uses a logical appeal: music helped lay the foundation for many later U.S.-Chinese exchanges.

---

14. Henry Kissinger, *White House Years* (Boston: Little, Brown, 1979), 779.

15. Richard Nixon, *The Memoirs of Richard Nixon* (New York: Grosset & Dunlap, 1978), 570.

16. "Joint Communiqué of the United States of America and the People's Republic of China," February 28, 1972.

The Music of Cultural Exchange

Following the signing of the 1972 communiqué, Zhou invited the American pianists Frances and Richard Hadden, who had lived in the city of Wuhan for some time, to perform in Beijing. Though the concert was not open to the public, it was the first classical music performance by foreigners since the beginning of the Cultural Revolution. A few months later, Premier Zhou granted permission to radio stations to play foreign music. These actions proved to be controversial and met with harsh criticism from Jiang Qing, who argued that no one should assume that such decadent sounds could be played on Chinese radio.[17]

Such events continued, however, and foreign musical ensembles began visiting Chinese concert halls. The London Philharmonic and the Vienna Philharmonic toured the country and collaborated with Chinese music circles. These international orchestra visits paved a path for Zhou's ultimate goal, which was to improve diplomatic relations with the United States. The pinnacle of these encounters took place in September 1973, when the Philadelphia Orchestra, led by the legendary Eugene Ormandy, visited China. Zhou and Jiang Qing had remembered that Ormandy helped to raise money for the medical service of China's Eighth Route Army in a 1940 benefit.[18]

Li Delun planned a warm welcome for the American group. With the approval of Zhou Enlai, the Central Philharmonic Chorus sang "America the Beautiful"—in English—a momentous symbol of camaraderie that moved many of the Americans to tears and eased lingering fears about visiting Communist China.[19]

The tour included six sold-out performances—four

Another subheading signals the third major section of the essay: the aftermath of the diplomatic rapprochement of the early 1970s.

Further evidence of U.S.-Chinese musical exchanges is presented. Chronological order continues to organize the essay.

Sources are introduced in support of the claim of goodwill created by the Philadelphia Orchestra's 1973 visit to China.

---

17. Nelson and Cai, *Rhapsody in Red*, 268.
18. Ibid.
19. Ibid.

concerts in Beijing and two in Shanghai—and a chance for the Philadelphia musicians to sit in during one of the Central Philharmonic's rehearsals. The repertoire for the first two Beijing concerts comprised symphonies by Mozart, Brahms, and American composer Roy Harris. Tactfully chosen encores included "March of the Workers and Peasants," a popular Chinese revolutionary song and a favorite of Zhou Enlai, and John Philip Sousa's "Stars and Stripes Forever."[20] The visit was heralded as a success by the U.S. media. Harold Schonberg, who chronicled the tour for the *New York Times*, wrote favorably of banquets and warm receptions after every concert.[21] Much publicity was given to the "continual development of better understanding between China and the United States,"[22] as quoted by Ling Ling, the vice president of the Friendship Association, and toasts "to friendship with China" over lavish eleven-course meals featuring Peking duck. Boris Sokoloff, the orchestra's manager, said, "The response has been overwhelming. The hospitality and friendship are unbelievable. The Chinese went all out for us. They are a warm, friendly, delightful people, no question about it."[23] Conductor Ormandy added that this was "the most significant trip that the Philadelphia Orchestra has ever made."[24]

A counter-argument is acknowledged: not everyone was impressed with the visits of Western orchestras.

Although the visit was very well received in China, Jiang Qing was less enthusiastic than her fellow citizens were about the music. She was extremely critical of what she considered "bourgeois" music and refused to listen to it or learn about composers who lived in eras when the bourgeoisie rose to power. Great composers such as Tchaikovsky, Schumann, and Debussy were ruled out. At

---

20. Ibid, 269.
21. Harold C. Schonberg, "Philadelphians a 'Big Success' in Their First Concert in China," *New York Times*, September 15, 1973, A2.
22. Nelson and Cai, *Rhapsody in Red,* 270.
23. Harold C. Schonberg, "Philadelphians End China Visit," *New York Times*, September 23, 1973, A1.
24. Ibid., A1.

the root of Jiang Qing's objections was, perhaps, her unwillingness to defer to Zhou Enlai, who had invited three major Western orchestras to China against her wishes. She decided to punish him for his music diplomacy initiatives by proclaiming that from now on China should receive minimal visits from arts groups of capitalist countries. This decision broadened into a campaign against all "bourgeois" music.

When Mao died in 1976, however, Jiang Qing's power faded, she and the other members of the Gang of Four were arrested, and the Cultural Revolution came to an end. Li Delun began rebuilding his Central Philharmonic, and the orchestra performed Beethoven's Fifth on March 26, 1977. The rapturous performance ushered in a new movement with new instruments, new educational outreach activities, and new foreign exchanges. In May 1978, for example, the Boston Symphony Orchestra's conductor Seiji Ozawa accepted an invitation to guest conduct Li Delun's Central Philharmonic. The repertoire featured Chinese, Japanese, and Western music.

The end of the Cultural Revolution allows for more musical exchanges.

Soon after, violinist Isaac Stern, who had been interested in making a trip to China since the rapprochement, wrote to Kissinger asking for help in arranging a visit.[25] In 1979, a delighted Stern received an invitation to make a China tour. Bringing along a film crew to shoot a documentary called *From Mao to Mozart: Isaac Stern in China*, Stern thanked the welcoming committee in Beijing by saying, "We have come here to meet with the Chinese people, to say hello through music, and as musicians, then friends."[26] In his memoir, published twenty years later, he wrote, "I was using music as a kind of passport into the country."[27]

---

25. Isaac Stern, *My First Seventy-nine Years* (New York: Knopf, 1999), 212.

26. *From Mao to Mozart: Isaac Stern in China*, DVD, directed by Murray Lerner. Performed by Isaac Stern and David Golub (New York: New Video Group, 2001).

27. Stern, *My First Seventy-nine Years*, 246.

Footage of the trip includes clips of a Chinese orchestra playing "Oh, Susanna!" with traditional Chinese instruments such as the *erhu* and *pipa* as well as Western instruments like percussion drums. Chinese musicians worked to make their guests welcome by playing American tunes—but with Chinese instruments.[28]

Quotations sum up the role of music in the rapprochement between the two countries.

In his memoir, Stern writes, "To have visited China was to have experienced an entirely different world from the one we knew. But it was a world of human beings, toward whom we came to feel great warmth and with whom we ultimately shared a common language—the humanity of music."[29] Stern describes the Chinese as inquisitive, eager, and willing to use musical exchanges to express their desires for identity as well as for friendship.

As Stern suggests, music and culture are always entwined. Music embodies cultural values and directions of thought through sound and performance. Domestic politics and foreign relations are also intimately related, as those in power exercise both in interrelated ways. But the two spheres—music and politics—are also often isolated from each other; we do not usually consider them mutually inclusive. My investigation began as a search for perception of the other through music but led me to realize that music has played a larger and more active role in politics than I thought possible.

The conclusion summarizes the author's findings and reinforces her thesis.

Moreover, the role that music has played in connecting Americans and Chinese people has grown. In the twentieth century, music said what politics and economics often could not say. History has shown that musical relations and political relations can and do benefit one another in significant ways, and the legacies of Xiao Youmei, Li Jinhui, the jazz musicians, Li Delun, and Isaac Stern live on. Orchestras regularly tour both countries, scholars exchange ideas, and young musicians have

---

28. From *Mao to Mozart*.
29. Stern, *My First Seventy-nine Years*, 252.

joined the next generation of cultural ambassadors. As music plays a greater role in U.S.-China relations, Chinese and Americans will fulfill the dreams of the pioneers who believed in the power of music.

BIBLIOGRAPHY

Cohen, Warren I. *America's Response to China*. New York: Columbia University Press, 2000.

From Mao to Mozart: Isaac Stern in China. DVD. Directed by Murray Lerner. Performed by Isaac Stern and David Golub. New York: New Video Group, 2001.

"I Did Not Want the Hot Words of TV." *Time*, October 5, 1970, 16. http://www.time.com/time/magazine/article/0,9171,904333,00.html# (accessed September 22, 2008).

"Joint Communiqué of the United States of America and the People's Republic of China." February 28, 1972.

Jones, Andrew F. *Yellow Music: Media Culture and Colonial Modernity in the Chinese Jazz Age*. Durham: Duke University Press, 2001.

Kissinger, Henry. *White House Years*. Boston: Little, Brown, 1979.

Nelson, Sheila, and Jindong Cai. *Rhapsody in Red: How Western Classical Music Became Chinese*. New York: Angora, 2004.

Nixon, Richard. *The Memoirs of Richard Nixon*. New York: Grosset & Dunlap, 1978.

Schonberg, Harold C. "Philadelphians a 'Big Success' in Their First Concert in China." *New York Times*, September 15, 1973.

———. "Philadelphians End China Visit." *New York Times*, September 23, 1973.

Stern, Isaac. *My First Seventy-nine Years*. New York: Knopf, 1999.

China: The Prizes and Pitfalls of Progress

LAN XUE

ABSTRACT

Pushes to globalize science must not threaten local innovations in developing countries, argues Lan Xue.

Developing countries such as China and India have emerged both as significant players in the production of high-tech products and as important contributors to the production of ideas and global knowledge. China's rapid ascent as a broker rather than simply a consumer of ideas and innovation has made those in the "developed" world anxious. A 2007 report by UK think tank Demos says that "U.S. and European pre-eminence in science-based innovation cannot be taken for granted. The centre of gravity for innovation is starting to shift from west to east."[1]

But the rapid increase in research and development spending in China—of the order of 20% per year since 1999—does not guarantee a place as an innovation leader. Participation in global science in developing countries such as China is certainly good news for the global scientific

This article was written by Lan Xue, a faculty member in the School of Public Policy and Management and the director of the China Institute for Science and Technology Policy, both at Tsinghua University in Beijing, China. It was published in the online edition of *Nature* in July 2008.

Illustrations by D. Parkins.

community. It offers new opportunities for collaboration, fresh perspectives, and a new market for ideas. It also presents serious challenges for the management of innovation in those countries. A major discovery in the lab does not guarantee a star product in the market. And for a country in development, the application of knowledge in productive activities and the related social transformations are probably more important than the production of the knowledge itself. By gumming the works in information dissemination, by misplacing priorities, and by disavowing research that, although valuable, doesn't fit the tenets of modern Western science, developing countries may falter in their efforts to become innovation leaders.

VICIOUS CIRCLE

China's scientific publications (measured by articles recorded in the Web of Science) in 1994 were around 10,000, accounting for a little more than 1% of the world total. By 2006, the publications from China rose to more than 70,000, increasing sevenfold in 12 years and accounting for almost 6% of the world total (see graph, next page). In certain technical areas, the growth has been more dramatic. China has been among the leading countries in nanotechnology research, for example, producing a volume of publications second only to that of the United States.

The publish-or-perish mentality that has arisen in China, with its focus on Western journals, has unintended implications that threaten to obviate the roughly 8,000 national scientific journals published in Chinese. Scientists in developing countries such as China and India pride themselves on publishing articles in journals listed in the Science Citation Index (SCI) and the Social Science Citation Index (SSCI) lists. In some top-tier research institutions in China, SCI journals have become the required outlet for research.

A biologist who recently returned to China from the United States was told by her colleague at the research institute in the prestigious Chinese Academy of Sciences (CAS) that publications in Chinese journals don't really count toward tenure or promotion. Moreover, the institute values only those SCI journals with high impact factors. Unfortunately, the overwhelming majority of the journals in SCI and SSCI lists are published in developed countries in English or other European languages. The language requirement and the high costs of these journals mean that few researchers in China will have regular access to the content. Thus as China spends

THE RISE OF CHINESE SCIENTIFIC PUBLICATIONS

more and publishes more, the results will become harder to find for Chinese users. This trend could have a devastating impact on the local scientific publications and hurt China's ability to apply newly developed knowledge in an economically useful way.

Several members of the CAS expressed their concerns on this issue recently at the 14th CAS conference in Beijing. According to Molin Ge, a theoretical physicist at the Chern Institute of Mathematics, Nankai University, Tianjin, as more high-quality submissions are sent to overseas journals, the quality of submissions to local Chinese journals declines, which lowers the impact of the local Chinese journals. This becomes a vicious circle because the lower the impact, the less likely these local journals are to get high-quality submissions.[2]

SETTING AGENDAS

Research priorities in developing countries may be very different from those in developed nations, but as science becomes more globalized, so too do priorities. At the national level, developing countries' research priorities increasingly resemble those of the developed nations, partly as a result of international competitive pressures. For example, after the United States announced its National Nanotechnology Initiative (NNI) in 2001, Japan and nations in Europe followed suit, as did South Korea, China, India, and Singapore. According to a 2004 report by the European Union,[3] public investment in nanotechnology had increased from €400 million (U.S.$630 million) in 1997 to more than €3 billion in 2004.

Part of the pressure to jump on the international bandwagon comes from researchers themselves. Scientists in the developing world maintain communications with those elsewhere. It is only natural that they want to share the attention that their colleagues in the developed Western world and Japan are receiving by pursuing the same hot topics. The research is exciting, fast-moving, and often easier to publish. At the same time, there are many other crucial challenges to be met in developing countries. For example, public health, water and food security, and environmental protection all beg for attention and resources. If people perceive these research areas as less intellectually challenging and rewarding, the issues will fail to receive the resources, support, and recognition they require. Without better agenda-setting practices, the scientific community will continue to face stinging criticism. It can send a satellite to Mars but not solve the most basic problems that threaten millions of lives in the developing world.

The introduction of Western scientific ideals to the developing world can generate an environment that is hostile to the indigenous research that prima facie does not fit those ideals. The confrontation between Western medicine and traditional Chinese medicine dates back to the early days of the twentieth century when Western medicine was first introduced in China. The debate reached a peak last year when a famous actress, Xiaoxu Chen, died from breast cancer. She allegedly insisted on treatment by Chinese traditional medicine, raising the hackles of some who claimed it to be worthless. Many Chinese still support traditional medicine and say that the dominance of Western medicine risks endangering China's scientific and cultural legacy.

A similar row erupted around earthquake prediction. In the 1960s and 1970s, China set up a network of popular earthquake-prediction stations, using simple instruments and local knowledge. For the most part, the network was decommissioned as China built the modern earthquake-monitoring system run by the China Earthquake Administration. When the system failed to predict the recent Sichuan earthquake, several people claimed that non-mainstream approaches had predicted its imminence. Scientists in the agency have tended to brush off such unofficial and individual predictions. To many this seems arrogant and bureaucratic.

It would be foolish and impossible to stop the globalization of science. There are tremendous benefits to science enterprises in different countries being integrated into a global whole. One should never think of turning back the clock. At the same time, it is possible to take some practical steps to minimize the harmful effects of this trend on local innovation.

Prioritizing for the People

First of all, there is a need to re-examine the governance of global science in recognition of the changing international geography of science. Many international norms and standards should be more open and accommodating to the changing environment in developing countries. For example, there is a need to re-evaluate the SCI and SSCI list of journals to include quality journals in the developing countries. In the long run, the relevant scientific community could also think about establishing an international panel to make decisions on the selection of journals for these indices, given their important influence. The recent move by Thomson Reuters, the parent company of ISI, to expand its coverage of the SCI list by adding 700 regional academic journals, is a step in the right direction.[4]

English has become the de facto global language of science. Developing countries should invest in public institutions to provide translation services so that global scientific progress can be disseminated quickly. Developing countries can learn from Japan, a world leader in collecting scientific information and making it available to the public in the local language. At the same time, there should also be international institutions to provide similar services to the global science community so that "results and the knowledge generated through research should be freely accessible to all," as advocated by Nobel Laureates John Sulston and Joseph Stiglitz.[5]

When setting agendas, governments in developing countries must be careful in allocating their resources for science to achieve a balance between following the science frontier globally and addressing crucial domestic needs. A balance should also be struck between generating knowledge and disseminating and using knowledge. In addition, the global science community has a responsibility to help those developing countries that do not have adequate resources to solve problems themselves.

Finally, special efforts should be made to differentiate between pseudo-science and genuine scientific research. For the latter, one should tolerate or even encourage such indigenous research efforts in developing countries even if they do not fit the recognized international science paradigm. After all, the real advantage of a globalized scientific enterprise is not just doing the same research at a global scale, but doing new and exciting research in an enriched fashion.

REFERENCES

1. Leadbeater, C. & Wilsdon, J. *The Atlas of Ideas: How Asian Innovation Can Benefit Us All* (Demos, 2007).
2. Xie, Y. et al. *Good submissions went overseas—Chinese S&T journals could not keep up with their overseas peers*, Chinese Youth Daily, 25 June 2008.
3. http://ec.europa.eu/nanotechnology/pdf/nano_com_en_new.pdf
4. http://scientific.thomsonreuters.com/press/2008/8455931/
5. Sulston, J. & Stiglitz, J. *Science is being held back by outdated laws*, The Times (5 July 2008).

7
Structuring Arguments

Structure in arguments defines which parts go where. But as you might imagine, people don't always agree about what parts an argument should include or what their arrangement might be. Traditionally, logical arguments have been described as using either an *inductive* or *deductive* structure, but in practice the two almost always work together.

• • •

Inductive reasoning is the process of generalizing on the basis of a number of specific examples: if you usually become sick after eating shellfish, for instance, you'll likely draw the inductive conclusion that you're allergic to such food. In making inductive arguments, you first present the evidence you have gathered and then present your inductive conclusion:

I get hives after eating crawdads.

My mouth swells up when I eat clams.

Shrimp triggers my asthma.

↓

Shellfish makes me ill.

Deductive reasoning, on the other hand, reaches a conclusion by assuming a general principle (called the *major premise*) and then applying that principle to a specific case (called the *minor premise*). The inductive generalization "Shellfish makes me ill," for example, could serve as the major premise for a deductive chain of reasoning that you may recognize from a logic class as a *syllogism*:

Shellfish makes me ill.

Lobster is a type of shellfish.

↓

Lobster will make me ill.

Most of us shorten syllogisms by leaving out the middle term when it seems obvious: "Since all shellfish makes me ill, I shouldn't eat the lobster on this buffet." Aristotle called syllogisms shortened this way *enthymemes* and thought that such concise, self-evident claims played a key role in persuasion. If you can construct sound inductive or deductive arguments and present them clearly in words or images, you will influence most audiences.

But arguments involve more than just the tight reasoning offered within syllogisms and enthymemes. In most rhetorical situations (see Chapter 1), you will also need to define claims, explain the contexts in which you are offering them, defend your assumptions, offer convincing evidence, deal with people who disagree with you, and more. That's a lot of parts to juggle and perspectives to keep in mind. In this chapter, we present three influential ways of thinking about how to structure arguments. Chances are you'll find yourself borrowing from all of them.

The Classical Oration

Nothing may seem more pointless to you than a structure of argument that was devised by Greek and Roman rhetoricians two thousand years ago for presenting cases in courts or making speeches to a senate. Yet the elements of *the classical oration* still influence our attitudes toward persuasion (especially of the political variety) because the oration taught speakers and writers to think of arguments as debates that have winners and losers. The oration has the following sequence of six parts, most of which will seem familiar to you, despite their Latin names:

> *Exordium:* The speaker/writer tries to win the attention and goodwill of an audience while introducing a subject or problem.

> *Narratio:* The speaker/writer presents the facts of the case, explaining what happened when, who is involved, and so on. The *narratio* puts an argument in context.

> *Partitio:* The speaker/writer divides up the subject, explaining what the claim is, what the key issues are, and in what order the subject will be treated.

Cicero, considered the greatest of ancient Roman orators

Confirmatio: The speaker/writer offers detailed support for the claim, using both logical reasoning and factual evidence.

Refutatio: The speaker/writer acknowledges and then refutes opposing claims or evidence.

Peroratio: The speaker/writer summarizes the case and moves the audience to action.

If you have ever written a paper in which you introduced a subject, stated a thesis, made a series of supporting arguments (often three, leading up to your best point), and drawn a conclusion, you've shown the influence of the classical oration. And you probably were expected in that paper to anticipate opposing arguments and deal with them.

The structure is powerful because it covers all the bases: readers or listeners want to know what your subject is, how you intend to cover it, and what evidence you have to offer. And you probably need a reminder to present a pleasing *ethos* when beginning a presentation and to conclude with enough *pathos* to win an audience over completely. Here, in outline form, is a five-part updated version of the classical pattern, which you may find useful on many occasions:

Introduction

- gains readers' interest and willingness to listen
- establishes your qualifications to write about your topic
- establishes some common ground with your audience
- demonstrates that you're fair and evenhanded
- states your claim

Background

- presents any necessary information, including personal narrative, that's important to your argument

Lines of argument

- presents good reasons, including logical and emotional appeals, in support of your claim

Alternative arguments

- examines alternative points of view and opposing arguments
- notes the advantages and disadvantages of these views
- explains why your view is better than others

Conclusion

- summarizes the argument
- elaborates on the implications of your claim
- makes clear what you want the audience to think or do
- reinforces your credibility and perhaps offers an emotional appeal

You may notice that the oration (and its contemporary variations) is composed with lines already drawn and the opinions of writers and speakers hardened. Greek lawyers or Roman senators knew what they had to do to prevail in a legal case or win an election. The oration gave orators on both sides of an issue a structure to achieve that success, generating material both in favor of an argument and against an opponent's point of view.

Not every piece of rhetoric, past or present, follows the structure of the oration or includes all its components. But you can likely identify some of its elements in successful arguments if you pay attention to their design. You no doubt recognize the words of the 1776 Declaration of Independence proclaiming the sovereignty of the United States:

> When in the Course of human events, it becomes necessary for one people to dissolve the political bands which have connected them with another, and to assume among the powers of the earth, the separate and equal station to which the Laws of Nature and of Nature's God entitle them, a decent respect to the opinions of mankind requires that they should declare the causes which impel them to the separation.
>
> We hold these truths to be self-evident, that all men are created equal, that they are endowed by their Creator with certain unalienable Rights, that among these are Life, Liberty, and the pursuit of Happiness—that to secure these rights, Governments are instituted among Men, deriving their just powers from the consent of the governed—That whenever any Form of Government becomes destructive to these ends, it is the Right of the People to alter or to abolish it and to institute new Government, laying its Foundation on such principles and organizing its powers in such form, as to them shall seem most likely to effect their Safety and Happiness. Prudence, indeed, will dictate that Governments long established should not be changed for light and transient causes; and accordingly all experience hath shewn that mankind are more disposed to suffer, while evils are sufferable, than to right themselves by abolishing the forms to which they are accustomed. But when a long train of abuses and usurpations, pursuing

invariably the same Object evinces a design to reduce them under absolute Despotism, it is their right, it is their duty, to throw off such Government and to provide new Guards for their future security.—Such has been the patient sufferance of these Colonies; and such is now the necessity which constrains them to alter their former Systems of Government. The history of the present King of Great Britain is a history of repeated injuries and usurpations, all having in direct object the establishment of an absolute Tyranny over these States. To prove this, let Facts be submitted to a candid world.

—Declaration of Independence, July 4, 1776

The Declaration opens with a brief *exordium* explaining to readers why the document is necessary, invoking a broad audience in acknowledging a need to show "a decent respect to the opinions of mankind." Important in this case, it also explains the assumptions on which the document rests. A *narratio* follows, offering background on the situation: because the government of George III has become destructive, the framers of the Declaration are obligated to abolish their allegiance to him. Arguably, the *partitio* begins with "The history of the present King of Great Britain is a history of repeated injuries and usurpations," followed by the longest part of the document (not reprinted here), a *confirmatio* that lists the "long train of abuses and usurpations" by George III.

This section is followed by a briefer *refutatio* addressed to the British people in which the signers argue that they have done all they could to address the crisis more conventionally: "We have warned them ["our British brethren"] . . . We have reminded them. . . . We have appealed to their native justice." All this was to no avail, of course. Not until the very end, however, do the signers assert their central claim, which amounts to a powerful *peroratio*: "That these United Colonies are, and of Right ought to be FREE AND INDEPENDENT STATES."

The authors might have organized this argument even more conventionally—for example, by beginning with the last two sentences of the excerpt and then listing the facts intended to prove the king's abuse and tyranny. But by choosing first to explain the purpose and "self-evident" assumptions behind their argument and only then moving on to demonstrate how these "truths" have been denied by the British, the authors forge an immediate connection with readers and build up to the memorable conclusion. The structure is both familiar and inventive—as your own use of key elements of the oration should be in the arguments you compose.

Rogerian Argument

During the first season of *Saturday Night Live* in 1975, comedian Gilda Radner introduced the character of Emily Litella, a feisty, public-spirited woman who aired her editorial opinions during Chevy Chase's "Weekend Update." Here's a transcript of such an episode, in which Litella objects to "busting" schoolchildren (her mishearing of the term *busing*, which referred to a controversial policy for integrating schools in the 1970s and 1980s):

> *Chevy Chase:* Weekend Update recognizes its obligation to present responsible opposing viewpoints to our editorials. Here to reply to a recent editorial is Emily Litella.
>
> *Emily Litella:* I'm here tonight to speak out against busting schoolchildren. Busting schoolchildren is a terrible, terrible thing. I hear this is going on all over the country. Mean policemen arrest little children and put them in jail in the wrong neighborhood, so they can't even play with their little friends. Imagine, busting schoolchildren! The food in jail isn't good, and even though they get bread, I don't believe they can get toast. Or nice cake. Now, who will tuck them in? Where will they hang their leggings? Where will they set up their little lemonade stands? Well, they don't have toys in jail, except maybe . . .
>
> *Chevy Chase:* [interrupting] Miss Litella?
>
> *Emily Litella:* Yes?
>
> *Chevy Chase:* I'm sorry. The editorial was on *busing* schoolchildren. Busing. Not busting.
>
> *Emily Litella:* Oh. I'm sorry. Never mind.
>
> —*Saturday Night Live* transcript, season 1, episode 7

What Emily embodied, week after week, was the inclination of even well-meaning citizens to misrepresent the positions of people with whom they disagree. Most of us probably don't mistake *canker* for *cancer* and *erection* for *election* as Ms. Litella hilariously did, but we may share her tendency to rush into arguments we don't entirely grasp, eager to score points against those we imagine to be opponents. At times, we may lack Emily's willingness to disengage when we're proven wrong.

The ease with which discussions of serious issues can turn into shouting matches moved scholars and teachers of rhetoric to consider whether the nonconfrontational principles applied by psychologist Carl Rogers in personal therapy sessions might also work in public situations.

Gilda Radner's Emily Litella character spoofed an earnest and concerned citizen.

In simple terms, Rogers believed that people involved in disputes should not respond to each other until they could fully, fairly, and even sympathetically state the other person's position. Scholars of rhetoric Richard E. Young, Alton L. Becker, and Kenneth L. Pike gave Rogers's approach this four-part structure when applied to rhetorical situations:

Introduction: The writer describes an issue, a problem, or a conflict. The description is rich enough to demonstrate that the writer fully understands and respects any alternative position or positions.

Contexts: The writer describes the contexts in which the alternative positions may be valid or legitimate.

Writer's position: The writer states his or her position on the issue and presents the circumstances in which that opinion would be valid.

Benefits to opponent: The writer explains to opponents how they would benefit from adopting his or her position.

The key to Rogerian argumentation is a willingness to think about opposing positions and to describe them fairly. In this respect, Rogerian argument differs significantly from the oration, which focuses on the conflicts between positions. In moving through a Rogerian structure, you have to acknowledge that alternatives to your claims exist and that they might be reasonable under certain circumstances. In admitting that your opponents deserve to be at the table, you are (at least theoretically) more likely to search for compromise. In tone, Rogerian arguments steer clear of heated and stereotypical language, emphasizing instead how all parties in a dispute might gain from working together.

Living in a society that encourages individualism and competition, you may find it hard to accept the Rogerian method as practical or even attractive. And don't hold your breath waiting for guests on *Hardball or The O'Reilly Factor* to start restating the opinions of their opponents accurately or to pay more than lip service to bipartisan compromise.

Rogerian-style moves toward understanding and cooperation are not always ineffectual or even new. Consider how Frederick Douglass tried to broaden the outlook of American audiences when he delivered a Fourth of July oration in 1852. Most nineteenth-century Fourth of July speeches followed a pattern of praising the Revolutionary War heroes and emphasizing freedom, democracy, and justice. Douglass, a former slave, had that tradition in mind as he delivered his address, praising the "great principles" that the "glorious anniversary" celebrates. But he also asked his (white) listeners to see the occasion from another point of view:

> Fellow-citizens, pardon me, allow me to ask, why am I called upon to speak here today? What have I, or those I represent, to do with your national independence? Are the great principles of political freedom and natural justice, embodied in the Declaration of Independence, extended to us? And am I, therefore, called upon to bring our humble offering to the national altar, and to confess the benefits and express devout gratitude for the blessings resulting from your independence to us? . . . I say it with a sad sense of the disparity between us. I am not included within the pale of this glorious anniversary! Your high independence only reveals the immeasurable distance between us. The blessings in which you, this day, rejoice, are not enjoyed in common. The rich inheritance of justice, liberty, prosperity and independence, bequeathed by your fathers, is shared by you, not by me. The sunlight that brought life and healing to you, has brought stripes and death to me. This Fourth of July is yours, not mine. You may rejoice, I must mourn.
>
> —Frederick Douglass, "What to the Slave Is the Fourth of July?"

Although his speech may seem confrontational, Douglass is inviting his audience to acknowledge a version of reality that they could have discovered on their own had they dared to imagine the lives of African Americans living in the shadows of American liberty. But the solution to the conflict between slavery and freedom, black and white, oppression and justice, was a long time in coming.

It arrived through the arguments of another African American orator. Speaking at the foot of the Lincoln Memorial in Washington, D.C., on August 28, 1963, Martin Luther King Jr. clearly had Douglass's address (and Abraham Lincoln's Emancipation Proclamation) in mind in the opening of his "I Have a Dream" speech, which bluntly describes the condition of blacks in the United States:

> Five score years ago, a great American, in whose symbolic shadow we stand today, signed the Emancipation Proclamation. This momentous decree came as a great beacon light of hope to millions of Negro slaves who had been seared in the flames of withering injustice. It came as a joyous daybreak to end the long night of their captivity.
>
> But one hundred years later, the Negro still is not free. One hundred years later, the life of the Negro is still sadly crippled by the manacles of segregation and the chains of discrimination. One hundred years later, the Negro lives on a lonely island of poverty in the midst of a vast ocean of material prosperity. One hundred years later, the Negro is still languished in the corners of American society and finds himself an exile in his own land.
>
> —Martin Luther King Jr.,
> "I Have a Dream"

Martin Luther King Jr. on the steps of the Lincoln Memorial

King goes on to delineate the many injustices that were still characteristic of U.S. society. Then, in one of the most brilliant perorations in the history of speechmaking, he invokes a dream of a future in which the United States would live up to its highest ideals, such as those articulated in the Declaration of Independence. The outcome he imagines is a Rogerian-style win/win deliverance for all:

> . . . when we allow freedom to ring, when we let it ring from every village and every hamlet, from every state and every city, we will be able

to speed up that day when all of God's children, black men and white men, Jews and Gentiles, Protestants and Catholics, will be able to join hands and sing in the words of the old Negro spiritual: "Free at last! Free at last! Thank God Almighty, we are free at last!"

—Martin Luther King Jr., "I Have a Dream"

Such moments in political life are rare, but the public claims to prefer nonpartisan and cooperative rhetoric to one-on-one, winner-take-all battles. Indeed, every election cycle includes pleas for a more civil national discourse—though sometimes we have to wait until the end of the campaigns for the true Rogerian notes to be sounded. Here, John McCain in his concession speech following the presidential election on November 5, 2008, urges his supporters to seek common ground with Barack Obama, the new president-elect:

I urge all Americans who supported me to join me in not just congratulating him, but offering our next president our goodwill and earnest effort to find ways to come together to find the necessary compromises to bridge our differences and help restore our prosperity, defend our security in a dangerous world, and leave our children and grandchildren a stronger, better country than we inherited.

In his victory speech that same night, Obama appeals directly to his opponents by endorsing the sentiments of the first Republican to win the White House, Abraham Lincoln:

As Lincoln said to a nation far more divided than ours, "We are not enemies, but friends. . . . Though passion may have strained, it must not break our bonds of affection." And, to those Americans whose support I have yet to earn, I may not have won your vote, but I hear your voices, I need your help, and I will be your president, too.

Perhaps such sentiments are just posturing and hypocrisy—the homage that vice pays to virtue. But they also hint that Rogerian rhetoric strikes a chord in many people, especially in a world that is ever more uneasy with confrontational rhetoric and increasingly open to issues of diversity.

It makes sense in structuring your own arguments to learn opposing positions well enough to state them accurately and honestly, to strive to understand the points of view of your opponents, to acknowledge those views fairly in your own work, and to look for solutions that benefit as many people as possible.

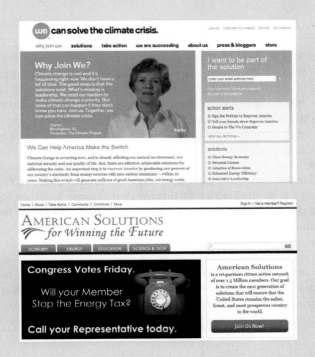

Not Just Words

Retired politicians Al Gore, a Democrat, and Newt Gingrich, a Republican, have both been associated with organizations that are seemingly designed to reach across partisan lines to solve problems. Gore's "We" focuses on issues of global warming, while Gingrich's "American Solutions" targets a host of problems, including the need to drill for more oil in the United States. Study the Web sites of these groups, and decide whether either can be described as Rogerian in its approach to argument. Do the sites persuade Americans to solve problems by working together, or do they merely use the language of bipartisanship to advance Democratic and Republican political agendas? Look for language that echoes the Rogerian emphasis on mutual understanding, cooperation, and compromise.

Toulmin Argument

Both the classical oration and Rogerian rhetoric provide general structures for argument, but a system of reasoning that was developed by British philosopher Stephen Toulmin offers advice for building convincing cases. In *The Uses of Argument* (1958), Toulmin presented structures to describe the way that ordinary people make reasonable arguments. Because Toulmin's system acknowledges the complications of life—those situations when people qualify their thoughts with words such as *sometimes, often, presumably, unless,* and *almost*—his method isn't as airtight as formal logic, the kind that uses syllogisms (see p. 171 in this chapter and p. 84 in Chapter 4). But for that reason, Toulmin logic has become a powerful and, for the most part, practical tool for understanding and shaping arguments in the real world. We use his concepts and terminology in subsequent chapters in Part 2.

You'll find Toulmin argument to be especially helpful as a way to come up with ideas and then to test them. Moreover, it will help you understand what goes where in many kinds of arguments. Perhaps most important, you'll acquire solid habits of analysis when you learn to think in Toulmin's terms.

Making Claims

In the Toulmin model, arguments begin with *claims*, which are debatable and controversial statements or assertions that you hope to prove. Notice that in this model the arguments depend on conditions set by others—your audience or readers. *It's raining* might be an innocent statement of fact in one situation; in another, it might provoke a debate: *No, it's not. That's sleet.* And so an argument begins, involving a question of definition.

Claims that are worth arguing tend to be controversial; there's no point worrying about points on which most people agree. For example, there are assertions in the statements *Twelve inches make a foot* and *Earth is the third planet from the sun.* But except in unusual circumstances, such claims aren't worth the time that it takes to argue over them.

Claims should also be debatable; they can be demonstrated using logic or evidence, the raw material for building arguments. Sometimes the line between what's debatable and what isn't can be thin. You push back your chair from the table in a restaurant and declare, *That was delicious!* A debatable point? Not really. If you thought the meal was out of sight, who can challenge your taste, particularly when your verdict affects no one but yourself?

But now imagine that you're a restaurant critic working for the local newspaper, leaning back from the same table and making the same observation. Because of your job, your claim about the restaurant's cannelloni has a different status and wider implications. People's jobs—including your own—might be at stake. *That was delicious!* suddenly becomes a claim that you have to support, bite by bite.

Many writers stumble when it comes to making claims because facing issues squarely takes thought and guts. A claim answers the question *So what's your point?* Some writers would rather ignore the question and avoid taking a stand. But when you make a claim worth writing about, you move slightly apart from the crowd and ask that it notice you.

Is there a danger that you might oversimplify an issue by making too bold a claim? Of course. But making that sweeping claim is a logical first step toward eventually saying something more reasonable and subtle. Here are some fairly simple, undeveloped claims:

> **The filibuster tactic in the legislatures of both the United States and Canada ought to be abolished.**
>
> **It's time to legalize the medical use of marijuana.**
>
> **NASA should launch a human expedition to Mars.**
>
> **Vegetarianism is the best choice of diet.**
>
> **Same-sex unions deserve the same protections as those granted to marriage between a man and a woman.**

Note that these claims are statements, not questions. There's nothing wrong with questions per se; in fact, they're often what you ask to reach a claim:

Questions	**What should NASA's next goal be? Should the space agency establish a permanent moon base? Should NASA launch more robotic interstellar probes? Can NASA even afford to send people to Mars?**
Statement	**NASA should launch a human expedition to Mars.**

Don't mistake one for the other.

Good claims often spring from personal experiences. Almost all of us know enough about something to merit the label *expert*—though we don't always realize it. If you're a typical first-year college student, for example, you're probably an expert about high school. You could make trustworthy claims (or complaints) about a range of consequential issues, including competency testing and the administration of athletic programs. And if you aren't a typical college student, the things that make you different—perhaps your experiences at work, in the military, or with a family—could make claims leap to mind. Whether you're a typical or nontypical college student, you might also know a lot about music, urban living, retail merchandising, inequities in government services, and so on—all fertile ground for authoritative, debatable, and personally relevant claims.

Offering Evidence and Good Reasons

A claim is just a lonely statement hanging in the wind—until it teams up with some evidence and good reasons. You can begin developing a claim by drawing up a list of reasons to support it or finding evidence that backs up the point. In doing so, you'll likely generate still more claims that are in need of more support; that's the way that arguments work.

Evidence and Reason(s) ⟶ So Claim

One student writer, for instance, wanted to gather good reasons in support of an assertion that his college campus needed more officially designated spaces for parking bicycles. He did some research—gathering statistics about parking-space allocation, numbers of people using particular designated slots, and numbers of bicycles registered on campus. Before he went any further with this argument, however, he listed his primary reasons for wanting to increase bicycle parking:

- **Personal experience:** At least twice a week for two terms, he was unable to find a designated parking space for his bike.

- **Anecdotes:** Several of his friends told similar stories. One even sold her bike as a result.

- **Facts:** He found out that the ratio of car to bike parking spaces was 100 to 1, whereas the ratio of cars to bikes registered on campus was 25 to 1.

- **Authorities:** The campus police chief had indicated in an interview with the college newspaper that she believed a problem existed for students who tried to park bicycles legally.

On the basis of his preliminary listing of possible reasons in support of the claim, this student decided that his subject was worth more research. He was on the way to amassing a set of good reasons that were sufficient to support his claim.

In some arguments that you read, claims might be widely separated from the reasons offered to support them. In shaping your own arguments, try putting claims and reasons together early in the writing process to create enthymemes. Think of these enthymemes as test cases or even as topic sentences:

> Bicycle parking spaces should be expanded because the number of bikes on campus far exceeds the available spots.

> It's time to lower the drinking age because I've been drinking since I was fourteen and it hasn't hurt me.

> Legalization of the medical use of marijuana is long overdue since it has been proven an effective treatment for symptoms associated with cancer.

> Violent video games should be carefully evaluated and their use monitored by the industry, the government, and parents because these games cause addiction and psychological harm to players.

As you can see, attaching a reason to a claim often spells out the major terms of an argument. In rare cases, the full statement is all the argument you'll need:

> Don't eat that mushroom: it's poisonous.

> We'd better stop for gas because the gauge has been reading empty for more than thirty miles.

More often, your work is just beginning when you've put a claim together with its supporting reasons and evidence. If your readers are capable (and you should always assume that they are), then they'll begin to question your statement. They might ask whether the reasons and evidence that you're offering really do support the claim: Should the drinking age be changed simply because you've managed to drink since you were fourteen? Should the whole state base its laws on what's worked for you? They might ask pointed questions about your evidence: Exactly how do you know that the number of bikes on campus far exceeds the number of spaces available? Eventually, you've got to address both issues—quality of assumptions and quality of evidence. The connection between claim and reason(s) is a concern at the next level in Toulmin argument. (For more on enthymemes, see Chapter 4, pp. 85–87.)

Anticipate challenges to your claims.

"I know your type, you're the type who'll make me prove every claim I make."

Determining Warrants

Crucial to Toulmin argument is appreciating that there must be a logical and persuasive connection between a claim and the reasons and data supporting it. Toulmin calls this connection the *warrant*. It answers the question *How exactly do I get from the data to the claim?* Like the warrant in legal situations (a search warrant, for example), a sound warrant in an argument gives you authority to proceed with your case.

The warrant tells readers what your (often unstated) assumptions are—for example, that any practice that causes serious disease should be banned by the government. If readers accept your warrant, you can then present specific evidence to develop your claim. But if readers dispute your warrant, you'll have to defend it before you can move on to the claim itself.

When you state a warrant accurately, you sometimes expose a fatal flaw in an argument. However, stating warrants can be tricky because they can be phrased in various ways. What you're looking for is the general principle that enables you to justify the move from a reason to a specific claim—the bridge connecting them. The warrant is the assumption that makes the claim seem plausible. It's often a value or principle that you share with your readers. Let's demonstrate this logical movement with an easy example:

Don't eat that mushroom: it's poisonous.

The warrant supporting this enthymeme can be stated in several ways, always moving from the reason (*it's poisonous*) to the claim (*Don't eat that mushroom*):

Anything that is poisonous shouldn't be eaten.

If something is poisonous, it's dangerous to eat.

Here's the relationship, diagrammed:

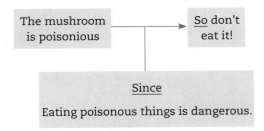

The mushroom is poisonious → So don't eat it!

<u>Since</u>

Eating poisonous things is dangerous.

Perfectly obvious, you say? Exactly—and that's why the statement is so convincing. If the mushroom in question is a death cap or destroying angel (and you might still need expert testimony to prove that it is), the warrant does the rest of the work, making the claim that it supports seem logical and persuasive.

Let's look at a similar example, beginning with the argument in its basic form:

We'd better stop for gas because the gauge has been reading empty for more than thirty miles.

In this case, you have evidence that is so clear (a gas gauge reading empty) that the reason for getting gas doesn't even have to be stated: the

POCKET NATURALIST™

MUSHROOMS

AN INTRODUCTION
TO FAMILIAR NORTH
AMERICAN SPECIES

Ravenel's
Stinkhorn

Fading Scarlet
Waxy Cap

Parasol
Mushroom

Chanterelle

Turkey Tail

WATERFORD PRESS

Fly Agaric
Amanita muscaria
To 7 in. (18 cm)
Cap: Yellow to red-orange cap
has white warts
Stalk: Whitish, frilled collar
Gills: Free, white to yellow
Spore Print: White
Habitat: Oak and coniferous forests.
Was once used, mixed with milk,
to poison house flies.

Destroying Angel
Amanita virosa
To 10 in. (25 cm)
Cap: White, smooth
Stalk: Basal bulb, collar
Gills: Free
Spore Print: White
Habitat: Mixed forests.
Young caps resemble edible
Agaricus mushrooms.

Death Cap
Amanita phalloides
To 5 in. (13 cm)
Cap: Smooth, greenish-yellow
Stalk: Widest at base, collar near top
Gills: Free
Spore Print: White
Habitat: All woods, especially under
oaks and conifers.

In a pocket field guide, a simple icon—a
skull and crossbones—makes a visual
argument that implies a claim, a reason,
and a warrant.

tank is almost empty. The warrant connecting the evidence to the claim is also compelling and pretty obvious:

> **If the fuel gauge of a car has been reading empty for more than thirty miles, then that car is about to run out of gas.**

Since most readers would accept this warrant as reasonable, they would also likely accept the statement the warrant supports.

Naturally, factual information might undermine the whole argument: the fuel gauge might be broken, or the driver might know from previous experience that the car will go another fifty miles even though the fuel gauge reads empty. But in most cases, readers would accept the warrant.

Let's look at a third easy case, one in which stating the warrant confirms the weakness of an enthymeme that doesn't seem convincing on its own merits:

> **Grades in college should be abolished because I don't like them!**

Moving from stated reason to claim, we see that the warrant is a silly and selfish principle:

> **What I don't like should be abolished.**

Most readers won't accept this assumption as a principle that is worth applying generally. It would produce a chaotic or arbitrary world, like that of the Queen of Hearts in *Alice's Adventures in Wonderland* ("Off with the heads of anyone I don't like!"). So far, so good. But how does understanding warrants make you better at writing arguments? The answer is simple: warrants tell you what arguments you have to make and at what level you have to make them. If your warrant isn't controversial, you can immediately begin to defend your claim. But if your warrant is controversial, you must first defend the warrant—or modify it or look for better assumptions on which to support the claim. Building an argument on a weak warrant is like building a house on a questionable foundation. Sooner or later, the structure will crack.

Let's consider how stating and then examining a warrant can help you determine the grounds on which you want to make a case. Here's a political enthymeme of a familiar sort:

> **Flat taxes are fairer than progressive taxes because they treat all taxpayers in the same way.**

Warrants that follow from this enthymeme have power because they appeal to a core American value—equal treatment under the law:

> **Treating people equitably is the American way.**
>
> **All people should be treated in the same way.**

You certainly could make an argument on these grounds. But stating the warrant should also raise a flag if you know anything about tax policy. If the principle is obvious and universal, then why are federal and many state income taxes progressive, requiring people at higher levels of income to pay at higher tax rates than people at lower income levels? Could the warrant not be as universally popular as it seems at first glance? To explore the argument further, try stating the contrary claim and warrants:

> **Progressive taxes are fairer than flat taxes because people with more income can afford to pay more, benefit more from government, and can shelter more of their income from taxes.**
>
> **People should be taxed according to their ability to pay.**
>
> **People who benefit more from government and can shelter more of their income from taxes should be taxed at higher rates.**

Now you see how different the assumptions behind opposing positions really are. In a small way, we've stated one basic difference between political right and political left, between Republicans and Democrats. If you decided to argue in favor of flat taxes, you'd be smart to recognize that some members of your audience might have fundamental reservations about your position. Or you might even decide to shift your entire argument to an alternative rationale for flat taxes:

> **Flat taxes are preferable to progressive taxes because they simplify the tax code and reduce the likelihood of fraud.**

Here, you have two stated reasons that are supported by two new warrants:

> **Taxes that simplify the tax code are desirable.**
>
> **Taxes that reduce the likelihood of fraud are preferable.**

Whenever possible, you'll choose your warrant knowing your audience, the context of your argument, and your own feelings. Moreover, understanding how to state a warrant and how to assess its potential makes subsequent choices better informed.

Examples of Claims, Reasons, and Warrants

Smoking causes serious diseases in smokers and endangers nonsmokers, as well. → <u>So</u> the federal government should ban smoking.

<u>Since</u>

The Constitution was established to "promote the general welfare," and citizens are thus entitled to protection from harmful actions by others.

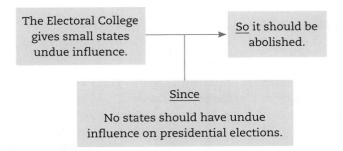

The Electoral College gives small states undue influence. → <u>So</u> it should be abolished.

<u>Since</u>

No states should have undue influence on presidential elections.

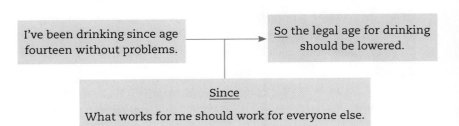

I've been drinking since age fourteen without problems. → <u>So</u> the legal age for drinking should be lowered.

<u>Since</u>

What works for me should work for everyone else.

Be careful, though, that you don't give your audience the impression that you're appealing to whatever warrants work to your advantage. If your readers suspect that your argument for progressive taxes really amounts to *I want to stick it to people who work harder than me*, your credibility may suffer a fatal blow.

Offering Evidence: Backing

As you might guess, claims and warrants provide only the skeleton of an argument. The bulk of a writer's work—the richest, most interesting part—remains to be done after the argument has been outlined. Claims and warrants that are clearly stated suggest the scope of the evidence that you now have to assemble.

An example will illustrate the point. Here's an argument in brief— suitably debatable and controversial, especially in tough times:

NASA should launch a human expedition to Mars because Americans need a unifying national goal.

Here's one version of the warrant that supports the enthymeme:

What unifies the nation ought to be a national priority.

To run with this claim and warrant, a writer first needs to place both in context because most points worth arguing have a rich history. Entering an argument can be like walking into a conversation that is already in progress. In the case of the politics of space exploration, the conversation has been a lively one that has been debated with varying intensity since the 1957 launch of the Soviet Union's *Sputnik* satellite (the first man-made object to orbit the earth) and sparked again after the losses of the U.S. space shuttles *Challenger* (1986) and *Columbia* (2003). A writer stumbling into this dialogue without a sense of history or economics won't get far. Acquiring background knowledge (through reading, conversation, and inquiry of all kinds) is the price that you have to pay to write

A depiction of the Mars Exploration Rover vehicle

on the subject. Without a minimum amount of information on this (or any comparable) subject, all the moves of Toulmin argument won't do you much good. You've got to do the legwork before you're ready to make a case. (See Chapter 3 for more on gaining authority.)

If you want examples of premature argument, listen to talk radio or C-SPAN phone-ins for a day or two. You'll soon learn that the better callers can hold a conversation with the host or guests, fleshing out their basic claims with facts, personal experience, and evidence. The weaker callers usually offer a claim that is supported by a morsel of data. Then such callers begin to repeat themselves, as if saying over and over again that "Republicans are fascists" or "Democrats are socialists" will make the statement true.

As noted earlier, there's no point in defending any claim until you've satisfied readers that any questionable warrants (like those about Republicans and Democrats above) on which the claim is based are defensible. In Toulmin argument, evidence you offer to support a warrant is called *backing*.

Warrant

What unifies the nation ought to be a national priority.

Backing

On a personal level, Americans want to be part of something bigger than themselves. (Emotional appeal as evidence)

In a country as regionally, racially, and culturally diverse as the United States, common purposes and values help make the nation stronger. (Ethical appeal as evidence)

In the past, big government investments such as the Tennessee Valley Authority, Hoover Dam, and *Apollo* moon program enabled many—though not all—Americans to work toward common goals. (Logical appeal as evidence)

In addition to evidence to support your warrant (backing), you'll need evidence to support your claim:

Argument in brief (enthymeme/claim)

NASA should launch a human expedition to Mars because Americans now need a unifying national goal.

Evidence

The American people are politically divided along lines of race, ethnicity, religion, gender, and class. (Fact as evidence)

A common challenge or problem often unites people to accomplish great things. (Emotional appeal as evidence)

Successfully managing a Mars mission would require the cooperation of the entire nation—and generate tens of thousands of jobs. (Logical appeal as evidence)

A human expedition to Mars would be a valuable scientific project for the nation to pursue. (Appeal to values as evidence)

As these examples show, you can draw from the full range of argumentative appeals to provide support for your claims. Appeals to values and emotions might be just as appropriate as appeals to logic and facts, and all such claims will be stronger if a writer presents a convincing ethos. Although it's possible to study such appeals separately, they work together in arguments, reinforcing each other. (See Chapter 3 for more on ethos.)

Finally, arguments can quickly shift downward from an original set of claims and warrants to deeper, more basic claims and reasons. In a philosophy course, for example, you might dig through many layers to reach what seem to be first principles. In general, however, you need to pursue an argument only as far as your audience demands, always presenting readers with adequate warrants and convincing evidence. There comes a point, as Toulmin himself acknowledges, at which readers have to agree to some basic principles, or else the argument becomes pointless.

Using Qualifiers

Toulmin's system works well in the real world because it acknowledges that *qualifiers*—words and phrases that place limits on claims, such as *usually*, *sometimes*, and *in many cases*—play an essential role in arguments. By contrast, formal logic requires universal premises (*All humans are mortal*, for example). Unfortunately, life doesn't lend itself well to many such sturdy truths. If we could argue only about these types of sweeping claims, we'd be silent most of the time.

Toulmin logic encourages you to limit your responsibilities in an argument through the effective use of qualifiers. You can save time if you qualify a claim early in the writing process. But you might not figure out how to limit a claim effectively until after you've explored your subject or discussed it with others.

Experienced writers cherish qualifying expressions because they make writing more precise and honest:

Qualifiers

few	more or less	often
it is possible	in some cases	perhaps
rarely	many	under these conditions
it seems	in the main	possibly
some	routinely	for the most part
it may be	most	if it were so
sometimes	one might argue	in general

Never assume that readers understand the limits you have in mind. By spelling out the terms of the claim as precisely as possible, you'll have less work to do, and your argument will seem more reasonable. In the following examples, the first claim in each pair is much harder to argue convincingly and responsibly—and tougher to research—than the second claim. (Notice that the second qualified claim doesn't use terms from the list above but instead specifies and limits the actions proposed.)

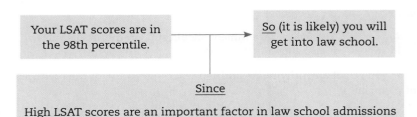

Unqualified Claim	People who don't go to college earn less than those who do.
Qualified Claim	*In most cases,* people who don't go to college earn less than those who do.
Unqualified Claim	Welfare programs should be cut.
Qualified Claim	*Ineffective federal* welfare programs should be *identified, modified,* and, *if necessary, eliminated.*

Understanding Conditions of Rebuttal

In *The Reader over Your Shoulder,* Robert Graves and Alan Hodge advise writers to imagine a crowd of "prospective readers" hovering over their shoulders, asking hard questions. At every stage in Toulmin argument (making a claim, offering a reason, or studying a warrant), you might consider conversing with those nosy readers, imagining them as skeptical, demanding, even a bit testy. They may well get on your nerves. But they'll likely help you foresee the objections and reservations that real readers will have regarding your arguments.

In the Toulmin system, potential objections to an argument are called *conditions of rebuttal.* Understanding and reacting to these conditions are essential to buttress your own claims where they're weak and also to understand the reasonable objections of people who see the world differently. For example, you may be a big fan of the Public Broadcasting Service (PBS) and the National Endowment for the Arts (NEA) and prefer that federal tax dollars be spent on these programs. So you offer the following claim:

Claim	The federal government should support the arts.

You need reasons to support this thesis, so you decide to present the issue as a matter of values:

Argument in Brief	The federal government should support the arts because it also supports the military.

Now you've got an enthymeme and can test the warrant, or the premises of your claim:

Warrant	If the federal government can support the military, then it can also support other programs.

But the warrant seems frail: something's missing to make a convincing case. Over your shoulder, you hear your skeptical friends wondering what wouldn't be fundable according to your very broad principle. They restate your warrant in their own mocking fashion: *Because we pay for a military, we should pay for everything!* You could deal with their objection in the body of your paper, but revising your claim might be a better way to parry the objections. You give it a try:

Revised Argument	If the federal government can spend huge amounts of money on the military, then it can afford to spend moderate amounts on arts programs.

Now you've got a new warrant, too:

Revised Warrant	A country that can fund expensive programs can also afford less expensive programs.

This is a premise that you feel more able to defend because you believe strongly that the arts are just as essential as a strong military is to the well-being of the country. (In fact, you believe that the arts are more important, but remembering those readers over your shoulder, you decide not to complicate your case by possibly overstating it.) To provide backing for this new and more defensible warrant, you plan to illustrate the huge size of the federal budget and the proportion of it that goes to various programs.

Although the warrant seems solid, you still have to offer strong grounds to support your specific and controversial claim. Once again, you cite statistics from reputable sources, this time comparing the federal budgets for the military and the arts. You break them down in ways that readers can visualize, demonstrating that much less than a penny of every tax dollar goes to support the arts.

But once more, you hear those voices over your shoulder, pointing out that the "common defense" is a federal mandate; the government is constitutionally obligated to support a military. Support for public television or local dance troupes is hardly in the same league. And the nation has run up so much debt bailing out banks and corporations that taxpayers won't be eager to subsidize *Swan Lake*, too.

Hmmm. You'd better spend a paragraph explaining all the benefits that the arts provide for the very few dollars spent, and maybe you should also suggest that such funding falls under the constitutional mandate to "promote the general welfare." Though not all readers will accept these grounds, they'll at least appreciate that you haven't ignored

Caroline Kennedy introduces Michelle Obama at the American Ballet Theatre's 2009 opening night spring gala at the Metropolitan Opera House in New York. Advocates of federal funding for the arts have often received political influential support from First Ladies.

their point of view. You gain credibility and authority by anticipating a reasonable objection.

As you can see, dealing with conditions of rebuttal is a natural part of argument. But it's important to understand rebuttal as more than mere opposition. Anticipating objections broadens your horizons and likely makes you more open to change. Recall the earlier section on Rogerian rhetoric: one of the best exercises for you or for any writer is to learn to state the views of others in your own favorable words. If you can do that, you're more apt to grasp the warrants at issue and the commonalities that you may share with others, despite differences.

Fortunately, today's wired world is making it harder to argue in isolation. Newsgroups and blogs on the Internet provide quick and potent responses to positions offered by participants in discussions. Email and instant messaging make cross-country connections feel almost like face-to-face conversations. Even the links on Web sites encourage people to think of communication as a network that is infinitely variable and open to many voices and different perspectives. Within the Toulmin system, conditions of rebuttal—the voices over the shoulder—remind us that we're part of this bigger world. (For more on arguments in electronic environments, see Chapters 14 and 15.)

Outline of a Toulmin Argument

Consider the claim that was mentioned on p. 191:

Claim	The federal government should ban smoking.
Qualifier	The ban would be limited to public spaces.
Good Reasons	Smoking causes serious diseases in smokers. Nonsmokers are endangered by secondhand smoke.
Warrants	The Constitution promises to "promote the general welfare." Citizens are entitled to protection from harmful actions by others.
Backing	The United States is based on a political system that is supposed to serve the basic needs of its people, including their health.
Evidence	Numbers of deaths attributed to secondhand smoke Lawsuits recently won against large tobacco companies, citing the need for reparation for smoking-related health care costs Examples of bans already imposed in many public places
Authority	Cite the surgeon general.
Conditions of Rebuttal	Smokers have rights, too. Smoking laws should be left to the states. Such a ban could not be enforced.
Response	The ban applies to public places; smokers can smoke in private. The power of the federal government to impose other restrictions on smoking (such as warning labels on cigarettes and bans on cigarette advertisements on television) has survived legal challenges. The experience of New York City, which has imposed such a ban, suggests that enforcement would not be a significant problem.

A Toulmin Analysis

You might wonder how Toulmin's method holds up when applied to an argument that is longer than a few sentences. Do such arguments really work the way that Toulmin predicts? After all, knowledgeable readers often don't agree on the core claim in a piece, let alone on its warrants. Yet such an analysis can be rewarding because it raises basic questions about purpose, structure, quality of evidence, and rhetorical strategy. In the following short argument, Alan Dershowitz, a professor at Harvard Law School, responds to a proposal by the school in late 2002 to impose a speech code on its students. Dershowitz's piece, originally published in the *Boston Globe* newspaper, is followed by an analysis of it in Toulmin's terms. Keep in mind what you've learned about analyzing arguments as you read this article.

Testing Speech Codes

ALAN M. DERSHOWITZ

We need not resort to hypothetical cases in testing the limits of a proposed speech code or harassment policy of the kind that some students and faculty members of Harvard Law School are proposing. We are currently experiencing two perfect test cases.

The first involves Harvard's invitation to Tom Paulin to deliver a distinguished lecture for which it is paying him an honorarium. Paulin believes that poetry cannot be separated from politics, and his politics is hateful and bigoted.

He has urged that American Jews who make aliya to the Jewish homeland and move into the ancient Jewish quarters of Jerusalem or Hebron "should be shot dead." He has called these Jews "Nazis" and has expressed "hatred" toward "them." "Them" is many of our students and graduates who currently live on land captured by Israel during the defensive war in 1967 or who plan to move there after graduation.

The Jewish quarters of Jerusalem and Hebron have been populated by Jews since well before the birth of Jesus. The only period in which they were Judenrein was between 1948 and 1967, when it was under Jordanian control, and the Jordanian government destroyed all the synagogues and ethnically cleansed the entire Jewish populations.

Though I (along with a majority of Israelis) oppose the building of Jewish settlements in Arab areas of the West Bank and Gaza, the existence of these settlements—which Israel has offered to end as part of an overall peace—does not justify the murder of those who believe they have a religious right to live in traditional Jewish towns such as Hebron.

Paulin's advocacy of murder of innocent civilians, even if it falls short of incitement, is a paradigm of hate speech. It would certainly make me uncomfortable to sit in a classroom or lecture hall listening to him spew his murderous hatred. Yet I would not want to empower Harvard to censor his speech or include it within a speech code or harassment policy.

Or consider the case of the anti-Semitic poet Amiri Baraka, who claims that "neo-fascist" Israel had advance knowledge of the terrorist attack on the World Trade Center and warned Israelis to stay away. This lie received a standing ovation, according to *The Boston Globe*, from "black students" at

Wellesley last week. Baraka had been invited to deliver his hate speech by Nubian, a black student organization, and [was] paid an honorarium with funds provided by several black organizations. Would those who are advocating restrictions on speech include these hateful and offensive lies in their prohibitions? If not, would they seek to distinguish them from other words that should be prohibited?

These are fair questions that need to be answered before anyone goes further down the dangerous road to selective censorship based on perceived offensiveness. Clever people can always come up with distinctions that put their cases on the permitted side of the line and other people's cases on the prohibited side of the line.

For example, Paulin's and Baraka's speeches were political, whereas the use of the "N-word" is simply racist. But much of what generated controversy at Harvard Law School last spring can also be deemed political. After all, racism is a political issue, and the attitudes of bigots toward a particular race is a political issue. Paulin's and Baraka's poetry purports to be "art," but the "N-word" and other equally offensive expressions can also be dressed up as art.

The real problem is that offensiveness is often in the eyes and experiences of the beholder. To many African Americans, there is nothing more offensive than the "N-word." To many Jews, there is nothing more offensive than comparing Jews to Nazis. (Ever notice that bigots never compare Sharon to Pinochet, Mussolini, or even Stalin, only to Hitler!)

It would be wrong for a great university to get into the business of comparing historic grievances or experiences. If speech that is deeply offensive to many African Americans is prohibited, then speech that is deeply offensive to many Jews, gays, women, Asians, Muslims, Christians, atheists, etc. must also be prohibited. Result-oriented distinctions will not suffice in an area so dominated by passion and historical experience.

Unless Paulin's and Baraka's statements were to be banned at Harvard—which they should not be—we should stay out of the business of trying to pick and choose among types and degrees of offensive, harassing, or discriminatory speech. Nor can we remain silent in the face of such hate speech. Every decent person should go out of his or her way to condemn what Tom Paulin and Amiri Baraka have said, just as we should condemn racist statements made last spring at Harvard Law School.

The proper response to offensive speech is to criticize and answer it, not to censor it.

ANALYSIS

Dershowitz uses an inverted structure for his argument, beginning with his evidence—two extended examples—and then extracting lessons from it. Indeed, his basic claim occurs, arguably, in the final sentence of the piece, and it's supported by three major reasons—although the third reason might be seen as an extension of the second:

> The proper response to offensive speech is to criticize and answer it, not to censor it, [because]
>
> - Clever people can always come up with distinctions that put their cases on the permitted side of the line and other people's cases on the prohibited side of the line.
> - It would be wrong for a great university to get into the business of comparing historic grievances or experiences.
> - [W]e should stay out of the business of trying to pick and choose among types and degrees of offensive, harassing, or discriminatory speech.

As Dershowitz presents them, the cases of Tom Paulin and Amiri Baraka suggest that smart people can always find reasons for defending the legitimacy of their offensive speech.

The closest that Dershowitz gets to stating a warrant for his argument may be in the following sentence:

> The real problem is that offensiveness is often in the eyes and experiences of the beholder.

He doesn't want individuals dictating the limits of free speech because if they did, freedom would likely be restrained by the "eyes and experiences" of specific people and groups and not protected by an absolute and unwavering principle. Dershowitz doesn't actually offer such a warrant, perhaps because he assumes that most readers will understand that protecting free speech is a primary value in American society.

Dershowitz establishes his ethos by making it clear that although he's offended by the speech of both Paulin and Baraka, he wouldn't censor them—even though Paulin says things that are especially offensive to him. An implicit ethical appeal is that if Dershowitz is willing to experience hate speech on his own campus, then surely the law school should be able to show such tolerance toward its students.

What Toulmin Teaches

Just as few of the arguments that you read are expressed in perfectly sequenced claims or clearly agreed-upon warrants, you might not think of Toulmin's terms as you build your own arguments. Once you're into your subject, you'll be too eager to make a point to worry about whether you're qualifying a claim or finessing a warrant. That's not a problem if you appreciate Toulmin argument for what it teaches:

- Claims should be stated clearly and qualified carefully. Arguments in magazines or newspapers often develop a single point, but to make that point they may run through a complex series of claims. They may open with an anecdote, use the story to raise the issue that concerns them, examine alternative perspectives on the subject, and then make a half-dozen related claims only as they move toward a conclusion. You have the same freedom to develop your own arguments, as long as you make sure that your claims are clear and reasonable.

- Claims should be supported with evidence and good reasons. Remember that a Toulmin structure provides the framework of an argument. Most successful arguments are thick with ideas and different kinds of evidence. You may not think of photographs or graphs as evidence, but they can serve that purpose. So can stories that may go on for many paragraphs or pages. Once you acquire the habit of looking for reasons and evidence, you'll be able to separate real supportive evidence from filler, even in arguments offered by professional writers. When you write arguments, you'll discover that it's far easier to make claims than to back them up.

- Claims and reasons should be based on assumptions that readers will likely accept. Toulmin's focus on warrants confuses a lot of people because it forces readers and writers to think about their assumptions—something that they would often prefer to avoid doing. It's tough for a writer, particularly in a lengthy argument, to stay consistent about warrants. At one point, a writer might offer a claim based on the warrant that makes "free speech" an absolute principle. But later, he might rail against those who criticize the president in wartime, making national morale a higher value than free speech. Because most people read at the surface, they may not consciously detect the discrepancy—although they may nonetheless sense at some level that something's wrong with the argument. Toulmin pushes you to

Organization

As you think about how to organize your writing, remember that cultural factors are at work: the patterns that you find satisfying and persuasive are probably ones that are deeply embedded in your culture. In the United States, many people (especially those in the academic and business worlds) expect a writer to "get to the point" as directly as possible and to articulate that point efficiently and unambiguously. The organizational patterns that are favored by U.S. engineers in their writing, for example, hold many similarities to the classical oration described some two thousand years ago. It's a highly explicit pattern that leaves little or nothing unexplained—introduction and thesis, background, overview of the parts that follow, evidence, other viewpoints, and conclusion. If a piece of writing follows this pattern, American readers ordinarily find it "well organized."

Predictably, student writers in the United States are expected to make their structures direct and their claims explicit, leaving little unspoken. Their claims usually appear early in an argument, often in the first paragraph.

But not all cultures take such an approach. Some expect any claim or thesis to be introduced subtly, indirectly, and perhaps at the end of a work, assuming that audiences will "read between the lines" to understand what's being said. Consequently, the preferred structure of arguments (and face-to-face negotiations, as well) may be elaborate, repetitive, and full of digressions. Those accustomed to such writing may find more direct Western styles overly simple, childish, or even rude.

When arguing across cultures, look for cues to determine how to structure your presentations effectively. Here are several points to consider:

- Do members of your audience tend to be very direct, saying explicitly what they mean? Or are they restrained, less likely to call a spade a spade? Consider adjusting your work to the expectations of the audience.
- Do members of your audience tend to respect authority or show consideration for the opinion of a group? They may find blunt approaches disrespectful or contrary to their expectations.
- Consider when to state your thesis: At the beginning? At the end? Somewhere else? Not at all?
- Consider whether digressions are a good idea, a requirement, or an element that's best avoided.

probe into the values that support any argument and to think of those values as belonging to particular audiences. You can't go wrong if you're both thoughtful and aware of your readers when you craft an argument.

- Effective arguments respectfully anticipate objections readers might offer. In the United States, public argument seems more partisan than ever today. Yet there's still plenty of respect for people who can make a powerful, even passionate case for what they believe without dismissing the objections of others as absurd or idiotic. They're also willing to admit the limits of their own knowledge. Toulmin argument appreciates that any claim can crumble under certain conditions, so it encourages a complex view of argument that doesn't demand absolute or unqualified positions. It's a principle that works for many kinds of successful and responsible arguments.

It takes considerable experience to write arguments that meet all these conditions. Using Toulmin's framework brings them into play automatically. If you learn it well enough, constructing good arguments can become a habit.

RESPOND•

1. Choose a controversial topic that is frequently in the news, and decide how you might structure an argument on the subject, using the general principles of the classical oration. Then look at the same subject from a Rogerian perspective. How might your argument differ? Which approach would work better for your topic? For the audiences you might want to address?

2. Following is a claim with five possible supporting reasons. State the warrant that would support each of the arguments in brief. Which of the warrants would need to be defended? Which one would a college audience likely accept without significant backing?

   We should amend the Constitution to abolish the Electoral College

   - because a true democracy is based on the popular vote, not the votes of the virtually unknown electors.

   - because under the Electoral College system the votes of people who have minority opinions in some states end up not counting.

   - because then Al Gore would have won the 2000 election.

- because the Electoral College is an outdated relic of an age when the political leaders didn't trust the people.

- because the Electoral College skews power toward small and midsize states for no good reason.

3. Claims aren't always easy to find. Sometimes they're buried deep within an argument, and sometimes they're not present at all. An important skill in reading and writing arguments is the ability to identify claims, even when they aren't obvious.

   Collect a sample of eight to ten letters to the editor of a daily newspaper (or a similar number of argumentative postings from a political blog). Read each item, and then identify every claim that the writer makes. When you've compiled your list of claims, look carefully at the words that the writer or writers use when stating their positions. Is there a common vocabulary? Can you find words or phrases that signal an impending claim? Which of these seem most effective? Which ones seem least effective? Why?

4. At their simplest, warrants can be stated as *X is good* or *X is bad*. Return to the letters to the editor or blog postings that you analyzed in exercise 3, this time looking for the warrant that is behind each claim. As a way to start, ask yourself these questions: If I find myself agreeing with the letter writer, what assumptions about the subject matter do I share with the letter writer? If I disagree, what assumptions are at the heart of that disagreement? The list of warrants you generate will likely come from these assumptions.

5. Using a paper that you're writing for this class (it doesn't matter how far along you are in the process), do a Toulmin analysis of the argument. At first, you may struggle to identify the key elements, and you might not find all the categories easy to fill. When you're done, see which elements of the Toulmin scheme are represented. Are you short of evidence to support the warrant? Have you considered the conditions of rebuttal? Next, write a brief revision plan: How will you buttress the argument in the places where it is weakest? What additional evidence will you offer for the warrant? How can you qualify your claim to meet the conditions of rebuttal? Having a clearer sense of the logical structure of your argument will help you revise more efficiently.

   It might be instructive to show your paper to a classmate and have him or her do a Toulmin analysis, too. A new reader will probably see your argument in a very different way and suggest revisions that may not have occurred to you.

8
Arguments of Fact

One roommate to another at the dorm cafeteria: "Stay away from trans fats: they're all artificial and toxic!" "Oh really?" says the other. "After dinner, let's check the facts on that."

For the umpteenth time, the *Times* is carrying a feature story about the real authorship of Shakespeare's plays. All the familiar claimants are mentioned—Francis Bacon, Christopher Marlowe, Ben Jonson, even Edward de Vere, seventeenth Earl of Oxford. But isn't it more likely that the author of *Hamlet*, *Macbeth*, and *Twelfth Night* was the person that audiences who first saw those plays thought wrote them—William Shakespeare of Stratford-upon-Avon?

Members of the faculty council are outraged to learn that the Athletic Department aims to raise $100 million to build an addition to the football stadium. The chair of the council complains in an editorial in the campus paper that the professionalization of college sports—football, in particular—is not consistent with the educational mission of the university as stated in its charter.

When an instructor announces a tough new attendance policy for her course, a student objects on the grounds that there is no evidence that students who regularly attend their lecture classes perform any better than those who do not. The instructor begs to differ.

A nutritionist notes that many people think that taking vitamin E daily will prevent colon cancer, heart attacks, cataracts, impotence in men, and wrinkles. The evidence available in many scientific studies suggests that they are probably wrong.

Understanding Arguments of Fact

Given the pressure on natural environments throughout the world, it's a triumph whenever a threatened plant or animal, such as the Peregrine falcon or the gray wolf, recovers enough to be removed from the endangered species list. Far more typically, species depart the list because they have become extinct. So imagine the excitement in April 2005 when an article in *Science* magazine carried the good news that the ivory-billed woodpecker, a strikingly handsome bird not seen for more than sixty years in American forests, had been spotted in Arkansas. The *Science* article staked its claim on the evidence of at least seven sightings by searchers and a brief, blurry videotape of a bird resembling the ivory-billed woodpecker flying away from a naturalist's canoe.

Was the argument sound? At least a few ornithologists remained doubtful, worried that eager colleagues may have mistaken a pileated

The ivory-billed woodpecker by John James Audubon, American naturalist and painter (1785–1851)

Cartoonist Bob Englehart of the *Hartford Courant* takes a jaundiced bird's-eye view of the ivory-billed's "rediscovery."

© 2005 Bob Englehart, The Hartford Courant, and PoliticalCartoons.com

woodpecker, a common bird with similar markings, for the extinct species. And cartoonists predictably had a field day with this elusive bird.

Some skeptics withdrew their objections to the claim after hearing audiotapes recorded in an Arkansas bottomland forest carrying the distinctive call and double-rap sound of the ivory-billed. But blue jays or nuthatches might have made the noises, experts also admitted. What would it take to seal the deal—to assure scientists and birders alike that the ivory-billed woodpecker really did survive in the wilds of Arkansas?

Researchers in Cornell University's computer-graphics program decided to try answering that question by spending more than two years developing a virtual version of the bird, based on hundreds of CAT scans of the only preserved ivory-billed woodpecker left in the world. After painstakingly tracking the virtual bird's flight and simulating the details of the original camera image, the researchers found that the wing patches in the videotape appeared to match those of an ivory-billed rather than a pileated woodpecker. But even this evidence is only enough for scientists to say "there's a good chance" that the ivory-billed is back.

"What we need is a photo," said Russell Chariff of the Cornell Lab of Ornithology to the *New York Times*, discussing the burden of proof as it existed in late 2005. True, a photograph might be faked, especially a digital image. But a clear shot of the woodpecker by a reputable researcher could indeed be the clincher—given all the other tantalizing but not quite conclusive evidence in this case.

In the meantime, bird enthusiasts are still out there in the Arkansas woods, hoping to bring this argument to a conclusion by confirming the bird's existence. Their dilemma will be like that of anyone trying to make a factual argument—to find sufficient evidence for a claim to satisfy a reasonably skeptical audience (in this case, of scientists, naturalists, and birders).

Factual arguments come in many varieties with different standards of proof. What they have in common is an attempt to establish whether something is or is not so—that is, whether a thing exists (*the ivory-billed*) or whether claims made about something are true (*The poverty rate is higher in Mississippi than in Texas*). At first glance, you might object that these aren't arguments at all but just a matter of looking things up and writing a report. And you'd be right to an extent: people don't ordinarily argue factual matters that are settled or agreed upon (*The earth orbits the sun*) or that might be decided with simple research (*Nelson Mandela was South Africa's first black president*) or the equivalent of a rule (*One foot equals 0.3048 meters*).

Transmitting facts, it would seem, should be free of the pressures and biases of argument. Yet facts become arguments when they're controversial in themselves or when they're used to challenge or change people's beliefs. A factual argument about the existence of a woodpecker has a kind of clean scientific logic to it, but there's passion in the debate because so many researchers want the bird to survive. And there's resistance among those who don't want to rush to judgment until the evidence is definitive—as it might one day be in this case.

Arguments of fact do much of the heavy lifting in our world. They report on what has been recently discovered or explore the implications of that new information and the conflicts it may engender. In recent years, for instance, we've seen plenty of contrary medical reports that raise questions about the safety or efficacy of prescription drugs, vitamin regimens, or surgical procedures. Such news has become so routine that the public is asking increasingly sophisticated questions about the studies, such as who sponsored them, who or what exactly was studied, over how many years, and among which populations. Healthy skepticism is the common attitude now, rather than simple acceptance of what the scientific community reports.

Some factual arguments make the public aware of information that's already available to anyone who is willing to do the work of finding it and studying its implications. Malcolm Gladwell, author of *The Tipping Point*, *Blink*, and *Outliers*, has exposed patterns in our cultural behavior that seem obvious after he's pointed them out. *Blink*, for example, argues that people routinely use gut feelings to make sound (as well as dubious) judgments, an argument that has important repercussions for business, education, and the military—if Gladwell is right.

But serious factual arguments—especially those that touch on public issues—almost always have consequences. *Can we rely on wind and solar power to solve our energy needs? Will the Social Security trust fund really go broke? Should you heed the latest warnings about salmonella in tomatoes?* Various publics, national or local, need well-reasoned factual arguments on subjects of this kind to make well-informed decisions. Such arguments educate audiences.

For the same reason, we need arguments that correct or challenge beliefs and assumptions that are held widely within a society on the basis of inadequate or incomplete information. Corrective arguments appear daily in the national media, often based on detailed studies that are written by scientists, researchers, or thinkers and that the public may not encounter. Many people, for example, believe that talking on a cell phone while driving is just like listening to the radio. But their intuition is not based on hard information: more and more scientific studies suggest that using a cell phone in a car is comparable to driving under the influence of alcohol. As a result, some states have banned the use of handheld cell phones in cars.

Factual arguments also routinely address broad questions about the history or myths that societies want to believe about themselves. For example, are the accounts that we have of the American founding—or the Civil War, Reconstruction, or the heroics of the "Greatest Generation" in World War II—indeed accurate? Or do the "facts" that we believe today sometimes reflect the perspectives and prejudices of earlier times or ideologies? Scholars and historians frequently claim to be completing the historical record or looking for new information and new ways of interpreting evidence. Such revisionist history is almost always controversial and rarely settled: the British and Americans will always tell different versions of what happened in North America in 1776.

It's especially important to have factual arguments that flesh out or correct what's narrowly or mistakenly reported—whether by news media, corporations, or branches of government. For good or ill, the words of public figures and the actions of institutions, from churches to news organizations, are now always on record and searchable. When, for example, the *New York Times* criticized federal officials for cutting money for flood-control measures in the Mississippi Delta prior to the New Orleans hurricane of 2005, critics of the *Times* quickly located editorials from the same paper in 1993 and 1997 criticizing spending proposals for flood control. Corrective arguments can sometimes play like a game of "Gotcha!" but they broaden readers' perspectives and help them make judgments on the basis of better information. (They also suggest that our institutions are often just as inconsistent, fallible, and petty as the rest of us.)

As you probably suspect, factual arguments have a way of adding interest and complexity to our lives, taking what might seem simple and adding new dimensions to it. In many situations, they're the precursors to other forms of analysis, especially causal and proposal arguments. Before we can explore causes or solve problems, we need to know the facts on the ground.

Heath Ledger's powerful embodiment of the Joker in *The Dark Knight* was the last role played by this talented actor, who died suddenly six months before the film was released in the summer of 2008. Amid a swirl of rumors and gossip, even meticulous medical work couldn't determine all the "facts" of his death.

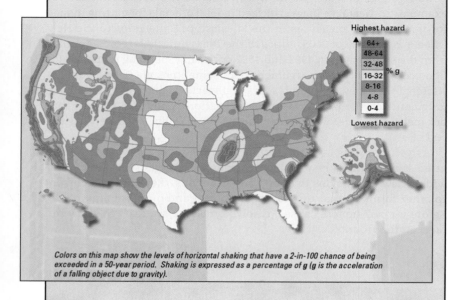

Highest hazard

64+
48-64
32-48
16-32 % g
8-16
4-8
0-4

Lowest hazard

Colors on this map show the levels of horizontal shaking that have a 2-in-100 chance of being exceeded in a 50-year period. Shaking is expressed as a percentage of g (g is the acceleration of a falling object due to gravity).

Not Just Words

Above is a National Seismic-Hazard Map, which was created by the U.S. Geological Survey from data collected over the last hundred years. Look closely at this map, and then offer several different factual claims that might be supported by the evidence you find there. Or go to the Web site of the Geological Survey at http://neic.usgs.gov/neis/eqlists/eqstats.html, and study some of its other data for earthquakes in the United States and worldwide.

Characterizing Factual Arguments

Factual arguments tend to be driven by perceptions and evidence. A writer first notes something new or different or mistaken and wants to draw attention to that fact. Or researchers notice a pattern that leads them to look more closely at some phenomenon or behavior, exploring questions such as *What if?* or *How come?* They're also motivated by simple human curiosity or suspicion: *If being fat is so unhealthy, why aren't mortality rates rising? Just how different are the attitudes of people in so-called red and blue states?*

Such observations can lead quickly toward *hypotheses*—that is, toward tentative and plausible statements of fact whose merits need to be examined more closely. *Maybe being a little overweight isn't as bad for people as we've been told. Maybe the differences between blue and red staters have been exaggerated by media types looking for a story.* To support such hypotheses, writers then have to uncover evidence that reaches well beyond the casual observations that triggered the initial interest—like a news reporter motivated to see whether there's a verifiable story behind a source's tip.

For instance, the authors of *Freakonomics*, Stephen J. Dubner and Steven Levitt, were intrigued by the National Highway Traffic Safety Administration's claim that car seats for children were 54 percent effective in preventing deaths in auto crashes for children below the age of four. In a *New York Times* op-ed column entitled "The Seat Belt Solution," they posed an important question about that factual claim:

> But 54 percent effective compared with what? The answer, it turns out, is this: Compared with a child's riding completely unrestrained.

Their initial question about that claim led them to a more focused inquiry, then to a database on auto crashes, and then to a surprising conclusion: for kids above age twenty-four months, those in car seats were statistically safer than those without any protection but weren't safer than those confined by seat belts (which are much simpler, cheaper, and more readily available devices). Looking at the statistics every which way, the authors wonder if children older than two years would be just as well off physically—and their parents less stressed and better off financially—if the government mandated seat belts rather than car seats for them.

What kinds of evidence typically appear in sound factual arguments? The simple answer might be "all sorts," but a case can be made that

Safer than a seat belt?

factual arguments try to rely on "hard evidence" more than on logic and reason (see Chapter 4). Even so, some pieces of evidence are harder and more convincing than others.

During the 2008 election campaign, the Republican vice presidential nominee, Alaska governor Sarah Palin, offered a number of facts to support her claims that she was a strong reformer who rejected earmarks—"pork-barrel" spending projects that members of Congress sponsor primarily to benefit their own districts or states. Palin insisted on numerous occasions, for example, that she had said "no thanks to that bridge to nowhere" (a proposal to build an expensive bridge to a sparsely populated island off the Alaska coast), but little hard evidence backed her up. In fact, journalists found considerable hard evidence—such as quotations from interviews and news photos and videos—showing that Palin had actually supported the project up until 2006, when support for it in Congress began to wane. Persistent attention to the facts of this case showed that what was being presented as "hard evidence" was very soft indeed. Eventually, Palin dropped this claim from her stump speech.

Fudging the facts? The Gravina Island bridge project proved a campaign issue to nowhere for Alaska governor Sarah Palin when she ran for vice president.

Developing a Factual Argument

Factual arguments on the same subject can bubble with outrage and anger or speak with the dispassionate drone of science. The following two claims circulated in the media shortly after Hurricane Katrina struck the Gulf Coast, and they suggest the range of factual argument in both substance and style. The first, by Ross Gelbspan, shows the sweeping claims and pithy style of fact-based editorial commentary. It's angry and speculative:

> The hurricane that struck Louisiana and Mississippi on Monday was nicknamed Katrina by the National Weather Service. Its real name is global warming. . . .
>   Although Katrina began as a relatively small hurricane that glanced off southern Florida, it was supercharged with extraordinary intensity by the high sea surface temperatures in the Gulf of Mexico.
>   The consequences are as heartbreaking as they are terrifying.

Unfortunately, few people in America know the real name of Hurricane Katrina because the coal and oil industries have spent millions of dollars to keep the public in doubt about the issue.

The reason is simple: To allow the climate to stabilize requires humanity to cut its use of coal and oil by 70 percent. That, of course, threatens the survival of one of the largest commercial enterprises in history.

—Ross Gelbspan, "Hurricane Katrina's Real Name"

The second claim, by William M. Gray and Philip J. Klotzback writing for the Department of Atmospheric Science at Colorado State University, addresses the same issue but provides its answers in a different style:

Many individuals have queried whether the unprecedented landfall of four destructive hurricanes in a seven-week period during August–September 2004 and the landfall of two more major hurricanes in the early part of the 2005 season is related in any way to human-induced climate changes. There is no evidence that this is the case. If global warming were the cause of the increase in United States hurricane landfalls in 2004 and 2005 and the overall increase in Atlantic basin major hurricane activity of the past eleven years (1995–2005), one would expect to see an increase in tropical cyclone activity in the other storm basins as well (i.e., West Pacific, East Pacific, Indian Ocean, etc.). This has not occurred. When tropical cyclones worldwide are summed, there has actually been a slight decrease since 1995. In addition, it has been well documented that the measured global warming during the 25-year period of 1970–1994 was accompanied by a downturn in Atlantic basin major hurricane activity over what was experienced during the 1930s through the 1960s.

—William M. Gray and Philip J. Klotzback, "Forecast of Atlantic Hurricane Activity for September and October 2005 and Seasonal Update through August"

Any factual argument that you might compose—from how you state your claim to how you present evidence and the language you use—will be shaped by the occasion for the argument and the audiences that you intend to reach. But we can offer some general advice to help you get started.

Identifying an Issue

Before you can offer a factual argument, you need to identify an issue or problem that will interest (or that you believe should interest) readers.

You might look, for example, for apparent contradictions or tensions in local or national communities—situations or phenomena that are out of the ordinary in the expected order of things. You might have read that the trailers given to victims of the Katrina disaster in 2006 turned out to contain toxic chemicals: what is the latest information on this issue, and what has happened to those who were living in the trailers? Or you might notice that many people you know are deciding not to attend college. How widespread is this change, and who are the people making this choice? Or you might explore questions that many people have already formulated but haven't yet examined in detail or that have been hotly contested for some time (such as whether cell phones are really as safe as claimed or whether we'll discover twenty years from now that a generation of Americans has slow-cooked its gray matter).

Whole books are written when authors decide to pursue factual questions, even those that have been explored before. But you want to be careful not to argue matters that pose no challenge to you or your audiences. You're not offering anything new if you try to persuade readers that smoking is harmful to their health. But perhaps knowing that Microsoft founder Bill Gates and New York mayor Michael Bloomberg together pledged millions to conduct antismoking campaigns around the world might lead you to uncover information about smoking on your own campus that might provoke thoughtful examinations of the issue. Perhaps you suspect that smoking is correlated in interesting ways to academic majors, gender, or ethnic identity. Would it be important to recognize these facts—if you could prove them?

Some quick preliminary research and reading might allow you to move from an intuition, a hunch, or mere interest to a hypothesis (a tentative statement of your claim): *Women in the liberal arts are the heaviest smokers on campus.* As noted earlier, factual arguments often provoke other kinds of analysis. Where might such a claim lead if you could find evidence to support it? You might find yourself moving irresistibly toward arguments about the cause of the phenomenon, but don't do this until you establish its basis in fact.

On the other hand, the large number of cigarette butts on the ground outside the business school might suggest that your hypothesis is questionable. It may be that men studying accounting and marketing blacken their lungs as thoroughly as do women in philosophy classes. What do you do now? Abandon your hypothesis or modify it. That's what hypotheses are for. They are works in progress.

Facts and Academic Arguments

As you might expect, facts play an instrumental role in academic arguments, whether for an essay in art history, a presentation in electrical engineering, or a proposal in human biology. Look how a communication scholar uses facts in an academic argument about privacy and social networking in the United States:

> According to three 2005 Pew Reports (Lenhart, 2005; Lenhart, et al., 2005; Lenhart and Madden, 2005), 87 percent of American teens aged 12–17 are using the Internet. Fifty-one percent of these teenagers state that they go online on a daily basis. Approximately four million teenagers or 19 percent say that they create their own weblogs (personal online journals) and 22 percent report that they maintain a personal Web page (Lenhart and Madden, 2005). In blogs and on personal Web sites, teenagers are providing so much personal information about themselves that it has become a concern. Today, content creation is not only sharing music and videos; it involves personal diaries.
>
> —Susan B. Barnes, "A Privacy Paradox: Social Networking in the United States"

Note that this researcher uses facts drawn from reports produced by the Pew Research Center, a well-known and respected organization. In each case, she tells readers exactly where she got her facts, and she provides a list of references at the end of the article to help readers locate the specific sources. Choose an assignment that you are working on now or have completed in the past that calls for the use of facts. Then examine your writing with an eye to how effective your facts are: Do you let readers know the sources of your facts? Are all the sources credible? What additional facts might improve this piece of writing?

Researching Your Hypothesis

How and where you research your subject will depend, naturally, on your subject. You'll certainly want to review Chapter 16, "What Counts as Evidence," and Chapter 19, "Evaluating and Using Sources," before constructing an argument of fact. Libraries and the Web will provide you deep resources on almost every subject. Your task will typically be to separate the best sources from all the rest. The word *best* here has many connotations: some reputable sources may be too technical for your audiences; some accessible sources may be pitched too low or be too far removed from the actual facts.

You'll be making judgments like this routinely. But don't hesitate to go to primary sources whenever you can. For example, when gathering a comment from a source on the Web, trace it whenever possible to its original site, and read the comment in its full context. When statistics are quoted, follow them back to the source that originally offered them to be sure that they're recent and reputable. Instructors and librarians can help you appreciate the differences. Understand that even sources with pronounced biases can furnish useful information, provided that you know how to use them, take their limitations into account, and then share what you know about the sources with your readers.

Sometimes, you'll be able to do primary research on your own, especially when your subject is local and you have the resources to do it. You might be able to conduct a competent survey of campus opinions and attitudes, for example, or you could study budget records to determine trends in faculty salaries, tuition, student fees, and so on. Primary research of this sort can be challenging because even the simplest surveys or polls have to be intelligently designed and executed in a way that samples a representative population (see Chapter 4). But the work could pay off in an argument that brings new information to readers.

Refining Your Claim

As you learn more about your subject, you might revise your hypothesis to reflect what you've discovered. In many cases, these revised hypotheses will grow increasingly complex and specific. Following are three versions of essentially the same claim, with each iteration offering more information to help readers assess its merit:

> Americans really did land on the moon, despite what some people think!

> Since 1969, when the *Eagle* supposedly landed on the moon, some people have been skeptical about the success of the USA's *Apollo* program.

New details about a subject often lead to new ways to support or refute a claim about it. Conspiracy theorists claim that the absence of visible stars in photographs of the moon landing is evidence that it was staged, but photographers know that the camera exposure needed to capture the foreground—astronauts in their bright space suits—would have made the stars in the background too dim to see.

Despite plentiful hard evidence to the contrary—from *Saturn* V launches witnessed by thousands to actual moon rocks tested by independent labs worldwide—some people persist in believing that NASA's moon landings were actually filmed on deserts in the American southwest as part of a massive propaganda fraud.

As you advance in your research, your hypothesis or thesis will likely pick up even more qualifying words and expressions, which help you to make reasonable claims. Qualifiers—words and phrases such as *some, most, few, for most people, for a few users, under specific conditions, usually, occasionally, seldom,* and so on—will be among your most valuable tools.

It sometimes is important to set your claim into a context that helps explain it to others who may find it untenable or hostile. For instance, professor of English Vincent Carretta anticipated strong objections after he uncovered evidence that Olaudah Equiano—the author of *The Interesting Narrative* (1789), a much-cited autobiographical account of his Middle Passage voyage and subsequent life as a slave—may have been born in South Carolina and not in western Africa. Speaking to the *Chronicle of Higher Education,* Carretta explains why Equiano may have made up African origins to serve a larger cause—a growing antipathy to slavery and slave markets:

> "Whether [Equiano] invented his African birth or not, he knew that what that movement needed was a first-person account. And because they were going after the slave trade, it had to be an account of someone who had been born in Africa and was brought across the Middle Passage. An African-American voice wouldn't have done it."
>
> —Jennifer Howard, "Unraveling the Narrative"

Carretta asks readers to see that the new facts that he has discovered about *The Interesting Narrative* do not diminish the work's historical significance. If anything, his work has added new dimensions to its meaning and interpretation.

Deciding Which Evidence to Use

In this chapter, we've blurred the distinction between factual arguments for scientific and technical audiences and those for the general public (in media such as magazines, blogs, and television documentaries). In the former, you might find exhaustive appendices of information, including charts, graphs, and full databases. Scientific claims themselves are usually stated with great economy and precision, followed by a thorough account of methods and results. The article reporting the discovery of the ivory-billed woodpecker makes its point in two sentences: "The ivory-billed woodpecker (*Campephilus principalis*), long suspected to be extinct, has been rediscovered in the Big Woods region of eastern Arkansas. Visual encounters during 2004 and 2005, and analysis of a video clip from April 2004, confirm the existence of at least one male." The evidence then follows.

Less scientific factual arguments—claims about our society, institutions, behaviors, habits, and so on—are seldom this clean and draw on evidence from a great many different sources. For example, when the National Endowment for the Arts (NEA) published a study entitled "Reading at Risk" in June 2004 to report "the declining importance of literature to our populace," it drew its conclusion by studying a variety of phenomena in a large population:

> This survey investigated the percentage and number of adults, age 18 and over, who attended artistic performances, visited museums, watched broadcasts of arts programs, or read literature. The survey sample numbered more than 17,000 individuals, which makes it one of the most comprehensive polls of art and literature consumption ever conducted.
>
> —National Endowment for the Arts, "Reading at Risk"

Still, you could imagine other ways to measure an interest in literature, some of which might include nontraditional (graphic novels, for instance) or electronic forms not examined in the NEA study. A phenomenon as broad as "literature" is difficult to define factually because few people can agree on its dimensions. So for any study, you'll have to make choices about what evidence to draw from and be prepared to defend those choices.

Alison Bechdel's *Fun Home*, a graphic novel, is considered literature by many but a "mere comic" by others.

By contrast, a factual argument about a specific literary work (rather than the larger phenomenon of reading) might be a significantly easier task to manage because you can find much of your evidence in the poem, play, or novel itself, supplemented by historical and biographical information on the life and times of the author. For instance, is *Frankenstein* (1831) really a story about the growing impact of science and industrialism on Europe? To answer the question, you could refer to passages in Mary Shelley's novel itself and to information from histories of the period during which it was written showing a society experiencing rapid technological change.

Often, you may have only a limited number of words or pages in which to make a factual argument. What do you do then? You need to present your best evidence as powerfully as possible. But that's not difficult. You can make a persuasive factual case with just a few examples: three or four often suffice to make a point. Indeed, going on too long or presenting even good data in a way that makes it seem uninteresting or pointless can undermine a claim.

Presenting Your Evidence

In *Hard Times* (1854), British author Charles Dickens poked fun at a pedagogue he named Thomas Gradgrind, who preferred hard facts before all things human or humane. When poor Sissy Jupe (designated "girl number twenty" in his classroom) is unable at his command to define *horse*, Gradgrind turns to his star pupil:

> "Bitzer," said Thomas Gradgrind. "Your definition of a horse."
> "Quadruped. Graminivorous. Forty teeth, namely twenty-four grinders, four eyeteeth, and twelve incisive. Sheds coat in the spring; in marshy countries, sheds hoofs, too. Hoofs hard, but requiring to be shod with iron. Age known by marks in mouth." Thus (and much more) Bitzer.
> "Now girl number twenty," said Mr. Gradgrind. "You know what a horse is."
>
> —Charles Dickens, *Hard Times*

But does Bitzer? Rattling off facts about a subject isn't quite the same thing as knowing it, especially when your goal is, as it is in an argument of fact, to educate and persuade audiences. So you must take care how you present your evidence.

Factual arguments, like any others, take many forms. They can be as simple and pithy as a letter to the editor (or Bitzer's definition of a horse) or as comprehensive and formal as a senior thesis or even a dissertation. The National Commission on Adult Literacy's 2008 report, "Reach Higher, America: Overcoming Crisis in the U.S. Workforce," has the design of a formal scientific report, with sixty-five references, ten appendices, and a dozen figures and tables. Like many such studies, it also includes a foreword, an executive summary, and a detailed table of contents. All these elements help establish the ethos of the work, making it seem serious, credible, well conceived, and thorough.

Considering Design and Visuals

Precisely because factual arguments often rely on evidence that can be measured, counted, computed, or illustrated, they benefit from thoughtful, even artful presentation of data. When you prepare a factual argument, consider how its design can enhance the evidence you have to offer. If you have an argument that can be translated into a table, chart, or graph (see Chapter 14), try it. If you have lots of examples, you might present them in a list (bulleted or otherwise) and keep the language in each item roughly parallel.

Photos and images have many uses in factual arguments, from technical illustration to imaginative re-creation. Today, even amateurs can manipulate digital images in the way that only spy agencies could in the not-so-distant past, erasing people from photographs, for example. But images retain their power to illustrate what readers might otherwise have to imagine—whether actual conditions of drought, poverty, or

Figure 1
88 Million Adults Have At Least One Education Barrier

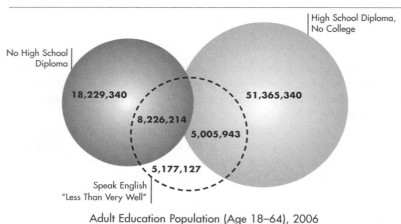

High School Diploma, No College

No High School Diploma

18,229,340   51,365,340

8,226,214

5,005,943

5,177,127

Speak English "Less Than Very Well"

Adult Education Population (Age 18–64), 2006

Source: *U.S. Census Bureau, 2006 American Community Survey (Public Use Microdata Samples); prepared by National Center for Higher Education Management Systems (NCHEMS). Unduplicated population = 88,003,964.*

This figure from the National Commission on Adult Literacy's report "Reach Higher, America: Overcoming Crisis in the U.S. Workforce" illustrates the report's use of visual elements to make information accessible.

Soldiers rescue a survivor from the rubble after an earthquake in Beichuan, China, on May 13, 2008. Photos help readers understand the details of factual arguments.

disaster like the earthquake that hit China in 2008, or the dimensions of the Roman forum as it existed in the time of Julius Caesar. Readers expect the arguments they read to include visual elements, and there's little reason not to offer this assistance.

Finally, consider how your opportunities for presenting information increase when you take an argument to the Web or use presentation software such as PowerPoint or Keynote. Not only can you use still images and illustrations, but you have access to video and audio resources as well. Readers interested in the ivory-billed woodpecker controversy, for example, could download both the video that purported to show the bird in flight and the audios of its call and knock.

Key Features of Factual Arguments

In drafting a factual argument, make sure you do the following:

- Describe a situation that leads you to raise questions about what the facts in a given situation might be.

- Make a claim that addresses the status of the facts as they're known. You'll usually be establishing, challenging, or correcting them. Your claim can be presented tentatively as a hypothesis or more boldly as a thesis.

- Offer substantial and authoritative evidence to support your claims.

In academic situations, a claim typically comes first, and the evidence trails after. But it's not unusual for arguments of fact to present evidence first and then build toward a claim or thesis. Such a structure invites readers to participate in the process by which a factual claim is made (or challenged). The argument unfolds with the narrative drive of a mystery story, with readers eager to know what point the evidence is leading to.

GUIDE to writing an argument of fact

● Finding a Topic

You're entering an argument of fact when you

- make a claim about fact or existence that's controversial or surprising: *Global warming is threatening Arctic species, especially polar bears.*
- correct an error of fact: *The overall abortion rate is not increasing in the United States, though rates are increasing in some states.*
- challenge societal myths: *Many Mexicans fought alongside Anglos in battles that won Texas its independence from Mexico.*

● Researching Your Topic

Solid research is the basis for most factual arguments. Use both a library and the Web to locate the information you need. One of your most valuable resources may be a research librarian. Take advantage of other human resources, too: don't hesitate to call experts or talk with eyewitnesses who may have special knowledge. For many factual arguments, you can begin research by consulting the following types of sources:

- newspapers, magazines, reviews, and journals (online and print)
- online databases
- government documents and reports
- Web sites, blogs, social networking sites, and listservs or newsgroups
- books
- experts in the field, some of whom might be right on your campus

In addition, your topic may require field research—a survey, a poll, or systematic observation. And whatever the sources, you will want to evaluate them carefully, making sure that each one is legitimate and credible.

● Formulating a Hypothesis

Don't rush into a thesis when you're developing a factual argument. Instead, begin with a hypothesis that expresses your beliefs at the beginning of the project but that may change as your work proceeds. You might even begin with a question to which you don't have an answer or with a broad, general interest in a subject:

- **Question:** Have higher admissions standards at BSU reduced the numbers of entering first-year students from small, rural high schools?
- **Hypothesis:** Higher admissions standards at BSU are reducing the number of students admitted from rural high schools, which tend to be smaller and less well funded than those in suburban and urban areas.

- **Question:** Have the iPod, the convenience of its iTunes, and comparable music sites reduced the amount of illegal downloading of music?
- **Hypothesis:** The iPod and its iTunes Web site may have done more than lawsuits by record companies to discourage illegal downloads of music.

- **Question:** How are prison guards who work on death row affected by their jobs?
- **Hypothesis:** A death-row assignment will desensitize prison guards to the prisoners held there.

● Examples of Arguable Factual Claims

- A campus survey that shows that far more students have read *Harry Potter and the Prisoner of Azkaban* than *Hamlet* indicates that our current core curriculum lacks depth.
- Evidence suggests that the European conquest of the Americas may have had more to do with infectious diseases than any superiority in technology or weaponry.
- In the long run, dieting may be more harmful than moderate overeating.

● Preparing a Proposal

If your instructor asks you to prepare a proposal for your project, here's a format that may help:

State your thesis completely. If you are having trouble doing so, try outlining it in Toulmin terms:

Claim:

Reason(s):

Warrant(s):

- Explain why the issue you're examining is important, and provide the context for raising the issue. Are you introducing new information, making available information better known, correcting what has been reported incorrectly, or complicating what has been understood more simply?

- Identify and describe those readers you most hope to reach with your proposal. Why is this group of readers most appropriate for your proposal? What are their interests in the subject?

- Discuss the kinds of evidence you expect to use in the project and the research the paper will require.

- Briefly identify the major difficulties you foresee in researching your argument.

- Describe the format or genre you expect to use: An academic essay? A formal report? A Web site? A wiki? Will you need charts, tables, graphs, other illustrations?

● Thinking about Organization

Factual arguments can be arranged many different ways. The simplest structure is to make a claim and then prove it. But even a basic approach needs an introductory section that provides a context for the claim and a concluding section that assesses the implications of the argument. A factual argument that corrects an error or provides an alternative view of some familiar concept or historical event will also need a section early on explaining what the error or the common belief is. Don't be stingy with details: be sure your opening answers the *who, what, where, when, how,* and (maybe) *why* questions that readers will bring to the case.

Some factual arguments offered in academic fields follow formulas and templates. For example, a typical paper in psychology will include an abstract, a review of literature, a discussion of method, an analysis, and a references list. You may be expected to follow a preexisting pattern for factual arguments or reports in many fields.

When you have more flexibility in the structure of your argument, pay attention to the arrangement of evidence and the transitions between key points. In many cases, it makes sense to lead with a strong piece of evidence or a striking example to interest readers in your subject and then to conclude with your strongest evidence.

Even if your argument isn't correcting an error or challenging a common belief, anticipate objections to it and find a place for them in the body of your argument. Ordinarily, you wouldn't want a factual argument in a public venue (in an op-ed piece or letter to the editor, for example) to end with your concessions or refutations. Such a strategy leaves readers thinking about the potential problems with your claim at the point when they should be impressed with its strengths. But if placed early in an argument, an acknowledgment of any problems in your analysis will usually enhance your ethos.

● Getting and Giving Response

All arguments benefit from the scrutiny of others. Your instructor may assign you to a peer group for the purpose of reading and responding to each other's drafts. If not, ask for responses from serious readers or consultants at a writing center. You can use the following questions to evaluate a draft. If you're evaluating someone else's draft, illustrate your points with examples. Specific comments are always more helpful than general observations.

The Claim

- Does the claim clearly raise a serious and arguable factual issue?
- Is the claim as clear and specific as possible?
- Is the claim qualified? If so, how?

Evidence for the Claim

- Is enough evidence provided to persuade the audience to believe the claim? If not, what kind of additional evidence is needed? Does any of the evidence provided seem inappropriate or otherwise ineffective? Why?
- Is the evidence in support of the claim simply announced, or are its significance and appropriateness analyzed? Is a more detailed discussion needed?
- Are any objections that readers might have to the claim or evidence adequately addressed?
- What kinds of sources are cited? How credible and persuasive will they be to readers? What other kinds of sources might be more credible and persuasive?
- Are all quotations introduced with appropriate signal phrases (such as "As Barbara Ehrenreich argues, . . .") and blended smoothly into the writer's sentences?
- Are all visuals titled and labeled appropriately? Have you introduced them and commented on their significance?

Organization and Style

- How are the parts of the argument organized? Is this organization effective, or would some other structure work better?

- Will readers understand the relationships among the claims, supporting reasons, warrants, and evidence? If not, what could be done to make those connections clearer? Are more transitional words and phrases needed? Would headings or graphic devices help?

- How might you use visual design elements to make your proposal more effective?

- Are there clear and effective transitions or links from point to point, paragraph to paragraph, and sentence to sentence? If not, how could they be improved?

- Is the style suited to the subject? Is it too formal? Too casual? Too technical? Too bland? How can it be improved?

- Which sentences seem particularly effective? Which ones seem weakest, and how could they be improved? Should some short sentences be combined, or should any long ones be separated into two or more sentences?

- How effective are the paragraphs? Do any seem too skimpy or too long? How can they be improved?

- Which words or phrases seem particularly effective, vivid, and memorable? Do any seem dull, vague, unclear, or inappropriate for the audience or the writer's purpose? Are definitions provided for technical or other terms that readers might not know?

Spelling, Punctuation, Mechanics, Documentation, Format

- Are there any errors in spelling, punctuation, capitalization, and the like?

- Is an appropriate and consistent style of documentation used for parenthetical citations and the list of works cited or references? (See Chapter 20.)

- Does the paper or project follow an appropriate format? Is it appropriately designed and attractively presented? How could it be improved? If it's a Web site, do all the links work?

RESPOND•

1. For each topic in the following list, decide whether the claim is worth arguing to a college audience, and explain why or why not:

   Hurricanes are increasing in number and ferocity.

   Many people die annually of cancer.

   Fewer people would die of heart disease each year if more of them paid attention to their diets.

   Japan might have come to terms more readily in 1945 if the Allies hadn't demanded unconditional surrender.

   Boys would do better in school if there were more men teaching in elementary and secondary classrooms.

   The economic recession will lead drivers to give up their gas-guzzling SUVs for more energy-efficient vehicles.

   There aren't enough high-paying jobs for college graduates these days.

   Hydrogen may never be a viable alternative to fossil fuels because it takes too much energy to change hydrogen into a usable form.

   Its opponents have grossly exaggerated the effects of the USA Patriot Act on free expression.

2. Working with a group of colleagues, generate a list of twenty favorite "mysteries" explored on cable TV shows, blogs, or tabloid newspapers. Here are three to get you started—the alien crash landing at Roswell, the existence of Atlantis, and the uses of Area 51. Then decide which—if any—of these mysteries might be resolved or explained in a reasonable factual argument and which ones remain eternally mysterious and improbable. Why are people attracted to such topics?

3. The Annenberg Public Policy Center at the University of Pennsylvania hosts FactCheck.org, a Web site that is dedicated to separating facts from opinion or falsehood in the area of politics. It claims to be politically neutral. Analyze one of its cases, either a recent controversial item listed on its homepage or another from its archives. Carefully study the FactCheck case you've chosen. Pay attention to the devices that FactCheck uses to suggest or ensure objectivity and the way that it handles facts and statistics. Then offer your own brief factual argument about the site's objectivity. A full case from FactCheck.org appears at the end of this chapter as a sample reading.

4. Because digital and electronic technologies have made still and video cameras cheap, small, and durable, they're being increasingly used in many situations to provide factual evidence. Security cameras survey

Police in New Orleans were videotaped arresting and beating a man they accused of being disorderly and drunk, a charge that the former teacher strongly disputed. The police were subsequently charged with battery.

more and more public spaces, from convenience stores to subway stations, to deter assaults or catch criminals in the act. Video recorders on police cars routinely tape encounters between officers and the public, putting both groups under scrutiny. Drivers can now get tickets in some states from cameras that catch them speeding or entering intersections after traffic lights have turned red. And the National Football League and some college leagues rely on instant replay to check calls by the officials that are disputed or questionable.

In all these circumstances, the cameras record what individuals on their own may not see or not remember well, presumably providing a better—though far from perfect—account of an event. (Overturning a call in a Big 10 football game, for example, requires "indisputable video evidence"; otherwise, the call by the referee stands.)

Does all this surveillance enhance our society or undermine it in some ways? Study just one type of surveillance, including any others you think of not mentioned here (baby monitors? cameras on cell phones?). Read up on the subject in the library or on the Web, and then make a factual argument based on what you uncover. For example, you might show whether and how people benefit from the technology, how it's being abused, or both.

The Psychological Experience of Security Officers Who Work with Executions

MICHAEL OSOFSKY

An abstract summarizes Osofsky's research. Abstracts are usually required in journal articles.

The Louisiana and Alabama "Execution Teams" were interviewed in order to understand the roles, experiences, and effects of carrying out the death penalty. One hundred twenty out of a possible one hundred twenty-four correctional officers were interviewed. Of those questioned, one hundred fifteen completed mental health inventories. The subjects were grouped based on their roles in order to gain a broader picture of the steps and their impact in carrying out the death penalty. Our results show that participants in the execution process stress "caring professionalism." There is an overwhelming emphasis on carrying out one's job at a high level. At the same time, officers are neither dehumanized nor callous, describing acting with respect and decency toward all involved. While their job is their prima facie duty, they experience stress and emotional reactions, frequently having a hard time carrying out society's "ultimate punishment."

Working with Professor Philip G. Zimbardo, Michael Osofsky wrote "The Psychological Experience of Security Officers Who Work with Executions" while he was a junior at Stanford University. His essay was published in the spring 2002 edition of the *Stanford Undergraduate Research Journal*. The paper provides an example of a factual argument with an indirect thesis: the study produces surprising insights into the lives and attitudes of officers who work with prisoners on death row. But it doesn't open with a thesis or even a hypothesis about the security officers. If the piece has a point of view to defend, it may lie in its opening account of arguments for and against the death penalty. Osofsky offers one rationale and a single sentence for the majority position in favor of the death penalty; he provides four arguments and a full paragraph to explicating the position of those who oppose the death penalty. Note that the documentation style in the paper does not conform to conventional MLA or APA style.

The topic of state-ordered executions invokes strong emotions from many people throughout the United States and around the world. In the past decade alone, dozens of countries have either placed a moratorium on executions or abolished the death penalty altogether.[1] Simultaneously, ambivalence is the term that best describes the overall attitude towards the death penalty.[2] On the one hand, the majority of the American public believes that serious offenders should be punished to the extent that they inflicted pain and suffering, namely retributive justice or the biblical concept of "an eye for an eye."[3]

Alternatively, a growing minority is horrified by the idea of state-ordered killing, regardless of the heinous nature of the crimes committed. In fact, an ABC Poll conducted in early 2001 found that public support for the death penalty had declined to 63%, a drop from 77% in 1996.[4] Many question whether the death penalty has any positive deterrent effect, citing evidence comparing states with and without capital punishment.[5] Others worry about the economic discrimination against the poor and even racist tendencies associated with the death penalty.[6] Additional opponents of capital punishment feel the punishment to be appalling, arguing that innocent individuals can be put to death.[7] Finally, many individuals question the lengthy appeals process that allows inmates to be executed years after their convictions. Over the course of ten, fifteen, or even twenty years on Death Row, inmates can be rehabilitated, the family of the victim(s) receive no closure, and prison guards can form a relationship with the inmate.[8–9]

A great deal of intrigue surrounds the members of an execution team. From stereotypes of a hooded executioner to the notion of multiple executioners with only one possessing the deadly bullet, little knowledge exists about the actual nature of how executions are carried out.[10–11]

The research essay opens by briefly examining arguments for and against the death penalty—setting the context for Osofsky's study of correctional officers involved in executions.

The point of the study is explicit: "to gain more understanding" of death row guards and the work they do.

Our interviews of execution team members at the Louisiana State Penitentiary at Angola and Holman State Prison in Alabama utilize an unprecedented number of subjects through full and uninhibited access to the staff involved. The current study was undertaken in order to gain more understanding about the unusual responsibilities and experiences of those who are directly involved with the legal termination of the lives of others.

The research methodology is described in detail.

One hundred and twenty correctional officers at the Louisiana State Penitentiary at Angola and Holman State Prison in Alabama were interviewed anonymously in order to understand broad areas of the execution process. The one to two hour interviews were conducted over the summers of 2000 and 2001. During 2000, interviews were conducted of fifty of fifty-two members of the Louisiana execution team. During 2001, fifty interviews were conducted of security officers who either work on Death Row or are a part of the execution process in Louisiana. An additional twenty interviews were carried out involving correctional officers who have worked with executions in Alabama. In addition to gathering demographic and background information, a number of questions were asked about the following topics: (1) The execution experience, including roles, reactions, preparation, emotions experienced, and changes over time; (2) Stresses related to their job and methods to cope with stress; (3) Support network and influence of work on relationships; (4) Aftermath of execution experience for the officer. Based on our interviews, we were able to recreate the step-by-step process of carrying out an execution. The process was largely similar in the two states, but differed due to both situational factors with the two facilities as well as the mode of execution employed in each state. (Louisiana uses lethal injection, while Alabama is one of two remaining states still employing the electric chair as its sole means of execution.)

Questions posed to death row officers examine their reactions to the "execution process." Osofsky seems to anticipate emotional reactions and stress.

The security officers were asked to complete three separate measures. During 2000, subjects completed the Beck Depression Inventory (BDI) and the first page of a Clinician Administered Post Traumatic Stress Disorder Scale (CAPS 1) for the DSM-IV, a life events checklist. The reported results from these two measures are primarily descriptive due to our desire to understand the execution process and psychological impacts of carrying out the death penalty. During 2001, we asked the officers to complete a questionnaire pertaining to issues of moral disengagement employed throughout the process. Interviews were tape recorded (without their names on the tapes) in order to guarantee that quotes, reactions, and attributed material were accurate.

After completing the interviews, we classified subjects into one of twelve roles: Wardens, classifications personnel, Death Row guards, death house/front gate security, liaisons to the press, mental health professionals, spiritual advisors, officers who sit with the victim's family, officers who sit with the inmate's family, the strapdown team, emergency medical technicians, and the Executioner.

Interview responses conveyed an interesting perspective on the death penalty relative to the existing literature on the subject. Consistent with current national polls, approximately two-thirds of officers indicate general support for the death penalty, stressing the heinous nature of the inmates' crimes and the impact on the victims and their families.

> Responses to the interviews suggest that guards reflect majority opinion about the death penalty in the United States.

All but three do not believe the death penalty is racially motivated. However, an equal number raised concerns that social class and poverty play major roles in determining who is executed.

"I've never seen a rich man executed," Death Row guard Willie W. asserted. The inmates on Death Row tend to come from poor, underprivileged backgrounds in which they had little access to basic necessities. Sarah S.,

> Officers do question the equity of the punishment.

the deputy warden, pointed out, "If they had educational opportunities, they wouldn't be here."

The execution team also noted that certain districts within the state are more likely to hand down a death sentence. This variation by district is a function of the District Attorneys, judges, and juries—standards that vary by city and state. A considerable number of the officers discussed their concern that many "lifers" have committed crimes that are as horrific as those committed by the inmates on Death Row. For this reason alone, several members of the execution team argued that either the sentences of those on Death Row should be commuted to life in prison or others should be on Death Row.

Further, we repeatedly heard that the death penalty simply takes too long to be carried out. Some described their identification with the inmates' pain in living and awaiting execution. Others discussed the high monetary cost to the state of the lengthy appeals process. Some worried that the victims cannot receive closure until the inmate is dead.

Ultimately, nearly every person we interviewed echoed two main components of the execution process. On the one hand, and most importantly, the security officers stressed their professionalism. Their duty is to carry out the laws of the United States, whatever those may be. They believe in their jobs, and try to do them as well as they possibly can. On the other hand, they act with decency and humanity toward the inmates. In their efforts to adjust and function successfully, they struggle internally. Although most attempt to suppress painful feelings, they state that if it ever becomes easy to participate in an execution, they would worry about themselves and their loss of humanity. Some deal with their stress by disassociative mechanisms. Some overtly exhibit their distress through transient or persistent stress, guilt, and even depression. Although many officers view Death Row inmates as the

---

Osofsky gives ample attention to a critical view of the death penalty expressed by "several" execution team members.

The study is not specific here about numbers. No charts or graphs summarize responses to interview questions.

Factual results here might furnish material for subsequent arguments: guards support implementation of the law yet struggle with the nature of their work.

"worst of the worst," all describe treating the inmates with decency. Death Row guard Charles S. said, "I treat them as I would want to be treated. I help them when I can and when my job permits." Strapdown team member Robert A. concurred, "They are people and deserve to be treated as such." While some prisoners do not repent or do so only superficially, the officers describe how many change, becoming cooperative in the process.

Certainly there are exceptions to the almost universal decency of the officers in this study; wrongful emotional and physical abuse can occur in a maximum-security penitentiary. Some guards have inappropriate motives for working at a prison. From our discussions it appears that most voluntarily leave or are weeded out over time. However, the officers we interviewed did not display hostility toward the inmates, but were concerned with maximizing humanity and dignity. Within the constraints needed to maintain security, they describe being kind to the inmates. Some describe feeling good about a number of inmates who shortly before their execution thank them for their compassion. If anything, after being involved on the death team, correctional officers become more reflective and take their job more seriously than ever.

Osofsky finds that most officials approach their stressful work with death row inmates humanely and reflectively.

WORKS CITED

Osofsky provides notes keyed to the text rather than the alphabetical bibliography more typical of a works cited page.

1. Prokosch E. *Human Rights v. The Death Penalty: Abolition and Restriction in Law and Practice*. New York: Amnesty International, 1998.
2. Finckenauer JO. Public Support for the Death Penalty: Retribution as Just Deserts or Retribution as Revenge? *Justice Quarterly* 1988; 5:81–100.
3. Gale ME. Retribution, Punishment and Death. *UC Davis Law Review* 1985; 18:973–1035.
4. Ellsworth P, Ross L. Public Opinion and Capital Punishment: A Close Examination of the Views of Abolitionists and Retentionists. *Crime and Delinquency* 1983; 29:116–169.
5. Reiman JH. *The Rich Get Richer and the Poor Get Prison*, 4th ed. Boston: Allyn and Bacon, 1985.
6. Jackson J. *Legal Lynching: Racism, Injustice and the Death Penalty*. New York: Marlowe, 1996.
7. Radelet ML, Bedau HA, Putnam CE. *In Spite of Innocence: Erroneous Convictions in Capital Cases*. Boston: Northeastern University Press, 1992.
8. Radelet ML, Vandiver M, Berardo F. Families, Prisons, and Men with Death Sentences: The Human Impact of Structured Uncertainty. *J of Family Issues* 1983; 4:595–596.
9. Goldhammer GE. *Dead End*. Brunswick: Biddle Publishing Company, 1994.
10. Mailer N. *The Executioner's Song*. Boston: Little, Brown, 1979.
11. Elliot RG. *Agent of Death: The Memoirs of an Executioner*. New York: Dutton, 1940.

What Is a Civil Union?

JESS HENIG AND LORI ROBERTSON

August 9, 2007

SUMMARY

When politicians say they support civil unions but not marriage for people of the same sex, what do they mean? We find three main differences between civil unions and marriage as it's traditionally viewed:

- **The right to federal benefits.** States that allow some type of same-sex union are able to grant only state rights. The Defense of Marriage Act passed in 1996 prohibits same-sex couples from receiving federal marriage rights and benefits.
- **Portability.** Because civil unions are not recognized by all states, such agreements are not always valid when couples cross state lines.
- **Terminology.** "Marriage" is a term that conveys societal and cultural meaning, important to both gay rights activists and those who don't believe gays should marry.

"What Is a Civil Union?" was written by Jess Henig and Lori Robertson, a staff writer and managing editor, respectively, of *Annenberg Political Fact Check*. It was originally published on FactCheck.org, whose mission statement says, "We are a nonpartisan, nonprofit, 'consumer advocate' for voters that aims to reduce the level of deception and confusion in U.S. politics. We monitor the factual accuracy of what is said by major U.S. political players in the form of TV ads, debates, speeches, interviews, and news releases. Our goal is to apply the best practices of both journalism and scholarship, and to increase public knowledge and understanding." The site is sponsored by the Annenberg Public Policy Center at the University of Pennsylvania and is not funded by corporations or political groups of any kind. Note that this article does include a list of sources, but they are not listed or cited within the text in any conventional way, such as MLA or APA style.

Since this article was published in 2007, additional states have legalized civil unions, domestic partnerships, or marriages between people of the same sex. In addition, in 2009 the Obama administration announced that certain federal benefits would be extended to same-sex couples, such as allowing same-sex partners to be added to the long-term-care insurance program for federal employees.

ANALYSIS

On Aug. 9, the Democratic presidential candidates will debate issues important to gay, lesbian, bisexual and transgender individuals. The forum in Los Angeles is sponsored by the Human Rights Campaign Foundation and the MTV Networks' Logo Channel. We expect the candidates will be asked about gay marriage and civil unions—a major issue that has sparked political passions on both the right and the left.

In a questionnaire that Human Rights Campaign, a gay rights advocacy group, sent to presidential candidates, all of the Democrats said they were in favor of civil unions for gay couples—a solution that is often touted as being functionally equivalent to marriage. Only Rep. Dennis Kucinich and former Sen. Mike Gravel said they would support gay marriage. But what exactly is the difference? FactCheck.org offers this primer on the subject.

Federal Recognition

The Defense of Marriage Act (DOMA), signed into law by President Bill Clinton in 1996, stipulated that for all federal legal purposes "marriage" is a union between one man and one woman. Because of that legislation, all federal laws pertaining to married couples apply exclusively to opposite-sex couples. States that have made civil unions legal, including Connecticut, New Hampshire, New Jersey, and Vermont, have granted state benefits to same-sex couples. These include state tax benefits, better access to family health plans, co-parenting privileges, automatic prefer-ence for guardianship and decision-making authority for a medically incapacitated partner, as well as protection under state divorce and sepa-ration laws. While each state law is somewhat different, they are similar in that they convey these state rights to gay couples; they do not and can-not grant federal rights and benefits.

California, Hawaii, Maine, Oregon, Washington, and the District of Columbia have domestic partnership laws, which are fundamentally simi-lar to civil unions. Massachusetts is the only state in which gays can legally marry, due to the 2003 Massachusetts Supreme Judicial Court ruling that said the state constitution didn't support discriminating against same-sex couples that wanted to wed. Like states that grant civil unions, Massachusetts extends all the state benefits of marriage to same-sex couples; unlike in other states, gay couples also can be issued a marriage license. However, married gay couples still are not eligible for federal benefits.

The Government Accountability Office lists 1,138 federal laws that pertain to married couples. Many in that long list may be minor or only relevant to small groups of citizens. However, a number of provisions are key to what constitutes a marriage legally in the United States:

- **Taxes.** Couples in a civil union may file a joint state tax return, but they must file federal tax returns as single persons. This may be advantageous to some couples, not so for others. One advantage for married couples is the ability to transfer assets and wealth without incurring tax penalties. Partners in a civil union aren't permitted to do that and thus may be liable for estate and gift taxes on such transfers.

- **Health insurance.** The state-federal divide is even more complicated in this arena. In the wake of the Massachusetts high court ruling, the group Gay & Lesbian Advocates & Defenders put together a guide to spousal health care benefits. GLAD's document is Massachusetts-specific but provides insight into how health insurance laws would apply to those in a civil union in other states. In general, GLAD says, it comes down to what's governed by state law and what's subject to federal oversight. If a private employer's health plans are subject to Massachusetts state insurance laws, benefits must be extended to a same-sex spouse. If the health plan is governed by federal law, the employer can choose whether or not to extend such benefits.

- **Social Security survivor benefits.** If a spouse or divorced spouse dies, the survivor may have a right to Social Security payments based on the earnings of the married couple, rather than only the survivor's earnings. Same-sex couples are not eligible for such benefits.

Other federal areas in which couples in civil unions don't have the same rights as married couples include immigration (a partner who's a foreign national can't become an American by entering into a civil union with someone) and veterans' and military benefits (only opposite-sex spouses have a right to pensions, compensation for service-related deaths, medical care, housing, and the right to burial in veterans' cemeteries). Gay couples, however, may actually benefit when applying for programs such as Medicaid or government housing that require low-income eligibility. A spouse's income is included in such applications, but a same-sex partner's income is not. One change has been made in federal law: A provision in the Pension Protection Act of 2006 allows same-sex couples to transfer 401(k) and IRA earnings to partners without penalty.

Brad Luna, director of communications at Human Rights Campaign, says there have been several unsuccessful lawsuits filed by same-sex couples who wish to receive federal benefits. "It's going to have to take the repeal of DOMA or a federal civil union law that would grant them that kind of federal recognition," he says.

Portable Unions

Since civil unions are legal only in certain states, they also can't be taken across state lines. If a couple gets married in Vermont, they can reasonably expect to still be married if they move to California; the same is not true for same-sex unions. While New Jersey law specifies that the state will recognize civil unions and domestic partnerships performed elsewhere, this is not true for all states that allow some form of same-sex partnership. And if civil partners move to a state that disallows all same-sex unions, they may find themselves with no legal standing whatsoever as a couple.

Most states have enacted DOMA legislation or passed constitutional amendments stipulating that marriage is a union exclusively between one man and one woman. In fact, only five states do not have laws on the books that prohibit same-sex marriage: Massachusetts, New Jersey, New Mexico, New York, and Rhode Island. The District of Columbia also does not have such a law. Both HRC and DOMAwatch.org, a project of the Alliance Defense Fund, which opposes gay marriage, have U.S. maps showing the breakdown of legislation by state.

The Meaning of "Marriage"

The least concrete difference between civil unions and marriage is also perhaps the most polarizing: the term "marriage" and the social and cultural weight it bears. For many, this is not just a semantic issue. Opponents are concerned that allowing gays to marry will dilute the term "marriage," threatening the institution it stands for. Supporters, meanwhile, feel that setting up a marriage-like institution for gays (such as civil unions) while defining marriage as fundamentally heterosexual is an example of flawed "separate but equal" legislation.

In an interview with FactCheck.org, Paul Cates of the Lesbian Gay Bisexual Transgender Project at the American Civil Liberties Union stressed the cultural significance of marriage: "You're not a little kid dreaming about your civil union day. It's your wedding day." When you want to commit to a partner, "you're not really thinking about the [legal] protections," he says. "It's the significance and what it means to be married and hold yourself out as married."

Opponents of gay marriage also recognize the social importance of the word. Jenny Tyree, associate analyst for marriage at Focus on the Family, a Christian organization headed by James C. Dobson, says her group "does not believe that marriage has to be redefined to care for all the people in society. We understand that every person has needs and people they want to care for. But these are pretty bold attempts to undermine the marriage institution."

Focus on the Family and other groups that oppose same-sex marriage are not just concerned with terminology. "Marriage is important because it's a time-honored enduring social institution that serves women, men and children," Tyree says. "And civil unions undermine marriage by reducing it to a bundle of rights and benefits." Despite difficulties like divorce, marriage "is still an institution that does what we need it to do for children," she adds.

Such views seem to be in the majority. A 2003 Pew Research Center survey showed that 56 percent of respondents agreed that gay marriage would undermine the traditional family.

As previously noted, even states that allow for same-sex civil unions or domestic partnerships—including California, Connecticut, Maine, Vermont, and Washington—have passed laws defining marriage as something that occurs between a man and a woman. Liberal-leaning politicians have made that distinction as well: Most of the Democratic candidates set to debate these issues support extending all the federal legal rights of married couples to same-sex couples—but they don't want to call that "marriage."

Update Aug. 9: Our article originally said that Jenny Tyree of Focus on the Family cited studies showing that children do better when raised by a married mother and father. Better than what, though? When we had a chance to do a little more checking, we found that research does seem to show that children raised by married biological parents are better off on average than those raised by cohabiting biological parents. In addition, other studies show that children raised by both parents fare better than children raised by one. Studies have also shown, though, that children raised by homosexual parents are just as emotionally and socially healthy as those raised by heterosexual parents. The Child Welfare League of America says of its position on same-sex parenting: "Studies using diverse samples and methodologies in the last decade have persuasively demonstrated that there are no systematic differences between gay or lesbian and non-gay or lesbian parents in emotional health, parenting skills, and attitudes toward parenting."

SOURCES

Connecticut General Assembly. Substitute Senate Bill No. 963. 14 Apr. 2005.

DOMAwatch.org, Alliance Defense Fund. Issues by State. 8 Aug. 2007.

Government Accountability Office. Defense of Marriage Act: Update to Prior Report. GAO.gov. 23 Jan. 2004.

Human Rights Campaign. State-by-State Information, national maps of marriage-related laws. HRC.org. 8 Aug. 2007.

New Hampshire General Court. House Bill 437-FN-LOCAL. 4 Apr. 2007.

New Jersey Legislature. Bill A3787. 21 Dec. 2006.

Vermont General Assembly. Act No. 91: An Act Relating to Civil Unions. 26 Apr. 2000.

9

Arguments of Definition

A traffic committee must define *small car* to enforce parking restrictions in a campus lot where certain spaces are marked "Small Car Only!" Owners of compact luxury vehicles, light trucks, and motorcycles have complained that their vehicles are being unfairly ticketed.

A panel of judges must decide whether computer-enhanced images will be eligible in a contest for landscape photography. At what point is an electronically manipulated image no longer a photograph?

A scholarship committee must determine whether the daughter of two European American diplomats, born while her parents were assigned to the U.S. embassy in Nigeria, will be eligible to apply for grants designated specifically for "African American students."

A young man hears a classmate describe hunting as a "blood sport." He disagrees and argues that hunting for sport has little in common with "genuine blood sports" such as cockfighting.

A committee of the student union is accused of bias by a conservative student group, which claims that the committee has brought a disproportionate share of left-wing speakers to campus. The committee defends its program by challenging the definition of *left wing* used to classify its speakers.

Understanding Arguments of Definition

Definitions matter. Just ask a scientist, a mathematician, an engineer, a lawyer, or maybe a politician.

During the early stages of the 2008 presidential campaign, some conservatives accused Barack Obama of a lack of patriotism. On one occasion, he was photographed standing a bit too casually during the national anthem, and on another a reporter noticed that he'd stopped wearing an American flag lapel pin. When questioned about the pin, he responded with a narrow definition of *patriotism*: "Shortly after 9/11 . . .

You may recall the argument started during the 2008 presidential primary season by this *Time* magazine photograph of Barack Obama, Bill Richardson, and Hillary Clinton standing for the national anthem.

that [pin] became a substitute for I think true patriotism, which is speaking out on issues that are of importance to our national security."

After hearing much criticism and perhaps realizing that his initial characterization of the term, with its emphasis on dissent, had omitted much that his fellow citizens understood by *patriotism*, Obama decided to try again. In Independence, Missouri, on June 30, 2008, he delivered a speech entitled "The America We Love," which proved to be an extended definition of the term. Among the definitions of *patriotism* that Obama offered were the following:

> For me, as for most Americans, patriotism starts as a gut instinct, a loyalty and love for country rooted in my earliest memories. I'm not just talking about the recitations of the Pledge of Allegiance or the Thanksgiving pageants at school or the fireworks on the Fourth of July, as wonderful as those things may be. Rather, I'm referring to the way the American ideal wove its way throughout the lessons my family taught me as a child.
>
> . . . That is why, for me, patriotism is always more than just loyalty to a place on a map or a certain kind of people. Instead, it is also loyalty to America's ideals—ideals for which anyone can sacrifice, or defend, or give their last full measure of devotion. I believe it is this loyalty that allows a country teeming with different races and ethnicities, religions and customs, to come together as one.
>
> . . . Of course, precisely because America isn't perfect, precisely because our ideals constantly demand more from us, patriotism can never be defined as loyalty to any particular leader or government or policy. As Mark Twain, that greatest of American satirists and proud son of Missouri, once wrote, "Patriotism is supporting your country all the time, and your government when it deserves it." We may hope that our leaders and our government stand up for our ideals, and there are many times in our history when that's occurred. But when our laws, our leaders or our government are out of alignment with our ideals, then the dissent of ordinary Americans may prove to be one of the truest expressions of patriotism.
>
> . . . In the end, it may be this quality that best describes patriotism in my mind—not just a love of America in the abstract, but a very particular love for, and faith in, the American people. That is why our heart swells with pride at the sight of our flag; why we shed a tear as the lonely notes of Taps sound. For we know that the greatness of this country—its victories in war, its enormous wealth, its scientific and cultural achievements—all result from the energy and imagination of the American people; their toil, drive, struggle, restlessness, humor and quiet heroism.

As you can see from these excerpts from Obama's much longer address, a term can be defined in many ways—by what it is, by what it isn't, by what it includes, by specific examples, by what authorities (such as Mark Twain) observe, and in this case, by feelings. And note that the expanded definition also preserves the more limited meaning that got Obama into trouble initially: "the dissent of ordinary Americans may prove to be one of the truest expressions of patriotism."

As Obama discovered, definitions matter because they are, in fact, arguments that define the concepts by which we live and operate. In the wake of Hurricane Katrina in 2005, for instance, the media were full of reports about the thousands of New Orleans residents who had fled their homes to escape the storm's horrors. In some early reports, those who had left New Orleans were labeled *refugees*. But that term rankled many native-born American citizens who were still in their home country and asked how they could be refugees, a term that was commonly used for people who were legally admitted to the United States from other countries.

As the media hastened to change its terminology to *evacuees*, however, some foreign refugees began voicing outrage at the implication that *refugee* was a derogatory term. The matter got more complicated when reporters pointed out that any legally designated foreign refugees who were affected by the hurricane would be eligible for benefits that were not available to other Katrina victims. In this case, the definition of one word meant a great deal for thousands of displaced people.

Arguments of definition can be important and contentious. They wield the power to say what someone or something is or can be. As such, these arguments can also include or exclude: a creature is an endangered species or it isn't; an act was harassment or it wasn't; a person deserves official refugee status or doesn't. Another way of approaching definitional arguments, however, is to think of what falls between *is* and *is not* in a definitional claim. In fact, some dynamic definitional disputes occur in this murky realm.

Consider the controversy over how to define *human intelligence*. Some argue that human intelligence is a capacity that is measured by tests of verbal and mathematical reasoning. In other words, it's defined by IQ and SAT scores. Others define *intelligence* as the ability to perform specific practical tasks. Still others interpret intelligence in emotional terms as a competence in relating to other people. Any of these positions could be defended reasonably, but perhaps the wisest approach would be to construct a definition of *intelligence* that is rich enough to incorporate all these perspectives—and maybe more.

Does the death penalty for juveniles like this one amount to "cruel and unusual punishment"?

Crucial political, social, and scientific terms—such as *intelligence* or *social justice*—are constantly "under construction" and are reargued and reshaped whenever they need to be updated for the times. In recent years, the Supreme Court has decided what the framers of the Constitution meant by phrases such as "cruel and unusual punishment" and "a well regulated militia." And astronomers have debated whether distant Pluto still fits the traditional definition of *planet*. (It doesn't.)

In case you're wondering, important arguments of definition can't be decided simply by running to a dictionary. Dictionaries themselves reflect the way that particular groups of people use words at a specified time and place. And like any form of writing, these reference books mirror the prejudices of their makers—as shown, perhaps most famously, in the entries of lexicographer Samuel Johnson (1709–1784), who gave the English language its first great dictionary. Johnson, no friend of the Scots, defined *oats* as "a grain which in England is generally given to horses, but in Scotland supports the people." (To be fair, he also defined *lexicographer* as "a writer of dictionaries, a harmless drudge.") Thus, it's possible to disagree with dictionary definitions or to regard them merely as starting points for arguments.

PATRIOTISM
MEANS SILENCE

A MESSAGE FROM THE OFFICE OF HOMELAND SECURITY

Not Just Words

Take a look at the images on this page and the facing one. What definition of *patriotism* can you infer from each one?

We The People **GayPatriot**
...the Internet home for the American gay conservative

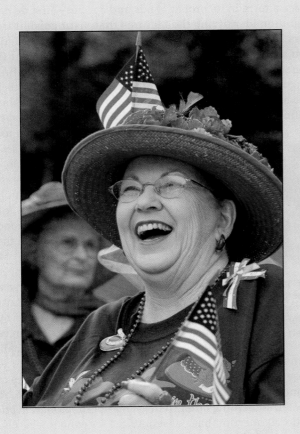

Kinds of Definition

Because there are different kinds of definitions, there are also different ways to make a definition argument. Fortunately, identifying a particular type of definition is less important than appreciating when an issue of definition is at stake. Let's explore some common definitional issues.

Formal Definitions

Formal definitions are what you find in dictionaries. Such definitions place a term in its proper genus and species—first determining its class and then identifying the features that distinguish it from other members of that class. That sounds complicated, but a definition will help you see the principle. To define *hybrid car*, you might first place it in a general class—*passenger vehicles*. Then the formal definition would distinguish hybrid cars from other passenger vehicles: *they can move using two or more sources of power, either separately or in combination.* So the full definition might look like this: *a hybrid car is a passenger vehicle* (genus) *that can operate using two or more sources of power, separately or in combination* (species).

Chevrolet Malibu: full hybrid or poseur? New York City mayor Michael Bloomberg (right) was convinced, ordering Malibus in 2008 for the city's fleets of taxis and official vehicles.

Many arguments involve deciding whether an object meets the criteria set by a formal definition. For instance, suppose that you are considering whether a Toyota Prius and a Chevrolet Malibu are actually hybrid cars. Both are clearly passenger cars, so the genus raises no questions. But not all vehicles that claim to be hybrids are powered by two sources: some of them are just electrically assisted versions of a regular gasoline car. That's the species question. Looking closely, you discover that a Prius can run on either gas or electric power alone. But does the Malibu have that flexibility? If not, should it be labeled something other than *hybrid*—perhaps, *mild hybrid*? This real definitional question has consequences for consumers who are concerned about gas prices.

Prince Charming considers whether an action would fulfill the conditions for an operational definition.

© www.cartoonstock.com

Operational Definitions

Operational definitions identify an object or idea by what it does or by what conditions create it. For example, someone's offensive sexual imposition on another person may not meet the technical definition of *harassment* unless it is considered *unwanted, unsolicited,* and *repeated.* These three conditions then define what makes an act that might be acceptable in some situations turn into harassment. But they might also then become part of a highly contentious debate: were the conditions actually present in a given case? For example, could an offensive act really be harassment if the accused believed sexual interest was mutual and therefore solicited?

Sometimes operational definitions may sound like descriptions or even narratives. In an article called "Moms Know . . . All about Operational Definitions," Kathy Parker gives this example: "From the age of six on, I knew the essence of an operational definition, even if the term itself was not known to me. I knew that chores were not considered 'complete' until I had taken the linens off my bed and put them in the laundry hamper, picked up toys and vacuumed my room. I also knew that there would be consequences if I ignored the definition of 'complete.'"

As you might imagine, arguments arise from operational definitions whenever people disagree about what the conditions define or whether these conditions have been fulfilled. Here are some examples of those types of questions:

Questions Related to Conditions

- Can institutional racism occur in the absence of specific and individual acts of racism?
- Can someone who is paid for their community service still be called a volunteer?
- Does someone who uses steroids to enhance home-run-hitting performance deserve the title Hall of Famer?

Questions Related to Fulfillment of Conditions

- Has an institution supported traditions or policies that have led to widespread racial inequities?
- Was the compensation given to a volunteer really "pay" or simply "reimbursement" for expenses?
- Should Player X, who used steroids prescribed for a medical reason, be ineligible for the Hall of Fame?

Definitions by Example

Resembling operational definitions are definitions by example, which define a class by listing its individual members. For example, one might define *smart phones* by describing the major examples of these products or define *heirloom tomatoes* by listing all those available at the local farmers' market.

A definition of *heirloom tomatoes* would include the Speckled Roman, the Olena Ukrainian, and the Yellow Brandywine.

Arguments of this sort focus on who or what may be included in a list that defines a category—*classic movies, worst natural disasters, groundbreaking painters.* Such arguments often involve comparisons and contrasts with the items that most readers would agree belong in this list. One might, for example, wonder why the status of planet is denied to asteroids, when both planets and asteroids are bodies that orbit the sun. A comparison between planets and asteroids might suggest that size is one essential feature of the eight recognized planets that asteroids don't meet. Or one might ask why Washington, D.C., is denied the status of a state. How does it differ from the fifty recognized American states?

Other Issues of Definition

Many issues of definition cross the line among the types described here and other forms of argument. For example, if you decided to explore whether banning pornography on the Internet violates First Amendment guarantees of free speech, you'd first have to establish definitions of *pornography* and *free speech.* You could refer either to legal definitions settled by, let's say, the Supreme Court or to other definitions closer to your own beliefs, perhaps offered by experts in Internet law. Then you'd have to argue that types of pornography on the Internet are or are not in the same class or that they share or do not share the characteristics of speech protected by the First Amendment. In doing so, you'd certainly find yourself slipping into an evaluative mode because matters of definition are often also questions of value. (See Chapter 10.)

When exploring an idea, don't worry about such slippage: it's a natural part of writing. But focus an argument on a central issue or question, and be honest in examining any definition you care to defend.

Developing a Definitional Argument

Definitional arguments don't just appear out of the blue; they evolve out of the occasions and conversations of daily life, both public and private. You might get into an argument over the definition of *ordinary wear and tear* when you return a rental car with some battered upholstery. Or you might be asked to write a job description for a new position to be created in your office: you have to define the position in a way that doesn't step on anyone else's turf on the job. Or maybe employees on your campus object to being defined as *temporary workers* when they've held their same jobs for years. Or someone derides one of your best friends as *just a nerd*. In a dozen ways every day, you encounter situations that are issues of definition. They're so frequent and indispensable that you barely notice them for what they are.

Formulating Claims

In addressing a question of definition, you'll likely formulate a *tentative claim*—a declarative statement that represents your first response to such situations. Note that such initial claims usually don't follow a single definitional formula.

Claims of Definition

A person paid to do public service is not a *volunteer.*

Institutional racism can exist—maybe even thrive—in the absence of overt civil rights violations.

Political bias has been consistently practiced by the mainstream media.

A *municipal fee* is often the same darn thing as a tax.

Napoleon Dynamite is one of many independent films to achieve *cult status*.

None of the claims listed here could stand on its own. Such claims often reflect first impressions and gut reactions. That's because stating a claim of definition is typically a starting point, a moment of bravura that doesn't last much beyond the first serious rebuttal or challenge. Statements of this sort aren't arguments until they're attached to reasons, data, warrants, and evidence. (See Chapter 7.)

Finding good reasons to support a claim of definition usually requires formulating a general definition by which to explore the subject. To be persuasive, the definition must be broad and not tailored to the specific controversy:

A volunteer is . . .

Institutional racism is . . .

Political bias is . . .

A tax is . . .

A cult film is . . .

Definitions and Academic Arguments

People within an academic field typically share a common and often highly technical vocabulary. Newcomers to any discipline (or major) have to understand how these key terms are defined: for instance, *affect* in psychology, *tort* in law, *persona* in literature, or *entropy* in engineering.

Scholars and researchers may spend considerable energy and time refining the definitions of technical items. But academics also create wholly new words to convey fresh observations and discoveries. Australian philosopher Glenn Albrecht, for example, recently

(continued)

(continued)

coined the term "solastalgia" to describe "a form of homesickness one gets when one is still at home" because familiar environments are being altered by global warming, war, terrorism, strip mining, urban gentrification, or other forces that alter a built environment. Here is Albrecht's academic definition of the term, as offered on his own blog:

> I suggest 'solastalgia' to describe the pain or sickness caused by the loss of, or inability to derive, solace connected to the present state of one's home environment. Solastalgia exists when there is recognition that the place where one resides and that one loves is under assault (physical desolation). It can be contrasted to the spatial and temporal dislocation and dispossession experienced as nostalgia. Solastalgia is the 'lived experience' of the loss of the value of the present as manifest in a feeling of dislocation; of being undermined by forces that destroy the potential for solace to be derived from the immediate and given. In brief, solastalgia is a form of homesickness one experiences when one is still at 'home'.
>
> —Glenn Albrecht, "Solastalgia: A New Psychoterratic Illness"

Clive Thompson, writing for *Wired* (January 2008), explains the newly defined term in language that is less academic:

> People are feeling displaced. They are suffering symptoms eerily similar to those of indigenous populations that are removed from their traditional homelands. But nobody is being relocated; they haven't moved anywhere. It's just that familiar markers of their area, the physical and sensory signals that define *home*, are vanishing. Their environment is moving away from them, and they miss it terribly.
>
> —Clive Thompson, "How the Next Victim of Climate Change Will Be Our Minds"

How does Albrecht's scholarly definition of solastalgia differ in style from Thompson's explanation of the phenomenon, which is aimed at the more general readership of *Wired*? Point to specific features of Albrecht's definition that mark it as academic writing.

Now consider how the following claims might be expanded with a general definition to become full-fledged definitional arguments:

Arguments of Definition

Someone paid to do public service is not a volunteer because volunteers are people who . . .

Institutional racism can exist even in the absence of overt violations of civil rights because, by definition, institutional racism is . . .

Political bias in the media is evident when . . .

A municipal fee is the same darn thing as a tax. Both fees and taxes are . . .

Napoleon Dynamite has achieved all the criteria of cult status: . . .

Notice, too, that some of the issues can involve comparisons between things—such as taxes and fees.

Crafting Definitions

Imagine that you decide to tackle the concept of paid volunteer in the following way:

Participants in the federal AmeriCorps program are not really volunteers because they receive "education awards" for their public service. Volunteers are people who work for a cause without receiving compensation.

In Toulmin terms, the argument looks like this:

Claim   Participants in AmeriCorps aren't volunteers . . .
Reason   . . . because they are paid for their service.
Warrant   People who are compensated for their services are, ordinarily, employees.

As you can see, the definition of *volunteers* will be crucial to the shape of the argument. In fact, you might think you've settled the matter with this tight little formulation. But now it's time to listen to the readers over your shoulder (see Chapter 7), who are pushing you further. Do the terms of your definition account for all pertinent cases of volunteerism—in particular, any related to the types of public service AmeriCorps members might be involved in? Consider, too, the word *cause* in your original state-ment of the definition:

> **Volunteers are people who work for a cause without receiving com-pensation.**

Cause has political connotations that you may or may not intend. You'd better clarify what you mean by *cause* when you discuss its definition in your paper. Might a phrase such as *the public good* be a more comprehen-sive or appropriate substitute for a *cause*? And then there's the matter of *compensation* in the second half of your definition:

> **Volunteers are people who work for a cause without receiving com-pensation.**

Aren't people who volunteer to serve on boards, committees, and com-missions sometimes paid, especially for their expenses? What about members of the so-called all-volunteer military? They're financially compensated for their years of service, and they enjoy benefits after they complete their tour of duty.

As you can see, you can't just offer up a definition as part of your argument and assume that readers will understand or accept it. Every part of the definition has to be weighed, critiqued, and defended. That means you'll want to investigate your subject in the library, on the Internet, and in conversation with others, including experts on your term. You might then be able to present your definition in a single para-graph, or you may have to spend several pages coming to terms with the complexity of the core issue.

After conducting research of this kind, you'll be in a better position to write an extended definition that explains to your readers what you believe makes a volunteer a volunteer, a tax a tax, and so on. At the end of this chapter, writer Lynn Peril provides just such a definition of the attitude that she claims is imposed on women in this country—what she calls "Pink Think."

Matching Claims to Definitions

Once you've formulated a definition that readers will accept—a demand-ing task in itself—you might need to look at your subject to see if it fits your general definition. It should provide evidence of one of the following:

- It is a clear example of the class defined.
- It clearly falls outside the defined class.

- It falls between two closely related classes or fulfills some conditions of the defined class but not others.
- It defies existing classes and categories and requires an entirely new definition.

It's possible that you might have to change your original claim at this point if the evidence you've gathered suggests that qualifications are necessary. It's amazing how often seemingly cut-and-dry issues of definition become blurry—and open to compromise and accommodation—when you learn more about them. That has proved to be the case as various campuses across the country have tried to define *hate speech* or *sexual harassment*—tricky matters. And even the Supreme Court has never said exactly what *pornography* is. Just when matters seem settled, new legal twists develop. Should virtual child pornography that is created with software be illegal, as is the real thing? Is a virtual image—even a lewd one—an artistic expression that is protected (as other works of art are) by the First Amendment?

Considering Design and Visuals

In thinking about how to present your argument of definition, don't forget that design—such as boldface and italics, headings, or links in online text—can contribute to (or detract from) its credibility and persuasiveness. Remember, too, that visuals like photographs, charts, and graphs can also help you make your case. Such items might demonstrate that the conditions for a definition have been met—as the widely circulated and horrific photographs from Abu Ghraib prison in 2004 helped to define *torture*. Or if you're working with a definitional claim about media bias, a chart might help to identify a characteristic of such prejudice, like a tendency among reporters to treat candidates in a political campaign differently. Note that such an item could also serve as evidence that the concept you are defining exists—often a matter of contention in arguments of definition.

Key Features of Definitional Arguments

In writing an argument of definition of your own, consider that it's likely to include the following parts:

- a claim involving a question of definition
- a general definition of some key concept

Positive Narratives in the Press
Percent of all assertions studied

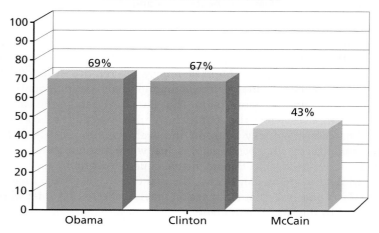

A chart from a study entitled "Character and the Primaries" might be used to define a characteristic of media bias. From Journalism.org, May 29, 2008, and the Project for Excellence in Journalism of the Pew Research Center

- a careful look at your subject in terms of that general definition
- evidence for every part of the argument, including visual evidence if appropriate
- a consideration of alternative views and counterarguments
- a conclusion drawing out the implications of the argument

It's impossible, however, to predict what emphasis each of those parts might receive or what the ultimate shape of an argument of definition will be.

Whatever form your definitional argument takes, be sure to share your draft with others who can examine its claims, evidence, and connections. Writers in isolation find it easy to think narrowly—and not to imagine that others might define *volunteer* or *institutional racism* in a completely different way. Be open to criticism and suggestions and look carefully at the terms of any definitions you offer. Do they really help readers distinguish one concept from another? Are the conditions offered sufficient or essential? Have you mistaken accidental features of a concept or object for more important features?

Don't hesitate to look to other sources for comparisons with your definitions. You can't depend on dictionaries to offer the last word about any disputed term, but you can begin with them, check encyclopedias and other reference works, and search the Web to find how your key terms are presented there. (In searching for the definition of *wetland*, for example, you could type *wetland definition* into a search engine like Google and get a limited number of useful hits.)

Finally, be prepared for surprises in writing arguments of definition. That's part of the delight in expanding the way you see the world. "I'm not a pig, I'm a sheepdog," thinks Babe in the 1995 film of the same name. Babe then goes right on to win a sheepdog competition. Such is the power of definition.

GUIDE to writing an argument of definition

● Finding a Topic

You're entering an argument of definition when you

- formulate a controversial or provocative definition: *In recent years, the American Dream meant a McMansion in a gated community with a deferential maid, gardener, and personal chef.*

- challenge a definition: *For most Americans today, the American Dream involves not luxury but the secure pensions, cheap energy costs, and health insurance that workers in the 1950s and 1960s enjoyed.*

- try to determine whether something fits an existing definition: *Expanding opportunity is (or is not) central to the American Dream.*

Look for issues of definition in your everyday affairs—for instance, in the way that jobs are classified at work, that key terms are described in your academic major, that politicians characterize the social issues that concern you, that you define yourself, or that others try to define you. Be alert to definitional arguments that may arise whenever you or others deploy adjectives such as *true, real, actual,* or *genuine: a true Texan, genuine environmental degradation, actual budget projections, authentic Mexican food.*

● Researching Your Topic

You can research issues of definition by using the following sources:

- college dictionaries and encyclopedias
- unabridged dictionaries
- specialized reference works and handbooks, such as legal and medical dictionaries
- your textbooks (check their glossaries)
- newsgroups and listservs that focus on particular topics

Be sure to browse in your library reference room. Also, use the search tools of electronic indexes and databases to determine whether or how often controversial phrases or expressions are occurring in influential materials—major online newspapers, journals, and Web sites.

When dealing with definitions, ask librarians to direct you to the most appropriate and reliable sources. For instance, in some cases, you may need to know what the legal definition of a term or concept is. A work such as *Black's Law Dictionary* or a database such as FindLaw may help. How the government defines terms may be important, too: you might check USA.gov.

● Formulating a Claim

After exploring your subject, begin to formulate a full and specific claim, a thesis that lets readers know where you stand and what issues are at stake. In moving toward this thesis, begin with the following types of questions of definition:

- questions related to genus: *Is assisting in suicide a crime?*

- questions related to species: *Is marijuana a harmful addictive drug or a useful medical treatment?*

- questions related to conditions: *Must the imposition of sexual attention be both unwanted and unsolicited to be considered sexual harassment?*

- questions related to fulfillment of conditions: *Has our college kept in place traditions or policies that might constitute racial discrimination?*

- questions related to membership in a named class: *Is any pop artist today in a class with Bob Dylan, the Beatles, Aretha Franklin, or the Rolling Stones?*

Your thesis should be a complete statement. In one sentence, you need to make a claim of definition and state the reasons that support your claim. In your paper or project itself, you may later decide to separate the claim from the reasons supporting it. But your working thesis should be a fully expressed thought. That means spelling out the details and the qualifications: *Who? What? Where? When? How many? How regularly? How completely?* Don't expect readers to fill in the blanks for you.

● Examples of Definitional Claims

- Assisting a gravely ill person in committing suicide should not be considered *murder* when the motive behind the act is to ease a person's suffering and not to do harm or to benefit from the death.

- Although marijuana is somewhat addictive, it should not be classified as a *dangerous drug* because it is less damaging to the individual and society than heroin or cocaine and because it helps people live more comfortably with life-threatening diseases.

- Flirting with the waitstaff in a restaurant should be considered *sexual harassment* when the activity is repeated, unsolicited, and obviously unappreciated.

- Giving college admission preference to all racial minorities can be an example of *class discrimination* because such policies may favor middle- and upper-class students who are already advantaged.

● Preparing a Proposal

If your instructor asks you to prepare a proposal for your project, here's a format that may help:

State your thesis completely. If you're having trouble doing so, try outlining it in Toulmin terms:

    Claim:

    Reason(s):

    Warrant(s):

- **Explain why this argument of definition deserves attention. What's at stake? Why is it important for your readers to consider?**

- **Specify whom you hope to reach through your argument and why this group of readers would be interested in it.**

- **Briefly discuss the key challenges that you anticipate in preparing your argument: Defining a key term? Establishing the essential and sufficient elements of your definition? Demonstrating that your subject will meet those conditions?**

- **Determine what strategies you'll use in researching your definitional argument. What sources do you expect to consult: Dictionaries? Encyclopedias? Periodicals? The Internet?**

- **Determine what visuals you will include in your definitional argument. How will each one be used?**

- **Consider what format you expect to use for your project: A conventional research essay? A letter to the editor? A Web page?**

● Thinking about Organization

Your argument of definition may take various forms, but it's likely to include elements such as the following:

- a claim involving a matter of definition: *Labeling Al Qaeda and similar groups as representatives of "Islamic fascism" is understandable but misleading.*

- an attempt to establish a definition of a key term: *Genuine fascism is a mass movement within a nation resulting from democracy gone wrong.*

- an explanation or defense of the terms of the definition: *Scholars agree that fascism is a modern mass movement distinguished by the primacy of the nation over the individual, the elimination of dissent, the creation of a single-party state, and the glorification of violence on behalf of a national cause.*

- an examination of the claim in terms of the definition and all its criteria: *Fascism is highly nationalistic, but Islam is hostile to nationalism; Islam is a religious movement, but fascism is a secular movement that is usually hostile to religion.*

- a consideration of alternative views and counterarguments: *It is true that Osama bin Laden appeals to violence on behalf of his cause of restoring the medieval Islamic empire and that some fascist regimes (like Franco's Spain) were closely allied to religious authorities. . . .*

● Getting and Giving Response

All arguments benefit from the scrutiny of others. Your instructor may assign you to a peer group for the purpose of reading and responding to each other's drafts. If not, ask for responses from serious readers or consultants at a writing center. You can use the following questions to evaluate a draft. If you're evaluating someone else's draft, be sure to illustrate your points with examples. Specific comments are always more helpful than general observations.

The Claim

- Is the claim clearly an issue of definition?
- Is the claim significant enough to interest readers?
- Are clear and specific criteria established for the concept being defined? Do the criteria define the term adequately? Using this definition, could most readers identify what's being defined and distinguish it from other related concepts?

Evidence for the Claim

- Is enough evidence furnished to explain or support the definition? If not, what kind of additional evidence is needed?

- Is the evidence in support of the claim simply announced, or are its significance and appropriateness analyzed? Is a more detailed discussion needed?

- Are all the conditions of the definition met in the concept being examined?

- Are any objections readers might have to the claim, criteria, evidence, or way the definition is formulated adequately addressed?

- What kinds of sources, including visual sources, are cited? How credible and persuasive will they be to readers? What other kinds of sources might be more credible and persuasive?

- Are all quotations introduced with appropriate signal phrases (such as "As Himmelfarb argues, . . .") and blended smoothly into the writer's sentences?

Organization and Style

- How are the parts of the argument organized? Is this organization effective, or would another structure work better?

- Will readers understand the relationships among the claims, supporting reasons, warrants, and evidence? If not, what could be done to make those connections clearer? Is the function of every visual clear? Have you related each visual to a particular point in your essay and explained its significance? Are more transitional words and phrases needed? Would headings or graphic devices help?

- Are the transitions or links from point to point, paragraph to paragraph, and sentence to sentence clear and effective? If not, how could they be improved?

- Is the style suited to the subject? Is it too formal? Too casual? Too technical? Too bland? How can it be improved?

- Which sentences seem particularly effective? Which ones seem weakest, and how could they be improved? Should some short sentences be combined, or should any long ones be separated into two or more sentences?

- How effective are the paragraphs? Do any seem too skimpy or too long? How can they be improved?

- Which words or phrases seem particularly effective, vivid, and memorable? Do any seem dull, vague, unclear, or inappropriate for the audience or the writer's purpose? Are definitions provided for technical or other terms that readers might not know?

Spelling, Punctuation, Mechanics, Documentation, Format

- Are there any errors in spelling, punctuation, capitalization, and the like?
- Is an appropriate and consistent style of documentation used for parenthetical citations and the list of works cited or references? (See Chapter 20.)
- Does the paper or project follow an appropriate format? Is it appropriately designed and attractively presented? How could it be improved? If it's a Web site, do all the links work?

RESPOND●

1. Briefly discuss the criteria that you might use to define the italicized terms in the following controversial claims of definition. Compare your definitions of the terms with those of your classmates.

   Graphic novels are *serious literature*.

   Burning a nation's flag is a *hate crime*.

   Conor Oberst defines *emo*.

   Matt Drudge and Arianna Huffington are *legitimate journalists*.

   College sports programs have become *big businesses*.

   Plagiarism can be an act of civil *disobedience*.

   Satanism is a *religion* properly protected by the First Amendment.

   Campaign contributions are acts of *free speech* that should not be regulated.

   The District of Columbia should not have all the privileges of an American *state*.

   Gay and lesbian couples should have the legal privileges of *marriage*.

2. This chapter opens with sketches of five rhetorical situations that center on definitional issues. Select one of these situations, and write definitional criteria using the strategy of formal definition. For example, identify the features of a photograph that make it part of a larger class (*art, communication method, journalistic technique*). Next, identify the features of a photograph that make it distinct from other members of that larger class. Then use the strategy of operational definition to establish criteria for the same object: what does it do? Remember to ask questions related to conditions (*Is a computer-scanned photograph still a photograph?*) and questions related to fulfillment of conditions (*Does a good photocopy of a photograph achieve the same effect as the photograph itself?*).

3. In an essay at the end of this chapter, Lynn Peril makes a variety of claims about a concept she identifies as *pink think*, which she defines in part as "a set of ideas and attitudes about what constitutes proper female behavior." After reading this selection, consider whether Peril has defined a concept that operates today. If you think "pink think" still exists, prove it by showing how some activities, behaviors, products, or institutions meet the definition of the concept. Write, too, about the power that this concept has to define behavior.

   Alternatively, define a concept of your own that applies to a similar kind of stereotypical behavior—for example, *dude think* or *surfer think* or *geek think*. Then argue that your newly defined concept does, in fact, influence people today. Be sure to provide clear and compelling examples of the concept in action as it shapes the way that people think and behave.

Are little girls who play the latest version of Mystery Date still buying into Lynn Peril's concept of "pink think"?

The Offbeat Allure of Cult Films

SAYOH MANSARAY

Opening paragraph includes a parodic definition of "great skills."

On a Saturday afternoon in February junior Clare Marshall and her family sit in her living room watching a film that Marshall is an avid fan of: *Napoleon Dynamite*. Marshall and her family say quotes along with the movie and laugh aloud at the hilarious parts. "Girls only want boyfriends who have great skills," Clare says, imitating Napoleon's trademark throaty drawl. "You know, like nun chuck skills, bow hunting skills . . . computer hacking skills."

Marshall is not the only teenager who likes films that are completely different from most movies in theaters. The teen followings of nonmainstream films like *Napoleon Dynamite* and *Donnie Darko* show that today's teens are looking for films that are "off the beaten path," according to English and Literature as Film teacher Mike Horne. Teens are gravitating toward these quirky movies, raising some of them to a cult-like status.

A tentative definition of "cult film" is offered.

The consensus among Blazers is that a cult movie is a quirky, different film that did not do well in theaters but has since gained a strong and faithful following on DVD or video. In recent years the definition of cult films has begun to evolve and broaden to include films that did not actually flop in theaters. Regardless of the specific definition, recent cult films are attracting teen fans.

Sayoh Mansaray wrote this article for *Silver Chips Online,* the online newspaper of Montgomery Blair High School in Silver Spring, Maryland, where she served as public relations codirector and factcheck supervisor. *Silver Chips Online,* which has won a number of awards, is all student-run and is partially sponsored by the *Washington Post.* Note that the article, like most pieces published in newspapers, does not document sources in any formal way.

A still from *Donnie Darko*, starring Jake Gyllenhaal (left)

"It Feels Real"

As Marshall continues to watch the film, a scene plays in which Napoleon talks to a girl on the phone. The girl has been forced by her mother to thank Napoleon for a picture he drew of her in hopes of getting a date. "It took me like three hours to finish the shading on your upper lip," Napoleon says to the girl, as Marshall quotes along with him.

Many teens, Marshall included, like cult films because they differ from other films in theaters. Horne says that teens gravitate to cult movies because they are not formulaic. "They are a little bit different, and they require some thought or interpretation," he says.

Junior Katrina Jabonete likes *Donnie Darko*, a film about a teen who is teetering on the edge of schizophrenia, because it is so beautifully twisted and darkly weird that the film opens itself to a thousand different interpretations. She believes that teens are drawn to cult movies because they aren't as clean or processed as mainstream flicks and because cult films are less likely to offer a concrete conclusion. Basically, they are more like real life. "[They] deal with problems and emotions in

Another characteristic of cult films is offered: they are "not formulaic" and they "require thought."

Reasons for the popularity of cult films are given.

a different, real way," she explains. "Teens relate to [these movies] because it feels real to them."

TIME WARP

While recent movies are gaining cult status, some students remain exclusively faithful to the classics, becoming part of groups that view their cult favorites over and over again.

Junior Linda Dye fits into this category. She thinks a cult movie is a film that is "so bad it's good." Take her favorite cult film, *The Rocky Horror Picture Show*, a 1975 musical about a group of gender-bending, quasi-alien, quasi-vampire, raving-lunatics-in-drag. "Ever since I first saw it, I've been completely in love with it," she gushes.

An example of a classic cult film is provided.

Dye is drawn to the film partially because the close-knit following allows her to interact with people she might never have known before. When Dye attended the annual *Rocky Horror* screening at the University of Maryland, she dressed up as one of the film's characters. In a bustier, a feather boa, and heels, Dye, along with the rest of the audience, yelled dialogue to the screen and made up her own lines as the movie played.

For Dye, this energy is what keeps her love for the film and its following alive. "You're sitting with these people you've never met, [but] by the end of the movie there's an energy—you're a community," she says.

"IF I HAD A TUMOR, I'D NAME IT MARLA"

Regardless of whether a movie is a classic or a recent hit, movie fans often display their love of films by quoting them. On snowy days, senior Robin Weiss likes to write one-liners from *Fight Club* like, "If I had a tumor, I'd name it Marla" and "We are a generation of men raised by women" on the icy windshields of random cars.

Marshall likes to answer questions with *Napoleon Dynamite* quotes. If a friend asks, "What are you doing today, Clare?" she might respond with a Napoleon line: "Whatever I feel like doing—gosh!"

Horne says that a major component of cult films is quotable dialogue. "Half the fun is reliving it with your friends," he says, smiling. Some fans can quote most of a movie, he adds. Senior Walker Davis, for example, knows most of the lines from *The Big Lebowski*.

According to Davis, cult films are never big budget productions, and no movie studio ever sets out to create a cult film—it just happens.

Many teens, like Marshall, just can't get enough of these films. Horne says that cult films are often bizarre, random, and edgy, which adds to their appeal. He says that people who watch cult films may have different motives than other moviegoers. "Many people look to film as an escape, [but] others are looking to find different thoughts," he says.

Quotable dialogue is a defining characteristic of a cult film.

Low-budget aspect of cult films, first mentioned in third paragraph, is reiterated here.

Pink Think

LYNN PERIL

From the moment she's wrapped in a pink blanket, long past the trau-matic birthday when she realizes her age is greater than her bust mea-surement, the human female is bombarded with advice on how to wield those feminine wiles. This advice ranges from rather vague proscriptions along the lines of "nice girls don't chew gum/swear/wear pants/fill-in-the-blank," to obsessively elaborate instructions for daily living. How many women's lives, for example, were enriched by former Miss America Jacque Mercer's positively baroque description of the proper way to put on a bathing suit, as it appeared in her guide *How to Win a Beauty Contest* (1960)?

> [F]irst, roll it as you would a girdle. Pull the suit over the hips to the waist, then, holding the top away from your body, bend over from the waist. Ease the suit up to the bustline and with one hand, lift one breast up and in and ease the suit bra over it. Repeat on the other side. Stand up and fasten the straps.

Instructions like these made me bristle. I formed an early aversion to all things pink and girly. It didn't take me long to figure out that many things young girls were supposed to enjoy, not to mention ways they were supposed to behave, left me feeling funny—as if I was expected to pound my square peg self into the round hole of designated girliness. I didn't know it at the time, but the butterflies in my tummy meant I had crested the first of many hills on the roller coaster ride of femininity—or, as I soon referred to it, the other f-word. Before I knew what was happening, I was hurtling down its track, seemingly out of control, and screaming at the top of my lungs.

After all, look what I was up against. The following factoids of feminin-ity date from the year of my birth (hey, it wasn't *that* long ago):

- In May of 1961, Betsy Martin McKinney told readers of *Ladies' Home Journal* that, for women, sexual activity commenced with intercourse

Lynn Peril is the publisher of the 'zine *Mystery Date*. This essay is excerpted from the introduction to *Pink Think,* a book that examines the influence of the feminine ideal.

and was completed with pregnancy and childbirth. Therefore, a woman who used contraceptives denied "her own creativity, her own sexual role, her very femininity." Furthermore, McKinney asserted that "one of the most stimulating predisposers to orgasm in a woman may be child-birth followed by several months of lactation." (Mmm, yes, must be the combination of episiotomy and sleep deprivation that does it.) Politely avoiding personal examples, she neglected to mention how many little McKinneys there were.

- During the competition for the title of Miss America 1961, five finalists were given two questions to answer. First they were asked what they would do if "you were walking down the runway in the swimsuit com-petition, and a heel came off one of your shoes?" The second question, however, was a bit more esoteric: "Are American women usurping males in the world, and are they too dominant?" Eighteen-year-old Nancy Fleming, of Montague, Michigan, agreed that "there are too many women working in the world. A woman's place is in the home with her husband and children." This, along with her pragmatic answer to the first question ("I would kick off both shoes and walk barefooted") and her twenty-three-inch waist (tied for the smallest in pageant history), helped Nancy win the crown.
- In 1961, toymaker Transogram introduced a new game for girls called Miss Popularity ("The True American Teen"), in which players competed to see who could accrue the most votes from four pageant judges—three of whom were male. Points were awarded for such attributes as nice legs, and if the judges liked a contestant's figure, voice, and "type." The prize? A special "loving" cup, of course! Who, after all, could love an unpopular girl?

These are all prime examples of "pink think." Pink think is a set of ideas and attitudes about what constitutes proper female behavior; a group-think that was consciously or not adhered to by advice writers, manufac-turers of toys and other consumer products, experts in many walks of life, and the public at large, particularly during the years spanning the mid-twentieth century—but enduring even into the twenty-first century. Pink think assumes there is a standard of behavior to which all women, no matter their age, race, or body type, must aspire.

"Femininity" is sometimes used as a code word for this mythical stan-dard, which suggests that women and girls are always gentle, soft, delicate, nurturing beings made of "sugar and spice and everything nice." But pink think is more than a stereotyped vision of girls and women as poor drivers who are afraid of mice and snakes, adore babies and small dogs, talk incessantly on the phone, and are incapable of keeping secrets. Integral to pink think is the belief that one's success as a woman is grounded in one's allegiance to such behavior. For example, a woman who fears mice isn't necessarily following the dictates of pink think. On the other hand, a woman who isn't afraid of mice but pretends to be because she thinks such helplessness adds to her appearance of femininity is toeing the pink think party line. When you hear the words "charm" or "personality" in the context of successful womanhood, you can almost always be sure you're in the presence of pink think.

While various self-styled "experts" have been advising women on their "proper" conduct since the invention of the printing press, the phenomenon defined here as pink think was particularly pervasive from the 1940s to the 1970s. These were fertile years for pink think, a cultural mindset and consumer behavior rooted in New Deal prosperity yet culminating with the birth of women's liberation. During this time, pink think permeated popular books and magazines aimed at adult women, while little girls absorbed rules of feminine behavior while playing games like the aforementioned Miss Popularity. Meanwhile, prescriptions for ladylike dress, deportment, and mindset seeped into child-rearing manuals, high school home economics textbooks, and guides for bride, homemaker, and career girl alike.

It was almost as if the men and women who wrote such books viewed proper feminine behavior as a panacea for the ills of a rapidly changing modern world. For example, myriad articles in the popular press devoted to the joys of housewifery helped coerce Rosie the Riveter back into the kitchen when her hubby came home from the war and expected his factory job back. During the early cold war years, some home economics texts seemed to suggest that knowing how to make hospital corners and a good tuna casserole were the only things between Our Way of Life and communist incursion. It was patriotic to be an exemplary housewife. And pink-thinking experts of the sixties and seventies, trying to maintain this ideal, churned out reams of pages that countered the onrushing tide of both the sexual revolution and the women's movement. If only all women behaved like our Ideal Woman, the experts seemed to say through the years, then everything would be fine.

You might even say that the "problem with no name" that Betty Friedan wrote about in *The Feminine Mystique* (1963) was a virulent strain of pink-thinkitis. After all, according to Friedan, "the problem" was in part engendered by the experts' insistence that women "could desire no greater destiny than to glory in their own femininity"—a pink think credo.

The pink think of the 1940s to 1970s held that femininity was necessary for catching and marrying a man, which was in turn a prerequisite for childbearing—the ultimate feminine fulfillment. This resulted in little girls playing games like Mystery Date long before they were ever interested in boys. It made home economics a high school course and college major, and suggested a teen girl's focus should be on dating and getting a boyfriend. It made beauty, charm, and submissive behavior of mandatory importance to women of all ages in order to win a man's attention and hold his interest after marriage. It promoted motherhood and housewifery as women's only meaningful career, and made sure that women who worked outside the home brought "feminine charm" to their workplaces lest a career make them too masculine.

Not that pink think resides exclusively alongside antimacassars and 14.4 modems in the graveyard of outdated popular culture: Shoes, clothing, and movie stars may go in and out of style with astounding rapidity, but attitudes have an unnerving way of hanging around long after they've outlived their usefulness—even if they never had any use to begin with.

10
Evaluations

"We don't want to go there for coffee. It's full of chemicals, it's not fair trade, and it's way overpriced."

The campus Labor Action Committee has been cochaired for four years by three students whose leadership has led to significant improvements in the way the university treats its workers. They're all graduating at once, leaving a leadership vacuum, so the group calls a special meeting to talk about what qualities it needs in its next leaders.

You've just seen *Citizen Kane* for the first time and want to share the experience with your roommate. Orson Welles's masterpiece is playing at the Student Union for only one more night, but the new *Incredible Hulk* is featured across the street in THX sound. Guess which movie your roomie wants to see? You intend to set him straight.

A senior is frustrated by the C she received on an essay written for a history class, so she makes an appointment to talk with the teaching assistant who graded the paper. "Be sure to review the assignment sheet first," the TA warns. Whoops: *now* the student notices that the back side of the sheet includes a checklist of requirements for the paper; she hadn't turned it over before.

"We have a lousy homepage," a sales representative observes at a district meeting. "What's wrong with it?" the marketing manager asks. "Everything," the sales rep replies, then quickly changes the subject when she notices the manager's furrowed brow. But the manager decides to investigate the issue. Who knows what an effective Web site looks like these days?

Understanding Evaluations

Here's the scene: you're going to be in New York City for only one night, and you want to indulge your love of musicals. You consult the *New Yorker* and find several possibilities, so you turn next to reviews, checking first with the *New York Times*. You don't have to read far before you come on a musical that sounds pretty fabulous: Lin-Manuel Miranda's *In the Heights*. "If you like the bubbly or sultry sounds of Latin music," the reviewer says, this one is for you. Since you are a big fan of Latin music, you read on:

> Under the enthusiastic guidance of the music director, Alex Lacamoire, the orchestra—band is really a better word—plays with a sense of excitement almost never heard emanating from a Broadway pit. (The standard amplification is less flattening to this music than to traditional scores.) Bright, piping fanfares from the trumpets punctuate the dance numbers; the merry tinkle of a steel drum laughs along with the jokes. The players below seem to be having as much fun as the performers onstage.
>
> That is saying plenty, for when this musical erupts in one of its expressions of collective joy, the energy it gives off could light up the George Washington Bridge for a year or two. The title song, for instance, is among the most galvanizing opening numbers in recent Broadway memory, as Usnavi gives the audience a guided tour, in briskly flowing rap, of the troubles that nip at the heels and the hopes that feed the imaginations of the neighborhood's inhabitants. . . .
>
> You could easily be cynical about the show's heartfelt belief in the possibility of a little love and a big lottery win making all things right. But then Mr. Miranda bounces back onstage, throwing down rhymes

A scene from *In the Heights*

and throwing his arms open wide as if to embrace the whole mezza-
nine. He seems to embody music's ability to make the trite seem true
again. And after all, this scrappy little musical about chasing your
dreams and finding your true home is Mr. Miranda's own dream come
true. He couldn't look more at home.

> —Charles Isherwood, "The View from Uptown:
> American Dreaming to a Latin Beat"

This reviewer offers you a number of reasons for choosing this particular musical—the quality of the sound ("bright, piping fanfares from
the trumpets" and "the merry tinkle of a steel drum"), the lead actor's
embodiment of "music's ability to make the trite seem true again," and
the collective joy of the dance ("the energy it gives off could light up the
George Washington Bridge for a year or two"). So you grab a ticket—and
months later see that the reviewer's evaluation of this show was matched
by the Tony Awards Committee.

Evaluations are everyday arguments. By the time you leave home in
the morning, you've likely made a dozen informal evaluations: you've
selected dressy clothes because you have a job interview in the afternoon

Lin-Manuel Miranda celebrating his Tony Award for best musical for *In the Heights*

with a law firm; you've chosen low-fat yogurt and fruit over the pancakes, butter, and syrup you really love; you've queued up the perfect playlist on your iPod for your hike to campus. In each case, you've applied criteria to a particular problem and then made a decision.

Some professional evaluations require more elaborate standards, evidence, and paperwork (imagine an aircraft manufacturer certifying a new jet for passenger service), but they don't differ structurally from the simpler choices that people make routinely. People love to voice their opinions, and they always have. In fact, a mode of ancient rhetoric—called the ceremonial, or *epideictic*—was devoted entirely to speeches of praise and blame. (See Chapter 1.)

Today, rituals of praise and blame are a significant part of American life. Adults who would choke at the notion of debating causal or definitional claims will happily spend hours appraising the Oakland Raiders, Boston Red Sox, or Detroit Pistons. Other evaluative spectacles in our culture include awards shows, beauty pageants, most-valuable-player presentations, lists of best-dressed or worst-dressed celebrities, "sexiest people" magazine covers, literary prizes, political opinion polls, consumer product magazines, and—the ultimate formal public gesture of evaluation—elections. Indeed, making evaluations is a form of entertainment in America and generates big audiences (think of *American Idol*) and revenues.

Evaluations and Academic Arguments

Evaluation is a hallmark of academic argument. You may already be familiar with two important forms of evaluation— postpublication book reviews and peer reviews of articles submitted to scholarly journals for publication (such reviews are most often "blind," in that the reviewer does not know the author's identity).

Take a look at part of one such evaluation, a book review by David Cole, a law professor at Georgetown University, of *Torture Team: Rumsfeld's Memo and the Betrayal of American Values* by Philippe Sands.

America's experiment with torture presents the Obama administration with one of its most difficult challenges: how should the nation account for the abuses that have occurred in the past, what are the appropriate remedies, and how can we ensure that such abuses not happen again? *Torture Team* offers new insight into what will surely be one of the leading human rights issues of the next several years. . . .

Because so many of the facts surrounding the torture policy are now well known, Sands's book is illuminating not so much for breaking new factual ground as for the human insight he brings to the events. Through his interviews, he tells a story about how ordinary human beings, all working within an institution designed to fight by the rules, felt tremendous pressure to bend the rules—and in most cases did so without apparent concern or self-doubt. A narrowly pragmatic ethos guided virtually all actors. The real arguments were for the most part not about whether coercive tactics were legally or morally acceptable, but about whether they worked. Some, especially those in the FBI, felt strongly that they were counterproductive, and that building rapport through noncoercive questioning was the only way to

(continued)

gain credible intelligence from captives. Others thought the idea of building rapport with al-Qaeda suspects was foolish; it could not be done. But with the courageous exception of Navy General Counsel Alberto Mora, few argued that coercive tactics were wrong because they were immoral and illegal, whether or not they worked. In America after September 11, idealists were few and far between, and an amoral, blinkered pragmatism ruled the day.

Sands is an unabashed idealist. He considers it the government lawyer's obligation to be the guardian of legality, even (and especially) where one's clients, the politically elected and appointed decision-makers, have decided that the law and the rules are inconvenient. Sands argues that torture is ineffective, and that building rapport with suspects is the better course. Indeed, he demonstrates in his own interviews the power of rapport to get subjects talking candidly. But in the end, his argument is not a pragmatic one—it is an argument of principle. The prohibition against torture is absolute, and expresses a fundamental norm about human decency, not a practical judgment about what produces results in interrogation.

—David Cole, "What to Do about Torturers"

Even an excerpt from this lengthy review in the *New York Review of Books* reveals the evaluative stance Cole takes: although the book does not add much to previously known facts about "America's experiment with torture," author Sands's compelling human insights and idealist principles make *Torture Team* worthy of careful consideration.

Criteria of Evaluation

Arguments of evaluation can produce simple rankings and winners or can lead to profound decisions about our lives, but they always involve standards. The particular standards we establish for judging anything—whether an idea, a work of art, a person, or a product—are called *criteria of evaluation.* Sometimes criteria are self-evident: an SUV that gets ten miles per gallon is a gas hog, and a piece of fish that smells even a little off shouldn't be eaten. But criteria are often complex when a potential subject is abstract: *What makes a professional referee effective? What features make a song a classic? What constitutes a living wage? How do we measure a successful foreign policy or college career?* Struggling to identify such difficult criteria of evaluation can lead to important insights into your values, motives, and preferences.

Why make such a big deal about criteria when many acts of evaluation seem effortless? We should be suspicious of our judgments even when we make them carelessly. It's irresponsible simply to think that stupid and uninformed opinions should carry the same weight as well-informed and well-reasoned opinions. Evaluations always require reflection, and when we look deeply into our judgments, we sometimes discover important *why* questions that typically go unasked:

- You challenge the grade you received in a course, but you don't question the practice of grading.
- You argue that buying a hybrid car makes more sense than keeping an SUV, but you don't ask whether taking alternative forms of transportation (like the bus or a bike) makes the most sense of all.
- You argue passionately that a Republican Congress is better for America than a Democratic alternative, but you fail to ask why voters get only two choices.

Push an argument of evaluation hard enough, and even simple judgments become challenging and intriguing.

In fact, for many writers, grappling with criteria is the toughest step in producing an evaluation. They've got an opinion about a movie or book or city policy, but they also think that their point is self-evident and widely shared by others. So they don't do the necessary work to specify the criteria for their judgments. If you know a subject well enough to evaluate it, your readers should learn something from you when you offer an opinion.

Do you think, for instance, that you could explain what (if anything) makes a veggie burger good? Though many people have eaten veggie burgers, they probably haven't spent much time thinking about them. But to evaluate them convincingly, it's not enough to claim merely that a good veggie burger is juicy or tasty. Such a claim is also not very interesting. The following criteria offered on the *Cook's Illustrated* Web site show that the writers have given the question quite a bit of thought:

> Store-bought veggie burgers border on inedible, but most homemade renditions are a lot of work. Could we develop a recipe that was really worth the effort? We wanted to create veggie burgers that even meat eaters would love. We didn't want them to taste like hamburgers, but we did want them to act like hamburgers, having a modicum of chew, a harmonious blend of savory ingredients, and the ability to go from grill to bun without falling apart.
>
> —*Cook's Illustrated*

After a lot of experimenting, *Cook's Illustrated* came up with a recipe that met these criteria.

Criteria of evaluation aren't static, either. They differ according to time and audience. Much market research, for example, is designed to find out what particular consumers want now and will want in the future—what their criteria are for buying a product. For a long time, such research indicated that consumers felt that TV was their major source of home entertainment and relegated computers to second place (and to the workplace). But that ranking began to change when online content became readily available. According to a *Los Angeles Times* article, researchers have concluded that "viewers want online video, and studios have decided they'd better give it to them, traditional corporate strategy be damned." This conclusion quickly led to some high-stakes ventures, including Hulu, an Internet video site: it's free, requires no registration or downloads, and gives viewers access to high-resolution top TV shows like Jon Stewart's *The Daily Show*.

One of Hulu's rivals, Veoh, reasons that the criteria of evaluation for such online video are still not completely understood. That is, while providers know that "viewers want online video," they don't yet know what the most *desirable* online video will be. In contrast to Hulu, which offers only a closed system of commercially produced video, Veoh is betting that viewers will continue to want the kind of user-generated content found on YouTube. So it provides both user-generated content and commercially produced shows like *CSI*. Only time will tell which of the new online video sites will better meet the criteria that users demand.

Characterizing Evaluation

One way of understanding evaluative arguments is to consider the types of evidence they use. A distinction we explored in Chapter 4 between hard evidence and arguments based on reason is helpful here. You may recall that we defined *hard evidence* as facts, statistics, testimony, and other kinds of arguments that can be measured, recorded, or even found—the so-called smoking gun in a criminal investigation. We defined *arguments based on reason* as those that are shaped by language, using various kinds of logic.

We can study arguments of evaluation the same way, looking at some as quantitative and others as qualitative. *Quantitative arguments* of evaluation rely on criteria that can be measured, counted, or demonstrated in some mechanical fashion (something is taller, faster, smoother, quieter, or more powerful than something else). In contrast, *qualitative arguments* rely on criteria that must be explained through words, relying on such matters as values, traditions, and emotions (something is more ethical, more beneficial, more handsome, or more noble than something else). A claim of evaluation might be supported by arguments of both sorts.

Fans can watch *Family Guy* on the Internet video site Hulu—but do their ideal criteria for online video also include user-generated content like YouTube?

Quantitative Evaluations

At first glance, quantitative evaluations seem to hold all the cards, especially in a society that is as enamored of science and technology as our own is. After you've defined a quantitative standard, making judgments should be as easy as measuring and counting—and in a few cases, that's the way things work out. *Who's the tallest or heaviest or loudest person in your class?* If your classmates allow themselves to be measured, you could find out easily enough, using the right equipment and internationally sanctioned standards of measurement—the meter, the kilo, or the decibel.

But what if you were to ask, *Who's the smartest person in class?* You could answer this more complex question quantitatively, using IQ tests or college entrance examinations that report results numerically. In fact, almost all college-bound students in the United States submit to this kind of evaluation, taking either the SAT or ACT to demonstrate their verbal and mathematical prowess. Such measures are widely accepted by educators and institutions, but they are also vigorously challenged. What do they actually measure? They predict likely academic success only in college, which is one kind of intelligence.

Quantitative measures of evaluation can be enormously useful, but even the most objective measures have limits. They've been devised by fallible people who look at the world from their own inevitably limited perspectives.

Qualitative Evaluations

Many issues of evaluation that are closest to people's hearts aren't subject to quantification. What makes a movie great? If you suggested a quantitative measure like length, your friends would probably hoot, "Get serious!" But what about box-office receipts, especially if they could be adjusted to reflect inflation? Would films that made the most money—an easily quantifiable measure—be the "best pictures"? That select group would include movies such as *Star Wars, The Sound of Music, Gone with the Wind, Titanic,* and *The Dark Knight.* An interesting group of films—but the best?

Or perhaps you want to argue that the Rotten Tomatoes Web site—with its ratings of films by the Rotten Tomatoes Community, by Top Critics, and by Approved Tomatometer Critics—offers a perfect way to

Not Just Words

Even what looks like totally objective counting can make a powerful evaluative argument. Look at this simple chart kept by the group Iraq Coalition Casualty Count. It offers a measure of U.S., British, and other coalition military fatalities in Iraq from March 20, 2003, when counting began, to July 8, 2009, when this chart was downloaded. What arguments of evaluation could be made based on these purely quantitative data?

MILITARY FATALITIES BY TIME PERIOD: IRAQ COALITION CASUALTY COUNT

Military Fatalities

Period	US	UK	Other*	Total	Days	Avg
7	195	3	0	198	353	0.56
6	1040	46	14	1100	534	2.06
5	933	32	21	986	412	2.39
4	715	13	18	746	318	2.35
3	580	25	27	632	216	2.93
2	718	27	59	804	424	1.90
1	140	33	0	173	43	4.02
Total	4321	179	139	4639	2300	2.02

*Other coalition countries.

Time Periods

Period 7: July 20, 2008–July 8, 2009
Period 6: February 1, 2007–July 19, 2008
Period 5: December 15, 2005–January 31, 2007
Period 4: January 31–December 14, 2005
Period 3: June 29, 2004–January 30, 2005
Period 2: May 2, 2003–June 28, 2004
Period 1: March 20, 2003–May 1, 2003

evaluate films. In the case of *Slumdog Millionaire*, Rotten Tomatoes Community members gave the film a "Tomatometer" score of 92 percent, while the Approved Critics and Top Critics both gave scores of 94 percent.

To argue for online ratings or box-office revenue as a criterion of film greatness, though, you'd have to offer a vigorous defense because many people in the audience would express serious doubts about either criterion. To define the criteria for "great movie," you'd probably look for the standards that serious critics use. You might consider the qualities that are shared by respected movies, such as their societal impact, cinematic technique, dramatic structures, casting, and so on. Most of these markers of quality could be defined with some precision but not measured or counted. Lacking hard numbers, you'd have to make your case rhetorically and convince the audience to accept your standards. A writer using qualitative measures could spend as much time defending criteria of evaluation as providing evidence that these standards are present in a particular film.

But establishing subtle criteria can make arguments of evaluation interesting. They require you, time and again, to challenge conventional wisdom. Look at the way Nick Gillespie in *Reasononline* reviews the last *Star Wars* movie, *Revenge of the Sith*:

> What might be called the continuing cultural hegemony of *Star Wars* is no small matter. With the possible exception of *The Lord of the Rings*, no other franchise has maintained a similar hold on the public imagination for so long a period of time. In a curious way, the first two installments in *The Godfather* saga did (as evidenced by the appropriation of its themes and motifs in everything from countless lesser mob movies to standup comedy to rap music). But it's undeniable that *Star Wars* is in the warp and woof of American culture, ranging from politics to toys to, of course, movies, novels, and comic books. It very much provides a backdrop, a framework, a system of reference for the ways we talk about things, whether we're talking about missile defense systems, visions of the future and technology, good vs. evil, you name it.
>
> This is all the more stunning given the generally acknowledged mediocrity of the *Star Wars* movies themselves. Indeed, it's a given that if *Star Wars* didn't start to go downhill sometime during the "Cantina Band" sequence in the very first flick, then the series actively started to suck wind harder than Billy Dee Williams in an action sequence by the start of the third release, *Return of the Jedi*, a film so bad that it may well be the space opera equivalent of *The Day the Clown*

Cried. (Personally, I lay in with those who peg the beginning of the end, if not the actual end of the end—or perhaps the high point—of the whole series to 1978's little-remembered yet still nightmare-inducing *The Star Wars Holiday Special,* which comes as close to the death-inducing video in *The Ring* as anything ever shown on non-premium cable.)

And yet, despite the craptacular nature of at least four out of six *Star Wars* movies, there's little doubt that no film event has been more anticipated than *Revenge of the Sith* (with the possible exception—and in France only—of the next *Asterix et Obelix* extravaganza).

—Nick Gillespie, "*Star Wars,* Nothing but *Star Wars*"

As Gillespie acknowledges, the *Star Wars* saga is full of flaws, some of them of a "craptacular" nature. And yet he goes on to make a much more subtle argument:

The enormous *Star Wars* industry—the movies, the cartoons, the toys, the pop-cult references—still generates interest, excitement, pleasure (this last is something that most critics, whether liberal or conservative

Does *Star Wars: The Clone Wars,* which premiered in August 2008, meet Nick Gillespie's criteria for continuing what he calls "a cultural conversation worth having"?

find absolutely terrifying), and, most important, a cultural conversation worth having. The series may well be crap—and a grave disappointment to critics who know so much better than the rest of us—but surely that's the least interesting thing about it.

Gillespie certainly knows that not everyone will agree with his assessment of the *Star Wars* saga, but his lengthy review makes clear to readers why he has come to the qualitative decision that the movies have nurtured "a cultural conversation worth having." Fans of the series are wondering whether that conversation will continue to be important in the animated continuation, *Star Wars: The Clone Wars.*

Developing an Evaluative Argument

Developing an argument of evaluation can seem like a simple process, especially if you already know what your claim is likely to be:

Citizen Kane is the finest film ever made by an American director.

Having established a claim, you would then explore the implications of your belief, drawing out the reasons, warrants, and evidence that might support it:

Claim	**Citizen Kane is the finest film ever made by an American director . . .**
Reason	**. . . because it revolutionizes the way we see the world.**
Warrant	**Great films change viewers in fundamental ways.**
Evidence	**Shot after shot, Citizen Kane presents the life of its protagonist through cinematic images that viewers can never forget.**

The warrant here is, in effect, a statement of criteria—in this case, the quality that defines "great film" for the writer.

In developing an evaluative argument, you'll want to pay special attention to criteria, claims, and evidence.

Formulating Criteria

Often neglected in evaluations is the discussion of criteria. Although even casual evaluations (*The band sucks!*) might be traced to reasonable criteria, most people don't bother defending their positions until they are challenged (*Oh yeah?*). Yet when writers address readers whom they understand or with whom they share core values, they don't defend most of their criteria in detail. A film critic like Roger Ebert isn't expected to restate all his principles every time he writes a movie review. Ebert assumes that his readers will—over time—come to appreciate his standards.

Still, the criteria can make or break a piece. In an essay from Salon .com's series of evaluative arguments called "Masterpieces," writer Stephanie Zacharek can barely contain her enthusiasm for the Chrysler Building in midtown Manhattan:

Why does this building make people happy?

> Architects, who have both intuition and training on their side, have some very good reasons for loving the Chrysler Building. The rest of us love it beyond reason, for its streamlined majesty and its inherent sense of optimism and promise for the future, but mostly for its shimmery, welcoming beauty—a beauty that speaks of humor and elegance in equal measures, like a Noel Coward play.
>
> How can a mere building make so many people so happy—particularly so many ornery New Yorkers, who often pretend, as part of their act, not to like anything? There may be New Yorkers who dislike the Chrysler Building, but they rarely step forward in public. To do so would only invite derision and disbelief.
>
> —Stephanie Zacharek,
> "The Chrysler Building"

It may seem odd to suggest that one measure of a great building is that it makes people happy. And so the writer has a lot to prove. She's got to provide evidence that a building can, in fact, be delightful. And she seems to do precisely that later in the same essay when she gives life even to the windows in the skyscraper:

> Looking at the Chrysler Building now, though, it's hard to argue against its stylish ebullience, or its special brand of sophisticated cheerfulness. . . . Particularly at night, the crown's triangular windows—lit up, fanned out and stacked high into the sky—suggest a sense of movement that has more in common with dance than with architecture: Those rows of windows are as joyous and seductive as a chorus line of Jazz Age cuties, a bit of sexy night life rising up boldly from an otherwise businesslike skyline.

The criteria that Zacharek uses lead to an inventive and memorable evaluation that perhaps teaches readers to look at buildings in a whole new way.

The iPhone 3GS

So don't take criteria of evaluation for granted. If you offer vague, dull, or unsupportable principles, expect to be challenged. You're most likely to be vague about your beliefs when you haven't thought enough about your subject. Push yourself at least as far as you imagine readers will. Imagine readers looking over your shoulder, asking difficult questions. Say, for example, that you intend to argue that anyone who wants to stay on the cutting edge of personal technology will obviously prefer Apple's iPhone 3GS because it's not only a great phone but a great handheld computer. But what does that mean? What makes the device "great"? Is it that it gives access to email and the wireless Web, has a widescreen iPod, has a hybrid GPS-Wi-Fi-cell tower triangulator that pinpoints your location on the iPhone's Google, and has an astonishing number of applications? These provide some criteria that you could defend. But should you get more—or less—technical? Do you need to assert very sophisticated criteria to establish your authority to write about the subject? These are appropriate questions to ask.

Making Claims

Claims can be stated directly or, in rare instances, strongly implied. For most writers, a direct evaluative claim with the statement carefully qualified works best. Consider the differences between the following three claims and how much greater the burden of proof for the first claim would be than the burden for the second and third ones:

> Margaret Cho is the most outrageous comedian around today.

> Margaret Cho is one of the three or four most outrageous comedians around today.

> Margaret Cho may come to be regarded as one of the most outrageous comedians of her time.

The most outrageous of them all? Margaret Cho in 2008 lamé mode.

The point of qualifying a statement isn't to make evaluative claims bland but to make them responsible and reasonable. Consider how *Pitchfork* critic Mary Pytlik evaluates a recent album, M.I.A.'s *Kala*:

In contrast to her comparatively sparkly and streamlined debut, *Kala* is clattering, buzzy, and sonically audacious. While it still sounds, for lack of a better word, as *digital* as its predecessor, the primarily Switch-produced album paradoxically reaches further than the produced-by-committee *Arular* in terms of its overall palette of sounds. From the disco bassline and gloopy Eurovision strings of the swimmy Bollywood cover "Jimmy" to the hairy didgeridoos and pitched-up elementary school raps (courtesy of Aboriginal schoolboy crew Wilcannia Mob) of "Mango Pickle Down River" to the bubbling synths of the gloriously woozy "20 Dollar," this represents a significant expansion of M.I.A.'s already big tent of sounds. It also signifies her expansion as a performer. Where *Arular* saw her make the best of her fairly limited vocal

Sri Lankan–British rapper M.I.A. has won critical praise for her genre-bending hip-hop music.

abilities, *Kala* finds her reaching further outward, either by singing sweetly, as she does capably on "Jimmy," by peppering her chatter with sudden, free-floating melodies ("20 Dollar"), or by simply putting even more emphasis on the elastic qualities of her usual sing-songy delivery, as she does on the pinched-nose baile funk of "World Town" and the celebratory first single "Boyz"—a triumph of her rhythmic patter if there ever was one.

—Mary Pytlik, "M.I.A.: *Kala*"

Pytlik offers evidence to prove the claim that M.I.A.'s new album is in many ways a "triumph," but she also qualifies that claim by noting that in *Kala* the singer has had to overcome some inherent weaknesses ("her fairly limited vocal abilities," "her usual sing-songy delivery"). Pointing to flaws as well as to successes is an easier task than trying to argue that this set of songs is flawless.

Presenting Evidence

The more evidence in an evaluation the better, provided that the evidence is relevant. For example, in evaluating the performance of two computers, the speed of their processors would be important, but the quality of their keyboards or the availability of service might be less crucial.

Just as important as relevance in selecting evidence is presentation. Not all pieces of evidence are equally convincing, nor should they be treated as such. Select the evidence that is most likely to impress your readers, and arrange the argument to build toward your best material. In most cases, that best material will be evidence that's specific, detailed, and derived from credible sources. Look at the details in these paragraphs of Sean Wilsey's review of *Fun Home: A Family Tragicomic*, a graphic novel by Alison Bechdel:

> If the theoretical value of a picture is still holding steady at a thousand words, then Alison Bechdel's slim yet Proustian graphic memoir, *Fun*

Home, must be the most ingeniously compact, hyper-verbose example of autobiography to have been produced. It is a pioneering work, pushing two genres (comics and memoir) in multiple new directions, with panels that combine the detail and technical proficiency of R. Crumb with a seriousness, emotional complexity and innovation completely its own. Then there are the actual words. Generally this is where graphic narratives stumble. Very few cartoonists can also write—or, if they can, they manage only to hit a few familiar notes. But *Fun Home* quietly succeeds in telling a story, not only through well-crafted images but through words that are equally revealing and well chosen. Big words, too! In 232 pages this memoir sent me to the dictionary five separate times (to look up "bargeboard," "buss," "scutwork," "humectant" and "perseverated").

A comic book for lovers of words! Bechdel's rich language and precise images combine to create a lush piece of work — a memoir where concision and detail are melded for maximum, obsessive density. She has obviously spent years getting this memoir right, and it shows. You can read *Fun Home* in a sitting, or get lost in the pictures within the pictures on its pages. The artist's work is so absorbing you feel you are living in her world.

—Sean Wilsey, "The Things They Buried"

The details in this passage are rich enough to make the case that Alison Bechdel's novel is one that pushes both comics and memoirs in new directions.

In evaluation arguments, don't be afraid to concede a point when evidence goes contrary to the overall claim you wish to make. If you're really skillful, you can even turn a problem into an argumentative asset, as Bob Costas does in acknowledging the flaws of baseball great Mickey Mantle in the process of praising him:

None of us, Mickey included, would want to be held to account for every moment of our lives. But how many of us could say that our best moments were as magnificent as his?

—Bob Costas, "Eulogy for Mickey Mantle"

Considering Design and Visuals

In thinking about how to present your evidence, don't forget to consider the visual aspects of doing so. Design features—such as headings for the

A direct visual representation of what you are evaluating, such as this page from Alison Bechdel's *Fun Home*, can be critical to an evaluation's success.

different criteria you're using or, in online evaluations, links to material related to your subject—can enhance your authority, credibility, and persuasiveness. Think, too, about how you might use visual evidence to good effect. For example, you might use a bar graph to show how your subject measures up to a similar one. In a review of *Fun Home*, Sean Wilsey might have used the page shown above from the book to illustrate his point that "*Fun Home* quietly succeeds in telling a story, not only through well-crafted images but through words that are equally revealing and well chosen. Big words, too!"

Key Features of Evaluations

In drafting an evaluation, you should consider three basic elements:

- an evaluative claim that makes a judgment about a person, an idea, or an object
- the criterion or criteria by which you'll measure your subject
- evidence that the particular subject meets or falls short of the stated criteria

All these elements will be present in arguments of evaluation, but they won't follow a specific order. In addition, you'll often need an opening paragraph to explain what you're evaluating and why. Tell readers why they should care about your subject and take your opinion seriously.

Nothing adds more depth to an opinion than letting others challenge it. When you can, use the resources of the Internet or more local online networks to get responses to your opinions. It can be eye-opening to realize how strongly people react to ideas or points of view that you regard as perfectly normal. When you're ready, share your draft with friends and classmates, asking them to identify places where your ideas need additional support, either in the discussion of criteria or in the presentation of evidence.

GUIDE to writing an evaluation

● Finding a Topic

You're entering an argument of evaluation when you

- make a judgment about quality: Citizen Kane *is probably the finest film ever made by an American director.*
- challenge such a judgment: Citizen Kane *is vastly overrated by most film critics.*
- construct a ranking or comparison: Citizen Kane *is a more intellectually challenging movie than* Casablanca.

Issues of evaluation arise daily—in the judgments you make about public figures or policies; in the choices you make about instructors and courses; in the recommendations you make about books, films, or television programs; in the preferences you exercise in choosing products, activities, or charities. Be alert to evaluative arguments whenever you read or use terms that indicate value or rank—*good/bad, effective/ineffective, best/worst, competent/incompetent, successful/unsuccessful.* Finally, be aware of your own areas of expertise. Write about subjects or topics about which others regularly ask your opinion or advice.

● Researching Your Topic

You can research issues of evaluation by using the following sources:

- journals, reviews, and magazines (for current political and social issues)
- books (for assessing judgments about history, policy, etc.)
- biographies (for assessing people)
- research reports and scientific studies
- books, magazines, and Web sites for consumers
- periodicals and Web sites that cover entertainment and sports
- blogs for exploring current affairs

Surveys and polls can be useful in uncovering public attitudes: *What books are people reading? Who are the most admired people in the country? What activities or businesses are thriving or waning?* You'll discover that Web sites, newsgroups, and blogs thrive on evaluation. Browse these public forums for ideas, and, when possible, explore your own topic ideas there. But remember that all sources need to be evaluated—especially those you plan to use in an evaluation argument. So examine each source carefully, making sure that it is legitimate and credible.

● Formulating a Claim

After exploring your subject, begin to formulate a full and specific claim, a thesis that lets readers know where you stand and on what criteria you'll base your judgments. Look for a thesis that's challenging enough to attract readers' attention, not one that merely repeats views already widely held. In moving toward this thesis, you might begin with questions like these:

- What exactly is my opinion? Where do I stand?
- Can I make my judgment more specific?
- Do I need to qualify my claim?
- According to what standards am I making my judgment?
- Will readers accept my criteria, or will I have to defend them, too?
- What major reasons can I offer in support of my evaluation?

Your thesis should be a complete statement. In one sentence, you need to make a claim of evaluation and state the reasons that support your claim. Be sure your claim is specific. Anticipate the questions readers might have: *Who? What? Where? Under what conditions? With what exceptions? In all cases?* Don't expect readers to guess where you stand.

● Examples of Evaluative Claims

- Though they may never receive Oscars for their work, Sandra Bullock and Keanu Reeves deserve credit as actors who have succeeded in a wider range of film roles than most of their contemporaries.
- Many computer users are discovering that Microsoft's Vista is more trouble than it is worth.
- Barack Obama's speech on race, delivered in Philadelphia on March 18, 2008, is the most honest presentation of this issue we have heard since Martin Luther King's time.

- Jimmy Carter has been highly praised for his work as a former president of the United States, but history may show that even his much-derided term in office laid the groundwork for the foreign policy and economic successes now attributed to later administrations.

- Because knowledge changes so quickly and people switch careers so often, an effective education today is one that trains people how to learn more than it teaches them what to know.

● Preparing a Proposal

If your instructor asks you to prepare a proposal for your project, here's a format that may help:

State your thesis completely. If you're having trouble doing so, try outlining it in Toulmin terms:

Claim:

Reason(s):

Warrant(s):

- **Explain why this issue deserves attention. What's at stake?**
- **Specify whom you hope to reach through your argument and why this group of readers would be interested in it.**
- **Briefly discuss the key challenges you anticipate: Defining criteria? Defending them? Finding quantitative evidence to support your claim? Developing qualitative arguments to bolster your judgment?**
- **Determine what research strategies you'll use. What sources do you expect to consult?**
- **Consider what format you expect to use for your project: A conventional research essay? A letter to the editor? A Web page?**

● Thinking about Organization

Your evaluation may take various forms, but it's likely to include elements such as the following:

- a specific claim: *Most trucks are unsuitable for the kind of driving Americans do.*
- an explanation or defense of the criteria (if necessary): *The overcrowding and pollution of American cities and suburbs might be relieved if more Americans*

drove small, fuel-efficient cars. Cars do less damage in accidents than heavy trucks and are also less likely to roll over.

- an examination of the claim in terms of the stated criteria: *Most trucks are unsuitable for the kind of driving Americans do because they are not designed for contemporary urban driving conditions.*

- evidence for every part of the argument: *Trucks get very poor gas mileage; they are statistically more likely than cars to roll over in accidents; . . .*

- consideration of alternative views and counterarguments: *It is true, perhaps, that trucks make drivers feel safer on the roads and give them a better view of traffic conditions. . . .*

● Getting and Giving Response

All arguments benefit from the scrutiny of others. Your instructor may assign you to a peer group for the purpose of reading and responding to each other's drafts. If not, ask for responses from some serious readers or consultants at a writing center. You can use the following questions to evaluate a draft. If you're evaluating someone else's draft, be sure to illustrate your points with examples. Specific comments are always more helpful than general observations.

The Claim

- Is the claim clearly an argument of evaluation? Does it make a judgment about something?

- Does the claim establish clearly what's being evaluated?

- Is the claim too sweeping? Does it need to be qualified?

- Will the criteria used in the evaluation be clear to readers? Do the criteria need to be defined more explicitly or precisely?

- Are the criteria appropriate ones to use for this evaluation? Are they controversial? Does evidence of their validity need to be added?

Evidence for the Claim

- Is enough evidence furnished to ensure that what's being evaluated meets the criteria established for the evaluation? If not, what kind of additional evidence is needed?

- Is the evidence in support of the claim simply announced, or are its significance and appropriateness analyzed? Is a more detailed discussion needed?

- Are any objections readers might have to the claim, criteria, or evidence adequately addressed?
- What kinds of sources, including visual sources, are cited? How credible and persuasive will they be to readers? What other kinds of sources might be more credible and persuasive?
- Are all quotations introduced with appropriate signal phrases (such as "As Will argues, . . .") and blended smoothly into the writer's sentences?

Organization and Style

- How are the parts of the argument organized? Is this organization effective, or would some other structure work better?
- Will readers understand the relationships among the claims, supporting reasons, warrants, and evidence? If not, what could be done to make those connections clearer? Are more transitional words and phrases needed? Would headings or graphic devices help?
- Are the transitions or links from point to point, paragraph to paragraph, and sentence to sentence clear and effective? If not, how could they be improved?
- Are all visuals carefully integrated into the text? Is each visual introduced and commented on to point out its significance? Is each visual labeled as a figure or a table and given a caption as well as a citation?
- Is the style suited to the subject? Is it too formal? Too casual? Too technical? Too bland? How can it be improved?
- Which sentences seem particularly effective? Which ones seem weakest, and how could they be improved? Should some short sentences be combined, or should any long ones be separated into two or more sentences?
- How effective are the paragraphs? Do any seem too skimpy or too long? How can they be improved?
- Which words or phrases seem particularly effective, vivid, and memorable? Do any seem dull, vague, unclear, or inappropriate for the audience or the writer's purpose? Are definitions provided for technical or other terms that readers might not know?

Spelling, Punctuation, Mechanics, Documentation, Format

- Are there any errors in spelling, punctuation, capitalization, and the like?

- Is an appropriate and consistent style of documentation used for parenthetical citations and the list of works cited or references? (See Chapter 20.)
- Does the paper or project follow an appropriate format? Is it appropriately designed and attractively presented? How could it be improved? If it's a Web site, do all the links work?

RESPOND●

1. Choose one item from the following list that you understand well enough to evaluate. Develop several criteria of evaluation that you could defend to distinguish excellence from mediocrity in the area. Then choose an item that you don't know much about and explain the research you might do to discover reasonable criteria of evaluation for it.

   fashion designers

   Navajo rugs

   musicals

   spoken word poetry

   UN secretaries-general

   NFL quarterbacks

   social networking sites

   TV journalists

   video games

   organic vegetables

   animated films

   universal health care plans

2. In the last ten years, there has been a proliferation of awards programs for movies, musicians, sports figures, and other categories. For example, before the Academy of Motion Picture Arts and Sciences hands out the Oscars, a half-dozen other organizations have given prizes to the annual crop of films. Write a short opinion piece assessing the merits of a particular awards show or a feature such as *People*'s annual "sexiest man" issue. What should a proper event of this kind accomplish? Does the event you're reviewing do so?

3. Local news and entertainment magazines often publish "best of" issues or articles that list readers' and editors' favorites in such categories as "best place to go on a first date," "best ice cream sundae," and "best dentist." Sometimes the categories are specific: "best places to say 'I was retro before retro was cool'" or "best movie theater seats." Imagine that you're the editor of your own local magazine and that you want to put out a "best of" issue tailored to your hometown. Develop ten categories for evaluation. For each category, list the evaluative criteria that you would use to make your judgment. Next, consider that because your criteria are warrants, they're especially tied to audience. (The criteria for "best dentist," for example, might be

tailored to people whose major concern is avoiding pain, to those whose children will be regular clients, or to those who want the cheapest possible dental care.) For several of the evaluative categories, imagine that you have to justify your judgments to a completely different audience. Write a new set of criteria for that audience.

4. Develop an argument using (or challenging) one of the criteria of evaluation presented in this chapter. You might explore one of the following topics:

   Immigrant workers deserve a fair wage and minimal benefits.

   A car should be energy efficient.

   Good songs remain in people's memories.

   Great films change viewers in fundamental ways.

   Good pets need not have fur and four legs.

   Great veggie burgers need just the right shape and texture.

5. For examples of powerful evaluation arguments, search the Web or your library for obituaries of famous, recently deceased individuals. Try to locate at least one such item, and analyze the types of claims it makes about the deceased. What criteria of evaluation are employed? What kinds of evidence does it present?

The Burden of Laughter: Chris Rock Fights Ignorance His Way

JACK CHUNG

Adorned in an expensive black leather jacket, the skinny comedian with the well-trimmed goatee spits out controversial insights in his angry, signature shrill voice. The hoots and hollers of the sold-out audience are intermingled with frenzied applause. The man of the hour, Chris Rock, is performing at the Apollo Theater in Harlem, only a few blocks away from where he grew up. This particular stand-up routine, entitled *Bigger and Blacker*, is Rock's third HBO special and it comes after the years of performing in smoky comic clubs, after his unfruitful years at *SNL*, after his landmark HBO special *Bring the Pain*, and after the two Emmy wins. It is 1999, and Chris Rock is on top of the comedic world.

Chris Rock! Chris Rock! Chris Rock! The comedian has become a household name in America, and he is seen everywhere from movies to talk shows to TV commercials to the documentary *Good Hair* that he presented at Sundance in 2009. More importantly, he has become arguably the most talked-about comedian of today, and he has intellectual defenders and critics who both agree

Evaluative claim stated and elaborated on

Jack Chung wrote "The Burden of Laughter: Chris Rock Fights Ignorance His Way" when he was a student in Alyssa O'Brien's first-year writing class at Stanford University. The essay (which has been shortened for use in this book) was later published in *The Boothe Prize Essays*, a volume devoted to outstanding undergraduate student writing. In commenting on this essay, O'Brien notes that it is "structured as a series of miniature performances" and that it "delves deep into the complicated history of Blackface minstrelsy, 'coon' stereotypes, and 'Jim Crow' humor" to evaluate Rock's use of humor and to argue forcefully for its effectiveness in "carrying on the tradition of a painful yet treasured humor that has long been intricately woven into the fabric of African American culture." Chung uses many sources for his essay and follows MLA style in citing them.

that the man holds a significant role in the debate over sociopolitical issues of race that rage across the nation. Interestingly, throughout the discussion of Rock's importance in affecting the public's perspective of race relations, the comedian himself has noticeably downplayed his role. He has persistently answered to both admirers and critics that he is nothing more than a "Jokeman," and that his only concern is to be funny (Rock, "Rock on a Roll" 3). However, whether or not Rock is sincere in devaluing his position as a social commentator, his comic material and activities off the stage suggest that he is indeed one of the forerunners in shaping Americans' perception of African Americans as a race, and he is a leader, though an unwilling one, in tearing down the stereotypes that both whites and black have of each other.

Evidence of claim that Rock's humor is painfully honest and often angry— a criterion by which it can be evaluated.

With his painfully honest and often angry humor, Rock upholds the traditional African-American humor that originates from the days of slavery, and he pioneers that humor to a new direction with his conscious efforts to portray the diversity of Black America. *Nothing more racist than an old black man. Because old black men went through real racism. He didn't go through that "I can't get a cab" shit. He was the cab. The white man would jump on his back and say, "Main Street." "Left, nigga! Left, you fuckin nigga!"* (Rock, *Bigger and Blacker*)

Forty minutes into his special *Bigger and Blacker*, Rock introduces this bit on the injustices that blacks suffered during the heyday of the civil rights era, and now there is a twinge of discomfort among the audience members, a discomfort echoed in Harvard psychologist A. Poussaint's assertion that such "street" comedy surely encourages the acceptance of white superiority rather than challenging it. *The New Republic* goes further by deriding it as humor that is "attempting to shuck, jive, grin, shout, and bulge [its] eyes all the way back to the days of minstrelsy" (Driver 29). Such criticism is not light, for it charges Rock's comedy with reverting to the Jim Crow humor of the nineteenth and early twentieth centuries, therefore

Counter-argument: Rock's humor does not tear down but rather perpetuates stereotypes.

undermining the progress that blacks have made in challenging such prejudiced images of themselves.

To support his argument that Chris Rock is reminiscent of the "coons" of the minstrel shows of the nineteenth century, Justin Driver gives a short history lesson of the blackface minstrels in his *New Republic* article. The minstrel shows were popularized in the 1830s by white performers who mimicked blacks by wearing black face paint, and eventually by the 1850s blacks had formed their own troupes of minstrels through which they presented the ignorant "coon" that shucked and jived (Driver 29). In this sense, Rock's buffoonish gestures can be seen as reminiscent of the minstrels, and his voice—"a high-pitched, piercing shrill that seems to work most effectively when shouted through a grotesquely enormous grin" (29)—is nothing more than a device to convey the profanity that is crucial to Rock's angry delivery (30).

Driver is not the only critic who finds Rock's profanity irrelevant; legendary comedian Bill Cosby, offended by the vulgar language in Rock's comedy, asked Rock to remove his comedy album from Rock's opening act of the *Bring the Pain* special (Kamp 9). However, another legendary comedian, Jerry Seinfeld, defends Rock's rhetorical usage of his voice by claiming, "It's the yelling that makes it special" (qtd. in Farley 67). Indeed, when Rock shouts out the vulgar words in his routine, it is almost as if they are *meant* to grate against the ear and create the caustic pain and laughter that Rock seeks. An exasperated Rock points this out to those who cannot comprehend his use of foul language in an interview by yelling, "You ignorant people, grow up. Cursing is used for emphasis; it's never the joke" (qtd. in Nelson 2).

Paradoxically, even with his supposed "reactionary" comedic style that conjures up images of the "coons" past, Chris Rock is extremely popular with black audiences. Justin Driver dismisses this popularity by stating that African Americans have come to enjoy such politically incorrect gestures of minstrelsy because they

Evidence in support of counterargument

A counter to the counterargument introduced

have endured "coon" comedy for such a long time (32). Dexter B. Gordon, author of the article "Humor in African American Discourse: Speaking of Oppression" in *Journal of Black Studies*, disagrees with Driver, and, although he never alludes to Chris Rock in his article, his analysis of African comic traditions makes the best argument in defense of Rock's rhetorical strategies on stage. Gordon argues that at its core, African-American humor is a diverse product that ranges from the quaint and delightful to the most often obscene, bitter, and sardonic (2). He goes on to claim that much of what Driver finds offensive in Rock's presentation—the jiving, the shouting, and the shuckin—are actually distinctive "games" of African-American culture (Gordon 3). And whereas Driver sees these characteristics as traits used to "assuage white concerns about the moral propriety of slavery" (Driver 30), Gordon sees them as "part of the humor that continues to fulfill the need for a sense of power in the midst of misery, the need for both a morale booster and amusement in Black culture" (Gordon 3). His assertion that "shuckin" and "jiving" is part of African-American lore supports the idea that Chris Rock's rhetorical strategies are not a return to "coon comedy"— rather they are part of a continuation of African-American humor that keeps intact its unique methods of delivering humor.

Evidence in support of the claim that Rock's humor reflects distinct African American culture and style

One of the reasons that Rock is so successful in transforming the boundless rage of his material into a product of uproarious laughter is his keen understanding that his humor carries the seriousness and shame that Gordon links to African-American humor. Gordon says, "At its base, then, African American humor is very serious" (2), and Rock reveals this insight when he reflects on his own work: "I don't think anything I ever said onstage isn't something I first said in a conversation being perfectly serious" (qtd. in Nelson 3). Gordon also mentions that an important aspect of African-American humor is self-deprecation (2), and Rock uses this tool in a sophisticated manner that is developed through various aspects

Another criterion introduced: self-deprecating humor with a distinct edge is characteristic of Rock's humor.

of his comedy. For instance, in his book, Rock tackles the controversial subject of the word "nigger" that both blacks and whites would prefer to shy away from, and he says, "Of course, 'nigger' is just a word. White people could call us anything, like 'butter.' 'Hey you fucking butter! Pick that cotton, butter!'" By discussing the "N" word in the comedic form of the word "butter," he reduces the dignity of blacks as the "N" word is originally meant to, but he does it in a way so that readers are able to comprehend that he mocks the word and not black people. He doesn't stop there, however; he carries that joke further in his TV show, *The Chris Rock Show*, by playing a pseudo-commercial in which blacks rave about a cereal called "Nigga Please." At first glance, the casual use of the word in the parody seems derogatory to black people, but Rock uses self-degradation and even extends it to social degradation to derail the vulgarity of the word "nigger." Of course, not all of the audience gets the complex joke, and some come away offended by the coarse satire, but Rock accepts this as part of his ongoing attempt to stray from the "good-natured" humor of Aristotle and Plato: "Somebody should always be offended. Somebody in your life should always be like, 'Why did you do that?' Always. That's just being a real artist. That's the difference between Scorsese and Disney" (qtd. in Farley 68). The quote by itself is a memorable sound bite, but when Rock says on stage that a white busboy would not change positions with even a rich black man, the quote becomes the centerpiece of a philosophy of a man who has dedicated his life to bring out the wincing grimace of his spectators.

The question then arises as to why Rock turns to potentially controversial humor in his comedic acts. Why is it that he's not afraid of the angry beehive he might stir up when he says on stage, "There ain't a white man in this room who'd change places with me"? Much of his bold and perhaps even reckless courage in choosing his subject matters comes from his own personal experience.

Use of controversial humor discussed: another characteristic of Rock's style

Biographical
information
introduced

As a teenager growing up in Brooklyn, New York, in the post–civil rights 1970s, Rock was sent to an all-white school in Bensonhurst by a mother who wanted a better education for her son (Farley 68). At the high school Rock claims that he was beaten regularly and called "nigger" every day by "white toxic waste" (Hammer 1, 3), and it is from such hellish torture that "he came away with a kind of sad wisdom that will never leave him and thoroughly inhibits his humor" (Schruers 40). Friend and actor Joe Pesci explains that Chris Rock feels entitled to poke fun of both blacks and whites because he experienced racism directly (qtd. in Nelson 2), and the result is a comedian who sounds off incisive remarks to both races. In *Rock This*, Rock says of white people, "Broke-ass white people have it bad. I'll bet you a set of black satin sheets that 80 percent of the Ku Klux Klan makes less than $13,000 a year" (29). It is debatable whether Rock truly has the liberty to denigrate another race based on his past school experience, but it is an unimportant debate; in answering the original question of the source of Rock's fearlessness, the point is that he feels he has the right to show the failings of both white and black people.

While Rock's schooling definitely led him to find humor in all groups of people, it did not affect his work as much as the loss of his father, who died in 1989 from a ruptured ulcer after spending 55 years of his life holding two jobs as a union trucker and a cab driver (Schruers 42). At the time of his father's death, Rock was a struggling comedian trying to make a name for himself: with his father's death, something changed. Looking back, Rock says, "The only time I ever wanted to give it up is when my dad died" (qtd. in Chappell 168). Rock, however, did not give up; instead, he came away from the experience with a new sense of urgency to take risks in his comedy before he had to face his own death. In a *Rolling Stone* interview with Fred Schruers, Rock shares some of his thoughts: "You could be played out tomorrow and it's no fault of your own. . . . Work as hard as you can . . . and go out swinging. If you're going to make mistakes, make aggressive mistakes" (qtd. in Schruers 64). This epiphany freed Rock to produce the edgy comedic sketches that paved his way to fame. In an ironic and cruel twist of fate, the death of Rock's father may have been a great gift; Rock was now finally ready to unleash his most insightful fury.

> There's, like, a civil war going on with black people, and there's two sides: there's black people . . . and there's niggas. And niggas have got to go! Every time black people want to have a good time, ign'ant-ass niggas fuck it up! Can't do shit without some ign'ant-ass niggas fuckin it up!
> (Rock, *Bring the Pain*)

"Niggas vs. Black People." The notorious comic sketch from his 1996 HBO special remains his most divisive and brilliant piece of work, and it is repeated and discussed to this day. When Chris Rock proclaimed this manifesto in front of a large viewing audience, he floored everyone, blacks and whites, by unveiling thoughts that blacks had of each other. *Can't do nothing! Can't keep a disco open more than three weeks. Grand opening closing!* The white media was amazed by this revelation that blacks were critical of some members of their own community, and they praised Rock for his daring monologue (Farley 69). Blacks, on the other hand, were divided on the piece; some loved it for what they saw as an honest portrayal while others hated it for the possibility that it could lead to even more stereotypical thinking among white people. The opinions on "Niggas vs. Black People" varied greatly, but no one could deny the importance of the piece in explaining Rock's views on race.

When Chris Rock presented "Niggas vs. Black People" in *Bring the Pain*, he believed that he was speaking to a mostly African-American audience about the "gangsta" blacks that other blacks despised for the negative image they portrayed to the media. Even after the backlash Rock received for the routine, he held steadfastly to his

Another criterion—risk taking—is central to Rock's humor.

The 1996 HBO sketch noted as meeting the evaluative criteria discussed notion that there were a minority of "Niggas" in the black community who undermine much of the positive values that the majority of black hold. Fellow comedian Mario Joiner agrees with Rock's perspective by commenting on the sketch, "Every black person can relate to it—hell, you got cousins you don't want to be around" (Kamp 6). Support also came in the form of Rock's mother in a 1998 *60 Minutes* interview with Ed Bradley when she defended her son's monologue by saying, "I love my people. I don't want to live next door to niggers either" ("Chris Rock: Comedy").

However, Ed Bradley, a black man himself, was unsatisfied by Ms. Rock's input on the matter and demanded to know the difference between "niggers" and black people. His grilling of the comedian's mother seemed to imply that he disapproved of Rock's performance because it fails to divide a clear line between the supposed two distinct groups of people, and the confusion may lead to racial stereotypical thinking in which all blacks are regarded as having some "nigga" characteristics.

Indeed, Justin Driver argues that Rock's well-intentioned but unconvincing separation of "niggas" from black people "legitimates [certain whites'] racist view of the world" (31). He then concludes his article by saying that Rock belongs to a group of comedians and rappers who feed stereotypes of blacks by "extolling negative behavior among African Americans as the only genuine blackness" and that his work "obscures the rich and varied truth about black life in America today" (33).

As adamant as some critics are in their belief that Rock tarnishes the image of blacks in the eyes of the rest of America, there are those who would counter that such bits as "Niggas vs. Black People" shed light on the elasticity of the black experience. In response to *The New Republic*'s searing criticism, *Time* writer Bruce Handy defends Rock by saying, "I would wager that Rock is making a point about how street culture celebrates boorish behavior, and how that can feed racist stereotypes, and how dispiriting that is" (67). With this statement, Handy directly contradicts Driver with his opinion that Rock does not perpetrate stereotypes with his comedy but rather seeks to help the black majority discard the negative labels brought on by the "gangsta" nihilism of a handful of blacks who are overly represented in television and music. Jill Nelson echoes similar sentiments when she says that the black majority that Rock supposedly wants to reveal to the public is a broad range of working-class people who seek to move forward, not backwards (1). In one particular segment of *Rock This*, Rock is especially apparent as the frustrated voice of the "silent black majority" when he exclaims, "White people don't know how to tell the difference between one black man and another. If they could, we'd all get along. . . . To white people, even Ed Bradley and Bryant Gumbel hanging out, waiting to cross the street together, is potentially scary" (11).

The debate continues, as critics charge Rock with encouraging stereotypes.

Even if Rock fights rather than encourages stereotyping, there remains the criticism of his "Niggas vs. Black People" riff that it exposes the taboo subjects spoken amongst only blacks to the public for full disclosure. In his interview with *60 Minutes*, Rock deduces that much of his criticism from black people on the use of the "N" word comes because he says it where white people could hear it ("Chris Rock: Comedy"). Professor and cultural critic Michael Eric Dyson registers his disapproval of Rock's revelation of black thought to white audiences when he says: "Rock signifies an unwillingness among the younger black generation to abide by the dirty-laundry theory. That theory suggests you don't say anything self-critical or negative about black people where white people can hear it. But the hip-hop generation believes in making money off the publication of private pain and agony" (qtd. in Farley 69).

Another critic disagrees, offering evidence in support of Rock.

Dyson's concerns seem legitimate, but *Time* writer Chris Farley contends that it is precisely because Rock refuses to uphold the "dirty-laundry theory" that his comedy becomes a powerful agent to advance blacks. He argues that although *Bring the Pain* was aired on HBO and not on BET, it was a comedy routine made about blacks, for blacks (Farley 69). It was a momentous event, for it was one of the first times that whites were ignored in the scheme of the situation, and Farley predicts that more undisclosed aspects of the black community will be revealed on the national stage because blacks no longer care about the image they may relay to white people (Farley 70).

Return to central claims of the essay

In the larger context of the history of African-American humor, Rock's "Niggas vs. Black People" follows the formula of bitter self-denigrating humor, but it is elevated to something African-American humor had not been before. Whereas in the past such humor had served as a quiet venting of anger and aggression for blacks who acknowledged white superiority, Rock shared that humor with his fellow African Americans in a medium that white audiences could observe but not play a role in, and the result was that much of the black inferiority complex associated with African-American culture was absolved. In speaking of the long range effects of such an emancipation, hip-hop mogul Russell Simmons chuckles, "Now [members of the mainstream media] have to live with [Rock] even though he makes them uncomfortable, and I think that's fabulous" (qtd. in Farley 70). For the first time, African-American humor disassociated itself from any kind of white involvement, and the pieces of such a shake-up are still falling today as African-American humor continually reshapes its role in black culture.

The breadth of passionate debate that Rock's comedy elicits from intellectuals is evidence enough that he is advancing discussion of the foibles of black America, but Rock continually insists that he has no political aims: "Really, really at the end of the day, the only important thing is being funny. I don't go out of my way to be political" (qtd. in Bogosian 58). His unwillingness to view himself as a black leader triggers Justin Driver to say, "[Rock] wants to be caustic and he wants to be loved" (32). Even supporters wistfully sigh, "One wishes Rock would own up to the fact that he's a damned astute social critic" (Kamp 7).

Rock's ultimate goals probed: is he only a jokeman, or is he a leader?

Although Rock would at first seem merely content to let his comic material speak for itself, his activities have shown him to be carrying out his mission to increase black diversity in the entertainment industry. In the fall of 1998, he started a college humor magazine entitled the *Illtop Journal* at Howard University to create an "infrastructure" through which young black talent could hone their humorous writing skills (Rock, "Rock on a Roll" 2; Kamp 3). He has also used *The Chris Rock Show* as a political forum for notable black leaders such as Jesse Jackson and Marion Barry to voice their opinions. When the show ended its run in year 2000, activist Reverend Al Sharpton remarked that there should be "a national day of mourning," for the show "provided a forum where people like

Evidence introduced to support view of Rock as a leader

me could talk to a different part of America that did not necessarily get exposure to us" ("Chris Rock Pulls Plug"). Regarding the purpose of the show, Rock himself has been proud of the way it broadened the range of black humor, and in the *Vanity Fair* interview, he boasts, "One thing we do well is, it's the only time in history you've seen a black guy do something dry" (qtd. in Kamp 9). Even though Rock may never admit that he is more than a comedian, he uses the *Illtop Journal* and *The Chris Rock Show* to reveal to America of the multiple dimensions of black life. Perhaps, then, Rock is not an unwilling leader as originally stated in one of the opening paragraphs but a leader in the disguise of a comedian.

Summation of argument

I think we need a new leader. We haven't had a leader in awhile. Someone to move you (Rock, *Bigger and Blacker*). With these words, Rock slowly works his way to the closing remarks of his race sketch in *Bigger and Blacker*. As he peers into the dark of the Apollo Theater, he must realize that the invisible faces staring back at him regard him as one such leader. He is not the leader in the mold of Martin Luther King Jr. or Barack Obama, but he is a leader nonetheless, for he carries with him the burden of carrying on the tradition of a painful yet treasured humor that has long been woven into the fabric of African-American culture. As the curtains draw down at the end of the show to drown out the standing ovation, Rock knows that his work for the day is done, but tomorrow he will arrive at his office of *The Chris Rock Show* to continue his work of portraying the eclectic characteristics of black people. The teaching never stops, and he does it under the façade of humor because he understands that the purpose of his humor, African-American humor, is to make "visible the invisible while masking its own anger and rage" (Gordon 11). Rock gives the adoring crowd one last crooked grin, and the audience is unsure whether the grin is a smile or a smirk as they watch his shadow trail off the stage.

WORKS CITED

Bogosian, Eric. "Chris Rock Has No Time for Your Ignorance." *New York Times Magazine* 5 Oct. 1997: 56–59. Print.

Chappell, Kevin. "Bigger, Better, and Hotter! Chris Rock Talks about Fame, Controversy, and the Challenge of Being No. 1." *Ebony* Oct. 1999: 162–70. Print.

"Chris Rock: Comedy, Life, and Career of Entertainer Chris Rock." *Sixty Minutes*. CBS, WCBS, New York, 6 Sept. 1998. Web. Transcript. 24 Feb. 2002.

"Chris Rock Pulls Plug on His HBO Show." *CNN.com*. Cable News Network, 8 Dec. 2000. Web. 26 Feb. 2002.

Driver, Justin. "The Mirth of a Nation: Black Comedy's Reactionary Hipness." *New Republic* 4 June 2001: 29–33. Print.

Farley, Christopher John. "Seriously Funny." *Time* 13 Sept. 1999: 66–70. Print.

Gordon, Dexter B. "Humor in African American Discourse: Speaking of Oppression." *Journal of Black Studies* 29 (Nov. 1998): 254–76. Web. 22 Feb. 2002.

Hammer, Steve. Interview. *NUVO Newsweekly*. Aug. 1994. Web. 22 Feb. 2002.

Handy, Bruce. "Chris Rock: Even When Cracking Jokes That Make Us Cringe, He Shows Us That Laughter Can Be the Best Revenge." *Time* 9 July 2001: 67. Print.

Kamp, D. "The Color of Truth." *Vanity Fair* Aug. 1999. Web. 19 Feb. 2002.

Nelson, Jill. "Alternative Rock." *US News* 10–12 July 1998. Web. 22 Feb. 2002.

Poussaint, Alvin F. Foreword. *African American Viewers and the Black Situation Comedy: Situating Racial Humor*. By Robin R. Means Coleman. New York: Garland, 2000. xi–xiv. Web. 22 Feb. 2002.

Rock, Chris, perf. *The Best of the Chris Rock Show*. Warner Home Video, 1999. DVD.

——, perf. *Bigger and Blacker*. HBO, 1999. DVD.

——, perf. *Bring the Pain*. HBO, 1996. DVD.

——. *Rock This!* Darby, PA: Diane, 1997. 6–31. Print.

——. "Rock on a Roll: Chris Rock Takes His Comedy Very Seriously." Interview by Keven Powell. *Papermag* Aug. 2000. Web. 23 Feb. 2002.

Schruers, Fred. "Chris Rock Star." *Rolling Stone* 2 Oct. 1997: 38–42, 64–65. Print.

With Friends Like These . . .

TOM HODGKINSON

I despise Facebook. This enormously successful American business describes itself as "a social utility that connects you with the people around you." But hang on. Why on God's earth would I need a computer to connect with the people around me? Why should my relationships be mediated through the imagination of a bunch of supergeeks in California? What was wrong with the pub?

And does Facebook really connect people? Doesn't it rather disconnect us, since instead of doing something enjoyable such as talking and eating and dancing and drinking with my friends, I am merely sending them little ungrammatical notes and amusing photos in cyberspace, while chained to my desk? A friend of mine recently told me that he had spent a Saturday night at home alone on Facebook, drinking at his desk. What a gloomy image. Far from connecting us, Facebook actually isolates us at our workstations.

Facebook appeals to a kind of vanity and self-importance in us, too. If I put up a flattering picture of myself with a list of my favorite things, I can construct an artificial representation of who I am in order to get sex or approval. ("I like Facebook," said another friend. "I got a shag out of it.") It also encourages a disturbing competitiveness around friendship: it seems that with friends today, quality counts for nothing and quantity is king. The more friends you have, the better you are. You are "popular," in the sense much loved in American high schools. Witness the cover line on Dennis Publishing's new *Facebook* magazine: "How to Double Your Friends List."

It seems, though, that I am very much alone in my hostility. At the time of writing Facebook claims 59 million active users, including 7 million in the UK, Facebook's third-biggest customer after the U.S. and Canada. That's 59 million suckers, all of whom have volunteered their ID card information and consumer preferences to an American business they

Tom Hodgkinson, author of *How to Be Idle* and *How to Be Free*, writes for *The Guardian*, the *Sunday Times*, and other British publications. "With Friends Like These" was published in January 2008 in *The Guardian*. (The correction on p. 334 appeared two days later.)

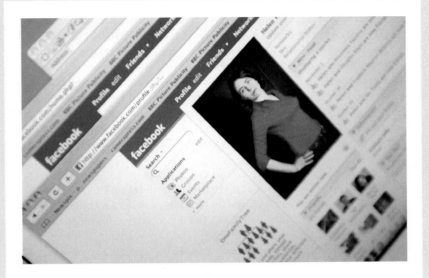

know nothing about. Right now, 2 million new people join each week. At the present rate of growth, Facebook will have more than 200 million active users by this time next year. And I would predict that, if anything, its rate of growth will accelerate over the coming months. As its spokesman Chris Hughes says: "It's embedded itself to an extent where it's hard to get rid of."

All of the above would have been enough to make me reject Facebook forever. But there are more reasons to hate it. Many more.

Facebook is a well-funded project, and the people behind the funding, a group of Silicon Valley venture capitalists, have a clearly thought out ideology that they are hoping to spread around the world. Facebook is one manifestation of this ideology. Like PayPal before it, it is a social experiment, an expression of a particular kind of neoconservative libertarianism. On Facebook, you can be free to be who you want to be, as long as you don't mind being bombarded by adverts for the world's biggest brands. As with PayPal, national boundaries are a thing of the past.

Although the project was initially conceived by media cover star Mark Zuckerberg, the real face behind Facebook is the forty-year-old Silicon Valley venture capitalist and futurist philosopher Peter Thiel. There are only three board members on Facebook, and they are Thiel, Zuckerberg and a third investor called Jim Breyer from a venture capital firm called Accel Partners (more on him later). Thiel invested $500,000 in Facebook when Harvard students Zuckerberg, Chris Hughes and Dustin Moskowitz went to meet him in San Francisco in June 2004, soon after they had launched the site. Thiel now reportedly owns 7 percent of Facebook, which, at Facebook's current valuation of $15 billion, would be worth more than $1 billion. There is much debate on who exactly were the original co-founders of Facebook, but whoever they were, Zuckerberg is the only one left on the board, although Hughes and Moskowitz still work for the company.

Thiel is widely regarded in Silicon Valley and in the U.S. venture capital scene as a libertarian genius. He is the co-founder and CEO of the virtual banking system PayPal, which he sold to eBay for $1.5 billion, taking $55 million for himself. He also runs a £3 billion hedge fund called Clarium Capital Management and a venture capital fund called Founders Fund. *Bloomberg Markets* magazine recently called him "one of the most successful hedge fund managers in the country." He has made money by betting on rising oil prices and by correctly predicting that the dollar would weaken. He and his absurdly wealthy Silicon Valley mates have recently been labeled "The PayPal Mafia" by *Fortune* magazine, whose reporter also observed that Thiel has a uniformed butler and a $500,000 McLaren supercar. Thiel is also a chess master and intensely competitive. He has been known to sweep the chessmen off the table in a fury when losing. And he does not apologize for this hypercompetitiveness, saying: "Show me a good loser and I'll show you a loser."

But Thiel is more than just a clever and avaricious capitalist. He is a futurist philosopher and neocon activist. A philosophy graduate from Stanford, in 1998 he cowrote a book called *The Diversity Myth*, which is a detailed attack on liberalism and the multiculturalist ideology that dominated Stanford. He claimed that the "multiculture" led to a lessening of individual freedoms. While a student at Stanford, Thiel founded a right-wing journal, still up and running, called *The Stanford Review*—motto: *Fiat Lux* ("Let there be light"). Thiel is a member of TheVanguard.org, an Internet-based neoconservative pressure group that was set up to attack MoveOn.org, a liberal pressure group that works on the Web. Thiel calls himself "way libertarian."

TheVanguard is run by one Rod D. Martin, a philosopher-capitalist whom Thiel greatly admires. On the site, Thiel says: "Rod is one of our nation's leading minds in the creation of new and needed ideas for public policy. He possesses a more complete understanding of America than most executives have of their own businesses."

This little taster from their Web site will give you an idea of their vision for the world: "TheVanguard.org is an online community of Americans who believe in conservative values, the free market and limited government as the best means to bring hope and ever-increasing opportunity to everyone, especially the poorest among us." Their aim is to promote policies that will "reshape America and the globe." TheVanguard describes its politics as "Reaganite/Thatcherite." The chairman's message says: "Today we'll teach MoveOn [the liberal Web site], Hillary and the leftwing media some lessons they never imagined."

So Thiel's politics are not in doubt. What about his philosophy? I listened to a podcast of an address Thiel gave about his ideas for the future. His philosophy, briefly, is this: since the seventeenth century, certain enlightened thinkers have been taking the world away from the old-fashioned nature-bound life, and here he quotes Thomas Hobbes' famous characterization of life as "nasty, brutish and short," and towards a new virtual world where we have conquered nature. Value now exists in imaginary things. Thiel says that PayPal was motivated by this belief: that you can find value not in real manufactured objects, but in the relations between human beings. PayPal was a way of moving money around the world with no restriction. *Bloomberg Markets* puts it like this: "For Thiel, PayPal was all about freedom: it would enable people to skirt currency controls and move money around the globe." Clearly, Facebook is another uber-capitalist experiment: can you make money out of friendship? Can you create communities free of national boundaries—and then sell Coca-Cola to them? Facebook is profoundly uncreative. It makes nothing at all. It simply mediates in relationships that were happening anyway.

Thiel's philosophical mentor is one René Girard of Stanford University, proponent of a theory of human behavior called *mimetic desire*. Girard reckons that people are essentially sheeplike and will copy one another without much reflection. The theory would also seem to be proved correct in the case of Thiel's virtual worlds: the desired object is irrelevant; all you need to know is that human beings will tend to move in flocks. Hence financial bubbles. Hence the enormous popularity of Facebook. Girard is a regular at Thiel's intellectual soirees. What you don't hear about in Thiel's philosophy, by the way, are old-fashioned real-world concepts such as art, beauty, love, pleasure and truth.

The Internet is immensely appealing to neocons such as Thiel because it promises a certain sort of freedom in human relations and in business, freedom from pesky national laws, national boundaries and suchlike. The Internet opens up a world of free trade and laissez-faire expansion. Thiel also seems to approve of offshore tax havens, and claims that 40 percent of the world's wealth resides in places such as Vanuatu, the Cayman Islands, Monaco and Barbados. I think it's fair to say that Thiel, like Rupert Murdoch, is against tax. He also likes the globalization of digital culture because it makes the banking overlords hard to attack: "You can't have a workers' revolution to take over a bank if the bank is in Vanuatu," he says.

If life in the past was nasty, brutish and short, then in the future Thiel wants to make it much longer, and to this end he has also invested in a firm that is exploring life-extension technologies. He has pledged £3.5 million to a Cambridge-based gerontologist called Aubrey de Grey, who is searching for the key to immortality. Thiel is also on the board of advisers of something called the Singularity Institute for Artificial Intelligence. From its fantastical Web site, the following: "The Singularity is the technological creation of smarter-than-human intelligence. There are several technologies . . . heading in this direction . . . Artificial Intelligence . . . direct brain-computer interfaces . . . genetic engineering . . . different technologies which, if they reached a threshold level of sophistication, would enable the creation of smarter-than-human intelligence."

So by his own admission, Thiel is trying to destroy the real world, which he also calls "nature," and install a virtual world in its place, and it is in this context that we must view the rise of Facebook. Facebook is a deliberate experiment in global manipulation, and Thiel is a bright young thing in the neoconservative pantheon, with a penchant for far-out techno-utopian fantasies. Not someone I want to help get any richer.

The third board member of Facebook is Jim Breyer. He is a partner in the venture capital firm Accel Partners, who put $12.7 million into Facebook in April 2005. On the board of such U.S. giants as Wal-Mart and Marvel Entertainment, he is also a former chairman of the National Venture Capital Association (NVCA). Now these are the people who are really making things happen in America, because they invest in the new young talent, the Zuckerbergs and the like. Facebook's most recent round of funding was led by a company called Greylock Venture Capital, who put in the sum of $27.5 million. One of Greylock's senior partners is called Howard Cox, another former chairman of the NVCA, who is also on the board of In-Q-Tel. What's In-Q-Tel? Well, believe it or not (and check out their Web site), this is the venture-capital wing of the CIA. After 9/11, the U.S. intelligence community became so excited by the possibilities of new technology and the innovations being made in the private sector that in 1999 they set up their own venture capital fund, In-Q-Tel, which "identifies and partners with companies developing cutting-edge technologies to help deliver these solutions to the Central Intelligence Agency and the broader U.S. Intelligence Community (IC) to further their missions."

The U.S. defense department and the CIA love technology because it makes spying easier. "We need to find new ways to deter new adversaries," defense secretary Donald Rumsfeld said in 2003. "We need to make the leap into the information age, which is the critical foundation of our transformation efforts." In-Q-Tel's first chairman was Gilman Louie, who served on the board of the NVCA with Breyer. Another key figure in the In-Q-Tel team is Anita K. Jones, former director of defense research and engineering for the U.S. department of defense, and—with Breyer—board member of BBN Technologies. When she left the U.S. department of defense, Senator Chuck Robb paid her the following tribute: "She brought the technology and operational military communities together to design detailed plans to sustain U.S. dominance on the battlefield into the next century."

Now even if you don't buy the idea that Facebook is some kind of extension of the American imperialist program crossed with a massive information-gathering tool, there is no way of denying that as a business, it is pure megagenius. Some Net nerds have suggested that its $15 billion valuation is excessive, but I would argue that if anything that is too modest. Its scale really is dizzying, and the potential for growth is virtually limitless. "We want everyone to be able to use Facebook," says the impersonal voice of Big Brother on the Web site. I'll bet they do. It is Facebook's enormous potential that led Microsoft to buy 1.6 percent for $240 million. A recent rumor says that Asian investor Lee Ka-Shing, said to be the ninth richest man in the world, has bought 0.4 percent of Facebook for $60 million.

The creators of the site need do very little bar fiddle with the program. In the main, they simply sit back and watch as millions of Facebook addicts voluntarily upload their ID details, photographs and lists of their favorite consumer objects. Once in receipt of this vast database of human beings, Facebook then simply has to sell the information back to advertisers, or, as Zuckerberg puts it in a recent blog post, "to try to help people share information with their friends about things they do on the Web." And indeed, this is precisely what's happening. On November 6 last year, Facebook announced that twelve global brands had climbed on board. They included Coca-Cola, Blockbuster, Verizon, Sony Pictures and Condé Nast. All trained in marketing bullshit of the highest order, their representatives made excited comments along the following lines:

"With Facebook Ads, our brands can become a part of the way users communicate and interact on Facebook," said Carol Kruse, vice president, global interactive marketing, the Coca-Cola Company.

"We view this as an innovative way to cultivate relationships with millions of Facebook users by enabling them to interact with Blockbuster in convenient, relevant and entertaining ways," said Jim Keyes, Blockbuster chairman and CEO. "This is beyond creating advertising impressions. This is about Blockbuster participating in the community of the consumer so that, in return, consumers feel motivated to share the benefits of our brand with their friends."

"Share" is Facebookspeak for "advertise." Sign up to Facebook and you become a free walking, talking advert for Blockbuster or Coke, extolling the virtues of these brands to your friends. We are seeing the commodification of human relationships, the extraction of capitalistic value from friendships.

Now, by comparison with Facebook, newspapers, for example, begin to look hopelessly outdated as a business model. A newspaper sells advertising space to businesses looking to sell stuff to their readers. But the system is far less sophisticated than Facebook for two reasons. One is that newspapers have to put up with the irksome expense of paying journalists to provide the content. Facebook gets its content for free. The other is that Facebook can target advertising with far greater precision than a newspaper. Admit on Facebook that your favorite film is *This Is Spinal Tap*, and when a *Spinal Tap*-esque movie comes out, you can be sure that they'll be sending ads your way.

It's true that Facebook recently got into hot water with its Beacon advertising program. Users were notified that one of their friends had made a purchase at certain online shops; 46,000 users felt that this level of advertising was intrusive, and signed a petition called "Facebook! Stop invading my privacy!" to say so. Zuckerberg apologized on his company blog. He has written that they have now changed the system from "opt-out" to "opt-in." But I suspect that this little rebellion about being so ruthlessly commodified will soon be forgotten: after all, there was a national outcry by the civil liberties movement when the idea of a police force was mooted in the UK in the mid-nineteenth century.

Furthermore, have you Facebook users ever actually read the privacy policy? It tells you that you don't have much privacy. Facebook pretends to be about freedom, but isn't it really more like an ideologically motivated virtual totalitarian regime with a population that will very soon exceed the UK's? Thiel and the rest have created their own country, a country of consumers.

Now, you may, like Thiel and the other new masters of the cyberverse, find this social experiment tremendously exciting. Here at last is the Enlightenment state longed for since the Puritans of the seventeenth century sailed away to North America, a world where everyone is free to express themselves as they please, according to who is watching. National boundaries are a thing of the past and everyone cavorts together in free-wheeling virtual space. Nature has been conquered through man's boundless ingenuity. Yes, and you may decide to send genius investor Thiel all your money, and certainly you'll be waiting impatiently for the public flotation of the unstoppable Facebook.

Or you might reflect that you don't really want to be part of this heavily funded program to create an arid global virtual republic, where your own self and your relationships with your friends are converted into commodities on sale to giant global brands. You may decide that you don't want to be part of this takeover bid for the world.

For my own part, I am going to retreat from the whole thing, remain as unplugged as possible, and spend the time I save by not going on Facebook doing something useful, such as reading books. Why would I want to waste my time on Facebook when I still haven't read Keats' "Endymion"? And when there are seeds to be sown in my own back yard? I don't want to retreat from nature, I want to reconnect with it. Damn air-conditioning! And if I want to connect with the people around me, I will revert to an old piece of technology. It's free, it's easy and it delivers a uniquely individual experience in sharing information: it's called talking.

The following correction was printed in the *Guardian's* Corrections and Clarifications column, Wednesday, January 16, 2008

The U.S. intelligence community's enthusiasm for hi-tech innovation after 9/11 and the creation of the In-Q-Tel, its venture capital fund, in 1999 were anachronistically linked in the article below. Since 9/11 happened in 2001 it could not have led to the setting up of In-Q-Tel two years earlier.

11
Causal Arguments

Concerned that middle-school students are consuming too much junk food and soda pop at lunch, a principal considers banning vending machines on her campus. But then she discovers how much revenue those machines generate for her school, and she quickly has second thoughts.

An experienced columnist tours Greenland with the minister of climate and energy and sees firsthand evidence of the effects of climate change on Greenland's ice sheet. He concludes that "we've added so many greenhouse gases to the atmosphere . . . that our kids are likely going to spend a good part of their adulthood . . . just dealing with the climate implications of our profligacy."

Researchers in Marin County, California, discover that the occurrence of breast cancer cases is significantly higher there than in any other urban area in California. They immediately begin work to investigate possible causes.

A large soft-drink manufacturer wants to increase its worldwide market share among teenage buyers. Its executives know that another company has been the overwhelming market leader for years—and they set out to learn exactly why.

Convinced of the strong and compelling causal link between second-hand smoke and lung cancer—as well as other diseases—New York mayor Michael Bloomberg and Microsoft's Bill Gates team up to contribute $375 million to support projects around the world that will raise tobacco taxes, help smokers quit, and ban advertising of tobacco products.

A state legislator notes that gasoline prices are consistently between twenty-five and fifty cents higher in one large city in the state than elsewhere. After some preliminary investigation, the legislator decides to bring a class action lawsuit on behalf of the people of this city, arguing that price fixing and insider deals are responsible for the price difference.

Understanding Causal Arguments

The eye-catching title image of a *National Geographic* story poses a simple question: "Why Are We So Fat?" You can probably guess that simple questions like this rarely have simple answers. But in this case, the author, Cathy Newman, argues that there are no real surprises:

> [I]n one sense, the obesity crisis is the result of simple math. It's a calories in, calories out calculation. The First Law of Fat says that anything you eat beyond your immediate need for energy, from avocados to ziti, converts to fat. . . . The Second Law of Fat: The line between being in and out of energy balance is slight. Suppose you consume a mere 5 percent over a 2,000-calorie-a-day average. "That's just one hundred calories; it's a glass of apple juice," says Rudolph Leibel, head of molecular genetics at Columbia University College of Physicians and Surgeons. "But those few extra calories can mean a huge weight gain." Since one pound of body weight is roughly equivalent to 3,500 calories, that glass of juice adds up to an extra 10 pounds over a year.
> —Cathy Newman, "Why Are We So Fat?"

And yet you know that there's more to it than that—as Newman's full story reveals. "Calories in, calories out" may explain the physics of weight

WHY ARE WE SO
fat?

And the answer is . . . ?

gain. But why in recent years have we so drastically shifted the equation from out to in? Because people instinctually crave fatty foods? Because we've grown addicted to fast food? Because fast-food restaurants and junk-food corner stores are the only ones available in some neighborhoods? Because we walk less? Because we've become Internet (or video game) addicts? Whatever the reasons for our increased tonnage, the consequences can be measured by everything from the width of airliner seats to the rise of diabetes in the general population. Many explanations are offered by scientists, social critics, and health gurus, and many are refuted. Figuring out what's going on is an importance exercise in cause-and-effect argument.

Causal arguments—from the consequences of poverty in Africa to the causes of terrorism around the globe—are at the heart of many major policy decisions, both national and international. But arguments about causes and effects also inform many choices that people make every day. Suppose that you need to petition for a grade change because you were unable to turn in a final project on time. You'd probably enumerate the reasons for your failure—the death of your cat, followed by an attack of the hives, followed by a crash of your computer—hoping that a committee reading the petition might see these explanations as tragic enough to change your grade. In identifying the causes of the situation, you're implicitly arguing that the effect (your failure to submit the project on time) should be considered in a new light. Unfortunately, the committee might accuse you of faulty causality (see pp. 527–29) and judge that your failure to complete the project is due more to procrastination than to the reasons you offer.

Causal arguments exist in many forms and frequently appear as part of other arguments (such as evaluations or proposals). It may help focus your work on causal arguments to separate them into three major categories:

- arguments that state a cause and then examine its effects

Cause A   ————————→ leads to   Effect B
                                            Effect C
                                            Effect D

- arguments that state an effect and then trace the effect back to its causes

Effect D   ————————→ results from   Cause A
                                              Cause B
                                            Cause C

- arguments that move through a series of links: A causes B, which leads to C and perhaps to D

Cause A →　leads to Cause B →　leads to Cause C →　leads to Effect D

ARGUMENTS THAT STATE A CAUSE AND THEN EXAMINE ITS EFFECTS

What would happen if openly homosexual men and women were allowed to join (or stay in) the American military? The possible effects of this "cause" could be examined in detail and argued powerfully. You could imagine very different cases (and consequences) presented by people on various sides of this hot-button issue. In such an argument, you'd be successful if you could show compellingly that the cause would indeed lead to the effects you describe. Or you could challenge the causal assumptions made by people you don't agree with.

Unfortunately, causes and effects are rarely this easy to determine.

Take a look at the opening of an article from the *Christian Science Monitor* on the increased production of ethanol from corn:

> Policymakers and legislators often fail to consider the law of unintended consequences. The latest example is their attempt to reduce the United States' dependence on imported oil by shifting a big share of the nation's largest crop—corn—to the production of ethanol for fueling automobiles.
>
> Good goal, bad policy. In fact, ethanol will do little to reduce the large percentage of our fuel that is imported (more than 60 percent),

and the ethanol policy will have ripple effects on other markets. Corn farmers and ethanol refiners are ecstatic about the ethanol boom and are enjoying the windfall of artificially enhanced demand. But it will be an expensive and dangerous experiment for the rest of us.

—Colin A. Carter and Henry I. Miller, "Hidden Costs of Corn-based Ethanol"

Note that the researchers here begin with a cause—raising the percentage of the corn crop used for ethanol—and then point to several effects of that cause that they will later explore. In this case, they say, some of these effects are clearly "unintended consequences."

ARGUMENTS THAT STATE AN EFFECT AND THEN TRACE ITS CAUSES

This type of argument might begin with a certain effect (for example, Hollywood's record-breaking slump in movie attendance in 2007) and then trace the effect or effects to the most likely causes (a rise in DVD sales, the increase in large-screen home theaters, the growing tendency

Cartoonist Mark Alan Stamaty portrays an effect and three of its causes.

© Mark Alan Stamaty

to stay home for entertainment because of the rise in gasoline prices, increasingly noisy cell-phone-using audiences, mediocre movies, and unimaginative remakes). Or you might examine the reasons that Hollywood executives offer for their industry's dip and decide whether their causal analyses pass muster.

Like other kinds of causal arguments, those tracing effects to a cause can have far-reaching significance. In 1962, for example, the scientist Rachel Carson seized the attention of millions with a famous causal argument about the effects that the overuse of chemical pesticides might have on the environment. Here's an excerpt from the beginning of her book-length study of this subject. Note how she begins with the effects before saying she'll go on to explore the causes:

> [A] strange blight crept over the area and everything began to change. Some evil spell had settled on the community: mysterious maladies swept the flocks of chickens; the cattle and sheep sickened and died. Everywhere was a shadow of death. The farmers spoke of much illness among their families. . . . There had been several sudden and unexplained deaths, not only among adults but even among children, who would be stricken suddenly while at play and die within a few hours. The roadsides, once so attractive, were now lined with browned and withered vegetation as though swept by fire. These, too, were silent, deserted by all living things. Even the streams were now lifeless. Anglers no longer visited them, for all the fish had died.
>
> In the gutters under the eaves and between the shingles of the roofs, a white granular powder still showed a few patches; some weeks before it had fallen like snow upon the roofs and lawns, the fields and streams. No witchcraft, no enemy action had silenced the rebirth of new life in this stricken world. The people had done it themselves. . . . What has silenced the voices of spring in countless towns in America? This book is an attempt to explain.
>
> —Rachel Carson, *Silent Spring*

Today, one could easily write a causal argument of the first type about *Silent Spring* and the environmental movement that it spawned.

ARGUMENTS THAT MOVE THROUGH A SERIES OF LINKS: A CAUSES B, WHICH LEADS TO C AND PERHAPS TO D

In an environmental science class, for example, you might decide to argue that a national law regulating smokestack emissions from utility plants is needed because of the following reasons:

1. Emissions from utility plants in the Midwest cause acid rain.
2. Acid rain causes the death of trees and other vegetation in eastern forests.
3. Powerful lobbyists have prevented midwestern states from passing strict laws to control emissions from these plants.
4. As a result, acid rain will destroy most eastern forests by 2020.

In this case, the first link is that emissions cause acid rain; the second, that acid rain causes destruction in eastern forests; and the third, that states have not acted to break the cause-and-effect relationship that is established by the first two points. These links set the scene for the fourth link, which ties the previous points together to argue from effect: unless X, then Y.

Characterizing Causal Arguments

Causal arguments tend to share several characteristics.

THEY ARE OFTEN PART OF OTHER ARGUMENTS.

Many causal arguments stand alone and address questions that are fundamental to our well-being: *Why are juvenile asthma and diabetes increasing so dramatically in the United States? What are the causes of the rise in cases of malaria in Africa, and what can we do to counter this rise? What will happen to Europe if its birthrate continues to decline?*

But causal analyses often work to further other arguments—especially proposals. For example, a proposal to limit the time that children spend playing video games might first draw on a causal analysis to establish that playing video games can have bad results—such as violent behavior, short attention spans, and decreased social skills. The causal analysis provides a rationale that motivates the proposal. In this way, causal analyses can be useful in establishing good reasons for arguments in general.

THEY ARE ALMOST ALWAYS COMPLEX.

The complexity of most causal relationships makes it difficult to establish causes and effects. For example, scientists and politicians continue to disagree over the extent to which acid rain is actually responsible for

Causal Claims and Academic Arguments

As this chapter demonstrates, making causal claims stick is almost always a delicate and difficult matter. Yet causal reasoning is important to academic arguments across the disciplines. Here, professor of communications Fred Turner looks at the relationship between the Burning Man phenomenon and forms of new media production emerging in Silicon Valley. Here is the abstract of Turner's article:

Every August for more than a decade, thousands of information technologists and other knowledge workers have trekked out into a barren stretch of alkali desert and built a temporary city devoted to art, technology and communal living: Burning Man. Drawing on extensive archival research, participant observation, and interviews, this paper explores the ways that Burning Man's bohemian ethos supports new forms of production emerging in Silicon Valley and especially at Google. It shows how elements of the Burning Man world—including the building of a socio-technical commons, participation in project-based artistic labor, and the fusion of social and professional interaction—help shape and legitimate the collaborative manufacturing processes driving the growth of Google and other firms. The paper thus develops the notion that Burning Man serves as a key cultural infrastructure for the Bay area's new media industries.

—Fred Turner, "Burning Man at Google: A Cultural Infrastructure for New Media Production"

Note the care with which Turner states his case. He is not arguing for a simple or direct cause-and-effect relationship. Rather, he says that he will argue that Burning Man is part of a web of events that have helped to shape certain processes. In academic arguments, writers treat causal relationships with special care.

the death of many eastern forests. Or consider the complexity of analyzing the causes of some kinds of food poisoning: in 2008, investigators spent months trying to discover whether tomatoes, cilantro, or jalapeno peppers were the cause of a nationwide outbreak of food poisoning.

Likewise, those trying to untangle the causes leading to a rise in teenage pregnancy are faced with a complex web of potential causes rather than a clear causal relationship. But when you can show that X definitely causes Y, you'll have a powerful argument at your disposal because causal arguments must take into account an enormous number of factors, conditions, and alternative possibilities. That's why, for example, great effort went into establishing an indisputable link between smoking and lung cancer. Once proven, decisive legal action could finally be taken to warn smokers.

THEY ARE OFTEN DEFINITION BASED.

One reason that causal arguments are complex is that they often depend on careful definitions. Recent figures from the U.S. Department of Education, for example, show that the number of high school dropouts is rising and that this rise has caused an increase in youth unemployment. But exactly how does the study define *dropout*? A closer look may suggest that some students (perhaps a lot) who drop out "drop back in" and complete high school or that some who drop out become successful business owners. Further, how does the study define *employment*? Until you can provide definitions that answer such questions, you should proceed cautiously with a causal argument.

THEY USUALLY YIELD PROBABLE RATHER THAN ABSOLUTE CONCLUSIONS.

Because causal relationships are almost always complex, they seldom can yield more than a high degree of probability and are almost always subject to critique or charges of false causality. (We all know smokers who defy the odds to live long, cancer-free lives.) Scientists in particular are wary of making causal claims—such as environmental factors cause infertility, for example, because it's highly unlikely that a condition as variable as infertility can be linked to any one single cause.

Even after an event, proving what caused it can be hard. During the campus riots of the late 1960s, for example, a commission was charged with determining the causes of riots on a particular campus. After two years of work and almost a thousand pages of evidence and reports, the commission was unable to pinpoint anything but a broad network of contributing causes and related conditions.

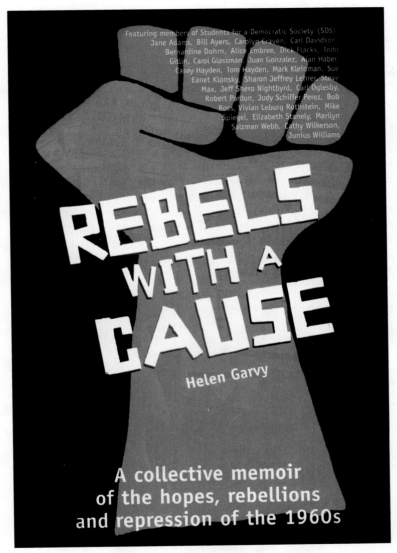

Featuring members of Students for a Democratic Society (SDS):
Jane Adams, Bill Ayers, Carolyn Craven, Carl Davidson,
Bernardine Dohrn, Alice Embree, Dick Flacks, Todd
Gitlin, Carol Glassman, Juan Gonzalez, Alan Haber,
Casey Hayden, Tom Hayden, Mark Kleinman, Sue
Eanet Klonsky, Sharon Jeffrey Lehrer, Steve
Max, Jeff Shero Nightbyrd, Carl Oglesby,
Robert Pardun, Judy Schiffer Perez, Bob
Ross, Vivian Leburg Rothstein, Mike
Spiegel, Elizabeth Stanely, Marilyn
Salzman Webb, Cathy Wilkerson,
Junius Williams

REBELS
WITH A
CAUSE

Helen Garvy

A collective memoir
of the hopes, rebellions
and repression of the 1960s

The poster for a documentary film based on this book features an interesting comment on causality: "It isn't the rebels who cause the troubles of the world; it's the troubles that cause the rebels." Some forty years after the campus riots of the late 1960s, scholars are still arguing over their causes.

Not Just Words

When Rachel Carson wrote *Silent Spring* to warn of the environmental dangers of pesticides (see p. 341), one of her targets was the widespread use of DDT in American agriculture. DDT was an effective pesticide, but used indiscriminately it had harmful long-term side effects for birds and other animals. Environmentalists succeeded in virtually banning the use of DDT in the rich industrialized countries. But now some developing nations are interested in restoring its use. Why? DDT kills or repels the mosquitoes responsible for malaria, one of the most insidious diseases in some African and Asian countries. As you might imagine, this controversy is a heated one, and arguments on either side go well beyond words. Look at the accompanying two images, and think about the argument that each one is making.

© Cox & Forkum Editorial Cartoons

Each of these images makes at least one complex argument about causes and effects relating to the use of pesticides such as DDT. Working with one or two classmates, study these images, and then make a list of the possible causal arguments that each one makes.

To demonstrate that A caused B, you must find the strongest possible evidence and subject it to the toughest scrutiny. But a causal argument doesn't fail just because you can't find a single compelling cause. In fact, causal arguments are often most effective when they help readers appreciate how tangled our lives and landscapes really are.

Developing Causal Arguments

Formulating a Claim

You might decide to write a wildly exaggerated or parodic causal argument for humorous purposes. Humorist Dave Barry does this when he explains the causes of El Niño and other weather phenomena: "So we see that the true cause of bad weather, contrary to what they have been claiming all these years, is TV weather forecasters, who have also single-handedly destroyed the ozone layer via overuse of hair spray." Most of the causal reasoning you do, however, will take a serious approach to subjects that you, your family, and your friends care about.

To begin creating a strong causal claim, try listing some of the effects—events or phenomena—that you'd like to know the causes of:

- What causes led to the decreasing numbers of salmon along the northwest coast?
- What's really responsible for rises and falls in gasoline prices?
- What has led to warnings of contamination along your favorite creek?
- Why has the divorce rate leveled off in recent decades?
- Why do so few young Americans vote, even in major elections?

Or try moving in the opposite direction, listing some phenomena or causes you're interested in and then hypothesizing what kinds of effects they may produce:

- What will happen if your campus institutes a coed policy on all dorm bathrooms?
- What will be the effects of a total crackdown on peer-to-peer file sharing?

You probably know that people make and sell cheap imitations of Prada's high-fashion handbags, shoes, and accessories. But what would cause someone to make a fake Prada store? A group of German artists built one outside the small west Texas town of Marfa. What effects do you imagine have resulted?

- What will happen if more liberal (or conservative) judges are appointed to the U.S. Supreme Court?
- What will happen if China and India become thriving industrialized nations?

Read a little about the causal issues that interest you most, and then try them out on friends and colleagues. Can they suggest ways to refocus or clarify what you want to do? Can they offer leads to finding information about your subject? If you've already asserted some cause-and-effect relationships, can they offer counterexamples or refutations? Finally, map out a rough statement about the causal relationship you want to explore:

A might cause (or might be caused by) B for the following reasons:

1.

2.

3.

Such a statement should be tentative because writing a causal argument will often be a research exercise in which you uncover facts, not assume them to be true. Often, your early assumptions (*Tuition was raised to renovate the stadium*) might be undermined by the facts you later discover (*Tuition doesn't fund the construction or maintenance of campus buildings*).

Developing the Argument

Once you've drafted a claim, you can explore cause-and-effect relationships, drawing out the reasons, warrants, and evidence that can support the claim most effectively:

Claim	Losing seasons caused the football coach to lose his job.
Reason	The team lost more than half its games for three seasons in a row.
Warrant	Winning is the key to success for major-team college coaches.
Evidence	For the last ten years, coaches with more than two losing seasons in a row have lost their jobs.
Claim	Certain career patterns cause women to be paid less than men.
Reason	Women's career patterns differ from men's, and in spite of changes in the relative pay of other groups, women's pay still lags behind that of men.
Warrant	Successful careers are made during the period between ages twenty-five and thirty-five.
Evidence	Women often drop out of or reduce work during the decade between ages twenty-five and thirty-five to raise families.

In further developing a causal argument, you can draw on many strategies that we've already touched on. In the article that the following passage is excerpted from, Stephen King uses dozens of examples—from *The Texas Chainsaw Massacre, The Gory Ones*, and *Invasion of the Body Snatchers* to *Night of the Living Dead, Psycho, The Amityville Horror*, and *The Thing*—to answer a causal question: why do people love horror movies?

> The mythic horror movie, like the sick joke, has a dirty job to do. It deliberately appeals to all that is worst in us. It is morbidity unchained, our most base instincts let free, our nastiest fantasies realized . . . and it all happens, fittingly enough, in the dark. For those reasons, good liberals often shy away from horror films. For myself, I like to see the most aggressive of them—*Dawn of the Dead*, for instance—as lifting a trap door in the civilized forebrain and throwing a basket of raw meat

Dawn of the Dead—satisfying uncivilized cravings since 1978

to the hungry alligators swimming around in that subterranean river beneath.

Why bother? Because it keeps them from getting out, man. It keeps them down there and me up here.

—Stephen King, "Why We Crave Horror Movies"

Another way to support (or undermine) a causal argument is through the use of analogies. The strength of such an argument lies in how closely you can relate the two phenomena being compared. In exploring why women consistently earn less pay than men even when they're performing the same jobs, Sarah Banda Purvis draws an analogy between working women and sports:

An analogy I use when describing my experiences as a female manager in corporate America is that I was allowed to sit on the bench but never given a chance to get on the field and play in the game.

—Sarah Banda Purvis, "What Do Working Women Want in the Twenty-first Century?"

She goes on to trace the effects that constantly being relegated to the "bench" has on earning power. If you find this analogy unsatisfactory, you might suggest that it falsely portrays the causal relationship of women and promotion. After all, benchwarmers are usually players who don't perform as well as those on the field. Surely Purvis doesn't want to suggest that women aren't moving up in the business world because they don't play the game as well as men.

Establishing causes for physical effects (like diseases) often calls for another means of support—testing *hypotheses*, or theories about possible causes. This kind of reasoning, which is often highly technical, helped researchers to identify a mystery disease that struck nearly fifty people in Quebec City. Puzzled by cases involving the same effects (nausea, shortness of breath, cough, stomach pain, weight loss, and a marked blue-gray skin coloration), doctors at first hypothesized that the common cause was severe vitamin deficiency. But the large number of cases within a short time made this explanation unlikely; after all, sudden epidemics of vitamin deficiency are rare. In addition, postmortem examinations of the twenty people who died revealed severe damage to the heart muscle and the liver, features inconsistent with the vitamin-deficiency hypothesis. So the doctors sought a clue to the mysterious disease in something the victims shared: all fifty had been beer lovers and had drunk a particular brew.

It seemed possible that the illness was connected to that brand, which was brewed in both Quebec City and Montreal. But Montreal had no outbreak of the disease. The hypothesis, then, was further refined: could the brewing processes be different in the two cities? Bingo. The Quebec brewery added a cobalt compound to its product to enhance the beer's foaminess; the Montreal brewery did not. Furthermore, the compound was first added only a month before the first victims became ill. Yet doctors in this case were still cautious about the causal connection because the cobalt hadn't been present in sufficient quantities to kill a normal person. Yet twenty had died. After persistent scientific analysis, the doctors decided that this fact must be related to the victims' drinking habits, which in some way reduced their resistance to the chemical. For those twenty people, a normally nonlethal dose of cobalt had proven fatal.

Not all the evidence in compelling causal arguments needs to be strictly scientific. Many causal arguments rely on *ethnographic observations*—the systematic study of ordinary people in their daily routines. How would you explain, for example, why some people step aside when they encounter someone head-on and others do not? In an argument that attempts to account for such behavior, investigators Frank Willis, Joseph Gier, and David Smith observed "1,038 displacements involving 3,141 persons" at a Kansas City shopping mall. In results that surprised the investigators, "gallantry" seemed to play a significant role in causing people to step aside for one another—more so than other causes that the investigators had anticipated (such as deferring to someone who's physically stronger or higher in status). Doubtless you've read of other such studies, perhaps in psychology courses.

Finally, you may want to consider using personal experiences in support of a causal argument. Indeed, people's experiences generally lead them to seek out or to avoid various causes and effects. If you're consistently praised for your prowess at ultimate Frisbee, you'll probably look for opportunities to produce that pleasant effect. If three times in a row you get sick after eating shrimp, you'll almost certainly identify the shellfish as the cause of your difficulties and stop eating it. Personal experience can also help build your credibility as a writer, gain the empathy of your listeners, and thus support your causal claim. Although one person's experiences cannot ordinarily be universalized, they can still argue eloquently for causal relationships. Leslie Marmon Silko uses personal experience to explain her shift from studying to become a lawyer to becoming a writer, photographer, and activist, arguing that the best way to seek justice isn't through the law but through the power of stories:

> When I was a sophomore in high school I decided law school was the place to seek justice. . . . I should have paid more attention to the lesson of the Laguna Pueblo land claims lawsuit from my childhood: The lawsuit was not settled until I was in law school. The U.S. Court of Indian Claims found in favor of the Pueblo of Laguna, but the Indian Claims Court never gives back land wrongfully taken; the court only pays tribes for the land. . . . The Laguna people wanted the land they cherished; instead, they got twenty-five cents for each of the six million acres stolen by the state. The lawsuit had lasted twenty years, so the lawyers' fees amounted to nearly $2 million.
>
> I completed three semesters in the American Indian Law School Fellowship Program before I realized that injustice is built into the Anglo-American legal system. . . . But I continued in law school until our criminal law class read an appeal to the U.S. Supreme Court to stop the execution of a retarded black man convicted of strangling a white librarian in Washington, D.C., in 1949. The majority on the Court refused to stop the execution, though it was clear that the man was so retarded that he had no comprehension of his crime. That case was the breaking point for me. I wanted nothing to do with such a barbaric legal system.
>
> My time in law school was not wasted: I had gained invaluable insights into the power structure of mainstream society, and I continue to follow developments in the law to calculate prevailing political

winds. It seems to me there is no better way to uncover the deepest values of a culture than to observe the operation of that culture's system of justice.

[But] I decided the only way to seek justice was through the power of stories.

—Leslie Marmon Silko, *Yellow Woman and a Beauty of Spirit:*
Essays on Native American Life Today

All these strategies—the use of examples, analogies, testing hypotheses, experimental evidence, and personal experience—can help you support a causal argument or undermine a causal claim you regard as faulty. However, you may still have to convince readers that the reasons you offer are indeed compelling. In terms of causal arguments, this may mean distinguishing among immediate, necessary, and sufficient reasons. In the case of the mysterious illness in Quebec City, the immediate reasons for illness were the symptoms themselves—nausea, shortness of breath, and so on. But they weren't the root causes of the disease. Drinking the particular beer in question served as a necessary reason: without the tainted beer, the illness wouldn't have occurred. However, the researchers had to search harder for the sufficient reason—the reason that causes the effect (the illness) if it's present. In the case of the Quebec City beer, that reason turned out to be the addition of cobalt.

Even everyday causal analysis can draw on this distinction among reasons. What caused you, for instance, to choose the college you wanted to attend? Immediate reasons might be the proximity of the school to your home or the college's rich curriculum in your major interest. But what are the necessary reasons—the ones without which your choice of that college could not occur? Adequate funds? Good test scores and academic record? The expectations of your family? You might even explore possible sufficient reasons, those that—if present—will guarantee the effect of your attending that college. In such a case, you may be the only person with enough information to determine what the sufficient reasons might be.

Considering Design and Visuals

You may find that the best way to illustrate a causal relationship is to present it visually. Consider the way that even a simple bar graph like the one on the facing page can make a point clearly and emphatically—in this case, showing the dramatic effects of lowered birthrates. The report that uses this figure explores the effects that such a change would

Figure 1. The comparative size of successive generations across time when fertility is constant at 1.3 births per woman

A simple graph can provide dramatic evidence for a causal claim—in this case, the effect of reduced fertility rates on a population.

have on the economies of the world. Or you might study the intriguing ways that editorial cartoonists embed causal relationships in some of their pieces, inviting readers to find causal connections as they interpret the images, as in the cartoon below.

Cartoonist Lisa Benson suggests that the push to develop alternative fuels has a serious effect on the world's supply of food.

Key Features of Causal Arguments

In drafting your own causal argument, you'll want to do the following:

- Thoroughly question every cause-and-effect relationship in the argument, both those you suggest yourself and others already in play.

- Show that the causes and effects you've suggested are highly probable and backed by evidence, or show what's wrong with the faulty causal reasoning you may be critiquing.

- Assess any links between causal relationships (what leads to or follows from what).

- Show that your explanations of any causal chains are accurate, or show where links in a causal chain break down.

- Show that plausible cause-and-effect explanations haven't been ignored or that the possibility of multiple causes or effects has been given due consideration.

In developing a causal argument, you'll address many of these items, though their order may vary. You may open an essay dramatically by describing an effect and then "flash back" to its multiple causes. Or you might open with a well-known phenomenon, identify it as a cause, and then trace its effects. Or you might begin by suggesting plausible explanations for an event that have been ignored for one reason or another. In any case, you should sketch an organizational plan and get reactions to it from your instructor, writing center consultants, and colleagues before proceeding to a full draft. When the draft is complete, you should again look for critical readers who are willing to test the strength of your causal argument.

GUIDE to writing a causal argument

● Finding a Topic

A little time spent brainstorming will turn up some good possibilities for causal arguments of several kinds, including those that grow out of your personal experiences. *Just exactly what led to the slump in my grades last term?* Beyond your own personal concerns, many public issues lend themselves to causal analysis and argument: *What factors have led to the near bankruptcy of the nation's major airlines? What will happen if the United States takes the lead in reducing greenhouse gas emissions? What effects have been caused by the ban on the use of trans fats in many cities' restaurants?* As you're brainstorming possibilities for your causal argument, don't ignore important current campus issues: *What have been the effects of the decision to admit a larger number of students each year? What are the likely outcomes of shifting the academic calendar from a quarter to a semester system? If, as some argue, there has been a significant increase of racism and homophobia on campus, what has caused that increase? What are its consequences?*

Finally, remember that it's fair game to question existing assumptions about causality for being inaccurate or not probing deeply enough into the reasons for a phenomenon. You can raise doubts about the facts or assumptions that others have made and perhaps offer a better causal connection. For example, some writers have argued that obsessive playing of violent video games leads to antisocial or violent behavior. Others have challenged this causal argument, noting that a large percentage of youth crime is carried out by those who play very few video games. What's going on here? Perhaps your research can provide an answer.

● Researching Your Topic

Causal arguments will lead you to many different resources:

- current news media—especially magazines and newspapers (online or in print)
- online databases
- scholarly journals

- books written on your subject (here you can do a keyword search, either in your library or online)
- blogs, Web sites, listservs, social networking sites, or newsgroups devoted to your subject

In addition, why not carry out some field research of your own? Conduct interviews with appropriate authorities on your subject, or create a questionnaire aimed at establishing a range of opinion on your subject. The information you get from interviews or from analyzing responses to a questionnaire can provide evidence to back up your claims.

● Formulating a Claim

First, identify the kind of causal argument that you expect to make—one moving from cause(s) to effect(s); one moving from effect(s) to cause(s); or one involving a series of links, with cause A leading to B, which then leads to C. (See pp. 337–42 for a review of these kinds of arguments.) Or you might be debunking an existing cause-and-effect claim.

Your next move may be to explore your own relationship to your subject. What do you know about the subject and its causes and effects? Why do you favor (or disagree with) the claim? What significant reasons can you offer in support of your position? In short, you should end this process of exploration by formulating a brief claim or thesis about a particular causal relationship. It should include (1) a statement that says, in effect, *A causes (or does not cause or is caused by) B*, and (2) a summary of the reasons supporting this causal relationship. Remember to make sure that your thesis is as specific as possible and that it's sufficiently controversial or interesting to hold your readers' interest. Recognize, too, that any such claim is tentative and is subject to change as your project develops and you learn more about your subject.

● Examples of Causal Claims

- Right-to-carry gun laws are, in part, responsible for increased rates of violent crimes in states that have approved such legislation.
- Sophisticated use of the Internet is now a must for any presidential candidate who hopes to win.
- The proliferation of images in film, television, and computer-generated texts is changing the way we read and process information.

- The many extensions of the copyright laws to protect and provide incentives to creators have diminished the right of the public to information, severely limited the fair-use doctrine, and added billions of dollars to the coffers of Disney and other huge entertainment conglomerates.
- Grade inflation is lowering the value of a college education.

Preparing a Proposal

If your instructor asks you to prepare a proposal for your project, here's a format that may help:

State the thesis of your argument completely. If you're having trouble doing so, try outlining it in Toulmin terms:

Claim:

Reason(s):

Warrant(s):

- Explain why this argument deserves attention. Why is it important for your readers to consider?
- Specify whom you hope to reach through your argument and why this group of readers is an appropriate audience. What interest or investment do they have in the issue? Why will they (or should they) be concerned?
- Briefly identify and explore the major challenges you expect to face in supporting your argument. Will demonstrating a clear causal link between A and B be particularly difficult? Will the data that you need to support the claim be hard to obtain?
- List the strategies that you expect to use in researching your argument. Will you be interviewing? Surveying opinion? Conducting library and online searches? Other?
- Briefly identify and explore the major counterarguments that you might expect in response to your argument.
- Consider what format, genre, or media will work best for your argument. Will you be preparing a Web site? A press release? An editorial for the local newspaper? A report for an organization you belong to?

● Thinking about Organization

Whatever genre or format you decide to use, your causal argument should address the following elements:

- a specific causal claim somewhere in the paper: *Devastating flash floods associated with El Niño were responsible for the dramatic loss of homes in central California in early 2003.*

- an explanation of the claim's significance or importance: *Claims for damage from flooding put some big insurance companies out of business; as a result, homeowners couldn't get coverage, and many who lost their homes had to declare bankruptcy.*

- evidence sufficient to support each cause or effect—or, in an argument based on a series of causal links, evidence to support the relationships among the links: *The amount of rain that fell in central California in early 2008 was 25 percent below normal, leading inexorably to drought conditions.*

- a consideration of alternative causes and effects and evidence that you understand these alternatives and have thought carefully about them before rejecting them: *Although some say that excessive and sloppy logging and poor building codes were responsible for the loss of homes, the evidence supporting these alternative causes is not convincing.*

● Getting and Giving Response

All arguments can benefit from the scrutiny of others. Your instructor may assign you to a peer group for the purpose of reading and responding to each other's drafts. If not, ask for responses from some serious readers or consultants at a writing center. You can use the following questions to evaluate a draft. If you're evaluating someone else's draft, be sure to illustrate your points with examples. Specific comments are always more helpful than general observations.

The Claim

- What's most effective about the claim? What are its strengths?
- Is the claim sufficiently qualified?
- Is the claim specific enough to be clear? How could it be narrowed and focused?
- How strong is the relationship between the claim and the reasons given to support it? How could that relationship be made more explicit?

- Is it immediately evident why the claim is important? How could it be rephrased in a way that more forcefully and clearly suggests its significance?
- Does the claim reveal a causal connection? How could it be revised to make the causal links clearer?

Evidence for the Claim

- What's the strongest evidence offered for the claim? What, if any, evidence needs to be strengthened?
- Is enough evidence offered that these particular causes are responsible for the effect that has been identified, that these particular effects result from the identified cause, or that a series of causes and effects are linked? If not, what kind of additional evidence is needed? What kinds of sources might provide this evidence?
- How credible and persuasive will the sources likely be to potential readers? What other kinds of sources might be more credible and persuasive?
- Is the evidence in support of the claim simply announced, or are its appropriateness and significance analyzed? Is a more detailed discussion needed?
- Have all the major alternative causes and effects as well as objections to the claim been considered? What support is offered for rejecting these alternatives? Where is additional support needed?

Organization and Style

- How are the parts of the argument organized? Is this organization effective, or would some other structure work better?
- Will readers understand the relationships among the claims, supporting reasons, warrants, and evidence? If not, what could be done to make those connections clearer? Are more transitional words and phrases needed? Would headings or graphic devices (diagrams, flowcharts, illustrations) help?
- Are the transitions or links from point to point, paragraph to paragraph, and sentence to sentence clear and effective? If not, how could they be improved?
- Is the style suited to the subject? Is it too formal? Too casual? Too technical? Too bland? Too geeky? How can it be improved?

- Which sentences seem particularly effective? Which ones seem weakest, and how could they be improved? Should some short sentences be combined, or should any long ones be separated into two or more sentences?

- How effective are the paragraphs? Do any seem too skimpy or too long? How can they be improved?

- Which words or phrases seem particularly effective, vivid, and memorable? Do any seem dull, unclear, or inappropriate for the audience or the writer's purpose? Are definitions provided for technical or other terms that readers might not know?

Spelling, Punctuation, Mechanics, Documentation, Format

- Are there any errors in spelling, punctuation, capitalization, and the like?

- Is an appropriate and consistent style of documentation used for parenthetical citations and the list of works cited or references? (See Chapter 20.)

- Does the paper or project follow an appropriate format? Is it appropriately designed and attractively presented? How could it be improved? If it's a Web site, do all the links work?

RESPOND •

1. The causes of some of the following events and phenomena are well known and frequently discussed. But do you understand them well enough to spell out the causes to someone else? Working in a group, see how well (and in how much detail) you can explain each of the following events or phenomena. Which explanations are relatively clear, and which seem more open to debate?

   earthquakes

   the Burning Man festival

   the collapse of communism in Eastern Europe in 1989

   arroyos

   the AIDS pandemic in Africa

   the popularity of the *Batman* films

   the swelling caused by a bee sting

   the mortgage crisis of 2008 and 2009

   the rise in cases of autism

   the destruction of the space shuttle *Columbia*

2. One of the fallacies of argument discussed in Chapter 17 is the *post hoc, ergo propter hoc* ("after this, therefore because of this") fallacy. Causal arguments are particularly prone to this kind of fallacious reasoning, in which a writer asserts a causal relationship between two entirely unconnected events. When Angelina Jolie gave birth to twins, for instance, the stock market rallied by nearly 600 points, but it would be difficult to argue that one caused the other.

   Because causal arguments can easily fall prey to this fallacy, you might find it useful to try to create and defend an absurd connection of this kind. Begin by asserting a causal link between two events or phenomena that likely have no relationship: *The enormous popularity of the iPhone is partially due to global warming.* Then spend a page or so spinning out an imaginative argument to defend the claim. It's OK to have fun with this exercise, but see how convincing you can be at generating plausible arguments.

3. Working with a group, write a big *Why?* on a sheet of paper or computer screen, and then generate a list of *why* questions. Don't be too critical of the initial list:

   Why?

   — *do people laugh?*

   — *do some animals form monogamous relationships?*

— *do college students binge drink?*

— *do teenagers drive fast?*

— *do babies cry?*

Generate as long a list as you can in fifteen minutes. Then decide which of the questions might make plausible starting points for intriguing causal arguments.

4. Here's a schematic causal analysis of one event, exploring the difference among immediate, necessary, and sufficient causes. Critique and revise the analysis as you see fit. Then create another of your own, beginning with a different event, phenomenon, incident, fad, or effect.

Event: Traffic fatality at an intersection

Immediate cause: An SUV that runs a red light, totals a Miata, and kills its driver

Necessary cause: Two drivers who are navigating Friday rush-hour traffic (if no driving, then no accident)

Sufficient cause: An SUV driver who is distracted by a cell-phone conversation

Cultural Stress Linked to Suicide

LIA HARDIN

May 31, 2007

Asian American women demonstrate a high rate of suicide when compared with women of other ethnicities, California State–Fullerton researcher Eliza Noh found in a recent empirical study.

The causal claim is introduced: several factors lead to mental health problems. Credentials of researchers are established.

Noh and Stanford mental health professionals Alejandro Martinez, the director of Counseling and Psychological Services (CAPS), and Rona Hu, director of the Acute Inpatient Unit at Stanford Hospital, told *The Daily* that parental pressure, cultural differences between the United States and Asian countries, and avoidance of mental health issues in Asian American families can contribute to the prevalence of mental health problems.

Examples of deaths attributed to the identified factors are given.

Following the death of graduate student Mengyao "May" Zhou earlier this year and the recent revelation that Azia Kim had been squatting in Stanford dorms for eight months despite the fact that she was not a student, suicide and mental health issues in the Asian American community have become widely discussed on the Stanford campus.

Citing the ongoing study, Noh said that the tendency of Asian American women to ignore or deny stress, depression, and other mental health problems can cause the larger anxieties that lead to suicide.

Expert testimony in support of claim is introduced.

"There are multiple factors that contribute to suicidality," Noh said. "[For Asian American women] there is this pressure to do well in school and that pressure comes

---

Lia Hardin wrote this article as a staff writer for her campus newspaper, the *Stanford Daily*. In it, she explores the factors that contribute to the relatively high rate of suicide among Asian American women. Because she is writing for a newspaper, Hardin does not provide any formal documentation of her sources but simply identifies the three authorities who supplied most of her information.

from their family members. There is a miscommunication or a lack of communication with their parents. There is a cultural division between them and their parents."

"They are expected to listen to their parents," she said, "to do well in school, not to ask questions and not to talk back."

All those cultural pressures can lead Asian American women to treat mental health issues like an elephant in the room, exacerbating existing problems and generating others.

A second expert researcher is cited.

Hu argued that, for many Asian American women, culturally related issues can contribute directly to mental health problems. She cited young women she knew who had been disowned by their families because of circumstances that parents interpreted as failures.

"The whole concept in the Asian family is that the family is not a democracy," Hu said. "Parents feel entitled to make decisions for their children, including what major or career to choose, or whom to marry. There's a line from a movie where they say, 'There's no word for *privacy* in Chinese.'"

"The sense of shame can be a big part of Asian American culture and that's something that Americans don't understand so much," she added. "If Hugh Grant is caught doing something [shameful,] he apologizes and goes on with his movie career. In Asia, shame can endure for generations. The default Asian coping mechanism is denial."

A third researcher is cited.

Martinez added that differences between education systems in America and Asian countries can lead to misunderstandings within families.

"Specifically in some Asian countries, people have to make career decisions almost when they get to high school," Martinez said. Coming from such a background, parents often misinterpret their children's decision to explore different fields in college.

"If someone did that in their country of origin, it would be a dramatic setback," he said. "They may not be familiar with how much flexibility is possible in the United States."

Martinez cited Korea's suicide rate, which is far higher than the United States.

"The consequences of someone getting a 'B' in a class at Stanford really aren't that great in the context of career decisions and career opportunities," he said. "In other cultures they can be significant."

Noh said that open discussion of mental health issues in the community, along with the availability of resources that can cater specifically to Asian Americans, can be used to counter the problem.

Ways to address the problem are introduced.

"There has to be some serious commitment on the part of the community," Noh said. "[Resources] need to be appropriate for Asian American students. Councilors should be trained in the languages that they speak and have some level of cultural awareness of [students'] backgrounds."

Without those specially tailored resources, she said, Asian American women in her study often chose to reject counseling and therapy altogether.

"The big fear was that they didn't want to go to strangers who didn't know about their situation," she said. "Asian Americans have the lowest rates of utilization of mental health services. There is something about traditional mental health services that doesn't appeal to Asian Americans."

Hu and Martinez said that Stanford has resources for Asian Americans available at campus mental health facilities.

Campus resources for addressing the problem are reviewed.

"We address this in two ways," Martinez said. "An important one is to have diversity on our staff. In addition to that, we do commit some of our resources to making sure that all of our staff have sensitivity to the communities that make up Stanford students."

Hu said that at the Stanford Hospital, some of the attending physicians and residents in psychiatry are Asian and that staff members fluent in Mandarin are available.

Hu and Noh both said that in addition to providing ethnicity-specific resources, fostering discussion of suicide and mental health is important because avoidance of the issue is pervasive in the Asian American community.

"Helping to de-stigmatize things is very helpful," Hu said. "I don't see people disowned so frequently in other cultures."

A final contributing factor to suicide: feeling alone and helpless.

"The number one factor that [study participants] felt in terms of contributing to suicide is that they felt alone and helpless and that they didn't have any place to turn," Noh said. "I've received lots of emails of thanks . . . from people happy that there is dialogue taking place."

Stinging Tentacles Offer Hint of Oceans' Decline

ELISABETH ROSENTHAL

BARCELONA, Spain—Blue patrol boats crisscross the swimming areas of beaches here with their huge nets skimming the water's surface. The yellow flags that urge caution and the red flags that prohibit swimming because of risky currents are sometimes topped now with blue ones warning of a new danger: swarms of jellyfish.

In a period of hours during a day a couple of weeks ago, 300 people on Barcelona's bustling beaches were treated for stings, and 11 were taken to hospitals.

From Spain to New York, to Australia, Japan and Hawaii, jellyfish are becoming more numerous and more widespread, and they are showing up in places where they have rarely been seen before, scientists say. The faceless marauders are stinging children blithely bathing on summer vacations, forcing beaches to close and clogging fishing nets.

But while jellyfish invasions are a nuisance to tourists and a hardship to fishermen, for scientists they are a source of more profound alarm, a signal of the declining health of the world's oceans.

Elisabeth Rosenthal is a physician as well as an award-winning journalist. She writes on energy, climate change, and other science-related topics, often for the *New York Times*, where this article was published in August 2008.

"These jellyfish near shore are a message the sea is sending us saying, 'Look how badly you are treating me,'" said Dr. Josep-María Gili, a leading jellyfish expert, who has studied them at the Institute of Marine Sciences of the Spanish National Research Council in Barcelona for more than 20 years.

The explosion of jellyfish populations, scientists say, reflects a combination of severe overfishing of natural predators, like tuna, sharks and swordfish; rising sea temperatures caused in part by global warming; and pollution that has depleted oxygen levels in coastal shallows.

These problems are pronounced in the Mediterranean, a sea bounded by more than a dozen countries that rely on it for business and pleasure. Left unchecked in the Mediterranean and elsewhere, these problems could make the swarms of jellyfish menacing coastlines a grim vision of seas to come.

"The problem on the beach is a social problem," said Dr. Gili, who talks with admiration of the "beauty" of the globular jellyfish. "We need to take care of it for our tourism industry. But the big problem is not on the beach. It's what's happening in the seas."

Jellyfish, relatives of the sea anemone and coral that for the most part are relatively harmless, in fact are the cockroaches of the open waters, the ultimate maritime survivors who thrive in damaged environments, and that is what they are doing.

Within the past year, there have been beach closings because of jellyfish swarms on the Côte d'Azur in France, the Great Barrier Reef of Australia, and at Waikiki and Virginia Beach in the United States.

In Australia, more than 30,000 people were treated for stings last year, double the number in 2005. The rare but deadly Irukandji jellyfish is expanding its range in Australia's warming waters, marine scientists say.

While no good global database exists on jellyfish populations, the increasing reports from around the world have convinced scientists that the trend is real, serious and climate-related, although they caution that jellyfish populations in any one place undergo year-to-year variation.

"Human-caused stresses, including global warming and overfishing, are encouraging jellyfish surpluses in many tourist destinations and productive fisheries," according to the National Science Foundation, which is issuing a report on the phenomenon this fall and lists as problem areas Australia, the Gulf of Mexico, Hawaii, the Black Sea, Namibia, Britain, the Mediterranean, the Sea of Japan and the Yangtze estuary.

In Barcelona, one of Spain's most vibrant tourist destinations, city officials and the Catalan Water Agency have started fighting back, trying desperately to ensure that it is safe for swimmers to go back in the water.

Each morning, with the help of Dr. Gili's team, boats monitor offshore jellyfish swarms, winds and currents to see if beaches are threatened and if closings are needed. They also check if jellyfish collection in the waters near the beaches is needed. Nearly 100 boats stand ready to help in an emergency, said Xavier Duran of the water agency. The constant squeal of Dr. Gili's cellphone reflected his de facto role as Spain's jellyfish control and command center. Calls came from all over.

Officials in Santander and the Basque country were concerned about frequent sightings this year on the Atlantic coast of the Portuguese man-of-war, a sometimes lethal warm-water species not previously seen regularly in those regions.

Farther south, a fishing boat from the Murcia region called to report an off-shore swarm of *Pelagia noctiluca*—an iridescent purplish jellyfish that issues a nasty sting—more than a mile long. A chef, presumably trying to find some advantage in the declining oceans, wanted to know if the local species were safe to eat if cooked. Much is unknown about the jellyfish, and Dr. Gili was unsure.

In previous decades there were jellyfish problems for only a couple of days every few years; now the threat of jellyfish is a daily headache for local officials and is featured on the evening news. "In the past few years the dynamic has changed completely—the temperature is a little warmer," Dr. Gili said.

Though the stuff of horror B-movies, jellyfish are hardly aggressors. They float haplessly with the currents. They discharge their venom automatically when they bump into something warm—a human body, for example—from poison-containing stingers on mantles, arms or long, threadlike tendrils, which can grow to be yards long.

Some, like the Portuguese man-of-war or the giant box jellyfish, can be deadly on contact. *Pelagia noctiluca*, common in the Mediterranean, delivers a painful sting producing a wound that lasts weeks, months or years, depending on the person and the amount of contact.

In the Mediterranean, overfishing of both large and small fish has left jellyfish with little competition for plankton, their food, and fewer predators. Unlike in Asia, where some jellyfish are eaten by people, here they have no economic or epicurean value.

The warmer seas and drier climate caused by global warming work to the jellyfish's advantage, since nearly all jellyfish breed better and faster in warmer waters, according to Dr. Jennifer Purcell, a jellyfish expert at the Shannon Point Marine Center of Western Washington University.

Global warming has also reduced rainfall in temperate zones, researchers say, allowing the jellyfish to better approach the beaches. Rain runoff from land would normally slightly decrease the salinity of coastal waters, "creating a natural barrier that keeps the jellies from the coast," Dr. Gili said.

Then there is pollution, which reduces oxygen levels and visibility in coastal waters. While other fish die in or avoid waters with low oxygen levels, many jellyfish can thrive in them. And while most fish have to see to catch their food, jellyfish, which filter food passively from the water, can dine in total darkness, according to Dr. Purcell's research.

Residents in Barcelona have forged a prickly coexistence with their new neighbors.

Last month, Mirela Gómez, 8, ran out of the water crying with her first jellyfish sting, clutching a leg that had suddenly become painful and itchy. Her grandparents rushed her to a nearby Red Cross stand. "I'm a little afraid to go back in the water," she said, displaying a row of angry red welts on her shin.

Francisco Antonio Padrós, a 77-year-old fisherman, swore mightily as he unloaded his catch one morning last weekend, pulling off dozens of jellyfish clinging to his nets and tossing them onto a dock. Removing a few shrimp, he said his nets were often "filled with more jellyfish than fish."

By the end of the exercise his calloused hands were bright red and swollen to twice their normal size. "Right now I can't tell if I have hands or not—they hurt, they're numb, they itch," he said.

Dr. Santiago Nogué, head of the toxicology unit at the largest hospital here, said that although 90 percent of stings healed in a week or two, many people's still hurt and itched for months. He said he was now seeing 20 patients a year whose symptoms did not respond to any treatment at all, sometimes requiring surgery to remove the affected area.

The sea, however, has long been central to life in Barcelona, and that is unlikely to change. Recently when the beaches were closed, children on a breakwater collected jellyfish in a bucket. The next day, Antonio López, a diver, emerged from the water. "There are more every year—we saw hundreds offshore today," he said. "You just have to learn how to handle the stings."

12
Proposals

A student looking forward to spring break proposes to two friends that they join a group that will spend the vacation helping to build a school in a Guatemalan village.

The members of a club for undergrad business majors talk about their common need to create informative, appealing résumés. After much talk, three members suggest that the club develop a Web site that will guide members in building such résumés and provide links to other resources.

A project team at a large architectural firm works for three months developing a response to an RFP (request for proposal) to convert a university library into a digital learning center.

The undergraduate student organization at a large state university asks the administration for information about how long it takes to complete a degree in each academic major. After analyzing this information, the group recommends a reduction in the number of hours needed to graduate.

Understanding and Categorizing Proposals

Think big, and be patient. You might be amazed by what you accomplish. Executive director of the Sierra Club Foundation and renowned environmentalist David Brower (1912–2000) long blamed himself for not standing firm against the Glen Canyon Dam project in northern Arizona—which in 1963 began holding back the waters of the Colorado River, flooding some of the most wild and beautiful canyons in the world to create a reservoir more than 100 miles long, Lake Powell. "I have worn sackcloth and ashes ever since, convinced that I could have saved the place if I had simply got off my duff," he wrote.

But he did more than penance. In a 1997 article entitled "Let the River Run through It," Brower made a blunt proposal:

> But as surely as we made a mistake years ago, we can reverse it now. We can drain Lake Powell and let the Colorado River run through the dam that created it, bringing Glen Canyon and the wonder of its side canyons back to life. We can let the river do what it needs to do downstream in the Grand Canyon itself.
>
> We don't need to tear the dam down, however much some people would like to see it go. Together the dam's two diversion tunnels can send 200,000 cubic feet of water per second downstream, twice as much as the Colorado's highest flows. Once again Grand Canyon would make its own sounds and, if you listened carefully, you would hear it sighing with relief. The dam itself would be left as a tourist attraction, like the Pyramids, with passers-by wondering how humanity ever built it, and why.
>
> —David Brower, "Let the River Run through It"

Droughts have shrunk Lake Powell dramatically in the years since Brower wrote this article, and the concrete arch of Glen Canyon Dam still holds fast against the Colorado River. But the logic of Brower's proposal has persisted. In 2008, film director Greg MacGillivray recalled Brower's proposal in his documentary film *Grand Canyon Adventure: River at Risk*, which followed author and photographer Wade Davis, environmentalist Robert Kennedy Jr., and their daughters Tara and Kick as they traveled down the Colorado. With voiceover by Robert Redford, this film defends Brower's proposal and demonstrates how the regulated flow of the Colorado relates to the current world water crisis.

Pointing out that the creation of the Glen Canyon Dam changed the flow of the Colorado forever, the film shows that the river, once a source of water and power for 25 million Americans, continues to suffer from the severe drought and overregulation. As MacGillivray says, "In our film, the Colorado becomes a metaphor for global water issues, revealing how interconnected our rivers, water supply, and human actions really are." This film ends with a proposal that is broader than Brower's—that every viewer take action to protect water now, from installing low-flow shower heads, to voting in ways that will help protect the Colorado, to thinking about water in completely new and much more serious ways.

Not all proposals are as dramatic or far-reaching as those made by Brower and *Grand Canyon Adventure*, but such arguments, whether casual

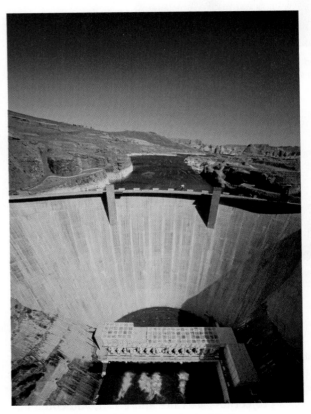

Glen Canyon Dam with a power plant at its base

Lake Powell, created by the dam, now stands at only 46 percent capacity: should it be drained?

Cracks five feet deep scar lakebeds that were formerly fed by the Colorado River.

or formal, are important in all of our lives. How many proposals do you make or respond to in one day? Your neighbor might suggest that you work together to clean up a park down the street, you and a colleague might collaborate on a project to save time and effort, you could call your best friend to check out a new movie, or you might approach your boss about implementing an idea you've just had. In each case, the proposal implies that some action should take place and suggests that there are sound reasons why it should.

In their simplest form, proposal arguments look something like this:

A should do B because of C.

┌──────── A ────────┐ ┌──────────── B ────────────┐
Our student government should endorse the Academic Bill of Rights

┌──────────────────── C ────────────────────┐
because students should not be punished in their courses for their reasonable political views.

Proposals come at us so routinely that it's not surprising that they cover a dizzyingly wide range of possibilities, from local and concrete practices (*A student should switch dorms immediately; A company should switch from one supplier of paper to another*) to broad matters of policy (*The U.S. Congress should act to reform immigration rules*). So it may help to think of proposal arguments as divided roughly into two kinds—those that focus on practices and those that focus on policies.

Here are several examples:

Proposals about Practices

- The college should allow students to pay tuition on a month-by-month basis.
- The NCAA should implement a playoff system to determine its Division I football champion.
- San Francisco should erect a more effective suicide-prevention barrier on the Golden Gate Bridge.

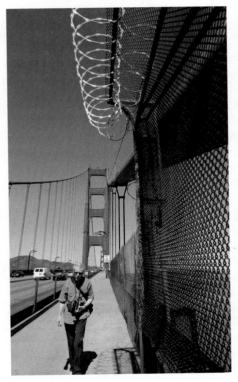

Existing suicide-prevention barriers on the Golden Gate Bridge often prove ineffective.

Proposals about Policies

- The college should adopt a policy guaranteeing a "living wage" to all campus workers.
- The state should repeal all English-only legislation.
- The police department should institute a policy to train officers in intercultural communication.

Characterizing Proposals

Proposals have three main characteristics:

- They call for action or response, often in response to a problem.
- They focus on the future.
- They center on the audience.

Proposals always call for some kind of action. They aim at getting something done—or sometimes at *preventing* something from being done. Proposals marshal evidence and arguments to persuade people to choose a course of action: *Let's build a completely green home; Let's oppose the latest Supreme Court ruling; Let's create a campus organization for first-generation college students.* But you know the old saying, "You can lead a horse to water, but you can't make it drink." It's usually easier to *convince* audiences what a good course of action is than to *persuade* them to take it (or pay for it). You can present a proposal as cogently as possible—but usually you can't make an audience take the action you propose.

Proposal arguments must appeal to more than good sense—as David Brower and Greg MacGillivray do. Ethos matters, too. It helps if a writer carries a certain gravitas (Brower was one of the great environmentalists of the twentieth century, and MacGillivray is well known for his searing environmental documentaries). If your word and experience are credible, then an audience is more likely to do what you propose.

In addition, proposal arguments focus on the future—what people, institutions, or governments should do over the upcoming weeks, months, or even decades. This orientation toward the future presents special challenges, since few of us have crystal balls. Proposal arguments must therefore offer the best evidence available to suggest that actions we recommend will achieve what they promise.

In 2008, for example, oil magnate T. Boone Pickens appeared in a series of television commercials presenting evidence that the United States must move beyond an unsustainable reliance on fossil fuel. In these TV spots, Pickens drew on his ethos, presenting himself as one who had been an "oilman all my life" but who now understood from the weight of evidence that he and the country had to move beyond oil. He asked viewers to watch for a proposal he would be making, and within a month, additional advertisements appeared in which Pickens proposed his own energy plan (the United States should move aggressively to harvest power from the wind) and offered evidence to suggest that doing so would provide major help in curing the "oil addiction." Putting his money where his mouth is, Pickens—a billionaire many times over—immediately ordered $2 billion worth of wind turbines.

It will take years, however, to see whether Pickens's crystal ball provided the best answer to America's dependence on oil. By mid-2009, technical problems had already forced him to cancel plans for a single huge "wind farm" in the Texas Panhandle and to explore other options in the Midwest and Canada.

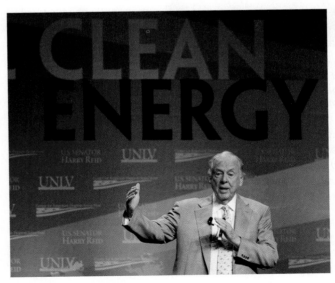

T. Boone Pickens defending his wind-power proposal

Finally, proposals have to focus on particular audiences, especially on people who can get something done. Sometimes, proposal arguments are written to general audiences. You can find these arguments, for example, in newspaper editorials and letters to the editor. And such appeals to a broad group make sense when a proposal—say, to finance new toll roads or build an art museum—must surf on waves of community support and financing. But such grand proposals also need to influence individuals (such as financiers, developers, public officials, and legislators) who have the power to make change actually happen. On your own campus, for example, a plan to alter admissions policies might be directed both to students in general and (perhaps in a different form) to the university president, members of the faculty council, and admissions officers. Identifying your potential audiences is critical to the success of any proposal.

Proposals have to take audience values into account. Shooting deer, even when they're munching on garden flowers, is unacceptable to most suburbanites.

An effective proposal also has to be compatible with the values of the audience. Some ideas may make good sense but cannot be enacted. For example, many American towns and cities have a problem with expanding deer populations. Without natural predators, the deer are moving closer to homes, dining on gardens and shrubbery, and endangering traffic. Yet one obvious and feasible solution—culling the herds through hunting—is usually not acceptable to the communities (perhaps too many people remember *Bambi*).

Developing Proposals

How do you develop an effective proposal? Start by showing that a problem needs a solution or that some need is not being met. Then make a proposal that addresses the problem or meets the need. Explain in detail why adopting your proposal will address the need or problem better than other solutions, and finally, show that the proposal is both feasible and acceptable. This might sound easy, but writing a proposal argument can be a process of discovery. At the outset, you think you know exactly what ought to be done, but by the end, you may see (and even recommend) other options.

Defining a Need or Problem

To make a proposal to solve a problem or meet a need, first establish that a need or problem exists. You'll typically describe the problem that you intend to address at the beginning of your project as a way to lead up to a specific claim. But in some cases, you could put the need or problem right after your claim as the major reason for adopting the proposal: *Let's ban cell phones on campus now. Why? Because we've become a school of walking zombies. No one speaks or even acknowledges the people they meet or pass on campus. Half of our students are so busy chattering to people that they don't participate in the community around them.*

The task of establishing a need or problem calls on you to do the following:

- Paint a picture of the need or problem in concrete and memorable ways.
- Show how the need or problem affects the audience for the argument as well as the larger society.
- Explain why the need or problem is significant.
- Explain why other attempts to address the issue may have failed.

In proposing that community service be required for students enrolled in state colleges, for example, you might begin by painting a picture of a self-absorbed "me first and only" society that values instant gratification. After evoking this dismal scene, you might trace the consequences of such behavior for your campus and community, arguing, for instance, that it fosters excessive competition, leaves many of society's most vulnerable members without helping hands, and puts the responsibility of assisting people solely in the hands of government—thereby adding to its size and cost and raising taxes for all. You might have to cite some authorities and statistics to prove that the problem you're diagnosing is real and that it touches everyone likely to read your argument. Then readers will be ready to hear your proposal.

Look at how Craig R. Dean, a lawyer and executive director of the Equal Marriage Rights Fund, prepares his claim—that the United States should legalize same-sex marriage—by explaining the significant problems that the existing ban on gay marriages creates:

In November 1990, my lover, Patrick Gill, and I were denied a marriage license because we are gay. In a memorandum explaining the District's decision, the clerk of the court wrote that "the sections of the District of Columbia code governing marriage do not authorize marriage between persons of the same sex." By refusing to give us the same legal recognition that is given to heterosexual couples, the District has degraded our relationship as well as that of every other gay and lesbian couple.

At one time, interracial couples were not allowed to marry. Gays and lesbians are still denied this basic civil right in the U.S.—and around the world. Can you imagine the outcry if any other minority group was denied the right to legally marry today? Marriage is more than a piece of paper. It gives societal recognition and legal protection to a relationship. It confers numerous benefits to spouses; in the District alone, there are more than 100 automatic marriage-based rights. In every state in the nation, married couples have the right to be on each other's health, disability, life insurance and pension plans. Married couples receive special tax exemptions, deductions and refunds. Spouses may automatically inherit property and have rights of survivorship that avoid inheritance tax. Though unmarried couples—both gay and heterosexual—are entitled to some of these rights, they are by no means guaranteed.

For married couples, the spouse is legally the next of kin in case of death, medical emergency or mental incapacity. In stark contrast, the family is generally the next of kin for same-sex couples. In the shadow of AIDS, the denial of marriage rights can be even more ominous. . . .

Some argue that gay marriage is too radical for society. We disagree. According to a 1989 study by the American Bar Association, eight to 10 million children are currently being reared in three million gay households. Therefore, approximately 6 percent of the U.S. population is made up of gay and lesbian families with children. Why should these families be denied the protection granted to other families? Allowing gay marriage would strengthen society by increasing tolerance. It is paradoxical that mainstream America perceives gays and lesbians as unable to maintain long-term relationships while at the same time denying them the very institutions that stabilize such relationships.

—Craig R. Dean, "Legalize Gay Marriage"

Notice, too, that Dean indicates that the problems faced by gays who seek to marry have consequences for all members of the potential audience—who also might face problems stemming from intolerance. Although homosexuals might benefit most directly from solving the problem he describes, ultimately everyone in society gains.

In describing the problem that your proposal argument intends to solve, you may also need to review earlier attempts to address it. Many issues have a long history that you can't afford to ignore. For example, if you were arguing for a college football play-off, you might point out that the current bowl championship series represents an attempt—largely unsuccessful—to crown a widely recognized national champion. Some problems seem to grow worse every time someone tinkers with them. You might pause before proposing any additional attempt at reform of the current system of financing federal election campaigns when you discover that previous reforms have resulted in more bureaucracy, more restrictions on political expression, and more unregulated money flowing into the system. *Enough is enough* is a potent argument when faced with such a mess.

Making a Strong and Clear Claim

After you've described and analyzed a problem or state of affairs, you're prepared to make a claim. Begin with your claim (a proposal of what X or Y should do) followed by the reason(s) that X or Y should act and the effects of adopting the proposal:

Claim	Communities should encourage the development of charter schools.
Reason	Charter schools are not burdened by the bureaucracy that is associated with most public schooling.
Effects	Instituting such schools will bring more effective education to communities and offer an incentive to the public schools to improve their programs.

Having established a claim, you can explore its implications by drawing out the reasons, warrants, and evidence that can support it most effectively:

Claim	In light of a recent U.S. Supreme Court decision that ruled that federal drug laws cannot be used to prosecute doctors who prescribe drugs for use in suicide, our state should immediately pass a bill legalizing physician-assisted suicide for patients who are terminally ill.

Reason	Physician-assisted suicide can relieve the suffering of those who are terminally ill and will die soon.
Warrant	The relief of suffering is desirable.
Evidence	Oregon voters have twice approved the state's Death with Dignity Act, which has been in effect since 1997, and to date the suicide rate has not risen sharply nor have doctors given out a large number of prescriptions for death-inducing drugs. Several other states are considering ballot initiatives in favor of doctor-assisted suicide.

In this proposal argument, the *reason* sets up the need for the proposal, whereas the *warrant* and *evidence* demonstrate that the proposal is just and could meet its objective. Your actual argument would develop each point in detail.

Showing That the Proposal Addresses the Need or Problem

An important but tricky part of making a successful proposal lies in relating the claim to the need or problem that it addresses. When gasoline prices soared in the summer of 2008, John McCain, then the Republican nominee for president, proposed to end the long-standing U.S. ban on offshore drilling for oil, a move that he had earlier opposed. McCain could certainly show that a problem existed: the economic effects of the highest-ever gas prices were being exacerbated by the spiraling cost of food and the housing and mortgage crisis. He and other advocates of dropping the ban had a harder time, however, showing that the action they proposed would actually address the problem. Indeed, experts from the Bush administration's Department of Energy said that adopting such a proposal would have little effect on the price of oil for at least twenty years. Later, McCain admitted that such drilling would have only "psychological effects," which, he said, would be "beneficial."

Sometimes a proposal calls for audiences to dream a little about how it fulfills a need or solves a problem that might not be immediately recognizable. That strategy was taken by President John F. Kennedy in a famous speech that he gave on September 12, 1962, explaining his proposal that the United States land a man on the moon by the end of the 1960s. Here are three paragraphs from his speech at Rice University, explaining why:

> We set sail on this new sea because there is new knowledge to be gained, and new rights to be won, and they must be won and used for

John and Cindy McCain promoting offshore oil drilling.

the progress of all people. For space science, like nuclear science and all technology, has no conscience of its own. Whether it will become a force for good or ill depends on man, and only if the United States occupies a position of pre-eminence can we help decide whether this new ocean will be a sea of peace or a new terrifying theater of war. I do not say that we should or will go unprotected against the hostile misuse of space any more than we go unprotected against the hostile use of land or sea, but I do say that space can be explored and mastered without feeding the fires of war, without repeating the mistakes that man has made in extending his writ around this globe of ours.

There is no strife, no prejudice, no national conflict in outer space as yet. Its hazards are hostile to us all. Its conquest deserves the best of all mankind, and its opportunity for peaceful cooperation may never come again. But why, some say, the moon? Why choose this as our goal? And they may well ask why climb the highest mountain? Why, 35 years ago, fly the Atlantic? Why does Rice play Texas?

We choose to go to the moon. We choose to go to the moon in this decade and do the other things, not because they are easy, but because they are hard, because that goal will serve to organize and measure the best of our energies and skills, because that challenge is one that we are willing to accept, one we are unwilling to postpone, and one which we intend to win, and the others, too.

—John F. Kennedy

Proposals and Academic Argument

Academic writers are often called to present proposals in the form of applications for grants. In fact, you may have an opportunity to write a grant proposal during your undergraduate years to secure funding from a campus organization for a favorite project. Here is the introduction to a grant proposal that was submitted to the National Science Foundation:

Integrative Approaches to Bilingual Cognition and Interaction

This project proposes a new initiative to integrate doctoral education and research in Computer Science and Psychology, with extension planned to Linguistics and Education. The project's specific focus will be the connections between cognitive models of language and cognitive models in human-computer interaction, with a particular emphasis on bilingualism. The principal research efforts will involve understanding (1) the nature of bilingual language processing, combining cognitive and computational methods, and (2) how to develop real-time conversational systems based on cognitively accurate models for bilingual populations, especially at time scales of 300 milliseconds and below. The project will play a major part in a university-wide initiative on research and education in the interdisciplinary field of language and cognition. The project will also serve as a model for integrating doctoral programs across college and departmental boundaries. Students served by this project will include significant numbers of Hispanics; over 70 percent of the University's 19,000 students are Mexican American, and another 12 percent are Mexican nationals. The project's full proposal provides a list of project participants, detailed rationale, description of methods, step by step outcomes, and an itemized budget.

Note that this introduction sets out the major research questions to be answered, connects the proposal to larger university efforts, identifies the population to be served by the project, and provides an overview of what is to come in the full proposal.

Showing That the Proposal Is Feasible

To be effective, proposals must be *feasible*—that is, the action proposed can be carried out in a reasonable way. Demonstrating feasibility calls on you to present evidence—from similar cases, from personal experience, from observational data, from interview or survey data, from Internet research, or from any other sources—showing that what you propose can indeed be done with the resources available. "Resources available" is key: if the proposal calls for funds, personnel, or skills beyond reach or reason, your audience is unlikely to accept it. When that's the case, it's time to reassess your proposal, modify it, and test any new ideas against these revised criteria. This is also when you can reconsider proposals that others might suggest are better, more effective, or more workable than yours. There's no shame in admitting that you may have been wrong. When drafting a proposal, ask friends to think of counterproposals. If your own proposal can stand up to such challenges, it's likely a strong one.

Using Personal Experience

If your own experience backs up your claim or demonstrates the need or problem that your proposal aims to address, then consider using it to develop your proposal (as Craig R. Dean does in the opening of his proposal to legalize gay marriage). Consider the following questions in deciding when to include your own experiences in making a proposal:

- Is your experience directly related to the need or problem that you seek to address or to your proposal about it?
- Will your experience be appropriate and speak convincingly to the audience? Will the audience immediately understand its significance, or will it require explanation?
- Does your personal experience fit logically with the other reasons that you're using to support your claim?

Be careful. If a proposal seems crafted to serve mainly your own interests, you won't get far.

Considering Design and Visuals

Because proposals often address specific audiences, they can take a
number of forms—a letter, memo, Web page, feasibility report, brochure,
or prospectus. Each form has different design requirements. Indeed, the

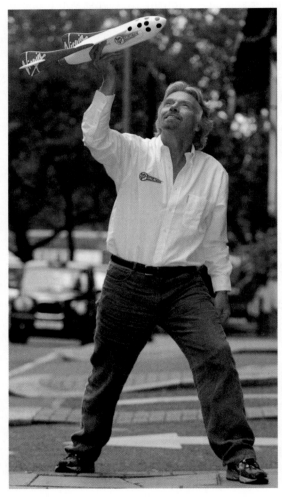

Richard Branson with a model of Virgin Galactic's
Mothership

design may add powerfully to—or detract significantly from—the effectiveness of the proposal. Even in a college essay that is written on a computer, its headings and subheadings, variations in type (such as boldface or italics), and white space and margins can guide readers through the proposal and enhance its persuasiveness. So before you produce a final copy of any proposal, plan its design.

A related issue to consider is whether a graphic image might help readers understand key elements of the proposal—what the challenge is, why it demands action, and what exactly you're suggesting—and help make the idea more attractive. That strategy is routinely used in professional proposals by architects, engineers, and government agencies. When British businessman Richard Branson updated his proposal to take people on (very expensive) trips into space, he presented an animated video explaining the concept of space tourism and showing what such a trip would be like. The brief animation made the proposal seem exciting, attractive, and possible and appeared on YouTube and other sites (you can check it out at http://www.virgingalactic.com).

Key Features of Proposals

In drafting a proposal, make sure you include:

- a description of a problem that needs a solution
- a claim that proposes a practice or policy that addresses a problem or need, is oriented toward action, is directed at the future, and is appropriate to your audience
- statements that clearly relate the claim to the problem or need
- evidence that the proposal will effectively address the need or solve the problem and that it's workable

To fully develop your proposal, you will need to address all these elements, though you may choose to arrange them in several ways. A proposal might open with a vivid description of a problem and even an image (such as photographs of beautiful canyons that were destroyed by the Glen Canyon Dam). Or it might open with your proposal itself, which perhaps is stunning or unexpected in its directness.

Organize your proposal carefully, and ask for responses to your organizational plan from your instructor and classmates.

Not Just Words

Every day, groups make proposals that need to be approved by community or government groups, which often wind up paying for them. Such proposals are typically presented in the most flattering and appealing way possible.

Take a look at the images associated with a proposed project, a huge sports, entertainment, and shopping complex planned for New Jersey.

The Meadowlands Xanadu Complex as it was planned to look on completion

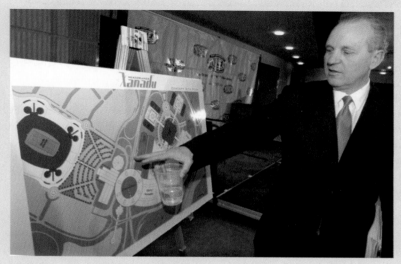

The site plan for Meadowlands Xanadu

These and a number of other images on the Web site for Meadowlands Xanadu support the proposed project by showing how traffic will flow in and around it, how it will serve its customers in five different venues, and how it will enhance the surrounding neighborhood and skyline. Look for similar examples of planned complexes or developments online. Is your community considering a new museum, library, stadium, or park, or is a local developer planning to turn a warehouse district into a shopping mall? Collect as much information as you can find about the proposal, and ask what it will offer to your community. Then design a brochure, poster, or Web site that would support or oppose the proposal. Be creative—and remember that design involves more than just images and photos.

GUIDE to writing a proposal

● Finding a Topic or Identifying a Problem

Your everyday experience often calls on you to consider problems and to make proposals—to change your academic major for important reasons, to add to the family income by starting a home-based business, or to oppose restricting new scholarships to specific student groups. In addition, your work or your job may require you to solve problems or make proposals to a boss, a board of directors, the local school board, someone you want to impress: the list could go on and on. You also can make proposals to online groups; with email one click away, the whole world can be the audience for your proposal.

In all these cases, you'll be calling for action or critiquing an action. Why not make an informal list of proposals that you'd like to explore in a number of different areas? Or do some freewriting on a subject of great interest to you, and see if it leads to a proposal. Either method of exploration is likely to turn up several possibilities for a good proposal argument.

● Researching Your Topic

Proposals often call for research. Even a simple one like *Let's start painting the house this weekend* raises questions that require some investigation: *Who has the time for the job? What sort of paint will be the best? How much will the job cost?* A proposal for adopting block scheduling at your local high school calls for careful research into evidence that supports the use of such a system. *Where has it been effective, and why?* And for proposals about social issues (for example, that information on the Internet should be freely accessible to everyone, even minors), extensive research would be necessary to provide adequate support.

For many proposals, you can begin your research by consulting the following types of sources:

- newspapers, magazines, reviews, and journals (online and print)
- online databases
- government documents and reports

- Web sites, blogs, social networking sites, listservs, or newsgroups
- books
- experts in the field, some of whom might be right on your campus

In addition, you might decide to carry out some field research—a survey of student opinions on Internet accessibility, for example, or interviews with people who are well informed about your subject.

Finally, remember that your proposal's success can depend on the credibility of the sources you use in support of it. As a result, you need to evaluate each source carefully (see Chapter 19).

● Formulating a Claim

As you think about and explore your topic, begin formulating a claim about it. To do so, come up with a clear and complete thesis that makes a proposal and states the reasons that this proposal should be followed. To start formulating a claim, explore and respond to the following questions:

- What do I know about the proposal that I'm making?
- What reasons can I offer to support my proposal?
- What evidence do I have that implementing my proposal will lead to the results I want?

● Examples of Proposal Claims

- Because we are in an economic crisis, because many people need help, and because President Obama's National Day of Service (January 19, 2009) was a success, schools and colleges should develop and implement service programs that all students can participate in.
- Every home should be equipped with a well-stocked emergency kit that can sustain inhabitants for at least three days in a natural disaster.
- Congress should repeal the Copyright Extension Act, since it disrupts the balance between incentives for creators and the right of the public to information as set forth in the U.S. Constitution.
- The Environmental Protection Agency must allow California and other states to establish tighter controls on greenhouse gases.

● Preparing a Proposal

If your instructor asks you to prepare a proposal for your project, here's a format that may help:

State the thesis of your proposal completely. If you're having trouble doing so, try outlining it in Toulmin terms:

Claim:

Reason(s):

Warrant(s):

- Explain the problem you intend to address and why your proposal is important. What's at stake in taking or not taking the action that you propose?
- Identify and describe those readers that you hope to reach with your proposal. Why is this group of readers most appropriate for your proposal? What are their interests in the subject?
- Briefly discuss the major difficulties that you foresee for your argument: Demonstrating that the action you propose is necessary? Demonstrating that it's workable? Moving the audience beyond agreement to action? Something else?
- List the research that you need to do. What kinds of sources do you need to consult?
- Note down the format or genre that you expect to use: An academic essay? A formal report? A Web site?

● Thinking about Organization

Proposals can take many different forms but generally include the following elements:

- a description of the problem you intend to address or the state of affairs that leads you to propose the action: *Our neighborhood has recently experienced a rash of break-ins and burglaries. Neighbors feel like captives in their homes, and property values are threatened.*
- a clear and strong proposal, including the reasons for taking the proposed action and the effects that taking this action will have: *Our neighborhood*

should establish a Block Watch program to reduce break-ins and vandalism and involve our kids in building neighborhood pride.

- a clear connection between the proposal and a significant need or problem: *Break-ins and vandalism have been on the rise in our neighborhood for the last three years in part because neighbors have lost contact with one another.*

- a demonstration of ways in which the proposal addresses the need: *A Block Watch program establishes a rotating monitor system for the streets in a neighborhood and a voluntary plan to watch homes.*

- evidence that the proposal will achieve the desired outcome: *Block Watch programs in three other local areas have significantly reduced break-ins and vandalism.*

- a consideration of alternative ways to achieve the desired outcome and a discussion of why these are not feasible: *We could ask for additional police presence, but funding would be hard to get.*

- a demonstration that the proposal is workable and practical: *Because Block Watch is voluntary, our own determination and commitment are all we need to make it work.*

● Getting and Giving Response

All arguments can benefit from the scrutiny of others. Your instructor may assign you to a peer group for the purpose of reading and responding to each other's drafts. If not, ask for responses from some serious readers or consultants at a writing center. You can use the following questions to evaluate a draft. If you're evaluating someone else's draft, be sure to illustrate your points with examples. Specific comments are always more helpful than general observations.

The Claim

- Does the claim clearly call for action? Is the proposal as clear and specific as possible?

- Is the proposal too sweeping? Does it need to be qualified? If so, how?

- Does the proposal clearly address the problem that it intends to solve? If not, how could the connection be strengthened?

- Is the claim likely to get the audience to act rather than just to agree? If not, how could it be revised to do so?

Evidence for the Claim

- Is enough evidence furnished to get the audience to support the proposal? If not, what kind of additional evidence is needed? Does any of the evidence provided seem inappropriate or otherwise ineffective? Why?

- Is the evidence in support of the claim simply announced, or are its significance and appropriateness analyzed? Is a more detailed discussion needed?

- Are any objections that readers might have to the claim or evidence adequately addressed?

- What kinds of sources are cited? How credible and persuasive will they be to readers? What other kinds of sources might be more credible and persuasive?

- Are all quotations introduced with appropriate signal phrases (such as "As Ehrenreich argues, . . .") and blended smoothly into the writer's sentences?

- Are all visuals titled and labeled appropriately? Have you introduced them and commented on their significance?

Organization and Style

- How are the parts of the argument organized? Is this organization effective, or would some other structure work better?

- Will readers understand the relationships among the claims, supporting reasons, warrants, and evidence? If not, what could be done to make those connections clearer? Are more transitional words and phrases needed? Would headings or graphic devices help?

- How have you used visual design elements to make your proposal more effective?

- Are the transitions or links—from point to point, paragraph to paragraph, and sentence to sentence—clear and effective? If not, how could they be improved?

- Is the style suited to the subject? Is it too formal? Too casual? Too technical? Too bland? How can it be improved?

- Which sentences seem particularly effective? Which ones seem weakest, and how could they be improved? Should some short sentences be combined, or should any long ones be separated into two or more sentences?

- How effective are the paragraphs? Do any seem too skimpy or too long? How can they be improved?
- Which words or phrases seem particularly effective, vivid, and memorable? Do any seem dull, vague, unclear, or inappropriate for the audience or the writer's purpose? Are definitions provided for technical or other terms that readers might not know?

Spelling, Punctuation, Mechanics, Documentation, Format

- Are there any errors in spelling, punctuation, capitalization, and the like?
- Is an appropriate and consistent style of documentation used for parenthetical citations and the list of works cited or references? (See Chapter 20.)
- Does the paper or project follow an appropriate format? Is it appropriately designed and attractively presented? How could it be improved? If it's a Web site, do all the links work?

RESPOND •

1. For each problem and solution, make a list of readers' likely objections to the solution offered. Then propose a more defensible solution of your own, and explain why you think it's more workable than the original solution.

   Problem Future shortfalls in the Social Security system
   Solution Raise the age of retirement to seventy-five.

   Problem Extended drought that has killed flowers in the city's parks
   Solution Ration the use of water throughout the city.

   Problem Increasing rates of obesity in the general population
   Solution Ban the sale of high-fat items in fast-food restaurants.

   Problem Increasing school violence
   Solution Authorize teachers and students to carry concealed handguns.

   Problem Increases in sexual assaults on and around campus
   Solution Establish an 8:00 p.m. curfew on weekends.

2. People write proposal arguments to solve problems and to change the way things are. But problems aren't always obvious: what troubles some people might be no big deal to others. To get an idea of the range of problems people face on your campus (some of which you may not even have thought of as problems), divide into groups, and brainstorm about things that annoy you on and around campus, including wastefulness in the cafeterias, 8:00 a.m. classes, and long lines for football or concert tickets. Ask each group to aim for at least twenty gripes. Then choose one problem, and as a group, discuss how you'd prepare a proposal to deal with it. Remember that you'll need to (a) make a strong and clear claim, (b) show that the proposal meets a clear need or solves a significant problem, (c) present good reasons that adopting the proposal will effectively address the need or problem, and (d) show that the proposal is workable and should be adopted.

3. In the essay "Send It Somewhere Special" (p. 411), Michael Benson proposes that we convert the International Space Station into an interplanetary spacecraft, turning it from "an Earth-orbiting caterpillar into an interplanetary butterfly." Using the Toulmin model discussed in Chapter 7, analyze the proposal's structure. What claim does Benson make, and what reasons does he give to support the claim? What warrants connect the reasons to the claim? What evidence does he provide? Alternatively, make up a rough outline of Benson's proposal, and track the reasons that he presents to support his claim.

A Call to Improve Campus Accessibility for the Mobility Impaired

MANASI DESHPANDE

INTRODUCTION

The paper opens with a personal example and dramatizes the issue of campus accessibility.

Wes Holloway, a sophomore at the University of Texas at Austin, never considered the issue of campus accessibility during his first year on campus. But when an injury his freshman year left him wheelchair-bound, he was astonished to realize that he faced an unexpected challenge: maneuvering around the UT campus. Hills that he had effortlessly traversed became mountains; doors that he had easily opened became anvils; and streets that he had mindlessly crossed became treacherous terrain. Says Wes: "I didn't think about accessibility until I had to deal with it, and I think most people are the same way."

Both problem and solution are previewed here, with more details provided in subsequent sections of the paper.

For the ambulatory individual, access for the mobility impaired on the UT campus is easy to overlook. Automatic door entrances and bathrooms with the universal handicapped symbol make the campus seem sufficiently accessible. But for many students and faculty at UT, including me, maneuvering the UT campus in a wheelchair is a daily experience of stress and frustration. Although the University has made a concerted and continuing effort to improve access, students and faculty with physical disabilities still suffer from discriminatory

---

Manasi Deshpande wrote this formidable essay for a course preparing her to work as a consultant in the Writing Center at the University of Texas at Austin. Note how she reaches out to a general audience to make an argument that might seem to have a narrow constituency. She also effectively uses headings to guide readers through the complexities of her proposal. This essay is documented using MLA style.

hardship, unequal opportunity to succeed, and lack of independence.

The University must make campus accessibility a higher priority and take more seriously the hardship that the campus at present imposes on people with mobility impairments. Administrators should devote more resources to creating a user-friendly campus rather than simply conforming to legal requirements for accessibility. The University should also enhance the transparency and approachability of its services for members with mobility impairments. Individuals with permanent physical disabilities would undoubtedly benefit from a stronger resolve to improve campus accessibility. Better accessibility would also benefit the more numerous students and faculty with temporary disabilities and help the University recruit a more diverse body of students and faculty.

ASSESSMENT OF CURRENT EFFORTS

The current state of campus accessibility leaves substantial room for improvement. There are approximately 150 academic and administrative buildings on campus (Grant). Eduardo Gardea, intern architect at the Physical Plant, estimates that only about nineteen buildings comply fully with the Americans with Disabilities Act (ADA). According to Penny Seay, Ph.D., director of the Center for Disability Studies at UT Austin, the ADA in theory "requires every building on campus to be accessible." However, as Bill Throop, associate director of the Physical Plant, explains, there is "no legal deadline to make the entire campus accessible"; neither the ADA nor any other law mandates that certain buildings be made compliant by a certain time. Though not bound by specific legal obligation, the University should strive to fulfill the spirit of the law and recognize campus accessibility as a pressing moral obligation.

While the University has made substantial progress in accessibility improvements, it has failed to make campus accessibility a priority. For example, the Campus Master Plan, published in 1999 by the University, does not include improvements in campus accessibility as one of its major goals for the design and architecture of the University. It mentions accessibility only once to recommend that signs for wayfinding comply with the ADA. The signs should provide "direction to accessible building entrances and routes" and "clear identification of special facilities" (Gleeson et al. 90). Nowhere does the Master Plan discuss the need to design these accessible building entrances, routes, and special facilities or how to fit accessibility improvements into the larger renovation of the campus.

THE BENEFITS OF CHANGE
Benefits for People with Permanent Mobility Impairments

Improving campus accessibility would significantly enhance the quality of life of students and faculty with mobility impairments. The campus at present poses discriminatory hardship on these individuals by making daily activities such as getting to class and using the bathroom unreasonably difficult. Before Wes Holloway leaves home, he must plan his route carefully to avoid hills, use ramps that are easy to maneuver, and enter the side of the building with the accessible entrance. As he goes to class, Wes must go out of his way to avoid poorly paved sidewalks and roads. Sometimes he cannot avoid them and must take an uncomfortable and bumpy ride across potholes and uneven pavement. If his destination does not have an automatic door, he must wait for someone to open the door for him because it is too heavy for him to open himself. To get into Burdine Hall, he has to ask a stranger to push him through the heavy narrow doors because his fingers would get crushed if he pushed himself. Once in the classroom, Wes must find a suitable place to sit, often far away from his classmates because stairs block him from the center of the room.

Other members of the UT community with mobility impairments suffer the same daily hardships as Wes.

The paper uses several layers of headings to organize its diverse materials.

The author outlines the challenges faced by a student with mobility impairment.

Accessibility problems are given a human face with numerous examples of the problems that mobility-impaired people face on campus.

According to Mike Gerhardt, student affairs administrator of Services for Students with Disabilities (SSD), approximately eighty students with physical disabilities, including twenty to twenty-five students using wheelchairs, are registered with SSD. However, the actual number of students with mobility impairments is probably higher because some students choose not to seek services from SSD. The current state of campus accessibility discriminates against all individuals with physical disabilities in the unnecessary hardship it imposes.

Beyond inflicting daily stress on people with mobility impairments, the poor accessibility on campus denies these individuals their independence. Students with physical disabilities must often ask for help from others, especially in opening doors without functional automatic door entrances. Bathrooms without access also deny these individuals their independence. Once when I needed to use a bathroom in Burdine Hall, I found that none of the stalls was accessible. To be able to use the bathroom in privacy, I had to ask a stranger to stand outside the bathroom and make sure no one entered.

The author offers her personal perspective on the subject—a factual appeal that has an emotional dimension.

The state of campus accessibility also denies people with physical disabilities an equal opportunity to succeed. In the summer of 2004, I registered for CH 204, a chemistry lab, because I planned to be a Human Biology major. The major requires students to take four labs. When I got to the lab on the first day of class, I found that I could not perform any tasks independently. The supposedly accessible lab bench was just as high as the other benches, so I could not write, take proper measurements, or handle equipment on the bench. I could not reach the sink. The lab was so cramped that I could hardly fit through the aisles, and I wheeled around in fear of bumping into someone carrying glass equipment. Services for Students with Disabilities informed me that it would not be able to provide me with an assistant. Though I was fully capable of performing the labs myself, the lack of accessibility made me unable to complete even the simplest tasks.

Even with an assistant, I would have lacked independence and felt unequal to my classmates. After this experience, I dropped both the class and the major.

Benefits for People with Temporary Mobility Impairments

In addition to helping the few members of the UT campus with permanent mobility impairments, a faster rate of accessibility improvement would also benefit the much larger population of people with temporary physical disabilities. Many students and faculty will become temporarily disabled from injury at some point during their time at the University. Sprained ankles, torn ACLs, and fractured legs all require use of crutches or a wheelchair. Judy Lu, a second-year Business Honors Program/Plan II/ Pre-med major, used crutches for two weeks when she sprained her ankle playing volleyball. She encountered difficulties similar to those facing people with permanent disabilities, including finding accessible entrances, opening doors without automatic entrances, and finding convenient classroom seating. Getting around campus on crutches "was not convenient at all," and her temporary disability required her to "plan ahead a whole lot more" to find accessible routes and entrances.

The author broadens the appeal of her proposal by showing how improved accessibility will benefit everyone on campus.

All members of the UT community face the risk of enduring an injury that could leave them with a temporary physical disability. According to Dr. Jennifer Maedgen, assistant dean of students and director of SSD, about 5 to 10 percent of the approximately 1,000 students registered with SSD at any given time have temporary disabilities. The number of students with temporary physical disabilities is largely underreported because many students do not know about SSD or do not feel the need for temporary academic accommodations. By improving campus accessibility, the University would reach out not only to its few members with permanent physical disabilities but in fact to all of its members, even those who have never considered the possibility of mobility impairment or the state of campus accessibility.

Numbers provide hard evidence for an important claim.

Benefits for the University

Better accessibility would also benefit the University as a whole by increasing recruitment of handicapped individuals and thus promoting a more diverse campus. When prospective students and faculty with disabilities visit the University, they might decide not to join the UT community because of poor access. On average, about 1,000 students, or 2 percent of the student population, are registered with SSD. Mike Gerhardt reports that SSD would have about 1,500 to 3,000 registered students if the University reflected the community at large with respect to disability. These numbers suggest that the University can recruit more students with disabilities by taking steps to ensure that they have an equal opportunity to succeed. Improving accessibility is one way to achieve a more diverse campus.

COUNTERARGUMENTS

Arguments against devoting more effort and resources to campus accessibility have some validity but ultimately prove inadequate. Some argue that accelerating the rate of accessibility improvements and creating more efficient services require too much spending on too few people. However, this spending actually enhances the expected quality of life of all UT community members rather than just the few with permanent physical disabilities. Unforeseen injury can leave anyone with a permanent or temporary disability at any time. In making decisions about campus accessibility, administrators must realize that having a disability is not a choice and that bad luck does not discriminate well. They should consider how their decisions would affect their campus experience if they became disabled. Despite the additional cost, the University should make accessibility a priority and accommodate more accessibility projects in its budget.

Others argue that more money would not accelerate change because the physical constraints of the campus limit the amount of construction that can take place. Mr. Gerhardt, for example, argues that "more money wouldn't make a difference" because ADA projects must be spaced over the long term to minimize disruption from construction. Other administrators, architects, and engineers, however, feel that money does play a significant role in the rate of ADA improvements. Although Mr. Throop of the Physical Plant acknowledges that the campus only has the capacity to absorb a certain amount of construction, he nonetheless feels that the Physical Plant "could do more if [it] had more monetary resources" and argues that the University "should fund [the Plant] more." Dr. Maedgen of SSD agrees, saying that the main constraint to making the campus more accessible more quickly is "mostly money." Even though there is "a real desire to do it," the problem "tends to be fiscally oriented in nature."

RECOMMENDATIONS

Foster Empathy and Understanding for Long-Term Planning

The University should make campus accessibility a higher priority and work toward a campus that not only fulfills legal requirements but also provides a user-friendly environment for the mobility impaired. Increased effort and resources must be accompanied by a sincere desire to understand and improve the campus experience of people with mobility impairments. It is difficult for the ambulatory person to empathize with the difficulties faced by these individuals. Recognizing this problem, the University should require the administrators who allocate money to ADA projects to use wheelchairs around the campus once a year. This program would help them understand the needs of people using wheelchairs. It would also allow them to assess the progress of campus accessibility as afforded by their allocation of resources. Administrators must realize that people with physical disabilities are not a small, distant, irrelevant group; anyone can join their ranks at any time. Administrators

After establishing a case for enhanced campus accessibility, the author offers several suggestions for action.

should ask themselves if they would find the current state of campus accessibility acceptable if an injury forced them to use a wheelchair on a permanent basis.

In addition, the University should actively seek student input for long-term improvements to accessibility. The University is in the process of creating the ADA Accessibility Committee, which, according to the office of the Dean of Students' Web site, will "address institutionwide, systemic issues that fall under the scope of the Americans with Disabilities Act." This committee will replace the larger President's Committee on Students with Disabilities. Linda Millstone, the University's ADA coordinator, reports that the three student representatives on the President's Committee "were not engaged" and that even now she is "not hearing a groundswell of interest from students." The University should not take this apparent lack of interest to mean that its members with mobility impairments face no problems. According to Ms. Millstone, a survey done about two years ago indicated that students were "clueless" that the President's Committee even existed. This ignorance is not the fault of students but rather a failure of the University to make its accessibility efforts open and transparent. Students should play a prominent and powerful role in the new ADA Accessibility Committee. Since students with mobility impairments traverse the campus more frequently than most administrators, they understand the structural problems of the campus. The Committee should select its student representatives carefully to make sure that they are driven individuals committed to working for progress and representing the interests of students with disabilities. The University should consider making Committee positions paid so that student representatives can devote sufficient time to their responsibilities.

Improve Services for the Mobility Impaired

The University should also work toward creating more useful, transparent, and approachable services for its members with physical disabilities by making better use of online technology and helping students take control of their own experiences. Usefulness of services would decrease the dependence of people with physical disabilities on others and mitigate the stress of using a wheelchair on campus. Approachability would help these individuals take control of their campus experience by allowing more freedom of expression and encouraging self-advocacy. Transparency would allow people with mobility impairments to understand and appreciate the University's efforts at improving campus accessibility.

First, SSD can make its Web site more useful by updating it frequently with detailed information on construction sites that will affect accessible routes. The site should delineate alternative accessible routes and approximate the extra time required to use the detour. This information would help people with mobility impairments to plan ahead and avoid delays, mitigating the stress of maneuvering around construction sites.

The University should also develop software for an interactive campus map. The software would work like Mapquest or Google Maps but would provide detailed descriptions of accessible routes on campus from one building to another. It would be updated frequently with new ADA improvements and information on construction sites that impede accessible routes. In addition, the interactive map would rate building features such as entrances, bathrooms, and elevators on their level of accessibility. It would also report complaints received by SSD and the Physical Plant regarding access around and inside buildings. The software would undoubtedly ease the frustration of finding accessible routes to and from buildings.

Since usefulness and approachability of services are most important for students during their first encounters with the campus, SSD should hold formal one-on-one orientations for new students with mobility impairments. SSD should inform students in both oral and written format of their rights and responsibilities and make them aware of problems that they will encounter on the campus. For example, counselors should advise students to look at their classrooms well in advance and assess potential problems such as poor building access, the need for an elevator key, and the design of the classroom. Beyond making services more useful, these orientations would give students the impression of University services as open and responsive, encouraging students to report problems that they encounter and assume the responsibility of self-advocacy.

As a continuing resource for people with physical disabilities, the SSD Web site should include an anonymous forum for both general questions and specific complaints and needs. The forum should be restricted by the University of Texas Electronic Identification (UTEID) to students registered with SSD. Obviously, if a student has an urgent problem, he or she should visit or call SSD as soon as possible. However, for less pressing problems such as a nonfunctional automatic door button or the need for a curb cut, an anonymous forum would allow for an easy way to let administrators know of a problem. By looking at the forum, administrators and the Physical Plant can get a good idea of the most pressing accessibility issues on campus and notify students of when they will fix the reported problems. Many times, students notice problems but do not report them because they find visiting or calling SSD time-consuming or because they do not wish to be a burden. The anonymity and immediate feedback provided by the forum would allow for more freedom of expression and provide students an easier way to solve the problems they face.

Services for the mobility impaired should also increase their transparency by actively advertising current accessibility projects on their Web sites. My research has given me the strong impression that the administrators, architects, and engineers on the front lines of ADA improvements are devoted and hard-working. To a person with a mobility impairment, however, improvements to campus accessibility seem sluggish at best. In addition to actually devoting more resources to accessibility, then, the University should give its members with mobility impairments a clearer idea of its ongoing efforts to improve campus accessibility. Detailed online descriptions of ADA projects, including the cost of each project, would affirm its resolve to create a better environment for its members with physical disabilities.

CONCLUSION

Although the University has made good progress in accessibility improvements on an old campus, it must take bold steps to improve the experience of its members with mobility impairments. At present, people with permanent mobility impairments face unreasonable hardship, unequal opportunity to succeed, and lack of independence. The larger number of people with temporary disabilities faces similar hardships, and the University as a whole suffers from lack of diversity with respect to disability. To enhance the quality of life of all of its members and increase recruitment of disabled individuals, the University should focus its resources on increasing the rate of accessibility improvements and improving the quality of its services for the mobility impaired. Administrators must learn not to view people with disabilities as a "them" distinct from "us," instead recognizing that the threat of mobility impairment faces everyone.

As a public institution, the University has an obligation to make the campus more inclusive and serve as an example for disability rights. With careful planning and a genuine desire to respond to special needs, practical and cost-effective changes to the University campus can significantly improve the quality of life of many of its members and prove beneficial to the future of the University as a whole.

WORKS CITED

Gardea, Eduardo. Personal interview. 24 Mar. 2005.

Gerhardt, Michael. Personal interview. 8 Apr. 2005.

Gleeson, Austin, et al. *The University of Texas at Austin Campus Master Plan.* Austin: U of Texas, 1999. Print.

Grant, Angela. "Making Campus More Accessible." *Daily Texan Online.* 14 Oct. 2003. Web. 1 Mar. 2005.

Holloway, Wesley Reed. Personal interview. 5 Mar. 2005.

Lu, Judy Yien. Personal interview. 5 Mar. 2005.

Maedgen, Jennifer. Personal interview. 25 Mar. 2005.

Office of the Dean of Students, University of Texas at Austin. "ADA Student Forum." 6 Apr. 2005. Web. 23 Apr. 2005.

Seay, Penny. Personal interview. 11 Mar. 2005.

Throop, William. Personal interview. 6 Apr. 2005.

Send It Somewhere Special

MICHAEL BENSON

Consider the International Space Station, that marvel of incremental engineering. It has close to 15,000 cubic feet of livable space; 10 modules, or living and working areas; a Canadian robot arm that can repair the station from outside; and the capacity to keep five astronauts (including the occasional wealthy rubbernecking space tourist) in good health for long periods. It has gleaming, underused laboratories; its bathroom is fully repaired; and its exercycle is ready for vigorous mandatory workouts.

The only problem with this $156 billion manifestation of human genius—a project as large as a football field that has been called the single most expensive thing ever built—is that it's still going nowhere at a very high rate of speed. And as a scientific research platform, it still has virtually no purpose and is accomplishing nothing.

I try not to write this cavalierly. But if the station's goal is to conduct yet more research into the effects of zero gravity on human beings, well, there's more than enough of that already salted away in Russian archives, based on the many years of weightlessness that cosmonauts heroically logged in a series of space stations throughout the 1970s, '80s and '90s. By now, ISS crews have also spent serious time in zero gravity. We know exactly what weightlessness does and how to counter some of its atrophying effects. (Cue shot of exercycle.)

And if the station's purpose is to act as a "stepping stone" to places beyond—well, that metaphor, most recently used by NASA Administrator Michael Griffin, is pure propaganda. As any student of celestial mechanics can tell you, if you want to go somewhere in space, the best policy is to go directly there and not stop along the way, because stopping is a waste of precious fuel, time and treasure. Which is a pretty good description of the ISS, parked as it is in constant low Earth orbit.

Michael Benson, the author of *Beyond: Visions of the Interplanetary Probes*, writes frequently about space science. On July 13, 2008, "Send It Somewhere Special" appeared in the *Washington Post's* weekend Outlook section. Benson's proposal to retrofit the International Space Station as an interplanetary spacecraft proved to be highly controversial.

This is no doubt why, after the horrifying disintegration of the space shuttle *Columbia* in 2003, the Bush administration belatedly recognized that, if we're going to spend all that money on manned spaceflight, we should justify the risks by actually sending our astronauts somewhere. So NASA is now developing a new generation of rockets and manned spacecraft. By 2020, the Constellation program is supposed to take astronauts beyond low Earth orbit for the first time since *Apollo 17* returned from the moon in 1972. Yes, that'll be almost 50 years. Where will they go? To the moon—the only place humans have already visited.

Which leads us right back to the expensively orbiting ISS. It hasn't a fig-leaf's role left. The moon is the new "stepping stone," with Mars bruited as a next destination. Although NASA officials will never quite say so, their current attitude seems to be that the station is essentially a high-maintenance distraction, even a mistake. Their plan is to finish assembling the thing ASAP and hand the keys over to the Russians, Canadians, Europeans and Japanese, with minimal continuing U.S. involvement. This should happen by the shuttle's mandatory retirement in 2010. Meanwhile, we're still writing a lot of high-denomination checks and preparing the two remaining shuttles for risky flights to finish something we then plan to be largely rid of. This seems absurd. I have an alternative proposal:

Send the ISS somewhere.

The ISS, you see, is already an interplanetary spacecraft—at least potentially. It's missing a drive system and a steerage module, but those are technicalities. Although it's ungainly in appearance, it's designed to be boosted periodically to a higher altitude by a shuttle, a Russian *Soyuz* or one of the upcoming new Constellation program *Orion* spacecraft. It could fairly easily be retrofitted for operations beyond low-Earth orbit. In principle, we could fly it almost anywhere within the inner solar system—to any place where it could still receive enough solar power to keep all its systems running.

It's easy to predict what skeptics both inside and outside NASA will say to this idea. They'll point out that the new Constellation program is already supposed to have at least the beginnings of interplanetary ability. They'll say that the ISS needs to be resupplied too frequently for long missions. They'll worry about the amount of propellant needed to push the ISS's 1,040,000 pounds anywhere—not to mention bringing them all back.

There are good answers to all these objections. We'll still need the new Constellation *Ares* boosters and *Orion* capsules—fortuitously, they can easily be adapted to a scenario in which the ISS becomes the living-area and lab core of an interplanetary spacecraft. The *Ares* V heavy-lift booster could easily send aloft the additional supplies and storage and drive modules necessary to make the ISS truly deep-space-worthy.

The *Orion* crew exploration module is designed to be ISS-compatible. It could serve as a guidance system and also use its own rocket engine to help boost and orient the interplanetary ISS. After remaining dormant for much of the one-year journey to, say, Mars, it could then be available to conduct independent operations while the ISS core orbited the Red Planet, or to investigate an asteroid near Earth, for instance.

But, the skeptics will say, the new *Orion* capsule's engines wouldn't be nearly enough; a spacecraft as large as the ISS would need its own drive system. Here, too, we're in surprisingly good shape. The ISS is already in space; the amount of thrust it needs to go farther is a lot less than you might think. Moreover, a drive system doesn't have to be based on chemical rockets. Over the past two decades, both the U.S. and Japanese programs have conducted highly successful tests in space of ion-drive systems. Unlike the necessarily impatient rockets we use to escape Earth's gravity and reach orbit, these long-duration, low-thrust engines produce the kind of methodical acceleration (and deceleration) appropriate for travel once a spacecraft is already floating in zero gravity. They would be a perfect way to send the ISS on its way and bring it back to Earth again.

This leaves a lander. A lunar lander substantially larger than the spidery *Apollo*-era LEMs is currently on the drawing board. It's not nearly as far along in development as the *Ares* booster and *Orion* spacecraft components of the Constellation program—which is a good thing. While I question the need to return to the moon in the first place, I wouldn't exclude it as a possible destination, so I think we should modify the lander's design to make it capable of touching down on either the moon or Mars and then returning to the ISS with samples for study in its laboratories. Such landers could also investigate the moon's poles, where we think water may be present, or one of the near-Earth asteroids—which may have raw materials suitable for use by future generations of space explorers.

But, our skeptics will sputter, this will all cost far more money than the Constellation program. Who'll pay for it?

Actually, it will in effect save all the money we've already spent on the ISS. And the station is already an international project, with substantial financial and technological input from the Russians, Canadians, Europeans and Japanese. In recent years, the Chinese, who have developed their own human spaceflight capabilities, have made repeated overtures to NASA, hoping to be let in on the ISS project. They've been unceremoniously rebuffed by the Bush administration, but a new administration may be more welcoming. An interplanetary ISS—the acronym now standing for International Space Ship—would be a truly international endeavor, with expenses shared among all participating nations.

How likely is any of this to happen? Not very. A lot depends on the flexibility of a NASA that hasn't always been particularly welcoming to outside ideas. On the other hand, the agency also collaborates with outsiders all the time. So it's not impossible. The reason the ISS went from being a purely American, Reagan-era project ("Space Station Freedom") to one including the Russians and many other nations was a political decision by the Clinton administration. A similar political vision will be necessary here.

All the billions already spent on the space station would pay off—spectacularly—if this product of human ingenuity actually went somewhere and did something. But it would also serve as a compelling demonstration that we're one species, living on one planet, and that we're as capable of cooperating peacefully as we are at competing militaristically. Let's begin the process of turning the ISS from an Earth-orbiting caterpillar into an interplanetary butterfly.

STYLE AND PRESENTATION IN arguments

13

Style in Arguments

A classmate sitting with you in the library throws down a journal article that he has been reading. "Dry as dust," he complains. You know exactly what he means.

A person you know only slightly objects strenuously when you characterize her in-class comments as laced with irony, saying, "Sorry, you're wrong *again*. Irony's not my style." Since you'd meant this as a compliment, you decide to apologize and ask her how she would describe her style.

An architectural team working to design a new fast-food restaurant studies the most successful franchises of the last twenty-five years. What they find suggests that each franchise has a trademark architectural style, so they go to work seeking something new and distinctive—and something as unlike McDonald's design as possible.

A photographer looking to land the cover photo on *Vogue* takes a tour of college campuses. At each school, he sits patiently in the student union, watching as students pass by. He's looking for a face with "fresh new style."

A researcher trying to describe teen style crafted a questionnaire and distributed it to five hundred teens in three different cities. Why was she not surprised when the style mentioned favorably most often was "hip-hop style"?

● ● ●

Arguments have their own styles. One classical orator and statesman outlined three basic styles of communication, identifying them as *high* (formal or ornate), *middle* (understated and very clear), and *low* (everyday or humorous). High style in argument is generally formal, serious, even high-minded—an argument wearing its best tuxedo. Middle style marks most ordinary arguments, from the commonplace to the professional: these arguments have sturdy work clothes on. And low style is informal, colloquial, humorous—an argument with its shoes off and feet propped up. Even choice of font can help to convey a style: you could think of French Script, for example, as ornate or high, Garamond as understated or middle, and Comic Sans as everyday or low.

Such broad characterizations can give only a very general sense of an argument's style, however. To think more carefully about style in argument, consider the relationship among style and word choice, sentence structure, punctuation, and what we call special effects.

Style and Word Choice

The vocabulary that you choose for an argument helps to define its style, so your words should match the tone that you want to establish as well as the subject and purpose of your piece. For most academic arguments, formal language is appropriate. In an article that urges every member of society to care about energy issues, Chevron CEO Dave O'Reilly adopts a formal and serious tone: "We call upon scientists and educators, politicians and policy-makers, environmentalists, leaders of industry, and each one of you to be part of reshaping the next era of energy." Had he written "How 'bout everybody rallyin' round to mix up a new energy plan?," the effect would have been quite different.

Slang and colloquial terms can sometimes enliven an argument, but they also can bewilder readers. An article about arms-control negotiations that uses terms like *nukes* and *boomers* to refer to nuclear weaponry might confuse some readers and irritate others who assume that the shorthand betrays a callous attitude toward a serious subject. Be alert, too, to the use of jargon in arguments. Although *jargon* (the special vocabulary of members of a profession, trade, or field) serves as shorthand for experts, it can alienate readers who don't recognize technical words or acronyms.

Another key to an argument's style is its control of *connotation*, the unspoken associations that surround many words. Note, for example, the differences in connotation among the following three statements:

> Students from the Labor Action Committee (LAC) carried out a hunger strike to call attention to the below-minimum wages that are being paid to campus temporary workers, saying, "The university must pay a living wage to all its workers."

> Left-wing agitators and radicals tried to use self-induced starvation to stampede the university into caving in to their demands.

> Champions of human rights put their bodies on the line to protest the university's tightfisted policy of paying temporary workers scandalously low wages.

Here, the first sentence is the most neutral. It presents the facts and offers a quotation from one of the students. The second sentence uses loaded terms like "agitators," "radicals," and "stampede" to create a negative image of this event, while the final sentence uses other loaded words to create a positive view. As these examples demonstrate, words matter.

Finally, arguments that use concrete and specific words rather than abstract and general ones will make a more vivid impact on readers and listeners. Responding to a claim that American students are falling behind their counterparts in Asia and Europe, Jay Mathews uses memorable language to depict the stereotype:

> Most commentary on the subject leaves the impression that China and India are going to bury the United States in an avalanche of new technology. Consider, for example, a much-cited 2005 *Fortune* article that included the claim that China turned out 600,000 engineers in the previous year, India graduated 350,000, and poor, declining America could manage only 70,000. The cover of *Fortune* showed a buff Chinese

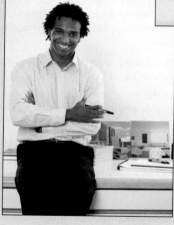

Not Just Words

Choose one of the images above, and study it for a few minutes. How would you describe the style of the person depicted—just by thinking about choice of pants, stance, and so on? How does the photograph help to convey that style? Consider the composition, the use of color, and so on.

beach bully looming over a skinny Uncle Sam. The headline said, "Is the U.S. a 97-Pound Weakling?"

—Jay Mathews, "Bad Rap on the Schools"

Mathews could have used more general language (such as "Most commentators imply that foreign countries are going to produce much more new technology than the United States"), but his concrete language ("bury," "avalanche," and "buff Chinese beach bully looming over a skinny Uncle Sam") makes this passage more memorable and creates a style that moves readers along.

Sentence Structure and Argument

Choices about sentence structure also can define the style of an argument. A series of sentences needs variety to keep readers involved. Writers of effective arguments take this maxim to heart, working to vary sentence patterns and lengths.

Varying sentence length can be especially effective. Here's George Orwell in a famous passage from his essay "Politics and the English Language," moving easily between sentences of varying length to make an upbeat point:

> A man may take to drink because he feels himself to be a failure, and then fail all the more completely because he drinks. It is rather the same thing that is happening to the English language. It becomes ugly and inaccurate because our thoughts are foolish, but the slovenliness of our language makes it easier for us to have foolish thoughts. The point is that the process is reversible.
>
> —George Orwell, "Politics and the English Language"

Here is Ronald Reagan on July 12, 1987, standing at Berlin's Brandenburg Gate before the wall that still separated Western and Soviet sectors in the city and delivering a strong appeal that leads to three short, powerful imperatives:

> There is one sign the Soviets can make that would be unmistakable, that would advance dramatically the cause of freedom and peace. General Secretary Gorbachev, if you seek peace, if you seek prosperity for the Soviet Union and Eastern Europe, if you seek liberalization: Come here to this gate! Mr. Gorbachev, open this gate! Mr. Gorbachev, tear down this wall!
>
> —Ronald Reagan

Paying attention to the way that sentences begin can similarly help to build an argument's effectiveness. In the article by Chevron CEO O'Reilly mentioned on page 418, we find the following paragraph:

> Demand is soaring like never before. As populations grow and economies take off, millions in the developing world are enjoying the benefits of a lifestyle that requires increasing amounts of energy. In fact, some say that in 20 years the world will consume 40% more oil than it does today. At the same time, many of the world's oil and gas fields are maturing. And new energy discoveries are mainly occurring in places where resources are difficult to extract, physically, economically, and even politically. When growing demand meets tighter supplies, the result is more competition for the same resources.
>
> —Dave O'Reilly

Look at how much less effective this passage becomes when the sentences all begin in the same way—that is, with the subject first:

> Demand is soaring like never before. Millions in the rapidly developing world are enjoying the benefits of a lifestyle that requires increasing amounts of energy. Some say that in 20 years the world will consume 40% more oil than it does today. Many of the world's oil and gas fields are maturing. New energy discoveries are mainly occurring in places where resources are difficult to extract, physically, economically, and even politically. Growing demand and tighter supplies result in more competition for the same resources.

The second version omits all transitions ("In fact," "At the same time") and openings that vary the subject-first order ("As populations grow," "When growing demand meets tighter supplies"), which makes the passage much less interesting to read, harder to understand, and less persuasive as an argument.

Effective arguments can also make good use of parallel structures in sentences. In a review of a biography of writer Henry Roth, Jonathan Rosen includes the following description:

> His hands were warped by rheumatoid arthritis; the very touch of his computer keyboard was excruciating. But he still put in five hours a day, helped by Percocet, beer, a ferocious will, and the ministrations of several young assistants.
>
> —Jonathan Rosen, "Writer, Interrupted"

In the first sentence, Rosen chooses a coordinate structure, with the first clause about Roth's arthritic hands perfectly balanced by the following clause describing the results of putting those hands on a keyboard. In the second sentence, Rosen uses a series of parallel specific nouns and noun phrases ("Percocet," "beer," "the ministrations") to build up a picture of Roth as extremely persistent.

Punctuation and Argument

In a memorable comment, actor and director Clint Eastwood said, "You can show a lot with a look. . . . It's punctuation." Eastwood is right about punctuation's effect, either in acting or in arguing. As you read and write arguments, consider choices of punctuation closely. Here are some ways in which punctuation helps to enhance style.

The semicolon is a handy punctuation mark since it signals a pause that is stronger than a comma but not as strong as a period. Here, Mary Gordon uses a semicolon in an argument about "the ghosts of Ellis Island":

> Immigration acts were passed; newcomers had to prove, besides moral correctness and financial solvency, their ability to read.
> —Mary Gordon, "More than Just a Shrine"

"You can show a lot with a look. . . . It's punctuation."

Gordon could have put a period after "passed," separating this passage into two sentences. But she chooses a semicolon instead, giving the sentence an abrupt rhythm that suits her topic—laws that imposed strict requirements on immigrants.

Semicolons can also make passages easier to read, as in the following example:

> Every year, whether the Republican or the Democratic party is in office, more and more power drains away from the individual to feed vast reservoirs in far-off places; and we have less and less say about the shape of events which shape our future.
>
> —William F. Buckley Jr., "Why Don't We Complain?"

Writers also use end punctuation to good effect. Although the exclamation point can be distracting and irritating if overused (think of those email messages you get from friends that fairly bristle with them), it can be helpful if used infrequently. Exclamation points are especially good for indicating a speaker's tone. For example, in an argument about the treatment of prisoners at Guantánamo, consider how Jane Mayer evokes the sense of desperation in some of the suspected terrorists:

> As we reached the end of the cell-block, hysterical shouts, in broken English, erupted from a caged exercise area nearby. "Come here!" a man screamed. "See here! They are liars! . . . No sleep!" he yelled. "No food! No medicine! No doctor! Everybody sick here!"
>
> —Jane Mayer, "The Experiment"

The question mark is another handy mark of punctuation. In a fairly negative review of Steven Spielberg's *War of the Worlds*, David Denby uses a series of questions to drive home the point he's been making:

> As the scenes of destruction cease, one has to ponder the oddity of a science-fiction movie without science, or even routine curiosity. Who are the aliens? What is their chemical makeup and how might they be vulnerable? What does the attack mean? Nobody raises any of these issues.
>
> —David Denby, "Stayin' Alive"

Two other punctuation marks are often important in establishing the style of an argument. While sometimes used interchangeably, the colon and the dash have different effects. The colon often introduces explanations or examples and separates elements from one another. Alison Lurie uses a colon in this way:

> The men may also wear the getup known as Sun Belt Cool: a pale beige suit, open-collared shirt (often in a darker shade than the suit), cream-colored loafers and aviator sunglasses.
> —Alison Lurie, "The Language of Clothes"

A dash or a pair of dashes, on the other hand, is often used to insert comments or highlight material within a sentence. Notice how columnist Maureen Dowd uses dashes to set off her point about the Bush administration's claim that it doesn't need search warrants to spy on individuals suspected of terrorist connections:

> Even when [Vice President Dick Cheney] can easily—and retroactively— get snooping warrants, he doesn't want their stinking warrants. Warrants are for sissies.
> —Maureen Dowd, "Looking for a Democratic Tough Guy, or Girl"

In the following example, *New York Times Book Review* critic Joel Conarroe uses dashes to mock their overuse by sportswriter Roger Angell and to show how they can slow the pace of the prose:

> Mr. Angell is addicted to dashes and parentheses—small pauses or digressions in the narrative like those moments when the umpire dusts off home plate or a pitcher rubs up a new ball—that serve to slow an already deliberate movement almost to a standstill.
> —Joel Conarroe, "Ode on a Rainbow Slider"

As these examples suggest, punctuation is often key to creating the rhythm of an argument. Take a look at how Maya Angelou uses a dash along with another punctuation mark—ellipsis points—to indicate a pause or hesitation, in this case one that builds anticipation:

> Then the voice, husky and familiar, came to wash over us—"The winnah, and still heavyweight champeen of the world . . . Joe Louis."
> —Maya Angelou, "Champion of the World"

Creating rhythms can be especially important in online communication when writers are trying to invest their arguments with emotion or emphasis. Some writers still use asterisks in online communication to convey the sense that italic type creates in print texts: "You *must* respond to this email today!" Others use emoticons or other new characters (from the ubiquitous smiley face ☺ to combinations like g2g for "got to go") to establish a particular rhythm, tone, and style. In some online writing, experimentation is acceptable, but in an argument where the stakes are high, writers use conventional style to avoid alienating their audiences.

Special Effects: Figurative Language and Argument

Look at any magazine or Web site, and you'll see how figurative language works on behalf of arguments. When a writer says that "the digital revolution is whipping through our lives like a Bengali typhoon," she's making an implicit argument about the speed and strength of the digital revolution. When another writer calls Disney World a "smile factory," she begins a stinging critique of the way pleasure is "manufactured" there.

Just what is figurative language? Traditionally, the terms *figurative language* and *figures of speech* refer to language that differs from the ordinary—language that calls up, or "figures," something else. But all language could be said to call up something else. The words *table* and *war*, for example, aren't themselves a table or a war; rather, they call up these concepts in our imaginations in different forms. Thus, just as all language is by nature argumentative, so are all figures of speech. Far from being mere decoration or embellishment (something like icing on the cake of thought), figures of speech are indispensable to language use.

Figurative language brings two major strengths to arguments. First, it aids understanding by drawing parallels between an unknown and a known. For example, to describe DNA as they had identified it, scientists Watson and Crick used two familiar examples—a helix (spiral) and a zipper. Today, arguments about computer technologies are filled with similar uses of figurative language. Indeed, Microsoft likens its entire word processing system to an office (as in Microsoft Office) to make its software features understandable and familiar to users. Second, figurative language makes arguments memorable. A person argued that slang should be used in formal writing because "slang is language that takes off its coat, spits on its hands, and gets to work." In a brief poem that carries a powerful argument, Langston Hughes uses figurative language to explore the consequences of unfulfilled dreams:

What happens to a dream deferred?

Does it dry up
Like a raisin in the sun?
Or fester like a sore—
And then run?
Does it stink like rotten meat?
Or crust and sugar over—
Like a syrupy sweet?

Maybe it just sags
Like a heavy load.

Or does it explode?
—Langston Hughes, "Harlem—A Dream Deferred"

You may be surprised to learn that during the European Renaissance, schoolchildren sometimes learned and practiced using as many as 180 figures of speech. Such practice seems unnecessary today, especially because figures of speech come naturally to native speakers of the English language. People speak of "chilling out," "taking flak," "nipping a plot in the bud," "getting our act together," "blowing your cover," "marching to a different drummer," "seeing red," "smelling a rat," "being on cloud nine," "throwing in the towel," "tightening our belts," "rolling in the aisles," and "turning the screws": you get the picture. In fact, you and your friends probably have favorite figures of speech that you use every day. Try taking a quick inventory. Listen to everything that's said around you for one day, and jot down any figurative language you hear.

Figures of speech have traditionally been classified into two main types: *tropes* involve a change in the ordinary signification, or meaning, of a word or phrase, and *schemes* involve a special arrangement of words. We can't provide a complete catalog of figures and their special effects in this chapter, but here is a brief listing—with examples—of some of the most familiar kinds. They can be used to very good effect in the arguments you write.

Tropes

METAPHOR

One of the most pervasive uses of figurative language, *metaphor* implies a comparison between two things and thereby clarifies and enlivens many arguments. In the following passage, novelist and poet Benjamin Saenz uses several metaphors to describe his relationship to the southern border of the United States:

> It seems obvious to me now that I remained always a son of the border, a boy never quite comfortable in an American skin, and certainly not comfortable in a Mexican one. My entire life, I have lived in a liminal space, and that space has both defined and confined me. That liminal space wrote and invented me. It has been my prison, and it has also been my only piece of sky.
>
> —Benjamin Saenz, "Notes from Another Country"

In another example, Ron Rosenbaum uses an artful series of comparisons to describe how much he dislikes Billy Joel in an unambiguously titled article from *Slate*:

> Which brings me to Billy Joel—the Andrew Wyeth of contemporary pop music—and the continuing *irritation* I feel whenever I hear his

Billy Joel: schlock 'n' roll?

tunes, whether in the original or in the multitude of elevator-Muzak versions. It is a kind of mystery: Why does his music make my skin crawl in a way that other bad music doesn't? Why is it that so many of us feel it is possible to say Billy Joel is—well—just *bad*, a blight upon pop music, a plague upon the airwaves more contagious than West Nile virus, a dire threat to the peacefulness of any given elevator ride, not rock 'n' roll but schlock 'n' roll?

—Ron Rosenbaum, "The Worst Pop Singer Ever"

Language use is so filled with metaphors that these powerful, persuasive tools often zip by unnoticed, so be on the lookout for effective metaphors in everything you read. For example, when a reviewer of new software that promises complete filtering of advertisements on the World Wide Web refers to the product as "a weedwhacker for the Web," he's using a metaphor to advance an argument about the nature and function of that product. Enjoy the metaphor, but think about it, too.

SIMILE

A *simile* is a figure of speech that uses *like* or *as* to compare two things. The device is pervasive in both written and spoken language. Eminem's song "Like Toy Soldiers," for example, compares human beings to toy soldiers who "all fall down," are "torn apart," and "never win" but fight on anyway. A radio announcer says that the UCLA men's basketball team is so eager for the NCAA playoffs that its players are "like pit bulls on pork chops." One of our grandmothers used to say, "Prices are high as a cat's back" or, as a special compliment, "You look as pretty as red shoes." Here's a formal written example from an article in the *New Yorker* magazine:

You can tell the graphic-novels section in a bookstore from afar, by the young bodies sprawled around it like casualties of a localized disaster.

—Peter Schjeldahl, "Words and Pictures: Graphic Novels Come of Age"

And here's a carefully crafted zinger by John McCain, playing off Barack Obama's celebrity status during the 2008 presidential campaign:

Taking in my opponent's performances is a little like watching a big summer blockbuster, and an hour in, realizing that all the best scenes were in the trailer you saw last fall.

Similes play a major part in many arguments, as you can see in this excerpt from a brief *Wired* magazine review of a new magazine for women:

> Women's magazines occupy a special niche in the cluttered infoscape of modern media. Ask any *Vogue* junkie: no girl-themed Web site or CNN segment on women's health can replace the guilty pleasure of slipping a glossy fashion rag into your shopping cart. Smooth as a pint of chocolate Häagen-Dazs, feckless as a thousand-dollar slip dress, women's magazines wrap culture, trends, health, and trash in a single, decadent package. But like the diet dessert recipes they print, these slick publications can leave a bad taste in your mouth.
>
> —Tiffany Lee Brown, "En Vogue"

Here, three similes are in prominent display—"smooth as a pint of chocolate Häagen-Dazs" and "feckless as a thousand-dollar slip dress" in the third sentence and "like the diet dessert recipes" in the fourth. Together, the similes add to the writer's image of mass-market women's magazines as a mishmash of "trash" and "trends."

ANALOGY

Analogies compare two things, often point by point, to show similarity (as in *Many are tempted to draw an analogy between the computer and the human brain*) or to argue that if two things are alike in one way they are probably alike in other ways as well. Often extended to several sentences, paragraphs, or even whole essays, analogies can clarify and emphasize points of comparison. In considering the movie *Hustle and Flow*, a reviewer draws an analogy between the character DJay and the late, great musician, composer, and bandleader Duke Ellington:

> As [actor] Howard develops DJay's frustration and rue, he avoids the obvious, the overemphatic. His self-mocking performance is so ironically refined and allusive that one might think that Duke Ellington himself had slipped into an old undershirt and hit the fetid streets of Memphis.
>
> —David Denby, "Stayin' Alive"

And in an argument about the failures of the aircraft industry, another writer uses an analogy for potent contrast:

> If the aircraft industry had evolved as spectacularly as the computer industry over the past twenty-five years, a Boeing 767 would cost five

hundred dollars today, and it would circle the globe in twenty minutes on five gallons of fuel.

—*Scientific American*

Analogies applied to politics are so common that *The New Republic* writer Michael Schaffer poked fun of them in a piece that shows how such comparisons work structurally. Here are examples for both Barack Obama and John McCain:

Obama is: John F. Kennedy in 1960

Evidence: Appeal to new generation; first member of long-discriminated group to win; glamorous wife; support of Ted and Caroline Kennedy.

Representative media quote: "Today, for a brief shining hour, the young got to see what we saw—not the gauzy images of 'Camelot,' but the living spirit of The New Frontier." —Chris Matthews, *Hardball*

Political cartoonist Michael Ramirez demonstrates how analogies work visually in arguing in favor of drilling in the Arctic National Wildlife Refuge (ANWR).

By permission of Michael Ramirez and Creators Syndicate, Inc.

McCain is: Theodore Roosevelt in 1904

Evidence: Reformist history; past quarrels with party insiders.

Representative media quote: "Apart from their superficial similarities—the wreathing, weather-beaten face, the stocky build, the cowboy affectations—they do have some important traits in common. An obsession with things military, great personal courage, a genial way with reporters and an almost gravitational instinct toward the center of any political controversy." —Roosevelt biographer Edmund Morris, *Chicago Tribune*

—Michael Schaffer, "Political Analogies Are Like Toothbrushes"

CULTURAL CONTEXTS FOR ARGUMENT

Formality and Other Style Issues

Style is always affected by language, culture, and rhetorical tradition. Effective style therefore varies broadly across cultures and depends on the rhetorical situation—purpose, audience, and so on.

At least one important style question needs to be considered when arguing across cultures: what level of formality is most appropriate? In the United States, a fairly informal style is often acceptable and even appreciated. Many cultures, however, tend to value formality.

If you're in doubt, it's wise to err on the side of formality, especially in communicating with elders or with those in authority:

- Take care to use proper titles as appropriate (*Ms.*, *Mr.*, *Dr.*, and so on).
- Don't use first names unless you've been invited to do so.
- Steer clear of slang, jargon, and hip expressions. When you're communicating with members of other cultures, slang may not be understood, or it may be seen as disrespectful.
- Avoid potentially puzzling cultural allusions, such as sports analogies or musical references.

Beyond formality, stylistic preferences vary widely. When arguing across cultures or languages, the most important stylistic issue might be clarity. When you're communicating with people whose native languages are different from your own, analogies and similes almost always aid in understanding. Likening something unknown to something familiar can help make your argument forceful—and understandable.

OTHER TROPES

Several other tropes deserve special mention.

Signifying, in which a speaker cleverly and often humorously needles the listener, is a distinctive trope that is found extensively in African American English. In the following passage, two African American men (Grave Digger and Coffin Ed) signify on their white supervisor (Anderson), who has ordered them to discover the originators of a riot:

> "I take it you've discovered who started the riot," Anderson said.
>
> "We knew who he was all along," Grave Digger said.
>
> "It's just nothing we can do to him," Coffin Ed echoed.
>
> "Why not, for God's sake?"
>
> "He's dead," Coffin Ed said.
>
> "Who?"
>
> "Lincoln," Grave Digger said.
>
> "He hadn't ought to have freed us if he didn't want to make provisions to feed us," Coffin Ed said. "Anyone could have told him that."
>
> —Chester Himes, *Hot Day, Hot Night*

In these *Boondocks* strips, Huey signifies on Jazmine, using indirection, ironic humor, and two surprising twists.

Coffin Ed and Grave Digger demonstrate the major characteristics of effective signifying—indirection, ironic humor, fluid rhythm, and a surprising twist at the end. Rather than insulting Anderson directly by pointing out that he's asked a dumb question, they criticize the question indirectly by ultimately blaming a white man (and not just any white man but one they're supposed to revere). This twist leaves the supervisor speechless, teaching him something and giving Grave Digger and Coffin Ed the last word—and the last laugh.

You'll find examples of signifying in the work of many African American writers. You may also hear signifying in NBA basketball, where it's an important element of trash talking. What Grave Digger and Coffin Ed do to Anderson, Allen Iverson regularly does to his opponents on the court.

Take a look at the example of signifying from a *Boondocks* cartoon (see the figure on p. 433). Note how Huey seems to be sympathizing with Jazmine and then, in two surprising twists, reveals that he has been needling her all along.

Hyperbole is the use of overstatement for special effect, a kind of pyrotechnics in prose. The tabloid papers and gossip magazines whose headlines scream at shoppers in the grocery checkout line are champions of hyperbole. (Journalist Tom Wolfe once wrote a satirical review of a *National Enquirer* writers' convention that he titled "Keeps His Mom-in-Law in Chains Meets Kills Son and Feeds Corpse to Pigs.") Everyone has seen these overstated arguments and perhaps marveled at the way they sell.

Hyperbole is also the trademark of serious writers. In a column arguing that men's magazines fuel the same kind of neurotic anxieties about appearance that have long plagued women, Michelle Cottle uses hyperbole and humor to make her point:

> What self-respecting '90s woman could embrace a publication that runs such enlightened articles as "Turn Your Good Girl Bad" and "How to Wake Up Next to a One-Night Stand"? Or maybe you'll smile and wink knowingly: What red-blooded hetero chick wouldn't love all those glossy photo spreads of buff young beefcake in various states of undress, ripped abs and glutes flexed so tightly you could bounce a check on them? Either way you've got the wrong idea. My affection for *Men's Health* is driven by pure gender politics. . . . With page after page of bulging biceps and Gillette jaws, robust hairlines and silken skin, *Men's Health* is peddling a standard of male beauty as unforgiving and

unrealistic as the female version sold by those dewy-eyed pre-teen waifs draped across covers of *Glamour* and *Elle*.

—Michelle Cottle, "Turning Boys into Girls"

As you might imagine, hyperbole can easily backfire, so it pays to use it sparingly and for an audience whose reactions you can predict with confidence. American journalist H. L. Mencken ignored this advice in 1921 when he used relentless hyperbole to savage the literary style of President Warren Harding. Note that in doing so, he says that he's offering a "small tribute," making the irony even more notable:

> I rise to pay my small tribute to Dr. Harding. Setting aside a college professor or two and half a dozen dipsomaniacal newspaper reporters, he takes the first place in my Valhalla of literati. That is to say, he writes the worst English that I have ever encountered. It reminds me of a string of wet sponges; it reminds me of tattered washing on the line; it reminds me of stale bean-soup, of college yells, of dogs barking idiotically through endless nights. It is so bad that a sort of grandeur creeps into it. It drags itself out of the dark abysm (I was about to write abscess!) of pish, and crawls insanely up the topmost pinnacle of posh. It is rumble and bumble. It is flap and doodle. It is balder and dash.
>
> —H. L. Mencken, "Gamalielese"

Understatement, on the other hand, requires a quiet, muted message to make its point effectively. In her memoir, Rosa Parks—the civil rights activist who made history in 1955 by refusing to give up her bus seat to a white passenger—uses understatement so often that it becomes a characteristic of her writing and a mark of her ethos. She refers to Martin Luther King Jr. simply as "a true leader," to Malcolm X as a person of "strong conviction," and to her own lifelong efforts as simply a small way of "carrying on."

Understatement can be particularly effective in arguments that might seem to call for its opposite. When Watson and Crick published their first article on the structure of DNA (p. 426), they felt that they had discovered the secret of life. (Imagine what the *National Enquirer*'s headlines might have been for this story.) Yet in an atmosphere of extreme scientific competitiveness, they closed their article with a vast understatement that emphasizes the importance of their discovery: "It has not escaped our notice that the specific pairing we have postulated immediately suggests a possible copying mechanism for the genetic material." A half century later, considering the profound developments that have taken place in genetics, including the cloning of animals, the power of this understatement still resonates strongly.

Rhetorical questions don't really require answers. Rather, they help assert or deny something about an argument. Most of us use rhetorical questions frequently. Think of the times that you've said, "Who cares?" or "Why me?" or "How should I know?" These are all rhetorical questions. Rhetorical questions also show up in written arguments. In a review of a book-length argument about the use and misuse of power in the Disney dynasty, Linda Watts uses a series of rhetorical questions to introduce part of the book's argument:

> If you have ever visited one of the Disney theme parks, though, you have likely wondered at the labor—both seen and unseen—necessary to maintain these fanciful environments. How and when are the grounds tended so painstakingly? How are the signs of high traffic erased from public facilities? What keeps employees so poised, meticulously groomed, and endlessly cheerful?
>
> —Linda S. Watts, review of *Inside the Mouse*

And Debra Saunders opens her argument for the legalization of medical marijuana with a rhetorical question:

> If the federal government were right that medical marijuana has no medicinal value, why have so many doctors risked their practices by recommending its use for patients with cancer or AIDS?
>
> —Debra Saunders, "Feds Should Respect Court's Ruling for Docs"

Antonomasia is probably most familiar to you from sports coverage: "His Airness" means Michael Jordan; "The Great One," Wayne Gretzky; "The Sultan of Swat," Babe Ruth. But it's also used in fields like politics, sometimes neutrally (Arnold Schwarzenegger as "The Governator"), sometimes as a

Baseball player Roger Clemens became know as "The Rocket" because of his powerful pitching.

compliment (Ronald Reagan as "The Great Communicator"), and sometimes as a crude and sexist put-down (Sarah Palin as "Caribou Barbie"). Such shorthand substitutions of a descriptive word or phrase for a proper name can pack arguments into just one phrase. What does calling Jordan "His Airness" argue about him?

Irony, the use of words to convey a meaning in tension with or opposite to their literal meanings, also works powerfully in arguments. One of the most famous sustained uses of irony in literature occurs in Shakespeare's *Julius Caesar* as Marc Antony punctuates his condemnation of Brutus with the repeated ironic phrase "But Brutus is an *honourable* man." Publications such as *The Onion* and the online *Ironic Times* are noted for their satiric treatment of politics and popular culture, scoring points while provoking a chuckle.

Schemes

Schemes, figures that depend on word order, can add syntactic "zing" to arguments. Here, we present the ones that you're likely to see most often.

Parallelism involves the use of grammatically similar phrases or clauses for special effect:

> For African Americans, the progress toward racial equality over the last half century was summed up in a widely quoted sequence: "Rosa sat so that Martin could walk. Martin walked so that Obama could run. Obama ran so that our children could fly."

> Current government programs don't protect poor people very well against the cost of becoming sick. They do much better at protecting sick people against the risk of becoming poor.
> —Michael Kinsley, "To Your Health"

> The laws of our land are said to be "by the people, of the people, and for the people."

Antithesis is the use of parallel structures to mark contrast or opposition:

> That's one small step for a man, one giant leap for mankind.
> —Neil Armstrong

> Marriage has many pains, but celibacy has no pleasures.
> —Samuel Johnson

Those who kill people are called murderers; those who kill animals, sportsmen.

Inverted word order, in which the parts of a sentence or clause are not in the usual subject-verb-object order, can help make arguments particularly memorable:

Into this grey lake plopped the thought, I know this man, don't I?

—Doris Lessing

Hard to see, the dark side is.

—Yoda

Good looking he was not; wealthy he was not; but brilliant—he was.

As with anything else, however, too much of such a figure can quickly become, well, too much.

Anaphora, or effective repetition, can act like a drumbeat in an argument, bringing the point home. Here is an emotional section from Ronald Reagan's June 6, 1984, address to the aging World War II veterans who assembled in Normandy, France, for the fortieth anniversary of D-Day:

Behind me is a memorial that symbolizes the Ranger daggers that were thrust into the top of these cliffs. And before me are the men who put them there.

These are the boys of Pointe du Hoc. These are the men who took the cliffs. These are the champions who helped free a continent. These are the heroes who helped end a war.

—Ronald Reagan

In an argument about the future of Chicago, Lerone Bennett Jr. similarly uses repetition to link Chicago to innovation and creativity:

[Chicago]'s the place where organized Black history was born, where gospel music was born, where jazz and the blues were reborn, where the Beatles and the Rolling Stones went up to the mountaintop to get the new musical commandments from Chuck Berry and the rock'n'roll apostles.

—Lerone Bennett Jr., "Blacks in Chicago"

And speaking of the Rolling Stones, here's Dave Barry using repetition comically in his comments on their 2002 tour:

Recently I attended a Rolling Stones concert. This is something I do every two decades. I saw the Stones in the 1960s, and then again in the 1980s. I plan to see them next in the 2020s, then the 2040s, then the 2060s, at their 100th anniversary concert.

—Dave Barry, "OK, What Will Stones Do for 100th Anniversary?"

Reversed structures for special effect have been used widely in political argumentation. President John F. Kennedy's inaugural address in 1961 charged citizens to "ask not what your country can do for you; ask what you can do for your country." Like the other figures we've listed here, this one can help make arguments memorable:

> The Democrats won't get elected unless things get worse, and things won't get worse until the Democrats get elected.
>
> —Jeane Kirkpatrick

> Your manuscript is both good and original. But the part that is good is not original, and the part that is original is not good.
>
> —Samuel Johnson

RESPOND●

1. Turn to something you read frequently—a blog, a sports or news magazine, or a friend's page on Twitter—and look closely at the sentences. What seems distinctive about them? Do they vary in terms of their length and the way that they begin? If so, how? Do they use parallel structures or other structural devices to good effect? How easy to read are they, and what accounts for that ease?

2. Try your hand at writing a brief movie review for your campus newspaper, experimenting with punctuation as one way to create an effective style. Consider whether a series of questions might have a strong effect, whether exclamation points would add or detract from the message you want to send, and so on. When you've finished the review, compare it to one written by a classmate, and look for similarities and differences in your choices of punctuation.

3. In the following advertising slogans, identify the types of figurative language used—metaphor, simile, analogy, hyperbole, understatement, rhetorical question, antonomasia, irony, parallelism, antithesis, inverted word order, anaphora, or reversed structure.

   "Good to the last drop." (Maxwell House coffee)

   "It's the real thing." (Coca-Cola)

   "Melts in your mouth, not in your hands." (M&M's)

   "Be all that you can be." (U.S. Army)

   "Breakfast of champions." (Wheaties)

   "Double your pleasure; double your fun." (Doublemint gum)

"Got milk?" (America's Milk Processors)

"Let your fingers do the walking." (the Yellow Pages)

"Think small." (Volkswagen)

"Like a Rock." (Chevy trucks)

"Real bonding, real popcorn, real butter, real good times." (Pop-Secret Popcorn)

4. Some writers or public speakers are well known for their use of tropes and schemes. (Tom Wolfe and Jesse Jackson come to mind.) Using the Internet, find the text of an essay or a speech by someone who uses figures of speech liberally. Pick a paragraph that seems particularly rich in figures, and rewrite it, eliminating every trace of figurative language. Then read the two paragraphs—the original and your revised version—aloud to your class. With your classmates' help, imagine rhetorical situations in which the figure-free version would be most appropriate.

5. Now find an example of prose that seems dry and nonfigurative (such as a technical manual, instructions for operating appliances, or a legal document). Rewrite part of the piece in the most figurative language that you can come up with. Then try to list rhetorical situations in which this newly figured language might be most appropriate.

14
Visual Arguments

You know that you shouldn't buy camping gear just because you see it advertised in a magazine. But what's the harm in imagining yourself in Yosemite National Park with the sun setting, the camp stove open, and the tent up? That could be *you* there in Mariposa Grove, just like the tanned campers in the ad. What was the brand name of that gear again, and what's the company's URL?

A student government committee is meeting to talk about campus safety. One member has prepared a graph showing a steady increase in on-campus robberies over the last five years and has brought several photographs that bring these crimes vividly to life.

A photographer is banned from accompanying U.S. Marines in an Afghan war zone because he has posted photographs on a Web site showing dead American soldiers who were killed by a suicide bomber. Supporters of the photographer believe that his images provide a visual argument against the conflict. Those who oppose his act believe that he is exploiting dead heroes for a political purpose.

You've never heard of the sponsoring time-share resort. But its impressive letter is printed on thick bond paper with smart color graphics, and hey, the company's CEO is offering you a free weekend at its Palm Beach facility just to consider investing in a time-share. In addition, the firm's Web site seems professional: it's quick-loading and easy to navigate. Somebody's on the ball. Perhaps you should take the firm up on its offer.

A shiny silver convertible passes you effortlessly on a steep slope along a curving mountain interstate highway. It's moving too fast for you to read the nameplate, but on the grill you see a three-pointed star. Maybe after you graduate from law school and your student loans are paid off?

The Power of Visual Arguments

We don't need to be reminded that visual images have clout. Just think for a moment about where you were on September 11, 2001, when you first saw images of the hijacked planes that slammed into the World Trade Center towers. Or remember the images of the August 2005 floodwaters in New Orleans and the desperate citizens who were driven to rooftops in the wake of Hurricane Katrina. Or maybe you recall the dramatic opening ceremonies of the 2008 Summer Olympics in Beijing. Images like these stick in our memories.

Yet even in mundane moments, visual images—from T-shirts to billboards to movie and computer screens—influence us. Everyone seems to be trying to get our attention with images as well as words. Some argue that images today pack more punch than words, especially for the "millennial" generation that has grown up doing much of its reading onscreen. As technology makes it easier for people to create and transmit images, images become more compelling than ever, brought to us via Blu-ray and high-definition television on our smartphones and computers, on our walls, in our pockets, and even in our cars.

But visual arguments weren't invented by YouTube, and they've always had power. The pharaohs of Egypt lined the banks of the Nile River with statues of themselves to assert their authority, and Roman emperors had their portraits stamped on coins for the same reason.

What arguments does an image of *Air Force One* in flight usually make? What arguments were provoked by the scene above, a low-altitude pass over New York City by an identical backup plane—with no public notice in advance—on April 27, 2009?

Some thirty thousand years ago, people in the south of France created magnificent cave paintings, suggesting that people have long used images to celebrate and to communicate.

For the authors of this book, two events marked turning points in the growing power of media images. The first occurred in 1960 when presidential candidates John F. Kennedy and Richard M. Nixon met in a nationally televised debate. Kennedy, robust and confident in a dark suit, faced a pale and haggard Nixon who had recently recovered from an illness. Kennedy looked cool and "presidential"; Nixon did not. Many viewers believe that the contrasting images that Kennedy and Nixon presented on that evening changed the direction of the 1960 election campaign and led to Kennedy's narrow victory. The debate also established television as the chief medium for political communication in the United States until the rise of the Internet.

Richard M. Nixon and John F. Kennedy in a televised debate, 1960

The second event is more recent—the introduction in the early 1980s of personal computers with graphic interfaces. These machines, which initially seemed strange and toylike, operated with easy-to-use icons and pictures rather than through complicated commands made up of letters, numbers, and symbols. Subtly at first and then with the force of a tsunami, graphic computers (the only kind that people use now) moved society further away from an age of print into an era of electronic, image-saturated communications.

At the end of the opening decade of a new millennium, people have adjusted to a world of seamless, multichannel, multimedia communications. The prophet of this time was Marshall McLuhan, who over forty years ago proclaimed that "the medium is the massage," with the play on *message* and *massage* intentional. Certainly images massage us all the time, and anyone reading and writing today has to be prepared to deal with arguments that shuffle more than words.

Not Just Words

One of the best-known photographs that appeared after the September 11, 2001, terrorist attacks was shot by Thomas Franklin. It shows three firefighters hoisting the American flag in the wreckage of the World Trade Center as dust settles around them. In 2002, the image was used on a fund-raising stamp that sold for forty-five cents, with proceeds going to the Federal Emergency Management Agency. Part of the picture's appeal was its resemblance to another famous American image—Joe Rosenthal's photo of U.S. Marines raising the flag on Iwo Jima in 1945. That image was made into a three-cent stamp that became the best-selling U.S. stamp for many years.

Take a look at the two images, and consider how they're composed. What attracts your attention? How do your eyes move over the images? What immediate impression do they create? Also notice other features of the stamps—tinting, text placement, font, and wording. What argument do these stamps make about America?

Shaping the Message

Images make arguments of their own. A photograph, for example, isn't a faithful representation of reality; it's reality shaped by the photographer's point of view. You can see photographic and video arguments at work everywhere, particularly during political campaigns. Staff photographers place candidates in settings that show them in the best possible light (shirtsleeves rolled up and surrounded by smiling children and red-white-and-blue bunting), and their opponents look for opportunities to present the other side's candidates in a bad way. Closer to home, you may well have selected photographs that show you at your best to include on MySpace or Facebook.

Those who produce images shape the messages that those images convey, but those who "read" those images are by no means passive. Human vision is selective. To some extent, we actively shape what we see and have learned to see things according to their meanings within our culture. People don't always see things the same way, which explains why eyewitnesses to the same event often report it differently. Even instant replays don't always solve disputed calls on football fields. The visual images that surround us today and argue forcefully for our attention, time, and money are constructed to invite, perhaps even coerce, us into seeing them in just one way. But since we all have our own frames of reference, we resist such pressures. So visual arguments might best be described as a give-and-take, a dialogue, or even a tussle.

Analyzing Visual Elements of Arguments

Analyzing the visual elements of arguments is a challenge, especially when you encounter multimedia appeals on the Web. Here are some questions that can help you recognize and analyze visual and multimedia arguments:

About the Creators and Distributors

- Who created this visual text? Who distributed it?
- What can you find out about these people and other work that they have they done?

- What does the creator's attitude seem to be toward the image?
- What do the creator and the distributor intend its effects to be? Do they have the same intentions?

About the Medium

- Which media are used for this visual text? Images only? Words and images? Sound, video, graphs, or charts?
- How are the media used to communicate words and images? How do various media work together?

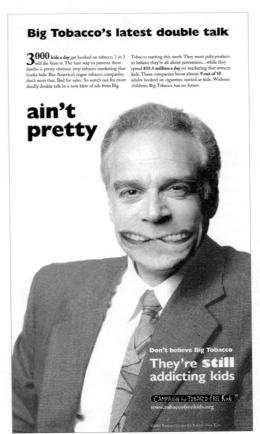

Big Tobacco's latest double talk

3,000 kids a day get hooked on tobacco. 1 in 3 will die from it. The best way to prevent these deaths is pretty obvious: stop tobacco marketing that hooks kids. But America's rogue tobacco companies don't want that. Bad for sales. So watch out for more deadly double talk in a new blitz of ads from Big Tobacco starting this week. They want policymakers to believe they're all about prevention...while they spend **$15.5 million a day** on marketing that attracts kids. These companies know almost **9 out of 10** adults hooked on cigarettes started as kids. Without children, Big Tobacco has no future.

ain't pretty

Don't believe Big Tobacco

They're still addicting kids

CAMPAIGN for TOBACCO-FREE Kids
www.tobaccofreekids.org

Analyzing Visual Elements: The Creators and Distributors

"Ain't Pretty" is one of a series of print ads created and distributed by the Campaign for Tobacco-Free Kids, which the *New York Times Magazine* describes as "the country's leading anti-tobacco lobby." The campaign itself represents a coalition of more than one hundred organizations (listed on its Web site) working together to discourage and prevent smoking, from the Academy of General Dentistry and the American Federation of Teachers to the Church of Jesus Christ of Latter-Day Saints and the Sierra Club. But whose view of Big Tobacco does the image in the ad represent? Only that of the Campaign for Tobacco-Free Kids, or that of all the individual members of the coalition? What sorts of reactions might the image evoke?

Analyzing Visual Elements: The Medium

In summer 2008, Democratic Speaker Nancy Pelosi recessed the House of Representatives rather than allow an up or down vote on an energy bill that authorized drilling for oil off American coastlines. She also ordered the lights and C-SPAN cameras turned off in the chamber as she headed off on a five-week vacation. Republican representatives remained in the darkened chamber and responded with a multimedia protest. As they argued about energy issues, they used cell phone and video cameras to record the shutdown and then communicated with constituents via podcasts, blogs, and a Twitter feed. These online media allowed the protesters to gain public attention, despite a lack of coverage by mainstream news outlets. Protesters for democracy in Iran later used similar techniques.

- What effect does the medium have on the message of the visual text? How would the message be altered if different media were used?

- What role is played by the words that accompany the visual text? How do they clarify, reinforce, blur, or contradict the image's message?

About Viewers and Readers

- What does the visual text assume about its viewers and about what they know and agree with?

- What overall impression does the visual text create in you?

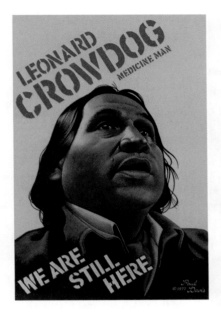

Analyzing Visual Elements: The Viewers and Readers

In 1977, Paul Davis created this poster celebrating Native American political activist Leonard Crowdog. The poster uses simple language and a strong image to express solidarity among Native Americans (and their political allies) and to affirm Crowdog's call for renewal of Native American traditions. In what ways can visual arguments invoke their audiences or even become a part of their cultural histories? With what visual items (such as posters or CD art) do you identify?

- What positive or negative feelings about individuals, scenes, or ideas does the visual intend to evoke in viewers?

About Content and Purpose

- What argumentative purpose does the visual text convey? What is it designed to convey?
- What cultural values does the visual evoke? The good life? Love and harmony? Sex appeal? Youth? Adventure? Economic power or dominance? Freedom? Does the visual reinforce these values or question them? What does the visual do to strengthen the argument?
- What emotions does the visual evoke? Are these the emotions that it intends to evoke?

About Design

- How is the visual text composed? What's your eye drawn to first? Why?
- What's in the foreground? In the background? What's in or out of focus? What's moving? What's placed high, and what's placed low?

Analyzing Visual Elements: The Content and Purpose

An Associated Press photograph of Republican vice-presidential candidate Sarah Palin at a campaign rally in Bethlehem, Pennsylvania, started a controversy in October 2008, as news organizations and commentators raised questions about the content and purpose of the image. Some found it sexist and prurient, but others called it upbeat or emblematic of a new kind of feminism. Did the photographer and AP (which has been accused of both left- and right-wing bias in its overall political coverage) have a political agenda in taking and distributing the shot? Or did people read their own arguments into it?

What's to the left, in the center, and to the right? What effect do these placements have on the message?

- Is any information (such as a name, face, or scene) highlighted or stressed to attract your attention?
- How are light and color used? What effects are they intended to have on you? What about video? Sound?
- What details are included or emphasized? What details are omitted or deemphasized? To what effect? Is anything downplayed, ambiguous, confusing, distracting, or obviously omitted? To what end?
- What, if anything, is surprising about the design of the visual text? What do you think is the purpose of that surprise?
- Is anything in the visual repeated, intensified, or exaggerated? Is anything presented as "supernormal" or idealistic? What effects are intended by these strategies, and what effects do they have on you as a viewer? How do they clarify or reinforce (or blur or contradict) the message?

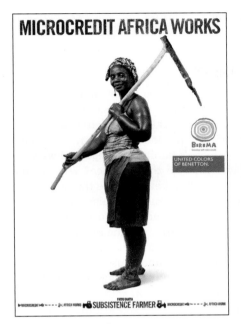

Analyzing Visual Elements: The Design

For years, United Colors of Benetton has launched memorable advertising campaigns with themes of political and social justice. Controversial in both content and design, its ads—like this one from a series that supports African economic development—compel audiences to think about issues not directly related to the fashions sold by Benetton. How does your eye construct this ad? What do you notice first? Do the parts make sense when you put them together?

- How are you directed to move within the argument? Are you encouraged to read further? Click on a link? Scroll down? Fill out a form? Provide your email address? Place an order?

Using Visuals in Your Own Arguments

You can and sometimes should use visuals in your writing. Many college classes now call for projects to be posted on the Web, which almost always involves the use of images. Other courses invite or require students to make multimedia presentations using software such as PowerPoint or even old-fashioned overhead projectors with transparencies.

On the following pages, we sketch out some basic principles of visual rhetoric. To help you appreciate the argumentative character of visual texts, we examine them under some of the same categories that we use for written and oral arguments earlier in this book (Chapters 2, 3, and 4).

You may be surprised by some of the similarities that you'll see between visual and verbal arguments.

Visual Arguments That Appeal to Emotion

People tend to be suspicious of arguments supported by multimedia elements because they can be used to manipulate our senses. In fact, many advertisements, political documentaries, rallies, marches, and even church services do use visuals to trigger emotions. Who hasn't teared up at a funeral when members of a veteran's family are presented with an American flag and a bugler plays "Taps" in the distance? Who hasn't been moved emotionally by a powerful film performance that is accompanied by a heart-wrenching musical score? You might also have seen or heard about *Triumph of the Will*, a 1935 propaganda film authorized by the National Socialists that powerfully depicts Hitler as the benign savior of the German people and a hero of superhuman dimensions. It's a chilling reminder of how images can be manipulated and abused.

You can't flip through a magazine without being cajoled or seduced by images of all kinds—most of them designed in some way to attract your eye and attention. Sometimes emotions can support the legitimate claims that you hope to advance. Emotions certainly run high at sporting events or ceremonies that honor human achievements, such as high school and college graduations.

APPRECIATE THE EMOTIONAL POWER OF IMAGES

Images can bring a text or presentation to life. Sometimes images have the power to persuade by sheer pathos. This was the case with photographs that showed 1960s civil rights demonstrators being assaulted by police dogs and water hoses and that showed the 2005 victims of Hurricane Katrina, which led many people to contribute to relief campaigns. You have an advantage if you can present images that make arguments almost entirely on their own.

But images you select for a presentation may be equally effective if the visual text works well with other components of the argument. Indeed, a given image might support many different kinds of arguments. Consider the famous *Apollo 8* photograph of our planet as a big blue marble hanging above the horizon of the moon. You might use this image to introduce an argument about the need for additional investment in the space program. Or it might become part of an argument about the need

A striking image, like this *Apollo 8* photograph of the earth shining over the moon, can support many different kinds of arguments.

to preserve our frail natural environment or an argument against nationalism: *From space, we are one world.* You could make any of these claims without the image, but the photograph—like most images—might touch members of your audience more powerfully than words alone could.

APPRECIATE THE EMOTIONAL POWER OF COLOR

Color has great power. Consider the color red. It attracts hummingbirds— and traffic cops. It excites the human eye in ways that other colors don't. You can make a powerful statement with a red dress or a red car because the color evokes emotions—but so do black, green, pink, and even brown. Our response to color is part of our biological and cultural makeup. So it makes sense to consider what colors are compatible with the kinds of arguments you're making. You might find that the best choice is black on a white background.

In most situations, you can be guided in your selection of colors by your own good taste, by designs you admire, or by the advice of friends or helpful professionals. Some design and presentation software will even help you choose colors by offering dependable "default" shades or an array of preexisting designs and compatible colors (for example, of presentation slides).

The colors that you choose for a design should follow certain commonsense principles. If you're using background colors on a political poster, Web site, or slide, the contrast between words and background should be vivid enough to make reading easy. For example, white letters on a yellow background are not usually legible. Similarly, any bright background color should be avoided for a long document because reading is easiest with dark letters against a light or white background. Avoid complex patterns, even though they might look interesting and be easy

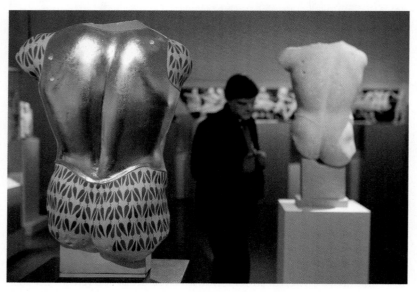

The ancient statues that you see in museums are usually white or pale gray. But evidence suggests that the Greeks and Romans painted these figures brightly, as you can see in this original (right) and painted copy (left) in an Athens museum. Buildings, too, were far more colorful than the white marble facades that we see in Hollywood re-creations of Athens or Rome. How might your appreciation of these buildings change if you imagined them in color?

to create. Often, they interfere with other more important elements of a presentation.

When you use visuals in your college projects, test them on prospective readers. That's what professionals do because they appreciate how delicate the choices about visual and multimedia texts can be. These responses will help you analyze your own arguments and improve your success with them.

Visual Arguments Based on Character

What does visual argument have to do with ethos or character? Consider two argumentative essays submitted to an instructor. One is scrawled in thick pencil on pages ripped from a spiral notebook, and little curls of paper dangle from the left margin. The other is neatly typed on bond paper and in a form that the professor likely regards as "professional." Is there much doubt about which argument will (at least initially) get the more sympathetic reading?

You might object that appearances shouldn't count for so much, and you would have a point. The argument scratched in pencil could be the stronger piece, but it is at a disadvantage because its author has sent the wrong signals. Visually, the writer seems to be saying, "I don't much care about this message or the people I'm sending it to." At times, you might want to send exactly such a signal to an audience, but the visual rhetoric of your piece ought to be a deliberate choice and not an accident. Also

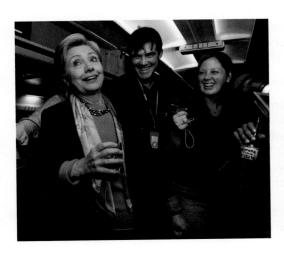

Near the end of her campaign for the 2008 presidential nomination of her party, Hillary Clinton loosened up a bit with reporters. Many thought that images such as this one enhanced her ethos by making her seem down to earth and likable.

These three images are used to convey authority and credibility. Do the Obama pre-presidential seal, the corporate logo of McDonald's, and the state seal of Louisiana accomplish their goals? Why or why not?

keep control of your own visual image. In most cases, when you present an argument, you want to appear authoritative and credible.

LOOK FOR IMAGES THAT REINFORCE YOUR AUTHORITY AND CREDIBILITY

For a brochure about your new small business, for instance, you might be considering images of your office, state-of-the-art equipment, and competent staff to reassure consumers that your company has the resources to do its job. Similarly, for a Web site about a company or organization that you represent, you would include its logo or emblem because such images provide credibility. That's why university Web sites often include the seal of the institution somewhere on the homepage or why the president of the United States travels with a presidential seal to hang on the speaker's podium. An emblem or a logo can convey a wealth of cultural and historical implications.

CONSIDER HOW DESIGN REFLECTS YOUR CHARACTER

Almost every design element sends signals about character and ethos, so be sure to think carefully about them. For example, the type fonts that you select for a document can mark you as warm and inviting or as efficient and contemporary. The warm and inviting fonts often belong to a family called *serif*. The serifs are those little flourishes at the ends of the strokes that make the fonts seem handcrafted and artful:

warm and inviting (Bookman Old Style)

warm and inviting (Times New Roman)

warm and inviting (Bookman)

Cleaner, modern fonts go without those little flourishes and are called *sans serif*. These fonts are cooler, simpler, and, some argue, more readable on a computer screen (depending on screen resolution):

efficient and contemporary (Helvetica)

efficient and contemporary (Arial Black)

efficient and contemporary (Lucida Sans)

You may also be able to use decorative fonts. These are appropriate for special uses but not for long texts:

decorative and special uses (Zapf Chancery)

decorative and special uses (Goudy Handtooled BT)

Other typographic elements shape your ethos as well. The size of type can make a difference. If your text or headings are boldfaced and too large, you'll seem to be shouting. Tiny type, on the other hand, might make you seem evasive:

Lose weight! Pay nothing!*

*Excludes the costs of enrollment and required meal purchases. Minimum contract: 12 months.

Similarly, your choice of color—especially for backgrounds—can make a statement about your taste, personality, and common sense. For instance, you'll create a bad impression with a Web page whose dark background colors or busy patterns make reading difficult. If you want to be noticed, you might use bright colors—the same sort that would make an impression in clothing or cars. But subtle background shades are a better choice in most situations.

Don't ignore the power of illustrations and photographs. Because they reveal what you visualize, images can communicate your preferences, sensitivities, and inclusiveness. Conference planners, for example, are careful to create brochures that represent all participants, and they make sure that the brochure photos don't show only women, only men, or only members of one racial or ethnic group.

Even your choice of medium says something important about you. Making an appeal on a Web site sends signals about your technical skills, contemporary orientation, and personality. If you direct people to a

Olympic champion Michael Phelps learned a quick lesson about ethos when a drug-related incident tarnished his reputation, costing him an endorsement deal with Kellogg's. His photograph had already appeared on boxes of Kellogg's Corn Flakes and Wheaties.

© Dave Granlund/Cagle Cartoons, Inc.

Facebook or Flickr page, be sure that the images and items there present you in a favorable light.

Presentations that rely on an overhead projector, an LCD projector with software, or photocopied handouts give different impressions about the presenters. When reporting on a children's story that you're writing, the most effective medium of presentation might be cardboard and paper made into an oversized book and illustrated by hand.

FOLLOW DESIGN CONVENTIONS

Many kinds of writing have required design conventions. When that's the case, follow them to the letter. It's no accident that lab reports for science courses are sober and unembellished. Visually, they reinforce the professional ethos of scientific work. The same is true of a college research paper. You might resent the tediousness of placing page numbers in the right place or aligning long quotations just so, but these visual details help convey your competence. So whether you're composing a term paper, résumé, screenplay, or Web site, look for authoritative models and follow them.

Visual Arguments Based on Facts and Reason

People tend to associate facts and reason with verbal arguments, but here, too, visual elements play an essential role. Indeed, it's hard to imagine a compelling presentation these days that doesn't rely, to some degree, on visual elements to enhance or even make the case.

Many readers and listeners now expect ideas to be represented graphically. Not long ago, media critics ridiculed the colorful charts and graphs in newspapers like *USA Today*. Now, comparable features appear in even the most traditional publications because they work: they convey information efficiently. And viewers have adjusted to the multiple data streams that cable news, weather, and finance channels routinely broadcast around talking heads on split screens.

ORGANIZE INFORMATION VISUALLY

A design works well when readers can look at an item and understand what it does. A brilliant, much-copied example of such an intuitive design is a seat adjuster invented many years ago by Mercedes-Benz (see below). It's shaped like a tiny seat. Push any element of the control, and the real seat moves the same way—back and forth, up and down. No instructions are necessary.

Good visual design can work the same way in an argument by conveying information without elaborate instructions. Titles, headings, subheadings, enlarged quotations, running heads, and boxes are some common visual signals.

When you present headings in the same type font, size, and color, you're showing that the information under these headings is in some way related. Use headings when they'll guide your readers through your document. For

Mercedes-Benz's seat adjuster

complex and very long pieces, you may use both headings and subheadings. So in a conventional term paper, headings and subheadings group information that's connected or parallel. Similarly, on a Web site, two or three types of headings might group chunks of related information.

You should also decide how text should be arranged on a page by searching for relationships among items that should look alike. In this book, for example, bulleted lists are used to offer specific guidelines, and boxes titled "Not Just Words" have colored backgrounds and present visual arguments. You might use a list or a box to set off information that should be treated differently from the rest of the presentation, or you might visually mark it in other ways—by shading, color, or typography.

An item presented in large type or under a large headline should be more important than one that gets less visual attention. Place illustrations carefully: what you position front and center will appear more important than items in less conspicuous places. On a Web site, key headings should usually lead to subsequent pages on the site.

You take a risk if you violate the expectations of your audience or if you present a visual text without coherent signals. Particularly for Web-based materials, which may be accessible to people around the world, you can't make many assumptions about what seems coherent in diverse cultures. So you need to think about the roadmap that you're giving viewers whenever you present them with a visual text.

Remember, too, that design principles evolve and change from medium to medium. A printed text or an overhead slide, for example, ordinarily works best when its elements are easy to read, simply organized, and surrounded by restful white space. But some types of Web pages seem to thrive on visual clutter. They attract and hold their audiences' attention by packing a wide variety of information onto a relatively limited screen. Look closely, and you'll probably find the logic in these designs.

USE VISUALS TO CONVEY DATA EFFICIENTLY

Words are powerful and capable of precision and subtlety. But some information is conveyed more efficiently by charts, graphs, drawings, maps, or photos than by words. When making an argument, especially to a large group, consider what information should be delivered in nonverbal form.

Cable television news shows, like many Web pages, seem to thrive on visual clutter, packing a lot of information into a relatively small place. Split screens, news "crawls" across the bottom, and sports scores (or electoral votes) in small type at the top make for a busy look but let viewers with varied interests (and limited patience and attention spans) see at a glance the information they want.

A **pie chart** is an effective way of comparing parts to the whole. You might use a pie chart to illustrate the ethnic composition of your school, the percentage of taxes paid by people at different income levels, or the consumption of energy by different nations. Pie charts depict such information memorably, as those on p. 462 show.

A **graph** is an efficient device for comparing items over time or according to other variables. You could use a graph to trace the rise and fall of test scores over several decades or to show college enrollment by sex, race, and Hispanic origin, as in the bar graph on p. 462.

Diagrams or **drawings** are useful for drawing attention to details. You can use drawings to illustrate complex physical processes or designs of all sorts. After the 2001 attack on the World Trade Center, for example, engineers used drawings and diagrams to help citizens understand precisely what led to the total collapse of the buildings.

You can use **maps** to illustrate location and spatial relationships—something as simple as the distribution of office space in your student union or as complex as the topography of Utah. Such information would be far more difficult to explain using words alone.

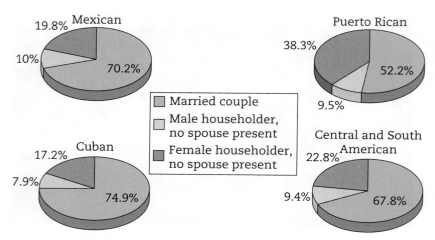

Family households by type and Hispanic origin group, 2002

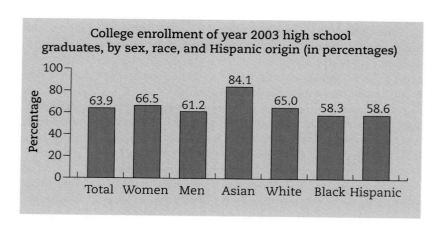

FOLLOW PROFESSIONAL GUIDELINES FOR PRESENTING VISUALS

Charts, graphs, tables, and illustrations play such an important role in many fields that professional groups have come up with guidelines for labeling and formatting these items. You need to become familiar with those conventions as you advance in a field. A guide such as the *Publication Manual of the American Psychological Association* (6th edition) or the *MLA Handbook for Writers of Research Papers* (7th edition) describes these rules in detail.

REMEMBER TO CHECK FOR COPYRIGHTED MATERIAL

You also must be careful to respect copyright rules when using visual items that were created by someone else. It's relatively easy these days to download visual texts of all kinds from the Web. Some of these items—such as clip art or government documents—may be in the *public domain*, meaning that you're free to use them without requesting permission or paying a royalty. But other visual texts may require permission, especially if you intend to publish your work or use the item commercially. And remember: anything you place on a Web site is considered "published." (See Chapter 18 for more on intellectual property.)

RESPOND●

1. The December 2002 issue of the *Atlantic Monthly* included the following poem and the photograph that may have inspired it (shown on p. 464). Look carefully at the image, read the poem several times, at least once aloud. Working with another person in your class, discuss how the words of the poem and the image interact with one another. What difference would it make if you hadn't seen the photo before reading this text? Write a brief report of your findings, and bring it to class for discussion.

A waterfall of black chains
looms behind the man in the stovepipe hat.
Cigar. Wrinkled clothes. This is
Isambard Kingdom Brunel.
Who could not stop working. Slept
and ate at the shipyard.
The largest ship in the world.
Driven to outdo himself.

This photograph of the engineer Isambard
Kingdom Brunel was taken by Robert Howlett
in 1857 and is included in the National Portrait
Gallery's collection in London.

Fashioned from iron plate and
powered by three separate means.
Able to sail to Ceylon and back
without refueling. Fated
to lay the Atlantic cable, the India cable.
Untouched in size for forty years.
The Great Leviathan. The Little Giant,
Isambard Kingdom Brunel.
Builder of tunnels, ships, railroads, bridges.
Engineer and Genius of England.
He should have built churches, you know.
Everything he prayed for came true.
—John Spaulding, "The Launching Chains of the *Great Eastern*"

2. Find an advertisement that has both verbal and visual elements.
   Analyze the ad's visual argument by answering some of the questions

on pp. 446–51, taking care to "reread" its visual elements as carefully as you would its words. After you've answered each question as thoroughly as possible, switch ads with a classmate, and analyze the new argument in the same way. Then compare your own and your classmate's responses to the two advertisements. If they're different—and there's every reason to expect that they will be—how do you account for the differences? What effect does the audience have on the argument's reception? What differences appear between your own active reading and your classmate's?

3. You've no doubt noticed how visual design and textual material are presented on the Web. In the best Web pages, text and images work together rather than simply compete for space. Even if you've never used the Web, you still know a great deal about graphic design from newspapers and magazines. Your own college papers use design principles to create effective texts.

    Find three or four Web pages or magazine pages that you think exemplify good visual design—and then find three or four that don't. When you've picked the good and bad designs, draw a rough sketch of each page's physical layout. Where are the graphics? Where is the text? What are the size and position of text blocks relative to graphics? How is color used? Can you discern common design principles among the pages, or does each good page work well in its own way? Write a brief explanation of what you find, focusing on the way that the visual arguments influence audiences.

4. Go to the Web page for the Pulitzer Prize archives at http://pulitzer.org. Pick a year to review, and then study the images of the winners in three categories—editorial cartooning, spot news photography, and feature photography. (Click on "Works" to see the images.) Choose one image that you believe makes a strong argument, and write one paragraph that describes the image and the argument that it makes.

15
Presenting Arguments

In the wake of a devastating earthquake, political leaders take to the airwaves to promise quick action and material support for survivors. Local church leaders search for words to console their congregations and give them hope.

To protest the installation of more traffic cameras at intersections, an activist distributes a PowerPoint presentation online detailing just how little revenue the devices generate for cities that use them and how much they earn for the companies that operate them.

At a campus rally, a spoken-word poet performs a piece against racism and homophobia.

For a course on Elizabethan drama, a student creates a multimedia presentation to demonstrate that Shakespeare's strong female characters reflect the power wielded by Elizabeth I.

During their wedding in Vancouver, a couple exchanges special vows that they've worked together to create.

Sometimes the choice of how to deliver an argument to an audience is made for you: the boss says, "Write a report," or an instructor says, "Build a Web site." But often, you'll need to decide on your own the form of presentation that best fits your topic, purpose, and audience. The following advice can help you make good choices.

Print Presentations

For many arguments that you make in college, print remains the best medium of delivery. Print texts are more permanent than most Web-based materials, they're inexpensive and easy to produce, and they offer a precise way to express abstract ideas or to set down complicated chains of reasoning. But in making an argument in print, writers face an embarrassment of riches. Printed documents used to be created in standard formats—black print on 8½ x 11 white paper read left to right, top to bottom—but today's print texts come in a dizzying array of shapes, sizes, and colors.

As you think about presenting textual arguments, here are some issues to consider:

- What overall tone do you want to create in this written argument? What's the purpose of your argument, and to whom is it addressed?

- What format will get your message across most effectively? A formal report with a table of contents and an executive summary? A newsletter? A triple-fold brochure?

- What fonts will make your argument most readable? Will varying the font or type size help guide readers through your text? Will it draw attention to what's most important?

- Will you use subheads as another guide to readers? If so, what size type will you select for them? Will you use all caps, boldface, or italics? In any case, be consistent in the style and the structure of subheads (all nouns, for example, or all questions).

- Should you use colors other than black ink and white paper in presenting your argument? If so, what colors best evoke your tone and purpose? What colors will be most appealing to your audience?

- How will you use white or blank space in your argument? To give readers time to pause? To establish a sense of openness or orderliness?

- Will you use visuals in your print argument? If so, how will you integrate them smoothly into the text? (For more on the role of visuals in arguments, see Chapter 14.)

Oral and Multimedia Presentations

Students tell us that they're frequently being asked to make oral presentations in their classes these days—but also complain that they're rarely given instructions about how to do so. And students returning from summer internships in a range of fields from engineering to the arts report that their employers simply expect them to be proficient at delivering arguments orally and to accompany such presentations with the appropriate illustrative materials.

It's hard to generalize here, but capable presenters attribute their success to several crucial elements:

- They have thorough knowledge of their subjects.

- They pay attention to the values, ideas, and needs of their listeners.

- They use structures and styles that make their spoken arguments easy to follow.

- They realize that oral arguments are interactive (live audiences can argue back!).

- They appreciate that most oral presentations involve visuals, and they plan accordingly.

- They practice, practice—and then practice some more.

Oral Arguments in Discussions

Most of the oral arguments that you'll make in college will occur in ordinary discussions. You are arguing all the time, whether in exploring the meaning of a poem in English class, arguing against a textbook's interpretation of an economic phenomenon, or trying to reform a student government policy on funding political organizations. In such

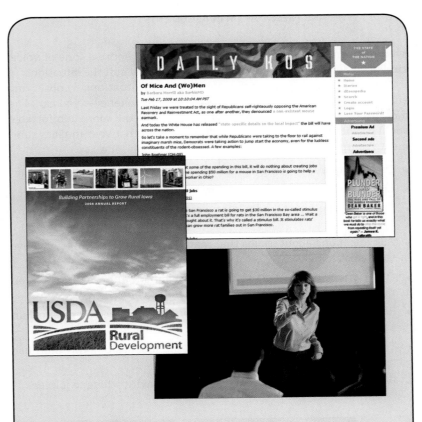

Not Just Words

The figures above illustrate three different modes of presentation—an informative blog, a printed report, and an oral or multimedia presentation for a live audience. Spend time talking with a classmate about the choices that were involved in selecting each of these methods of presentation, and then report your findings to the class.

everyday contexts, many people automatically choose a tone of voice, kind of evidence, and length of speaking time that suit the situation.

You can improve your performance in such situations by observing effective speakers and by joining conversations whenever you can. The more that you participate in lively discussions, the more comfortable you'll be with speaking your mind. To make sure that your in-class comments count, follow these tips:

- Do the required reading so that you know what you're talking about.
- Listen with a purpose, and jot down important points.
- Speak to the point under discussion so that your comments are relevant.
- Ask questions about issues that matter to you: others probably have the same thoughts.
- Occasionally offer brief summaries of points that have already been made to make sure that everyone is "on the same page."
- Respond to questions or comments by others in specific rather than vague terms.
- Try to learn the names of people in the discussion, and then use them.
- When you are already part of a discussion, invite others to join in.

CULTURAL CONTEXTS FOR ARGUMENT

Speaking Up in Class

Speaking up in class is viewed as inappropriate or even rude in some cultures. In the United States, however, doing so is expected and encouraged. Some instructors even assign credit for such class participation.

Formal Oral and Multimedia Presentations

When asked to make a formal presentation in class or on the job, consider the context carefully. Note how much time you have to prepare and how long the presentation should be. You want to use your slot effectively and not infringe on the time of others. Consider also what visual aids, handouts, or other materials might make the presentation successful. Will you have to use an overhead projector or just a blackboard? Or can you use PowerPoint or other presentation software?

Check out where your presentation will take place. In a classroom with fixed chairs? A lecture or assembly hall? An informal sitting area? Will you have a lectern? Other equipment? Will you sit or stand? Remain in one place or move around? What will the lighting be, and can you adjust it? Sometimes oral presentations are group efforts. When that's the case, plan and practice accordingly. The work will need to be divvied up, and you will need to work out who speaks when. Finally, note any criteria for evaluation: how will your live oral argument be assessed?

In addition to these logistical matters, consider these rhetorical elements whenever you make a formal presentation:

Purpose

- Determine your major argumentative purpose. Is it to inform? To convince or persuade? To explore? To make a decision? To entertain? Something else?

Audience

- Who is your audience? An interested observer? A familiar face? A stranger? What will be the mix of age groups, men and women, and so on? Are you a peer of the audience members? Think carefully about what they already know about your topic and what opinions they're likely to hold.

Structure

- Structure your presentation so that it's easy to follow, and plan an introduction that gets the audience's attention and a conclusion that makes your argument memorable. You'll find more help with structure on p. 473.

Arguments to Be Heard

Even if you deliver a live presentation from a printed text, be sure to compose a script that is to be *heard* rather than *read*. Such a text—whether in the form of note cards, an overhead list, or a fully written-out script—should feature a strong introduction and conclusion, an unambiguous structure with helpful transitions and signposts, concrete diction, and straightforward syntax.

STRONG INTRODUCTIONS AND CONCLUSIONS

Like readers, listeners remember beginnings and endings best. Work hard, therefore, to make these elements of your spoken argument especially memorable. Consider including a provocative or puzzling statement, opinion, or question; a memorable anecdote; a powerful quotation; or a vivid visual image. If you can refer to the interests or experiences of your listeners in the introduction or conclusion, then do so.

Look at the introduction to Toni Morrison's acceptance speech to the Nobel Academy when she won the Nobel Prize for Literature:

> "Once upon a time there was an old woman. Blind but wise." Or was it an old man? A guru, perhaps. Or a griot soothing restless children. I have heard this story, or one exactly like it, in the lore of several cultures. "Once upon a time there was an old woman. Blind. Wise."
>
> —Toni Morrison

Here, Morrison uses a storytelling strategy, calling on the traditional "Once upon a time" to signal to her audience that she's doing so. Note also the use of repetition and questioning. These strategies raise interest and anticipation in her audience: how will she use this story in accepting the Nobel Prize?

Toni Morrison accepting the Nobel Prize for Literature in 1993

CLEAR STRUCTURES AND SIGNPOSTS

For a spoken argument, you want your organizational structure to be crystal clear. So offer an overview of your main points toward the beginning of the presentation, and make sure that you have a clearly delineated beginning, middle, and end. Throughout the report or lecture, remember to pause between major points and to offer signposts to mark your movement from one topic to the next. They can be transitions as obvious as *next, on the contrary,* or *finally.* Such words act as memory points in your spoken argument and thus should be explicit and concrete: *The second crisis point in the breakup of the Soviet Union occurred hard on the heels of the first,* rather than *The breakup of the Soviet Union came to another crisis.* You can also keep listeners on track by repeating key words and concepts and by using unambiguous topic sentences to introduce each new idea.

STRAIGHTFORWARD SYNTAX AND CONCRETE DICTION

Avoid long, complicated sentences, and as much as possible, use straightforward syntax (subject-verb-object, for instance, rather than an inversion of that order). Remember, too, that listeners can hold onto concrete verbs and nouns more easily than they can grasp a steady stream of abstractions. So when you need to deal with abstract ideas, try to illustrate them with concrete examples.

Take a look at the following text that student Ben McCorkle wrote about *The Simpsons*, first as he prepared it for an essay and then as he adapted it for a live oral and multimedia presentation:

Print Version

The Simpson family has occasionally been described as a "nuclear" family, which obviously has a double meaning: first, the family consists of two parents and three children, and, second, Homer works at a nuclear power plant with very relaxed safety codes. The overused label *dysfunctional,* when applied to the Simpsons, suddenly takes on new meaning. Every episode seems to include a scene in which son Bart is being choked by his father, the baby is being neglected, or Homer is sitting in a drunken stupor transfixed by the television screen. The comedy in these scenes comes from the exaggeration of commonplace household events (although some talk shows and news programs would have us believe that these exaggerations are not confined to the madcap world of cartoons).

—Ben McCorkle, "The Simpsons: A Mirror of Society"

Oral Version (with a visual illustration)

What does it mean to describe the Simpsons as a *nuclear* family? Clearly, a double meaning is at work. First, the Simpsons fit the dictionary meaning—a family unit consisting of two parents and some children. The second meaning, however, packs more of a punch. You see, Homer works at a nuclear power plant [pause here] with *very* relaxed safety codes!

Still another overused family label describes the Simpsons. Did everyone guess I was going to say *dysfunctional*? And like "nuclear,"

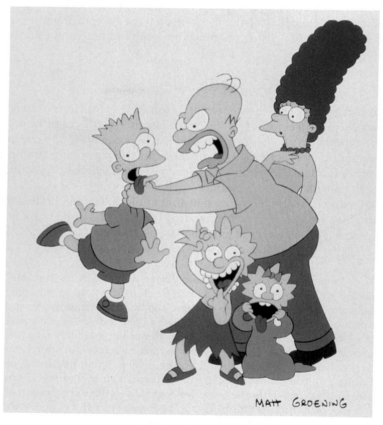

MATT GROENING

Homer Simpson in a typical pose

when it comes to the Simpsons, "dysfunctional" takes on a whole new meaning.

Remember the scene when Bart is being choked by his father? How about the many times the baby is being neglected? Or the classic view—Homer sitting in a stupor transfixed by the TV screen!

My point here is that the comedy in these scenes often comes from double meanings—and from a lot of exaggeration of everyday household events.

Note that the revised version presents the same information as the original, but this time it's written to be *heard*. The revision uses helpful signposts, some repetition, a list, italicized words to prompt the speaker to give special emphasis, and simple syntax so that it's easy to listen to.

Arguments to Be Remembered

You can probably think of oral and multimedia arguments that still stick in your memory—a song like Bruce Springsteen's "Born in the USA," for instance, or Paris Hilton's hilarious riff on a 2008 John McCain campaign ad. Such arguments are memorable in part because they offer us intriguing ideas (Hilton's energy policy!) that are reinforced by figures of speech and devices of language (her reference to a "wrinkly, white-haired guy"). One especially powerful strategy in oral arguments is deliberate repetition, especially when linked with parallelism and climactic order. (See Chapter 13 for more on using figurative language to make arguments more vivid and memorable.)

REPETITION, PARALLELISM, AND CLIMACTIC ORDER

Whether they're used alone or in combination, repetition, parallelism, and climactic order are especially appropriate for spoken arguments that sound a call to arms or that seek passionate engagement from the audience. Perhaps no person in the twentieth century used them more effectively than Martin Luther King Jr., whose sermons and speeches helped to spearhead the civil rights movement. Standing on the steps of the Lincoln Memorial in Washington, D.C., on August 23, 1963, with hundreds of thousands of marchers before him, King called on the nation to make good on the "promissory note" represented by the Emancipation Proclamation.

Look at the way that King uses repetition, parallelism, and climactic order in the following paragraph to invoke a nation to action:

> It is obvious today that America has defaulted on this promissory note insofar as her citizens of color are concerned. Instead of honoring this sacred obligation, America has given the Negro people a bad *check* which has come back marked "*insufficient funds.*" But *we refuse to* believe that the bank of justice is bankrupt. *We refuse to believe that* there are *insufficient funds* in the great vaults of opportunity of this nation. So *we have come* to cash this *check*—a *check* that will give us upon demand the riches of freedom and the security of justice. *We have also come* to this hallowed spot to remind America of the fierce urgency of now. This is no *time* to engage in the luxury of cooling off or to take the tranquilizing drug of gradualism. *Now is the time to* rise from the dark and desolate valley of segregation to the sunlit path of racial justice. *Now is the time to* open the doors of opportunity to all of God's children. *Now is the time to* lift our nation from the quicksands of racial injustice to the solid rock of brotherhood.
> —Martin Luther King Jr., "I Have a Dream" (emphasis added)

The italicized words highlight the way that King uses repetition to drum home his theme. But along with that repetition, he sets up a powerful set of parallel verb phrases, calling on all "to rise" from the "dark and desolate valley of segregation" to the "sunlit path of racial justice" and "to open the doors of opportunity" for all. The final verb phrase ("to lift") leads to a strong climax as King moves from what each individual should do to what the entire nation should do: "to lift our nation from the quicksands of racial injustice to the solid rock of brotherhood." These stylistic choices, together with the vivid image of the "bad check," help to make King's speech powerful, persuasive—and memorable.

You don't have to be as highly skilled as King to take advantage of the power of repetition and parallelism. Simply repeating a key word in your argument can impress it on your audience, as can arranging parts of sentences or items in a list in parallel order.

The Role of Visuals in Oral and Multimedia Arguments

Visual materials—chart, graphs, posters, slides, and PowerPoint screens—often figure prominently in oral arguments and should be carefully prepared. Don't think of them as add-ons but rather as major tools for conveying your message and supporting your claims. In many cases, a picture can truly be worth a thousand words.

Be certain that any visuals that you use are large enough to be seen by all members of your audience. If you use slides or overhead projections, the information on each frame should be simple, clear, and easy to process. For audience members to read information on a transparency, this means using 36 point type for major headings, 24 point for subheadings, and at least 18 point for all other text. For slides, use 24 point for major headings, 18 point for subheadings, and at least 14 point for other text.

The same rule of clarity and simplicity holds true for posters, flip charts, and chalkboards. And remember not to turn your back on your audience while you refer to these visuals. If you prepare supplementary materials (such as bibliographies or other handouts) for the audience, don't distribute them until the audience actually needs them. Or wait until the end of the presentation so that they don't distract listeners from your spoken argument.

If you've watched many PowerPoint presentations, you're sure to have seen some bad ones. But nothing is more deadly than a speaker who stands up and reads from each screen. It is fine to use presentation slides to furnish an overview for a presentation and to give visual signposts to listeners. But never read the slides word for word—or even put much prose on a screen. You'll just put your audience to sleep.

For an oral and multimedia presentation, one student used the PowerPoint slides shown on pp. 478, 480, and 482 to compare Frank Miller's graphic novel *Sin City* and its movie adaptation. Notice that the student uses text throughout, but in moderation. Next take a look at the written script (written to be heard) that the student developed for this presentation. The student does not read from the slides; rather, the slides illustrate the points that he's making orally. The text on the slides sums up—and occasionally supplements—his oral presentation. This careful use of text makes the student's argument clear and easy to follow.

His choices in layout and font size also aim for clarity but without sacrificing visual appeal. The choice of white and red text on a black background is appropriate for the topic—a stark black-and-white graphic novel and its shades-of-gray movie version. But be aware that light writing on a dark background can be hard to read and that dark writing on a white or cream-colored background is almost always a safer choice.

(Note that if your presentation shows or is based on source materials—either text or images—your instructor may want you to include a slide that lists the sources at the end of the presentation.)

From Frames to Film:
Graphic Novels on the Big Screen

Presentation by Sach Wickramasekara
PWR 2-06, Professor Lunsford
Wallenberg Hall Room 329
March 8, 2006

Introduction

A frame from the *Sin City* graphic novel.

"Instead of trying to make it [*Sin City*] into a movie which would be terrible, I wanted to take cinema and try and make it into this book."

- Robert Rodriguez, DVD Interview

The same scene from the *Sin City* movie.

[Opening Slide: Title]

Hi, my name is Sach.

[Change Slide: Introduction]

Take a look at this pair of scenes. Can you tell which one's from a movie and which one's from a graphic novel? How can two completely different media produce such similar results? Stay tuned; you're about to hear how.

[Pause]

Today I'll be analyzing *Sin City's* transition from a graphic novel to the big screen. The past decade has seen an increasing trend of comic books and graphic novels morphing into big-budget movies, with superhero flicks such as *Spider-Man* and *X-Men* headlining this list. However, until recently, movies borrowed from their comic book licenses but never stuck fully to their scripts. That all changed with *Sin City,* and I'll show you how dedication to preserving the look and feel of the graphic novel is what makes the screen version of *Sin City* neither a conventional graphic novel nor a conventional movie, but a new, innovative art form that's a combination of the two.

[Body]

[Change Slide—Technology]

Part of what makes *Sin City* so innovative is the technology powering it. The movie captures the look of the graphic novel so

Technology

Right: The original scene from the graphic novel.

Left: The scene is filmed with live actors on a green screen set.

Right: The final version of the scene, after the colors have been changed to shades of black and white. Notice the sapphire shade of the convertible, and how it stands out from the background.

Audio and Voice

"When I read the books, I felt that they were fantastic exactly as they were . . . . I loved that the dialogue didn't sound like movie dialogue." - Robert Rodriguez

JUST ONE HOUR TO GO. MY LAST DAY ON THE JOB. EARLY RETIREMENT. NOT MY IDEA. DOCTOR'S OR- DERS. HEART CONDITION. *ANGINA*, HE CALLS IT.

"Just one hour to go. My last day on the job. Early retirement. Not my idea. Doctor's orders. Heart condition. Angina, he calls it."

- *Sin City* movie

well by filming actors on a green screen and using digital imagery to put detailed backdrops behind them. Computer technology also turns the movie's visuals into shades of black and white with rare dashes of color splashed in, reproducing the noir feel of the original novels. Thus, scenes in *Sin City* have a photorealistic yet stylized quality that differentiates them from both the plain black-and-white images of the comics and the real sets used in other movies.

[Change Slide—Audio and Voice]

Pretty pictures are all well and good, but everyone knows that voice is just as important in a movie, especially because the media of comics and film use words so differently. The *Sin City* movie reproduces many sections of the novel that have a first-person narrator as monologues, and the script is lifted word for word from Miller's originals. This gives the dialogue an exaggerated quality that is more fantastic than realistic, which is exactly what director Robert Rodriguez intended. Here is an example from the film. "*Just one hour to go. My last day on the job. Early retirement. Not my idea. Doctor's orders. Heart condition. Angina, he calls it.*" A text box monologue fits perfectly in comics, where you read it and hear the character's voice in your head, but you wouldn't expect to hear it within an actual film. This contrast in narrative styles between the spoken word and how it is used is another factor that makes *Sin City* such an original work.

[Change Slide—Time and Structure]

Films are based on movement and sound, but comics divide movement into a series of "freeze-frame" images and represent

Time and Structure

Film: Movement – Sound – Time
Comics: Images – Text – Space

Dwight

Sin City ———→ Marv

Hartigan

Sin City revolves around the gallant
Dwight, the street thug Marv, and the
detective Hartigan. Each has his own
story, which does not cross the path of
the others apart from sharing the same
setting and a few minor characters.

Works Consulted

Goldstein, Hillary. "Five Days of Sin." *IGN.com*. 1 Apr. 2006. IGN Entertainment. Web.
12 Feb. 2006.
"The Making of *Sin City*." *Sin City* DVD preview page. Buena Vista Online Entertainment.
Web. 4 Feb. 2006.
Miller, Frank. *The Big Fat Kill*. Milwaukie: Dark Horse Books, 1994. Print.
---.*The Hard Goodbye*. Milwaukie: Dark Horse Books, 1991. Print.
---.*That Yellow Bastard*. Milwaukie: Dark Horse Books, 1996. Print.
Otto, Jeff. "*Sin City* Review." *IGN.com: Filmforce*. 29 Mar. 2005. IGN Entertainment.
Web. 10 Feb. 2006.
Robertson, Barbara. "The Devil's in the Details." *Computer Graphics World*. Apr. 2005:
18. *Expanded Academic ASAP*. Web. 11 Feb. 2006.
Sin City. Dir. Robert Rodriguez. Perf. Bruce Willis, Jessica Alba, Mickey Rourke, and
Clive Owen. Dimension, 2005. DVD.

sound as text. If you freeze the *Sin City* movie at certain frames, the scene might look identical to what is portrayed in the graphic novel. Press the play button again, and the characters appear to jump to life and begin moving within the frame. Thus, it's easy to view *Sin City* as a beautifully depicted, real-time graphic novel, where time is the factor that makes the story move forward, instead of space separating the different panels of the graphic novel.

[Pause]

Like the graphic novel by Frank Miller that it's based on, the *Sin City* movie is composed of a series of stories with different protagonists such as Marv, Dwight, and the detective Hartigan. These separate tales share only their settings and several secondary characters. Therefore, the movie feels episodic, rather than continuous like a feature-length film. Just as Miller's originals were a compilation of short stories linked by their setting, *Sin City* has the unique feel of being three short films linked by Miller's vision of an alternate universe.

[Change Slide—Works Consulted]

[Pause]

Sin City has opened the doors for future comic adaptations, none more anticipated than *Sin City 2* itself. There hasn't been a lot of info. on this movie, but apparently it'll be based on a brand new story that Frank Miller is writing. It'll be intriguing to see director Rodriguez adapt a graphic novel that hasn't even been written yet, so keep an eye out for this one. Any questions?

The best way to test the effectiveness of your visuals is to try them out on friends, family members, classmates, or roommates. If they don't get the meaning of the visuals right away, revise and try again.

Remember, finally, that visuals and accompanying media tools can help make your presentation accessible but that some members of your audience may not be able to see your presentation or may have trouble seeing or hearing them. Here are a few key rules to remember:

- Use words to describe projected images. Something as simple as *That's Franklin Roosevelt in 1944* can help even sight-impaired audience members appreciate what's on a screen.

- Consider providing a written handout that summarizes your presentation or putting the text on an overhead projector—for those who learn better by reading *and* listening.

- If you use video, take the time to label sounds that might not be audible to audience members who are hearing impaired. (Be sure your equipment is caption capable and use the captions; they can be helpful to everyone when audio quality is poor.)

Some Oral and Multimedia Presentation Strategies

In spite of your best preparation, you may feel some anxiety before a live presentation. This is natural. (According to one Gallup poll, Americans often identify public speaking as a major fear and as scarier than possible attacks from outer space.) Experienced speakers say that they have strategies for dealing with anxiety—and even that a little anxiety (and accompanying adrenaline) can act to a speaker's advantage.

The most effective strategy seems to be thoroughly knowing your topic and material. Confidence in your own knowledge goes a long way toward making you a confident speaker. In addition to being well prepared, you may want to try some of the following strategies:

- Practice a number of times, running through every part of the presentation. Leave nothing out, even audio or visual clips. Work with the equipment that you intend to use so that you are familiar with it. It also may help to visualize your presentation, imagining the scene in your mind as you run through your materials.

- Time your presentation to make sure you stay within your allotted slot.

- Tape yourself (video, if possible) at least once so that you can listen to your voice. Tone of voice and body language can dispose audiences for—or against—speakers. For most oral arguments, you want to develop a tone that conveys commitment to your position as well as respect for your audience.

- Think about how you'll dress for your presentation, remembering that audience members usually notice how a speaker looks. Dressing for an effective presentation depends on what's appropriate for your topic, audience, and setting, but most experienced speakers choose clothes that are comfortable, allow easy movement, and aren't overly casual. Dressing up a little indicates that you take pride in your appearance, have confidence in your argument, and respect your audience.

- Get some rest before the presentation, and avoid consuming too much caffeine.

- Relax! Consider doing some deep-breathing exercises. Then pause just before you begin, concentrating on your opening lines.

- Maintain eye contact with members of your audience. Speak to them, not to your text or to the floor.

- Most speakers make a stronger impression standing than sitting, so stand if you have that option. Moving around a bit may help you maintain good eye contact.

- When using presentation slides, stand to the side so that you don't block the view. Look at the audience rather than the slide.

- Interact with the audience whenever possible; doing so will often help you relax and even have some fun.

Finally, remember to allow time for audience responses and questions. Keep your answers brief so that others may join the conversation. And at the very end of your presentation, thank the audience for its attention to your arguments.

A Note about Webcasts: Live Presentations over the Web

This discussion of live oral and multimedia presentations has assumed that you'll be speaking before an audience that's in the same room with you. Increasingly, though—especially in business, industry, and science—the presentations you make will be live, but you won't be in the same physical space as the audience. Instead, you might be in front of a camera that will capture your voice and image and relay them via the Web to attendees who might be anywhere in the world. In another type of Webcast, participants can see only your slides or the software that you're demonstrating, using a screen-capture relay without cameras, and you're not visible but still speaking live.

In either case, as you learn to adapt to Webcast environments, most of the strategies that work in oral and multimedia presentations for an audience that's physically present will continue to serve you well. But there are some significant differences:

- Practice is even more important in Webcasts, since you need to be able to access online any slides, documents, video clips, names, dates, and sources that you provide during the Webcast.

- Because you can't make eye contact with audience members, it's important to remember to look into the camera (if you are using one), at least from time to time. If you're using a stationary Webcam, perhaps one mounted on your computer, practice standing or sitting without moving out of the frame and yet without looking stiff.

- Even though your audience may not be visible to you, assume that if you're on camera, the Web-based audience can see you. If you slouch, they'll notice. Also assume that your microphone is always live. Don't mutter under your breath, for example, when someone else is speaking or asking a question.

Web-Based Presentations

Even without the interactivity of Webcasts, most students have enough access to the Web to use its powers for effective presentations, especially in Web sites and blogs.

Web Sites

Students are increasingly creating Web sites for themselves, working hard at their self-presentation and showcasing their talents and accomplishments. They are also creating Web sites for extracurricular organizations, for work, or for class assignments and creating pages for themselves on MySpace or Facebook.

In planning any Web site, you'll need to pay careful attention to your rhetorical situation—the purpose of your site, its intended audience, and the overall impression that you want to make. To get started, you may want to visit several sites that you admire, looking for effective design ideas and ways of organizing navigation and information. Creating a map or storyboard for your site will help you to think through the links from page to page.

Experienced Web designers cite several important principles for Web-based presentations. The first of these is *contrast*, which is achieved through the use of color, icons, boldface, and so on; contrast helps guide readers through the site. The second principle, *proximity*, calls on you to keep together the parts of a page that are closely related, again for ease of reading. *Repetition* means using a consistent design throughout the site for the elements (such as headings and links) that help readers move smoothly through the site. Finally, designers concentrate on an *overall impression* or mood for the site, which means that the site's colors and visuals should help to create that impression rather than challenge or undermine it.

Here are some additional tips that may help you design your site:

- The homepage of your site should be eye-catching, inviting, and informative. Use titles and illustrations to make clear what the site is about.

- Think carefully about two parts of every page—the navigation area (menus or links) and the content areas. You want to make these two areas clearly distinct from one another. And make sure you *have* a navigation area for every page, including links to the key sections of the site and a link back to the homepage. Ease of navigation is one key to a successful Web site.

- Either choose a design template that is provided by Web-writing tools (like DreamWeaver), or create a template of your own that ensures that the elements of each page are consistent.

- Remember that some readers may not have the capacity to download heavy visuals or to access elements like Flash. If you want to reach a wide audience, stick with visuals that can be downloaded easily.

- Remember to include Web contact information on every page, but not your personal address or phone number.

Blogs

No Web texts have captured the public imagination more swiftly than blogs, which are now too numerous to count. Blogs take the idea of a personal Web page and give it the interactivity of a listserv, allowing readers to make comments and respond both to the blogger and to one another. Many if not most blogs contain primarily the writer's ideas and musings, but others have become prominent sources of news and opinion in politics, entertainment, and other fields.

In many ways, these blogs offer an alternative to traditional newspapers, TV networks, and periodicals, now somewhat derisively described by bloggers as the mainstream media (MSM). Blogs have broken important news stories and given more breadth to the political spectrum. As such, blogs create an ideal space for building communities, engaging in arguments, and giving voice to views and opinions of ordinary, everyday folks. We seldom see these people writing or being written about in major print media—many of which now sponsor blogs themselves as part of their electronic versions.

Blogs also have downsides. They're idiosyncratic, can be self-indulgent and egoistic, and can distort issues by spreading misinformation very quickly.

Blogs appear to be changing the ways that people communicate and redistributing power in ways that we still don't fully understand. If you're a reader of blogs, be sure to read carefully. The information on blogs

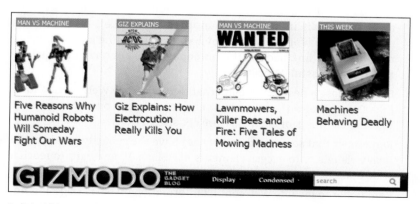

Political blogs get plenty of attention, but many of the most popular sites focus on technology, social networks, and cultural phenomena.

hasn't been critically reviewed in the way that traditional print sources review their stories. Nevertheless, blogs have reported many instances of the mainstream media's failure to live up to their own standards.

If you're a blogger, you know that the rules of etiquette for blogging and conventions for blogs are still evolving. In the meantime, you'll be wise to join the spirit of any blog that you contribute to, be respectful in your comments (even very critical ones), and think carefully about the audience that you want to reach in every entry you make.

RESPOND ●

1. Take three or four paragraphs from an essay that you've recently written. Then, following the guidelines in this chapter, rewrite the passage to be heard by a live audience. Finally, make a list of every change that you made.

2. Find a print presentation that you find particularly effective. Study it carefully, noting how its various elements—format, type sizes, typefaces, color, white space, visuals, and overall layout—work to deliver its message. If you find a particularly ineffective print presentation, carry out the same analysis to figure out why it's bad. Finally, prepare a five-minute presentation of your findings to deliver in class.

3. Attend a lecture or presentation on your campus, and observe the speaker's delivery. Note the strategies that the speaker uses to capture and hold your attention (or not). What signpost language and other guides to listening can you detect? How well are visuals integrated into the presentation? What aspects of the speaker's tone, dress, eye contact, and movement affect your understanding and appreciation (or lack of it)? What's most memorable about the presentation, and why? Finally, write up an analysis of this presentation's effectiveness.

4. Go to a Web site that you admire or consult frequently. Then answer the following questions: Why is a Web site—a digital presentation— the best way to present this material? What advantages over a print text or a live oral and multimedia presentation does the Web site have? What would you have to do to "translate" the argument(s) of this site into print or live oral format? What might be gained or lost in the process?

PART 4

CONVENTIONS OF argument

16
What Counts as Evidence

A person who cycles from home to work thinks that she notices some animosity from drivers of cars along her route. She decides to conduct some careful observations to test her hypothesis, and if it proves to be accurate, she'll design a survey to find out how other cyclists respond to and manage such animosity.

A business consultant wants to identify characteristics of effective team-work so that he can convince his partners to adopt these characteristics as part of their training program. To begin gathering evidence for this argument, the consultant decides to survey members of three effective teams and then conduct in-depth interviews with each member.

To support his contention that people are basically honest, an economist points to the detailed records kept by a vendor who sells muffins on the honor system in downtown offices. The merchant discovers that only a small percentage of people take advantage of him. The numbers also show that executives cheat more than middle-management employees.

For an argument aimed at showing that people still often unconsciously think of occupations as either masculine or feminine, a student decides to carry out an experiment. She will ask fifty people chosen at random to draw pictures of a doctor, a police officer, a nurse, a CEO, a lawyer, and a secretary—and see which are depicted as men and which as women. The results of this experiment will become evidence for (or against) the argument.

Trying to convince her younger brother to give up his out-of-date Mac in favor of a PC laptop, a college student mentions her three years of personal experience using a PC for her college coursework.

In arguing that Wikipedia is a reliable source of information, a student writer provides evidence for this claim by citing sixteen library sources that review and critique "the people's encyclopedia."

● ● ●

Evidence and the Rhetorical Situation

As the examples above demonstrate, people use all kinds of evidence in making and supporting claims. But this evidence doesn't exist in a vacuum. Instead, the quality of evidence—how it was collected, by whom, and for what purposes—may become part of the argument itself. Evidence may be persuasive in one time and place but not in another; it may convince one kind of audience but not another; it may work with one type of argument but not the kind you are writing.

To be most persuasive, evidence should match the time and place in which you make your argument. For example, arguing that a twenty-first-century Marine general should employ tactics of delay and strategic retreat because that strategy worked effectively for George Washington is likely to fail if Washington's use of the tactic is the only evidence provided. After all, a military maneuver that was effective in 1776 for an outnumbered band of revolutionaries is likely to be irrelevant today for a much different fighting force. In the same way, a writer may achieve excellent results by citing her own experiences and an extensive survey of local teenagers as evidence to support a new teen center for her small-town community, but she may have less success in using the same

The need for evidence depends a lot on the rhetorical situation.

© John Ditchburn/INKCINCT Cartoons

evidence in arguing for a teen center in a distant, large inner-city area where her personal authority may count for less.

College writers also need to consider the fields that they're working in. In disciplines such as experimental psychology or economics, *quantitative data*—the sort that can be observed and counted—may be the best evidence. In many historical or literary or philosophical studies, however, the same kind of data may be less appropriate or persuasive, or even impossible to come by. As you become more familiar with a particular discipline, you'll gain a sense of what it takes to prove a point or support a claim. The following questions will help you understand the rhetorical situation of a particular discipline:

- How do other writers in the field use *precedence*—examples of actions or decisions that are very similar—and authority as evidence? What or who counts as an authority in this field? How are the credentials of authorities established?

- What kinds of data are preferred as evidence? How are such data gathered and presented?
- How are statistics or other numerical information used and presented as evidence? Are tables, charts, or graphs commonly used? How much weight do they carry?
- How are definitions, causal analyses, evaluations, analogies, and examples used as evidence?
- How does the field use firsthand and secondhand sources as evidence?
- Is personal experience allowed as evidence?
- How are quotations used as part of evidence?
- How are images used as part of evidence, and how closely are they related to the verbal parts of the argument being presented?

As these questions suggest, evidence may not always travel well from one field to another.

Firsthand Evidence and Research

Firsthand evidence comes from research that you have carried out or been closely involved with, and much of this kind of research requires you to collect and examine data. Here, we discuss the kinds of firsthand research that are most commonly conducted by student writers.

Observations

"What," you may wonder, "could be easier than observing something?" You just choose a subject, look at it closely, and record what you see and hear. If observing were easy, however, all eyewitnesses would provide reliable accounts. Yet experience shows that several people who have observed the same phenomenon generally offer different, sometimes even contradictory, evidence on the basis of those observations. (When TWA Flight 800 exploded off the coast of New Jersey in 1996, eyewitnesses gave various accounts, some claiming that they saw what might have been a missile streaking toward the passenger jet. The official report found that an internal electrical short likely ignited vapors in a fuel tank.) Trained observers say that recording an observation accurately requires intense concentration and mental agility.

Before you begin an observation, decide exactly what you want to find out, and anticipate what you're likely to see. Do you want to observe an action that is repeated by many people (such as people at the checkout line in a grocery store for an argument that the store should install a new software program that automates pricing)? A sequence of actions (such as the stages that are involved in student registration, which you want to argue is far too complicated)? The interactions of a group (such as meetings of the campus interfaith group, which you hope will create a code of principles to guide difficult discussions)? Once you have a clear sense of what you'll observe and what questions you'll try to answer through the observation, use the following guidelines to achieve the best results:

- Make sure that the observation relates directly to your claim.
- Brainstorm about what you're looking for, but don't be rigidly bound to your expectations.
- Develop an appropriate system for collecting data. Consider using a split notebook or page: on one side, record the minute details of your observations; on the other, record your thoughts or impressions.
- Be aware that the way you record data will affect the outcome, if only in respect to what you decide to include in your observational notes and what you leave out.
- Record the precise date, time, and place of the observation.

In the following excerpt, *New York Times* media critic Virginia Heffernan uses information that she has drawn from careful study and observation to argue that Kanye West has created "a masterpiece blog" and an "online gallery of art and design" in a stunning "Web site that would improbably cross memoir and mall":

> The site looks nothing like the Web forays of other rap figures: Nas, Lil Wayne and 50 Cent use shadowy photographs of themselves in dark-alley spaces leavened mostly by sparkling Champagne bottles and fist-size diamonds.
>
> By contrast, the conceit of Kanye UniverseCity is a crayon-colored cartoon cityscape—an ever-expanding metropolis on the order of Shanghai. Click on features of the city, and up come chances to live the Kanye life, which is stylish, roguish, worldly, tech-savvy and socially responsible. Naturally you can buy its trappings and contribute to its causes. (West has recently turned his attention to traumatized veterans of the war in Iraq.) . . .

Kanye West's kanyeuniversecity.com—evidence that's easy to observe

West's site is also just fun. On the blog, West serves as an all-seeing coolhunter, turning up a range of favorite things—German art installations, limited-edition Parisian fashion, an iPod remote control worn like a wedding ring. ("Avant garde" is a category on the site.) For now, West styles himself as a hip and male answer to Oprah Winfrey, a cultural curator with incalculable influence over an audience that he alone has united. And if Oprah, whose O Magazine pushes cashmere sweaters and melamine bowls, is the Smithsonian, West is the Whitney.

—Virginia Heffernan, "Kanye on Keyboards"

Interviews

Some evidence is best obtained through direct interviews. If you can talk with an expert—in person, on the phone, or online—you might obtain information you couldn't have gotten through any other type of research. In addition to an expert opinion, you might ask for firsthand accounts, biographical information, or suggestions of other places to look or other people to consult. The following guidelines will help you conduct effective interviews:

- Determine the exact purpose of the interview, and be sure it's directly related to your claim.
- Set up the interview well in advance. Specify how long it'll take, and if you wish to tape-record the session, ask permission to do so.
- Prepare a written list of both factual and open-ended questions. (Brainstorming with friends can help you come up with good questions.) Leave plenty of space for notes after each question. If the interview proceeds in a direction that you hadn't expected but that seems promising, don't feel that you have to cover every one of your questions.
- Record the subject's full name and title, as well as the date, time, and place of the interview.
- Be sure to thank those people whom you interview, either in person or with a follow-up letter or email message.

Newspapers often use interviews to add perspective to stories or to check the authenticity of claims. Steve Fainuru, a reporter for the *Washington Post*, uses that technique to weigh the validity of an internal U.S. Army report that found flaws in the Stryker, a military transport vehicle used in Iraq:

> But in more than a dozen interviews, commanders, soldiers and mechanics who use the Stryker fleet daily in one of Iraq's most dangerous areas unanimously praised the vehicle. The defects outlined in the report were either wrong or relatively minor and did little to hamper the Stryker's effectiveness, they said.
>
> "I would tell you that at least 100 soldiers' lives have been saved because of the Stryker," said Col. Robert B. Brown, commander of the 1st Brigade, 25th Infantry Division, Stryker Brigade Combat Team, which uses about 225 Strykers for combat operations throughout northern Iraq. "That's being conservative," he said.
>
> —Steve Fainuru, "Soldiers Defend Faulted Strykers"

Note how the story uses a dramatic quotation to represent the opinion expressed in the interviews. A more academic study might include the full transcript of the interviews to give readers access to more firsthand data.

Surveys and Questionnaires

Surveys usually require the use of questionnaires. Questions should be clear, easy to understand, and designed so that respondents' answers can be easily analyzed. Questions that ask respondents to say "yes" or "no" or to rank items on a scale (1 to 5, for example, or "most helpful" to "least helpful") are particularly easy to tabulate. Because tabulation can take time and effort, limit the number of questions you ask. Note also that people often resent being asked to answer more than about twenty questions, especially online.

Here are some other guidelines to help you prepare for and carry out a survey:

- Write out your purpose in conducting the survey, and make sure that its results will be directly related to your purpose.
- Brainstorm potential questions to include in the survey, and ask how each relates to your purpose and claim.
- Figure out how many people you want to contact, what the demographics of your sample should be (for example, men in their twenties or an equal number of men and women), and how you plan to reach these people.
- Draft questions that are as free of bias as possible, making sure that each calls for a short, specific answer.
- Think about possible ways that respondents could misunderstand you or your questions, and revise with these points in mind.
- Test the questions on several people, and revise those questions that are ambiguous, hard to answer, or too time-consuming to answer.
- If your questionnaire is to be sent by mail or email or posted on the Web, draft a cover letter explaining your purpose and giving a clear deadline. For mail, provide an addressed, stamped return envelope.
- On the final draft of the questionnaire, leave plenty of space for answers.
- Proofread the final draft carefully. Typos will make a bad impression on those whose help you're seeking.
- After you've done your tabulations, set out your findings in clear and easily readable form, using a chart or spreadsheet if possible.

In arguing that the effects of Hurricane Katrina are still being felt by New Orleans residents more than three years after the event, the Kaiser

A key requirement of survey questions is that they be easy to understand.

"Next question: I believe that life is a constant striving for balance, requiring frequent tradeoffs between morality and necessity, within a cyclic pattern of joy and sadness, forging a trail of bittersweet memories until one slips, inevitably, into the jaws of death. Agree or disagree?"

Family Foundation drew on data from an extensive survey that revealed a "still struggling population" that feels "forgotten by the nation and its leaders":

> Overall, the study finds about four in 10 residents who lived through the storm report that their lives are still very or somewhat disrupted— only marginally better than the share who reported this level of disruption in Fall 2006.

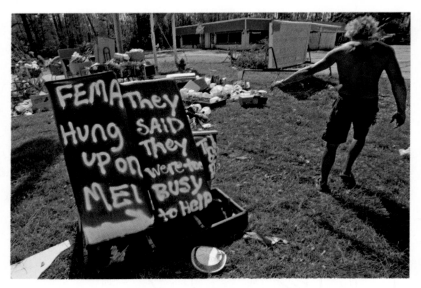

A photo taken in New Orleans in January 2008. A visual can provide evidence for a statistical survey.

Designed and analyzed by Foundation researchers, the survey was fielded house-to-house and by telephone in Spring 2008 among 1,294 residents of Orleans Parish. The survey is the second of at least three that the Foundation will conduct to track residents' experiences and views as the city rebuilds after Hurricane Katrina and the subsequent levee breaches that devastated huge sections in August 2005. By providing an over-time assessment of residents' experiences, priorities, goals and concerns, the Foundation hopes to give people a continuing chance to report on how the recovery effort is affecting them, to inform leaders of the public's priorities and to maintain national attention on the efforts to rebuild New Orleans.

—Kaiser Family Foundation, "New Orleans Three Years after the Storm: The Second Kaiser Post-Katrina Survey, 2008"

Experiments

Some arguments can be supported by evidence that is gathered through experiments. In the sciences, data from experiments conducted under rigorously controlled conditions are highly valued. For other kinds of writing, more informal experiments may be acceptable, especially if they're intended to provide only part of the support for an argument.

If you want to argue, for instance, that the recipes in *Gourmet* magazine are impossibly tedious to follow and take far more time than the average person wishes to spend preparing food, you might ask five or six people to conduct an experiment—following two recipes from a recent issue and recording and timing every step. The evidence that you gather from this informal experiment could provide some concrete support—by way of specific examples—for your contention.

But such experiments should be taken with a grain of salt (maybe organic in this case). They may not be effective with certain audiences, and if they can easily be attacked as skewed or sloppily done ("The people you asked to make these recipes couldn't cook a Pop-Tart"), then they may do more harm than good.

In a blog entry (with accompanying video) on TheNextWeb.com, Joop Dorresteijn reports on an experiment that he and a colleague carried out:

> Established blogs like ReadWriteWeb and Techcrunch proudly show a Feedburner chicklet that displays the site's popularity. But beware—since people are more likely to subscribe to a site with a larger number of readers, some sites manipulate the counter.
>
> Every once and a while co-editor Patrick and I stumble on a shady looking website with a ton of readers. That made us wonder whether Feedburner is hackable. I've sacrificed my personal blog for a hacking experiment and the result; *faking your subscriber count IS possible!*
>
> We found an easy way to hack Feedburner (not the obvious hack that simply steals a chicklet from a popular site). Looking at the subscriber count at some sites, we see we're not the first ones who found out, but we are the first ones to write it down. All it takes is an OPML file, a Netvibes Universe, and a good night's sleep.
>
> —Joop Dorresteijn, "Feedburner Hack: How to Get
> 2500 Subscribers Overnight"

The author goes on to explain that this experiment has gotten swift results: as of this posting, Google is working on a solution to the problem. In the meantime, Dorresteijn says, "the hack still works."

Personal Experience

Personal experience can serve as powerful evidence when it's appropriate to the subject, to your purpose, and to the audience. If it's your only evidence, however, personal experience usually won't be sufficient to carry the argument. Nevertheless, it can be effective for drawing in listeners or readers, as N'Gai Croal does in arguing that the video games with the greatest potential are those that appeal to the nongeek:

> I still get questions every now and then from people looking for advice on how to get their hands on a Nintendo Wii. But more and more, I'm hearing stories from people who've already scored one and are still rhapsodizing about it months after taking possession of the slim white console. The gushing comes from some of the most unexpected people. The grill man at my favorite New York burger joint told me last week that in his household, he mows down zombies in Resident Evil 4, his wife works out using Wii Fit, and he's introducing his son to the classic games of his youth via the Wii's download service. Similarly, a cardiologist friend of mine and his medical-resident girlfriend use Wii Golf to unwind; when they have friends over on the weekends, the same relaxing game turns into a fierce competition.
>
> As someone who covers videogames for *Newsweek*, I've marveled at how quickly the tastes of nontraditional players have moved from the margins of the industry toward the center. This is happening at the same time that geek tastes have taken center stage in other areas of pop culture: witness the summer movie schedule, which looks like new-release Wednesdays at your local comic-book shop.
>
> —N'Gai Croal, "You Don't Have to Be a Nerd"

CULTURAL CONTEXTS FOR ARGUMENT

Using Personal Experience

Personal experience counts in making academic arguments in some but not all cultures. Showing that you have personal experience with a topic can carry strong persuasive appeal with many English-speaking audiences, however, so it will probably be a useful way to argue a point in the United States. As with all evidence used to make a point, evidence based on your own experience must be pertinent to the topic, understandable to the audience, and clearly related to your purpose and claim.

Personal experience provides evidence for the popularity of Wii bowling (at least among humans).

Secondhand Evidence and Research

Secondhand evidence comes from sources beyond yourself—books, articles, films, online documents, photographs, and so on.

Library Sources

Your college library has printed materials (books, periodicals, reference works) as well as computer terminals that provide access to electronic catalogs, indexes, and other libraries' catalogs via the Internet. Although this book isn't designed to give a complete overview of library resources, we can make some important distinctions and pose a few key questions that can help you use the library most efficiently.

Two Important Distinctions

- Remember the distinction between *library databases* and the *Internet/ Web*. Your library's computers hold important resources that aren't on the Web or aren't available to you except through the library's system. The most important of these resources is the library's catalog of its

Not Just Words

Images often play a role in providing evidence for arguments. In documenting human-rights abuses in the conflict in Darfur province in Sudan, researchers with Human Rights Watch gave paper and crayons to hundreds of children and invited them to draw while the researchers interviewed the children's parents and neighbors. The children's drawings were published in *The Smallest Witnesses: The Conflict in Darfur through Children's Eyes*, a moving argument that claims that the government of Sudan is guilty of ethnic cleansing and crimes against humanity. The children's powerful drawings also led to many exhibitions and a series of videotaped presentations. Take a look at the drawings below, and then talk with classmates about what would be lost if the authors had offered only verbal descriptions of what the children drew.

Picture of janjaweed and their weapons

A drawing of a typical execution

Bombing by government forces

holdings (mostly books), but college libraries also pay to subscribe to scholarly databases—guides to journal and magazine articles, the *Lexis/Nexis* database of news stories and legal cases, and compilations of statistics, for example—that you can use for free. You should consult these electronic sources through your college library, perhaps even before turning to the Web.

- Remember the distinction between *subject headings* and *keywords*. The *Library of Congress Subject Headings* (LCSH) are standardized words and phrases that are used to classify the subject matter of books and articles. Library catalogs and databases usually use the LCSH headings to index their contents by author, title, publication date, and subject headings. When you do a subject search of the library's catalog, you're searching only one part of the electronic record of the library's books, and you need to use the exact wording of the LCSH. These subject headings are available in your library. On the other hand, searches with keywords use the computer's ability to look for any term in any field of the electronic record. Keyword searching is less restrictive than searching by subject headings, but it requires you to think carefully about your search terms to get good results. In addition, you need to use certain techniques to limit (or expand) your search. These include combining keywords with *and*, *or*, *not*, parentheses, and quotation marks or using similar procedures that are built into the catalog's or database's search mechanism.

Some Questions for Beginning Research

- What kinds of sources do you need to consult? Check your assignment to see whether you're required to consult different kinds of sources. If you'll use print sources, find out whether they're readily available in your library or whether you must make special arrangements (such as an interlibrary loan) to use them. If you need to locate nonprint sources (such as audiotapes, videotapes, artwork, or photos), find out where those are kept and whether you need special permission to examine them.

- How current do your sources need to be? If you must investigate the latest findings about, say, a new treatment for HIV/AIDS, you'll probably want to check periodicals, medical journals, and the Web. If you want broader, more detailed coverage and background information, you may need to depend more on books. If your argument deals with a specific time period, you may need to examine newspapers, magazines, and books written during that period.

- How many sources should you consult? Expect to look over many more sources than you'll end up using, and be sure to cover all major perspectives on your subject. The best guideline is to make sure you have enough sources to support your claim.

- Do you know your way around the library? If not, ask a librarian to help you locate the following resources in the library—general and specialized encyclopedias; biographical resources; almanacs, yearbooks, and atlases; book and periodical indexes; specialized indexes and abstracts; the circulation computer or library catalog; special collections; audio, video, and art collections; and the interlibrary loan office.

Online Sources

Many important resources for argument are now available in databases, either online or on CD-ROM, and many libraries now share the resources of their electronic catalogs through *WorldCat*. Like library catalogs and databases, the Internet and Web offer two ways to search for sources related to your argument—one using subject categories and one using keywords.

A subject directory organized by categories (such as you might find at http://dir.yahoo.com) allows you to choose a broad category like "Entertainment" or "Science" and then click on increasingly narrow categories like "Movies" or "Astronomy" and then "Thrillers" or "The Solar System" until you reach a point where you're given a list of Web sites or the opportunity to do a keyword search.

With the second kind of Internet search option, a search engine, you start right off with a keyword search—filling in a blank, for example, on the opening page of http://www.google.com. Because the Internet contains vastly more material than even the largest library catalog or database, exploring it with a search engine requires careful choices and combinations of keywords. For an argument about the fate of the antihero in contemporary films, for example, you might find that *film* and *hero* produce far too many possible matches, or hits. You might further narrow the search by adding a third keyword—say, *American* or *current*. In doing such searches, you'll need to observe the search logic that is followed by a particular database. Using *and* between keywords (*movies and heroes*) usually indicates that both terms must appear in a file for it to be called up. Using *or* between keywords usually instructs the computer to locate every file in which either one word or the other shows up, and using *not* tells the computer to exclude files containing a particular word from the search results (*movies not heroes*).

Using Evidence Effectively

You may gather an impressive amount of evidence on your topic—from firsthand interviews, from careful observations, and from intensive library and online research. But until that evidence is woven into the fabric of your own argument, it's just a pile of data. You still have to turn that data into information that will be persuasive to your intended audiences.

CULTURAL CONTEXTS FOR ARGUMENT

Defining Evidence

How do you decide what evidence will best support your claims? The answer depends, in large part, on how you define *evidence*. Differing notions of what counts as evidence can lead to arguments that go nowhere fast.

Journalists are often called on to interview those whose view of what constitutes effective evidence differs markedly from their own. When Italian journalist Oriana Fallaci interviewed the Ayatollah Khomeini, Iran's supreme leader, in 1971, she argued in a way that's common in North American and Western European cultures: she presented claims that she considered to be adequately backed up with facts ("Iran denies freedom to people. . . . Many people have been put in prison and even executed, just for speaking out in opposition"). In response, Khomeini relied on very different kinds of evidence— analogies ("Just as a finger with gangrene should be cut off so that it will not destroy the whole body, so should people who corrupt others be pulled out like weeds so they will not infect the whole field") and, above all, the authority of the Qur'an. Partly because of these differing

(continued)

beliefs about what counts as evidence, the interview ended unsuccessfully.

People in Western nations tend to give great weight to factual evidence, but even in those countries, what constitutes evidence can differ radically. This is so, for example, in debates in the United States between proponents of evolutionary theory and supporters of what is termed "intelligent design." In arguing across cultural divides, whether international or otherwise, you need to think carefully about how you're accustomed to using evidence—and about what counts as evidence to other people (without surrendering your own intellectual principles).

Here are some questions to help you review the types of evidence on which you're building your argument:

- Do you rely on facts? Examples? Firsthand experience?
- Do you include testimony from experts? Which experts are valued most (and why)?
- Do you cite religious or philosophical texts? Proverbs or everyday wisdom?
- Do you use analogies and metaphors as evidence? How much do they count?

Once you've determined what counts as evidence in your own arguments, ask the same questions about the use of evidence by members of other cultures.

Considering Audiences

The ethos that you bring to an argument (see Chapter 3) is crucial to your success in connecting with your audience. You want to present yourself as reliable and credible, but you also need to think about the way that your evidence relates to your audience. Is it appropriate to this particular group of readers or listeners? Does it speak to them in ways that they'll understand and respond to? Does it acknowledge their concerns?

It's hard to give definite advice for making sure that your evidence fits an audience. But in general, timeliness is important to audiences: the more up-to-date your evidence, the better. In addition, evidence that represents typical rather than extreme circumstances usually is more convincing. For example, in arguing for a campuswide security escort service after 10 p.m., a writer who cites the actual number of students who have recently been threatened or attacked on their way across campus after dark will be in a stronger position than one who cites only one sensational attack that occurred four years ago.

Building a Critical Mass

Throughout this chapter, we've stressed the need to discover as much evidence as possible in support of your claim. If you can find only one or two pieces of evidence—only one or two reasons or illustrations to back up your contention—then you may be on weak ground. Although there's no definite way of saying how much evidence is enough, you should build toward a critical mass by having several pieces of evidence all pulling in the direction of your claim.

And remember that *circumstantial evidence* (that is, indirect evidence that suggests that something occurred but doesn't prove it directly) may not be enough if it is the only evidence that you have. After seven years of intensive investigation into the anthrax killings that came shortly after September 11, 2001, the FBI was set to bring a case against scientist

Police removing mail suspected of containing anthrax from a box in New York City in October 2001

Bruce Ivins. But the evidence was all circumstantial: there was no "smoking gun," no direct, firsthand evidence of Ivins's guilt. After he committed suicide, the FBI closed the case, even though many critics demanded a trial to test whether a critical mass of evidence had been obtained.

If your evidence for a claim relies solely on circumstantial evidence, on personal experience, or on one major example, you should extend your search for additional sources and good reasons to back up your claim—or modify the claim. Your initial position may have been wrong. For example, if your claim that violent video games are leading young people to violent acts rests only on your personal experience or on indirect, circumstantial evidence (that several young people who had committed violent acts also had video games in their homes), then you don't have very strong support for your claim.

Arranging Evidence

Review your evidence, deciding which pieces support specific points in the argument. In general, try to position your strongest pieces of evidence in key places—near the beginning of paragraphs, at the end of the introduction, or toward a powerful conclusion. In addition, try to achieve a balance between, on the one hand, your own argument and your own words, and on the other hand, the sources that you use or quote in support of the argument. The sources of evidence are important props in the structure, but they shouldn't overpower the structure (your argument) itself.

RESPOND ●

1. What counts as evidence depends in large part on the rhetorical situation. One audience might find personal testimony compelling in a given case, whereas another might require data that only experimental studies can provide. Imagine that you want to argue that advertisements should not include demeaning representations of chimpanzees and that the use of primates in advertising should be banned. You're encouraged to find out that a number of companies such as Honda and Puma have already agreed to such a ban, so you decide to present your argument to other companies' CEOs and advertising officials. What kind of evidence would be most compelling to this group? How would you rethink your use of evidence if you were writing for the campus newspaper, for middle schoolers, or for animal-rights group

members? What can you learn about what sort of evidence each of these groups might value—and why?

2. Finding, evaluating, and arranging evidence in an argument is often a discovery process. Sometimes you're concerned not only with digging up support for an already established claim but also with creating and revising tentative claims. Surveys and interviews can help you figure out what to argue, as well as provide evidence for a claim.

Interview a classmate with the goal of writing a brief proposal argument about the career that he or she should pursue. The claim should be something like *My classmate should be doing X in five years from now.* Limit yourself to ten questions. Write them ahead of time, and don't deviate from them. Record the results of the interview (written notes are fine; you don't need a tape recorder). Then interview another classmate with the same goal in mind. Ask the same first question, but this time let the answer dictate the next nine questions. You still get only ten questions.

Which interview gave you more information? Which one helped you learn more about your classmate's goals? Which one better helped you develop claims about his or her future?

3. Imagine that you're trying to decide whether to take a class with a particular professor but you don't know if he or she is a good teacher. You might already have an opinion, based on some vaguely defined criteria and dormitory gossip, but you're not sure if that evidence is reliable. You do some digging on RateMyProfessor.com and then decide to observe a class before you make your final decision.

Visit a class in which you aren't currently enrolled, and make notes on your observations following the guidelines given in this chapter (pp. 496–97). You probably need only a single visit to take the notes, though you would probably take longer to write a thorough evaluation of the professor.

Write a short evaluation of the professor's teaching abilities on the basis of your observations. Then write an analysis of your evaluation. Is it honest? Fair? What other kinds of evidence might you need if you wanted to make an informed decision about the class and the teacher? What evidence is available to you in terms of local files of teaching evaluations, online teaching evaluation sites, and so on?

17
Fallacies of Argument

"Just what you'd expect an eco-alarmist like that to say."

"If you don't give me an A in this class, I won't get into medical school!"

"Ask not what your country can do for you; ask what you can do for your country."

"No blood for oil!"

"All my friends have iPhones."

"9/11 changed everything."

• • •

Certain types of argumentative moves are so controversial that they're traditionally classified as *fallacies*—arguments that are flawed by their very nature or structure. But you might find it more interesting to think of them as *flashpoints* or *hotspots* because they instantly raise questions about the ethics of argument—that is, whether a particular strategy of argument is fair, honest, or principled. You should avoid fallacies in your own writing and challenge them in arguments that you hear or read. But it's important to appreciate that one person's fallacy may well be another person's perceptive insight.

Consider, for example, the fallacy termed *ad hominem* ("to the man") argument. It describes a strategy of attacking the character of people that you disagree with rather than the substance of their arguments: *So you think that Reverend Jeremiah Wright is a racist, a radical, and an anti-Semite? Well, you're just a white-bread, redneck bigot yourself.* Many people have blurted out such insults at some time in their lives and later regretted them.

In some situations, however, a person's moral fiber actually *is* central to an argument. The problem arises in deciding when such arguments are legitimate and when they are fallacious. You're very likely to think of personal attacks on people that you admire as *ad hominem* slurs and those on people that you disagree with as reasonable criticisms. As you can imagine, debates about character can become polarizing. Consider 50 Cent and Kanye West or maybe MSNBC's Keith Olbermann and all the people that he labels as "the worst person in the world." (For more on arguments based on character, see Chapter 3.)

Sometimes fallacies are errors that you can detect and expose in someone else's work, but often they are strategies that hurt everyone (including the person using them) because they make productive argument more difficult. Fallacies muck up the frank but civil conversations that people should be able to have—regardless of their differences.

To help you understand fallacies of argument, we've classified them according to three rhetorical appeals discussed in earlier chapters—emotional arguments, ethical arguments, and logical arguments (see Chapters 2, 3, and 4).

Fallacies of Emotional Argument

Emotional arguments can be powerful and suitable in many circumstances, and most writers use them frequently. However, writers who pull on their readers' heartstrings or raise their blood pressure too often can violate the good faith on which legitimate argument depends.

Readers won't trust a writer who can't make a point without frightening someone, provoking tears, or stirring up hatred.

Scare Tactics

Scare tactics are common in everything ranging from ads for life insurance to threats of audits by the Internal Revenue Service. Politicians, advertisers, and public figures sometimes peddle their ideas by scaring people and exaggerating possible dangers well beyond their statistical likelihood. Such ploys work because it's usually easier to imagine something terrible happening than to appreciate its statistical rarity. Why do many people fear flying more than they fear driving? More people die from auto accidents every year, but such accidents don't fire up our imaginations as spectacularly as air disasters do.

Scare tactics can also be used to stampede legitimate fears into panic or prejudice. People who genuinely fear losing their jobs can be persuaded to fear that immigrants might work for less money. People who are living on fixed incomes can be convinced that minor modifications of entitlement programs represent dire threats to their standard of living. Such tactics have the effect of closing off thinking because people who are scared often act irrationally. Even well-intended fear campaigns—like those directed against the use of illegal drugs, smoking, or unprotected sex—can misfire if their warnings prove too shrill. People just stop listening.

Either-Or Choices

One way to simplify arguments and give them power is to reduce the options for action to only two choices. One option (or the preferred existing policy) might be drawn in warm, favorable terms, whereas the other is cast as a dangerous alternative. That's the nature of the choices that President George W. Bush offered in an August 20, 2005, radio address to the nation:

> **Our troops know that they're fighting in Iraq, Afghanistan, and elsewhere to protect their fellow Americans from a savage enemy. They know that if we do not confront these evil men abroad, we will have to face them one day in our own cities and streets, and they know that the safety and security of every American is at stake in this war, and they know we will prevail.**

The parental ultimatum—a classic form of the *either-or* argument

"They say we can go there for Thanksgiving or they can cut us out of the will. Our choice."

Sometimes neither alternative is pleasant: that's the nature of many ultimatums. For instance, the Allies in World War II offered the Axis powers only two choices as the conflict drew to a close—either continued war and destruction or unconditional surrender. No third option was available.

Either-or choices can be well-intentioned strategies to get something accomplished. Parents use them all the time ("Eat your broccoli, or you won't get dessert"). But they become fallacious arguments when they reduce a complicated issue to excessively simple terms or when they're designed to obscure legitimate alternatives.

For instance, to suggest that renewable power sources such as wind and solar represent the only long-term solution to our energy needs may have rhetorical power, but the choice is too simple. Energy shortages can be fixed in any number of ways, *including* wind and solar power. But to

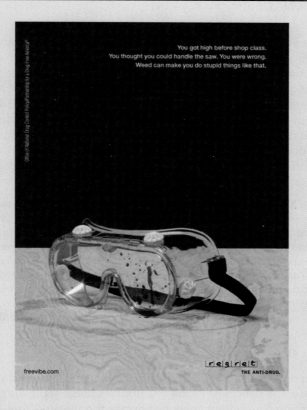

Not Just Words

Look at the advertisement above. Is it a scare tactic? A legitimate warning? Something in between? How effective do you think this ad would be for college students or for people who use marijuana or might be tempted to? What effect does the text in the upper right-hand corner have on your answers to these questions? What about the text at the bottom? Do graphic images like this and sponsor labels like "Partnership for a Drug-Free America" make the campaign against marijuana and other illegal drugs more effective—or less so? How does this ad compare with the one about drunk driving on p. 104?

promote such renewable resources as the *only* reasonable option risks losing the support of people who know better.

But *either-or* arguments—like most scare tactics—are often purposefully designed to seduce those who don't know much about a subject. That's another reason that the tactic violates principles of civil discourse. Argument should enlighten people by making them more knowledgeable and more capable of acting intelligently and independently. We usually don't have to choose one side over the other. Here, Paris Hilton pokes fun at opposing political camps for debating energy issues in *either-or* terms by offering her own alternative:

> Ok, so here's my energy policy. Barack wants to focus on new technologies to cut foreign oil dependency and McCain wants offshore drilling. Well, why don't we do a hybrid of both candidates' ideas? We can do limited offshore drilling with strict environmental oversight, while creating tax incentives to get Detroit making hybrid and electric cars. That way, the offshore drilling carries us until the new technologies kick in, which will then create new jobs and energy independence. Energy crisis solved.
>
> —Paris Hilton, funnyordie.com

Slippery Slope

The slippery-slope fallacy describes an argument that portrays today's tiny misstep as tomorrow's slide into disaster. Some arguments that aim at preventing dire consequences do not take the slippery-slope approach (for example, the parent who corrects a child for misbehavior now is acting sensibly to prevent more serious problems as the child grows older). A slippery-slope argument becomes wrongheaded when a writer exaggerates the likely consequences of an action, usually to frighten readers. As such, slippery-slope arguments are also scare tactics. For instance, defenders of civil liberties often depict any action by Western democracies to use eavesdropping technologies domestically to track terrorists as assaults on freedom of speech reminiscent of those of the KGB.

In recent years, the issue of same-sex marriage has similarly encouraged slippery-slope arguments:

> Anyone else bored to tears with the "slippery slope" arguments against gay marriage? Since few opponents of homosexual unions are brave enough to admit that gay weddings just freak them out, they hide behind the claim that it's an inexorable slide from legalizing gay

marriage to having sex with penguins outside JC Penney's. The problem is it's virtually impossible to debate against a slippery slope.
—Dahlia Lithwick, "Slippery Slop"

Ideas and actions do have consequences, but they aren't always as dire
as writers fond of slippery-slope tactics would have you believe.

Sentimental Appeals

Sentimental appeals are arguments that use tender emotions excessively
to distract readers from facts. Often, such appeals are highly personal

This calendar is designed to elicit sympathy for the penguins on its cover
and inspire donations to the wildlife organization that protects them. But
sometimes sentimental images of threatened species are attached to much
less worthy sales pitches—for soda or camping gear, for example.

and individual and focus attention on heartwarming or heart-wrenching situations that make readers feel guilty if they challenge an idea, a policy, or a proposal. Emotions become an impediment to civil discourse when they keep people from thinking clearly.

Yet sentimental appeals are a major vehicle of television news, where tugging at viewers' heartstrings can mean high ratings. For example, when a camera documents the day-to-day sacrifices of parents who are trying to meet their mortgage payments in a tough economy, their on-screen struggles can represent the spirit of an entire class of people threatened by callous bankers. Another family, also behind in its mortgage payments, might be shown living large in an oversized house while legislators ask for public funds to bail such people out. In either case, the conclusion the reporter wants you to reach is supported by powerful images that evoke emotions in support of that conclusion. But though the individual stories presented may stir genuine emotions, they seldom give a complete picture of a complex social or economic issue.

Bandwagon Appeals

Bandwagon appeals are arguments that urge people to follow the same path that everyone else is taking. Many American parents seem to have an innate ability to refute bandwagon appeals. When their kids whine, *Everyone else is going camping overnight without chaperones,* the parents reply, *And if everyone else jumps off a cliff (or a railroad bridge or the Empire State Building), you will too?* The children stomp and groan—and then try a different line of argument.

Unfortunately, not all bandwagon approaches are transparent. Although people like to imagine themselves as independent thinkers, they can be seduced by ideas that are repeated obsessively in the mass media—the intellectual equivalent of a feeding frenzy. Even legitimate issues that are raised by a news event may be transformed into a bandwagon when powerful media and political voices all shout the same thing. In recent decades, bandwagon issues have included the war on drugs, the nuclear freeze movement, the campaign against drunk driving, campaign finance reform, illegal immigration, the defense of marriage, and bailouts for banks and businesses. These issues are all too complex to permit the suspension of judgment that bandwagon tactics require.

Rather than think independently about where to go, it's often easier to get on board the bandwagon with everyone else.

Fallacies of Ethical Argument

Not surprisingly, readers give their closest attention to authors whom they respect or trust. So writers usually want to present themselves as honest, well informed, likable, or sympathetic in some way. But *trust me* is a scary warrant. Not all the devices that writers use to gain the attention and confidence of readers are admirable. (For more on appeals based on character, see Chapter 3.)

Appeals to False Authority

One effective strategy for supporting an idea is to draw on the authority of widely respected people, institutions, and texts. In fact, many academic research papers find and reflect on the work of reputable authorities and introduce these authorities through direct quotations, citations (such as footnotes), or allusions. (For more on assessing the reliability of sources, see Chapter 19.) False authority, however, occurs when writers offer themselves or other authorities as sufficient warrant for believing a claim:

Claim	X is true because I say so.
Warrant	What I say must be true.
Claim	X is true because Y says so.
Warrant	What Y says must be true.

Few readers would accept a claim that states authority quite so baldly as in these formulas. Nonetheless, claims of authority drive many persuasive campaigns. American pundits and politicians are fond of citing the U. S. Constitution and its Bill of Rights (Canadians have their Charter of Rights and Freedoms) as ultimate authorities, a reasonable practice when the documents are interpreted respectfully. However, the rights and liberties claimed sometimes aren't in the texts themselves or don't mean what the speakers think they do. And most constitutional matters are debatable—as volumes of court records prove.

Likewise, religious believers often base arguments on books or traditions that wield great authority within a particular religious community. However, the power of these texts is usually limited outside that group and less capable of persuading others solely on the grounds of their authority.

Institutions can be cited as authorities, too. Serious attention should be paid to claims that are supported by respected authorities—such as the Centers for Disease Control, the National Science Foundation, the *Wall Street Journal*, and the *Globe and Mail*. But information and opinions should not be accepted simply because they are put forth by such offices and agencies. To quote a Russian proverb made famous by Ronald Reagan, "Trust, but verify."

Dogmatism

A writer who asserts or assumes that a particular position is the only one that is conceivably acceptable within a community is expressing dogmatism. Indeed, dogmatism is a fallacy of character because the tactic undermines the trust that must exist between those who make and listen to arguments. When people speak or write dogmatically, they imply that no arguments are necessary: the truth is self-evident. You're probably listening to a dogmatic opinion when someone begins a sentence with *No rational person would disagree that . . .* or *It's clear to anyone who has thought about it that. . . .*

Even so, some arguments present positions and claims that are so outrageous or absurd that they're beyond civil discourse and are unworthy of serious attention. For example, attacks on the historical reality of the Holocaust fall into this category. But few subjects that can be defended with facts, testimony, and good reasons ought to be off the table in a free society. In general, whenever someone suggests that raising an issue for debate is somehow "unacceptable," "inappropriate," or "outrageous"—whether on the grounds that it's racist, sexist, unpatriotic, blasphemous, insensitive, or offensive in some other way—you should be suspicious.

Ad Hominem Arguments

As explained earlier, *ad hominem* (from the Latin for "to the man") arguments are attacks directed at the character of a person rather than at the claims he or she makes. The theory is simple: when you destroy the credibility of your opponents, you either destroy their ability to present reasonable appeals or distract from the successful arguments they may be offering. Here, for example, Christopher Hitchens questions whether former secretary of state Henry Kissinger should be appointed to head an important government commission in 2002:

> But can Congress and the media be expected to swallow the appointment of a proven coverup artist, a discredited historian, a busted liar, and a man who is wanted in many jurisdictions for the vilest of offenses?
>
> —Christopher Hitchens, "The Case against Henry Kissinger"

There's not much doubt about where Hitchens stands. Liberal critics of Rush Limbaugh's politics rarely fail to note his problems with the drug OxyContin; conservative detractors of Speaker of the House Nancy Pelosi can't resist mentioning that the district she represents is that far-left haven San Francisco.

In such cases, *ad hominem* tactics turn arguments into two-sided affairs with good guys and bad guys, and that's unfortunate, since character often *does* matter in argument. People expect the proponent of peace to be civil, a secretary of the treasury to pay his taxes, and the champion of family values to be a faithful spouse. But it's fallacious to attack an idea by uncovering the foibles of its advocates or by attacking their motives, backgrounds, or unchangeable traits.

Fallacies of Logical Argument

You'll encounter a problem in any argument when the claims, warrants, or pieces of evidence in it are invalid, insufficient, or disconnected. In theory, such problems seem easy enough to spot, but in practice, they can be camouflaged by a skillful use of words or images. Indeed, logical fallacies pose a challenge to civil argument because they often seem reasonable and natural, especially when they appeal to people's self-interests. Whole industries (such as online psychics) depend on one or more of the logical fallacies for their existence. Political campaigns, too, rely on them to prop up the current staple of democratic advertising—the fifteen-second TV spot.

Hasty Generalization

Among logical fallacies, only faulty causality might be as prevalent as hasty generalization. A hasty generalization is an inference drawn from insufficient evidence: *Because my Honda broke down, then all Hondas must be junk.* It also forms the basis for most stereotypes about people or institutions: because *a few* people in a large group are observed to act in a certain way, *all* members of that group are inferred to behave similarly. The resulting conclusions are usually sweeping claims of little merit: *Women are bad drivers; men are slobs; Scots are stingy; Italians are lecherous; English teachers are nitpicky; scientists are nerds.* You could, no doubt, expand this roster of stereotypes by the hundreds.

To draw valid inferences, you must always have sufficient evidence—a random sample of a population, a selection large enough to represent fully the subjects of your study, an objective methodology for sampling the population or evidence, and so on (see Chapter 16). And you must qualify your claims appropriately. After all, people do need generalizations to make reasonable decisions in life. Such claims can be offered legitimately if placed in context and tagged with appropriate qualifiers—*some, a few, many, most, occasionally, rarely, possibly, in some cases, under certain circumstances, in my limited experience.*

"Google must be anti-American because the company decorates its famous logo for occasions such as the anniversary of *Sputnik*, Earth Day, and Persian New Year but not Memorial Day in the United States." A hasty generalization? Check "holiday logos" at Google, and decide for yourself.

You should be especially alert to the fallacy of hasty generalization when you read reports and studies of any kind, especially case studies that are based on carefully selected populations. Be alert for the fallacy in the interpretation of poll numbers, too. Everything from the number of people selected to the time the poll was taken to the exact wording of the questions may affect its outcome.

Faulty Causality

In Latin, the fallacy of faulty causality is described by the expression *post hoc, ergo propter hoc*, which translates as "after this, therefore because of this." Odd as the translation may sound, it accurately describes what faulty causality is—the fallacious assumption that because one event or action follows another, the first causes the second. Consider a lawsuit commented on in the *Wall Street Journal* in which a writer sued Coors (unsuccessfully), claiming that drinking copious amounts of the company's beer had kept him from writing a novel.

Some actions do produce reactions. Step on the brake pedal in your car, and you move hydraulic fluid that pushes calipers against disks to create friction that stops the vehicle. If you are the chair of the Federal Reserve Board, you drop interest rates to lower the cost of borrowing to increase the growth of the economy in order to reduce unemployment— you hope. Causal relationships of this kind are reasonably convincing because one can provide evidence of relationships between the events sufficient to convince most people that an initial action did, indeed, cause subsequent actions.

In other cases, however, a supposed connection between cause and effect turns out to be completely wrong. For example, doctors now believe that when an elderly person falls and is found to have a broken leg or hip, the break usually caused the fall rather than the other way around. And as the Federal Reserve example suggests, causality can be especially difficult to control or determine when complex economic, political, or social relationships are involved.

That's why suspiciously simple or politically convenient causal claims should always be subject to scrutiny. By mid-2008, it was apparent that the military situation in the long-running Iraq War had changed significantly, with American casualties down dramatically and violence throughout the still-occupied country significantly reduced. The Bush administration credited that improvement to a military strategy called the surge—which involved a change in counterinsurgency tactics of American troops and a temporary increase in their numbers. Critics of the war, however, claimed that the surge only appeared to work because it had occurred just as Sunni tribal leaders decided to turn against Al Qaeda and support the Iraqi government. Whose causal claim was right? Perhaps that of both camps, as a writer for the *Washington Post* explains:

> The arrival of additional U.S. forces signaled renewed resolve. Sunni tribal leaders, having glimpsed the dismal future in store for their people under a regime controlled by al-Qaeda in Iraq and fearful of abandonment, were ready to throw in their lot with the coalition. The surge did not create the first of the tribal "awakenings," but it was the catalyst for their expansion and eventual success. The tribal revolt took off

after the arrival of reinforcements and as U.S. and Iraqi units fought to make the Iraqi people secure.

—Peter Mansoor, "How the Surge Worked"

The final word on this complicated causal relationship will probably be written by military historians decades from now when more facts are known and can be interpreted with fewer partisan pressures.

Begging the Question

There's probably not a teacher in the country who hasn't heard the following argument: *You can't give me a C in this course; I'm an A student.* For a member of Congress accused of taking kickbacks, a press secretary makes a version of the same argument: *Representative X can't be guilty of accepting such bribes; she's an honest person.* In both cases, the problem with the claim is that it's made on grounds that cannot be accepted as true because those grounds are in doubt. How can the student claim to be an A student when he just earned a C? How can the accused bribe taker defend herself on the grounds of honesty when that honesty is now suspect? Setting such arguments in Toulmin terms helps to expose the fallacy:

Claim	You can't give me a C in this course . . .
Reason	. . . because I'm an A student.
Warrant	An A student is someone who can't receive Cs.
Claim	Representative X can't be guilty of accepting bribes . . .
Reason	. . . because she's an honest person.
Warrant	An honest person cannot be guilty of accepting bribes.

With the warrants stated, you can see why begging the question—assuming as true the very claim that's disputed—is a form of circular argument that is divorced from reality. If you assume that an A student can't receive Cs, then the first argument stands. But no one is an A student *by definition*; that standing is earned by performance in individual courses. Likewise, even though someone with a record of honesty is unlikely to accept bribes, a claim of honesty isn't an adequate defense against specific charges. An honest person won't accept bribes, but merely claiming that someone is honest doesn't make her so. (For more on Toulmin argument, see Chapter 7.)

A wannabe resists believing "I'm a writer because I say I am." Begging the question can deceive ourselves as well as others.

"I don't usually tell people I'm a writer because
I've never actually written anything."

Equivocation

The finest definition of *equivocation* and its most famous literary examples come from Shakespeare's tragedy *Macbeth*. In the drama, three witches, representing the fates, make prophecies that favor the ambitious Macbeth but that prove disastrous when understood more fully. He's told, for example, that he has nothing to fear from his enemies "till Birnam wood / Do come to Dunsinane" (*Mac.* 5.5.44–45). Although it seems impossible that trees could move, they indeed appear to move when enemy soldiers cut down branches from the forest of Birnam for camouflage and march on Macbeth's fortress. Catching on to the game, Macbeth starts "to doubt the equivocation of the fiend / That lies like truth" (5.5.43–44). An equivocation is an argument that gives a lie an honest appearance; it's a half-truth.

Equivocations are usually juvenile tricks of language. Consider the plagiarist who copies a paper word for word from a source and then declares (honestly, she thinks) that "I wrote the entire paper myself"— meaning that she physically copied the piece on her own. But the plagiarist is using *wrote* equivocally—in a limited sense—and knows that most

people understand the word to mean both composing as well as mere copying of words. Many public figures are fond of parsing their words carefully so that no certain meaning emerges. In the 1990s, Bill Clinton's "I never had sex with that woman" claim became notorious when the then-president defined *sex* in a narrow way. In the first decade of the twenty-first century, critics of the Bush administration said its many denials that *torture* was being used on U.S. prisoners abroad amounted to a long series of equivocations.

Baseball star Alex Rodriguez admitted that he had taken performance-enhancing drugs during the 2003 season, but said that "I don't know exactly what" and hinted that they may have been legal substances. Some expert observers think that's an equivocation—a dishonest play on the word *know*—since he tested positive for drugs that can't be obtained legally in the United States.

Non Sequitur

A non sequitur is an argument in which claims, reasons, or warrants fail to connect logically; one point doesn't follow from another. As with other fallacies, children are notably adept at framing non sequiturs. Consider this familiar form: *You don't love me or you'd buy me that bicycle!* It might be more evident to harassed parents that no connection exists between love and Huffys if they were to consider the implied warrant:

Claim	You must not love me . . .
Reason	. . . because you haven't bought me that bicycle.
Warrant	Buying bicycles for children is essential to loving them.

A five-year-old might endorse that warrant, but no responsible adult would because love doesn't depend on buying bicycles. Activities more logically related to love might include feeding and clothing children, taking care of them when they're sick, providing shelter and education, and so on.

Non sequiturs occur when writers omit a step in an otherwise logical chain of reasoning, assuming that readers agree with what may be a highly contestable claim. For example, it's a non sequitur simply to argue that the comparatively poor performance of American students on international mathematics examinations means that the country should spend more money on math education. Such a conclusion might be justified if a correlation were known or found to exist between mathematical ability and money spent on education. But the students' performance might be poor for reasons other than education funding, so a writer should first establish the nature of the problem before offering a solution.

The Straw Man

Those who resort to the "straw-man" fallacy attack an argument that isn't really there. It's much weaker or more extreme than the one that the opponent is actually making. The speaker or writer "sets up a straw man" in this way to create an argument that's easy to knock down, proceeds to do so, and then claims victory over the opponent—whose real argument was quite different. In a February 20, 2009, *Weekly Standard* column, Republican political commentator Fred Barnes suggests that President Obama is fond of the device:

> Obama may not be eloquent, but he is glib and clever and at times persuasive. One of his favorite rhetorical devices is setting up a straw man, then knocking it down. He invoked this classic ploy subtly in his inaugural address, crudely in his press conference. "We will restore science to its rightful place," Obama said at his inauguration. Really? Where had science been? "We are ready to lead once more," he said, as if we—America—hadn't been. He may have disapproved of the prior administration's policies in the world, but that doesn't mean it wasn't

leading. Also in his inaugural speech, Obama said, "we can no longer afford indifference to suffering outside our borders." When were we indifferent? Not in Obama's lifetime.

—Fred Barnes, "Obama's First Month"

A lot of "straw-man" arguments have been advanced in the recent debates over evolution and intelligent design. Some who argue against intelligent design say that its advocates attribute life to the actions of a white-haired deity in the sky. Some who argue against evolutionary theory allege that its adherents hold that evolution is all chance—implying that a structure as complicated as the human eye came into existence randomly. But in both instances, such speakers are refuting arguments that their opponents haven't actually made. At least in their public political or legal statements, supporters of intelligent design don't make claims about who or what the "intelligent designer" is. And supporters of evolution contend that the process is driven by random mutations in genes but that organisms evolve only if such mutations make them better adapted to their environment (such as by increasing their ability to detect light) and thus more likely to reproduce. Both sides are attacking weak arguments that their opponents aren't actually making. As a result, both sides are ignoring the tougher issues.

Faulty Analogy

Comparisons give ideas greater presence; they also may help to clarify one concept by measuring it against another that is more familiar. Consider how quickly you make a judgment about Britney Spears after reading this comparison with Madonna:

> [R]egardless of how hard she tries, Britney's not Madonna. To be fair, Madonna wasn't Madonna at first either, but emulating someone else—even if they're as successful as Madonna—usually doesn't work in the end.
>
> —Erik J. Barzeski

When comparisons are extended, they become *analogies*—ways of understanding unfamiliar ideas by comparing them with something that's already known. People understand the world around them largely through comparisons, metaphors, and analogies. But useful as such comparisons are, they may prove false either taken on their own and pushed too far, or taken too seriously. At this point, they become *faulty analogies*—inaccurate or inconsequential comparisons between objects or concepts. For instance,

Russian deputy foreign minister Sergei Ivanov startled observers on August 13, 2008, when he justified his country's military incursion into the tiny neighboring country of Georgia by claiming a comparison to the 9/11 terrorist attacks:

> We just reacted because we didn't have any other option. Any civilized country would act the same way. I may remind you, September the 11th, the reaction was similar. American citizens were killed. You know the reaction.
>
> —Sergei Ivanov

RESPOND●

1. The following list of political slogans or phrases may be examples of logical fallacies. Discuss each item to determine what you may know about the slogan. Then decide which, if any, fallacy might be used to describe it.

   "Leave no child behind." (George Bush policy and slogan)

   "It's the economy, stupid." (sign on the wall at Bill Clinton's campaign headquarters)

   "Nixon's the one." (campaign slogan)

   "Remember the Alamo." (battle cry)

   "Make love, not war." (antiwar slogan during the Vietnam War)

   "A chicken in every pot." (campaign slogan)

   "No taxation without representation." (American colonial slogan)

   "Loose lips sink ships." (slogan from World War II)

   "Guns don't kill, people do." (NRA slogan)

   "If you can't stand the heat, get out of the kitchen." (attributed to Harry S. Truman)

   "We are the ones we've been waiting for. We are the change that we seek." (Obama campaign statement)

2. We don't want you to argue fallaciously, but it's fun and good practice to frame argumentative fallacies in your own language. Pick an argumentative topic—maybe one that you've used for a paper in this class—and write a few paragraphs making nothing but fallacious arguments in each sentence. Try to include all the fallacies of emotional, ethical, and logical argument that are discussed in this chapter.

3. Choose a paper you've written for this or another class, and analyze it carefully for signs of fallacious reasoning. Once you've tried analyzing your own prose, find an editorial, a syndicated column, and a political speech, and look for the fallacies in them. Which fallacies are most common in the four arguments? How do you account for their prevalence? Which are the least common? How do you account for their absence? What seems to be the role of audience in determining what's a fallacy and what isn't?

4. Arguments on the Web are no more likely to contain fallacies than are arguments in any other medium, but the fallacies can take on different forms. The hypertextual nature of Web arguments and the ease of including visuals with text make certain fallacies more likely to occur there. Find a Web site that is sponsored by an organization (the Future of Music Coalition, perhaps), business (Coca-Cola, Pepsi), or other group (the Democratic or Republican National Committee), and analyze the site for fallacious reasoning. Among other considerations, look at the relationship between text and graphics and between individual pages and the pages that surround or are linked to them. How does the technique of separating information into discrete pages affect the argument? Then consider sending an e-mail message to the site's creators, explaining what you found and proposing ways the arguments in the site could be improved.

5. Political blogs such as wonkette.com, andrewsullivan.com, DailyKos .com, and InstaPundit.com typically provide quick responses to daily events and detailed critiques of material in other media sites, including national newspapers. Study one active political blog for a few days to determine whether and how the blogger critiques the material he or she links to. Does the blogger point to fallacies in arguments? If so, does he or she explain them or just assume readers understand them or will figure them out? Summarize your findings in an oral report to your class.

18

Intellectual Property, Academic Integrity, and Avoiding Plagiarism

On a college campus, a student receives a warning: she has been detected using peer-to-peer music file-sharing software. Has she been practicing fair use, or is she guilty of copyright infringement?

A student writing an essay about the effect of Title IX of the Education Amendments of 1972 on college athletic programs finds some powerful supporting evidence for his argument on a Web site. Can he use this information without gaining permission?

Day-care centers around the country receive letters arguing that they'll be liable to lawsuit if they use representations of Disney characters without explicit permission or show Disney films "outside the home."

A tattoo artist claims ownership of the butterfly design on a movie star's arm and protests when his work appears in an advertisement without permission. The actor argues that it's her arm.

Haute couture houses—angered by the prevalence of cheap knockoffs of their dresses, handbags, and shoes—ask Congress to pass legislation protecting their apparel designs for three years.

Musicians argue against other musicians, saying that the popular use of "sampling" in songs amounts to a form of musical plagiarism.

● ● ●

In agricultural and industrial eras, products that could provide a livelihood were likely to be concrete things—crops, tools, machines. But in our current age of information, intellectual property is one of society's most important products—hence the importance of and controversies surrounding what counts as "property" in an information age.

Perhaps the framers of the U.S. Constitution foresaw that the bases of the nation's economy would shift. To accommodate these kinds of changes, they expressed in the Constitution a delicate balance between the public's need for information and the worker's need to be encouraged to create products—both material and intellectual. Thus, the Constitution (in article 1, section 8, clause 8), empowers Congress

> [t]o promote the progress of Science and useful Arts, by securing for limited Times to Authors and Inventors the exclusive Right to their respective Writings and Discoveries.

This passage allows for limited protection (copyright) of the expression of ideas ("Writings and Discoveries"), and over time that limit has been extended to lifetime plus seventy years.

Why is this historical information important to student writers? First, writers need to know that ideas cannot be copyrighted: only the expression of those ideas is protected. Second, some works fall out of copyright and can be used without paying a fee. Third, the current debates over who owns online materials—materials that may never take any concrete form—will be resolved in ways that will directly affect students and teachers. For up-to-date information about copyright law, see the U.S. Copyright Office site (http://copyright.gov).

Crediting Sources in Arguments

Giving full credit to your sources enhances your ethos in argumentative writing. In the first place, saying "thanks" to those who've helped you suggests gratitude and candidness, qualities that audiences like. Second,

Who owns the guardian angel on David Beckham's back—the athlete or the tattoo artist, Louis Molloy, who created it?

acknowledging your sources demonstrates that you have "done your homework," understand what others have written about the topic, and encourage others to join the conversation as well. Finally, citing sources reminds you to think critically about how well you've used them. Are they timely and reliable? Have you referenced them in a biased or overly selective way? Have you used them accurately, double-checking all quotations and paraphrases? Thinking through such questions will improve your work.

Citing Sources and Recognizing Plagiarism

In many ways, "nothing new under the sun" is more than just a cliché. Most of what you think or write is built on what you've previously read or experienced. And trying to recall every source of influence, even for just one day, would leave you little time to say anything. Luckily, you'll seldom, if ever, be called on to list every influence on your life. But you do have responsibilities in school and professional situations to acknowledge any intellectual property you've borrowed to create arguments. If you don't, you may be accused of *plagiarism*—claiming as your own the words or intellectual work of others.

Avoiding plagiarism is important because in Western culture using someone else's language and ideas without acknowledgment is considered dishonest. Plagiarism can have devastating consequences—especially, though not only, in school.

Inaccurate or Incomplete Citation of Sources

You may be accused of plagiarism if you use a paraphrase that's too close to the original wording or sentence structure of your source material (*even* if you cite the source), if you leave out the parenthetical reference for a quotation (*even* if you include the quotation marks themselves), or if you don't indicate clearly the source of an idea you obviously didn't come up with on your own. And the accusation can be made even if you didn't intend to plagiarize. This kind of inaccurate or incomplete citation of sources often results either from carelessness or from not learning how to use citations accurately and fully.

Here, for example, is the first paragraph from an essay by Russell Platt published in the *Nation* (http://www.thenation.com/doc/20051003/platt):

> Classical music in America, we are frequently told, is in its death throes: its orchestras bled dry by expensive guest soloists and greedy musicians unions, its media presence shrinking, its prestige diminished, its educational role ignored, its big record labels dying out or merging into faceless corporate entities. We seem to have too many well-trained musicians in need of work, too many good composers going without commissions, too many concerts to offer an already satiated public.
>
> —Russell Platt, "New World Symphony"

To cite this passage correctly in MLA style, you could quote directly from it, using both quotation marks and some form of attribution. Either of the following versions would be acceptable:

> Russell Platt has doubts about claims that classical music is "in its death throes: its orchestras bled dry by expensive guest soloists and greedy musicians unions" ("New World").

Not Just Words

Like words, images and designs can also be claimed as intellectual property. As we explain in this chapter, you can download a photograph you find on the Web and use it, with appropriate documentation, in an academic paper. But you'd probably need permission from the copyright holder to use it online, even for an academic Web project.

Logos and other visual designs are similarly protected. The T-shirts and ball caps with your school's symbol and colors likely have a royalty cost built in, with the money going back to the institution. For commercial and artistic reasons, institutions and corporations protect their designs, logos, symbols, and signs.

How, then, can the *Onion, Saturday Night Live,* or Adbusters.org take familiar designs and logos and use them in their publications, shows, or Web sites? It's unlikely that Benetton approved a spoof (see facing page) suggesting that its famous series of socially conscious ads are just about making money. Yet there it is on Adbusters.org, along with dozens of other like-minded parodies.

The answer is in the word *parody.* The U.S. Supreme Court has decided that parody falls within fair-use provisions of copyright law and that satire is protected by the First Amendment's protection of free speech, at least when such a lampoon targets public figures. You can explore these decisions easily on the Web (search for "Parody" and "Supreme Court").

Working in a small group, create a parody of a familiar visual item or advertising campaign, perhaps beginning with an image from the Web. Be sure to take advantage of any skills people in your group may have with software such as Photoshop, which will enable you to change or manipulate images. Or use paper: cutting and pasting still works. Design a parody that makes a thoughtful point.

But is classical music in the United States really "in its death throes," as some critics of the music scene suggest (Platt)?

You might also paraphrase Platt's paragraph, putting his ideas entirely in your own words but giving him due credit:

A familiar story told by critics is that classical music faces a bleak future in the United States, with grasping soloists and unions bankrupting orchestras and classical works vanishing from radio and television, school curricula, and the labels of recording conglomerates. The public may not be able or willing to support all the talented musicians and composers we have today (Platt).

All of these sentences with citations would be keyed to a works-cited entry at the end of the paper that would look like the following in MLA style:

Platt, Russell. "New World Symphony." *The Nation.* The Nation, 3 Oct. 2005. Web. 15 Oct. 2009.

How might a citation go wrong? As we indicated, omitting either the quotation marks around a borrowed passage or an acknowledgment of the source is grounds for complaint. Neither of the following sentences provides enough information for a correct citation:

But is classical music in the United States really in its death throes, as some critics of the music scene suggest (Platt)?

But is classical music in the United States really "in its death throes," as some critics of the music scene suggest?

Just as faulty is a paraphrase such as the following, which borrows the words or ideas of the source too closely. It represents plagiarism, though it identifies the source from which almost all the ideas—and a good many words—are borrowed:

In "New World Symphony," Russell Platt observes that classical music is thought by many to be in bad shape in America. Its orchestras are being sucked dry by costly guest artists and insatiable unionized musicians, its place on TV and radio is shrinking, its stature is diminished, its role in education is largely ignored, and its big record contracts are declining too. The problem may also be that we have too many well-trained musicians who need employment, too many good composers going without jobs, too many concerts for a public that prefers *Desperate Housewives.*

Even the original observation at the end of the paragraph isn't enough to change the fact that the paraphrase is just Platt's original, lightly stirred.

Because the consequences of even unintentional plagiarism can be severe, it's important to understand how it can happen and how you can guard against it. In a January 2002 article published in *Time* magazine, historian Doris Kearns Goodwin explains how someone else's writing wound up unacknowledged in her book. The book in question, nine hundred pages long and with 3,500 footnotes, took Goodwin ten years to write.

DOONESBURY   *BY GARRY TRUDEAU*

A Doonesbury cartoon on intellectual property pokes fun at best-selling historian and presidential biographer Stephen Ambrose, who was found to have plagiarized passages from at least twelve authors in at least six of his books—and in his doctoral dissertation.

During these ten years, she says, she took most of her notes by hand, organized the notes into boxes, and—after the draft was completed—returned to her sources to check that all the material from them was correctly cited. "Somehow in this process," Goodwin claims, "a few books were not fully rechecked," and so she omitted some necessary quotation marks in material she didn't acknowledge. Reflecting back on this experience, Goodwin says that discovering such carelessness in her own work was troubling—so troubling that in the storm of criticism that ensued over the discovery of these failures to cite properly, she resigned from her position as a member of the Pulitzer Prize Committee.

Acknowledging Your Use of Sources

The safest way to avoid charges of plagiarism is to acknowledge all of your sources, with the following three exceptions:

- common knowledge, which is a specific piece of information most readers will know (that Barack Obama won the 2008 presidential election, for instance)
- facts available from a wide variety of sources (that the Japanese bombed Pearl Harbor on December 7, 1941, for example)
- your own findings from field research (observations, interviews, experiments, or surveys you have conducted), which should be presented as your own

For all other source material, you should give full credit: place quotation marks around any quoted material, cite your sources according to the documentation style you're using, and include them in a list of references or works cited. Material to be credited includes all of the following:

- direct quotations
- facts that are not widely known
- arguable statements
- judgments, opinions, and claims that have been made by others
- images, statistics, charts, tables, graphs, or other illustrations that appear in any source
- collaboration—that is, the help provided by friends, colleagues, instructors, supervisors, or others

For more on using and documenting sources, see Chapters 19 and 20.

Using Copyrighted Internet Sources

If you've done any surfing on the Internet, you know that it opens the door to worldwide collaborations: you can contact individuals and groups around the globe and have access to whole libraries of information. As a result, writing (especially online writing) often is made up of a patchwork of materials that are woven from many sources. But when you gather information from Internet sources and use it in your own work, it's subject to the same rules that govern information gathered from other types of sources.

Even if the material does not include a copyright notice or symbol ("© 2009 by John J. Ruszkiewicz and Andrea A. Lunsford," for example), it's likely to be protected by copyright laws, and you may need to request permission to use part or all of it. Although they're currently in flux, "fair-use" legal precedents still allow writers to quote brief passages from published works without permission from the copyright holder if the use is for educational or personal, noncommercial reasons and if full

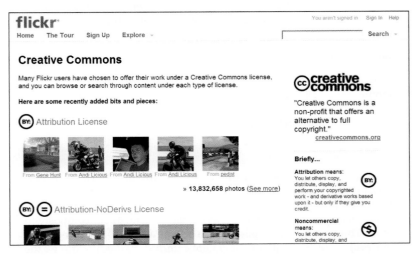

A growing number of works such as photographs, music, and video are published online under so-called Creative Commons license that often eliminates the need to request permission. These works—marked with a Creative Commons license at Flickr, for example—are made available to the public under this alternative to copyright, which grants blanket permission to reuse or remix work under certain terms if credit is given to the work's creator.

credit is given to the source. For personal communications (such as email) or for listserv postings, however, you should ask permission of the writer before you include any of his or her material in your own argument. For graphics, photos, or other images that you wish to reproduce in your text, you should also request permission from the creator or owner if the text is going to be disseminated beyond your classroom— especially if it's going to be published online.

Here are some examples of student requests for permission:

From: sanchez.32@stanford.edu
To: litman@mindspring.com
CC: lunsford.2@stanford.edu
Subject: Request for permission

Dear Professor Litman:

I am writing to request permission to quote from your essay "Copyright, Owners' Rights and Users' Privileges on the Internet: Implied Licences, Caching, Linking, Fair Use, and Sign-on Licences." I want to quote some of your work as part of an article I am writing for the *Stanford Daily* to explain the complex debates over ownership on the Internet and to argue that students at my school should be participating in these debates. I will give full credit to you and will cite the URL where I first found your work (msen.com/~litman/dayton/htm).

Thank you very much for considering my request.

Raul Sanchez

From: fox.360@stanford.edu
To: fridanet@aol.com
CC: lunsford.2@stanford.edu
Subject: Request for permission

Dear Kimberley Masters:

I am a student at Stanford University writing to request your permission to download and use a photograph of Frida Kahlo in a three-piece suit (fridanet/suit.htm#top) as an illustration in a project about Kahlo that I and two other students are working on in our composition class. This project will be posted on a school Web site. In the report on our project, we will cite members.aol.com/fridanet/kahlo.htm as the URL, unless you wish for us to use a different source.

Thank you very much for considering our request.

Jennifer Fox

CULTURAL CONTEXTS FOR ARGUMENT

Understanding Plagiarism

Not all cultures accept Western notions of plagiarism, which rest on a societal agreement that language can be owned by writers. Indeed, in many countries and in some communities within the United States, using the words of others is considered a sign of respect and an indication of knowledge—and attribution is not expected or required. In writing arguments in the United States, however, you should credit all materials except those that are common knowledge, that are available in a wide variety of sources, or that are your own findings from field research.

Acknowledging Collaboration

We've already noted the importance of acknowledging the inspirations and ideas you derive from talking with others. Such help counts as one form of collaboration, and you may also be involved in more formal kinds of collaborative work—preparing for a group presentation to a class, for example, or writing a group report. Writers generally acknowledge all participants in collaborative projects at the beginning of the presentation, report, or essay. In print texts, the acknowledgment is often placed in a footnote or brief prefatory note.

The seventh edition of the *MLA Handbook for Writers of Research Papers* (2009) calls attention to the growing importance of collaborative work and gives the following advice on how to deal with issues of assigning fair credit all around:

> Joint participation in research and writing is common and, in fact, encouraged in many courses and in many professions. It does not constitute plagiarism provided that credit is given for all contributions. One way to give credit, if roles were clearly demarcated or were unequal, is to state exactly who did what. Another way, especially if roles and contributions were merged and shared, is to acknowledge all concerned equally. Ask your instructor for advice if you are not certain how to acknowledge collaboration.

RESPOND•

1. Not everyone agrees that intellectual material is property that should be protected. The slogan "information wants to be free" has been showing up in popular magazines and on the Internet, often with a call to readers to take action against protection such as data encryption and further extension of copyright.

   Using a Web search engine, look for pages where the phrase "free information" appears. Find several sites that make arguments in favor of free information, and analyze them in terms of their rhetorical appeals. What claims do the authors make? How do they appeal to their audience? What's the site's ethos, and how is it created? After you've read some arguments in favor of free information, return to this chapter's arguments about intellectual property. Which arguments do you find most persuasive? Why?

2. Although this text is concerned principally with ideas and their written expression, other forms of intellectual property are also legally protected. For example, scientific and technological developments are protectable under patent law, which differs in some significant ways from copyright law.

   Find the standards for protection under U.S. copyright law and U.S. patent law. You might begin by visiting the U.S. copyright Web site (http://copyright.gov). Then imagine that you're the president of a small, high-tech corporation and are trying to inform your employees of the legal protections available to them and their work. Write a paragraph or two explaining the differences between copyright and patent, and suggest a policy that balances employees' rights to intellectual property with the business's needs to develop new products.

3. Define *plagiarism* in your own terms, making your definition as clear and explicit as possible. Then compare your definition with those of two or three other classmates, and write a brief report on the similarities and differences you noted in the definitions. You might research terms such as *plagiarism, academic honesty,* and *academic integrity* on the Web.

4. Spend fifteen or twenty minutes jotting down your ideas about intellectual property and plagiarism. Where do you stand, for example, on the issue of music file sharing? On downloading movies free of charge? Do you think these forms of intellectual property should be protected under copyright law? How do you define your own intellectual property, and in what ways and under what conditions are you willing to share it? Finally, come up with your own definition of *academic integrity*.

19
Evaluating and Using Sources

As many examples in this text have shown, the effectiveness of an argument often depends on the quality of the sources that support or prove it. You'll need to carefully evaluate and assess all your sources, including those that you gather in libraries, from other print sources, in online searches, or in your own field research.

Remember that different sources can contribute in different ways to your work. In most cases, you'll be looking for reliable sources that provide accurate information or that clearly and persuasively express opinions that might serve as evidence for a case you're making. At other times, you may be looking for material that expresses ideas or attitudes—how people are thinking and feeling at a given time. You might need to use a graphic image, a sample of avant-garde music, or a controversial YouTube clip that doesn't fit neatly into categories such as "reliable" or "accurate" yet is central to your argument. With any and all such sources and evidence, your goals are to be as knowledgeable about them and as

When might a tattle-tale actually be a reliable source—and how would you know?

"I'm *not* being a tattle-tale! — I'm being a reliable source!"

responsible in their use as you can be and to share honestly what you learn about them with readers.

You don't want to be naïve in your use of any source material. Most of the evidence that is used in arguments on public issues—even material from influential and well-known sources—comes with considerable baggage. Scientists and humanists alike have axes to grind, corporations have products to sell, bureaucracies have power to maintain, politicians have policies and candidacies to promote, journalists have reputations to make, media owners and editors have readers, listeners, viewers, and advertisers to attract and to avoid offending. All of these groups produce and use information to their own benefit, and it's not (usually) a bad thing that they do so. You just have to be aware that when you take information from a given source, it will often carry with it at least some of the enthusiasms, assumptions, and biases (conscious or not) of the people who produce and disseminate it. Teachers and librarians are not exempted from this caution.

To correct for these biases, draw on as many reliable sources as you can manage when you're preparing to write. You shouldn't assume that

CNN's Nancy Grace, a former prosecutor, has been accused of allowing her pro-prosecution bias to influence her commentary.

all arguments are equally good or that all the sides in a controversy can be supported by the same weight of evidence and good reasons. But you want to avoid treading so narrowly among sources that you miss essential issues and perspectives. That's easy to do when you read only sources that agree with you or when the sources that you read all seem to carry the same message.

Especially when writing on political subjects, you should be aware that the sources you're reading or viewing almost always support particular beliefs and goals. That fact has been made apparent in recent years by bloggers—from all parts of the political spectrum—who put the traditional news media under daily scrutiny, exposing errors, biases, and omissions. Even so, political bloggers (mostly amateur journalists, although many are professionals in their own fields) have their own agendas, but unlike most writers in mainstream news outlets, they often admit their biases openly and frankly.

Evaluating Sources

Print Sources

Since you want information to be reliable and persuasive, it pays to evaluate each potential source thoroughly. The following principles can help you evaluate print sources:

- *Relevance.* Begin by asking what a particular source will add to your argument and how closely the source is related to your argumentative claim. For a book, the table of contents and the index may help you decide. For an article, look for an abstract that summarizes the contents. If you can't think of a good reason for using the source, set it aside. You can almost certainly find something better.

- *Credentials of the author.* Sometimes the author's credentials are set forth in an article, in a book, or on a Web site, so be sure to look for them. Is the author an expert on the topic? To find out, you can gather information about the person on the Internet using a search engine like Yahoo! or Ask.com. Another way to learn about the credibility of an author is to search Google Groups for postings that mention the author or to check the Citation Index to find out how others refer to this author. If you see your source cited by other sources you're using, look at how they cite it and what they say about it that could provide clues to the author's credibility.

- *Stance of the author.* What's the author's position on the issue(s) involved, and how does this stance influence the information in the source? Does the author's stance support or challenge your own views?

- *Credentials of the publisher or sponsor.* If your source is from a newspaper, is it a major one (such as the *Wall Street Journal* or the *Washington Post*) that has historical credentials in reporting, or is it a tabloid? Is it a popular magazine like *O: The Oprah Magazine* or a journal sponsored by a professional group, such as the *Journal of the American Medical Association?* If your source is a book, is the publisher one you recognize or has its own Web site?

- *Stance of the publisher or sponsor.* Sometimes this stance will be obvious: a magazine called *Save the Planet!* will take a pro-environmental stance, whereas one called *America First!* will probably take a conservative stance. But other times, you need to read carefully between the lines to identify particular positions and see how the stance affects the message the source presents. Start by asking what the source's goals are: what does the publisher or sponsoring group want to make happen?

- *Currency.* Check the date of publication of every book and article. Recent sources are often more useful than older ones, particularly in the sciences. However, in some fields (such as history and literature), the most authoritative works are often the older ones.

- *Accuracy.* Check to see whether the author cites any sources for the information or opinions in the article and, if so, how credible and current they are.

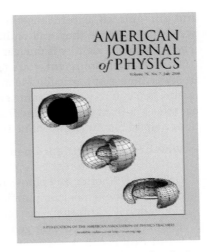

Note the differences between the cover of *Popular Science* and that of a physics journal.

- *Level of specialization.* General sources can be helpful as you begin your research, but later in the project you may need the authority or currency of more specialized sources. Keep in mind that highly specialized works on your topic may be difficult for your audience to understand.
- *Audience.* Was the source written for a general readership? For specialists? For advocates or opponents?
- *Length.* Is the source long enough to provide adequate details in support of your claim?
- *Availability.* Do you have access to the source? If it isn't readily accessible, your time might be better spent looking elsewhere.
- *Omissions.* What's missing or omitted from the source? Might such exclusions affect whether or how you can use the source as evidence?

Electronic Sources

You'll probably find working on the Internet both exciting and frustrating, for even though this tool is enormously useful, it contains information of widely varying quality. Because it is a source that's mostly open and unregulated, careful researchers look for corroboration before accepting evidence they find online, especially if it comes from a site whose sponsor's identity is unclear.

In such an environment, you must be the judge of the accuracy and trustworthiness of particular electronic sources. In making these judgments, you can rely on the same criteria and careful thinking that you use to assess print sources. In addition, you may find the following questions helpful in evaluating online sources:

- Who has posted the document or message or created the site? An individual? An interest group? A company? A government agency? Does the URL offer any clues? Note especially the final suffix in a domain name—.*com* (commercial), .*org* (nonprofit organization), .*edu* (educational institution), .*gov* (government agency), .*mil* (military), or .*net* (network). Also note the geographical domains that indicate country of origin—as in .*ca* (Canada) or .*ar* (Argentina). The homepage or first page of a site should tell you something about the sponsorship of the source, letting you know who can be held accountable for its information. (You may need to click on an "About Us" button.) Finally, links may help you learn how credible and useful the source is. Click on some links to see if they lead to legitimate and helpful sites.

- What can you determine about the credibility of the author or sponsor? Can the information in the document or site be verified in other sources? How accurate and complete is it? On a blog, for example, look for a link that identifies the creator of the site (some blogs are managed by multiple authors). Also review the links the blog offers. They'll often help you understand both the perspective of the site and its purposes.

- Who can be held accountable for the information in the document or site? How well and thoroughly does it credit its own sources?

- How current is the document or site? Be especially cautious of undated materials. Most reliable sites are updated regularly.

- What perspectives are represented? If only one perspective is represented, how can you balance or expand this point of view? Is it a straightforward presentation, or could it be a parody or satire?

Several years ago, the Stanford Persuasive Technology Lab argued that Google News might become the "most credible Web site of them all." The lab listed twenty-five reasons in support of this conclusion, including the timeliness of the information, the lack of a single viewpoint or ideology, and the ad-free policy. Since then, however, liberals have charged that Google News gives more coverage to conservative stories than it should, and conservatives have claimed that it excludes some important right-leaning sources. And yet computer algorithms, not human editors, select the stories in Google News. For readers who are sensitive to media perspectives, even machines have biases. But humans do create the machines and the algorithms.

Field Research

If you've conducted experiments, surveys, interviews, observations, or any other field research in developing and supporting an argument, make sure to review your results with a critical eye. The following questions can help you evaluate your own field research:

- Have you rechecked all data and all conclusions to make sure they're accurate and warranted?
- Have you identified the exact time, place, and participants in all your field research?
- Have you made clear what part you played in the research and how, if at all, your role could have influenced the results or findings?
- If your research involved other people, have you gotten their permission to use their words or other materials in your argument? Have you asked whether you can use their names or whether the names should be kept confidential?

Using Sources

As you locate, examine, and evaluate sources in support of an argument, remember to keep a careful record of where you've found them. For print sources, you should keep a working bibliography either on your computer or in a notebook you can carry with you. For each book, write the name of the author, the title of the book, the city of publication, the publisher, the date of publication, and the place that you found it (the section of the library, for example, and the call number for the book). For each article, write the name of the author, the title of the article, the title of the periodical, and the volume, issue, and exact page numbers. Include any other information you may later need in preparing a works-cited list or references list.

For electronic sources, keep a careful record of the information you'll need in a works-cited list or references list. Write the author and title information, the name of the database or other online site where you found the source, the full electronic address (URL), the date the document was first produced, the date it was published on the Web or most recently updated, and the date you accessed and examined it. The simplest way to ensure that you have this information is to print a copy of the source, highlight source information, and write down any other pertinent information.

Signal Words and Introductions

Because your sources are crucial to the success of your arguments, you need to introduce them carefully to your readers. Doing so usually calls for using a signal phrase of some kind in the sentence to introduce the source. Typically (but not always), the signal phrase precedes the quotation:

> According to noted primatologist Jane Goodall, the more we learn about the nature of nonhuman animals, the more ethical questions we face about their use in the service of humans.

> The more we learn about the nature of nonhuman animals, the more ethical questions we face about their use in the service of humans, according to noted primatologist Jane Goodall.

> The more we learn about the nature of nonhuman animals, according to noted primatologist Jane Goodall, the more ethical questions we face about their use in the service of humans.

In each of these sentences, the signal phrase tells readers that you're drawing on the work of a person named Jane Goodall and that this person is a "noted primatologist."

Now look at an example that uses a quotation from a source in more than one sentence:

> In *Job Shift*, consultant William Bridges worries about "dejobbing and about what a future shaped by it is going to be like." Even more worrisome, Bridges argues, is

the possibility that "the sense of craft and of professional vocation . . . will break down under the need to earn a fee" (228).

The signal verbs "worries" and "argues" add a sense of urgency to the message Bridges offers and suggest that the writer either agrees with— or is neutral about—Bridges's points. Other signal verbs have a more negative slant, indicating that the point being introduced in the quotation is open to debate and that others (including the writer) might disagree with it. If the writer of the passage above had said, for instance, that Bridges "unreasonably contends" or that he "fantasizes," these signal verbs would carry quite different connotations from those associated with "argues."

In some cases, a signal verb may require more complex phrasing to get the writer's full meaning across:

Bridges recognizes the dangers of changes in work yet refuses to be overcome by them: "The real issue is not how to stop the change but how to provide the necessary knowledge and skills to equip people to operate successfully in this New World" (229).

As these examples illustrate, the signal verb is important because it allows you to characterize the author's or source's viewpoint as well as your own—so choose these verbs with care.

Some Frequently Used Signal Verbs

acknowledges	claims	emphasizes	remarks
admits	concludes	expresses	replies
advises	concurs	hypothesizes	reports
agrees	confirms	interprets	responds
allows	criticizes	lists	reveals
argues	declares	objects	states
asserts	disagrees	observes	suggests
believes	discusses	offers	thinks
charges	disputes	opposes	writes

Quotations

To support your argumentative claims, you'll want to quote (that is, to reproduce an author's precise words) in at least three kinds of situations—when the wording is so memorable or expresses a point so well

JACQUES STEINBERG
ATTACK DOG

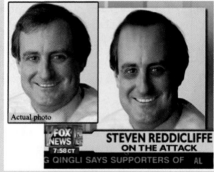

STEVEN REDDICLIFFE
ON THE ATTACK

Not Just Words

What's wrong with these pictures? During a segment of *Fox & Friends*, a television news and opinion show, hosts Steve Doocy and Brian Kilmeade called *New York Times* reporter Jacques Steinberg and editor Steven Reddicliffe "attack dogs" and displayed photos of the two men. When Media Matters for America (http://mediamatters.org/index), the progressive research and information Web site, took a closer look, it found that the photos of the two journalists seemed to have been digitally altered. Take a look at the photos: What differences do you see between the before and after pictures? How do they affect your perception of the reporters? How could you determine how the photos were altered and who was responsible for doing so? To what degree does the digital alteration undermine the authority of *Fox & Friends* as a source? How trustworthy do you find Media Matters for America to be?

Of course, anyone with a computer and Photoshop software can alter images or create fabrications. But as filmmaker Errol Morris demonstrates in an argument entitled "Photography as a Weapon," sometimes you don't even need to alter an image: all you have to do is change the caption. As an example, Morris shows grainy photos displayed in 2002 as part of the Bush administration's "proof" that Iraq had weapons of mass destruction. Different captions, he says, would have been just as credible as the "real" ones since viewers couldn't really tell what they were looking at anyway.

Morris sums up by asking whether photographs "provide illustration of a text or an idea of evidence of some underlying reality or both? And if they are evidence, don't we have to know that the evidence is *reliable*, that it can be trusted?" These are questions you should ask yourself about any photographs you want to use in your writing.

that you cannot improve it or shorten it without weakening it, when the author is a respected authority whose opinion supports your own ideas particularly well, and when an author challenges or disagrees with others in the field.

Direct quotations (such as a memorable phrase in your introduction or a detailed eyewitness account) can be effective in capturing your readers' attention. In an argument, quotations from respected authorities can help build your ethos as someone who has sought out experts in the field. Finally, carefully chosen quotations can broaden the appeal of your argument by drawing on emotion as well as logic, appealing to the reader's mind and heart. A student who is writing on the ethical issues of bullfighting, for example, might introduce an argument that bullfighting is not a sport by quoting Ernest Hemingway's comment that "the formal bull-fight is a tragedy, not a sport, and the bull is certain to be killed" and might accompany the quotation with an image such as the one below.

A tragedy, not a sport?

The following guidelines can help you make sure that you quote accurately:

- If the quotation extends over more than one page in the original source, note the placement of page breaks in case you decide to use only part of the quotation in your argument.
- Label the quotation with a note that tells you where and how you think you'll use it.
- Make sure you have all the information necessary to create an in-text citation as well as an item in your works-cited list or references list.
- When using a quotation in your argument, introduce the author(s) of the quotation, and follow the quotation with commentary of your own that points out the significance of the quotation.
- Copy quotations carefully, reproducing the punctuation, capitalization, and spelling exactly as they are in the original.
- Enclose the quotation in quotation marks (don't rely on your memory to distinguish your own words from those of your source). If in doubt, recheck all quotations for accuracy.
- Use square brackets if you introduce words of your own into the quotation or make changes to it ("And [more] brain research isn't going to define further the matter of 'mind'").
- Use ellipsis marks if you omit material ("And brain research isn't going to define . . . the matter of 'mind'").
- If you're quoting a short passage (four lines or less in MLA style; forty words or less in APA style), it should be worked into your text, enclosed by quotation marks. Long quotations should be set off from the regular text. Begin such a quotation on a new line, indenting every line one inch or ten spaces (MLA) or a half inch or five to seven spaces (APA). Set-off quotations do not need to be enclosed in quotation marks.

Paraphrases

Paraphrases involve putting an author's material (including major and minor points, usually in the order they're presented in the original) into your own words and sentence structures. Here are guidelines that can help you paraphrase accurately:

- When using a paraphrase in your argument, identify the source of the paraphrase, and comment on its significance.

- Collect all the information necessary to create an in-text citation as well as an item in your works-cited list or references list. For online sources without page numbers, record the paragraph, screen, or other section number(s) if indicated.

- If you're paraphrasing material that extends over more than one page in the original source, note the placement of page breaks in case you decide to use only part of the paraphrase in your argument.

- Label the paraphrase with a note suggesting where and how you intend to use it in your argument.

- Include all main points and any important details from the original source, in the same order in which the author presents them.

- Leave out your own comments, elaborations, or reactions.

- State the meaning in your own words and sentence structures. If you want to include especially memorable or powerful language from the original source, enclose it in quotation marks.

- Recheck to make sure that the words and sentence structures are your own and that they express the author's meaning accurately.

Summaries

A summary is a significantly shortened version of a passage or a whole chapter of a work that captures the main ideas in your own words. Unlike a paraphrase, a summary uses just enough information to record the points you want to emphasize. Summaries can be extremely valuable in supporting arguments. Here are some guidelines to help you prepare accurate and helpful summaries:

- When using a summary in an argument, identify the source, and add your own comments about why the material in the summary is significant for the argument that you're making.

- Collect all the information necessary to create an in-text citation as well as an item in your works-cited list or references list. For online sources without page numbers, record the paragraph, screen, or other section number(s) if available.

- If you're summarizing material that extends over more than one page, indicate page breaks in case you decide to use only part of the summary in your argument.

- Label the summary with a note that suggests where and how you intend to use it in your argument.
- Include just enough information to recount the main points you want to cite. A summary is usually much shorter than the original.
- Use your own words. If you include any language from the original, enclose it in quotation marks.
- Recheck to make sure that you've captured the author's meaning accurately and that the wording is entirely your own.

CULTURAL CONTEXTS FOR ARGUMENT

Identifying Sources

Although some language communities and cultures expect audiences to recognize the sources of important documents and texts, thereby eliminating the need to cite them directly, conventions for writing in North America call for careful attribution of any quoted, paraphrased, or summarized material. When in doubt, explicitly identify your sources.

Visuals

If a picture is worth a thousand words, then using pictures calls for caution: one picture might overwhelm or undermine the message you're trying to send in your argument. However, as you've seen in Chapter 14, visuals can powerfully affect audiences and help them to understand or accept your arguments. In choosing visuals to include in your argument, each one needs to make a strong contribution to your message and be appropriate and fair to your subject or topic and your audience.

When you use visuals in your written arguments, treat them as you would any other sources you integrate into your text. Like quotations, paraphrases, and summaries, visuals need to be introduced and commented on in some way. In addition, label (as "Figure" or as "Table") and number ("Figure 1," "Figure 2," and so on) all visuals, provide a caption that includes source information and describes the visual, and cite the source in your references list or works-cited list. Even if you create a visual (such as a bar graph) by using information from a source (the results, say, of a Gallup Poll), you must cite the source. If you use a photograph you took yourself, cite it as a personal photograph.

Below is a visual that accompanied the introduction to an article entitled "An S.U.V. Traffic Jam" that appeared in the business section of the *New York Times* on August 13, 2008. Note that the caption indicates the way the visual is related to the argument (the bunch of car keys hanging from a salesman's neck indicates the many sport-utility vehicles that are sitting on sales lots throughout the country) and that a credit line identifies the source of the visual (this photograph was taken by Fabrizio Costantini for the *Times*). If you were going to use this as the first visual in an essay, you would include the source, describe the image in relationship to your topic, and label it "Figure 1." As long as you use this image only in a print text for your instructor and classmates, you're allowed fair use of it. Before you can post your argument and this image on the Web or otherwise publish the image for a wider audience, however, you need to request permission from the copyright owner (see Chapter 18, pp. 545–46).

Fabrizio Costantini for The New York Times
Kevin Whims, an account representative for Dealer Specialties shown at Matthews-Hargreaves Chevrolet in Royal Oak, Mich., had more ignition keys than customers Friday.

RESPOND●

1. Select one of the essays at the end of Chapters 8 to 12. Write a brief summary of the essay that includes both direct quotations and para-phrases. Be careful to attribute the ideas properly, even when you paraphrase, and to use signal phrases to introduce quotations. Then trade summaries with a partner, comparing the passages you selected to quote and paraphrase and the signal phrases you used to introduce them. How do your choices create an ethos for the original author that differs from the one your partner has created? How do the signal phrases shape a reader's sense of the author's position? Which sum-mary best represents the author's argument? Why?

2. Return to the Internet sites you found in exercise 1 of Chapter 18 (p. 548) that discuss free information. Using this chapter's criteria for evaluating electronic sources, judge each of those sites. Select three that you think are most trustworthy, and write a paragraph summa-rizing their arguments and recommending them to an audience un-familiar with the debate.

3. Choose a news Web site that you have visited. Then, using the guide-lines discussed in this chapter, spend some time evaluating its credi-bility. You might begin by comparing it with Google News or another site that has a reputation for being reliable.

20
Documenting Sources

What does documenting sources have to do with argument? First, the sources that a writer chooses form part of any argument, showing that he or she has done some homework, knows what others have said about the topic, and understands how to use these items as support for a claim. Similarly, the list of works cited or references makes a statement, saying, "Look at how thoroughly this essay has been researched" or "Note how up-to-date I am!"

Even the choice of documentation style makes an argument in a subtle way. You'll note in the instructions that follow, for example, that the Modern Language Association (MLA) style requires putting the date of publication of a print source at or near the end of a works-cited list entry, whereas the American Psychological Association (APA) style places that date near the beginning of a reference-list citation. Pay attention to such fine points of documentation style, always asking what these choices suggest about the values of scholars and researchers who use a particular system of documentation.

MLA Style

Documentation styles vary from discipline to discipline, with one format favored in the social sciences and another in the natural sciences, for example. Widely used in the humanities, MLA style is fully described in the *MLA Handbook for Writers of Research Papers* (7th edition, 2009). In this discussion, we provide guidelines drawn from the *MLA Handbook* for in-text citations, notes, and entries in the list of works cited.

In-Text Citations

MLA style calls for in-text citations in the body of an argument to document sources of quotations, paraphrases, summaries, and so on. For in-text citations, use a signal phrase to introduce the material, often with the author's name *(As LaDoris Cordell explains, . . .).* Keep an in-text citation short, but include enough information for readers to locate the source in the list of works cited. Place the parenthetical citation as near to the relevant material as possible without disrupting the flow of the sentence, as in the following examples.

1. Author Named in a Signal Phrase

Ordinarily, use the author's name in a signal phrase to introduce the material, and cite the page number(s) in parentheses.

> Loomba argues that Caliban's "political colour" is black, given his stage representations, which have varied from animalistic to a kind of missing link (143).

2. Author Named in Parentheses

When you don't mention the author in a signal phrase, include the author's last name before the page number(s) in the parentheses.

> Oil from shale in the western states, if it could be extracted, would be equivalent to six hundred billion barrels, more than all the crude so far produced in the world (McPhee 413).

3. Two or Three Authors

Use all authors' last names.

> Gortner, Hebrun, and Nicolson maintain that "opinion leaders" influence other people in an organization because they are respected, not because they hold high positions (175).

4. Four or More Authors

The MLA allows you to use all authors' last names or to use only the first author's name with *et al.* (in regular type, not italicized). Although either format is acceptable when applied consistently throughout a paper, in an argument it is better to name all authors who contributed to the work.

> Similarly, as Goldberger, Tarule, Clinchy, and Belenky note, their new book builds on their collaborative experiences (xii).

5. Organization as Author

Give the full name of a corporate author if it's brief or a shortened form if it's long.

> In fact, one of the leading foundations in the field of higher education supports the recent proposals for community-run public schools (Carnegie Corporation 45).

6. Unknown Author

Use the full title of the work if it's brief or a shortened form if it's long.

> "Hype," by one analysis, is "an artificially engendered atmosphere of hysteria" ("Today's Marketplace" 51).

7. Author of Two or More Works

When you use two or more works by the same author, include the title of the work or a shortened version of it in the citation.

> Gardner presents readers with their own silliness through his description of a "pointless, ridiculous monster, crouched in the shadows, stinking of dead men, murdered children, and martyred cows" (*Grendel* 2).

8. Authors with the Same Last Name

When you use works by two or more authors with the same last name, include each author's first initial in the in-text citation.

> Father Divine's teachings focused on eternal life, salvation, and socioeconomic progress (R. Washington 17).

9. Multivolume Work

Note the volume number first and then the page number(s), with a colon and one space between them.

Aristotle's "On Plants" is now available in a new translation edited by Barnes (2: 1252).

10. Literary Work

Because literary works are often available in many different editions, you need to include enough information for readers to locate the passage in any edition. For a prose work such as a novel or play, first cite the page number from the edition you used, followed by a semicolon; then indicate the part or chapter number (114; ch. 3) or act or scene in a play (42; sc. 2).

In *The Madonnas of Leningrad*, Marina says "she could see into the future" (7; ch. 1).

For a poem, cite the stanza and line numbers. If the poem has only line numbers, use the word line(s) in the first reference (lines 33–34) and the number(s) alone in subsequent references.

On dying, Whitman speculates "All that goes onward and outward, nothing collapses, / And to die is different from what any one supposed, and luckier" (6.129-30).

For a verse play, omit the page number, and give only the act, scene, and line numbers, separated by periods.

Before he takes his own life, Othello says he is "one that loved not wisely but too well" (5.2.348).

As *Macbeth* begins, the witches greet Banquo as "Lesser than Macbeth, and greater" (1.3.65).

11. Works in an Anthology

For an essay, short story, or other short work within an anthology, use the name of the author of the work, not the editor of the anthology; but use the page number(s) from the anthology.

In the end, if the black artist accepts any duties at all, that duty is to express the beauty of blackness (Hughes 1271).

12. Sacred Text

To cite a sacred text, such as the Qur'an or the Bible, give the title of the edition you used, the book, and the chapter and verse (or their equivalent), separated by a period. In your text, spell out the names of books. In a parenthetical reference, use an abbreviation for books with names of five or more letters (for example, *Gen.* for Genesis).

> He ignored the admonition "Pride goes before destruction, and a haughty spirit before a fall" (*New Oxford Annotated Bible,* Prov. 16.18).

13. Indirect Source

Use the abbreviation *qtd. in* to indicate that what you're quoting or paraphrasing is quoted (as part of a conversation, interview, letter, or excerpt) in the source you're using.

> As Catherine Belsey states, "to speak is to have access to the language which defines, delimits and locates power" (qtd. in Bartels 453).

14. Two or More Sources in the Same Citation

Separate the information for each source with a semicolon.

> Adefunmi was able to patch up the subsequent holes left in worship by substituting various Yoruba, Dahomean, or Fon customs made available to him through research (Brandon 115-17; Hunt 27).

15. Entire Work or One-Page Article

Include the citation in the text without any page numbers or parentheses.

> The relationship between revolutionary innocence and the preservation of an oppressive postrevolutionary regime is one theme Milan Kundera explores in *The Book of Laughter and Forgetting.*

16. Work without Page Numbers

If the work isn't numbered by page but has numbered sections, parts, or paragraphs, include the name and number(s) of the section(s) you're citing. (For *paragraphs*, use the abbreviation *par.* or *pars.;* for *section*, use *sec.;* for *part*, use *pt.*)

> Zora Neale Hurston is one of the great anthropologists of the twentieth century, according to Kip Hinton (par. 2).

17. Electronic or Nonprint Source

Give enough information in a signal phrase or parenthetical citation for readers to locate the source in the list of works cited. Usually give the author or title under which you list the source.

> In his film version of *Hamlet*, Zeffirelli highlights the sexual tension between the prince and his mother.

> Describing children's language acquisition, Pinker explains that "what's innate about language is just a way of paying attention to parental speech" (Johnson, sec. 1).

Explanatory and Bibliographic Notes

The MLA recommends using explanatory notes for information or commentary that doesn't readily fit into your text but is needed for clarification, further explanation, or justification. In addition, the MLA allows bibliographic notes for citing several sources for one point and for offering thanks to, information about, or evaluation of a source. Use a superscript number in your text at the end of a sentence to refer readers to the notes, which usually appear as endnotes (with the heading *Notes*, not underlined or italicized) on a separate page before the list of works cited. Indent the first line of each note five spaces, and double-space all entries.

TEXT WITH SUPERSCRIPT INDICATING A NOTE

> Stewart emphasizes the existence of social contacts in Hawthorne's life so that the audience will accept a different Hawthorne, one more attuned to modern times than the figure in Woodberry.[3]

NOTE

> [3] Woodberry does, however, show that Hawthorne was often unsociable. He emphasizes the seclusion of Hawthorne's mother, who separated herself from her family after the death of her husband, often even taking meals alone (28). Woodberry seems to imply that Mrs. Hawthorne's isolation rubbed off on her son.

List of Works Cited

A list of works cited is an alphabetical listing of the sources you cite in your essay. The list appears on a separate page at the end of your argument, after any notes, with the heading *Works Cited* centered an inch from the top of the page; don't underline or italicize it or enclose it in quotation marks. Double-space between the heading and the first entry, and double-space the entire list. (If you're asked to list everything you've read as background—not just the sources you cite—call the list *Works Consulted*.) The first line of each entry should align on the left; subsequent lines indent one-half inch or five spaces. See p. 585 for a sample works-cited page.

BOOKS

The basic information for a book includes four elements, each followed by a period:

- the author's name, last name first
- the title and subtitle, italicized
- the publication information, including the city, a shortened form of the publisher's name (such as Harvard UP), and the publication date
- the medium of publication (*Print*)

For a book with multiple authors, only the first author's name is inverted.

1. One Author

Castle, Terry. *Boss Ladies, Watch Out: Essays on Women, Sex, and Writing.* New York: Routledge, 2002. Print.

2. Two or More Authors

Jacobson, Sid, and Ernie Colón. *The 9/11 Report: A Graphic Adaptation.* New York: Hill, 2006. Print.

3. Organization as Author

American Horticultural Society. *The Fully Illustrated Plant-by-Plant Manual of Practical Techniques.* New York: American Horticultural Society and DK Publishing, 1999. Print.

4. Unknown Author

National Geographic Atlas of the World. New York: National Geographic, 1999. Print.

5. Two or More Books by the Same Author

List the works alphabetically by title. Use three hyphens for the author's name for the second and subsequent works by that author.

Lorde, Audre. *A Burst of Light*. Ithaca: Firebrand, 1988. Print.

---. *Sister Outsider*. Trumansburg: Crossing, 1984. Print.

6. Editor

Rorty, Amelie Oksenberg, ed. *Essays on Aristotle's Poetics*. Princeton: Princeton UP, 1992. Print.

7. Author and Editor

Shakespeare, William. *The Tempest*. Ed. Frank Kermode. London: Routledge, 1994. Print.

8. Selection in an Anthology or Chapter in an Edited Book

List the author(s) of the selection or chapter; its title; the title of the book in which the selection or chapter appears; Ed. and the name(s) of the editor(s); the publication information; and the inclusive page numbers of the selection or chapter.

Brown, Paul. "'This thing of darkness I acknowledge mine': *The Tempest* and the Discourse of Colonialism." *Political Shakespeare: Essays in Cultural Materialism*. Ed. Jonathan Dillimore and Alan Sinfield. Ithaca: Cornell UP, 1985. 48–71. Print.

9. Two or More Works from the Same Anthology

Include the anthology itself in the list of works cited.

Gates, Henry Louis, Jr., and Nellie McKay, eds. *The Norton Anthology of African American Literature*. New York: Norton, 1997. Print.

Then list each selection separately by its author and title, followed by a cross-reference to the anthology.

Karenga, Maulana. "Black Art: Mute Matter Given Force and Function." Gates and McKay 1973–77.

Neal, Larry. "The Black Arts Movement." Gates and McKay 1960–72.

10. Translation

Hietamies, Laila. *Red Moon over White Sea.* Trans. Borje Vahamaki. Beaverton, ON: Aspasia, 2000. Print.

11. Edition Other Than the First

Lunsford, Andrea A., and John J. Ruszkiewicz. *Everything's an Argument.* 5th ed. Boston: Bedford, 2010. Print.

12. One Volume of a Multivolume Work

Byron, Lord George. *Byron's Letters and Journals.* Ed. Leslie A. Marchand. Vol. 2. London: Murray, 1973–82. Print. 12 vols.

13. Two or More Volumes of a Multivolume Work

Byron, Lord George. *Byron's Letters and Journals.* Ed. Leslie A. Marchand. 12 vols. London: Murray, 1973–82. Print.

14. Preface, Foreword, Introduction, or Afterword

Kean, Thomas H., and Lee H. Hamilton. Foreword. *The 9/11 Report: A Graphic Adaptation.* By Sid Jacobson and Ernie Colón. New York: Hill, 2006. ix-x. Print.

15. Article in a Reference Work

Kettering, Alison McNeil. "Art Nouveau." *World Book Encyclopedia.* 2002 ed. Print.

16. Book That Is Part of a Series

Include the series title and number after the publication information.

Moss, Beverly J. *A Community Text Arises.* Cresskill: Hampton, 2003. Print. Language and Social Processes Ser. 8.

17. Republication

Scott, Walter. *Kenilworth.* 1821. New York: Dodd, 1996. Print.

18. Government Document

United States. Cong. House Committee on the Judiciary. *Impeachment of the President.* 40th Cong., 1st sess. H. Rept. 7. Washington: GPO, 1867. Print.

19. Pamphlet

An Answer to the President's Message to the Fiftieth Congress. Philadelphia: Manufacturer's Club of Philadelphia, 1887. Print.

20. Published Proceedings of a Conference

Edwards, Ron, ed. *Proceedings of the Third National Folklore Conference.* 26-27 Nov. 1988. Canberra, Austral.: Australian Folk Trust, 1988. Print.

21. Title within a Title

Tauernier-Courbin, Jacqueline. *Ernest Hemingway's* A Moveable Feast: *The Making of a Myth.* Boston: Northeastern UP, 1991. Print.

PERIODICALS

The basic entry for a periodical includes four elements, each followed by a period:

- the author's name, last name first
- the article title, in quotation marks
- the publication information, including the periodical title (italicized), the volume and issue numbers (if any), the date of publication, and the page number(s)
- the medium of publication (Print)

For works with multiple authors, only the first author's name is inverted. Note that the period following the article title goes inside the closing quotation mark. Finally, note that the MLA omits *the* in titles such as *The New Yorker.*

22. Article in a Journal

Give the issue number, if available.

Anderson, Virginia. "'The Perfect Enemy': Clinton, the Contradictions of Capitalism, and Slaying the Sin Within." *Rhetoric Review* 21 (2002): 384-400. Print.

Radavich, David. "Man among Men: David Mamet's Homosocial Order." *American Drama* 1.1 (1991): 46-66. Print.

23. Article That Skips Pages

Seabrook, John. "Renaissance Pears." *New Yorker* 5 Sept. 2005: 102+. Print.

24. Article in a Monthly Magazine

Wallraff, Barbara. "Word Count." *Atlantic* Nov. 2002: 144-45. Print.

25. Article in a Weekly Magazine

Reed, Julia. "Hope in the Ruins." *Newsweek* 12 Sept. 2005: 58-59. Print.

26. Article in a Newspaper

Friend, Tim. "Scientists Map the Mouse Genome." *USA Today* 2 Dec. 2002: A1. Print.

27. Editorial or Letter to the Editor

Posner, Alan. "Colin Powell's Regret." Editorial. *New York Times* 9 Sept. 2005: A20. Print.

28. Unsigned Article

"Court Rejects the Sale of Medical Marijuana." *New York Times* 26 Feb. 1998, late ed.: A21. Print.

29. Review

Ali, Lorraine. "The Rap on Kanye." Rev. of *Late Registration,* by Kanye West. *Newsweek* 5 Sept. 2005: 72-73. Print.

ELECTRONIC SOURCES

Most of the following models are based on the MLA's guidelines for citing electronic sources in the *MLA Handbook* (7th edition, 2009), as well as on up-to-date information available at its Web site (http://mla.org). The MLA no longer requires the use of URLs but assumes that readers can locate a source by searching using the author, title, and other publication information given in the citation. The basic MLA entry for most electronic sources should include the following elements:

- name of the author, editor, or compiler
- title of the work, document, or posting
- information for print publication, if any

- information for electronic publication
- medium of publication (e.g., *Web*, CD-ROM, etc.)
- date of access

30. Document from a Professional Web Site

When possible, include the author's name; the title of the document, in quotations; the name of the Web site, italicized; the sponsor or publisher; the date of publication; the medium consulted (*Web*); and the date you accessed the site.

"A History of Women's Writing." *The Orlando Project: An Integrated History of Women's Writing in the British Isles.* U of Alberta, 2000. Web. 14 Mar. 2006.

31. Entire Web Site

Include the name of the person or group who created the site, if relevant; the title of the site, italicized, or (if there is no title) a description such as *Home page*, not italicized; the publisher or sponsor of the site; the date of publication or last update; the medium consulted (*Web*); and the date of access.

Bowman, Laurel. *Classical Myth: The Ancient Source.* U of Victoria, 7 Mar. 2007. Web. 12 Sept. 2008.

Mitten, Lisa. *Native American Sites.* Lisa A. Mitten, 16 Sept. 2008. Web. 3 Dec. 2008.

32. Course, Department, or Personal Web Site

For a course Web site, include the instructor's name; the title of the site, italicized; a description of the site (such as *Course home page*, *Dept. home page*, or *Home page*—not italicized); the sponsor of the site (academic department and institution); dates of the course or last update to the page; the medium; and date of access. For an academic department, list the name of the department; a description; the academic institution; the date the page was last updated (use *n.d.* for no date, not italicized); the medium (*Web*); and the date of access.

Dept. of English. Home page. Amherst Coll., n.d. Web. 5 Apr. 2007.

Lunsford, Andrea A. Home page. Stanford U, 27 Mar. 2003. Web. 17 May 2008.

Lunsford, Andrea A. *Memory and Media.* Course home page. Dept. of English, Stanford U, Sept.–Dec. 2002. Web. 13 Mar. 2006.

33. Online Book

Cite an online book as you would a print book. After the print publication information (if any), give the title of the Web site or database in which the book appears, italicized; the medium (*Web*); and the date of access.

> Riis, Jacob A. *How the Other Half Lives: Studies among the Tenements of New York.* Ed. David Phillips. New York: Scribner's, 1890. *The Authentic History Center.* Web. 26 Mar. 2009.

Treat a poem, essay, or other short work within an online book as you would a part of print book. After the print publication information (if any), give the title of the Web site or database, italicized; the medium (*Web*); and the date of access.

> Dickinson, Emily. "The Grass." *Poems: Emily Dickinson.* Boston: Roberts Brothers, 1891. *Humanities Text Initiative American Verse Project.* Web. 6 Jan. 2008.

34. Article in an Online Journal

For an article in an online journal, cite the same information that you would for a print journal. If the online article does not have page numbers, use *n. pag.* (not italicized). Then add the medium consulted (*Web*) and the date of access.

> Johnson, Eric. "The 10,000-Word Question: Using Images on the World-Wide Web." *Kairos* 4.1 (1999): n. pag. Web. 20 Mar. 2007.

35. Article in an Online Magazine or Newspaper

For an article in an online magazine or newspaper, cite the author; the title of the article, in quotation marks; the name of the magazine or newspaper, italicized; the sponsor of the Web site; the date of publication; the medium (*Web*); and the date you accessed the article.

> Broad, William J. "In Ancient Fossils, Seeds of a New Debate on Warming." *New York Times.* New York Times, 7 Nov. 2006. Web. 12 Jan. 2009.

> McIntosh, Jill. "Test Drive: 2009 Subaru Forester 2.5X Touring." *Canadian Driver.* CanadianDriver Communications, 23 July 2008. Web. 30 Aug. 2008.

36. Posting to a Discussion Group

Begin with the author's name; the title of the posting, in quotation marks (if there is no title, use the description *Online posting*, not italicized); the name of the Web site, italicized; the sponsor or publisher of the site (use *N.p.*, not italicized, if there is no sponsor); the date of the posting; the medium; and the date of access.

> Kent, Robert. "Computers Legalized, Net Still Banned for Cubans." *Freenet Chat.* The Free Network Project, 5 May 2008. Web. 15 Nov. 2008.

37. Work from an Online Database or a Subscription Service

For a work from an online database, list the author's name; the title of the work, in quotation marks; any print publication information; the name of the database, italicized; the medium consulted (*Web*); and the date of access.

> "Bolivia: Elecciones Presidenciales de 2002." *Political Database of the Americas.* Web. 12 Nov. 2006.

> Penn, Sean, and Jon Krakauer. "*Into the Wild* Script." *Internet Movie Script Database.* Web. 12 June 2008.

For a work from an online service to which your library subscribes, include the same information as for an online database. After the information about the work, give the name of the database, italicized; the medium; and the date you accessed the work.

> "Breaking the Dieting Habit: Drug Therapy for Eating Disorders." *Psychology Today* Mar. 1995: 12+. *ProQuest.* Web. 30 Nov. 2008.

If you're citing an article from a subscription service to which you subscribe (such as AOL), use the following model:

> Weeks, W. William. "Beyond the Ark." *Nature Conservancy* Mar.-Apr. 1999. *America Online.* Web. 30 Nov. 2008.

38. Email Message

Include the writer's name; the subject line, in quotation marks; *Message to* [recipient's name] (not italicized); the date of the message; and the medium of delivery (*E-mail*). (Note that MLA style is to hyphenate *e-mail.*)

> Moller, Marilyn. "Seeing Crowns." Message to Beverly Moss. 3 Jan. 2003. E-mail.

39. Computer Software or Video Game

Include the title, italicized; the version number (if given); publication information; and the medium. If you are citing material downloaded from a Web site, include the title and version number (if given), but instead of publication information, add the publisher or sponsor of the Web site; the date; the medium (*Web*); and the date of access.

> *The Sims 2.* Redwood City: Electronic Arts, 2004. CD-ROM.

> *Web Cache Illuminator.* Vers. 4.02. NorthStar Solutions, n.d. Web. 12 Nov. 2007.

40. CD-ROM, Diskette, or Magnetic Tape, Single Issue

> McPherson, James M., ed. *The American Heritage New History of the Civil War.* New York: Viking, 1996. CD-ROM.

41. Periodically Revised CD-ROM

Include the author's name; publication information for the print version of the text (including its title and date of publication); the medium (*CD-ROM*); the title of the database (italicized); the name of the company producing it; and the publication date of the database (month and year, if possible).

> Heyman, Steven. "The Dangerously Exciting Client." *Psychotherapy Patient* 9.1 (1994): 37–46. CD-ROM. *PsycLIT.* SilverPlatter. Nov. 2006.

42. Multidisc CD-ROM

> *The 1998 Grolier Multimedia Encyclopedia.* Danbury: Grolier Interactive, 1998. CD-ROM. 2 discs.

OTHER SOURCES (INCLUDING ONLINE VERSIONS)

43. Unpublished Dissertation

> Fishman, Jenn. "'The Active Republic of Literature': Performance and Literary Culture in Britain, 1656–1790." Diss. Stanford U, 2003. Print.

44. Published Dissertation

> Baum, Bernard. *Decentralization of Authority in a Bureaucracy.* Diss. U of Chicago, 1959. Englewood Cliffs: Prentice, 1961. Print.

45. Article from a Microform

> Sharpe, Lora. "A Quilter's Tribute." *Boston Globe* 25 Mar. 1989: 13. Microform. *NewsBank: Social Relations* 12 (1989): fiche 6, grids B4–6.

46. Personal, Published, or Broadcast Interview

For a personal interview, list the name of the person interviewed, the label *Personal interview* (not italicized), and the date of the interview.

> Mullin, Joan. Personal interview. 2 Sept. 2008.

For a published interview, list the name of the person interviewed; the title (if any) or if there is no title, use the label *Interview by [interviewer's name]* (not italicized); then add the publication information, including the medium.

> Marshall, Andrew. "The Marshall Plan." Interview by Douglas McGray. *Wired.* CondéNet, Feb. 2003. Web. 17 Mar. 2007.

> Taylor, Max. "Max Taylor on Winning." *Time* 13 Nov. 2000: 66. Print.

For a broadcast interview, list the name of the person interviewed, the label *Interview* (not italicized), and the name of the interviewer (if relevant); then list information about the program, the date of the interview, and the medium.

> Fairey, Shepard. "Spreading the Hope: Street Artist Shepard Fairey." Interview by Terry Gross. *Fresh Air.* Natl. Public Radio. WBUR, Boston. 20 Jan. 2009. Radio.

If you listened to an archived version online, after the site's sponsor (if known), add the date of the interview, the medium (*Web*), and the date of access.

> Fairey, Shepard. "Spreading the Hope: Street Artist Shepard Fairey." Interview by Terry Gross. *Fresh Air.* Natl. Public Radio. 20 Jan. 2009. Web. 13 Feb. 2009.

47. Letter

Treat a published letter like a work in an anthology, but include the date of the letter.

> Jacobs, Harriet. "To Amy Post." 4 Apr. 1853. *Incidents in the Life of a Slave Girl.* Ed. Jean Fagan Yellin. Cambridge: Harvard UP, 1987. 234-35. Print.

48. Film

> Jenkins, Tamara, dir. *The Savages.* Perf. Laura Linney and Philip Seymour Hoffman. 2007. Fox Searchlight. Web. 4 Mar. 2008.

> *The Lord of the Rings: The Return of the King.* Dir. Peter Jackson. Perf. Elijah Wood, Ian McKellen. New Line Cinema, 2003. Film.

49. Television or Radio Program

"Box Office Bombshell: Marilyn Monroe." *A&E Biography.* Narr. Peter Graves. Writ. Andy Thomas, Jeff Schefel, and Kevin Burns. Dir. Bill Harris. Arts and Entertainment Network. 23 Oct. 2002. Television.

Schorr, Daniel. "Week in Review with Daniel Schorr." *Weekend Edition.* Natl. Public Radio. KQED, San Francisco. 20 Dec. 2008. Radio.

50. Sound Recording

Black Rebel Motorcycle Club. "Howl." *Howl.* RCA Records, 2005. CD.

Massive Attack. "Future Proof." *100th Window.* Virgin, 2003. CD.

51. Work of Art or Photograph

List the artist or photographer; the work's title, italicized; the date of composition (if unknown, use *n.d.*); and the medium of composition (*Oil on canvas, Bronze, Photograph*). Then cite the name of the museum or other location and the city. To cite a reproduction in a book, add the publication information. To cite artwork found online, omit the medium of composition, and after the location add the title of the database or Web site, italicized; the medium consulted (*Web*); and the date of access.

Chagall, Marc. *The Poet with the Birds.* 1911. Minneapolis Inst. of Arts. Artsmia.org. Web. 6 Oct. 2003.

General William Palmer in Old Age. 1810. Oil on canvas. National Army Museum, London. *White Mughals: Love and Betrayal in Eighteenth-Century India.* William Dalrymple. New York: Penguin, 2002. 270. Print.

Ulmann, Doris. *Man Leaning against a Wall.* 1930. Photograph. Smithsonian American Art Museum, Washington, DC.

52. Lecture or Speech

Jobs, Steve. Baccalaureate Address. Stanford University, Stanford, CA. 18 June 2005. Address.

53. Performance

Anything Goes. By Cole Porter. Perf. Klea Blackhurst. Shubert Theatre, New Haven. 7 Oct. 2003. Performance.

54. Map or Chart

The Political and Physical World. Map. Washington: Natl. Geographic, 1975. Print.

55. Cartoon

Brodner, Steve. Cartoon. *Nation* 31 Mar. 2003: 2. Print.

56. Advertisement

Chevy Avalanche. Advertisement. *Time* 14 Oct. 2002: 104. Print.

On p. 584, note the formatting of the first page of a sample essay written in MLA style. On p. 585, you'll find a sample works-cited page written for the same student essay.

Sample First Page for an Essay in MLA Style

Lesk 1

Emily Lesk

Professor Arraéz

Electric Rhetoric

15 November 2008

Red, White, and Everywhere

America, I have a confession to make: I don't drink Coke. But don't
call me a hypocrite just because I am still the proud owner of a bright
red shirt that advertises it. Just call me an American. Even before
setting foot in Israel three years ago, I knew exactly where I could find
one. The tiny T-shirt shop in the central block of Jerusalem's Ben Yehuda
Street did offer other designs, but the one with a bright white "Drink
Coca-Cola Classic" written in Hebrew cursive across the chest was what
drew in most of the dollar-carrying tourists. While waiting almost twenty
minutes for my shirt (depicted in Fig. 1), I watched nearly every
customer ahead of me ask for "the Coke shirt, *todah rabah*
[thank you very much]."

At the time, I never thought it strange that I wanted
one, too. After having absorbed sixteen years of Coca-Cola
propaganda through everything from NBC's Saturday morning
cartoon lineup to the concession
stand at Camden Yards (the Baltimore Orioles' ballpark), I associated the
shirt with singing along to the "Just for the Taste of It" jingle and with
America's favorite pastime, not with a brown fizzy beverage I refused to
consume. When I later realized the immensity of Coke's

Fig. 1. *Hebrew Coca-Cola T-shirt.*
Personal photograph. Despite my
dislike for the beverage, I bought
this Coca-Cola T-shirt in Israel.

Sample List of Works Cited for an Essay In MLA Style

Works Cited

Coca-Cola Santa pin. Personal photograph by the author. 9 Nov. 2008.

"The Fabulous Fifties." *Beverage Industry* 87.6 (1996): 16. *General OneFile*. Web. 2 Nov. 2008.

"Fifty Years of Coca-Cola Television Advertisements." *American Memory*. Motion Picture, Broadcasting and Recorded Sound Division, Lib. of Cong. 29 Nov. 2000. Web. 5 Nov. 2008.

"Haddon Sundblom and Coca-Cola." *Thehistoryofchristmas.com.* 10 Holidays, 2004. Web. 2 Nov. 2008.

Hebrew Coca-Cola T-shirt. Personal photograph by the author. 8 Nov. 2008.

Ikuta, Yasutoshi, ed. *'50s American Magazine Ads.* Tokyo: Graphic-Sha, 1987. Print.

Pendergrast, Mark. *For God, Country, and Coca-Cola: The Definitive History of the Great American Soft Drink and the Company That Makes It.* 2nd ed. New York: Basic, 2000. Print.

I Need a Hero

Seeking a bomb-throwing, passionate, visionary, liberal Scalia for a seat on the Supreme Court.

By Dahlia Lithwick
Posted Tuesday, Feb. 3, 2009, at 7:04 PM ET

Folks are wondering what kind of thumbprint Barack Obama should be leaving on the U.S. Supreme Court. It's hardly a theoretical question. Justice John Paul Stevens will soon be 89. Justice Ruth Bader Ginsburg is 75. And while both have insisted they aren't going anyplace anytime soon, the rumor mill continues to whisper that Justice David Souter (a mere 'tween at 69) is also thinking about packing it in.

The prospect of a liberal slot on the court being filled by a liberal president has some liberals dreaming big—as was evidenced in a piece last weekend, by Adam Liptak, asking whether President Obama should appoint someone "who by historical standards is a full-throated liberal, a lion like Justice William J. Brennan Jr. or Justice Thurgood Marshall?"

Today's high court is balanced between four conservatives and four moderate liberals. Moderate-conservative Anthony Kennedy remains the deciding vote in hotly contested cases. But liberals have long fussed that despite this 4-1-4 lineup, the court has still lurched far to the right of mainstream American thinking. One of the most vocal proponents of this view is

Not Just Words

Like the article from Slate.com shown above, many online texts acknowledge their sources not with parenthetical citations or lists of references but with direct electronic links to the sources themselves. What are the implications of documenting sources in this nonverbal way? Links make it easy to check what a source actually says and the context in which it occurs. But is there a downside for the writer or the reader in not having the source's name appear within the text and a list of sources at the end? Might the colors and underlining used to indicate links distract the reader from the writer's point or emphasize the source more than the writer's own ideas? What happens if the source is revised or deleted after it is linked in a text?

APA Style

The *Publication Manual of the American Psychological Association* (6th edition, 2010) provides comprehensive advice to student and professional writers in the social sciences. Here we draw on the *Publication Manual*'s guidelines to provide an overview of APA style for in-text citations, content notes, and entries in the list of references.

In-Text Citations

APA style calls for in-text citations in the body of an argument to document sources of quotations, paraphrases, summaries, and so on. These in-text citations correspond to full bibliographic entries in the list of references at the end of the text.

1. Author Named in a Signal Phrase

Generally, use the author's name in a signal phrase to introduce the cited material, and place the date, in parentheses, immediately after the author's name. For a quotation, the page number, preceded by *p.* (neither underlined nor italicized), appears in parentheses after the quotation. For electronic texts or other works without page numbers, paragraph numbers may be used instead, preceded by the abbreviation *para.* For a long, set-off quotation, position the page reference in parentheses one space after the punctuation at the end of the quotation.

> According to Brandon (1993), Adefunmi opposed all forms of racism and believed that black nationalism should not be a destructive force.

> As Johnson (2005) demonstrates, contemporary television dramas such as *ER* and *Lost* are not only more complex than earlier programs but "possess a quality that can only be described as subtlety and discretion" (p. 83).

2. Author Named in Parentheses

When you don't mention the author in a signal phrase, give the name and the date, separated by a comma, in parentheses at the end of the cited material.

> *The Sopranos* has achieved a much wider viewing audience than ever expected, spawning a cookbook and several serious scholarly studies (Franklin, 2002).

3. Two Authors

Use both names in all citations. Use *and* in a signal phrase, but use an ampersand (&) in parentheses.

Associated with purity and wisdom, Obatala is the creator of human beings, whom he is said to have formed out of clay (Edwards & Mason, 1985).

4. Three to Five Authors

List all the authors' names for the first reference. In subsequent references, use just the first author's name followed by *et al.* (in regular type, not underlined or italicized).

Lenhoff, Wang, Greenberg, and Bellugi (1997) cite tests that indicate that segments of the left brain hemisphere are not affected by Williams syndrome whereas the right hemisphere is significantly affected.

Shackelford (1999) drew on the study by Lenhoff et al. (1997).

5. Six or More Authors

Use only the first author's name and *et al.* (in regular type, not underlined or italicized) in every citation, including the first.

As Flower et al. (2003) demonstrate, reading and writing involve both cognitive and social processes.

6. Organization as Author

If the name of an organization or a corporation is long, spell it out the first time, followed by an abbreviation in brackets. In later citations, use the abbreviation only.

First Citation: (Federal Bureau of Investigation [FBI], 2002)

Subsequent Citations: (FBI, 2002)

7. Unknown Author

Use the title or its first few words in a signal phrase or in parentheses (in the example below, a book's title is italicized).

The school profiles for the county substantiate this trend (*Guide to secondary schools,* 2003).

8. Authors with the Same Last Name

If your list of references includes works by different authors with the same last name, include the authors' initials in each citation.

> G. Jones (1998) conducted the groundbreaking study of retroviruses, whereas P. Jones (2000) replicated the initial trials two years later.

9. Two or More Sources in the Same Citation

List sources by the same author chronologically by publication year. List sources by different authors in alphabetical order by the authors' last names, separated by semicolons.

> While traditional forms of argument are warlike and agonistic, alternative models do exist (Foss & Foss, 1997; Makau, 1999).

10. Specific Parts of a Source

Use abbreviations (*p.*, *pt.*, and so on) in a parenthetical citation to name the part of a work you're citing. However, *chapter* is not abbreviated.

> Pinker (2003, p. 6) argued that his research yielded the opposite results.

> Pinker (2003, Chapter 6) argued that his research yielded the opposite results.

11. Online Document

To cite a source found on the Internet, use the author's name and date as you would for a print source, and indicate the chapter or figure of the document, as appropriate. If the source's publication date is unknown, use *n.d.* ("no date"). To document a quotation, include paragraph numbers if page numbers are unavailable. If an online document has no page or paragraph numbers, provide the heading of the section and the number of the paragraph that follows.

> Werbach argued convincingly that "despite the best efforts of legislators, lawyers, and computer programmers, spam has won. Spam is killing email" (2002, p. 1).

12. Email and Other Personal Communication

Cite any personal letters, email messages, electronic postings, telephone conversations, or personal interviews by giving the person's initial(s) and last name, the identification, and the date. Do not list email in the references list, and note that APA style uses a hyphen in the word *e-mail*.

> E. Ashdown (personal communication, March 9, 2003) supported these claims.

Content Notes

The APA recommends using content notes for material that will expand or supplement your argument but otherwise would interrupt the text. Indicate such notes in your text by inserting superscript numerals. Type the notes themselves on a separate page headed *Footnotes* (not underlined, italicized, or in quotation marks) centered at the top of the page. Double-space all entries. Indent the first line of each note five to seven spaces, and begin subsequent lines at the left margin.

TEXT WITH SUPERSCRIPT INDICATING A NOTE

Data related to children's preferences in books were instrumental in designing the questionnaire.[1]

NOTE

[1]Rudine Sims Bishop and members of the Reading Readiness Research Group provided helpful data.

List of References

The alphabetical list of sources cited in your text is called *References*. (If your instructor asks you to list everything you've read as background—not just the sources you cite—call the list *Bibliography*.) The list of references appears on a separate page or pages at the end of your paper, with the heading *References* (not underlined, italicized, or in quotation marks) centered one inch from the top of the page. Double-space after the heading, and begin your first entry. Double-space the entire list. For print sources, APA style specifies the treatment and placement of four basic elements—author, publication date, title, and publication information. Each element is followed by a period.

- *Author:* List all authors with last name first, and use only initials for first and middle names. Separate the names of multiple authors with commas, and use an ampersand (&) before the last author's name.
- *Publication date:* Enclose the publication date in parentheses. Use only the year for books and journals; use the year, a comma, and the month or month and day for magazines and newspapers. Do not abbreviate

the month. If a date is not given, put *n.d.* ("no date," not italicized) in the parentheses. Put a period after the parentheses.

● *Title:* Italicize titles and subtitles of books and periodicals. Do not enclose titles of articles in quotation marks. For books and articles, capitalize only the first word of the title and subtitle and any proper nouns or proper adjectives. Capitalize all major words in the title of a periodical.

● *Publication information:* For a book published in the United States, list the city of publication and state abbreviation. For books published outside the United States, identify city and country. Provide the publisher's name, dropping *Inc.*, *Co.*, or *Publishers.* If the state is already included within the publisher's name, do not include the postal abbreviation for the state. For a periodical, follow the periodical title with a comma, the volume number (italicized), the issue number (if provided) in parentheses and followed by a comma, and the inclusive page numbers of the article. For newspaper articles and for articles or chapters in books, include the abbreviation *p.* ("page") or *pp.* ("pages").

The following APA-style examples appear in a "hanging indent" format, in which the first line aligns on the left and the subsequent lines indent one-half inch or five spaces.

BOOKS

1. One Author

Jones, L. H. (2004). *William Clark and the shaping of the West.* New York, NY: Hill and Wang.

2. Two or More Authors

Steininger, M., Newell, J. D., & Garcia, L. (1984). *Ethical issues in psychology.* Homewood, IL: Dow Jones-Irwin.

3. Organization as Author

Use the word *Author* (neither underlined nor italicized) as the publisher when the organization is both the author and the publisher.

Linguistics Society of America. (2002). *Guidelines for using sign language interpreters.* Washington, DC: Author.

4. Unknown Author

National Geographic atlas of the world. (1999). Washington, DC: National
Geographic Society.

5. Book Prepared by an Editor

Hardy, H. H. (Ed.). (1998). *The proper study of mankind.* New York, NY: Farrar,
Straus.

6. Selection in a Book with an Editor

Villanueva, V. (1999). An introduction to social scientific discussions on class. In
A. Shepard, J. McMillan, & G. Tate (Eds.), *Coming to class: Pedagogy and
the social class of teachers* (pp. 262-277). Portsmouth, NH: Heinemann.

7. Translation

Perez-Reverte, A. (2002). *The nautical chart* (M. S. Peaden, Trans.). New York, NY:
Harvest. (Original work published 2000)

8. Edition Other Than the First

Wrightsman, L. (1998). *Psychology and the legal system* (3rd ed.). Newbury Park,
CA: Sage.

9. One Volume of a Multivolume Work

Will, J. S. (1921). *Protestantism in France* (Vol. 2). Toronto, Ontario, Canada:
University of Toronto Press.

10. Article in a Reference Work

Chernow, B., & Vattasi, G. (Eds.). (1993). Psychomimetic drug. In *The Columbia
encyclopedia* (5th ed., p. 2238). New York, NY: Columbia University Press.

If no author is listed, begin with the title.

11. Republication

Sharp, C. (1978). *History of Hartlepool.* Hartlepool, United Kingdom: Hartlepool
Borough Council. (Original work published 1816)

12. Government Document

U.S. Bureau of the Census. (2001). *Survey of women-owned business enterprises.* Washington, DC: Government Printing Office.

13. Two or More Works by the Same Author

List the works in chronological order of publication. Repeat the author's name in each entry.

Rose, M. (1984). *Writer's block: The cognitive dimension.* Carbondale: Southern Illinois University Press.

Rose, M. (1995). *Possible lives: The promise of public education in America.* Boston, MA: Houghton Mifflin.

PERIODICALS

14. Article in a Journal Paginated by Volume

Kirsch, G. E. (2002). Toward an engaged rhetoric of professional practice. *Journal of Advanced Composition, 22,* 414-423.

15. Article in a Journal Paginated by Issue

Carr, S. (2002). The circulation of Blair's Lectures. *Rhetoric Society Quarterly, 32*(4), 75-104.

16. Article in a Monthly Magazine

Baker, C. (2008, September). Master of the universe. *Wired, 16*(9), 134-141.

17. Article in a Newspaper

Nagourney, A. (2002, December 16). Gore rules out running in '04. *The New York Times,* pp. A1, A8.

18. Letter to the Editor or Editorial

Erbeta, R. (2008, December). Swiftboating George [Letter to the editor]. *Smithsonian, 39*(9), 10.

19. Unsigned Article

Guidelines issued on assisted suicide. (1998, March 4). *The New York Times*, p. A15.

20. Review

Avalona, A. (2008, August). [Review of the book *Weaving women's lives: Three generations in a Navajo family*, by L. Lamphere]. New Mexico, *86*(8), 40.

21. Published Interview

Shor, I. (1997). [Interview with A. Greenbaum]. *Writing on the Edge, 8*(2), 7-20.

22. Two or More Works by the Same Author in the Same Year

List two or more works by the same author published in the same year alphabetically by title (excluding *A*, *An*, or *The*), and place lowercase letters (*a*, *b*, etc.) after the dates.

Murray, F. B. (1983a). Equilibration as cognitive conflict. *Developmental Review, 3*, 54-61.

Murray, F. B. (1983b). Learning and development through social interaction. In L. Liben (Ed.), *Piaget and the foundations of knowledge* (pp. 176-201). Hillsdale, NJ: Erlbaum.

ELECTRONIC SOURCES

The following models are based on the APA's *Publication Manual* (6th edition). A change for handling electronic sources involves the use of a digital object identifier (DOI) when available (instead of a URL) to locate an electronic source. The DOI is a unique number assigned to an electronic text (article, book, or other item) and intended to give reliable access to it. A second change is that a date of retrieval is no longer necessary unless a source changes very frequently. The basic APA entry for most electronic sources should include the following elements:

- name of the author, editor, or compiler
- date of electronic publication or most recent update
- title of the work, document, or posting
- publication information, including the title, volume or issue number, and page numbers

- the DOI (digital object identifier—see above) of the document, if one is available
- a URL, only if a DOI is not available, with no angle brackets and no closing punctuation.

23. World Wide Web Site

To cite a whole site, give the address in a parenthetical reference. To cite a document from a Web site, include information as you would for a print document, followed by a note on its retrieval. Provide a date of retrieval only if the information is likely to change frequently.

American Psychological Association. (2000). DotComSense: Commonsense ways to protect your privacy and assess online mental health information. Retrieved from http://helping.apa.org/dotcomsense

Mullins, B. (1995). Introduction to Robert Hass. Readings in contemporary poetry at Dia Center for the Arts. Retrieved from http://www.diacenter.org/prg/poetry/95_96/intrhass.html

24. Article from an Online Periodical

For an article you read online, provide either a DOI or the URL of the periodical's home page preceded by *Retrieved from*.

Lambert, N. M., Graham, S. M., & Fincham, F. D. (2009). A prototype analysis of gratitude: Varieties of gratitude experiences. *Personality and Social Psychology Bulletin, 35,* 1193-1207. doi:10.1177/0146167209338071

Palmer, K. S. (2000, September 12). In academia, males under a microscope. *The Washington Post.* Retrieved from http://www.washingtonpost.com

25. Article or Abstract from a Database

For an article you find on a database, provide a DOI if one is available. If the online article does not have a DOI, locate the home page for the journal in which the article appears and provide that URL. You need not identify the database you have used.

Kennedy, C., & Covell, K. (2009). Violating the rights of the child through inadequate sexual health education. *International Journal of Children's Rights, 17*(1), 143-154. doi:10.1163/092755608X278939

Hayhoe, G. (2001). The long and winding road: Technology's future. *Technical Communication, 48*(2), 133-145. Retrieved from http://www.stc.org/pubs/techcommGeneral01.asp

26. Software or Computer Program

McAfee Office 2000. (Version 2.0) [Computer software]. (1999). Santa Clara, CA: Network Associates.

27. Online Government Document

Cite an online government document as you would a printed government work, adding the date of access and the URL. If you don't find a date, use *n. d.*

Finn, J. D. (1998, April). *Class size and students at risk: What is known? What is next?* Retrieved from United States Department of Education website http://www.ed.gov/pubs/ClassSize/title.html

28. Posting to a Discussion Group

Include an online posting in the references list only if you're able to retrieve the message from a mailing list's archive. Provide the author's name; the date of posting, in parentheses; and the subject line from the posting. Include any information that further identifies the message in square brackets. For a Listserv message, end with the retrieval statement, including the name of the list and the URL of the archived message.

Troike, R. C. (2001, June 21). Buttercups and primroses [Msg 8]. Message posted to the American Dialect Society's ADS-L electronic mailing list, archived at http://listserv.linguistlist.org/archives/ads-1.html

29. Newsgroup Posting

Include the author's name, the date and subject line of the posting, the access date, and the name of the newsgroup.

Wittenberg, E. (2001, July 11). Gender and the Internet [Msg 4]. Retrieved from news://comp.edu.composition

30. Email Message or Synchronous Communication

Because the APA stresses that any sources cited in your list of references must be retrievable by your readers, you shouldn't include entries for email messages or synchronous communications (MOOs, MUDs); instead, cite these sources in your text as forms of personal communication (see p. 589). And remember that you shouldn't quote from other people's email without asking their permission to do so.

OTHER SOURCES

31. Technical or Research Reports and Working Papers

Wilson, K. S. (1986). Palenque: *An interactive multimedia optical disc prototype for children* (Working Paper No. 2). New York: Center for Children and Technology, Bank Street College of Education.

32. Unpublished Paper Presented at a Meeting or Symposium

Welch, K. (2002, March). *Electric rhetoric and screen literacy.* Paper presented at the meeting of the Conference on College Composition and Communication, Chicago.

33. Unpublished Dissertation

Seward, D. E. (2008). *Civil voice in Elizabethan parliamentary oratory: The rhetoric and composition of speeches delivered at Westminster in 1566* (Unpublished doctoral dissertation). University of Texas at Austin, Austin, TX.

34. Poster Session

Mensching, G. (2002, May). *A simple, effective one-shot for disinterested students.* Poster session presented at the National LOEX Library Instruction Conference, Ann Arbor, MI.

35. Motion Picture, Video, or DVD

Jackson, P. (Director). (2003). *The lord of the rings: The return of the king.* [Motion picture]. Los Angeles: New Line Cinema.

36. Television Program, Single Episode

Imperioli, M. (Writer), & Buscemi, S. (Director). (2002, October 20). Everybody hurts [Television series episode]. In D. Chase (Executive producer), *The Sopranos.* New York: Home Box Office.

37. Sound Recording

Begin with the writer's name, followed by the date of copyright. Give the recording date at the end of the entry (in parentheses, after the period) if it's different from the copyright date.

> Ivey, A., Jr., & Sall, R. (1995). Rollin' with my homies [Recorded by Coolio]. On *Clueless* [CD]. Hollywood, CA: Capitol Records.

RESPOND •

1. The MLA and APA styles differ in several important ways, both for in-text citations and for lists of sources. You've probably noticed a few: the APA lowercases most words in titles and lists the publication date right after the author's name, whereas the MLA capitalizes most words and puts the publication date at the end of the works cited entry. More interesting than the details, though, is the reasoning behind the differences. Placing the publication date near the front of a citation, for instance, reveals a special concern for that information in the APA style. Similarly, the MLA's decision to capitalize titles isn't arbitrary: that style is preferred in the humanities for a reason. Find as many consistent differences between the MLA and APA styles as you can. Then, for each difference, try to discover the reasons these groups organize or present information in that way. The MLA and APA style manuals themselves may be of help. You might also begin by determining which academic disciplines subscribe to the APA style and which to the MLA.

2. Working with another person in your class, look for examples of the following sources: an article in a journal, a book, a film, a song, and a TV show. Then make a references page or works-cited entry for each one, using either MLA or APA style.

GLOSSARY

academic argument writing that is addressed to an audience well informed about the topic, that aims to convey a clear and compelling point in a somewhat formal style, and that follows agreed-upon conventions of usage, punctuation, and formats.

accidental condition in a definition, an element that helps to explain what's being defined but isn't essential to it. An accidental condition in defining a bird might be "ability to fly" because most, but not all, birds can fly. (See also *essential condition* and *sufficient condition*.)

ad hominem **argument** a fallacy of argument in which a writer's claim is answered by irrelevant attacks on his or her character.

analogy an extended comparison between something unfamiliar and something more familiar for the purpose of illuminating or dramatizing the unfamiliar. An analogy might, say, compare nuclear fission (less familiar) to a pool player's opening break (more familiar).

anaphora a figure of speech involving repetition, particularly of the same word at the beginning of several clauses.

antithesis the use of parallel structures to call attention to contrasts or opposites, as in *Some like it hot; some like it cold.*

antonomasia use of a title, epithet, or description in place of a name, as in *Your Honor* for *Judge.*

argument (1) a spoken, written, or visual text that expresses a point of view; (2) the use of evidence and reason to discover some version of the truth, as distinct from *persuasion*, the attempt to change someone else's point of view.

artistic appeal support for an argument that a writer creates based on principles of reason and shared knowledge rather than on facts and evidence. (See also *inartistic appeal*.)

assumption a belief regarded as true, upon which other claims are based.

assumption, cultural a belief regarded as true or commonsensical within a particular culture, such as the belief in individual freedom in American culture.

audience the person or persons to whom an argument is directed.

authority the quality conveyed by a writer who is knowledgeable about his or her subject and confident in that knowledge.

background the information a writer provides to create the context for an argument.

backing in Toulmin argument, the evidence provided to support a *warrant*.

bandwagon appeal a fallacy of argument in which a course of action is recommended on the grounds that everyone else is following it.

begging the question a fallacy of argument in which a claim is based on the very grounds that are in doubt or dispute: *Rita can't be the bicycle thief; she's never stolen anything.*

causal argument an argument that seeks to explain the effect(s) of a cause, the cause(s) of an effect, or a causal chain in which A causes B, B causes C, C causes D, and so on.

ceremonial argument an argument that deals with current values and addresses questions of praise and blame. Also called *epideictic*, ceremonial arguments include eulogies and graduation speeches.

character, appeal based on a strategy in which a writer presents an authoritative or credible self-image to convince an audience to accept a claim.

claim a statement that asserts a belief or truth. In arguments, most claims require supporting evidence. The claim is a key component in *Toulmin argument.*

classical oration a highly structured form of an argument developed in ancient Greece and Rome to defend or refute a thesis. The oration evolved to include six parts—*exordium, narratio, partitio, confirmatio, refutatio,* and *peroratio.*

confirmatio the fourth part of a classical oration, in which a speaker or writer offers evidence for the claim.

connotation the suggestions or associations that surround most words and extend beyond their literal meaning, creating associational effects.

Slender and *skinny* have similar meanings, for example, but carry different connotations, the former more positive than the latter.

context the entire situation in which a piece of writing takes place, including the writer's purpose(s) for writing; the intended audience; the time and place of writing; the institutional, social, personal, and other influences on the piece of writing; the material conditions of writing (whether it's, for instance, online or on paper, in handwriting or print); and the writer's attitude toward the subject and the audience.

conviction the belief that a claim or course of action is true or reasonable. In a proposal argument, a writer must move an audience beyond conviction to action.

credibility an impression of integrity, honesty, and trustworthiness conveyed by a writer in an argument.

criterion in evaluative arguments, the standard by which something is measured to determine its quality or value.

definition, argument of an argument in which the claim specifies that something does or doesn't meet the conditions or features set forth in a definition: *Pluto is not a major planet.*

deliberative argument an argument that deals with action to be taken in the future, focusing on matters of policy. Deliberative arguments include parliamentary debates and campaign platforms.

delivery the presentation of a spoken argument.

dogmatism a fallacy of argument in which a claim is supported on the grounds that it's the only conclusion acceptable within a given community.

either-or choice a fallacy of argument in which a complicated issue is misrepresented as offering only two possible alternatives, one of which is often made to seem vastly preferable to the other.

emotional appeal a strategy in which a writer tries to generate specific emotions (such as fear, envy, anger, or pity) in an audience to dispose it to accept a claim.

enthymeme in Toulmin argument, a statement that links a claim to a supporting reason: *The bank will fail* (claim) *because it has lost the support of its largest investors* (reason). In classical rhetoric, an enthymeme is a syllogism with one term understood but not stated: *Socrates is mortal because he is a human being.* (The understood term is: *All human beings are mortal.*)

epideictic argument see *ceremonial argument*.

equivocation a fallacy of argument in which a lie is given the appearance of truth, or in which the truth is misrepresented in deceptive language.

essential condition in a definition, an element that must be part of the definition but, by itself, isn't enough to define the term. An essential condition in defining a bird might be "winged": all birds have wings, yet wings alone don't define a bird since some insects and mammals also have wings. (See also *accidental condition* and *sufficient condition*.)

ethical appeal see *character, appeal based on*, and *ethos*.

ethnographic observation a form of field research involving close and extended observation of a group, event, or phenomenon; careful and detailed note-taking during the observation; analysis of the notes; and interpretation of that analysis.

ethos the self-image a writer creates to define a relationship with readers. In arguments, most writers try to establish an ethos that suggests authority and credibility.

evaluation, argument of an argument in which the claim specifies that something does or doesn't meet established criteria: *The Nikon D3x is the most sophisticated digital SLR camera currently available.*

evidence material offered to support an argument. See *artistic appeal* and *inartistic appeal*.

example, definition by a definition that operates by identifying individual examples of what's being defined: *sports car—Corvette, Viper, Miata, Boxster.*

exordium the first part of a classical oration, in which a speaker or writer tries to win the attention and goodwill of an audience while introducing a subject.

experimental evidence evidence gathered through experimentation; often evidence that can be quantified (for example, a survey of students before and after an election might yield statistical evidence about changes in their attitudes toward the candidates). Experimental evidence is frequently crucial to scientific arguments.

fact, argument of an argument in which the claim can be proved or disproved with specific evidence or testimony: *The winter of 1998 was the warmest on record for the United States.*

fallacy of argument a flaw in the structure of an argument that renders its conclusion invalid or suspect. See ad hominem *argument, bandwagon appeal, begging the question, dogmatism, either-or choice, equivocation, false authority, faulty analogy, faulty causality, hasty generalization,* non sequitur, *scare tactic, sentimental appeal, slippery slope,* and *straw man.*

false authority a fallacy of argument in which a claim is based on the expertise of someone who lacks appropriate credentials.

faulty analogy a fallacy of argument in which a comparison between two objects or concepts is inaccurate or inconsequential.

faulty causality a fallacy of argument making the unwarranted assumption that because one event follows another, the first event causes the second. Also called *post hoc, ergo propter hoc,* faulty causality forms the basis of many superstitions.

firsthand evidence data—including surveys, observations, personal interviews, etc.—collected and personally examined by the writer. (See also *secondhand evidence.*)

flashpoint see *fallacy of argument.*

forensic argument an argument that deals with actions that have occurred in the past. Sometimes called judicial arguments, forensic arguments include legal cases involving judgments of guilt or innocence.

formal definition a definition that identifies something first by the general class to which it belongs *(genus)* and then by the characteristics that distinguish it from other members of that class *(species): Baseball is a game* (genus) *played on a diamond by opposing teams of nine players who score runs by circling bases after striking a ball with a bat* (species).

genus in a definition, the general class to which an object or concept belongs: *baseball is a sport; green is a color.*

grounds in Toulmin argument, the evidence provided to support a claim and reason—that is, an *enthymeme.*

hard evidence support for an argument using facts, statistics, testimony, or other evidence the writer finds.

hasty generalization a fallacy of argument in which an inference is drawn from insufficient data.

hyperbole use of overstatement for special effect.

hypothesis an expectation for the findings of one's research or the conclusion to one's argument. Hypotheses must be tested against evidence, opposing arguments, and so on.

immediate reason the cause that leads directly to an effect, such as an automobile accident that results in an injury to the driver. (See also *necessary reason* and *sufficient reason*.)

inartistic appeal support for an argument using facts, statistics, eyewitness testimony, or other evidence the writer finds *rather than creates*. (See also *artistic appeal*.)

intended readers the actual, real-life people whom a writer consciously wants to address in a piece of writing.

invention the process of finding and creating arguments to support a claim.

inverted word order moving grammatical elements of a sentence out of their usual order (subject-verb-object/complement) for special effect, as in *Tired I was; sleepy I was not*.

invitational argument a term used by Sonja Foss to describe arguments that are aimed not at vanquishing an opponent but at inviting others to collaborate in exploring mutually satisfying ways to solve problems.

invoked readers the readers directly addressed or implied in a text, which may include some that the writer didn't consciously intend to reach. An argument that refers to *those who have experienced a major trauma*, for example, invokes all readers who have undergone this experience.

irony use of language that suggests a meaning in contrast to the literal meaning of the words.

line of argument a strategy or approach used in an argument. Argumentative strategies include appeals to the heart (emotional appeals), to character (ethical appeals), and to facts and reason (logical appeals).

logical appeal a strategy in which a writer uses facts, evidence, and reason to make audience members accept a claim.

metaphor a figure of speech that makes a comparison, as in *The ship was a beacon of hope*.

narratio the second part of a classical oration, in which a speaker or writer presents the facts of a case.

necessary reason a cause that must be present for an effect to occur; for example, infection with a particular virus is a necessary reason for the development of AIDS. (See also *immediate reason* and *sufficient reason*.)

non sequitur a fallacy of argument in which claims, reasons, or warrants fail to connect logically; one point doesn't follow from another: *If you're really my friend, you'll lend me five hundred dollars.*

operational definition a definition that identifies an object by what it does or by the conditions that create it: *A line is the shortest distance between two points.*

parallelism use of similar grammatical structures or forms for pleasing effect: *in the classroom, on the playground, and at the mall.*

partitio the third part of a classical oration, in which a speaker or writer divides up the subject and explains what the claim will be.

pathos, appeal to see *emotional appeal.*

peroratio the sixth and final part of a classical oration, in which a speaker or writer summarizes the case and moves the audience to action.

persuasion the act of seeking to change someone else's point of view.

precedents actions or decisions in the past that have established a pattern or model for subsequent actions. Precedents are particularly important in legal cases.

premise a statement or position regarded as true and upon which other claims are based.

propaganda an argument advancing a point of view without regard to reason, fairness, or truth.

proposal argument an argument in which a claim is made in favor of or opposing a specific course of action: *Sport-utility vehicles should have to meet the same fuel economy standards as passenger cars.*

purpose the goal of an argument. Purposes include entertaining, informing, convincing, exploring, and deciding, among others.

qualifiers words or phrases that limit the scope of a claim: *usually; in a few cases; under these circumstances.*

qualitative argument an argument of evaluation that relies on nonnumerical criteria supported by reason, tradition, precedent, or logic.

quantitative argument an argument of evaluation that relies on criteria that can be measured, counted, or demonstrated objectively.

reason in writing, a statement that expands a claim by offering evidence to support it. The reason may be a statement of fact or another claim. In *Toulmin argument*, a *reason* is attached to a *claim* by a *warrant*, a statement that establishes the logical connection between claim and supporting reason.

rebuttal an answer that challenges or refutes a specific claim or charge. Rebuttals may also be offered by writers who anticipate objections to the claims or evidence they offer.

rebuttal, conditions of in Toulmin argument, potential objections to an argument. Writers need to anticipate such conditions in shaping their arguments.

refutatio the fifth part of a classical oration, in which a speaker or writer acknowledges and refutes opposing claims or evidence.

reversed structures a figure of speech that involves the inversion of clauses: *What is good in your writing is not original; what is original is not good.*

rhetoric the art of persuasion. Western rhetoric originated in ancient Greece as a discipline to prepare citizens for arguing cases in court.

rhetorical analysis an examination of how well the components of an argument work together to persuade or move an audience.

rhetorical questions questions posed to raise an issue or create an effect rather than to get a response: *You may well wonder, "What's in a name?"*

Rogerian argument an approach to argumentation based on the principle, articulated by psychotherapist Carl Rogers, that audiences respond best when they don't feel threatened. Rogerian argument stresses trust and urges those who disagree to find common ground.

scare tactic a fallacy of argument presenting an issue in terms of exaggerated threats or dangers.

scheme a figure of speech that involves a special arrangement of words, such as inversion.

secondhand evidence any information taken from outside sources, including library research and online sources. (See also *firsthand evidence*.)

sentimental appeal a fallacy of argument in which an appeal is based on excessive emotion.

simile a comparison that uses *like* or *as*: *My love is like a red, red rose* or *I wandered lonely as a cloud.*

slippery slope a fallacy of argument exaggerating the possibility that a relatively inconsequential action or choice today will have serious adverse consequences in the future.

species in a definition, the particular features that distinguish one member of a *genus* from another: *Baseball is a sport* (genus) *played on a diamond by teams of nine players* (species).

spin a kind of political advocacy that makes any fact or event, however unfavorable, serve a political purpose.

stance the writer's attitude toward the topic and the audience.

stasis theory in classical rhetoric, a method for coming up with appropriate arguments by determining the nature of a given situation: *a question of fact*; *of definition*; *of quality*; or *of policy*.

straw man a fallacy of argument in which an opponent's position is misrepresented as being more extreme than it actually is, so that it's easier to refute.

sufficient condition in a definition, an element or set of elements adequate to define a term. A sufficient condition in defining God, for example, might be "supreme being" or "first cause." No other conditions are necessary, though many might be made. (See also *accidental condition* and *essential condition.*)

sufficient reason a cause that alone is enough to produce a particular effect; for example, a particular level of smoke in the air will set off a smoke alarm. (See also *immediate reason* and *necessary reason.*)

syllogism in formal logic, a structure of deductive logic in which correctly formed major and minor premises lead to a necessary conclusion:

Major premise All human beings are mortal.

Minor premise Socrates is a human being.

Conclusion Socrates is mortal.

testimony a personal experience or observation used to support an argument.

thesis a sentence that succinctly states a writer's main point.

Toulmin argument a method of informal logic first described by Stephen Toulmin in *The Uses of Argument* (1958). Toulmin argument describes the key components of an argument as the *claim*, *reason*, *warrant*, *backing*, and *grounds*.

trope a figure of speech that involves a change in the usual meaning or signification of words, such as *metaphor*, *simile*, and *analogy*.

understatement a figure of speech that makes a weaker statement than a situation seems to call for. It can lead to powerful or to humorous effects.

values, appeal to a strategy in which a writer invokes shared principles and traditions of a society as a reason for accepting a claim.

warrant in *Toulmin argument*, the statement (expressed or implied) that establishes the logical connection between a claim and its supporting reason.

Claim	Don't eat that mushroom;
Reason	it's poisonous.
Warrant	What is poisonous should not be eaten.

ACKNOWLEDGMENTS

Chapter-Opening Art

Part 1 (left to right): © Brandon D. Cole/Corbis; AP Photo/Alex Brandon; AP Photo/ Office de Tourisme de Chartres; Desmond Kwande/AFP/Getty Images; AP Photo/ Seth Wenig.
Part 2 (left to right): Imaginechina via AP Images; © Warner Bros./Courtesy Everett Collection; Courtesy of Reuben H. Fleet Science Center; AP Photo/PA, Fiona Hanson; ©Foodcollection/age footstock.
Part 3 (left to right): © Peter Foley/Pool/epa/Corbis; Louisa Gouliamaki/AFP/Getty Images; AP Photo/Alex Brandon; © Carlos Barria/Reuters/Corbis; Fox Broadcasting/ Photofest © & ™ Fox.
Part 4 (left to right): Phil Cole/Getty Images; Juan Castillo/AFP/Getty Images; Fabrizio Costantini/The New York Times/Redux; © Tim Greyhavens/IPNstock.com; AP Photo/Ron Frehm.

Text

Daniel Ben-Ami. Excerpt from "Why People Hate Fat Americans." From *Spiked* (the London-based independent online publication), September 9, 2005. Copyright © *spiked* 2000–2009. All rights reserved. Reprinted by permission. www .spikedonline.com.
Michael Benson. "Send It Somewhere Special." From *The Washington Post*, Outlook section, July 13, 2008 issue. Copyright © 2008 by Washington Post Writers Group. Reproduced with permission of Washington Post Writers Group in the format Textbook by Copyright Clearance Center.
Richard Bernstein. "The Days After: A View from Abroad." From *The New York Times*, New York Times Blog Section, September 4, 2005 issue. Copyright © 2005 The New York Times. All rights reserved. Used by permission and protected by the Copyright Laws of the United States. The printing, copying, redistribution, or retransmission of the material without express written permission is prohibited.
Derek Bok. "Protecting Freedom of Expression at Harvard." Originally published in *The Boston Globe*, May 25, 1991. Copyright © 1991. Reprinted by permission of the author.
David Brower. Excerpts from "Let the River Run Through It." From *Sierra Magazine* (March/April 1997) by The New York Times Company. Reprinted with permission.
"Character and the Primaries" chart. From Journalism.org, May 29, 2008, and the Project for Excellence in Journalism of the Pew Research Center. © 2008–2009 Project for Excellence in Journalism. Reprinted by permission.
Colin A. Carter and Henry I. Miller. "The Hidden Costs of Corn-Based Ethanol." Opening of the article from *The Christian Science Monitor*, May 21, 2007 edition. Copyright © 2007, The Christian Science Monitor. Reprinted by permission of the publisher. All rights reserved.
David Cole. "What to Do about Torturers." Excerpt from David Cole's review of *Torture Team: Rumsfeld's Memo and the Betrayal of American Values* by Philippe

Langston Hughes. "Harlem (2)" ["What happens to a dream deferred . . ."], from *The Collected Poems of Langston Hughes* by Langston Hughes, edited by Arnold Rampersad with David Roessel, Associate Editor. Copyright © 1994 by the Estate of Langston Hughes. Used by permission of Alfred A. Knopf, a division of Random House, Inc.

Charles Isherwood. "The View From Uptown: American Dreaming to a Latin Beat." From *The New York Times*, March 10, 2008 issue. Copyright © 2008 The New York Times. All rights reserved. Used by permission and protected by the Copyright Laws of the United States. The printing, copying, redistribution, or retransmission of the material without express written permission is prohibited.

Armen Keteyian. Excerpt from "Bats Should Crack, Not Skulls." From *Sporting News*, June 24, 2002. Copyright © 2002 by Armen Keteyian. Reprinted by permission of the author.

Martin Luther King Jr. Excerpt from "I Have a Dream" speech. Copyright © 1963 Dr. Martin Luther King Jr.; copyright renewed 1991 Coretta Scott King. Reprinted by arrangement with the Heirs to the Estate of Martin Luther King Jr., c/o Writers House as agent for the proprietor, New York, NY.

Michael Lassell. "How to Watch Your Brother Die." Copyright © 1985 by Michael Lassell. Reprinted with the permission of the author.

Yiyun Li. Excerpt from "Passing Through." From *The New York Times Magazine* September 5, 2005 issue. Copyright © 2005 by The New York Times. All rights reserved. Reprinted by permission and protected by the Copyright Laws of the United States. The printing, copying, redistribution, or retransmission of the material without express written permission is prohibited.

James Lindgren. Excerpt from a review of "Arming America" by Michael Bellesile. First published in the *Yale Law Review*, vol. 111 (June 2002). Reprinted by permission of The Yale Law Journal Company and William S. Hein Company.

Myriam Marquez. "Why and When We Speak Spanish." Originally published in the *Orlando Sentinel*, June 29, 1999 issue. Copyright © 1999 Orlando Sentinel. Reproduced with permission of the Orlando Sentinel in the format Textbook via Copyright Clearance Center.

Cathy Newman. Excerpt from "Why Are We So Fat?" From *National Geographic* magazine, August 2004. Copyright © Cathy Newman/National Geographic Image Collection. Reprinted with permission of National Geographic Society.

Michael Osofsky. Excerpt from "The Psychological Experience of Security Officers Who Work with Executions." From *Stanford Undergraduate Research Journal* (May 2002). Reprinted with permission of the author in the format Textbook via Copyright Clearance Center.

Lynn Peril. Excerpt from "Introduction." From *Pink Think: Becoming a Woman in Many Uneasy Lessons* by Lynn Peril. Copyright © 2002 by Lynn Peril. Used by permission of W.W. Norton & Company.

Mark Pytlik. Excerpt from review of M.I.A.'s album, *Kala*. From Pitchforkmedia .com. Reprinted by permission of Pitchfork Media, Inc. All rights reserved. www.pitchforkmedia.com/article/record_review/44983-kala.

Elisabeth Rosenthal. "Stinging Tentacles Offer Hint of Oceans' Decline." From *The New York Times*, August 3, 2008 issue. Copyright 2008 The New York Times Co. All rights reserved. Used by permission and protected by the Copyright Laws of the

Illustrations

Redux; p. 34: Evelyn Hockstein/Polaris Images; p. 37: www.bumperart.com; p. 39: Courtesy of www.adbusters.com; p. 41: AP Photo/Alex Brandon; p. 42: (l) Cover from *Rolling Stone*, March 30, 2008. Photo by Tim O'Brien © Rolling Stone LLC 2009/ All Rights Reserved. Reprinted by Permission; (r) Drawing by Barry Blitt, *The New Yorker* Magazine © Conde Nast Publications; p. 43: Courtesy of www.adbusters .com; p. 47: From *Newsweek*, May 1, 2006, © 2006 Newsweek, Inc. All rights reserved. Used by permission and protected by the Copyright Laws of the United States. The printing, copying, redistribution, or retransmission of the Material without express written permission is prohibited; p. 50: (l) Courtesy of www.bumperart .com; (r) Courtesy of www.cafepress.com; p. 53: © Uli Deck/epa/Corbis; p. 54: AP Photo/Ajit Solanki; p. 50: (t) www.globalcompact.org; (r) courtesy of www .globalcompactcritics.net and www.somo.nl; Photo by Meet the Press via Getty Images; Norbert Von Der Groben/Contra Costa Times/Newscom; p. 61: (c) Paramount Classics/courtesy Everett Collection; p. 63: © Kim Ludbrook/epa/Corbis; p. 68: (l-r) © Kimberly White/Reuters/Corbis; Jay Laprete/AP Photos/Wide World; Brendan Smialowski/Getty Images for Meet The Press; © Ted Soqui/Corbis; p. 70: AP Photo/ Elise Amendola; p. 71: Poster courtesy of Despair, Inc; Photo © Ancil Nance/Getty Images; p. 72: © Sepah News/Handout/Document Iran/Corbis; p. 73: © 2002 CBS Worldwide Inc./Photofest; p. 80: Michelle Healy and Sam Ward for USA *Today*; p. 82: © Brandon D. Cole/Corbis; p. 89: AP Photo/Seth Wenig; p. 92: AP/Photo Mark Stahl; p. 96: (l) Robert Galbraith/Reuters/Landov; (r) Dimitrios Kambouris/WireImage/ Getty Images; p. 99: Courtesy of www.stickergiant.com; p. 100: Courtesy of Faye M. Anderson, Citizen Journalist; p. 102: Beth Hall/Bloomberg News/Landov; p. 104: Texas Dept. of Transportation/Sherry Matthews Advocacy Marketing; p. 108: © Denis Balibouse/Reuters/Corbis; p. 112: Shelley Eades/San Francisco Chronicle; p. 113–114: Copyright © Zombie; p. 118: Steve Liss/Time & Life Pictures/Getty Images; p. 121: Courtesy of Milena Ateya; p. 134: (t) TBWA Hunt Lascaris; p. 135: Illustration Credit: Tami Tolpa; p. 137: Adapted with permission of International Headache Society; p. 140: Erich Lessing/Art Resource, NY; p. 145: Rick Nease/MCT/ Landov; p. 150: Courtesy of Claire Liu; p. 155: © Bettmann/Corbis; p. 172: © The Art Archive/Corbis; p. 177: Courtesy of The Everett Collection; p. 179: AP images; p. 181: (t) Courtesy of wecansolveit.org; (b) www.AmericanSolutions.com; p. 188: *Mushrooms: An Introduction to Familiar North American Species*, text by James Kavanagh, illustrations by Raymond Leung. Used by permission of Waterford Press; p. 192: Courtesy NASA/JPL-Caltech; p. 198: Timothy A. Clary/AFP/Getty Images; p. 209: Ivory-billed Woodpecker, from *Birds of America*, 1829 (colored engraving) (see 195912 for detail), Audubon, John James (1785–1851)/Victoria & Albert Museum, London, UK/The Bridgeman Art Library; p. 213: © Warner Bros./Courtesy Everett Collection; p. 214: Courtesy USGS, National Earthquake Information Center; p. 216: Michael Newman/PhotoEdit; p. 217: (l) Marc Lester/MCT/Landov; (r) William Thomas Cain/Getty Images; p. 222: © Corbis; p. 224: Cover of FUN HOME: A Family Tragicomic by Alison Bechdel. Jacket art copyright © 2006 Alison Bechdel. Reprinted by permission of Houghton Mifflin Harcourt Publishing Company. All rights reserved; p. 226: U.S. Census Bureau; p. 227: Imaginechina via AP Images; p. 235: Mel Evans/AP Images; p. 236: Courtesy of Michael Osofsky; p. 250: Joshua Lott/ Reuters/Landov; p. 254: Brad Roberts www.lowdiameter.com; p. 250: Steve Liss; p. 255: (t) www.gaypatriot.com; (b) Robin Nelson/PhotoEdit; p. 256: Emile Wamsteker/General Motors via Getty Images; p. 257: www.cartoonstock.com;

p. 275: (t) courtesy of Graham Trievel; (b) Gilpatrick McDermott; p. 259: © Foodcollection/age footstock; p. 277: Flower Films/Gaylord/Adam Fields Production/ The Kobal Collection/Robinette, Dale; p. 285: Sara Krulwich/The New York Times/ Redux; p. 287: Theo Wargo/WireImage/Getty Images; p. 292: Courtesy of Hulu.com. Reprinted by permission; p. 294: Courtesy of www.icasualties.org; p. 296: © Warner Bros./Courtesy Everett Collection; p. 298: Index Stock/Photolibrary; p. 299: Courtesy of Apple; p. 300: © Cho Taussig/Courtesy Everett Collection; p. 301: Jim Dyson/Getty Images; p. 313: Courtesy of Jack Chung; p. 321: Jeff Gentner/Getty Images; p. 327: Linda Nylind/Guardian News & Media Ltd 2007; p. 333: AP Photo/Paul Sakuma; p. 337: Karen Kasmauski/National Geographic/Getty Images; p. 345: Courtesy of Helen Garvy and Shire Press and Films; p. 346: Photo courtesy IISD/Earth Negotiations Bulletin; p. 349: AP Photo/Matt Slocum; p. 351: Courtesy of the Everett Collection; p. 355: (t) Peter McDonald, Australian Demographic and Social Research Institute, The Australian National University; p. 369: Dani Cardona/Reuters/Corbis; p. 375: Lester Lefkowitz/Getty Images; p. 376: (t) From *Grand Canyon Adventure: River at Risk*, courtesy MacGillivray Freeman Films; (b) Kevin Moloney/The New York Times/Redux; p. 377: AP Photo/Paul Sakuma; p. 379: Ethan Miller/Getty Images; p. 380: Ron Sanford/Photo Researchers; p. 385: AP Photo/Mary Altaffer; p. 388: AP Photo/PA, Fiona Hanson; p. 390: Courtesy of Xanadu Meadowlands; p. 391: AP Photo/Mike Derer; p. 399: Courtesy of Manasi Deshpande; p. 420: (tl) Picturenet/ Veer; (tr) DesignPics Inc., Index Stock/Photolibrary; (b) Collage Photography/Veer; p. 423: Warner Brothers/Photofest; p. 428: Henny Rae Abrams/Getty Images; p. 436: © Peter Foley/Pool/epa/Corbis; p. 440: AP Photo/Milk Processors of America; p. 443: Courtesy The White House; p. 444: © Bettmann/Corbis; Mick Roessler/Photolibrary; p. 445: National Postal Museum; p. 447: Courtesy of the Campaign for Tobacco-Free Kids; p. 448: © Rob Bluey; p. 449: National Portrait Gallery, Smithsonian Institution/ Art Resource, NY; p. 450: © Carlos Barria/Reuters/Corbis; p. 451: United Colors of Benetton/Photo by James Mollison; p. 453: NASA; p. 454: Louisa Gouliamaki/AFP/ Getty Images; p. 455: AP Photo/Elise Amendola; p. 456: (l) AP Photo/Alex Brandon; (m) Courtesy McDonalds; (r) Louisiana Office of Tourism; p. 459: Ron Kimball Stock; p. 461: Mary Kate Denny/Photo Edit; p. 462: U.S. Census Bureau; p. 464: National Portrait Gallery London; p. 469: (l) U.S. Department of Agriculture; (t) http://www .dailykos.com; (br) Comstock/Punchstock; p. 472: AP/Wide World Photos; p. 474: Fox Broadcasting/Photofest © & ™ Fox; p. 478–482: © Frank Miller; p. 488: Courtesy of Gawker Media; p. 498: Kanye West/Mascotte Holdings, LLC.; p. 502: AP Photo/ Mark Humphrey; p. 505: Ryan Collerd/The NY Times/Redux; p. 506–507: Human Rights Watch; p. 512: AP Photo/Ron Frehm; p. 519: Office of National Drug Control Policy; p. 521: © Tim Greyhavens/IPNstock.com; p. 527: Courtesy of Google, Inc. Reprinted with permission; p. 531: (t) Al Messerschmidt/Getty Images; (b) V.J. Lovero/Sports Illustrated/Getty Images; p. 538: Phil Cole/Getty Images; p. 540: Courtesy www.adbusters.org; p. 545: (l) Gene Hunt/Flickr; (m) andi licious/Flickr; (r) pedist/Flickr; p. 551: AP Photo/Reed Saxon; p. 553: (l) Printed with permission from *Popular Science* ® Bonnier Corporation. Copyright 2009. All rights reserved. (r) Reprinted with permission from *American Journal of Physics*, vol. 6, no. 7, July 2008. American Association of Physics Teachers; p. 558: (t) (m) Courtesy of www .mediamatters.org; (b) U.S. Department of State; p. 560: Juan Castillo/AFP/Getty Images; p. 564: Fabrizio Costantini/The New York Times/Redux; p. 586: Slate.com. Reprinted with permission.

INDEX

abstracts
  citing, 595
  for journal articles, 236
academic arguments, 133–69
  and causal claims, 342
  definitions in, 261–62
  developing, 141–46
  and evaluations, 288–89
  examples of, 134–39, 150–69
  features of, 15, 139
  issues explored in, 133–39,
    141–42
  and proposals, 386
  reviewing, 146
  visuals for, 134, 140, 144–46
ad hominem arguments, 525–26
advertisements
  as academic arguments, 134
  citing, 583
  credibility, establishing, 102
  as emotional appeals, 104
  as persuasive, 7, 10
  scare tactics, 519
  sentimental appeals, 521–22
  visual elements, analyzing, 447,
    451
afterword, citing, 574
Albrecht, Glenn, 261–62
analogies
  in causal arguments, 351–52

elements of, 430–31
  logical appeals based on, 90
anaphora, 438
Angelou, Maya, 425
anthology, work from, citing, 568,
  573
antithesis, 437–38
antonomasia, 436–37
APA style, 586–98
  content notes, 590
  electronic sources, 589, 594–97
  References, 590–98
  in-text citations, 587–89
appeals
  emotional, 33, 38–51
  ethical, 34, 52–68
  logical, 34–35, 69–93
arguments. *See also* specific types
  of arguments and specific
  topics
  academic, 133–69
  audiences for, 27–32
  causal, 24–25, 335–72
  cultural contexts, 32–33
  definitional, 22–23, 249–83
  emotional appeals, 38–51
  ethical appeals, 52–68
  evaluations, 23–25, 284–334
  evidence, 493–513
  factual, 21–22, 208–48

fallacies of, 515–35
images with. *See* visuals
logical appeals, 69–93
occasions for, 15–21
persuasion compared to, 7
presentation methods, 466–89
proposals, 25–26, 373–414
purposes of, 5–15
rhetorical analysis, 95–130
rhetorical situations for, 35
structure of, 170–207
style, 417–40
visual, 441–65
Aristotle
argument classification by, 15
enthymemes, 85–87
on logical appeals, 69–70, 74,
84–85, 109
Armstrong, Neil, 437
artistic appeals, 70
art works, citing, 582
asterisks, 425–26
Ateya, Milena, "Curse and a
Blessing, A," 121–23
audience, 27–32
for academic arguments, 143
appeals to, 33–35
context, considering, 30–32
culture and addressing.
See culture
emotional appeal as connection
to, 44–45
and evidence used, 511–12
intended and invoked, 28–30
objections of. *See* objections to
arguments
pronouns, addressing with,
30, 63
for proposals, 380
real, 30
for rhetorical analysis, 101–3
and visual arguments, 448–49
authority of writer. *See* credibility

authors, citing
APA style, 587–89, 591–92
MLA style, 567–70, 572–74
backing, in Toulmin argument,
193–94, 199
bandwagon appeals, 522
Barnes, Fred, 532–33
Barnes, Susan B., 220
Barry, Dave, 49, 348, 438
Barzeski, Erik J., 533
Becker, Alton L., 177
begging the question, 529
Bell, Darrin, 10
Belle, Deborah, 31
Ben-Ami, Daniel, 10–11
Bennett, Lerone, Jr., 438
Benson, Michael, "Send It
Somewhere Special," 411–14
Bernstein, Richard, 59
bibliographic notes, MLA style, 571
blogs, 488–89
Bok, Derek, "Protecting Freedom
of Expression at Harvard,"
118–20
books, citing
MLA style, 572–74
online books, 578
boxes, 460
Branson, Richard, 388–89
Brower, David, 374–75
Brown, Tiffany Lee, 430
Buckley, William F., Jr., 424
"Burden of Laughter: Chris Rock
Fights Ignorance His Way,
The" (Chung), 313–25
Burke, Timothy, 105–6
Bush, George W., 49, 517

"Call to Improve Campus
Accessibility for the Mobility
Impaired, A" (Deshpande),
399–410
captions, for visuals, 563–64

Carson, Rachel, 341, 346
Carter, Colin A., 340
cartoons, citing, 583
causal arguments, 335–72
    categories of, 338–43
    developing, 348–55
    examples of, 365–72
    features of, 343–48, 356
    issues explored in, 335–37, 357
    reviewing, 360–62
    visuals for, 340, 345–47, 349,
        354–55
    writing, guidelines for, 357–62
cause and effect
    in academic arguments, 342
    examining. *See* causal
        arguments
    knowing, value of, 24–25
CD-ROM, citing, 580
ceremonial arguments, 18–20, 287
chapter of book, citing, 573, 589, 592
character
    arguments based on. *See* ethical
        appeals
    visual arguments based on,
        455–58
charts
    citing, 583
    as visuals, 461–62
Chavez, Linda, 87–88
"China: The Prizes and Pitfalls of
    Progress" (Lan Xue), 164–69
Chisholm, Latisha, 19–20
Chung, Jack, "Burden of Laughter:
    Chris Rock Fights Ignorance
    His Way, The," 313–25
Churchill, Winston, 40–41
Cicero, 172
circumstantial evidence, 512–13
claims
    in academic arguments, 142
    of authority, in ethical appeals,
        57–59

in causal arguments, 348–50,
    358–59, 360–61
in definitional arguments,
    260–61, 263–65, 269–72
in evaluations, 297, 300–301,
    306–8
in factual arguments, 221–23,
    228, 232
features of, 182–83
in proposals, 383–84, 393, 395
qualifiers to, 195–96, 222,
    300–301
in rhetorical analysis, 107–10,
    124–25, 127–28
support of. *See* evidence
in Toulmin argument, 182–84,
    199, 203, 204
classical oration, 172–75
    example of, 174–75
    structure of, 173–74
climactic order, in oral and
    multimedia presentations,
    475–76
Cloud, John, 25–26
Cole, David, 288–89
collaboration, acknowledging,
    547
colloquial terms, 419
colons, 424–25
color, 453–55, 457, 477
common knowledge, 544
common sense, 70
Conarroe, Joel, 425
concrete and specific words, 419
conditions of rebuttal
    credibility established with,
        63–64
    Toulmin argument, 196–99
conference proceedings, citing, 575
connotation, 419
content notes, APA style, 590
context
    and audience, 30–32

context (*continued*)
  cultural. *See* culture
  rhetorical situation, 35
convince, arguments to, 9–10
copyright and permissions
  legal aspects, 537, 541
  online sources, 463, 545–46
  visuals, 463, 541, 564
corporate authors, citing, 568, 572,
    588, 591
Costas, Bob, 49, 302
Cottle, Michelle, 434–35
credibility
  of authors, evaluating, 552
  and claims, 183–84
  and credentials of writer, 58–59
  cultural contexts, 64
  and documenting sources, 144,
    537–38
  establishing in ethical appeals,
    59–64
  and humor, 59–60
  losing, 70, 72–73
  and personal experience, 83–84
  reader objections, anticipating,
    198
  and respecting readers, 101–3
  and style, 111, 116
  and tone, 63–64, 106
  and visuals, 6, 9–10, 13–14, 61,
    102, 303, 456, 558–59
criteria, for evaluations, 289–91,
    297–300
Croal, N'Gai, 504
"Cultural Stress Linked to Suicide"
    (Hardin), 365–68
culture
  of audience, considering, 28–30
  and class participation, 470
  credibility, establishing with,
    58–59
  and ethical appeals, 64–65
  and evidence, 510–11

  norms of, recognizing, 32–33
  personal experience in
    arguments, 504
  plagiarism, concept of, 547
  shared, and logical appeals,
    87–89
  sources, identifying, 563
  and structure of arguments, 205
  and style, 432
"Curse and a Blessing, A" (Ateya),
    121–23

dashes, 425
data. *See* facts
databases
  citing, 579, 595
  library, 505, 508
Davis, Paul, 449
Dean, Craig R., 382–83, 387
debates, classical oration, 172–75
decision-making, arguments to aid,
    12–13
Declaration of Independence,
    174–75
deductive reasoning, 84, 171
definitional arguments, 249–83
  developing, 260–65
  examples of, 276–83
  features of, 22–23, 265–67
  issues explored in, 250–55, 268
  reviewing, 271–73
  types of, 256–60
  visuals for, 253–55, 265–66
  writing, guidelines for, 268–73
definitions
  in academic arguments, 261–62
  in causal arguments, 344
  crafting, 263–64
  by example, 258–59
  formal, 256–57
  operational, 257–58
degree, logical appeals based on,
    88–90

deliberative arguments, 17–18

Denby, David, 424, 430

Dershowitz, Alan M., "Testing Speech Codes," 201–2

Deshpande, Manasi, "Call to Improve Campus Accessibility for the Mobility Impaired, A," 399–410

design features. *See also* visuals
    academic arguments, 145–46
    character reflected in, 456–58
    color, 453–55, 457
    conventions, following, 458–59
    evaluations, 302–3, 310
    factual arguments, 226–27
    in oral and multimedia presentations, 477
    organization of, 459–60
    print presentations, 467–68
    proposals, 388–89
    visual arguments, 449–51
    Web sites, 487

diagrams, 461

Dickens, Charles, 225

dictionaries, definitions, bias in, 253

digital object identifier (DOI), 594–95

Dilulio, John J., Jr., 76

discussion group posting, citing, 578–79, 596

dissertations, citing, 580, 597

documentation of sources
    for academic arguments, 144
    APA style, 586–98
    credibility strengthened by, 144, 537–38
    exclusions from, 544
    material requiring, 544
    MLA style, 567–85
    visuals, 563–64

Dodick, David W., 135–36

dogmatism, 524–25

Dorresteijn, Joop, 503

Douglass, Frederick, 178

Dowd, Maureen, 425

Dowdle, Hillarie, 134

drawings, 461

Dreher, Rod, 81–82

Drum, Kevin, 116

Dubner, Stephen J., 215

DVDs, citing, 597

edited books, citing, 573

editions of works, citing, 574, 592

editorials, citing, 576, 593

editors, citing, 573, 592

Ehrenreich, Ben, 17

either-or choices, 517–18, 520

electronic sources. *See* online sources

ellipsis marks, 561

email messages, citing, 579, 589, 596–97

emoticons, 426

emotional appeals, 38–51
    arguments, sustaining with, 46–48, 103–4
    audience, connecting to, 44–45
    fallacies of, 516–22
    features of, 33, 40–43
    humor in, 48–50
    rhetorical analysis based on, 103–5
    using, 50
    visuals for, 34, 39, 42–43, 46–47, 104, 108, 445, 447, 453

enthymemes, 85–87, 171, 185, 188–89

epideictic arguments, 18–20, 287

equivocation, 530–31

ethical appeals, 52–68
    authority, claiming, 57–59
    credibility, establishing, 59–64
    cultural contexts, 64
    fallacies of, 523–26
    features of, 34, 53–57

motives in, 65–67
rhetorical analysis based on,
    105–6
visuals for, 54–55, 61
ethnographic observation, in causal
    arguments, 352–53
ethos. See ethical appeals
evaluations, 284–334
    and academic arguments,
        288–89
    criteria of, 289–91, 297–300
    developing, 297–304
    examples of, 313–34
    features of, 23–25, 304
    issues explored in, 285–88, 305
    qualitative and quantitative,
        292–97
    reviewing, 304, 308–10
    visuals for, 294, 303
    writing, guidelines for, 305–10
evidence, 493–513
    for academic arguments, 143–44
    audience, considering, 511–12
    backing, 193–94
    in causal arguments, 350, 352,
        361
    circumstantial, 512–13
    cultural contexts, 510–11
    for definitional arguments,
        264–65, 272
    in evaluations, 297, 301–2
    experiments as, 502–3
    facts as, 76–77
    in factual arguments, 215–16,
        223–25, 232
    hard, 69–75, 216, 292
    interviews to obtain, 498–99
    library sources, 505, 508–9
    in logical appeals, 69–84
    observations to obtain, 496–98
    online sources, 509–10
    organizing, 513
    personal experience as, 503–4

in proposals, 387, 396
questionnaires, 500–502
in rhetorical analysis, 109–10
and rhetorical situation, 494–96
statistics as, 78–79
surveys and polls as, 79–82
testimonies and narratives as,
    82–83
in Toulmin argument, 184–85,
    192–94, 199, 204
visuals as, 502, 506–7
example, definition by, 258–59
exclamation points, 424
experiments, 502–3
exploratory arguments, 11–12

facts
    arguments based on. *See* factual
        arguments; logical appeals
    as evidence, 76–77
    in factual arguments, 220
    visual arguments based on,
        459–63
factual arguments, 208–48
    developing, 217–25
    examples of, 236–48
    features of, 21, 227–28
    issues explored in, 211–13
    reviewing, 232–33
    visuals for, 214, 226–27
    writing, guidelines for, 229–33
Fainuru, Steve, 499
fair-use, 545
fallacies, 515–35
    of emotional arguments,
        516–22
    of ethical arguments, 523–26
    of logical arguments, 526–34
Fallows, James, 11
false authority, appeals to, 523–24
faulty analogy, 533–34
faulty causality, 527–29
feasibility, in proposals, 387

field research
  evaluating, 555
  types of, 352–53, 496–503
figurative language, 426–37
  schemes, 427, 437–39
  tropes, 428–37
  use in arguments, 426–27
films, citing, 581, 597
firsthand evidence, 496–504
font size and type, 145, 418, 456–57, 477
forensic arguments, 16–17
foreword, citing, 574
formal definitions, 256–57
formality, level of, and culture, 432
formal logic, 84
Foss, Sonja, 5
Fox, Stuart, 25
Franklin, Thomas, 445
Friedman, Thomas L., 90
future, arguments about, 17–18

Gargus, J. Jay, 135–36
Gelbspan, Ross, 217–18
Gillespie, Nick, 295–97
Gingrich, Newt, 181
Gladwell, Malcolm, 5, 212
Goadsby, Peter, 136–37
Goodwin, Doris Kearns, 543–44
Gordon, Mary, 423
Gore, Al, 60, 181
government documents, citing
  online sources, 596
  print sources, 574, 593
graphs, 355, 461–62
Gray, William M., 218
Griffin, Cindy, 5

hard evidence, 69–75, 216, 292
Hardin, Lia, "Cultural Stress Linked to Suicide," 365–68
hasty generalization, 526–27

headings, and organization, 145, 459–60
Heffernan, Virginia, 497–98
Heir, Theron, 10
Henig, Jess, "What Is a Civil Union?" 243–48
Hilton, Paris, 520
Himes, Chester, 433
historical events, arguments about, 16–17
Hitchens, Christopher, 525
Hodgkinson, Tom, "With Friends Like These … ," 326–34
hooks, bell, 30
Howard, Jennifer, 223
Hughes, Langston, 427
humor
  credibility established with, 59–60
  in emotional appeals, 48–50
  of enthymemes, 86
hyperbole, 434–35
hypotheses
  in causal arguments, 352
  in factual arguments, 215, 221–22, 229–30
  in rhetorical analysis, 124–25

inartistic appeals, 69–70
indirect sources, citing, 569
inductive reasoning, 171
informal logic, 84–87
informative arguments, 8–9
intellectual property. See copyright and permissions; documentation of sources
intended readers, 28–30
Internet sources. See online sources
interviews
  citing, 581, 594
  to obtain evidence, 496–98
  as research tool, 358

in-text citations
APA style, 587–89
MLA style, 567–71
introductions
in oral and multimedia presentations, 472
to source material, 556–57
introduction to work, citing, 574
inverted word order, 438
invitational arguments, 5
invoked readers, 28–30
irony, 437
Isherwood, Charles, 286
Ivanov, Sergei, 534
Ivins, Molly, 24

jargon, 419
Jobs, Steve, 44
Johnson, K. C., 46–48
Johnson, Samuel, 50, 253, 437, 439
journal articles, citing
online sources, 578
print sources, 575

Kennedy, John F., 384–85, 439, 443–44
Keteyian, Armen, 79–80
keyword searches, 508–10
King, Martin Luther, Jr., 179–80, 475–76
King, Stephen, 350–51
Kinsley, Michael, 437
Kirkpatrick, Jeane, 439
Kleege, Georgina, 45
Klotzback, Philip J., 218
Kuban, Adam, 66

Lan Xue, "China: The Prizes and Pitfalls of Progress," 164–69
Lassell, Michael, 14
lectures or speeches, citing, 582
Lessing, Doris, 438

letters (personal communication), citing, 581, 589
letters to the editor, citing, 576, 593
Levitt, Steven, 215
Library of Congress Subject Headings (LCSH), 508
library sources, 505, 508–9
Lindgren, James, 74–75
lists, bulleted, 226, 460
literary works, citing, 568
Lithwick, Dahlia, 521
Liu, Claire, "Music in U.S.-China Diplomacy," 150–63
logic. *See* reasoning
logical appeals, 69–93
and common sense, 70
cultural assumptions and values, considering, 87–88
evidence in, 69–84
fallacies of, 526–34
features of, 34–35, 69–70
reasoning in, 84–87
rhetorical analysis based on, 107–9
statements and proof in, 74–75, 109
structure for. *See* logical structures
sustaining with emotions, 46–48, 103–4
visuals for, 71, 80, 85, 89, 92
logical structures, 88–93
analogies, 90
degree, 88–90
precedent, 91–93
logos. See logical appeals
Lurie, Alison, 425

McCain, John, 180, 384–85, 429
McCorkle, Ben, 473
McLuhan, Marshall, 444

magazine articles, citing
  online sources, 578
  print sources, 576, 593
Mairs, Nancy, 66
Makau, Josina, 5
Mansaray, Sayoh, "Offbeat Allure of
  Cult Films, The," 276–79
Mansoor, Peter, 529
maps
  citing, 583
  as visuals, 461
Matthews, Chris, 431
Matthews, Jay, 419, 421
Mayer, Jane, 424
mediation, arguments for, 14–15
Mencken, H. L., 435
metaphors, 428–29
microform articles, citing, 580
Miller, Henry I., 340
MLA style, 567–85
  electronic sources, 576–80
  example of, 584–85
  explanatory and bibliographic
    notes, 571
  in-text citations, 567–71
  Works Cited, 572–83, 585
Morris, David J., 16
Morrison, Toni, 472
motives
  for ethical appeals, 65–67
  for rhetorical analysis, 99–100
multimedia presentations. See
  oral and multimedia
  presentations
multivolume works, citing, 568, 574,
  592
Murray, Charles, 9
"Music in U.S.-China Diplomacy"
  (Liu), 150–63

narratives, as evidence, 82–83
Newman, Cathy, 336
newsgroup posting, citing, 596

newspaper articles, citing
  online sources, 578
  print sources, 576, 593
Nixon, Richard M., 443–44
non sequitur, 531–32

Obama, Barack, 41–42, 78, 180,
  250–52
objections to arguments
  to claims, 185–86
  and factual arguments,
    231–32
  in Rogerian argument, 177–78
  in Toulmin argument, 196–99
observations
  ethnographic, 352–53
  guidelines for, 496–98
"Offbeat Allure of Cult Films, The"
  (Mansaray), 276–79
online sources
  APA style citation, 589, 594–97
  copyright and permissions, 463,
    545–46
  documenting with hyperlinks,
    586
  evaluating, 109, 553–55
  as evidence, 509–10
  information from, recording, 556
  MLA style citation, 576–80
  searching, 509–10
operational definitions, 257–58
oral and multimedia presentations,
  468–86
  in-class comments, 468, 470
  cultural contexts, 470
  for factual arguments, 227
  introductions, 472
  language devices for, 475–76
  organization, 473
  prepared text, presenting from,
    471
  presentation strategies, 484–85
  signposts, 473, 475

success, criteria for, 468
syntax, 473–75
visuals in, 476–84
Webcasts, 485–86
oration, classical, 172–75
O'Reilly, Dave, 418, 422
organization
  academic arguments, 144–45
  causal arguments, 360, 361–62
  classical pattern, 173–74
  definitional arguments, 271, 272
  of design features, 459–60
  evaluations, 307–8, 309
  of evidence, 513
  factual arguments, 231–33
  and headings, 145, 459–60
  oral and multimedia presenta-
    tions, 473
  proposals, 394–95, 396
  rhetorical analysis, 126–29
  Toulmin argument, 199
Orwell, George, 421
Osofsky, Michael, "Psychological
  Experience of Security
  Officers Who Work with
  Executions," 236–42
outline, of classical oration, 173–74

Palin, Sarah, 216–17
pamphlets, citing, 575
parallelism
  antithesis in, 437–38
  elements of, 437
  in oral and multimedia presen-
    tations, 475–76
  for rhetorical power, 116
  in sentences, 422–23
paraphrasing
  guidelines for, 562
  source material, 542, 561–62
Parker, Kathy, 258
past, arguments about, 16–17
pathos. See emotional appeals

peer review. *See* reviewing
  arguments
performance, citing, 582
Peril, Lynn, "Pink Think," 280–83
periodicals (articles), citing
  APA style, 593–95
  MLA style, 575–76, 578
  online sources, 578, 595
permissions. *See* copyright and
  permissions
personal experience
  in causal arguments, 353
  cultural contexts, 504
  as evidence, 503–4
  in proposals, 387
  testimonies and narratives,
    82–84
persuasion
  argument compared to, 7
  and emotional appeals, 42
persuasive arguments, push to
  action in, 10–11
pie charts, 461–62
Pike, Kenneth L., 177
"Pink Think" (Peril), 280–83
plagiarism, 539–44
  cultural contexts, 547
Platt, Russell, 539
policies, proposals about, 378
Pollan, Michael, 45
polls. *See* surveys and polls
poster sessions, citing, 597
Powell, Colin, 70, 72
PowerPoint, 476–84
practices, proposals about, 377
prayer, arguments in form of,
  14–15
precedent, logical appeals based on,
  91–93
precedents, 16
preface, citing, 574
premise, major and minor, 171
present, arguments about, 18–19

presentation methods, 466–89
    oral and multimedia, 468–86
    print, 467–68
    Web-based, 486–89
print presentations, 467–68
print sources, evaluating, 551–53
pronouns, addressing readers with,
    30, 63
proofreading, procedure for, 146
propaganda, 7
proposals, 373–414
    and academic arguments, 386
    causal argument in, 343
    developing, 380–89
    examples of, 399–414
    features of, 25–26, 110–11,
        378–80, 389
    issues presented in, 373–76, 392
    reviewing, 395–97
    types of, 377–78
    visuals for, 375–77, 380, 388–91
    writing, guidelines for, 392–97
proposals for assignments
    for causal arguments, 359
    for definitional arguments,
        270
    for evaluations, 307
    for factual arguments, 230–31
    for proposals, 394
    for rhetorical analysis, 126
"Protecting Freedom of Expression
    at Harvard" (Bok), 118–20
"Psychological Experience of
    Security Officers Who Work
    with Executions" (Osofsky),
    236–42
public domain, 463
public occasions, ceremonial
    arguments, 18–20
punctuation, to enhance style,
    423–26
Purvis, Sarah Banda, 351
Pytlik, Mary, 300–301

qualifiers
    in evaluations, 300–301
    in factual arguments, 222
    in Toulmin argument, 182,
        194–96, 199
qualitative evaluations, 292–97
quantitative evaluations, 292–94
question marks, 424
questionnaires, 500–502
questions
    hypothesis, exploring with, 230
    in questionnaires, 500
    rhetorical, 436
    in statis theory, 21–27
quotations
    accuracy, guidelines for, 561
    long, MLA and APA styles, 561
    source information, 539, 542,
        557, 560–61

radio programs, citing, 582
Ramirez, Michael, 431
Rand, Ayn, 88
Reagan, Ronald, 19, 421, 438
real readers, 30
reasoning
    deductive, 84, 171
    enthymemes, 85–87, 171, 185,
        188–89
    errors in, 84
    formal logic, 84
    inductive, 171
    informal logic, 84–87
    in logical appeals, 84–87
    syllogisms, 84, 171
reasons
    in causal arguments, 350
    in proposals, 383–84
    in Toulmin argument, 184–85,
        199, 204
rebuttal, in Toulmin argument,
    63–64, 196–99
References, APA style, 590–98

reference work, article in, citing, 574, 592
repetition
anaphora, 438
in oral and multimedia presentations, 475–76
for rhetorical power, 116
Web site design, 487
republication, citing, 574, 592
research
academic arguments, 141–42
causal arguments, 357–58
data gathered. *See* evidence
definitional arguments, 268–69
evaluations, 305–6
factual arguments, 221, 229
proposals, 392–93
rhetorical analysis, 124
research reports, citing, 597
respect for audience, 101–3
response, in Toulmin argument, 199
reversed structures, 439
reviewing arguments
academic arguments, 146
causal arguments, 360–62
definitional arguments, 266–67, 271–73
evaluations, 304, 308–10
factual arguments, 232–33
proposals, 395–97
rhetorical analysis, 109–11, 127–29
reviews, citing, 576, 594
rhetoric, Aristotle on, 15
rhetorical analysis, 95–130
audience, identifying, 101–3
composing, 97–103
emotional appeal as basis, 103–5
ethical appeal as basis, 105–6
examples of, 117–23
issues explored in, 95–98, 105, 109, 111, 124–29
logical appeal based on, 107–9

reviewing, 109–11, 127–29
of visuals, 111–15, 117
writing, guidelines for, 124–29
rhetorical questions, 436
rhetorical situation
and arguments, 35
and evidence, 494–96
rhetorical stance, and academic arguments, 142–43
ridicule, versus humor, 50
Robertson, Lori, "What Is a Civil Union?" 243–48
Rogerian argument, 176–81
examples of, 178–79
features of, 7, 177–78
structure of, 177–78
visuals for, 181
Rogers, Carl, 7, 176–77
Rose, Mike, 59
Rosen, Christine, 5
Rosen, Jonathan, 422
Rosenbaum, Ron, 428–29
Rosenthal, Elizabeth, "Stinging Tentacles Offer Hint to Oceans' Decline," 369–72

sacred texts, citing, 569
Saenz, Benjamin, 428
Saunders, Debra, 436
scare tactics, 517, 519
Schafer, Jack, 31
Schaffer, Michael, 431–32
schemes, 427, 437–39
Schjeldahl, Peter, 429
script, in oral and multimedia presentations, 477–83
search engines, 509
secondhand evidence, 505–10
semicolons, 423–24
"Send It Somewhere Special" (Benson), 411–14
sentence structure, varying, 421–23
sentimental appeals, 521–22

series, book in, citing, 574
Shriver, Lionel, 105
signal phrases
  in factual arguments, 232
  source material, introducing, 556, 567
  in-text citations, 571, 587
signal verbs, 557
signifying, 433–34
signposts, oral and multimedia presentations, 473, 475
Silko, Leslie Marmon, 354
similes, 429–30
Skolnick, Gilad, 92
slang, 419, 426
slippery slope, 520–21
software, citing, 579–80, 596
Solomon, Jack, 102
sound recordings, citing, 582, 597
sources
  bias, recognizing, 550–51
  citing. *See* documentation of sources
  collaboration, acknowledging, 547
  copyright and permissions, 541, 545–46
  evaluating, 551–55
  identifying, cultural context, 563
  incomplete citation, 542–43
  paraphrasing, 542, 561–62
  plagiarism, avoiding, 539–44
  quoting, 539, 542, 557, 560–61
  signal phrases to introduce, 556
  signal verbs with, 557
  summary of information from, 562–63
  visuals, 563–64
  working bibliography for, 555–56
Spaulding, John, 464
square brackets, 561
stasis theory, exploratory questions in, 21–27

statements and proof, in all arguments, 74–75, 109
statistics
  as evidence, 78–79
  surveys and polls, 79–80
Steinhardt, Alana, 31
Stevenson, Adlai, 70, 72
Stevenson, Seth, 95–97, 103
"Stinging Tentacles Offer Hint to Oceans' Decline" (Rosenthal), 369–72
Story, Louise, 31
straw-man fallacy, 532–33
structure of arguments, 170–207
  classical oration, 172–75
  cultural contexts, 205
  inductive and deductive arguments, 171
  logical structures, 88–93
  Rogerian argument, 176–81
  Toulmin argument, 85, 182–200
style, 417–40
  academic arguments, 145
  causal arguments, 361–62
  and credibility, 111, 116
  cultural contexts, 432
  definitional arguments, 272–73
  evaluations, 309
  factual arguments, 233
  figurative language, 426–37
  high, middle, and low, 418
  proposals, 396–97
  punctuation, 423–26
  rhetorical analysis, 111, 116–17, 128–29
  sentence structure, 421–23
  visuals to convey, 420
  word choice, 418–21
  word order, 437–40
subject directories, 509
subject headings, 508
subscription service, online, citing, 579

Sullivan, Andrew, 60–62, 77
summary, writing, 562–63
superscript
    for APA content notes, 590
    for MLA bibliographic notes, 571
surveys and polls
    as evidence, 79–82
    questionnaires, 500–502
    as research tool, 305–6
Swift, Jonathan, 65
syllogisms, 84, 171
symposium paper, citing, 597
synchronous communication,
    citing, 596–97
syntax, oral and multimedia
    presentations, 473–75

Talbot, Margaret, 83
Taylor, Stuart, 46–48
television programs, citing, 582, 597
testimonies, as evidence, 82–83
"Testing Speech Codes"
    (Dershowitz), 201–2
thesis
    causal arguments, 359
    definitional arguments, 269, 270
    evaluations, 306
    rhetorical analysis, 124–25
Thomas, Lewis, 62
Thomas, Ryan, 18
Thompson, Clive, 262
tone
    academic arguments, 145
    credibility established with,
        63–64, 106
    rhetorical analysis, 111
    Rogerian argument, 178
Toobin, Jeffrey, 116
topic selection
    academic arguments, 141
    causal arguments, 357
    definitional arguments, 268
    evaluations, 305

factual arguments, 218–19, 229
    proposals, 381–83, 392
    rhetorical analysis, 124
Toulmin, Stephen, 182
Toulmin argument, 85, 182–200
    analysis of, 203–4
    claims in, 182–84, 199, 203, 204
    conditions of rebuttal, 196–99
    contributions of, 204, 206
    for evaluations, 297, 307
    evidence in, 192–94, 199, 204
    example of, 201–5
    outline of, 199
    qualifiers in, 182, 194–96, 199
    reasons in, 184–85, 199, 204
    visuals for, 188
    warrants, 203, 204
    warrants in, 186–94, 199
translations, citing, 574, 592
tropes, 428–37
Trudeau, Gary, 543
Turner, Fred, 342

understatement, 435–36
undistributed middle term, 84

value or rank, terms related to, 305
values
    cultural, 87–88
    and proposals, 380
verbs, signal, 557
video games, citing, 579–80
videos, citing, 597
visual arguments, 441–65
    analysis of, 446–51
    character-based, 455–58
    emotional power of, 452–55
    fact and reason-based, 459–63
    power of, 442–45
    shaping messages, 446
visuals
    academic arguments, 134, 140,
        144–46

captions, 563–64
causal arguments, 340, 345–47, 349, 354–55
citing, 582
citing sources for, 563–64
copyright/permissions, 463, 541, 564
and credibility, 6, 9–10, 13–14, 303, 456, 558–59
definitional arguments, 253–55, 265–66
emotional appeals, 34, 39, 42–43, 46–47, 104, 108, 445, 447
ethical appeals, 54–55, 61
evaluations, 302–3, 303
as evidence, 502, 506–7
factual arguments, 214, 226–27
as form of argument, 6, 9–10, 13–14
labeling and formatting, guides to, 463
logical appeals, 71, 80, 85, 89, 92
oral and multimedia presentations, 476–84
placement of, 460
proposals, 375–77, 380, 388–91
rhetorical analysis, 111–15, 117
Rogerian argument, 181
style conveyed in, 420
Toulmin argument, 188

warrants
in causal arguments, 350
in evaluations, 297

in proposals, 384
in Toulmin argument, 186–94, 199, 203, 204
Watts, Linda S., 436
Weathers, Diane, 101–2
Web-based presentations, 486–89
blogs, 488–89
Webcasts, 485–86
Web sites, 486–87
Web sites
citing, 577, 595
creating, 486–87
"What Is a Civil Union?" (Henig and Robertson), 243–48
Williams, Terry Tempest, 58
Wilsey, Sean, 302
Winfrey, Oprah, 63–64
"With Friends Like These…" (Hodgkinson), 326–34
Wong, Elizabeth, 12–13
word choice, 418–21
word order, inverted, 438
working bibliography, 555–56
Works Cited, MLA style, 572–83, 585
WorldCat, 509

Young, Richard E., 177

Zacharek, Stephanie, 298–99
Zawodniak, Christian, 83–84